# CLINICIAN'S
# HANDBOOK
## BEHAVI
## ASSESS

D0933427

WITHDRAWN

# CLINICIAN'S HANDBOOK OF ADULT BEHAVIORAL ASSESSMENT

EDITED BY

## MICHEL HERSEN
*Pacific University*
*Forest Grove, Oregon*

AMSTERDAM • BOSTON • HEIDELBERG • LONDON
NEW YORK • OXFORD • PARIS • SAN DIEGO
SAN FRANCISCO • SINGAPORE • SYDNEY • TOKYO

Academic Press is an imprint of Elsevier

Elsevier Academic Press
30 Corporate Drive, Suite 400, Burlington, MA 01803, USA
525 B Street, Suite 1900, San Diego, California 92101-4495, USA
84 Theobald's Road, London WC1X 8RR, UK

This book is printed on acid-free paper.

**Library of Congress Cataloging-in-Publication Data**
Clinician's handbook of adult behavioral assessment / edited by Michel Hersen.
    p.  cm.
   Includes bibliographical references and index.
   ISBN 0-12-343013-5 (pbk. : alk. paper) 1. Behavioral assessment—Handbooks, manuals, etc.
 2. Psychological tests—Handbooks, manuals, etc.  I. Hersen, Michel.  II. Title.

   RC473.B43C585 2006
   616.89′075–dc22                                   2005014581

**British Library Cataloguing in Publication Data**
A catalogue record for this book is available from the British Library

ISBN13: 978-0-12-343013-7
ISBN10: 0-12-343013-5

For all information on all Elsevier Academic Press publications
visit our Web site at www.books.elsevier.com

Printed in the United States of America
06  07  08  09  10  9  8  7  6  5  4  3  2  1

# CONTENTS

## PART I

## GENERAL ISSUES

## 1

## OVERVIEW OF BEHAVIORAL ASSESSMENT WITH ADULTS

WILLIAM O'DONOHUE, KENDRA K. BEITZ, AND MICHELLE BYRD

# 2

## PSYCHOMETRIC CONSIDERATIONS

### STEPHEN N. HAYNES

# 3

## ANALOGUE AND VIRTUAL REALITY ASSESSMENT

### JOHAN ROSQVIST, ALECIA SUNDSMO, CHELSEA MACLANE, KIRSTEN CULLEN, DARCY CLOTHIER NORLING, MANDY DAVIES, AND DANIELLE MAACK

# 4

## BEHAVIORAL INTERVIEWING

### STEVEN L. SAYERS AND THOMAS J. TOMCHO

# 5

## ACTIVITY MEASUREMENT

### WARREN W. TRYON

# 6

## STRUCTURED AND SEMISTRUCTURED INTERVIEWS

### DANIEL L. SEGAL, FREDERICK L. COOLIDGE, ALISA O'RILEY, AND BENJAMIN A. HEINZ

# 7

## SELF ASSESSMENT

SANDRA T. SIGMON AND STEPHANIE M. LAMATTINA

# 8

## PSYCHOPHYSIOLOGICAL ASSESSMENT

KEVIN T. LARKIN

# PART II

## EVALUATION OF SPECIFIC DISORDERS AND PROBLEMS

# 9

## ANXIETY AND FEAR

### F. DUDLEY MCGLYNN, TODD A. SMITHERMAN, AND AMANDA M. M. MULFINGER

# 10

## DEPRESSION

### PAULA TRUAX, AARON TRITCH, AND BARB CARVER

# 11

## SOCIAL SKILLS DEFICIT

### NINA HEINRICHS, ALEXANDER L. GERLACH, AND STEFAN G. HOFMANN

# 12

## EATING DISORDERS

### TIFFANY M. STEWART AND DONALD A. WILLIAMSON

# 13

## ALCOHOL AND DRUG ABUSE

### PETER M. MILLER

# 14

## MARITAL DYSFUNCTION

### GARY R. BIRCHLER AND WILLIAM FALS-STEWART

# 15

## SEXUAL DEVIATION

### NATHANIEL McCONAGHY

# 16

## PSYCHOTIC BEHAVIOR

### NIRBHAY N. SINGH AND MOHAMED SABAAWI

# 17

## AGGRESSIVE BEHAVIOR

JENNIFER LANGHINRICHSEN-ROHLING, MATTHEW T. HUSS,
AND MARTIN L. ROHLING

# 18

## SLEEP DYSFUNCTION

SHAWN R. CURRIE

# 19

## BORDERLINE PERSONALITY DISORDER

WENDI L. ADAMS, TRACY JENDRITZA, AND SOONIE A. KIM

# PART III

## SPECIAL ISSUES

# 20

### TECHNOLOGY INTEGRATION AND BEHAVIORAL ASSESSMENT

DAVID C. S. RICHARD AND ANDREW GLOSTER

# 21

### EVALUATING OLDER ADULTS

BARRY A. EDELSTEIN, ERIN L. WOODHEAD, EMILY H. BOWER, AND ANGELA J. LOWERY

# 22

## BEHAVIORAL NEUROPSYCHOLOGY

MICHAEL D. FRANZEN, GLEN E. GETZ, AND KARIN SCHEETZ WALSH

# 23

## ETHICAL/LEGAL ISSUES

WILLIAM FREMOUW, JILL JOHANSSON-LOVE,
ELIZABETH TYNER, AND JULIA STRUNK

# 24

## BEHAVIORAL ASSESSMENT OF WORK-RELATED ISSUES

DEREK R. HOPKO, SANDRA D. HOPKO, AND C. W. LEJUEZ

# 25

## ASSESSMENT OF VALUE CHANGE IN ADULTS
## WITH ACQUIRED DISABILITIES

ELIAS MPOFU AND THOMAS OAKLAND

# CONTRIBUTORS

*Numbers in parentheses indicate the pages on which the authors' contributions begin.*

**Wendi L. Adams** (431), Portland Dialectical Behavior Therapy Program, Portland, Oregon 97239

**Kendra K. Beitz** (3), Department of Psychology, Eastern Michigan University, Ypsilanti, Michigan 48197

**Gary R. Birchler** (297), Department of Psychiatry, School of Medicine, University of California—San Diego, La Jolla, California 92093

**Emily H. Bower** (497), Department of Psychology, West Virginia University, Morgantown, West Virginia 26506

**Michelle Byrd** (3), Department of Psychology, University of Nevada, Reno, Nevada 89557

**Barb Carver** (209), School of Professional Psychology, Pacific University, Portland, Oregon 97205

**Frederick L. Coolidge** (121), Department of Psychology, University of Colorado, Colorado Springs, CO 80918

**Kirsten Cullen** (43), Clinical Psychology Program, Pacific University, Portland, Oregon 97205

**Shawn R. Currie** (401), Addiction Centre, Foothills Medical Centre, Calgary, Alberta, T2N 2T9, Canada

**Mandy Davies** (43), Clinical Psychology Program, Pacific University, Portland, Oregon 97205

**Barry A. Edelstein** (497), Department of Psychology, West Virginia University, Morgantown, West Virginia 26506

**William Fals-Stewart** (297), Research Triangle Institute, Research Triangle Park, North Carolina 27709

**Michael D. Franzen** (529), Department of Psychiatry, Allegheny General Hospital, Pittsburgh, Pennsylvania 15212

**William J. Fremouw** (547), Department of Psychology, West Virginia University, Morgantown, West Virginia 26506

**Alexander L. Gerlach** (235), Psychologisches Institut I, Psychologische Diagnostik und Klinische Psychologie, 48149 Muenster, Germany

**Glen E. Getz** (529), Department of Psychology, Allegheny General Hospital, Pittsburgh, PA 15212

**Andrew Gloster** (461), Department of Psychology, Eastern Michigan University, Ypsilanti, Michigan 48197

**Stephen N. Haynes** (17), Department of Psychology, University of Hawaii, Honolulu, Hawaii 96822

**Nina Heinrichs** (235), Institute of Psychology, Department of Clinical Psychology, Psychotherapy, and Assessment, Technical University of Braunschweig, 38106 Braunschweig, Germany

**Benjamin A. Heinz** (121), Department of Psychology, University of Colorado, Colorado Springs, CO 80918

**Stefan G. Hofmann** (235), Department of Psychology, Boston University, Boston, Massachusetts 02215

**Derek R. Hopko** (567), Department of Psychology, University of Tennessee, Knoxville, Tennessee 37996

**Sandra D. Hopko** (567), Cariten Assist Employee Assistance Program, Knoxville, Tennessee 37922

**Matthew T. Huss** (371), Creighton University, Department of Psychology, Omaha, Nebraska 68178

**Tracy Jendritza** (431), Portland Dialectical Behavior Therapy Program, Portland, Oregon 97239

**Jill Johansson-Love** (547), Department of Psychology, West Virginia University, Morgantown, West Virginia 26506

**Soonie A. Kim** (431), Portland Dialectical Behavior Therapy Program, Portland, Oregon 97239

**Stephanie M. LaMattina** (145), Department of Psychology, University of Maine, Orono, Maine 04469

**Jennifer Langhinrichsen-Rohling** (371), Department of Psychology, University of South Alabama, Mobile, Alabama 36688

**Kevin T. Larkin** (165), Department of Psychology, West Virginia University, Morgantown, West Virginia 26506

**C. W. Lejuez** (567), Department of Psychology, University of Maryland, College Park, Maryland 20742

**Angela J. Lowery** (497), Department of Psychology, West Virginia University, Morgantown, West Virginia 26506

**Danielle Maack** (43), Clinical Psychology Program, Pacific University, Portland, Oregon 97205

**Chelsea MacLane** (43), Clinical Psychology Program, Pacific University, Portland, Oregon 97205

**Nathanial McConaghy** (325), School of Psychiatry, University of New South Wales, Paddington, New South Wales 2021, Australia

**F. Dudley McGlynn** (189), Department of Psychology, Auburn University, Auburn University, Alabama 36849

**Peter M. Miller** (279), Center for Drug and Alcohol Programs, Department of Psychiatry and Behavioral Sciences, Medical University of South Carolina, Charleston, South Carolina 29425

**Elias Mpofu** (601), Department of Counselor Education, Counseling Psychology and Rehabilitation Services, Pennsylvania State University, University Park, Pennsylvania 16802

**Amanda M. M. Mulfinger** (189), Department of Psychology, Auburn University, Auburn University, Alabama 36849

**Darcy Clothier Norling** (43), Clinical Psychology Program, Pacific University, Portland, Oregon 97205

**William O'Donohue** (3), Department of Psychology, University of Nevada, Reno, Nevada 89557

**Alisa O'Riley** (121), Department of Psychology, University of Colorado, Colorado Springs, CO 80918

**Thomas Oakland** (601), Department of Educational Foundations, University of Florida, Gainesville, Florida 32611

**David C. S. Richard** (461), Department of Psychology, Rollins College, Winter Park, Florida 32789

**Martin L. Rohling** (371), Department of Psychology, University of South Alabama, Mobile, Alabama 36688

**Johan Rosquvist** (43), Counseling Psychology Program, Pacific University, Portland, Oregon 97205

**Mohamed Sabaawi** (349), Human Potential Consulting Group, Alexandria, Virginia 22314

**Steven L. Sayers** (63), Department of Psychiatry Philadelphia Veterans Affairs Medical Center and University of Pennsylvania School of Medicine, Philadelphia, Pennsylvania 19104

**Daniel L. Segal** (121), Department of Psychology, University of Colorado, Colorado Springs, CO 80918

**Sandra T. Sigmon** (145), Department of Psychology, University of Maine, Orono, Maine 04469

**Nirbhay N. Singh** (349), ONE Research Institute, Chesterfield, Virginia 23832

**Todd A. Smitherman** (189), Department of Psychology, Auburn University, Auburn University, Alabama 36849

**Tiffany M. Stewart** (253), Pennington Biomedical Research Center, Baton Rouge, Louisiana 70808

**Julia Strunk** (547), Department of Psychology, West Virginia University, Morgantown, West Virginia 26506

**Alecia Sundsmo** (43), Clinical Psychology Program, Pacific University, Portland, Oregon 97205

**Thomas J. Tomcho** (63), Philadelphia Veterans Affairs Medical Center, Philadelphia, Pennsylvania 19104

**Aaron Tritch** (209), School of Professional Psychology, Pacific University, Portland, Oregon 97205

**Paula Truax** (209), School of Professional Psychology, Pacific University, Portland, Oregon 97205

**Warren W. Tryon** (85), Department of Psychology, Fordham University, Bronx, New York 10458

**Elizabeth Tyner** (547), Department of Psychology, West Virginia University, Morgantown, West Virginia 26506

**Karin Scheetz Walsh** (529), Mount Washington Pediatric Hospital, Baltimore, Maryland 21210

**Donald A. Williamson** (253), Pennington Biomedical Research Center, Baton Rouge, Louisiana 70808

**Erin L. Woodhead** (497), Department of Psychology, West Virginia University, Morgantown, West Virginia 26506

# PREFACE

Several texts and handbooks on behavioral assessment have been published, most of them now outdated. Many new developments in this field cut across strategies, computerization, virtual reality techniques, and ethical and legal issues. Over the years many new assessment strategies have been developed and existing ones refined. In addition, it is now important to include a functional assessment and document case conceptualization and its relation to assessment and treatment planning. In general, texts and tomes on behavioral assessment tend to give too little emphasis to work, peer, and family relationships. Many of the existing texts are either theoretical/research in focus or clinical in nature. Nowhere are the various aspects of behavioral assessment placed in a comprehensive research/clinical context, nor is there much integration as to conceptualization and treatment planning. The *Clinician's Handbook of Adult Behavioral Assessment* was undertaken to correct these deficiencies of coverage in a single reference work.

This volume on adult assessment contains 25 chapters in three sections, beginning with general issues, followed by evaluation of specific disorders and problems, and closing with special issues. To ensure cross-chapter consistency in the coverage of disorders, these chapters follow a similar format, including an introduction, assessment strategies, research basis, clinical utility, conceptualization and treatment planning, a case study, and summary. Special issue coverage includes computerized assessment, evaluating older adults, behavioral neuropsychology, ethical-legal issues, work-related issues, and value change in adults with acquired disabilities.

Many individuals have contributed to the development of this work. First, I thank the contributors for sharing their expertise with us. Second, I once again thank Carole Londeree, my excellent editorial assistant, and my graduate student assistants (Cynthia Polance and Gregory May) for their technical expertise. And finally, but hardly least of all, I thank Nikki Levy, my publisher at Elsevier, for understanding the value and timeliness of this project.

*Michel Hersen*
*Forest Grove, Oregon*

PART I

# GENERAL ISSUES

# 1

## OVERVIEW OF BEHAVIORAL ASSESSMENT WITH ADULTS

WILLIAM O'DONOHUE

*Department of Psychology*
*University of Nevada*
*Reno, Nevada*

KENDRA K. BEITZ

*Department of Psychology*
*Eastern Michigan University*
*Ypsilanti, Michigan*

MICHELLE BYRD

*Department of Psychology*
*University of Nevada*
*Reno, Nevada*

## INTRODUCTION

Behavioral assessment can be best understood by explicating its relationship to three contexts: (1) its role with respect to the general purposes of assessment in science; (2) its role with respect to traditional assessment; and (3) its current and historical roles in behavior therapy and applied behavior analysis. This chapter will examine behavioral assessment in these three contexts as well as discuss issues such as: (a) some of the common difficulties posed in the task of accurate measurement; (b) controversies concerning how behavioral assessment instruments ought to be evaluated; and (c) the ethics of behavioral assessment.

*Clinician's Handbook of Adult Behavioral Assessment*

3

## PLACING BEHAVIORAL ASSESSMENT
## IN CONTEXT

### MEASUREMENT IN SCIENCE AND SCIENTIFIC
### CLINICAL PRACTICE

Measurement can be seen to be one of the most fundamental activities of science. Results of measurement provide five clinicians with the basic data or facts that can be used for them to make relevant clinical decisions. Scientists have to be able to accurately detect the presence or absence of something (for example, "Are there bacteria present in this sample?"). Thus, detection is a measurement process and as such can be deceptively difficult. Advances in instrumentation often are necessary before something can be detected (for instance, the invention of the telescope revealed other planets as well as irregularities on the surface of the moon). Clinically, the behavior therapist is sometimes interested in a detection task (for example, "Is my patient still using drugs?" "Does this individual have pedophilic interests?" "Is this patient having suicidal thoughts?"). Detection can be difficult because the target may be covert (e.g., as in fantasies) and/or the patient may have an interest in providing distorted information (e.g., as with substance abusers) or may even be difficult for the client to know and therefore report accurately (e.g., when he or she first started smoking). Screening instruments such as the Prime MD or HEAR are examples of attempts to detect the presence or absence of a wide variety of problems.

In addition to being either present or absent, some entities allow for quantification. Things are not simply hot or cold; they have a temperature. Another measurement task, then, is to accurately measure quantity. One problem in behavioral science is the frequent lack of clarity as to whether some entity can be quantified. Although it is obvious that cigarette smoking can be quantified (10 cigarettes/day vs. 20/day), it is not clear whether something like sex drive can be (what scale would this even be measured on—can we compare quantities of male vs. female sex drive?). Sechrest (1963) has provided a cogent criticism of some existing measures, such as the Beck Depression Inventory (BDI), because although some tests give the illusion of quantification (a BDI score of 36 vs. one of 18), they really do not provide much quantifiable information. We cannot say that the first score represents "twice" the depression of the latter score; moreover, we cannot even say that a higher score represents "more" depression, for this would assume that each question has the identical weight for the composite depression score. For example, if the BDI is "only" 18, does this mean that the patient is no longer suicidal? Does it mean that she is less dysphoric? These critical dimensions are weighted the same as ones that might be regarded as less indicative of depression (e.g., sex drive). All these reasonable questions cannot be answered from such numbers. It is possible for the score to lower, but some of what are generally considered to be the more serious symptoms of depression can actually increase in the "lower" composite score when individual items are considered.

Quantification is important because many of the questions we are curious about depend on it. Correlation questions (roughly, questions about the preservation of rank order) can depend on it. Correlation questions are interesting because they provide information about the "relatedness" of variables; a correlation of zero rules out a causal relationship. We need to know basic questions of more or less when we see if rank order is preserved. Clinically, we are often interested in reducing or increasing something (e.g., reducing smoking or increasing assertive behavior) and thus are interested in quantity.

Measurement is foundational to science in its focus on detection (presence or absence) and its focus on quantity in correlation or causal questions. It is also, then, fundamental to clinical science. We often want to know whether clinical problems are present or absent (and we may use screening devices to accomplish this), or we may want to know therapy status (perhaps to see if we are on the right track or even if termination is possible) and thus we may be interested in measuring quantity (e.g., number of cigarettes smoked).

## BEHAVIORAL ASSESSMENT AND TRADITIONAL ASSESSMENT

Assessment has played a key but changing role in the history of psychology and clinical psychology. Initially, because psychology had not gone clinical yet, assessment occurred only in the context of basic research. Therefore, in the late 19th and early 20th centuries, psychologists such as Ebbinghaus (Hergenhahn, 2001) were interested in the number of correctly recalled nonsense symbols, and Watson and Raynor (Morris, 2000) were interested in the amount of fear-and-approach behavior of Little Albert. At times, psychologists were assessing variables that might have some clinical interest, but they were not using this information to make diagnoses (or other clinically relevant problem statements) or to develop and implement treatment plans. Psychologists and others in this period were interested in intellectual testing, sometimes to address basic issues, such as racial differences, and sometimes, more practically, to help predict and understand school performance. Thus, intelligence tests, such as the Stanford Binet, were developed around the turn of the century.

Such tests set the stage for the first quasi-clinical use of tests by psychologists. They were employed in educational settings but functioned to help identify developmentally delayed individuals and in general to understand and predict academic performance. This was critical because psychologists began to be seen as professionals who had specialized measurement technologies that were useful for such practical questions. These tests often met standards that can be seen as some of the first recognition and implementation of contemporary psychometrics. They were standardized in administration and scoring; they were evaluated on the extent of the validity of inferences made from them (e.g., correlation coefficients were reported between the preservation of rank order of these test scores and class rank).

Two other very different developments in traditional testing occurred around the time of World War II. The first was the use of psychological testing to attempt to discern cognitive and personality capabilities to determine aptitude for different positions in the military. This can be seen as a further development of educational aptitude testing. The other was the development of projective testing as part of the growth of psychoanalytic psychotherapy during this period.

One important aspect to note is that assessment was born in the context of controversy. Intelligence testing existed in the practical controversies concerning racial differences in intelligence as well as in the controversies concerning the relative importance of nature vs. nurture. When one side of the debate did not like the data produced by a study, one avenue of attack was the quality (either psychometric or assumptions involved in the test) of the test utilized in the study. Projective testing also became controversial (see Garb, Wood, & Lilenfeld, 2002). It was controversial both within psychodynamic theory, as different branches began to disagree about what important constructs ought to be involved in testing (e.g., id impulses vs. ego-based constructs), as well as outside psychodynamic theory, as scholars began to question the interrater reliability and validity of these tests.

This raises an important and thorny issue in measurement: What in traditional psychometric theory is considered construct validity? Measurement, because, it also involves a causal process (it is a reaction to the test stimulus), can be coherent only if the constructs are well formed. One cannot answer the question, for example, of how long a piece of string is. "Piece of string" is a construct that does not carve nature at its joints.

However, after WWII, partly because the needs of casualties from the war overwhelmed psychiatry, psychologists began to go beyond their role as tester to a role that involved actually delivering therapy. Thus, they had needs to assess questions that were relevant to conducting therapy, such as diagnostic questions and outcome status. This produced a burgeoning of test development and, unfortunately, somewhat less of a growth of psychometric evaluation of these tests.

## BEHAVIORAL ASSESSMENT

Goldfried and Kent (1977, p. 409), in a classic statement of the differences between traditional and behavioral assessment, noted:

> Whereas traditional tests of personality involve the assessment of hypothesized personality constructs which, in turn, are used to predict overt behavior, the behavioral approach entails more of a direct sampling of the criterion behaviors themselves. In addition to requiring fewer inferences than traditional tests, behavioral assessment procedures are seen as being based on assumptions more amenable to direct empirical test and more consistent with empirical evidence.

When behavior therapy and behavior modification came on the scene in the 1950s and 1960s, these represented a paradigmatic shift from existing therapies. Behavior therapy was concerned with different issues, and behavioral assessment reflected this divergent focus. Some of the more striking differences included:

1. Less interest in formal diagnosis, particularly *DSM* diagnosis, partly as a result of the interrater reliability of these, the predictive validity of these, but most importantly concerns with moving away from more simple statements concerning problems with observable behavior.

2. An intense interest (especially among those influenced most heavily by B. F. Skinner) in the rate of responding as the most important variable to be measured. Skinner thought this variable was the one most prone to revealing order, and thus journals such as the *Journal of Applied Behavioral Analysis* reported study after study using this as the key variable.

3. Less interest in the construct of personality (see, for example, Ullmann & Krasner, 1969) and its related constructs (needs, dynamic processes, conflicts).

4. More interest in measuring variables related to causal inference in therapy outcome studies, e.g., therapist adherence, process mechanisms, follow-up measurements.

5. More interest in *in vivo* samples of behavior in settings such as home, school, and workplace.

6. More interest in directly measuring a behavioral excess or deficit rather than some other construct (rate of smoking could be defined as a behavioral excess).

One of the more remarkable changes since the 1960s is that behavior therapy, and hence behavioral assessment, has become much more accepting and concerned with traditional psychiatric diagnoses as found in the *DSM-IV*. One can see behavior therapists talking about treating problems such as Major Depression, and Panic Disorder with Agoraphobia, PTSD, and Erectile Dysfunction. This represents a change in the paradigm, although few have addressed the implications of this or even noted its occurrence. One influence that brought this about no doubt was use of the *DSM* by the National Institutes of Health, the Centers for Disease Control, and other major federal funding sources. Thus, if behavior therapists wanted grant funds to do research, they needed to adopt the language of the grantees. However, it has moved us some from a direct focus on observable behavior to the use of a system that can have unknown interrater reliability and unknown or poor predictive validity.

## COMMON SOURCES OF MEASUREMENT ERROR IN BEHAVIORAL ASSESSMENT

While behavioral assessment differs from traditional modes of assessment in several notable ways described previously in this chapter, the quality of data may still be compromised due to several sources of error, some shared by traditional assessments and others unique to behavioral strategies. Generally, psychometric theory regards all obtained measurement to be a function of both "signal" and error. The issues become: how much error, what the sources of this error are, and how it can be minimized. Although space does not permit a complete review of the possible sources of error and the suggested steps to prevent or ameliorate these problems (and comprehensive reviews are available elsewhere), we will now provide an overview of common sources of measurement error in observational and self-report methods of assessment, the two most frequently applied assessment strategies within the behavioral paradigm.

## BEHAVIORAL OBSERVATION

While behavioral observation offers many advantages over more inferential sources of data, these assessment strategies also come with distinct data quality pitfalls. The first source of error inherent in behavioral observation is the degree to which the behavior of interest itself has been adequately operationally defined prior to the formal assessment period. That is, whoever is observing the behavior must be able to differentiate problematic from other behaviors and specify important characteristics of the behavior. Related, the coding system must, to the extent possible, be specific, clear, practical for the setting, and user friendly. Codes should not be so complex or multifaceted that they cannot be assigned in the appropriate time frame, usually real time (coding video and audiotaped observations provide a unique advantage in this respect because they can be replayed ad infinitum). The use of handheld computers may be helpful in entering data accurately and efficiently while being nonobtrusive.

Particularly when observations occur in a natural setting relatively unknown to the investigator or therapist developing the coding system, it may be difficult to construct a comprehensive system that contains sufficient codes to adequately capture the universe of possible behaviors to be observed validly and reliably. Therefore, when observations are being conducted in a novel setting, piloting the coding system first and revising/expanding as necessary is of the utmost importance. Alterations in the target behaviors being coded, the method of sampling (e.g., time sampling vs. continuous monitoring), and the recording device itself may need to be made to improve the validity and reliability of the data collected. This iterative process may be compared to classic scale development and will most likely demand a great deal of time and care.

Once the variables of interest have been identified, well defined, and translated into a workable coding system, the next greatest threat to data quality are the coders themselves. Coders must be adequately trained in the coding system and, if they are observing in a naturalistic environment, in appropriate decorum so as to minimize the reactivity of clients (see later). However, it should be noted that excellent coder training may well involve withholding important information about the research (i.e., hypotheses, assignment to treatment condition) to protect the integrity of assigned ratings by limiting coder bias to the extent possible.

To safeguard reliability, when multiple coders are observing the same behavior, as is often the case, interobserver agreement should be calculated during the training period, and formal assessment should not begin until an adequate and predetermined level of agreement is reached (typically .8). When agreement falls short of the predetermined level, great care should be taken to review the discrepancies in detail, discussing the rationale for having given the codes with a master coder (either the developer of the coding system or someone facile with the system and previously trained to criterion). Interobserver agreement should be periodically randomly checked during data collection to protect against observer drift.

The third source of measurement error in behavioral observation is an artifact of the environment itself. Specifically, the extent to which the behavior observed is representative of the universe of behavior of interest greatly affects the validity of the sample. Day-to-day variations in the environment may result in significantly skewed data. To control for, or at least better understand, this source of variance, as much descriptive data about the observation conditions as possible should be gathered for each session (e.g., date, time, coders, clients observed, any coding anomalies). For example, we recently reviewed and attempted to analyze a set of codes made on consecutive days of children in a school setting. However, halfway through one week's worth of observations we noted significant changes in disruptive behavior and could not pinpoint the source of this drastic upward trend, for students and staff had remained constant. It was only on careful review of the descriptive documentation that we realized the observations occurred during the traumatic week of September 11, 2001.

Finally, clients being observed are themselves a primary source of measurement error, due to reactivity (Baird & Nelson-Gray, 1999; Hayes & Horn, 1982). That is, clients may knowingly or unknowingly alter their behavior as a consequence of being observed, limiting generalizability. While reactivity is not preventable, particularly when coders are not members of the environment being sampled, allowing ample time for habituation to occur prior to formal data collection is thought to be protective. However, reactivity may also result in genuine improvements in the target behavior because, by virtue of being observed, the client may become more mindful of his or her behavior and employ change strategies (Clum & Curtin, 1993; Bornstein, Hamilton, & Bornstein, 1986). Whether an outside observer is being used or one is observing his own behavior, reactivity remains a significant source of measurement error.


## SELF-REPORT DATA

Self-report may take many forms, including interviews, questionnaires, and self-monitoring devices. Relying on clients to report on their own behavior, while perhaps the most common assessment strategy, also invites a number of sources of error variance shared by nonbehavioral approaches to assessment.

First and foremost, many self-report strategies have not been developed using standard methods of test construction; therefore, their psychometric properties may not be known. Without this basic information about an assessment instrument, the quality of the data obtained using the instrument is questionable at best. In addition, if the self-report instrument is administered in a nonstandard manner, the information obtained may not be comparable to established norms or other benchmarks. Intake interviews, which are typically unstructured and the personal product of each individual clinician, are perhaps the most egregious example of these problems. Unfortunately, it is also common practice to base the majority of clinical decision making solely on this inherently unreliable and perhaps invalid source of information, emphasizing the need for utilizing multiple assessment methods.

Not only are the specific strategies employed in self-reporting vulnerable to measurement errors, but, in addition, even when the assessment instruments are themselves psychometrically sound and administered properly, the potential for biased reporting is still great. Clients may attempt to characterize their behavior such that it will be more socially acceptable, by inaccurately reporting on the behavior of interest. Clients may under- or overestimate rates of problematic behaviors during the course of treatment, to create the impression that therapy is either going well or not, depending on their motives to either curtail or extend therapy. Clients may also report inaccurately to try to manage the therapist's feelings. For example, they may give a report indicative of therapeutic progress, with the hope that the therapist will feel efficacious and hold them in positive regard.

When monitoring their own behavior, even when not attempting to project a particular image of themselves, clients may unintentionally be inaccurate in their data collection. As in behavioral observation, clients must be sufficiently trained in a sound data-collection system before they can be expected to provide reliable and valid estimates of their behavior. Furthermore, clients must be motivated to comply with the data-monitoring plan, for this form of homework is frequently a source of noncompliance in a therapeutic relationship.

Data quality becomes further jeopardized when clients are asked to retrospectively report on their behavior without having done self-monitoring in real time, as is commonly the case with questionnaires and behavioral interviews. The fallibility of memory or estimation in accurate reporting has been well documented (e.g., Nelson-Gray, D.L. Herbert, J.D. Herbert, Farmer, Badawi, & Lin, 1990; Farmer & Nelson-Gray, 1990).

In addition, self-report measures may create forced choices that do not map onto the client's experience. For example, the widespread use of formats such as multiple-choice questions and Likert scales, while helpful in standardizing responses, may also require higher levels of inference on the part of the client when their own response does not "fit" the available choices.

## EVALUATING ASSESSMENT STRATEGIES

There are myriad behavioral assessment strategies currently available, including interviews, rating scales, self-/other-report questionnaires, direct observation systems, and self-monitoring systems (Nelson-Gray, 2003). There are several ways to evaluate the quality of assessment strategies when selecting among them. As a first step, one should identify the purpose of the assessment and the level of analysis of interest. For instance, the goal of psychological testing is to interpret results in terms of nomothetic data, whereas the goal of psychological assessment is to generate a unifying description of an individual in terms of test results and the individual's history, behavior, and the like (Hunsley, 2002). Cone (1998) suggests five common reasons for conducting assessment: (1) to describe or classify an individual or a part of an individual's behavior, (2) to understand a phenomenon, (3) to predict behavior at some other time or place, (4) to control an aspect of an individual or an individual's behavior, and (5) to monitor differences in behavior over time. Testing or assessment data can also be used to guide treatment selection (Barrios & Hartmann, 1986). Once the intended purpose of assessment is identified, it allows us to select the appropriate assessment strategy; then we must evaluate the adequacy of different methods (Cone, 1998). The following are criteria used to judge the quality of assessment. The relative importance of each criterion is dependent on who we are and the conditions under which we are assessing.

### PSYCHOMETRIC STANDARDS

Psychometrics is based on the concepts of reliability and validity, and from a traditional point of view these are the standards by which to evaluate the quality of assessment. Reliability concerns the stability of assessment data (Haynes & O'Brien, 2002); validity concerns how well an assessment measures what it purports to evaluate (Nunnally & Bernstein, 1994). Accuracy, which should not be confused with reliability, is the "extent to which observed values approximate the 'true' state of nature" (Johnston & Pennypacker, 1993, p. 138).

Psychometric properties help us estimate how confident we can be when drawing inferences from assessment data (Haynes & O'Brien, 2002). Depending on the purpose of assessment and the subject matter being evaluated, psychometric considerations vary (Cone, 1998). An assessor must determine the relative importance of the different types of validity (e.g., face, content, construct, ecological, incremental) and reliability (e.g., interrater agreement, internal consistency, temporal stability, alternate form) in each situation. For instance, if the stability of behavior is of interest, a test should have high test–retest reliability, whereas test–retest reliability may be irrelevant when measuring behaviors that are expected to be highly variable (i.e., states). In addition to reliability and validity, Cone (1998) suggests that accuracy is essential and should be established before using a behavioral assessment measure to determine facts about behavior.

## GUIDELINES

Another way to evaluate the quality of assessment is to ascertain the degree to which assessment strategies meet relevant guidelines. For instance, the American Psychological Association *Standards for Educational and Psychological Testing* (1985) outline *primary standards*, which are those that should be met by all tests; *secondary standards*, which are desirable but not required; and *conditional standards*, which vary with application. Standards are provided for test construction and evaluation, which, for example, require tests to have validity, have reliability, be developed on a strong scientific basis, and provide information on how to interpret scores, recommended use, and special qualifications. Professional standards outline general principles of test use and also test use in clinical, school, counseling, and occupational settings, in addition to use of tests for program evaluation and professional licensure and certification. Standards are provided when working with different populations, such as testing linguistic minorities and handicapped individuals. Finally, standards are provided for administration procedures, including test administration, scoring, and reporting and how to protect the rights of test takers. In addition to the *Standards for Educational and Psychological Testing*, various organizations or entities may have other standards, guidelines, or recommendations that are relevant for certain populations (e.g., children or the elderly) or situations (e.g., forensic contexts). Depending on the purpose of assessment, different standards may be more or less important, but assessment strategies that meet relevant standards are better than those that do not.

## GENERALIZABILITY

Any observation of behavior represents a random sample from the hypothetical domain of all possible behaviors. Given that, how dependable are behavioral measurements such that one set of measurements of an individual's behavior generalizes to other assessments of that individual? In accordance with generalizability theory (Chronbach, Gleser, Nanda, & Rajaratnam, 1972), multiple sources of error operate simultaneously when assessing behavior. Cone (1977) suggests that observer, item, time, method, setting, and dimension are all domains relevant to behavioral assessment that can influence measurement scores. In other words, are scores consistent across observers, within all parts of the measure, between different forms of a measure, using different methods, across different settings, and over time? Given that a key tenet of behavioral assessment is that behavior be evaluated in context, the ability to generalize to other contexts becomes an important criterion for evaluating the quality of behavioral assessment strategies.

## TREATMENT VALIDITY/UTILITY

Treatment validity or utility refers to the degree to which assessment data contribute to increased treatment effectiveness or have a positive influence on the treatment (Hayes, Nelson, & Jarrett, 1987; Silva, 1993). Assessment strategies can meet psychometric standards, such as reliability, validity, and accuracy. However, they may not be useful for guiding the therapy process and evaluating treatment outcome. There is a plethora of competing psychosocial interventions currently available, not to mention that numerous treatments are available for the same problem (e.g., depression). Assessments that assist practitioners in case formulation and treatment selection have an obvious advantage. Therefore, if the goal of assessment is to enhance treatment outcomes, the treatment validity/utility of assessment becomes an important qualitative consideration when selecting among assessments.

## INCREMENTAL VALIDITY

In most situations, several assessment strategies are suitable given the purpose of assessment. There is a tendency for assessors to use multiple instruments, methods, and, often, informants (Hunsley, 2003). Simply because a measure is reliable and valid does not mean it is incrementally useful for achieving a particular assessment goal (i.e., treatment planning, predicting behavior, etc.; Haynes & O'Brien, 2002). Therefore, combing multiple sources of information is not justified without evidence of incremental validity (Hunsley, 2003). Incremental validity is defined several ways, and Hunsley (2003) notes, "All definitions have a common emphasis on the extent to which a measure adds to the prediction of a criterion beyond what can be predicted with other data" (p. 443). An assessment instrument or process can have incremental validity if it increases predictive efficiency (Sechrest, 1963), improves predictions as compared to more or less costly sources of information (Elliott, O'Donohue, & Nickerson, 1993), or provides unique data (Haynes & O'Brien, 2000). Also, measures can have negative incremental validity, such that adding and utilizing a particular measure worsen inferences. Thus, when using multiple assessment strategies, incremental validity becomes an important quality indicator.

## OTHER CONSIDERATIONS

A number of other factors may be important when determining the adequacy of an assessment strategy. For instance, when trying to predict or make a decision about a client, the *clinical utility* of assessment should be considered. Clinical utility concerns the degree to which assessment data enhance the validity of clinical judgments (Haynes & O'Brien, 2002). Cost may be another important consideration. *Cost* is traditionally defined in terms of economic issues, but it also includes other resource variables, such as assessor time, client time, and psychological resources needed to engage the process (Yates, 1996). The importance of sensitivity/specificity or false-positive/false-negative rates varies, depending on the goal of assessment. When assessment data are used to make recommendations that may have serious, negative consequences for the client (e.g., involuntary commitment), specificity is important and false-positive rates should be extremely low. Conversely, if the goal is to screen for a particular behavior, with the intent of following up with more detailed assessment (i.e., funneling strategy), sensitivity should be high and false-negative rates should be low. *Sensitivity to change* is the degree to which an assessment measures true changes in target variables over time (Haynes & O'Brien, 2002). Measures that are highly sensitive to change can provide useful information during the intervention process about whether or not the intervention is impacting behavioral targets as intended.

## THE ETHICS OF BEHAVIORAL ASSESSMENT

Behavioral assessment requires some unique extensions and interpretations of the APA Code of Ethics (2002). More specifically, these ethical guidelines, while a helpful starting place, were designed to direct traditional approaches to assessment and frequently do not speak as clearly to behavioral assessment techniques, which frequently rely on multiple sources of data, idiographic data-collection procedures, observation in naturalistic settings, and more active involvement of clients/subjects themselves in collecting data *in vivo*. Unfortunately, although many excellent volumes on behavioral assessment have been written, few have directly addressed the application of ethical principles to behavioral assessment. The following paragraphs will attempt to highlight particular sections of the code of which behavioral scientist-practitioners must be mindful.

In Standard 9.02(b), psychologists are instructed to use instruments with established psychometric properties for the population being tested. While behavior therapists are often able to do so, particularly when survey methods are employed, when more idiographic methods (such as direct observation) are used, it is sometimes impossible to establish reliability and validity prior to collecting data. Consistent with the code, behavior therapists must take care to describe the strengths and limitations of these approaches to any consumers of the assessment results. In particular, oral and written reports generated as products of behavioral assessments should describe threats to reliability, validity, and accuracy (see previous sections) unique to the methods employed. However, reports should also emphasize the inherent benefits of less inferential ways of knowing. Behavioral assessments may, in fact, be perceived as more credible by some audiences. For example, for legal purposes, behavioral methods reporting observable data may generate more clear and understandable estimates of phenomena than those provided by more traditional means.

Because behavioral assessment frequently involves direct observation of a person in his or her context or natural environment, obtaining informed consent also becomes more complex. Standard 9.03 of the Code addresses the issue of informed consent. One specific consideration is that persons other than the identified subject or client may be observed (and even coded) as a by-product of observing the behavior of interest. Informed consent may need to be obtained from these third parties. Not only does this complicate obtaining informed consent, but it may also pose a threat to client confidentiality when the purpose of observation (at least in general terms) needs to be revealed.

An additional ethical consideration in conducting behavioral assessment relates to Standard 9.07, which states that assessment techniques should not be used by unqualified persons. From the behavioral perspective, clients/subjects are generally considered experts in their own behavior and are, therefore, inherently qualified to observe and record data on themselves, though they have, obviously, not been formally trained. Furthermore, students of behavior analysis at various levels of training are often engaged in behavioral observation, while these same students may not be considered competent to conduct clinical interviews or to administer standardized tests. Supervising clinicians must be certain that observers are adequately trained and supervised to complete these tasks in an ethical and professional manner for the purpose of training.

We would urge behavior therapists to establish minimal standards for use of tests in addressing particular questions. It is problematic that there is no separate code of ethics for behavior therapists for this matter. It would also be useful if behavior therapists were to help create useful tools so that others could easily understand the evidence for the validity of inferences to be made from behavioral assessment procedures. Compiling criteria of adequacy and then listing assessment procedures that meet these criteria would be a step in the right direction.

## SUMMARY

In conclusion, as in any type of assessment, behavioral assessment requires diligent attention to ethical principles and guidelines to be conducted competently. Obviously, behavioral practitioners are required to know and adhere to the ethical guidelines provided by the APA. However, they must also remain mindful of the specific applications of the code to behavioral strategies, as discussed earlier. Furthermore, behavioral ethicists should be encouraged to develop specific guidelines for the ethical application of behavioral assessments (as have been written for the use of behavior analytic treatment techniques).

## REFERENCES

American Psychological Association. (1985). *Standard for educational and psychological testing*. Washington, DC: Author.

Baird, S., & Nelson-Gray, R. O. (1999). Direct observation and self-monitoring. In S.C. Hayes, D.H. Barlow & R. O. Nelson-Gray, *The Scientist Practitioner* (2nd ed., pp. 353–386). New York: Allyn & Bacon.

Barrios, B., & Hartmann, D. P. (1986). The contribution of traditional assessment: Concepts, issues, and methodologies. In R. O. Nelson & S. C. Hayes (Eds.), *Conceptual foundations of behavioral assessment* (pp. 81–110). New York: Guilford Press.

Bornstein, P., Hamilton, S., & Bornstein, M. (1986). Self-monitoring procedures. In A. Ciminero, K. Calhoun & W. Adams (Eds.), *Handbook of Behavioral Assessment* (pp. 176–222). New York, NY: John Wiley & Sons.

Chronbach, L. J., Gleser, G. C., Nanda, H., & Rajaratam, N. (1972). *The dependability of behavioral measurements: Theory of generalizability for scores and profiles.* New York: John Wiley and Sons.

Clum, G. A., & Curtin, L. (1993). Validity and reactivity of a system of self-monitoring suicide ideation. *Journal of Psychopathology & Behavioral Assessment 15(4),* 375–385.

Cone, J. D. (1977). The relevance of reliability and validity for behavioral assessment. *Behavior Therapy, 8,* 411–426.

Cone, J. D. (1998). Psychometric considerations: Concepts, contents, and methods. In A. S. Bellack & M. Herson (Eds.), *Behavioral assessment: A practical handbook* (4th ed., pp. 22–46). Boston: Allyn & Bacon.

Elliott, A. N., O'Donohue, W. T., & Nickerson, M. A. (1993). Incremental validity: A recommendation. *Clinical Psychology Review, 13,* 207–221.

Farmer, R., & Nelson-Gray, R. O. (1990). Personality disorders and depression: Theoretical issues, empirical findings, and methodological considerations. *Clinical Psychology Review 10,* 453–576.

Garb, H. N., Wood, J. M., & Lilienfeld, S. O. (2002). Effective use of projective techniques in clinical practice: Let the data help with selection and interpretaion. *Professional Psychology: Research and practice 33(5),* 454–463.

Goldfried, M. R., & Kent, R. N. (1972). Traditional versus behavioral personality assessment: A comparison of methodological and theoretical assumptions. *Psychological Bulletin, 77(6),* 409–420.

Goldfreid, M. R., & Kent, R. N. (1977). Traditional versus behavioral personality assessment: A comparison of methodological and theoretical assumptions. *Psychological Bulletin, 77,* 409–420.

Hayes, S. C., Nelson, R. O., & Jarrett, R. B. (1987). The treatment utility of assessment: A functional approach to evaluating assessment quality. *American Psychologist, 42,* 963–974.

Haynes, S. N., & O'Brien, W. H. (2002). *Principles and practice of behavioral assessment.* New York: Kluwer Academic.

Hergenhahn, B. R. (2001). *An introduction to the history of psychology.* Belmont, CA: Wadsworth/Thomson Learning.

Hunsley, J. (2002). Psychological assessment and psychological testing: A closer examination. *American Psychologist, 57,* 139–140.

Hunsley, J. (2003). Introduction to the special section on incremental validity and utility in clinical assessment. *Psychological Assessment, 15,* 443–445.

Johnston, J. M., & Pennypacker, H. S. (1993). *Strategies and tactics of human behavioral research* (2nd ed.). Hillsdale, NJ: Erlbaum.

Nelson-Gray, R. O. (2003). Treatment utility of psychological assessment. *Psychological Assessment, 15,* 521–531.

Nelson-Gray, R. O., Herbert, D. L., Herbert, J. D., Farmer, R., Badawi, I., & Lin, K. (1990). Estimation vs. counting in behavioral assessment. *Behavioral Assessment 12,* 157–178.

Nunnally, J. C., & Bernstein, I. H. (1994). *Psychometric theory.* New York: McGraw-Hill.

Sechrest, L. (1963). Incremental validity: A recommendation. *Educational & Psychological Measurement, 23,* 153–158.

Silva, F. (1993). *Psychometric foundations and behavioral assessment.* Newbury Park, CA: Sage Publications.

Ullman, L. P., & Kasner, L. (1969). *A psychological approach to abnormal behavior.* Oxford, England: Prentice Hall.

Yates, B. T. (1996). Analyzing costs, procedures, processes, and outcomes in human services. *Applied Social Research Method Series* (Vol. 42).

# 2

# PSYCHOMETRIC CONSIDERATIONS

STEPHEN N. HAYNES

*Department of Psychology*
*University of Hawaii at Manoa*
*Honolulu, Hawaii*

## INTRODUCTION

### THE FUNDAMENTAL ROLE OF MEASUREMENT IN CLINICAL SCIENCE

Measurement is the foundation of clinical science. Measurement is necessary for us to understand individual differences, such as why some persons and not others become depressed following divorce, enjoy high levels of life satisfaction even when experiencing chronic pain, and start using drugs at an early age.

Measurement also underlies our ability to understand variance over time and situations. Measurement is necessary for us to understand why a child is disobedient with one parent and not another, why a person has panic episodes on some days and not others, and why depressive episodes of a client can vary in intensity and duration. Measurement is also necessary for us to identify variables that moderate and mediate behavior problems and life satisfaction and to develop effective interventions to reduce behavior problems and promote life satisfaction.

Given the pivotal role of measurement, it is essential that measures we use in research and clinical practice be the best available. Without quality data on the variables of interest—measures that are valid, accurate, relevant, and comprehensive—we cannot develop and test explanatory models for or effective strategies for intervening with behavior disorders and enhancing quality of life.

Psychometry provides the methodological and conceptual bases for evaluating quality of data from our measurement procedures. Psychometry assists us in selecting the best assessment instruments and in evaluating data derived from them.

## INFORMATION SOURCES

Psychometric concepts, definitions, and methods that are most important vary across disciplines and across scholars within disciplines. This chapter reviews psychometric concepts that are relevant to one application of clinical science—behavioral assessment. In preparing the chapter, I assumed that readers have been exposed to the basic concepts and methods of psychometry, such as reliability and validity, test construction methods, and the principles and methods of behavioral assessment. Overviews of psychometric concepts can be found in Nunnally and Bernstein (1994) and Anastasi and Urbina (1997). Behavioral assessment concepts and methods are discussed in Hersen (2004) and books by Haynes and O'Brien (2000), Haynes and Heiby (2004), Bellack and Hersen (1998), and Shapiro and Kratochwill (2000).

The psychometric foundations of behavioral assessment encompass a more diverse content than can be addressed in this chapter. Other aspects of psychometry in behavioral assessment have been discussed in Cone (1998), Haynes, Nelson, and Blaine (1999), Haynes and O'Brien (2000, Ch. 10), Haynes and Waialae (1994), Strube (1990), and Suen and Rzasa (2004). Books by Silva (1993) and Suen and Ary (1989) are particularly scholarly discussions of reliability, accuracy, and validity applied to behavioral observation. Definitions of psychometric terms also vary across users, and Table 2.1 presents definitions of some frequently used psychometric terms, many of which appear in this chapter.

## CONDITIONAL RELEVANCE OF PSYCHOMETRIC
## CONCEPTS AND CHAPTER FOCUS

The relevance of psychometric principles for evaluating the quality of obtained measures varies as a function of the assumptions and methods associated with the psychological assessment system within which they are applied. For example, some psychometric principles, such as stability over time, that are relevant to the evaluation of measures of personality traits are less relevant to the evaluation of a behavioral observation measure. An indication of temporal instability over a 2-week period indicates measurement error when the target is a presumably stable variable, such as "neuroticism," but instability does not necessarily (but could) indicate measurement error with a target, such as "rate of self-injurious behavior," that would be expected to vary across time.

This chapter addresses a subset of psychometric principles, concepts, issues, and methods that are relevant to behavioral assessment. I discuss the evolving concepts of validity, generalizability, temporal stability, content validity, the conditional and dynamic nature of validity, applications in individualized assessment, and sources of error. To provide a context for the discussion of psychometric principles in behavioral assessment, the chapter briefly describes the assessment methods and outcome with one family.

TABLE 2.1 Psychometric Concepts

---

**Generalizability:** The degree to which measures from an assessment instrument can be assumed to be indicative of (correlate with) measures obtained (a) from other samples, (b) in other situations, (c) at other times, (d) from other assessment instruments, (e) of other behaviors, or (f) in other situations or contexts.

**Reliability**

**reliability:** The part of a measure that is due to systematic effects and therefore persists across persons or time under constant measurement conditions.

**homogeneity:** The conceptual similarity of a set of assessment instrument elements, such as questionnaire items or behavior codes.

**internal consistency:** The degree of consistency among elements within an assessment instrument.

**interobserver (interrater) agreement:** The degree of similarity between scores (or ratings, diagnoses, behavior rates) obtained from different assessors evaluating the same events, often at the same time.

**temporal stability (test–retest reliability):** The stability of obtained scores over time.

**Validity**

**validity:** The degree to which a measure reflects what it is supposed to. Often is used to mean "construct validity."

**accuracy:** The extent to which obtained measures approximate the "true" state of a phenomenon.

**agreement:** The degree of correspondence between the output of two or more assessment instruments; the degree of overlap between two more independently obtained measures.

**concurrent:** Any index of validity obtained when different measures of the same construct are administered on the same assessment occasion.

**construct:** Comprises the evidence and rationales supporting the trustworthiness of assessment instrument measures and inferences, in terms of explanatory concepts that account for both the obtained data and relations with other variables.

**content:** The degree to which elements of an assessment instrument are relevant to and representative of the targeted construct, for a particular assessment purpose. The *relevance* of an assessment instrument is the degree to which its elements are appropriate for measuring the targeted construct, for a given assessment purpose. The *representativeness* of an assessment instrument is the degree to which its elements proportionately sample the facets of the targeted construct. It is important to specify the construct that the instrument is intended to tap and to match the content of the instrument to that construct.

**convergent:** The degree to which data from an assessment instrument are coherently related to other measures of the same or similar constructs; the magnitude of covariance among scores from two assessment instruments that measure the same or similar constructs.

**criterion-referenced (criterion-related validity; criterion validity):** The degree to which measures from an assessment instrument correlate with scores from previously validated instruments that measure the construct of interest or with a criterion of practical value.

**discriminant (divergent):** The degree to which measures from an assessment instrument are distinct from measures of dissimilar constructs.

**discriminative:** The degree to which measures from an assessment instrument can differentiate individuals in groups, formed from independent criteria, known to vary on the measured construct.

**incremental:** The incremental value of acquired data; the degree to which additional assessment data increase the power, sensitivity, specificity, and predictive efficacy of judgments.

**postdictive:** The degree to which scores from an assessment instrument correlate with scores from another, validated assessment administered at a previous point in time.

---

*(continues)*

TABLE 2.1   (*continued*)

**predictive:** The degree to which measures from an assessment instrument correlate with measures from another, validated assessment administered at a later point in time; the time frame of measurement is less important than the criterion in determining if validation is predictive.

**treatment:** The degree to which data from an assessment instrument contributes to enhanced treatment outcome.

**Power and Sensitivity**

**power (of a measure):** The predictive accuracy of a measure from an assessment instrument; the overall proportion of persons accurately classified on the basis of obtained measures.

**positive predictive power:** The proportion of individuals identified by a measure as having a disorder or displaying a behavior who truly have the disorder or display the behavior.

**negative predictive power:** The proportion of individuals identified by a measure as not having a disorder or displaying a behavior who truly do not.

**sensitivity:** The probability that a person with a particular attribute will be so identified by a particular measure.

**sensitivity to change:** The degree to which measures reflect true changes in (the dynamic aspects of) the targeted variable.

**specificity:** The probability that a person without a particular attribute will be so identified by a particular measure.

Adapted from Haynes and O'Brien (2000).

## THE NATURE OF PSYCHOMETRY AND VALIDITY

Psychometry is the evaluative processes applied to psychological assessment data (Rust & Golombok, 1989). Psychometric indices, such as reliability and validity coefficients, provide information about the quality of data. Psychometry was developed from early efforts to measure presumably stable intellectual and personality traits, such as "intelligence" and "neuroticism," and educational abilities, such as mathematics comprehension and reading ability (see historical discussions in Bechtold, 1959).

In these early applications, dimensions of psychometric evaluation, such as reliability and validity, were invoked to estimate the degree to which the outcomes from an assessment instrument reflected variance in the targeted construct—e.g., the degree to which a test of reading ability truly reflected a person's reading ability. Psychometric investigations also helped to identify sources of error in the obtained measures. The evaluative dimensions of psychometry have guided the development, refinement, selection, application, and interpretation of thousands of psychological assessment instruments (see overviews of traditional applications of psychometry in the four-volume *Handbook of Psychological Assessment*; Hersen, 2004).

The commonly accepted definition of *validity* has evolved to incorporate a wider range of evidence and broader foci. For example, in educational assessment, many scholars and teachers became concerned that some assessment results were being used to place a disproportionate number of children from socially disadvantaged backgrounds and children with disabilities in less effective educational settings. As a result, *validity* began to include not only the degree to which a measure reflected the attribute being measured, but also the social consequences of measures, the judgments and decisions that were based on them. Also, the concept of *construct validity* was broadened to include a wide array of data on the degree to which a measure was related or not to other theoretically associated measures (see discussions by Messick, 1994, 1998).

Acknowledging the ethical, social, and political importance of judgments based on assessment data, I agree with recent proposals by Borsboom, Mellenbergh, and van Heerden (2004) for a more restrictive use of the term *validity*. How measures are used, the decisions and judgments based on measures, and their social implications are important concerns. But these concerns are independent of the validity of the measure on which they are based. Bad decisions can be based on valid data.

Evidence of the degree of covariance between measures of related constructs (e.g., covariance between measures of marital satisfaction and interpersonal problem-solving skills) are also useful but are only indirect measures of the validity of a measure. A measure of depression may not be optimally valid, because it contains irrelevant items, yet still significantly discriminate between persons who are and who are not seeking treatment for depression.

Thus, the quality of data, which is the focus of psychometry, depends on many factors. It depends on the methods and instruments used in the assessment, the strategy of assessment, and the precision and validity of the data from the instruments. In this chapter, the concept of *validity* is used more restrictively: *The validity of a measure is the degree to which changes on a dimension of an attribute produce changes in a measure of that attribute dimension* (e.g., Boorsboom et al., 2004).[1]

This seemingly straightforward definition presents challenges in clinical assessment. How do you know, for example, that a change in a teacher's report on the rate of self-injurious behaviors of a child has been produced by changes in the rate of self-injurious behaviors of the child? In the absence of a true criterion, we rely on *multivariate convergent validation*—we can never preclude sources of error in our measures. It is possible that changes in the reported rate of self-injurious behaviors reflect changes in the amount of time the teacher watched the child or reflect changes in what behaviors the teacher considered "self-injurious." We are confident in the validity of a measure to the degree that it covaries with other measures of the same phenomenon. A converging report from another observer (*interobserver agreement*) reduces the chance that

---

[1] I have devoted only a few sentences to a complex issue. Borsboom et al. discuss the definition of validity in logical positivist, realist, postmodernist, constructivist, metaphysical, empiricist, and ontological contexts.

measured changes reflected inattention or changes in the definition of the target behavior.

In psychological assessment we expand our domain of interest in validation to include the validity of inferences and judgments based on measures. For example, assume that we have a perfectly valid measure of how a parent responds when a child disobeys his or her request in a clinic play situation (e.g., the *conditional probabilities* of a positive or negative response by the parent when the child refuses a request)—changes in the parent's responses in that situation and differences between parents in their responses are perfectly reflected in our observation measures. However, in many such cases, our main interest is in inferring how the parent responds to the child's disobedient behavior at home. We use the clinic-based measure to estimate (i.e., use as a *marker* of) those functional relations.

Validity for this clinic-based measure now has two domains—the degree to which measures reflect behavior in the clinic and the degree to which measures reflect behavior in the home. How valid are our inferences and clinical judgments, based on clinic observations, about the response of the parent to the child's disobedience at home? *A measure may be valid in one domain and not in others.* As discussed later, psychometric processes are also relevant for validation of and identifying sources of error in the inferences and judgments from measures.

## A BRIEF CASE STUDY TO INTRODUCE THE APPLICABILITY OF PSYCHOMETRIC PRINCIPLES IN BEHAVIORAL ASSESSMENT

The assessment case described here provides a context for subsequent discussions of the relevance of psychometric principles and methods.

### REFERRAL PROBLEM AND METHODS

Mr. and Mrs. Jordan sought help from an outpatient mental health center for their 8-year-old son, Jeffrey, who had been increasingly oppositional and aggressive at home and school—he was disobedient and sassy to his parents and frequently pushing and hitting other children. The assessment team used *multiple methods* and *multiple sources* to specify Jeffrey's behavior problems and to identify factors that might be maintaining those problems. (An overview of family assessment methods and guiding concepts can be found in Dishion & Granic, 2004.)

The assessors first interviewed both parents, surveying their concerns about his behavior, their family interactions associated with his tantrums and aggressive behaviors, Jeffrey's positive attributes, and their goals in coming to the center. They followed with a more focused interview about the contexts, antecedent conditions and stimuli, and specific consequences of the tantrums and aggressive behaviors. Additionally, the assessors interviewed the parents about their marital and other family relationships and parenting strategies. Each parent also independently completed a behavior problem checklist on Jeffrey and his younger sister, Kara, and questionnaires on family and marital interactions.

At a follow-up visit in the clinic the assessors made formal and informal behavioral observations. They observed interactions between the parents and their son in several structured situations: They asked them to play a game together, to work together on a school assignment, and then asked the parents to have Jeffrey put the toys back on the shelves himself and sit quietly while the parents read. The assessors interviewed Jeffrey's teacher, who also completed a behavior problem checklist, and they administered an intelligence test to Jeffrey. They also observed Jeffrey during recess—a time often associated with aggressive behaviors. Based on information gained at that point, the teacher and the mother were asked to track instances of oppositional/defiant and aggressive behaviors for five days (i.e., *natural observation*).

## BEHAVIORAL CASE FORMULATION: SUMMARY

Guided by quantitative and qualitative information from these assessment methods, the assessors hypothesized that Jeffrey was frequently oppositional, defiant toward his parents and teachers and aggressive in the home and at school toward his sister and peers (i.e., hypothesized about the *conditional nature of his behavior problems*). They described the form of these behaviors and estimated their frequency (e.g., oppositional and defiant behavior were characterized by yelling insults, refusal to comply to requests and occurred two to five times per day) and the situations in which they were most likely to occur (e.g., requests that Jeffrey cease an activity he was enjoying and to do something else). The assessors also noted the escape and avoidance functions of his tantrums and that positive and negative contingencies were applied inconsistently by the parents and teacher to oppositional or aggressive behaviors. The parents had learned to avoid challenging or redirecting his activities because of his aversive responses.

Jeffrey had an above-average IQ (full-scale 110 on a WISC) but was performing below average on most academic tasks in the classroom. In the classroom he was frequently inattentive to work and was verbally disruptive. He had few friends at school or at home and appeared not to initiate social contacts with other children, other than through physical aggression or shouted commands. He enjoyed computer games, TV cartoons, and sports activities with his dad.

Data from interviews and questionnaires also identified marital distress and conflicts between Mr. and Mrs. Jordan, centering on parenting strategies, finances, and lack of shared activities. During an analogue problem-solving task, the assessors observed communication deficiencies that were likely interfering with effective parenting (see discussion of empirically supported couple assessment in Snyder, Heyman, & Haynes, in press). It was also discovered during the interview that Mrs. Jordan had a history of severe mood fluctuations. Her elevated moods were often accompanied by increased sleeplessness, excessive spending, more time away from home, and difficulties at her job as an accountant. There was also a low rate of positive interactions between Jeffrey and his parents (other than the narrow band of activities with his dad previously described). The presence in class of three other children with significant behavior problems and the class size (20 students) presented additional challenges to the teacher (a focus on systems issues).

## BEHAVIORAL CASE FORMULATION: THE FUNCTIONAL ANALYSIS

There are many applications of behavioral assessment, such as treatment outcome evaluation and basic research in psychopathology, but in this case the goal of assessment was to develop a clinical case formulation in order to plan the best treatment strategy for Jeffrey and his family. The summary of inferences from these data, supplemented by findings from the empirical literature on the behavior problems identified in the assessment, forms the clinical case formulation. There are several models of behavioral case formulation (see Nezu, Nezu, Peacock, & Girdwood, 2004), but here we focus on the *functional analysis*—the identification of important, modifiable causal variables associated with a behavior problem (e.g., Haynes & O'Brien, 2000; Haynes & Williams, 2003).

Figure 2.1 illustrates a functional analysis of Jeffrey (a functional analytic clinical case model; FACCM[2]). Note that the FACCM illustrates 11 variables that are important for case formulation and treatment design: the identification of multiple behavior problems, the estimated importance of and functional relations[3] between behavior problems, sequelae of behavior problems, causal and noncausal functional relations applicable to those behavior problems, the estimated strength of functional relations, and the estimated modifiability of and relations between the causal variables. These case formulation variables help estimate the magnitude of effects of an intervention that successfully modifies the various hypothesized causal variables.[4]

---

[2] A functional analysis is one form of behavioral clinical case formulation. Overviews of clinical case formulation models in behavioral assessment and therapy can be found in Haynes and O'Brien (2000) and Nezu et al. (2004). An expanded discussion of the functional analysis as a model for clinical case formulation can be found in Haynes and O'Brien (2000), Haynes and Williams (2003).

[3] A *functional relation* is a mathematically describable relationship (e.g., correlation, conditional probability) among two or more variables.

[4] The magnitudes of effect associated with the modification of a causal variable in an FACCM can be estimated arithmetically using path analyses, as discussed in Haynes (1994) and Haynes, Richard, and O' Brien (1996).

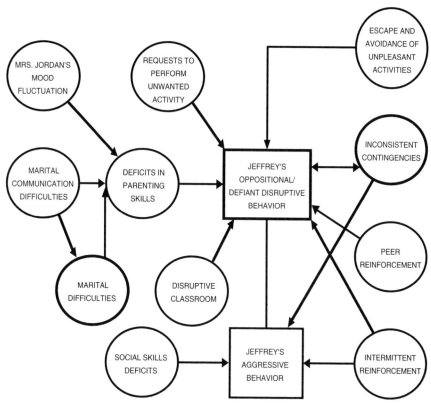

FIGURE 2.1    A functional analytic clinical case model (FACCM) of Jeffrey's family. Squares indicate behavior problems and circles represent causal variables. Arrows indicate the direction of causal relationships. Elaborated FACCMs depict the strengths of relationships, the modifiability of causal variables, and the importance of behavior problems; these are described in Haynes and O'Brien (2000). FACCMs summarize clinical judgments, based primarily on inferences from data collected in the assessment, augmented by research findings on relevant topics.

The goal of this case description is to illustrate the broad applicability of psychometric principles: All facets of the assessment and the judgments based on it are subject to evaluation. Psychometry addresses questions such as these: How confident can we be that the assessors used the best assessment methods and instruments and used the best sources for information? Did the assessors correctly identify and estimate the frequency and intensity of his behavior problems, identify the most important maintaining variables for Jeff's behavior problems, and correctly estimate the degree to which each of the causal variables affected the behavior problems? These are questions about behavioral assessment that can be addressed empirically, and psychometry is the empirical science of psychological assessment.

## APPLICABILITY AND UTILITY OF PSYCHOMETRIC PRINCIPLES IN BEHAVIORAL ASSESSMENT

As noted earlier in this chapter, psychometry is the evaluative process applied to all facets of psychological assessment. Psychometric principles guide the evaluation of published data on the validity and reliability of measures, the selection of the best assessment methods and instruments for a particular assessment occasion, the evaluation of the validity of data obtained during assessment, the comprehensiveness and temporal relevance of our assessment strategy, the identification and reduction of error in our assessments, the validity of clinical judgments based on assessment data, and the cost-benefits of an assessment strategy. The following sections discuss psychometric principles and methods in the context of its many applications in behavioral assessment.

### SELECTING ASSESSMENT METHODS AND INSTRUMENTS

Psychometric principles guide the evaluation of published data about measures derived from assessment methods and instruments.[5] The family assessment just described is most likely to provide valid and useful information to the degree that the questionnaires, interviews, and observation instruments used had been shown in previous research to provide data that were valid and relevant for families who resemble this one.

An important issue in selecting assessment instruments is the degree to which the results of prior research are relevant to a specific assessment occasion. In the case presented earlier, we are interested in the degree to which data on the quality of potentially useful assessment instruments (remember, the psychometric data pertain only to *measures* from an instrument, not the instrument itself) are relevant to this child, family, and school. The relevance of prior psychometric data depends on how closely the facets of the assessment—the subject characteristics, assessment contexts, functions of assessment, and assessment strategies—in prior psychometric research match those of this assessment occasion.[6]

---

[5] An *assessment instrument* refers to a specific procedure for deriving data on the behavior of a person or persons on a specific assessment occasion (e.g., a specific self-report depression questionnaire, a specific marital interacting observation and coding system).

An *assessment method* refers to a class of procedures for deriving data on the behavior or a person or persons (e.g., self-report questionnaires, behavioral observations in the natural environment, interviews).

An *assessment strategy* refers to the overall plan of action for deriving assessment data. It can include a particular set of assessment instruments and methods, instructions to the client, assessment settings, time-sampling parameters, and the place where measurement occurs (Haynes & O'Brien, 2000).

[6] de Gruijter and van der Kamp (1991) discuss applications of generalizability theory to assessment.

For this family assessment case, we would be interested in the degree to which the empirical literature supported the validity of the parent and teacher report measures when used for aggressive behaviors, for children of this age, sex, and ethnicity, and for behavior problems at this level of severity.

Often, an assessor can select from an array of potential instruments. The differential relevance of prior psychometric research on multiple measures is often difficult to ascertain because of the many facets within which relevance can be estimated. Prior research may support the use of a measure for a person of this age and sex, but another measure may have more support for a measure for a person exhibiting a particular level of problem severity. *Ultimately, the assessor must select that measure for which psychometric data are most strongly supportive for the most important facets of the assessment occasion.*

The same considerations apply when we draw conclusions from published research. For example, confidence in the conclusions from a published study (confidence in the generalizability of the findings) about the effectiveness of an enhancement program for distressed couples or about sources of distress for those couples depends on the degree to which the measures on which those inferences are based were appropriate (i.e., valid and relevant) for the assessment context. Often, researchers offer conclusions based on data from measures of undemonstrated validity.

The importance of psychometric data that are specifically relevant to an assessment occasion calls attention to the *conditional nature of validity*, discussed in greater detail in a subsequent section of this chapter. A principle repeatedly emphasized in this chapter is that validity is not an unconditional trait of a measure: *The validity of a measure can vary across target behaviors, time, subjects, assessment conditions, assessors, and the goals of assessment.*

## EVALUATING AND STRENGTHENING THE VALIDITY OF DATA OBTAINED DURING PSYCHOLOGICAL ASSESSMENT

Psychometric principles help us to evaluate and strengthen the validity of the measures we obtain from our clinical or research assessments. In order to establish confidence in the elements of the case formulation, as illustrated in Figure 2.1, we must estimate and strengthen, for example, the validity of our estimates of the rate of Jeffrey's defiant or aggressive behaviors and the source of marital distress for Mr. and Mrs. Jordan.

Unlike some other disciplines, in the behavioral sciences there are no "true" criteria against which to judge the validity of our measures and inferences. For many measures, especially *fundamental units*, in the physical sciences, there are standards against which an obtained measure can be compared. Thus, the absolute measure of a meter has been designated to be the distance light travels in a vacuum in 0.0000003 seconds. A second (as a unit of time) has been designated to be the time it takes for 9,192,631,770 cycles of resonance vibration of the cesium-133 atom (Darton & Clark, 1994). These are absolute criteria against which measures from other rulers and clocks can be compared.

There are no absolute standards to evaluate measures of depression, aggression, self-injury, or other variables and constructs in the behavioral sciences. Given the lack of absolute criteria, and invoking the definition of validity from page 19, how can we estimate the degree to which changes in our measure of Jeffrey's aggressive behavior are a function of true changes in Jeffrey's aggressive behavior? Our measures could also reflect error in the assessment instrument, such as observer bias or unsystematic error.

### Convergent Validation

We often estimate the validity of behavioral assessment data through *convergent validation*—we examine the degree of covariance between different measures of the same phenomenon. For example, we are confident in the validity of a questionnaire measure of how Jeffrey's parents respond to his problem behaviors to the degree that the data from this questionnaire converge with data on the same behavior from other measures, such as analogue observations, daily monitoring, and interviews.

Examining converging evidence from multiple sources recalls the multitrait-multimethod strategies of construct validation presented by Campbell and Fisk in 1959. Burns & Haynes (in press), reviewed several applications of multimethod and multitrait concepts and strategies.

Reliance on convergent validation in psychological assessment reemphasizes the importance of selecting the best instruments at the beginning of the assessment process. It is easier to estimate the validity of assessment data when the estimate is based on magnitudes of covariance with other measures that have received substantial and relevant psychometric support.

Magnitudes of covariances between measures can be difficult to interpret because many aspects of the evaluation can affect them. For example, data on Jeffrey's rate of aggressive behavior from two sources—parent daily monitoring and external observers in the home—can be highly correlated, and both can be valid in terms of the definition of validity offered earlier—both measures can change as a function of changes in the targeted behavior. However, there can be low agreement between these two measures even though they are highly correlated (remember that correlation is an index only of the linear relation between two variables). In this context, which source provides an accurate measure of the rate of Jeffrey's aggressive behavior in the home? Additional convergent validation measurements would be necessary to estimate the relative accuracy of these two measures.

I use *convergent validation* in a restrictive sense. For example, it is not unusual to draw validity inferences from the degree of covariation between a measures and "theoretically related phenomena." For example, the degree to which an analogue observational measure of critical comments among family members is correlated with self-reported emotional responses is interesting. But it does not directly address the degree to which critical comments were validly measured.

## Conditional Nature of Validity Inferences

As discussed in an article on psychometric foundations of analogue observation (Haynes, 2001), *accuracy* (in this case referring to the *generalizability* of clinic data to the home; de Gruijter & van der Kamp, 1991) is not always important. For example, if data from clinic-based analogue observation is highly correlated with, but does not accurately reflect, the rates of Jeffrey's aggressive behavior in the home, data from analogue observations can still be used to measure the degree of change in aggressive behavior at home. In this example the goal of the assessment is to measure *change in the rate* (or some other dimension such as duration), not *the rate of* occurrence. This is another example of the conditional relevance of psychometric dimensions—accuracy is more important for some assessment goals than for others.

In another aspect of the conditional nature of validity inferences, an assessment instrument, such as analogue observation, may not provide an accurate measure of the rate of a behavior but may provide an accurate estimate of functional relations. Thus, we may not be able to accurately estimate Jeffrey's rate of oppositional behavior in the home but could accurately estimate the probability that Jeffrey's oppositional behavior will be followed by a positive parental response in the home.

## Reliability Evaluation—Generalizability and the Strengthening of Validity Inferences

Many potential sources of error variance can be examined through *generalizability* evaluations. For example, we may be interested in estimating the degree to which observation data can be generalized across observers. In this case, we examine the agreement between observers (i.e., *interobserver agreement*). We may also be interested in estimating the degree to which data from an interview can be generalized across interviewers (*interinterviewer agreement*) or data from a questionnaire can be generalized across time (*temporal stability*).

These evaluations are often considered *reliability evaluations*, or an examination of *score precision*. Regardless of labels, they have the same goal—to help estimate the maximum proportion of variance in a measure that can be attributable to true changes in the targeted variable. For a variable that is presumed to be stable across the test–retest interval, temporal stability coefficients set the upper limits of validity. A test–retest reliability coefficient of .7 suggests that at least 51% of the variance in the targeted variable reflects error. Low rates of agreement between observers suggest that we cannot have confidence in the validity of measures obtained from an observer because a high proportion of variance is associated with observers rather than with the behavior being observed.

We are again exposed to the conditional relevance of psychometric principles. *Temporal stability*, for example, is a useful indicator of error when stability across time is expected. Temporal stability of observation data can suggest the degree to which data from one observation session can be expected to be generalizable to other sessions (given constant conditions). However, in this case temporal stability indices cannot be used to indicate the precision of the data. Low test–retest coefficients can reflect error in the observation system, or they can reflect true changes in the behaviors observed. These two sources of variance can only be differentiated with multivariate convergent validation. For example, if several observation measures at two observation sessions indicate similar changes, we can be more confident that variance in measures reflects true changes in the targeted behaviors.

## EVALUATING THE CONTENT VALIDITY OF ASSESSMENT FOCI AND CASE FORMULATIONS

Psychometric principles also help us evaluate the comprehensiveness of our assessment strategy and the validity of our case formulations. One unique application of pretreatment behavioral assessment is the construction of a clinical case formulation, as illustrated in Figure 2.1. Although we may have validly measured variables and functional relations targeted in our assessment, did we attempt to measure all important variables and functional relations? Note that in our case study we did not examine family nutrition, parents' substance use, or life stressors experienced by the parents. What if Mr. and Mrs. Jordan's ability to monitor Jeffrey was severely impaired during periods of alcohol use and we failed to identify that important functional relation?

Application of psychometry to clinical judgments is congruent with the definition of validity offered earlier. The functional analysis should reflect (i.e., be produced by) the client's behaviors and causal variables affecting those behaviors. Our functional analysis is valid to the extent that it includes all important variables, excludes irrelevant variables, and accurately estimates the importance, modifiability, and strength of relations between variables.

Congruent with psychometric methods applied to individual measures, we can estimate the validity of a functional analysis through two methods. First, we can use *multivariate convergent validation* methods, as described before. We are confident in the validity of our functional analysis to the degree that its elements are supported through measures from multiple methods, instruments, and sources.

Second, we can estimate validity of a functional analysis through manipulation of the hypothesized causal variables and observing the effects on behavior problems. If our functional analysis indicates that inconsistent parental contingencies is one causal factor for Jeffrey's oppositional behavior and increased consistency of parental contingencies is not followed by decreases in the rate of oppositional behavior within an expected time frame, our functional analysis is invalid (presuming other causal factors are constant).

In the case of a failure to validate through manipulation, it is difficult to know which aspect of the functional analysis is invalid. In our example, our hypothesis about the role of parental inconsistent contingencies may be valid, but perhaps we missed the operation of an important moderator variable (e.g., the medication state of Jeffrey or the behavior of peers).

Comprehensiveness and relevance of our clinical assessment strategy and resulting functional analysis indicate their *content validity*—the degree to which the targets of assessment are appropriately relevant and representative for the arrays of a client's behavior problems and their maintaining variables.

In reference to our original definition of validity, a case formulation is valid to the degree that the characteristics of behavior problems (importance, dimensions), the functional relations between behavior problems, the causal variables affecting those problems, and the strength and direction of causal relations for a person are accurately estimated. Our measures can be valid, yet the case formulation can be invalid if it fails to include important variables or includes unimportant variables.

## EVALUATING AND SELECTING TIME-SAMPLING STRATEGIES

Many of the variables and functional relations measured in behavioral assessment are dynamic (implications of the dynamic aspects of phenomena were discussed by Hume in 1748). Unstable variables are exemplified by changes across time in the rate with which spouses criticize or express appreciation to each other, a client's mood level, the likelihood that a client will purge following a meal, and sleep onset latencies. These variables can change, in systematic and unsystematic ways, rapidly or slowly, and to different degrees, over time.

Causal variables, causal relations for behavior problems, and treatment goals can also change over time (see an extended discussion of the dynamic nature of causal models and assessment implications in Haynes, 1992). The factors that trigger or maintain a client's alcohol intake, a child's inattention to academic material in the classroom, conflicts within a relationship, and opposition of an adolescent to parental requests can change across time.

In addition to reducing the value of temporal stability estimates of reliability, the dynamic nature of many variables places burdens on the timing of measurements and how assessment instruments are constructed. Timing of measurements and how instruments are constructed to capture dynamic characteristics of variables depend on the goals of the assessment and the inferences to be drawn. For example, we may be interested in long-term, broadband changes in behavior, such as year-to-year changes in cognitive abilities following head trauma. With this assessment goal, aggregate measures (e.g., aggregating several "speed of processing" measures) that are acquired infrequently provide satisfactory measures and more frequent monitoring of more specific abilities may not be cost beneficial. In other assessment contexts, we may be more interested in the measurement of changes in a narrower range of variables across shorter time periods. With these assessment goals, we can use more specific measures (e.g., measures of mood fluctuations associated with blood-glucose changes) acquired multiple times per day.

In the measurement of dynamic variables, an important psychometric evaluative dimension is *sensitivity to change.* This evaluative dimension has two components—the degree to which true change in a variable or functional relation is captured by a measure and the latency between change in the variable and change in the measure.

Sensitivity to change is affected by characteristics of the assessment instrument, the assessment method (such as analogue observation vs. self-report questionnaire), and the temporal parameters of the assessment strategy (e.g., how often and on what time schedule an instrument is administered). For example, external observers may detect small changes in the rate of classroom-disruptive behavior across minutes, while a teacher's report of the same behavior may not reflect such small changes and may not reflect changes immediately. Conversely, data from the teacher can more rapidly reflect behavior changes that occur when observers are not present.

In the first case, data from the observations would be more sensitive to change in behavior than would data from the teacher's report. Measures from the teacher report might be less sensitive to change because they reflect both relevant and irrelevant sources of variance. The teacher's report of the rate of classroom-disruptive behavior could be affected by the teacher's memory of the child's behavior on previous days, inattention to the target child due to distractions in the classroom, and changes in the mood of the teacher across time. Sensitivity to change of a measure is inversely related to the proportion of variance in a measure that is associated with irrelevant sources.

## IDENTIFYING, MEASURING, PREVENTING, AND CONTROLLING FOR SOURCES OF ERROR IN BEHAVIORAL ASSESSMENT

Psychometric principles help us to identify, measure, prevent, and control for sources of error in our assessment data. Data from our family assessment would reflect errors to the degree that the interviewer asked questions in a leading fashion, that the parents behaved differently toward Jeffrey because they were being observed, and that the marital satisfaction questionnaire failed to tap important facets of relationship functioning from the culture within which this family operated (the Jordan's had recently immigrated to the United States from Eastern Europe). These potential sources of error could result in *biased assessment results*—systematic error in the data, which, in turn, could lead to biased case formulations and intervention foci.

Prior psychometric research on assessment methods and instruments helps identify potential sources of measurement error. There is substantial empirical literature on sources of error in various assessment methods, such as the reactive effects of assessment (particularly self-monitoring and observation), biased memory in retrospective self-report, instrumentation errors in psychophysiological assessment, and inclusion of irrelevant items during questionnaire construction (see, for example, the four-volume series on behavioral, projective, personality, and neuropsychological assessment by Hersen, 2004).

This literature can guide assessment strategies to reduce the impact of error. We know, for example, that reactive effects of observation are more pronounced in earlier than later observation sessions and that interobserver agreement (an indirect measure of observer precision or accuracy) tends to remain higher when observers believe that their agreement will be periodically checked (see reviews of multiple sources of error in Haynes, 1978; Shapiro & Kratochwill, 2000).

Psychometric principles suggest which evaluative procedures are helpful in detecting and reducing error. We examine agreement between diagnosticians and interviewers, agreement between observers, temporal stability (test–retest reliability), and agreement across methods (convergent validation); and we calibrate psychophysiological instruments (criterion-related validity assessment). All are designed to estimate and reduce the degree to which obtained data reflect specific sources of error variance and, hopefully, convince those who will use the data of their validity.

### ESTIMATING THE COST-BENEFITS AND INCREMENTAL VALIDITY AND UTILITY OF ASSESSMENT STRATEGIES, ASSESSMENT INSTRUMENTS, AND MEASURES

Validity is an essential but insufficient indication of the *utility* of a measure. Given that a measure has been shown to be a valid indicator of a behavior, event, or functional relation, we are also interested in its relative or incremental validity and contribution to clinical judgments—*its incremental validity and utility* (Haynes & Lench, 2003).

Incremental validity has two facets. First is the degree to which a measure provides an index of a phenomenon that is more valid than other measures. For example, does a newly developed instrument provide a more valid measure, compared to existing measures, of depressed mood or alcohol use?

Second is the degree to which a measure contributes to predictive efficacy when added to already existing or more readily obtainable measures. Given what we know about the Jordan's family interactions from interviews, questionnaires, and analogue observations, will additional questionnaires or self-monitoring add to our clinical case formulation—will the additional measures increase the proportion of variance that we can account for in family interactions?

Another consideration is the *relative cost-benefits* of a measure (Yates & Taub, 2003). Assuming that a measure has a satisfactory degree of validity, is the cost of acquiring the measure warranted by its benefits? *Cost* refers to time, money, treatment delays, dropouts, and other negative effects associated with assessment.

A *benefit* refers to the ultimate outcome, such as enhanced validity of a case formulation in clinical applications or more accurate identification of functional relations in research applications.

Yates and Taub (2003) noted that costs involve multiple facets with different metrics. They suggested that costs can be reduced to the common metric of money. One can then calculate the costs of assessor and client time and the occupational impairment associated with treatment delays for different assessment strategies and instruments.

Incremental and cost-benefit evaluations are multifaceted and demanding additions to standard psychometric evaluations. A special section on *incremental validity* was published in *Psychological Assessment* (2003, Vol. 15, No. 4), edited by John Hunsley.

## DIFFERENTIAL RELEVANCE OF ELEMENTS OF PSYCHOMETRY IN BEHAVIORAL ASSESSMENT

As noted several times in the preceding sections, psychometry includes multiple dimensions of evaluation, such as interobserver agreement, internal consistency, and predictive validity (see Table 2.1 for an overview), and these dimensions are differentially applicable across the goals, methods, instruments, and measures in behavioral assessment. The relevance of a psychometric dimension for an assessment occasion also depends on the goals of assessment—the inferences to be drawn and the generalizations to be made from the data—and the characteristics of the variables measured.

For example, *discriminative validity*, the degree to which a measure discriminates between persons or events classified on the basis of an external criterion (Haynes & O'Brien, 2000; Table 2.1) can be a useful psychometric dimension in the evaluation of measures from self-report questionnaires, when the goal of the assessment is classification. To illustrate, Kubany, Leisen, and Kaplan (2000) examined the degree to which scores on the Distressing Events Questionnaire discriminated between persons with and without a diagnosis of PTSD. For this assessment goal, data on discriminative validity are relevant to our confidence that the measure performs a diagnostic function, as it was intended.

However, the degree to which a measure can correctly classify persons is less important for most applications of behavioral assessment because the goals of behavioral assessment are less often focused on classification (see the review of *DSM* and behavioral assessment by Nelson-Grey & James, 2004). More often, the goals of behavioral assessment are to measure changes in behavior problems across time, to measure approximations to treatment goals, or to estimate functional relations associated with behavior problems or goals.

For example, in observing a couple in a clinic setting while they are discussing a conflict in their relationship (Heyman & Slep, 2004), the assessor is likely most interested in the sequence of exchanges leading to an argument, the rate of positive and negative verbal and nonverbal behaviors, and their emotional reactions during the exchange. To investigate one source of possible error variance, we would examine the level of agreement between two observers. The degree to which the couple could be classified as distressed or not or the internal consistency of the behavioral measures would be less useful in evaluating this assessment method for its intended purpose (see review of couple assessment in Snyder, Heyman, & Haynes, in press).

We noted other examples where the relevance of psychometric dimensions depends on the characteristics of the measured events. For example, the *temporal stability* across short time periods is important in the evaluation of psychophysiological measures of a client's blood pressure responses while quietly sitting. Indices of systematic or unsystematic changes across times of blood pressure measurement (e.g., readings taken every 60 seconds for 15 minutes) can help estimate the number of blood pressure samples necessary to provide a reliable estimate of subjects' resting blood pressure. These data also indicate the degree of confidence warranted in the generalizability of any subset of blood pressure samples.

In contrast, temporal stability is less important in the evaluation of data from observations of parent–child interactions across several scenarios in a clinic setting (e.g., instructions to the parent to play a game that the child chooses, instructions to the parent to have the child put away toys in the clinic room). In this assessment occasion, the variables that affect behavior rates and functional relations can vary across assessment settings[7] and temporal stability estimates are less useful in evaluating the quality of the data.

Similar considerations apply to the relevance of *internal consistency* and interelement correlations. When a measure is formed by aggregating several elements, such as a ratio-scale measure of aggression formed by summing several items on a questionnaire, the degree to which the items of the scale covary is a useful indication of the internal consistency of the items. If the items all are intended to contribute to a measure of aggression (in this case "aggression" is a latent variable and the items are "signs" of aggression), they all should intercorrelate highly. The failure of one to correlate highly with others suggests that that item may be reflecting some other construct. Thus psychometric dimensions such as Cronbach alpha, split-half reliability, interitem correlations, item-total correlations, and factor structure are useful in evaluating the quality of the measure.

Some instruments in behavioral assessment provide samples of events and are not assumed to provide an aggregated measure of a latent variable. For example, the goal of a questionnaire may be to sample the traumatic life experiences to

---

[7] Indices of temporal consistency within a setting could be useful in determining the optimal duration of each setting, the duration necessary to provide a reliable index of behavior rates or functional relations.

which a person has been exposed. It is not presumed that exposure to one event (e.g., the death of a close friend) would be correlated with exposure to another event (e.g., an automobile accident). Thus, the measures of internal consistency used for "sign" measures are less relevant for evaluating the quality of the data from this instrument. Instead we may be interested in its *content validity* (the degree to which the items were all traumatic life events and the degree to which the domain of potential traumatic life events was sampled) and temporal stability.

The differential relevance of psychometric principles across assessment methods, measures, and targets is summarized by an important principle: Inferences about the validity of a measure should be based on the results of psychometric evaluations that are consistent with the characteristics of the assessment goals and of the phenomena being measured. Data from psychometric evaluations are useful for evaluation of the quality of a measure to the degree that they inform about the validity of the measure for its intended inference.

## CONDITIONAL AND DYNAMIC NATURE OF PSYCHOMETRIC INFERENCES AND EVALUATING PSYCHOMETRIC INDICES

The concepts of generalizability and the conditional nature of psychometric indices mandate a cautious analysis of published validity data. As noted throughout the chapter, data on a measure's reliability, accuracy, incremental validity, and other dimensions of psychometric evaluation are conditional and generalizable within limited domains—they must be interpreted within the constraints of the original investigation. Results from a psychometric study are not necessarily generalizable to other populations, settings, times, response modes, other measures from the same instrument, or other psychometric evaluative indices. *Psychometric indices have limited domains of validity.*

For example, the degree to which a behavior-problem checklist accurately measures aggressive behaviors of children can depend on the age of the child, the culture within which the family functions, the relationship between the respondent and child, the severity of problems being measured, and the state of the respondent. The checklist might be valid as a brief screening measure but not as a treatment-outcome measure, when used by a parent but not by a teacher, for mild but not severe problems, or when used in the school but not in the home.

Differential validity of a measure across facets or modes of a construct can be particularly challenging. Most constructs measured in clinical assessment have multiple facets. Consider the multiple facets of aggression (e.g., verbal aggression, throwing objects, severe physical aggression, anger) and social assertion skills (e.g., initiating conversations with strangers, refusing unreasonable requests, emotional responses during social interactions). An assessment instrument may provide a valid measure of some but not other facets and modes of a construct.

It is also difficult for a single measure to provide valid indices of multiple facets. Summary scores from an assessment instrument (e.g., a score that is the sum of cognitive, behavioral, and biological facets of depression) can over- or underrepresent individual facets of a construct, and it is difficult to attribute variance in scores to changes in particular facets.

The conditional nature of psychometric indices means that *validity is not an invariant trait of a measure* (Haynes & Waialae, 1994). It is even less a trait of the instrument from which the measure is obtained. Most assessment instruments provide multiple measures, which can differ in their validity, across the many dimensions noted earlier. As discussed in Haynes and O'Brien (2000), the degree to which data from those validity evaluations are relevant to our assessment goals is constrained by the similarity between the original validation methods (e.g., samples, timing, focus, goals) and our assessment occasion. In selecting assessment instruments to use in clinical practice or research, evaluating the validity of assessment data from clinical practice and research, and in constructing and validating assessment instruments, we must carefully consider the conditions, populations, settings, target variables, response modes and dimensions, and goals of intended assessment.

Another corollary is that *validity indices are not stable over time*. Because our understanding of behavior disorders and the variables that affect them evolves, the validity of assessment instruments must degrade over time. Consider the evolution of ideas about childhood depression and anxiety, PTSD, and personality disorders. Historical instruments are unlikely to capture newly understood facets of these disorders.

## VALIDITY AND THE INDIVIDUALIZED AND IDIOGRAPHIC ASSESSMENT

The methods, instruments, measures, and assessment contexts in behavioral assessment are often specially designed for an individual (see discussions of idiographic assessment in Haynes & O'Brien, 2000, and Silva, 1993). This individualized (i.e., idiographic) focus reflects an emphasis on the study of individuals over time, often within controlled single-subject designs, best exemplified by the works of B. F. Skinner and scholars in experimental and applied behavior analysis (see historical discussion by Kazdin, 1978).

In clinical applications, individualized assessment can occur in several ways. First, the assessment strategy and elements of assessment instruments can be individualized. For example, the array of assessment instruments selected, the time samples used in behavioral observations, the items selected from a questionnaire, or the scenarios used in role-play assessment can be designed individually for a client. The self-monitoring methods used by Jeffrey's parents and teacher are examples. Second, the measures obtained from an instrument can be individually selected. For example, the MMPI can provide many scale scores, and those of particular relevance for a client can be selected. Third, clinical judgments can be based on criteria selected specially for an individual. For example, criteria for independent self-help skills on goal-attainment scales can be different across patients in an inpatient psychiatric facility.

In this discussion of idiographic measures and psychometry, we address mostly individually constructed assessment instruments, such as individually constructed self-monitoring forms, questionnaires, and observation settings. The goal of psychometry with these instruments is the same as with nomothetically based instruments—we want to establish confidence in the validity of obtained measures and to understand sources of error variance, to strengthen the validity of inferences based on them.

With individually constructed instruments, all dimensions of psychometric evaluation are relevant—reliability, discriminant validity, etc. *Content validity* is a particularly important evaluative dimension. Given that the goal of idiographic assessment is to measure those behaviors and events that are most relevant to the targeted behavior problems, treatment goals, and causal variables for each client, we are concerned with the degree to which the behaviors and events sampled by the instrument are those most relevant to the client and that the instrument not include irrelevant elements. For example, does an audiotaped presentation of an auto accident designed to elicit psychophysiological responses of an accident victim with PTSD in order to measure treatment progress capture the most salient features of the accident?

As discussed earlier in this chapter, psychometric principles also apply to clinical judgments. Confidence in judgments from idiographic measures can be strengthened by the same multimethod, convergent validation strategies discussed earlier. We are confident in the validity of a judgment to the degree that the judgment is based on data from multiple, high-quality methods, instruments, informants, and measurement occasions. Unlike nomothetic measures, confidence in the validity of an individualized measure can rarely be strengthened by reference to published studies; confidence-building methods, such as convergent validation, must be built into the assessment strategy.

## SUMMARY

This chapter began by emphasizing the central role of measurement in research and clinical applications. Measures obtained through the assessment process guide all subsequent inferences about variables that affect behavior disorders, clinical case formulation, and treatment outcome. The central role of measurement explains the importance of psychometry: Psychometry is the science of measurement, and it provides the methods and concepts to help evaluate and interpret measures.

Several psychometric concepts relevant to behavioral assessment were discussed throughout the chapter—validity, internal consistency, generalizability, content validity, sensitivity to change, convergent validation, incremental validity, and temporal stability. The concept of validity has evolved to be more inclusive but I recommend a more restrictive definition—the degree to which changes on a dimension of an attribute produce changes in a measure of that attribute dimension. I also suggested that this definition can be applied to the evaluation of clinical judgments as well as the measures upon which judgments are based. Content validity is a particularly central evaluative dimension with clinical case formulations.

Validity inferences are conditional. An instrument can provide valid measures for some but not other persons, for behavior in some settings but not others, at one time but not another, for one dimension of an attribute but not another. Previously published data on the validity of a measure are relevant to the degree that they are congruent with the goals and characteristics of the assessment. The conditional nature of validity mandates careful selection of instruments, careful interpretation of data from them, and a humble ambience regarding the validity and potential generalizability of one's own assessment data.

Given lack of definitive criteria with which to judge validity of most measures obtained in behavioral assessment, the main method of examining the validity of measures, identifying sources of error, and in making the best judgments is convergent validation. Validity of a measure is most often inferred by the degree of convergence between it and alternative measures of the same phenomena.

I also noted that validity is a necessary but insufficient basis for judging the utility of a measure. Incremental validity of a measure, the degree to which it enhances our predictive validity contributes to estimates of its potential utility.

The dynamic nature of validity was also emphasized. Because our understanding of human behavior changes over time, the validity of measures that reflect prior understandings must diminish

## REFERENCES

Anastasi, A., & Urbina, S. (1997). *Psychological testing*. Englewood Cliffs, NJ: Prentice Hall.

Bechtold, H. P. (1959). Construct validity: A critique. *American Psychologist, 14,* 619–629.

Bellack, A. S., & Hersen, M. (Eds.). (1998). *Behavioral assessment: A practical handbook* (4th ed.). Boston: Allyn & Bacon.

Borsboom, D., Mellenbergh, G. J., & van Heerden, J. (2004). The concept of validity. *Psychological Review, 111,* 1061–1072.

Burns, G. L., & Haynes, S. N. (in press). Clinical psychology: Construct validation with multiple sources of information and multiple settings. In M. Eid & E. Diener (Eds.), *Handbook of psychological measurement: A multimethod perspective*. Washington, DC: American Psychological Association.

Cone, J. (1998). Psychometric considerations: Concepts, contents, and methods. In A. S. Bellack & M. Hersen (Eds.), *Behavioral assessment—A practical handbook* (4th ed., pp. 22–46). Boston: Allyn & Bacon.

Darton, M., & Clark, J. (1994). *The Macmillan dictionary of measurement.* New York: Maxwell Macmillan International.

de Gruijter, D. N. M., & van der Kamp, L. J. Th. (1991). Generalizability theory. In R. K. Hambleton & J. N. Zaal (Eds.), *Advances in educational and psychological testing* (pp. 45–68). Norwell, MA: Kluwer Academic.

Dishion, T. J., & Granic, I. (2004). Naturalistic observation of relationship processes. In S. N. Haynes & E. H. Heiby (Eds.), *Behavioral assessment.* New York: John Wiley & Sons.

Haynes, S. N. (1978). *Principles of behavioral assessment.* New York: Guilford Press.

Haynes, S. N. (1992). *Models of causality in psychopathology: Toward synthetic, dynamic and nonlinear models of causality in psychopathology.* Boston: Allyn & Bacon.

Haynes, S. N. (1994). Clinical judgment and the design of behavioral intervention programs: Estimating the magnitudes of intervention effects. *Psichologia Conductual, 2,* 165–184.

Haynes, S. N. (2001). Clinical applications of analogue observation: Dimensions of psychometric evaluation. *Psychological assessment, 13,* 73–85.

Haynes, S. N., & Heiby, E. H. (Eds.). (2004). *Behavioral assessment.* New York: John Wiley & Sons.

Haynes, S. N., & Lench, H. C. (2003). Incremental validity of new clinical assessment measures. *Psychological Assessment, 15,* 456–466.

Haynes, S. N., Nelson, K., & Blaine, B. (1999). Psychometric foundations of assessment research. In J. N. Butcher, G. N. Holmbeck, & P. C. Kendall (Eds.), *Handbook of research methods in clinical psychology.* Boston: Allyn & Bacon.

Haynes, S. N., & O'Brien, W. O. (2000). *Principles and practice of behavioral assessment.* New York: Allyn & Bacon.

Haynes, S. N., Richard, D., & O'Brien, W. B. (1996). The functional analysis in behavior therapy: Estimating the strength of causal relationships for the design of treatment programs. *Gedragstherapie, 4,* 289–314.

Haynes, S. N., & Waialae, K. (1994). Psychometric foundations of behavioral assessment. In R. Fernández-Ballestros (Ed.), *Evaluacion conductual hoy* [Behavioral assessment today]. Madrid, Spain: Ediciones Piramide.

Haynes, S. N., & Williams, A. W. (2003). Clinical case formulation and the design of treatment programs: Matching treatment mechanisms and causal relations for behavior problems in a functional analysis. *European Journal of Psychological Assessment, 19,* 164–174.

Hersen, M. (2004). *Handbook of psychological assessment.* New York: John Wiley & Sons.

Heyman, R. W., & Slep, A. M. (2004). Analogue behavioral observation. In S. N. Haynes & E. M. Heiby (Eds.), *Behavioral assessment* (pp. 162–180). New York: John Wiley & Sons.

Hume, D. (1748). *Philosophical essays concerning human understanding.* London: Nachdruck der Ausgabe.

Kazdin, A. E. (1978). *History of behavior modification.* Baltimore: University Park Press.

Kubany, E., Leisen, M. B., & Kaplan, A. (2000). Validation of a brief measure of posttraumatic stress disorder: The Distressing Events Questionnaire (DEQ). *Psychological Assessment, 12,* 197–209.

Messick, S. (1994). Foundations of validity: Meaning and consequences in psychological assessment. *European Journal of Psychological Assessment, 10,* 1–9.

Messick, S. (1998). Test validity: A matter of consequence. *Social Indicators Research, 45,* 35–44.

Nelson-Gray, R. O., & Paulson, J. P. (2004). Behavioral assessment and the DSM system. In S. N. Haynes & E. H. Heiby (Eds.), *Behavioral assessment.* New York: John Wiley & Sons.

Nezu, A. M., Nezu, C. M., Peacock, M. A., & Girdwood, C. P. (2004). Case formulation in cognitive-behavior therapy. In S. N. Haynes & E. H. Heiby (Eds.), *Behavioral assessment.* New York: John Wiley & Sons.

Nunnally, J. C., & Bernstein, I. H. (1994). *Psychometric theory.* New York: McGraw-Hill.

Rust, J., & Golombok, S. (1989). *Modern psychometrics: The science of psychological assessment.* New York: Routledge.

Shapiro, E. W., & Kratochwill, T. R. (Eds.). (1988). *Behavioral assessment in schools: Conceptual foundations and practical applications.* New York: Guilford Press.

Shapiro, E. S., & Kratochwill, T. R. (Eds.). (2000). *Behavioral assessment in schools: Theory, research, and clinical foundations.* New York: Guilford Press.

Silva, F. (1993). *Psychometric foundations and behavioral assessment.* Newbury Park, CA: Sage Publications.

Snyder, D., Heyman, R., & Haynes, S. N. (in press). Couples assessment. *Psychological Assessment.*

Strube, M. J. (1990). Psychometric principles: From physiological data to physiological constructs. In J. T. Cacioppo & L. G. Tassinary (Eds.), *Principles of psychophysiology: Physical, social and inferential elements* (pp. 34–57). New York: Cambridge University Press.

Suen, H. K., & Ary, D. (1989). *Analyzing quantitative behavioral data.* Hillsdale, NJ: Erlbaum.

Suen, H. K., & Rzasa, S. E. (2004). Psychometric foundations of behavioral assessment. In S. N. Haynes & E. H. Heiby (Eds.), *Behavioral assessment* (pp. 86–102). New York: John Wiley & Sons.

Yates, B. T., & Taub, J. (2003). Assessing the costs, benefits, cost-effectiveness, and cost–benefit of psychological assessment: We should, we can, and here's how. *Psychological Assessment, 15,* 478–495.

# 3

---

# ANALOGUE AND VIRTUAL
# REALITY ASSESSMENT

---

JOHAN ROSQVIST

*Counseling Psychology Program*

ALECIA SUNDSMO
CHELSEA MACLANE
KIRSTEN CULLEN
DARCY CLOTHIER NORLING
MANDY DAVIES
DANIELLE MAACK

*Clinical Psychology Program*
*Pacific University*
*Portland, Oregon*

## INTRODUCTION

The dawn of formal behavioral assessment included behavioral observation and experimental manipulation in naturalistic and analogue settings. Many researchers, practitioners, and graduate students alike can readily recall the early studies of Pavlov and Skinner as primary exemplars of these early, fundamental techniques. In earlier times the process of behavioral assessment was presented as a simple one, involving little or no inference and often focusing on collecting data by observation or mechanical devices (Sturmey, 1996). Today, the field has continued to use these kinds of techniques. But behavioral assessment has developed greatly in some new ways (e.g., assessment of daily living abilities in patients with traumatic brain injury or stroke through virtual reality assessment [Lee et al., 2003] or gauging how well patients are able to move about and pick up objects as indicative of ADHD through virtual reality assessment [Lee & Weekrakoon, 2001; Rizzo et al., 2000]). Additionally it has further refined old standards (e.g., functional assessment developing into a sophisticated hypothesis-testing mechanism) to become more complex and subtle. Barrios (1988) reported on the changing nature of behavioral assessment when commenting that it now is not uncommon to see behavioral analysis integrating multiple sources of information into a multidimensional system for understanding, describing, predicting, and controlling human behavior and related experiences (Cone, 1978).

Although the field of behavioral assessment has progressed into a hypothesis-testing procedure, professionals who rely on such methodology still hold to the primary assumption that the best and most precise way to continue to develop and evolve is through application of an approach based on the scientific method and the principles of science generally. It is this rigorous, scientific approach that many researchers and practitioners alike believe will lead to reliable and valid models of various behavioral disorders through a stronger emphasis on testability (i.e., refutable) and parsimony (i.e., minimizing inference and excessive, unnecessary explanatory mechanisms) of such models. The empirical basis of the scientific method and approach, therefore, mandates its users to focus on research-based hypotheses, to measure variables precisely, to explore potential sources of error through the use of multiple sources of information, and to make inferences solely on the basis of behavioral or environmental changes. It can be postulated that through close ties to these punctilious mandates it will be possible to distinguish the field of behavioral assessment from other forms of clinical assessment.

Behavioral assessment rests on three primary postulates. First, all behaviors are learned; therefore, they can also be unlearned and replaced by new, more adaptive behaviors. Second, relationships between behavior and environment are functional. This is not to say that they are healthy relationships, merely that the relationships are serving some purpose that perpetuates the existence of the behaviors. Third, these relationships between behaviors and environment are idiographic and dynamic in nature. Consequently, nomothetic inferences are not as useful in defining, predicting, controlling, or otherwise evaluating these relationships. Once foundations for behavioral assessment have been established, it is important to explicate more thoroughly what is actually involved in the process of behavioral assessment, to better appreciate its scholarly emphasis and its systematic application to behavior disorders.

An advantage to idiographic assessment methods is that the (idiosyncratic) individual is compared to him- or herself rather than to other people, as occurs in nomothetic methods. While this can provide more individualized assessments and focus on unique facets to a particular person and individual changes, it is harder to interpret idiographic data in terms of how that particular behavior conforms to or deviates from how most others would act in a similar situation. Often it is most useful to compare a behavior to the individual while also comparing it to a larger population. For example, if someone has three panic attacks this week, using just idiographic assessment it could be determined if that represented an improvement, a relapse, or no change. Using just nomothetic procedures it could be determined that three panic attacks per week represented "clinical impairment." However, more information is provided if it is known that while three panic attacks per week is still within the clinical range, this represented a great reduction from the person's recent historical trend of having between 20 and 30 panic attacks per week. Mumma (2001) suggests that to avoid potential pitfalls of both approaches (such as ignoring data we have no reference for or overestimating the importance of an idiosyncratic behavior) and to benefit from the positive aspects of both approaches (such as reducing the impact of biases and getting individualized data), it becomes necessary to use an integration of idiographic and nomothetic methods. Beyond making intuitive sense, this approach has been shown to have clinical effectiveness in several cases and to enhance clinical decision making.

In promoting thorough clinical decision making, behavioral assessment involves three foci of measurement: change, functionality, and individuality. In measuring change, behavioral assessment emphasizes ongoing tracking of changes in observable behavior. Measurement of change is useful not only in the initial assessment of the problem(s), but also to track treatment progress and to establish when treatment has been sufficiently "successful" to stop or end active interventions. Measurement of functionality occurs through the analysis of the settings, contexts, and consequences of behavior. Such thorough functional analysis is pivotal to case formulation because it identifies setting events (i.e., precipitating, antecedent) that control patients' problem behaviors. The central role of behavioral assessment is in the foundation and provision of sound clinical description and measurement. Finally, individual measurement refers to the idiographic nature of behavioral assessment. It is imperative that these phenomena (i.e., behavior change and functional relationships) be measured individually in order to establish an individually meaningful baseline for each patient from which practitioners can measure any subsequent change. Functional analysis, with its emphasis on measurement, posits that measurement furnishes predictive power, from which flows any and all capacity for true control. Experimental manipulation (i.e., control and measurement) of behaviors is the backbone of treatment planning, treatment intervention, and treatment progress measurement.

Behavioral assessment, therefore, is a scientific approach to psychological assessment that emphasizes the use of minimally inferential measures, the use of measures that have been validated in ways appropriate for the assessment context, the assessment of functional relations, and the derivation of judgments based on measurement in multiple situations, from multiple methods and sources, and across multiple times (Heiby & Haynes, 2004). Thus, its goals are multifold. It carefully measures treatment process and outcome (i.e., not focusing on a diagnosis per se). It identifies and measures specific patient goals, strengths, and reinforcers. It facilitates research about learning theory and pathology through an emphasis on empiricism and contextualism (i.e., settings, contexts, and consequences). It provides data for designing individualized intervention programs through a focus on contemporaneous functional relations between behavior and the environment and then evaluates multivariate and mediating effects of such programs. In emphasizing learning, it identifies causal variables for problem behavior(s) and goals (e.g., extended social systems). Unlike projective and personality assessment, behavioral assessment aims to provide a distinct cost-efficiency advantage, for functional analysis represents perhaps the most parsimonious way of offering helpful descriptions, predictions, and control. To optimize cost efficiency while emphasizing accuracy, behavioral assessment is still conducted largely in analogue settings, such as a hospital or clinic setting versus patients' natural environments (e.g., their homes, places of employment).

## ANALOGUE ASSESSMENT

Analogue assessments are indirect measurement procedures that reflect how individuals may behave in real-life situations (Hintze, Stoner, & Bull, 2000). Analogue assessments purposely control some part of either a behavior of interest or the environment in which the behavior occurs (Hintze et al.). As a result, analogue assessments aim to evaluate behavior in a theoretical situation that is developed to mimic a real-life (natural) situation. It is proposed that how individuals behave in contrived situations is an accurate measurement of how individuals would behave in their natural environments; therefore, such responses to artificial cues serve as predictors of how individuals are likely to behave in real life (Hintze et al.).

Naturalistic direct observation, on the other hand, is the direct observation of a target behavior in an individual's natural environment (Skinner, Rhymer, & McDaniel, 2000). Direct observation requires a trained individual to observe behaviors and record the behaviors and/or events. With naturalistic direct observation, practitioners and researchers can accurately observe how an individual behaves under naturally occurring reinforcers and consequences (Norton & Hope, 2001). Naturalistic observation can involve considerable time and often is very expensive. In addition, individuals may react to the presence of the observer, and thus may decrease the validity of the observation (Norton & Hope). However, it is unethical to conduct the observation without the consent of the individual. In addition, target behaviors often occur at a low frequency (e.g., only during public speaking) or in a highly specific situation (e.g., only in the bathroom) that make it difficult to observe directly. In addition, internal cognitions and emotions cannot be directly observed and thus make it hard to measure such constructs. Finally, naturalistic observers must be highly trained, because the process of constructing observation systems is extremely complex. As a result of the many problems associated with naturalistic observation, it is rarely used in clinical or research settings (Norton & Hope).

Similar to the nomothetic versus idiographic debate is whether to use structured or unstructured methods. The structure of an assessment tool can be rated on a continuum. When the evaluator reads a test manual verbatim and records the person's responses with minimal reaction to the subject's responses, it is a structured assessment; gathering information with no systematic approach or asking what a particular person wants to discuss is an unstructured assessment.

Most commonly (outside of the highly structured research realm), semistructured instruments are used. These assessments either use structured tools or tools that are intended to be semistructured. The evaluator will observe certain behaviors or ask certain questions of all participants. Depending on the responses, the evaluator then seeks follow-up data that seem pertinent for the individual patient (but may not be necessary to gather for other patients). While structured assessments are best for diagnostic classification (Dunner, 1993), unstructured assessments can provide richer information about how a person is behaving and the variables causing and maintaining the behaviors (Lohrmann-O'Rourke & Yurman, 2001). Analogue behavioral observation (ABO; Heyman & Smith Slep, 2004), when applied in clinical settings, is often unstructured (Mash & Foster, 2001). However, a more structured approach can be used within a clinical setting, and the unstructured approaches can also yield useful information (Mash & Foster). As with the idiographic and nomothetic methods, it is often optimal to use both structured and unstructured assessment methods. More structure reduces risks of data contamination and of neglecting to assess a certain behavior. The unstructured aspects allow tailoring to the individual client and the variable being measured.

Given the many constraints of naturalistic observation, many researchers and practitioners employ analogue assessment procedures instead, as common practice. Analogue assessments allow assessors to simplify complicated behaviors and to observe isolated aspects of more global behavioral repertoires in more controllable and convenient assessment situations (Kratochwill, Sheridan, Carlson, & Lasecki, 1999). Because analogue assessments are less direct than naturalistic observation, however, it is important that practitioners and researchers make a distinction between how an individual behaves in the contrived situation and how he or she behaves in real life. Practitioners and researchers must be wary of making large decisions or drawing conclusions based on analogue assessment data alone (Hintze et al., 2000).

Kratochwill et al. (1999) identify five forms of analogue assessment: paper and pencil, audiotape, videotape, enactment, and role-play. Other researchers have identified only four types of analogue assessments, combining enactment and role-play into the same category (Nay, 1977). Enactments and role-plays are likely the most common analogue assessment procedure. The subject is asked to respond to a contrived situation that is hypothetically arranged (Hintze et al., 2000). An enactment involves a contrived situation in which the individual is asked to respond to the hypothetical situation as he or she would in real life. For example, a practitioner or researcher may create a friendly work environment and then ask the group to interact. In contrast, a role-play involves contriving or scripting the behavior of an individual. For example, an individual may be asked to behave as if he or she was meeting a new coworker. Paper-and-pencil analogues involve having an individual respond to a stimulus that is presented in a written format (Hintze et al.). Videotape analogues involve having an individual respond to a stimulus that is presented visually, and an audiotape analogue involves having an individual respond to an auditory stimulus (Hintze et al.).

## BEHAVIORAL AVOIDANCE TEST

The Behavioral Avoidance Test (BAT: Lang & Lazovik, 1963; Van Hasselt, Hersen, Bellack, Rosenblum, & Lamparski, 1979) is one of the most common analogue outcome measures used in enactment and role-plays. The aim of the BAT is to expose an individual to a feared object or environment under controlled and replicable conditions, in order to observe and collect information relating to the behavioral response (Barrett, Healy, & March, 2003). It was first used to assess fear and avoidance behavior in adults with a specific phobia and is now used as a measure of treatment outcome across many different diagnoses. The BAT generally follows one of two variations in structure (Hintze et al., 2000). One variation involves a situational enactment, where an individual is brought into close proximity with the anxiety- or depression-producing stimulus. Systematic direct observational data is recorded on preestablished criteria (e.g., frequency, duration, intensity, latency). The criteria are determined by what is most salient to the individual's fear- or depression-provoking stimulus. In addition, the individual may complete self-report measures or self-observations on his or her level of discomfort during the contrived situation. In the other variation, an individual performs each step of a graded hierarchy of observable behaviors that brings the individual closer and closer to the depression- or anxiety-producing stimulus (Hintze et al.). Outcome measures can include direct observations, self-report, and compliance of the individual.

The BAT has many different advantages. First, it provides an observable measure of fear and behavior avoidance (Barrett et al., 2003). In addition, it is an inexpensive, objective, and simple assessment measure (Barrett et al.). It also allows for a multimodal assessment of various diagnoses (Barrett et al.). A number of disadvantages have been identified in the literature regarding the use of the BAT for assessing behavioral avoidance. One criticism is that there is no standard way in which to conduct the BAT. Another criticism is the notion that demand characteristics may impact an individual's behavior during the simulated situation (Barrett et al.). In addition, the fear and avoidance associated with a number of anxiety disorders is often associated with a specific situation (Barrett et al.). When a BAT is conducted in a clinic setting, it may not accurately portray the extent of the clients' fear or avoidance response. As a result, the BAT may not provide researchers and practitioners with an accurate portrayal of real-life behavior (Taylor, 1995). However, Sirbu, Ruscio, and Ollendick (2004) used a Behavioral Avoidance Test in more realistic virtual environments to more accurately assess their patients by placing them in a virtual environment and measuring their avoidance of certain stimuli. In such virtual environments, psychologists may be able to better measure patients' "true" heart rate and skin conductance during exposure to pseudo-natural (virtual) environments as a means to measure their arousal as it might occur in natural settings, away from the office (Wiederhold, Jang, Kim, & Wiederhold, 2002). In virtual BATs, practitioners can also see what clients react to and are privy to the images that provoke their patients, rather than hearing the client's description of the images (Riva et al., 2003).

## CARBON DIOXIDE CHALLENGE TEST
## (CO$_2$ CHALLENGE TEST)

The inhalation of carbon dioxide (CO$_2$) concentrations has been shown to provoke panic attacks in patients with panic disorder (Sanderson & Wetzler, 1990). Among the numerous agents capable of inducing a panic attack in patients with Panic Disorder, the administration of CO$_2$ concentrations offers significant advantages, such as being easily administered and being well tolerated (Valença, Nardi, Nascimento, Zin, Versiani, 2002). The two most common forms are prolonged (15 minutes) inhalation of 5% CO$_2$ and one or two vital capacity inhalations of 35% CO$_2$ and 65% O$_2$. The 35% technique has been found to differentiate between patients with Panic Disorder and control groups (Valença et al.).

## ROLE-PLAY

Role-plays are among the most common analogue assessments used in clinical practice. Role-plays involve a simulation, in a clinical setting, of an interaction between the patient and another individual or a group. The patient is told to behave as he or she would in real life and is encouraged to participate in the interaction. The basic question of validity involves whether or not a client's observed behavior during the simulated situation actually corresponds to his or her behavior observed in a natural situation (Norton & Hope, 2001). Several studies have reported moderate-to-excellent correspondence on measures of social skill (Kern, 1991; Wessberg, Marriotto, Conger, Farrell, & Conger, 1979) and anxiety (Wessberg et al.) obtained from nonclinical samples in role-play interactions. A few studies have looked at the correspondence between analogue and naturalistic observation measured in clinical samples. Moderate-to-good correlations have been observed in these studies (Curran, 1982; Bellack, Hersen, & Lamparski, 1979).

Although there is some evidence for the correspondence between role-played and naturalistic behavior, performance appears to be somewhat superior in role-played situations (Norton & Hope). Although evidence is limited for the correspondence between role-plays and naturalistic behavior, many researchers have found support for the ability to discriminate defined groups using observational data from role-play methods (Norton & Hope). Specifically, comparisons of psychiatric and nonclinical individuals consistently show differences between the two groups on global ratings of social skill and anxiety (Curran).

## TIME-SAMPLING METHODS

Time sampling involves dividing the observation period into intervals and observing (and recording) behaviors during that part of the interval. The intervals are discontinuous. An obvious practical advantage to this technique is that psychologists are human. It is impossible and impractical to try to attend to every behavior at once. Not only do people not want to be observed 100% of the time, but if we are looking for a variety of behaviors it is easier to miss some than if we are just paying attention to a reasonable number of factors at once. Of course, that raises the question of accuracy and whether the results of the time-sampling observation can be generalized beyond the observation interval. Hintze and Matthews (2004) looked at off-task behaviors of 14 students in a fifth-grade class. Observations were conducted by graduate students trained in determining on- and off-task behaviors by following certain protocols and demonstrating 90% reliability with a master protocol during training. Hintze and Matthews found that the time-sampling methods were reliable for a student with consistent behaviors but inadequate for students with varying behavior patterns. Kearns, Edwards, and Tingstrom (1990) found that misleading information was more likely with longer-interval (as compared to shorter-interval) observation periods during classroom behavior observations. While time-sampling techniques are quite useful and can provide accurate data, careful attention must be paid to the times of observation and the behaviors sampled. Even more important is to assess the individual. That is, a time-sampled approach for someone who is fairly routine in his or her reactions to stimuli would be appropriate, whereas it would not be the best method for someone who is erratic in his or her behavior and has not demonstrated set ways of responding. Gershuny (2004) further suggests that we collect information using a variety of time-sampling techniques (e.g., a random discrete time log and a continuous diary) and then compare the results, analyze the extraneous variables for each condition, and see what emerges. This would optimize the information gathered using time-sampling methods.

There are a few procedural and structural issues to consider when conducting role-plays that may have a great impact on the generalizability and accuracy of the data collected. First, the nature of the instructions provided to the clients prior to the role-play may greatly affect the quality of performance exhibited during the role-play (Norton & Hope, 2001). Practitioners and researchers employing role-play methods should give great thought to the goals of the assessment and script the instructions to match the determined goals (Norton & Hope). In addition, role-play assessment procedures are both standardized and individualized. There are advantages and disadvantages to each, depending on the goal of the assessment. Standardized role-plays facilitate the comparison between the performance of the identified patient and the performance of other individuals, which may help the researcher or practitioner to gauge the degree of anxiety or impairment relative to other, similar patients (Norton & Hope). Standardized role-plays also allow for comparison to normative data for both clinical and nonclinical populations (Norton & Hope). Despite these advantages, standardized role-plays may not fit well with the needs of patients. Individualized role-play scenarios can more easily match the patients' presenting difficulties (Norton & Hope). Inclusion of important cultural and personal aspects, such as sexual orientation and religious affiliation, ensures that the role-play is relevant to the client (Norton & Hope). It may be best to seek convergence from a combination of scenarios.

Other considerations, such as the use of role-play partners and immediate versus delayed or recorded assessment, can individually and mutually affect the validity of inferences derived from the role-play scenario (Norton & Hope, 2001). In addition, the level of assessment data collected (i.e., molar or molecular) allows for different conclusions (Norton & Hope). Molar-level assessments provide a more general assessment of functioning and may serve as the ultimate goal of treatment, whereas a molecular-level assessment provides a more specific assessment of an individual's strengths and weaknesses within the identified situation and can help in establishing treatment goals (Norton & Hope). All of these factors contribute to the validity and reliability of the data collected from the role-play data. It is of great importance that researchers and clinicians carefully consider these procedural and structural factors to ensure the validity and reliability of the gathered assessment data.

Analogue assessment methods allow clinicians and researchers to gather important indirect information across a variety of psychological constructs (Hintze et al., 2000). Such methods can be replicated to monitor progress in treatment and are easily incorporated into the treatment process because they are often already a part of the treatment efforts (Hintze et al.). In addition, analogue assessments are able to tap behavior that cannot be observed by naturalistic observation, such as behavior that occurs at a low frequency or behavior that occurs only in a highly specific situation.

## BENEFITS AND DRAWBACKS OF
## ANALOGUE ASSESSMENT

Despite the many advantages of analogue assessment procedures, there are a few important limitations. It remains questionable as to how generalizable an individual's observed behavior during an analogue assessment is to his or her natural behavior. A greater inference will need to be made than when naturalistic observation is employed. In addition, the majority of analogue assessment procedures are not standardized. As a result, the reliability and validity of the information gathered may be challenged (Hintze et al., 2000). The psychometric properties of most analogue methods are less developed than for other forms of assessment. Analogue assessment measures may best serve as a screening and monitoring of treatment effectiveness and should not be used to make very important decisions. Hintze and colleagues recommend that other assessment methods, such as semistructured interviews and systematic direct observation, be employed when using analogue assessment procedures in order to control for the analogue methods' limited scope.

## VALIDITY AND CLINICAL UTILITY ISSUES

Of course, no matter how much data one had collected or how much time one spent gathering it, if the data were not valid (that is measuring what it is supposed to measure), the data would be useless. If invalid data were analyzed, the results would first of all be inaccurate and therefore have no clinical utility; this would also be an unethical way to conduct psychological research. For example, if one were observing behaviors that are commonly associated with Attention-Deficit/Hyperactivity Disorder (ADHD) in an analogue setting, such findings can implicate diagnosis, treatment (including possibly stimulant medication), and qualification for certain programs (such as an Individualized Education Plan). Errors not only would impact one's research and possible future as a psychologist but could also significantly interfere with someone's life. In order for data to be valid in an analogue assessment, there needs to be interrater reliability. That is, anyone trained to look for certain behaviors must be able to consistently determine what does and does not meet predetermined requirements. It is necessary to be accurate in one's measurements and to be sure that what is being measured is actually a component of ADHD rather than something else. For example, all observers must be sure that the behavior one is rating is specific to the diagnosis of ADHD rather than something that may look similar but is very different (e.g., a child having a reaction to successfully trading his peanut butter sandwich and apple for three chocolate bars for lunch). Beyond a potential monumental impact on someone's life, inaccurate research can harm the field of psychology (not to mention one's own professional reputation). Others may believe what findings/research one shares with them and act on those (inaccurate/false) premises. Incidentally, research has suggested that evaluation of ADHD symptoms should be carried out in natural settings using analogue methods rather than just laboratory assessment methods (Barkley, 1991).

Beyond accuracy of the particular data being measured, validity requires that results be reproducible. Variations in technique of behavioral avoidance tasks (which are often done in an analogue setting) can lead to different results and conclusions (Bernstein & Nietzel, 1973). However, when well-defined procedures are followed in a behavioral avoidance task, sound convergent and discriminant validity and treatment sensitivity have been demonstrated in adults (Steketee, Chambless, Tran, Worden, & Gillis, 1996); good sensitivity has been shown in both adolescents and children (Barrett et al., 2003); and test–retest validity has been shown in children (Hamilton & King, 1991). Due to the nature of clinical analogue assessment and individualization of techniques, it is necessary to provide a clear, succinct outline of what procedures will be used. Modification of previously used procedures should not be assumed to be equivalent. When carried out properly, analogue behavioral observation assessment can be very useful in revealing important functional relationships that can inform effective treatment (Haynes, 2001).

Kurt Lewin (1951) once wrote, "There's nothing so practical as a good theory" (p. 169). He was right. Beyond good theory (which stems from good research) is good treatment. Individual case conceptualization involves conducting a functional analysis of what causes and maintains problems. It is in a sense an individualized theory, which is going to be systematically tested throughout treatment. The theory may change and is different for each patient; however, it remains a guideline to assess treatment goals and help ensure that both the patient and the practitioner stay on track. Analogue behavioral observation (ABO) is one method of generating sound case conceptualizations or theories about why a client is acting in an undesired manner and how to best stop the problem behavior or start an absent (yet desired) behavior. ABO allows clinicians to test theories about their clients (Heyman & Smith Slep, 2004).

First, ABO identifies the problem behavior specific to a particular client. Through unstructured and structured assessment methods, primarily observation, the problem behavior becomes evident. By manipulating the environment (as in ABO but not in naturalistic observation), theories explaining problem behaviors can be tested. Variables can be altered and the resulting change or lack of change in the target behaviors can be observed and recorded. If the theory is proven not to hold true (i.e., falsifiable) in a certain situation, it can be altered. Although structured, the theory remains flexible and is able to be altered; disproved suspicions are just as valuable as supported hypotheses. Therefore, it is easy to agree with Lewin that "there's nothing so practical as a good theory," and it would add something further useful to suggest that there's nothing so practical as a good theory-testing tool. Without a good way to test theories, we cannot determine if a theory is good. Behavioral assessment can be that tool.


## VIRTUAL REALITY ASSESSMENT

Virtual reality (VR) uses technology to create a human–computer interaction paradigm that involves more than just a multimedia interactive display where patients can, for example, engage in exposure therapy through a computer-generated three-dimensional, ecologically valid virtual world within which behavioral responding can be accurately recorded (Rothbaum & Hodges, 1999). Most commonly, users wear a head-mounted display that has TV screens for visual input, stereo earphones for auditory input, and a head-tracking device for location and movement. Participants are immersed in the computer-generated environment through real-time computer graphics, body-tracking devices, visual displays (two television screens, one in front of each eye, most commonly programmed to show slightly different images to produce a stereoscopic display), and other sensory input the head-mounted display generates (Emmelkamp,

Bruynzeel, Drost, & Van Der Mast, 2001; Rothbaum & Hodges). Participants are able to see, hear, and interact in a three-dimensional virtual world that gives participants a sense of presence in the virtual environment, which helps reduce common forms of interference, since patients emit more "real" reactions (Ku et al., 2001). The importance of presence cannot be underscored enough. To illustrate its central role in VR, imagine standing at the top level of the Eiffel Tower and gazing out at the city of Paris in springtime. It is an enormous sprawling mass of amazing architecture, roadways, and traffic circles (roughly equivalent to quicksand!), small and large parks filled with fountains and the most beautiful greenery, and lots of that fantastic mystique commonly referred to as *je ne sais quoi*. At the top of the Eiffel Tower, all of this, combined with the height, the wind, and the *joie de vivre* that comes naturally with a visit to Paris, can be experienced, for real. In real life (IRL), the experience is almost indescribable, and unfortunately even the best pictures or videotape cannot adequately capture and properly relay the experience felt when standing at the top of the Eiffel Tower (i.e., presence!). A family member or friend who later viewed pictures or video taken at this location could get a sense of it but would not feel *present* there. Presence would be absent! With VR, that person could also feel present at the Eiffel Tower, even though he would be in, let's say, New Jersey, thousands of miles from the breathtaking experience. Whether for enjoyment or more therapeutic purposes, VR has greatly improved what can be experienced on a true analogue basis (i.e., no "real-world" stimuli are experienced).

Indeed, instrument-assisted assessment methods such as VR have dramatically reduced interference in numerous ways. For example, Barnard and colleagues (1991) found computer-assisted assessment of competency to stand trial to be a reliable and valid screener that saved time. In addition, Nicholson, Barnard, Robbins, and Hankins (1994) demonstrated that computer-assisted assessment accurately predicted outcomes for inmates. However, computer-aided assessment could have some inherent problems. For instance, G. Lee and Weekrakoon (2001) found no difference in the assessment of students with computer tools and pen-and-paper multiple-choice tools. However, students demonstrated more anxiety with the computer-based assessment (G. Lee & Weekrakoon). This suggests that when approaching the VR psychology environments, patients may experience anxiety; therefore, practitioners may initially expose patients to simple VR environments and proceed with the complete assessment following the baseline, "accustoming" assessment.

VR treatment and assessment have been used for multiple anxiety disorders (Generalized Anxiety Disorder [GAD], Obsessive-Compulsive Disorder [OCD], Post-Traumatic Stress Disorder [PTSD] (Difede and Hoffman, 2002), specific phobias (Jang et al., 2002), Panic Disorder and Agoraphobia, Social Phobia (Harris, Kemmerling, & North, 2002; Roy et al., 2003), Attention-Deficit/ Hyperactivity Disorder (ADHD; Rizzo et al., 2000), eating disorders (Gaggioli, Mantovani, Castelnuovo, Wiederhold, & Riva, 2003; Riva, Bacchetta, Baruffi, Rinaldi, & Molinari, 1999), obesity (Gaggioli et al.), male sexual disorders, schizophrenia, substance dependence, traumatic brain injury, stroke (Lee et al., 2003), and chronic pain (Gershon, Zimand, Lemos, Rothbaum, & Hodges, 2003; Glantz, Rizzo, & Graap, 2003; North, North, & Coble, 1998; Steele et al., 2003).

In terms of exposure therapy, in general the important process contributing to effective therapy involves activation of anxiety through contact with feared stimuli and experiencing habituation and extinction to a point that feared stimuli no longer elicit anxiety. VR environments evoke a sense of actual presence in feared situations, so a VR experience is very similar to actually experiencing the feared stimulus in a natural environment. Thus, treatment through VR can be as effective as traditional methods of exposure. This advantage holds true for assessment as well, where patients' reactions and responses can be evaluated so as to lend stronger credibility to the sense of true (not hypothetical) data being produced.

Indeed, one proposed benefit and strength of this method of assessment and treatment is that it is flexible and programmable to a degree that the therapist can present a wide variety of controlled stimuli that specifically suit patients' needs and goals (Riva et al., 1999). Within one VR device, many different situations and stimuli can be presented and modified. For example, this allows for "real" reactions to feared stimuli, and the therapist can accurately monitor and measure behavioral responses patients make while proceeding through assessment and treatment. In addition, the commonly used patient report of subjective distress (Subjective Units of Distress Scale: SUDS) is recorded in tandem with stimulus presentation to measure the decrease in anxiety during treatment as patients encounter and habituate to feared stimuli (Rothbaum & Hodges, 1999). Ultimately, VR provides ecologically valid stimulus environments within which behavioral responding can be more accurately recorded.

VR assessment and treatment have numerous advantages over assessment and exposure therapy in natural environments (Emmelkamp et al., 2001; Glantz et al., 2003; Ressler et al., 2004). Assessment and treatment can be completely and adequately conducted in an office setting rather than outside the sanctuary of such a setting, where the real environment can be unpredictable and patient confidentiality, comfort and safety cannot always be guaranteed. VR assessment and treatment enable a provider to precisely control what is presented to patients, and desired environments can be idiosyncratically tailored to the needs of each patient. Treatment sessions, when compared to traditional exposure therapy, are more cost effective and less time consuming because VR technology allows sessions to be more readily completed within a conventional therapy hour of 45–50 minutes, where naturalistic assessment and treatment can be extremely laborious and time consuming. Further, such more conventional length (shorter) sessions may translate to a better chance of full reimbursement by insurance companies that may otherwise restrict session length and location. VR may also be more realistic in certain instances by providing assessment and treatment opportunities that would perhaps be unethical or unsafe to do naturalistically. Since VR is more realistic than imagination alone, it may elicit more specific information during the assessment (North et al., 1998).

Another specific benefit over traditional assessment methods and exposure therapy is the possibility for unlimited repetitions of virtual scenes. In terms of exposure therapy, this repetition actually assists in gradually reducing anxiety, and it also contributes to reducing the cost and time needed (e.g., *in vivo* exposure for fear of flying). Increased safety and control and patient ability to adjust the intensity of the virtual experience as well as turn it on and off instantaneously are additional benefits. Because VR is safe, it may allow clients to feel more comfortable confronting the information, so patients who have difficulties imagining an anxiety-provoking situation may be assisted by VR technology (North et al., 1998).

## VIRTUAL ENVIRONMENTS: ROLE IN ELICITING NATURAL (REAL) RESPONSES

Exposure through virtual reality has become successful and often a treatment of choice because of its ability to elicit real-life responses and change in individuals who experience anxiety in feared situations. Specifically, the patient is exposed to a real-life feared situation through the VR human–computer interaction program, where psychologists may measure the patient's heart rate and skin conductance during exposure to virtual environments as a means to measure arousal (Wiederhold et al., 2002). The VR system integrates lifelike visuals and real sounds to create the reality (i.e., presence) of the actual feared environment. The therapist uses a keyboard to control the programmed situations and, in careful, controlled stages, exposes the patient to experiences that elicit higher levels of anxiety. Exposure through a virtual reality environment is just like experiencing the feared situation in real life; the encounter with the feared stimulus in VR elicits the same reaction as in real life. Having a sense of presence or immersion in the virtual environment allows patients to feel that the situation is really happening; thus, behavioral and physiological reactions that one would experience in a real-life situation are the same reactions experienced in VR. A significant advantage to real life, however, is that therapists can actually see what clients react to, and they are also privy to the images that provoke their patients rather than hearing the client's description of the images (Riva et al., 2003). Difede and Hoffman (2002), for example, demonstrated that VR successfully treated a patient whose symptoms had not successfully remitted after traditional *in vivo* exposure for PTSD developed after witnessing the World Trade Center bombing. This suggested that VR assessment and treatment may better address symptoms involving internal experiences, especially when attention is paid to what can and cannot be recreated in an analogue (or natural) setting.

Rothbaum and Hodges (1999) report that exposure therapy is effective in eliciting a fearful response by activating the fear structure through contact with a feared stimuli. Through continued exposure, the process of habituation and extinction (where the feared stimulus ceases to elicit anxiety) can modify the fear structure so that the feared stimulus is less threatening. It is reported that any method that activates and modifies the fear structure is predicted to reduce anxiety symptoms, and exposure through the virtual environment has shown not only to elicit real fear responses through contact with a feared stimulus, albeit computer simulated, but to improve target symptoms as well (Emmelkamp et al., 2001; Riva et al., 1999). J. H. Lee et al. (2003) suggest that virtual environments may be useful in the assessment of daily living abilities in patients with traumatic brain injury or stroke. Patients were placed in a virtual environment and assessed based on their ability to maneuver through the environment and pick things up (Lee & Weekrakoon, 2001). Patient exposure to a VR classroom environment has been shown to be effective in the diagnosis of ADHD (Rizzo et al., 2000). In addition, researchers have demonstrated that tracking the patient's body movement while in the virtual environment can aid in assessing for hyperactiv-· ity (Rizzo et al.). This measure of hyperactivity based on measuring bodily movement appears to be as reliable as or even more reliable than teacher or parent report.

## IMPROVEMENT ON ANALOGUE ASSESSMENT

Indeed, VR has a number of distinct advantages over more conventional analogue behavioral assessment and treatment options. For instance, there no longer exists a need to rely on patients' capacity for internal imagery, skill, or sophistication. Therefore, patients who have difficulty imagining anxiety-provoking situations may be assisted by VR technology (North et al., 1998). Actually, VR environments allow patients to explore automatic thoughts, images, worst-case-scenario worries, and other intangible ideas more completely (Riva, 1998; Riva et al., 2003). VR is also "safe," which may allow more patients to feel more comfortable confronting otherwise-distressing information, and VR is also more realistic than imagination alone and may elicit more specific information during assessment and treatment (North et al.). These improvements may also influence the classic predicament of dropout, for findings suggest that patients suffering from phobias may be more likely to seek and complete therapy with VR exposure than with regular (live) exposure (Difede & Hoffman, 2002). Patients' confidentiality is also better protected by conducting assessment and treatment activities in office settings, where they can approach multiple stimuli over and over without the risk of being conspicuous (Glantz et al., 2003). However tempting Paris in spring may seem, this also means that it can be done without having to travel to natural settings. For obvious reasons, this cuts down on cost, time, and challenges to confidentiality. It even becomes possible to visit places and experience stimuli simply not otherwise feasible naturally.

## CONCLUSIONS AND FUTURE DIRECTIONS

Behavioral assessment and treatment remain the mainstay used by a large proportion of practitioners and researchers. Both historical and current indicators have established behavioral assessment and treatment as both reliable and valid as well as time conscious, cost effective, and highly tolerable and respectful in multiple ways. Issues related to behavioral approaches (e.g., confidentiality) are being solved and mitigated by new technology, such as VR. Although remaining true to their foundations, behaviorally oriented methods are being refined and elaborated to increase their utility, range, and feasibility. Such approaches are today used for an increasing number of life circumstances, and they are continuously researched for use in new and innovative ways (e.g., delivering booster sessions online, whether by VR or something less sophisticated). For VR specifically, more attention is being paid to special education purposes. Brown, Standen, and Cobb (1998) developed the Learning in Virtual Environments (LIVE) program, in which new experiential and communication tools are being explored and carefully investigated to answer how certain skills learned in VR can transfer to the real world (Wiederhold & Wiederhold, 2005). Although VR is a promising new technology with behavioral applications, some fundamental problems still need solutions (e.g., motion sickness during virtual environment immersion). Motion sickness can be a detractor from the sense of immersion in the VR environment, especially for fear of driving (Glantz et al., 2003). Since VR environments have been implicated as a potentially optimal tool for assessment and treatment of fear of driving, such basic issues need common and practical solutions. Whether using more conventional functional assessment or virtual worlds to assess and treat idiosyncratic people, attention still needs to be paid to optimizing the blend of idiographic and nomothetic data. As hypothesis testing becomes ever refined, it will remain important not to lose touch with the real persons being helped. Human relationships will need to remain present at the heart of behavioral methods, or potential problems may arise (e.g., premature terminations, noncompliance). Nonetheless, such approaches are becoming increasingly efficacious, effective, and efficient.

Although approaches may have become more refined, behavioral methods are still in basis systematically reliant on special techniques to better understand and help a given individual, group, or social ecology (McReynolds, 1968). Let us never forget that through understanding and appreciation comes effective coping with problems (Walsh & Betz, 1995). These are the objectives of behavioral assessment and treatment.

## REFERENCES

Barkley, R. A. (1991). The ecological validity of laboratory and analogue assessment methods of ADHD symptoms. *Journal of Abnormal Child Psychology, 19,* 149–178.

Barnard, G. W., Thompson J. W., Freeman, W. C., Robbins, L., Gies, D., & Hankins, G. C. (1991). Competency to stand trial: Description and initial evaluation of a new computer-assisted assessment tool. *Bulletin of the American Academy of Psychiatry and the Law, 19,* 367–381.

Barrett, P., Healy, L., & March, J. S. (2003). Behavioral avoidance test for childhood obsessive-compulsive disorder: A home-based observation. *American Journal of Psychotherapy, 57,* 81–101.

Barrios, B. A. (1988). On the changing nature of behavioral assessment. In A. S. Bellack & M. Hersen (Eds.), *Behavioral assessment: A practical handbook* (3rd ed., pp. 3–41). New York: Pergamon Press.

Bellack, A. S., Hersen, M., & Lamparski, D. (1979). Role-play tests for assessing social skills: Are they valid? Are they useful? *Journal of Consulting and Clinical Psychology, 47,* 335–342.

Bernstein, D. A., & Nietzel, M. T. (1973). Procedural variation in behavioral avoidance tests. *Journal of Consulting and Clinical Practice, 41,* 165–174.

Brown, D. J., Standen, P. J., & Cobb, S. V. (1998). Virtual environments: Special needs and evaluative methods. In G. Riva, B. K. Wiederhold, & E. Molinari (Eds.), *Virtual environments in clinical psychology and neuroscience* (Vol. 58, pp. 91–102). Amsterdam: IOP Press.

Cone, J. D. (1978). The Behavioral Assessment Grid (BAG): A conceptual framework and a taxonomy. *Behavior Therapy, 9,* 882–888.

Curran, J. P. (1982). A procedure for the assessment of social skills: The Simulated Social Interactions Test. In J. P. Curran & P. M. Monti (Eds.), *Social skills training: A practical handbook for assessment and treatment* (pp. 313–347). New York: Guilford Press.

Difede, J., & Hoffman, H. G. (2002). Virtual reality exposure therapy for World Trade Center Post-Traumatic Stress Disorder: A case report. *CyberPsychology & Behavior, 5,* 529–535.

Dunner, D. L. (1993). Diagnostic assessment. *Psychiatric Clinics of North America, 16,* 431–441.

Emmelkamp, P. M., Bruynzeel, M., Drost, L., & Van Der Mast, C. (2001). Virtual reality treatment in acrophobia: A comparison with exposure in vivo. *CyberPsychology & Behavior, 4,* 335–339.

Gaggioli, A., Mantovani, T., Castelnuovo, G., Wiederhold, B., & Riva, G. (2003). Avatars in clinical psychology: A framework for the clinical use of virtual humans. *CyberPsychology & Behavior, 6,* 117–125.

Gershon, J., Zimand, E., Lemos, R., Rothbaum, B. O., & Hodges, L. (2003). Use of virtual reality as a distractor for painful procedures in a patient with pediatric cancer: A case study. *CyberPsychology & Behavior, 6,* 657–661.

Gershuny, J. (2004). Costs and benefits of time-sampling methodologies. *Social Indicators Research, 67,* 247–252.

Glantz, K., Rizzo, A., & Graap, K. (2003). Virtual reality for psychotherapy: Current reality and future possibilities. *Psychotherapy: Theory, Research, Practice, Training, 40,* 55–67.

Hamilton, D. I., & King, N. J. (1991). Reliability of a behavioral avoidance test for the assessment of dog phobic children. *Psychological Reports, 69,* 18.

Harris, S. R., Kemmerling, R. L., & North, M. M. (2002). Brief virtual reality therapy for public speaking anxiety. *CyberPsychology & Behavior, 5,* 543–550.

Haynes, S. N. (2001). Clinical applications of analogue behavioral observation: Dimensions of psychometric evaluation. *Psychological Assessment, 13,* 73–85.

Heiby, E. M., & Haynes, S. N. (2004). Introduction to behavioral assessment. In S. N. Haynes & E. M. Heiby (Eds.), *Comprehensive handbook of psychological assessment: Volume 3. Behavioral assessment* (pp. 3–18). Hoboken, NJ: John Wiley & Sons.

Heyman, R. E., & Smith Slep, A. M. (2004). Analogue behavioral observation. In S. N. Haynes & E. M. Heiby (Eds.), *Comprehensive handbook of psychological assessment: Volume 3. Behavioral assessment* (pp. 162–180). Hoboken, NJ: Wiley.

Hintze, J. M., & Matthews, W. J. (2004). The generalizability of systematic direct observation across time and setting: A preliminary investigation of the psychometrics of behavioral observation. *School Psychology Review, 33,* 258–270.

Hintze, J. M., Stoner, G., & Bull, M. H. (2000). In E. S. Shapiro & T. R. Kratochwill (Eds.), *Conducting school-based assessments of child and adolescent behavior* (pp. 55–77). New York: Guilford Press.

Jang, D. P., Ku, J. H., Choi, J. H., Wiederhold, B. K., Nam, S. W., Kim, I. Y., et al. (2002). The development of virtual reality therapy (VRT) system for the treatment of acrophobia and therapeutic case. *IEEE Transactions on Information Technology in Biomedicine, 6,* 213–217.

Kearns, K., Edwards, R., & Tingstrom, D. H. (1990). Accuracy of long momentary time-sampling intervals: Implications for classroom data collection. *Journal of Psychoeducational Assessment, 8,* 74–85.

Kern, J. M. (1991). An evaluation of a novel role-play methodology: The standardized idiographic approach. *Behavior Therapy, 22,* 13–29.

Kratochwill, T. R., Sheridan, S. M., Carlson, J., & Lasecki, K. L. (1999). Advances in behavioral assessment. In C. R. Reynolds & T. B. Gutkin (Eds.), *The handbook of school psychology* (pp. 350–382). New York: John Wiley & Sons.

Ku, J., Jang, D., Shin, M., Jo, H., Ahn, H., Lee, J., et al. (2001). Development of virtual environment for treating acrophobia. *Studies in Health Technology and Informatics, 81,* 250–252.

Lang, P. J., & Lazovik, A. D. (1963). Experimental desensitization of a phobia. *Journal of Abnormal and Social Psychology, 66,* 519–525.

Lee, G., & Weekrakoon, P. (2001). The role of computer-aided assessment in health professional education: A comparison of student performance in computer-based and paper-and-pen multiple-choice tests. *Medical Teacher, 23,* 152–157.

Lee, J. H., Ku, J., Cho, W., Hahn, W. Y., Kim, I. Y., Lee, S. M., et al. (2003). A virtual reality system for the assessment and rehabilitation of the activities of daily living. *CyberPsychology & Behavior, 6,* 383–389.

Lewin, K. (1951). *Field Theory in Social Science.* Chicago: University of Chicago Press.

Lohrmann-O'Rouke, S., & Yurman, B. (2001). Naturalistic assessment of and intervention for mouthing behaviors influenced by establishing operations. *Journal of Positive Behavior Interventions, 3,* 19–27.

Mash, E. J., & Foster, S. L. (2001). Exporting analogue behavioral observation from research to clinical practice: Useful or cost-defective? *Psychological Assessment, 13,* 86–98.

McReynolds, P. (1986). History of assessment in clinical and educational settings. In R. O. Nelson & S. C. Hayes (Eds.), *Conceptual foundations of behavioral assessment* (pp. 42–80). New York: Guilford Press.

Mumma, G. H. (2001). Increasing accuracy in clinical decision making: Toward an integration of nomothetic-aggregate and intraindividual-idiographic approaches. *Behavior Therapist, 24,* 77–94.

Nay, W. R. (1977). Analogue measures. In A. R. Ciminero, K. S. Calhoun, & H. E. Adams (Eds.), *Handbook of behavioral assessment* (pp. 233–277). New York: John Wiley & Sons.

Nicholson, R. A., Barnard, G. W., Robbins, L., & Hankins, G. (1994). Predicting treatment outcome for incompetent defendants. *Bulletin of the American Academy of Psychiatry and the Law, 22,* 367–377.

North, M. M., North, S. M., & Coble, J. R. (1998). Virtual reality therapy: An effective treatment for psychological disorders. In G. Riva & B. K. Wienerhold (Eds.), *Virtual environments in clinical psychology and neuroscience: Methods and techniques in advanced patient–therapist interaction. Studies in Health Technology and Informatics* (Vol. 58, pp. 112–119). Amsterdam: IOS Press.

Norton, P. J., & Hope, D. A. (2001). Analogue observation methods in the assessment of social functioning adults. *Psychological Assessment, 13,* 59–71.

Ressler, K. J., Rothbaum, B. O., Tannenbaum, L., Anderson, P., Graap, K., Zimand, E., Hodges, L., & Davis, M. (2004). Cognitive enhancers as adjuncts to psychotherapy. *Archives of General Psychiatry, 61,* 1136–1144.

Riva, G. (1998). Virtual reality in neuroscience: A survey. *Stud Health Tech Inform, 58,* 191–199.

Riva, G., Bacchetta, M., Baruffi, M., Rinaldi, S., & Molinari, E. (1999). Virtual reality–based experiential cognitive treatment of anorexia nervosa. *Journal of Behavior Therapy, 30,* 221–230.

Riva, G., Alcaniz, M., Anolli, L., Bacchetta, M., Banos, R., Buselli, C., et al. (2003). The VEPSY updated project: Clinical rationale and technical approach. *CyberPsychology & Behavior, 6,* 433–439.

Rizzo, A., Buckwalter, J., Bowerly, T., Van der Zaag, C., Humphrey, L., Neumann, U., et al. (2000). The virtual classroom: A virtual reality environment for the assessment and rehabilitation of attention deficits. *CyberPsychology & Behavior, 3,* 483–501.

Rothbaum, B. O., & Hodges, L. F. (1999). The use of virtual reality exposure in the treatment of anxiety disorders. *Behavior Modification, 23,* 507–525.

Roy, S., Klinger, E., Legeron, P., Lauer, F., Chemin, I., & Nugues, P. (2003) Definition of a VR-based protocol to treat social phobia. *CyberPsychology & Behavior, 6,* 411–419.

Sanderson, W. C., & Wetzler, S. (1990). Five percent carbon dioxide challenge: Valid analogue and marker of panic disorder? *Biological Psychiatry, 27,* 689–701.

Sirbu, C., Ruscio, A. M., & Ollendick, T. H. (2004, November). *Virtual reality versus in vivo one-session treatment for acrophobia.* Poster session presented at the annual meeting of the Association for Advancement of Behavior Therapy, New Orleans, LA.

Skinner, C. H., Rhymer, K. N., & McDaniel, E. C. (2000). In E. S. Shapiro & T. R. Kratochwill (Eds.), *Conducting school-based assessments of child and adolescent behavior* (pp. 21–54). New York: Guilford Press.

Steele E., Grimmer, K., Thomas, B., Mully, B., Fulton, I., & Hoffman, H. (2003). Virtual reality as a pediatric pain modulation technique: A case study. *CyberPsychology & Behavior, 6,* 633–638.

Steketee, G., Chambless, D. L., Tran, G. Q., Worden, H., & Gillis, M. M. (1996). Behavioral avoidance test for Obsessive-Compulsive Disorder. *Behavior Research and Therapy, 34,* 73–83.

Sturmey, P. (1996). *Functional analysis in clinical psychology.* Chichester, UK: John Wiley & Sons.

Taylor, S. (1995). Assessment of obsessions and compulsions: Reliability, validity, and sensitivity to treatment effects. *Clinical Psychology Review, 15,* 261–296.

Valença, A. M., Nardi, A. E., Nascimento, I., Zin, W. A., & Versiani, M. (2002). Respiratory panic disorder subtype and sensitivity to the carbon dioxide challenge test. *Brazilian Journal of Medical and Biological Research, 35,* 783–788.

Van Hasselt, V. B., Hersen, M., Bellack, A. S., Rosenblum, N. D., & Lamparski, D. (1979). Tripartite assessment of the effects of systematic desensitization in a multiphobic child: An experimental analysis. *Journal of Behavior Therapy & Experimental Psychiatry, 10,* 51–55.

Walsh, W. B., & Betz, N. (1995). *Tests and assessment* (3rd ed.). New York: Prentice Hall.

Wessberg, H. W., Marriotto, M. J., Conger, A. J., Farrell, A. D., & Conger, J. C. (1979). The ecological validity of role plays for assessing heterosocial anxiety and skill of male college students. *Journal of Consulting and Clinical Psychology, 47,* 525–535.

Wiederhold, B. K., Jang, D. P., Kim, S. I., & Wiederhold, M. D. (2002). Physiological monitoring as an objective tool in virtual reality therapy. *CyberPsychology and Behavior, 5,* 77–82.

Wiederhold, B. K., & Wiederhold, M. D. (2005). *Virtual reality therapy for anxiety disorders: Advances in evaluation and treatment.* Washington, DC: American Psychological Association.

# 4

# BEHAVIORAL

# INTERVIEWING

STEVEN L. SAYERS

*Department of Psychiatry*
*Philadelphia Veterans Affairs Medical Center and*
*University of Pennsylvania School of Medicine*
*Philadelphia, Pennsylvania*

THOMAS J. TOMCHO

*Philadelphia Veterans Affairs Medical Center*
*Philadelphia, Pennsylvania*

## INTRODUCTION

Why conduct a behavioral interview? The methods of behavioral assessment have progressed substantially in the past several decades, with the increased use of structured and semistructured interviews, the coding and analysis of standard videotaped assessments of communication behavior (Bakeman & Gottman, 1997), the field-based observational assessment of problem behavior of patients with disabilities (Sprague & Horner, 1995), and cognitive assessment methods (Riso et al., 2003). The behavioral interview, however, is still an essential step in problem identification and the first step in developing a formulation of a patient's problems. Guided by the patient's complaints, the interviewer attempts to discover the relations between the person's environment and his individual responses to it. However, there are no "standards" for conducting a behavioral interview, only a general consensus among behaviorally oriented clinicians and theorists about what the interview involves (Galassi & Perot, 1992; Miltenberger & Veltum, 1988). Furthermore, the issues that arise in each interview can be quite diverse. Thus, learning how to conduct a behavioral interview can be a daunting task. The goal of this chapter is to clarify what concepts should guide a behavioral interview, how this may affect the way the interview is conducted, and specifically how a behavioral interview can be implemented.

Because the behavioral interview is usually the first step in behavioral assessment, it provides the first opportunity for the behavior therapist to set the tone and direction of the therapy. The behavioral interviewer should consider carefully what is subtly communicated to the patient about what therapy will be like and how the patient will be regarded in this therapy. On the other hand, the behavioral interview also needs to yield specific information crucial to understanding why the patient presented for treatment and how to help him or her. We hope to make it clear that the skilled behavioral interviewer accomplishes these goals simultaneously.

This chapter is divided into four sections. First, we present a definition and description of behavioral interviewing. This covers the assumptions and theoretical principles of behavioral treatments that guide these methods as well as the content and range of behavioral interviewing. Second, we briefly discuss the empirical literature on the training and evaluation of behavioral interviewing. Third, we discuss the specifics of how to conduct a behavioral interview, including illustrative case examples. Finally, we review aspects of interviewing affected by the "participants"—the stable and interactional characteristics that each interviewer and each patient bring to the interview that determine the outcome of the assessment. We do not address several related topics that are covered elsewhere in this or other excellent volumes, such as interviewing adults for the identification of children's problems or other forms of behavioral assessment (i.e., observation or structured interviewing methods).

## GENERAL ISSUES IN BEHAVIORAL INTERVIEWING

Most broadly, a behavioral interview aims to assess the behavior of a patient in his or her world. A behavioral interviewer often explicitly focuses on problematic behavior but often includes behavioral strengths of the patient. Such an interview may focus on the frequency of problematic behavior, such as the amount of alcohol intake by the patient in the last month. Often, however, behavioral interviewing focuses on patterns of behavior, factors that increase or decrease the likelihood of the problematic behavior, and the context in which it occurs. It is important to note that behavioral interviewing is regarded as an indirect behavioral assessment method, as opposed to a direct method, such as observation (Cone, 1978). In general, indirect assessment methods are more convenient and less costly to use than direct methods. Indeed, one early survey found that interviewing is the most commonly used behavioral assessment method (Swan & MacDonald, 1978).

Behavioral interviewing reflects the viewpoint that a patient's difficulties can be understood through the learning principles that govern the individual's behavior. Essential to this idea is that the patient has learned inappropriate responses, or not learned appropriate responses, to specific situations or problems. This does not blame the patient for these problems—it merely provides the therapist and patient a way to understand and respond to these difficulties in search of a more satisfactory outcome. The interviewer applies concepts from operant conditioning, classical conditioning, and social learning perspectives to the information provided by the patient. Using these frameworks, the interviewer attempts to elicit information about the consequences of the behaviors of interest, whether they are primarily aversive, positive, or mixed, and how immediate or delayed these consequences are (Deffenbacher, 1992). The goal is to perform a functional analysis of the problem, that is, to understand what environmental conditions or events are functionally related to the patient's behavior so as to result in unhappiness with his or her life.

The difficulties that bring the patient to therapy are not always seen by him or her as potentially influenced by the patient's own behavior, but instead as something visited on an unsuspecting victim. In fact, this may be literally true in cases such as Post-Traumatic Stress Disorder (PTSD) that develops subsequent to an automobile accident or a sexual assault. However, the clinician still must use careful interviewing to understand the factors that may determine the maintenance of the PTSD symptoms in order to develop a plan for treating the patient. Thus, when a patient voices a complaint (e.g., "I'm always anxious since I had the accident"), the behavioral interviewer attempts to understand the "ABC's" of the problem (O'Leary & Wilson, 1975)—antecedents (A) to the problem behavior or situation, the behavioral responses (B) of the patient, and the consequences (C). For example, the patient who complains of PTSD symptoms is asked to describe antecedents, or the circumstances in which he or she feels anxious and any event that may precipitate this subjective state. Further, the patient is asked to describe his or her responses, which include subjective emotional states, overt behavioral responses (e.g., avoidance of the situation), and other covert phenomena, such as thoughts and interpretations of the situation. Consequences that are examined might be immediate (e.g., reduced anxiety after avoidance of a situation), self-generated (e.g., intrusive disturbing memories and images), or delayed (e.g., reduced social contact and reduced social support). The clinician attempts to rely on as little inference as possible in the process of this analysis— the patient is asked to report specifically on internal states and to describe situations in detail so that the clinician does not make an erroneous assumption about what actually happens to the patient outside the office.

To a great extent, the goal of the interview is to develop specific and detailed descriptions of observable events that are potentially connected to the problems the patient brings to the initial interview. Patients often can be vague in their complaints and are generally not skilled at observing the events in a highly specific way. Thus, the interviewer often needs to describe to patients why such behavioral specificity is important and help them to provide the data needed. In the end, this detailed information is used to tie in the patient's complaints to specific and measurable goals of the treatment as well as to evaluate the success of the treatment in achieving these goals.

Clinicians who use a behavioral interview acknowledge that problematic behavior has multiple determinants and that the most important determinants are often the most proximal in time. For instance, an individual with social conflicts has learned inappropriate social skills over a period of time, likely starting in the patient's early years. Whereas this might suggest to some an analysis of these early conditions, it is actually more important (and practical) to examine the current conditions that maintain these behaviors. Importantly, it is the current social context that the therapist and patient will examine in order to determine what behavior change is possible and likely to be effective in overcoming the patient's social difficulties. Furthermore, the behavioral interviewer assumes that the patient's stated problems, the problem behavior, and the environmental context that influences them is not a static model, but a dynamic and interactive system (O'Brien & Haynes, 1993). In other words, the patient's environment (particularly his *social* environment), provides antecedents and consequences to his behavior; in turn, the patient behaves in ways that may influence the behavior of others in his environment. Since for each person in this scenario there are potentially many influential factors that naturally change over time, the result can be a complex, multileveled model of the patient's behavior that can shift with these changing circumstances.

The interviewer can acknowledge the potential influence of biological and neurodevelopmental conditions on a patient's symptoms while still determining the environmental conditions functioning as stimuli or consequences of the patient's behavior. Patients whose social skills result from the negative symptoms of schizophrenia can still potentially be helped through teaching family members to provide structure and appropriate reinforcements for improvements in the patient's social behavior within the home (Mueser & Glynn, 1995). Low reinforcement of the patient's behavior on the part of family members may be understood as the result of having a relative with schizophrenia; however, determining that family members can provide more reinforcement to the patient's social behavior may be crucial in improving family relations and ultimately improving the course of the illness.

The behavioral interview can be thought of as comprehensive but not exhaustive, covering the ABCs of the problem, the history of the problem, and any other relevant information about the patient that has a bearing on treatment. The interviewer should assess cognitions, behaviors, affects, and the patient's social relationships as they relate to the problem. Lazarus (1973) provided a highly useful framework (and acronym) for areas needing assessment in preparation for therapy: behavior (B), affect (A), sensation (S), imagery (I), cognitions (C), interpersonal relationships, and the possible need for drugs (D), or BASIC ID. A thorough examination of each of these domains will help the clinician identify the factors that are influencing the problem. In other words, what does the patient do, feel, think, and imagine when X happens? What do others do? Who are the people he or she interacts with, and what do these contacts lead the patient to do, feel, or think? What influences do other people have on the problem? In addition, what does the patient believe is causing the problem, and what can be done about it? The history of the problem is also quite important—how long it has occurred, whether it has varied in intensity, and what the patient has done about it thus far. The history of the problem is relevant from a number of perspectives. It may be useful to know the circumstances that lead the patient to learning inappropriate responses so that the therapist can estimate what reinforcers may be needed to help the patient learn new responses. For example, a patient who has learned to be abrupt, demanding, and controlling in interactions with coworkers may have been positively reinforced by relative success in convincing others to acquiesce to him by using this interpersonal approach. The interviewer should attempt to understand the value of this acquiescence as a reinforcer, relative to the value of reinforcers associated with a more cooperative style. Likewise, the chronicity of any problem behavior may inform the therapist and patient how difficult it may be for the patient to learn a different approach.

One important reason that such a broad sweep of the patient's complaints is conducted is that the problem ultimately addressed in therapy may not be the initial problem cited by the patient. For example, a patient treated by one of the present authors initially complained of social anxiety. She reported a history of chronic acne that had resulted in severe facial scarring. She was predictably anxious about others' perceptions of her at dances and parties and had requested the therapist to teach her relaxation techniques. Upon further detailed questioning, it was apparent that her responses to others' initiations in social settings were often defensive and sarcastic. It also seemed that her pessimistic beliefs about the outcome of social encounters and her own angry affect going into these situations led to ineffective behavior on her part. The problem was then reformulated as a difficulty in responding to the casual social encounters that held potential for relationship development, which led to further assessment of her skills in that area. In the end, it was found that the patient's beliefs and behavior in social encounters were highly complex and self-defeating and that the initial statement of the problem had little bearing on the goals of treatment.

The role of the patient's history in a behavioral interview needs to be considered carefully. The vast majority of behavioral treatments focus primarily on current situations and events as determinants in the problematic behaviors of the patient. In contrast, the hallmark of psychodynamic approaches is the great emphasis on early childhood events as causes of the patient's current problems. The reason for the emphasis on recent events in behavioral treatment is straightforward—after all, only the most current situations are potentially modifiable, and it is only relevant for the patient to learn new behaviors to respond to current, rather than past, situations. As cognitive therapy has become better developed, more attention has been placed on the etiology of cognitions. Beck (1995) describes use of the patient's early history in ways that have been considered antithetical to the behavioral approach. Specifically, the patient is asked to recall the events in childhood associated with a particular target feeling or thought (e.g., feelings of depression or inadequacy when yelled at by mom). The therapist helps the patient to draw more realistic conclusions about these events and potentially changes the core belief interfering with that patient's current functioning. Interested readers should consult Beck for the methods associated with this type of assessment.

Nevertheless, traditional behavioral interviewing focuses primarily on the here and now of the problematic behavior. To that end, the behavioral interview also should cover other information relevant to the success of behavioral treatment. What is the overall life context of the problem? Do the mother–adolescent conflicts presented to the therapist, for example, pale in comparison to the fact that the family might soon have electric power and telephone services terminated? Patients may have life circumstances that prevent them from completing behavioral assignments, such as overwhelming parenting or job demands. Furthermore, the interviewer should be fully aware of the patient's education and socioeconomic status (SES); less highly educated and lower-SES patients may expect less active involvement in treatment and not assume the importance of assignments and other "homework." On the other end of the continuum, patients with very high SES may feel they are above doing "homework" for therapy—an inquiry about these attitudes also might prevent problems with the implementation of behavior therapy. Further discussion about complications in the behavioral assessment and treatment of a variety of disorders can be found in the interesting volume *Failures in Behavior Therapy* (Foa & Emmelkamp, 1983).

As with any comprehensive interview, the behavioral interview should address the current medical status of the patient. Many medical conditions have psychiatric consequences, and many medical conditions may mimic psychiatric conditions. This suggests that a complete medical evaluation may be necessary to eliminate either of these possibilities. Furthermore, psychiatric patients may be less adequately evaluated by primary care physicians, for a variety of reasons (O'Boyle & Concirpini, 1993). Thus, the behavioral interviewer should be aware of the role of medical complications in evaluation and treatment and work in conjunction with primary care physicians to clarify the patient's medical status.

## RESEARCH ON BEHAVIORAL INTERVIEWS

Relatively little research has been conducted on the content, reliability, and validity of behavioral interviewing for clinical problems. On the other hand, there have been a great of deal of studies on structured and semistructured approaches to interview assessment (see Chapter 6 by Daniel L. Segal). For example, numerous studies have examined the reliability and validity of the timeline follow-back method (Sobell et al., 1988) of assessing alcohol and other substance use. The method also has been tested extensively with other populations, including the assessment of gambling behavior (Hodgins & Makarchuk, 2003), sexual behavior (Weinhardt et al., 1998), and binge eating (Bardone, Krahn, Goodman, & Searles, 2000). Most of the literature supports the validity and reliability of using this method to assess frequencies of problematic behavior over a specified time period (see Bardone et al. for an exception with regard to binge eating). This literature thus provides some guidance as to useful strategies for assessing behavioral frequencies, such as using a systematic approach to assessing problem behaviors over time and using a calendar as a stimulus for recall (see the later description for details of this method).

Only a few interview guidelines have been developed for the content of behavioral interviews with adults that approach the specificity of the semistructured or structured approaches for assessing frequencies of specific behaviors. Miltenberger and Veltum (1988) examined methods for training relatively inexperienced psychology students in behavioral interviewing using a list of 30 target therapist responses (e.g., "[Interviewer] Uses an open-ended question to ask client what happens just following the occurrence of the problem behavior"). Keane, Black, Collins, and Vinson (1982) examined the training of pharmacy externs in behavioral interviewing using a list of open-ended questions regarding antecedents, behaviors, and consequences that was similar to that of Miltenberger and Veltum. The simulated interviews were conducted with assistants in the role of seizure patients; they focused on both the seizures and medication compliance. Although the guidelines in these studies do not represent structured interviews, they have the advantage of providing behavioral targets against which the interviewer's behavior can be judged.

The studies by Miltenberger and Veltum (1988) and Keane et al. (1982) demonstrate that with training, interviewers can learn to conduct behavioral interviews with a high degree of proficiency. However, modeling and behavioral rehearsal seem to be crucial training elements. Miltenberger and Veltum showed that psychology students with a basic understanding of behavioral analysis and no training used only 21% of the behavioral interviewing responses on the target list developed by the authors. After receiving written instruction, audiotaped modeling, and feedback regarding the responses necessary in a behavioral interview, the students used an average of 94% of these responses. Only trainees that received modeling of the skills improved to a high level—written instruction was insufficient. Keane et al. demonstrated the importance of behavioral rehearsal in addition to modeling for training interviewers. The pharmacy externs who received training exclusively with a modeling videotape improved relative to a control group in the number of target content areas addressed; however, the trainees who also received behavioral rehearsal training addressed a significantly greater number of target areas. In addition, interviewers trained with behavioral rehearsal improved in the general use of open-ended questions; this effect also generalized to interviews of actual patients.

Despite research on the training for behavioral interviewing, a limited number of studies have demonstrated the reliability of identifying key problems in the adult population, compared to interviewing of adults and children regarding child behavior problems (see Iwata, Wong, Riordan, Dorsey, & Lau, 1982; O'Neill, Horner, Albin, Storey, & Sprague, 1990). Nevertheless, some studies suggest that the reliability of the selection of target behaviors by different interviewers can be somewhat limited (Hay, Hay, Angle, & Nelson, 1979; F. E. Wilson & Evans, 1983). In the Hay et al. reliability study of behavioral interviews, interviewers identified similar numbers of problem areas. However, the reliability was low regarding the identification of specific areas cited as problems. Interviewers differed significantly regarding the number of problems asked about as well as in the reliability of recording the problem areas actually identified by the clients (i.e., when compared to transcripts of the interviews). Future studies should take these findings as a starting point in trying to establish the reliability and validity for behavioral interviews so that clinicians can have relatively greater faith in interview assessment when direct observational assessment is not possible.

## CONDUCTING A BEHAVIORAL INTERVIEW

### PRELIMINARY CONSIDERATIONS

Starting a behavioral interview is often the first step in the behavioral assessment process for a new patient. The interviewer may have a broad range of information available to him or her prior to the initial meeting with the patient, such as an existing chart in the case of inpatient work or a treatment summary provided by another mental health professional. In other instances, the interviewer may have little, if any, information beyond demographic information from a referral form. It is often better for the interviewer to have as much information available prior to the initial meeting as possible so that he or she can begin to develop hypotheses about the patient as well as tailoring the structure of the interview to the presenting problem. For example, if the interviewer is aware that the patient reports experiencing anxiety in social situations, he or she can be prepared to devote more time in the interview to the nature of the social situations that the patient encounters.

If the interview is the patient's initial contact with a mental health provider, the patient may approach the interview with numerous preconceived notions or questions about what may occur, which may influence the patient's responses to the interviewer's queries. "What will the interviewer look like?" "Will I be asked to lay on a couch and talk about my dreams or my mother?" "Will the therapist say anything to me, or just listen and scratch his chin?" "Will he cure me in one session?" Even patients with previous exposure to mental health professionals may be somewhat surprised by the goal-directed interaction style used by a behavioral interviewer. Often these beliefs of what will occur in a session are shaped by television and movie portrayals of therapists that frequently are stereotypical or comical and are not an accurate representation of what occurs in an interview or therapy session. It is useful for the interviewer to consider the preconceived notions a patient may bring into an initial session and the influence that such beliefs may have on the patient's responses.

In order to facilitate rapport, the interviewer should also consider some of the logistical and situational elements of the setting in which the interview will be conducted. Regardless of the setting, certain structural elements are highly important, such as having a private environment in which the potential for disturbance is minimized. Both the patient and the interviewer should be seated, ideally in chairs of equal height, and directly facing each other. To convey an open environment, the patient and interviewer should not be separated from one another by a desk or table. If the interviewer takes notes, it should be done in a manner that involves minimal distraction to the patient and maximizes the degree of eye contact maintained with the patient.

## BEGINNING THE INTERVIEW

At the outset, the interviewer should introduce herself, using the manner in which she would prefer to be addressed. It may be useful to briefly summarize for the patient the information the interviewer already has about the patient. In addition, the patient should be told that the purpose of the interview is to gather information about the problem so that the patient will be prepared for the direction of the interview. Then the interviewer will want to give the patient an opportunity to speak about his presenting concern and may ask the patient, "I know a little about you, but why don't you tell me in your own words what has brought you here today?" Although the specific wording may vary from setting to setting, such a transitional statement conveys some understanding of the patient's concerns and gives the patient the opportunity to state the concern in his own words. Additionally, it is often useful to provide the patient more structure by briefly outlining the format of interview. For example, the interviewer might say, "After hearing what you'd like help with, I will ask you about your history, which might help us understand the problem. Then we'll go over the problem in a more detailed manner. So what is it that you would like help with?" Although interviewers who will later serve as therapists to the patient may wish to discuss the general behavioral approach to therapy at this time, it may be more useful to save such a discussion until the end of the interview, thereby allowing the patient to discuss his or her concerns as early as possible in the session.

## DEVELOPING A PROBLEM LIST

As a first step to conducting a functional analysis of the problematic behavior, the interviewer uses open-ended questions to identify one or more problems (Miltenberger & Veltum, 1988). Patients may respond in many ways to an invitation to discuss why they sought an evaluation or therapy. Some may embark on a long, detailed story involving several years of history; others may answer the question by simply saying, "I'm anxious." Regardless of how the patient responds to the query, the interviewer should summarize the patient's disclosure and provide empathy to the patient. Not only does this indicate to the patient that the interviewer is listening, it also begins to establish rapport. Often this initial response by the patient generates an endless supply of subsequent issues to examine. Although some of the details of the situation described may remain unclear, it may be better to continue probing with open-ended questions, allowing the patient to direct the early stages of the interview. It may be best for the interviewer to save more specific closed-ended questions, which might yield more precise information, for later in the interview. The interviewer should inquire about other difficulties the patient may have. These are noted in turn, and the interviewer should continue asking about further problems until the patient indicates there are none.

As the patient continues to describe the reason he is in the interviewer's office, the interviewer should continue to summarize what is being said and provide empathy to him. After the patient concludes a general description of his problems, the interviewer should summarize the list of problems just presented. In addition, the interviewer may wish to make a comment about the process of the interview to this point. For example, the interviewer might comment on the patient's plight, showing some appreciation for the difficulty he might have had in sharing such information or deciding to address the problem by entering into therapy.

## IDENTIFY A PRIORITY PROBLEM AND DEVELOP A SPECIFIC BEHAVIORAL DESCRIPTION

What does the patient think is the most distressing problem or area of his life? It is important for the interviewer to prioritize his or her efforts by asking open-ended questions about the problem that is most troublesome or should be addressed first (Miltenberger & Veltum, 1988). This involves addressing the consequences of selecting the problem, how the patient's life would be improved or changed if the problem were to be addressed, and how motivated the patient would be to change in that area of his or her life. Often this is not a straightforward process. One older adult that one of the present authors worked with identified conflict with his wife, difficulty maintaining a healthy diet in the face of the onset of diabetes, and depression as important problems. After identifying and discussing difficulties with his wife extensively, the patient opted to focus on changing his eating habits. Although the marital conflict and the feelings of depression that he thought resulted from this conflict were seemingly key aspects of his life, he decided that his ill health and need to address his diet were more important and changeable. Thus, the interviewer faces difficult decisions in guiding patients, it is important to be systematic in discussions with patients so that the consequences of the direction in therapy are well understood.

The onset and history of the problem are the next aspects for the interviewer to address. Straightforward questions such as "When did you first have problems like the one we just discussed?" are often sufficient to elicit the context giving rise to the problem. Some patients, however, may respond to this inquiry with vagueness or with the statement that "things have always been this way." Such responses should prompt specific questions of various time points in the patient's history to stimulate the patient's memory. The interviewer should keep in mind that many patients are not accustomed to thinking systematically about their problems and that maintaining rapport is more important than obtaining detailed historical information in the first contact. It may also be convenient to inquire about family and social history at this point.

The interviewer then examines the topography of the problem, including its frequency, duration, intensity, and/or latency (i.e., in relation to any precipitating event) (Deffenbacher, 1992). In order to obtain estimates of specific problem behaviors, such as compulsive buying, it is useful to adopt strategies used in semi-structured timeline follow-back (TLFB) assessments. The key aspects of the TLFB method include the use of a calendar as well as a systematic review of each time period on the calendar, working backward to stimulate recall. First, the interviewer establishes the time period, such as one month, six months, depending on the predicted frequency and the clinical consideration regarding the type of behavior involved. The therapist then asks about key events in the patient's life during this period or holidays as marked on the calendar, in order to relate these events to the behavior in question. Then starting with the most current time period, the interviewer asks about the frequency of behavior for that period. Details about the behavior are established as clinically relevant—for example, how long the patient shopped, what time of day the buying occurred, and how much the patient spent during the last week. Working backward, one week (or month, depending on the context) at a time, the interviewer asks for the patient's estimate of the behavior for that period. If the patient has a calendar or appointment book of his or her own, then the patient is asked to use this as a cue for better recall. If recall is poor for a specific period, then the interview can ask nondirective general questions about the frequency ("Were you compelled to buy anything during the first half of the month, to the best of your memory?"). It is also useful to refer back to any other sources of information regarding frequency of the behavior, either earlier in the interview or from other reporters, to reconcile any differences in the frequency from these sources.

In addition to frequency, the interviewer should inquire about the situational specificity of the patient's behavior relevant to the problem (Kazdin, 1979). What shopping situations do not lead to compulsive buying? This may include the moods experienced by the patient, the activity prior to the behavior, the type of people involved in the problem, the time of day, the place or type of place, or the type of activity that may be required. In the example of the patient who was plagued with compulsive buying, the patient may not feel compelled to buy items when in need of specific personal items and his or her mood is good, or he or she may not feel drawn to buy items when accompanied by friends to a mall.

The interviewer then assesses the immediate antecedents and consequences of the problem behavior or event, including the responses of the environment (i.e., "What did others do when you did X?") as well as shifts in mood, cognition, imagery, and behavior on the part of the patient. For example, the interviewer might ask, "Can you close your eyes now, imagine the event, and tell me what thoughts or images crossed your mind?" Using open-ended questions, the interview should systematically and carefully assess these factors before, during, and after the event (Miltenberger & Veltum, 1988). As stated earlier, it is necessary to assess the immediate as well as the delayed consequences of a problem behavior or event, in order to ensure that all possible influential factors are identified (Deffenbacher, 1992).

The role of the patient's beliefs about his problems and, more generally, his worldview has been recognized from early on in the history of behavior therapy (Lazarus, 1971). At this point, it may be helpful to inquire about the patient's beliefs about the cause of his problems. In the most direct way, a patient's beliefs about his problems may lead to noncompliance to the clinician's request during therapy. For example, if a patient believes his depression is primarily determined by biological factors, the relevance of behavioral methods of intervention may not be immediately clear to the patient. Many patients will have already hinted about their beliefs about the cause of the problem during their initial description of the problem. The interviewer can use this information to prompt the patient to expand on these ideas. For example, the clinician may say, "You mentioned that you wondered whether there was something physically wrong with your body. Do you have an idea of what that might be? Was there anything other doctors have told you or something you read that might lead you to consider that possibility?" On another level, the clinician needs to understand the patient's worldview in order to guide the assessment and treatment appropriately. What are the patient's values connected to the problem? Did the reported problem arise from the patient's failure to achieve his or her own behavioral expectations in life? This type of information will help the clinician appreciate how the patient prioritizes problems and how willing he might be to achieve therapeutic goals. For example, the reduction of social conflict for one patient who expects himself to have a high level of social competence may take a different course than for a patient whose career achievement is tantamount.

After the presenting problem has been identified and redefined in behavioral terms, the interview should begin to widen the spectrum of questioning to other areas of the patient's life. Asking how the problematic behavior affects other areas of the patient's life, such as employment and social relationships not already discussed, will allow the interviewer to further understand the extent of difficulty the presenting problem is causing. As already noted, the patient's medical status should be addressed first by inquiring about when the patient last went to a medical doctor or had a medical examination or whether the patient had recently been sick. The reader can consult Morrison and Bellack (1987) or Harper (2004) for detailed information about psychological syndromes and medical difficulties.

Although the patient's report of difficulties is essential, it may also be necessary to collect information about the patient's behavior from outside sources. The interviewer may arrange to interview other individuals, such as relatives, who interact with the patient concerning the problem behavior. Patients with Obsessive-Compulsive Disorder, for example, may be sufficiently embarrassed or distressed about their symptoms to underestimate the frequency of their compulsive behaviors or the degree of impact of this maladaptive behavior on family relationships.

## ENDING THE BEHAVIORAL INTERVIEW

As the interview comes to a close, the interviewer should provide a summary to the patient of the information collected. The summary provides another opportunity for the interviewer to explain to the client the presenting problem in behavioral terms. Some interviewers may wish to describe explicitly the antecedent–behavior–consequence relationship to the patient as an element of treatment. The patient will leave the office having received a behaviorally based conceptualization of the presenting problem and a basic idea of how the problem may be addressed in treatment.

Not only will the summary demonstrate understanding to the patient, it can be a useful bridge into a discussion of the need for further assessment. Additional assessment may include asking the patient to monitor his or her behavior prior to the next session or, when appropriate, observations of the patient in situations in which the problematic behavior is occurring. The reasons for these techniques need to be addressed fully using the initial behavioral conceptualization of the problem. Patients unfamiliar with behavioral assessment and therapy may be surprised that treatment will involve tasks such as behavioral monitoring and other "homework" assignments. Some patients may be uncomfortable with such an approach to assessment and treatment; others may not be willing to engage in this type of treatment due to the time commitment sometimes involved. Other patients may be critical of behavioral interventions due to issues of freedom and control. The interviewer should be prepared to address these concerns.

Finally, the interviewer may wish to provide encouragement to the patient by commenting on the previous distress of the patient and applaud his or her courage for seeking help. In addition, the interviewer may want to leave the patient with a sense of optimism by discussing the existing empirical support for the behaviorally based treatment of the presenting problem.

## PERSON FACTORS IN THE BEHAVIORAL INTERVIEW

The behavioral interview is an interactive process whose product, the information relevant to the patient's complaint, is a function of the interaction of many elements. This interaction is influenced to a large extent by the characteristics of the patient and the interviewer. In addition, other elements of the process affect the end product, including the environmental setting of the interview and the manner in which additional information about the patient is collected. In this section, we focus on the effect that the actual participants in the interview, the interviewer and the patient, have on the interview.

## INTERVIEWERS' CHARACTERISTICS AND BEHAVIORS

There are several aspects of interviewing style about which the behavioral interviewer should take note. As described in a previous section, behavioral interviews can be more efficient when the patient is provided some structure to present difficulties. The interviewer is the "leader" in the interview; consistent with this metaphor, the patient cannot be forced to follow. Again, the interviewer must be prepared to follow the patient's lead at times, exercising the flexibility in the goals he or she has for the interview. We have placed great emphasis on the information one needs to gather in a behavioral interview, how to help the patient to provide detailed information, and how to help the patient understand his or her difficulties through a behavioral "lens." Many patients will already have definite ideas about their difficulties and the solutions, however, despite having consulted a clinician for an evaluation. Some patients will have a firm agenda for the initial session that may differ from the agenda of the interviewer. It is important to remember that there need not be a struggle for the control of the session, because patients who present in this way are doing so for reasons that are paramount to them and important for the interviewer to understand. This type of behavior may be, in itself, a relevant sample of the patient's behavior. The interviewer can inquire about the range and frequency of assertive/directive type of behavior by saying the following: "It sounds like you have a good idea about the things you feel I should know and how you want to present them. I'm wondering if this would be your approach in general, or if this is an uncommon circumstance? For example, are you fairly systematic like this at work when talking to a coworker or to your boss?" Furthermore, the patient's cognitions and affect related to his way of presenting can be assessed in the following way: "I was wondering what you thought might happen if you did not arrive as organized as you have been— some people are afraid they won't be able to get to everything across; others fear they will not be organized enough. What was your motivation?" Although this example illustrates the use of a decidedly broad, nonbehavioral term (i.e., "motivation"), the patient will likely respond with clues about his or her thoughts and feelings that can be followed up with questions by the interviewer.

Second, the effective interviewer must have well-developed listening skills (P. H. Wilson, Spence, & Kavanagh, 1989). This includes good eye contact, a relaxed but appropriate body posture, appropriate turn-taking in speaking, and summarizing and asking for clarification for the information conveyed by the patient. As mentioned briefly in the section labeled "Beginning the Interview," the interviewer can facilitate the development of rapport through structural aspects of the interview—the placement of chairs, appropriate posture, appropriate eye contact even if the therapist takes notes during the interview. In addition, the interviewer must be careful to exhibit appropriate turn-taking in speaking, particularly during the first statements on the part of the patient. Although interruptions may be necessary at a later point in order to guide the direction of the conversation, interruptions early in the interview can convey an exaggerated sense of hierarchy (i.e., "What I am saying is more important that what you are saying") and lack of respect for the problems as seen by the patient. Some patients may be initially reticent in describing their problems, and the interviewer can "help" patients along by allowing for pauses before speaking. Furthermore, the interviewer can facilitate the telling of the "story" by briefly summarizing what was related and asking for clarifications about particular elements. For example, an interviewer might say, "So the most recent instance of fighting with your brother was the most upsetting and led most directly to feeling separated from your family. What was different this time from the other times?"

The communication of warmth, positive regard, and genuineness through expression of accurate empathy is of paramount importance. This is a subtle and difficult-to-specify aspect of the patient–therapist relationship that was emphasized several decades ago by Rogers (1961). Indeed, current texts on interviewing continue to emphasize this basic process (Turner, Hersen, & Heiser, 2003), so there are a few points the behavioral interviewer should keep in mind. First, exhibiting accurate empathy and acceptance can be facilitated by the interviewer's focusing on the emotions and moods expressed by the patient in addition to the facts of the problem situation. When summarizing the patient's statements through paraphrasing, empathy and acceptance are conveyed when the emotions are highlighted, rather than facts. This is a fundamentally different process than summarizing and clarifying, as illustrated earlier, where gathering information is the goal. The effective interviewer uses one or the other of these types of reflections, depending on what is needed at that particular moment. If the interviewer judges that the patient is conveying something particularly intense or unpleasant, then exhibiting empathy about these feelings may facilitate rapport more readily than focusing on the facts of the situation.

Another aspect of interviewer behavior that can determine the direction of the interview is the relative use of open- vs. closed-ended questions (Craig, 1989). The most important feature of open- versus closed-ended questions is the degree of structure that is placed on the response. Thus, the more closed-ended the question, the more restrictive and directive it is regarding the patient's response. An open-ended question that provides a good deal of freedom for the patient's response might be: "Can you tell me about what it has been like for you when on dates in the past?" A question that provides more restrictions to the patient's response is the following: "When you were at the movie with Beth last Friday night, what thoughts and feelings were you having about the date?" The most closed-ended type of question calls for a yes/no or numerical response, as illustrated by the following: "How many drinks did you have on Monday? How about on Tuesday? (etc.)," or "Did you go to any parties this week?" The closed-ended questions tend to get specific responses, but they are "conversation stoppers." Open-ended questions may get specific *or* general answers and may or may not address the desired content area. However, they tend to draw out information that is particularly important to the patient. The behavioral interviewer should keep in mind the general response style of the patient and the nature of the information desired at that point in the interview when deciding to use closed- vs. open-ended questions. Typically, there will be more open-ended questions in the beginning of the interview than at the end as the interviewer narrows down the most important content areas to address.

Both novice and expert interviewers often forget that they have developed a highly specialized vocabulary for describing psychological difficulties and often may use these technical words with the patient. Jargon should be avoided because it is distracting and often confusing to the patient because of the existence of alternate meanings in everyday language. Examples of problematic terminology include: *affect, obsession,* and *reinforcement.* Using common wording instead of jargon is not "dumbing down" the presentation of ideas in a way that insults the patient's intelligence. The interviewer might recognize that if an idea or concept cannot be described in nontechnical language to an interested nonprofessional person, then it is unlikely to be a useful idea.

Use of humor in clinical interviewing has a controversial history. The psychoanalytic position on the use of humor suggests that it is inappropriately injecting one's own personality and psychological conflicts into the assessment session; indeed, (the patient's) humor should be the subject of psychotherapeutic interpretation. Similarly, self-disclosure has often been seen as taboo, in that it may disturb the "blank slate" that allows the transference relationship to form. However, the concepts of the interpretation of humor and of transference have limited utility in behavior therapy. In behavioral interviewing it is important to establish a rationale for the use of humor and self-disclosure. In general, humor and self-disclosure should be used judiciously, particularly because the interviewer may be unable to know how the statement may be viewed by the patient. If humor or self-disclosure is used, the clinician should always understand the goal. Reasonable goals for both humor and self-disclosure include the following: (1) to put the patient at ease, (2) to provide a release in the tension of the session, (3) to build rapport by demonstrating a commonality or empathy (specifically, self-disclosure), and (4) to build rapport by showing genuineness.

## PATIENTS' CHARACTERISTICS AND BEHAVIORS

Numerous factors or variables of the patient can influence the behavioral interview process. At the most elementary level, a patient's demographic characteristics can influence the information conveyed to the interviewer. Gender, age, race, religion, marital status, employment history, and socioeconomic conditions are just some of the variables that may affect the information given to a behavioral interviewer. These characteristics in part influence a patient's worldview, in that each patient's concerns are formed by her experiences. For example, the interviewer must recognize that the concerns voiced by a devout Catholic patient about the possibility of a marital separation may take on a radically different meaning than for the relationship separation voiced by a nonreligious individual who has never been married.

In addition, the manner in which these variables compare and contrast with those of the interviewer may influence the information collected. Some research suggests that the demographic differences between interviewer and interviewee influences report of sensitive behaviors. For example, Ford and Norris (1997), found that interviewer age and ethnicity affect report of sexual activity in participants 15–24 years of age; Hispanic women reported more sexual activity to younger interviewers. At a more descriptive level, it is easy to imagine how a depressed, unemployed patient who attends sessions casually dressed in jeans may be embarrassed or resentful in discussing his or her financial problems with an interviewer wearing a suit. Another example might be a Jewish patient who may be reluctant to discuss the role personal religious beliefs play in his or her anxiety with a non-Jewish interviewer. The interviewer should keep in mind the role of diversity in the interview process. Is the patient tailoring or limiting the presentation of his concerns to the interviewer based on the patient's concept of the interviewer's demographics? Although this may not be accurately anticipated, the interviewer should be sure to maintain an open and accepting stance so that the patient will be encouraged to reveal as much as needed to address the presenting problem. This stance can be communicated if the interviewer limits any skeptical tone or implication in his questions; alternatively, a persistent, interested, and inquisitive manner might be more productive.

Along these lines, the interviewer must be careful not to make assumptions about the patient based on superficial demographic characteristics, especially when the patient appears to be from a culture that differs from his own. The family of a schizophrenia patient treated by one of us had emigrated from Pakistan and the family constellation was unusually close-knit by American standards. However, in this case it was important to avoid assuming that the conventional wisdom was true (and the family members' report) that it is normative that Pakistani families are more close-knit. A detailed inquiry about the functioning of the family, the expectations of each family member, and the needs of the patient was necessary to help the patient function as well as possible.

The manner in which patients convey the information to the interviewer also can influence the interview process. Patients often have their own understandings or hypotheses about their presenting problems and the importance or relevance in their lives. Although these self-generated hypotheses have their own truth for the patient, patients also may have little understanding of how their presenting problem is affected by ongoing behavioral contingencies. As discussed earlier, some patients may describe vaguely the effects of the presenting problem on their behavior, whereas others may be able to spontaneously pinpoint antecedents and consequences to their problems. Given the possible range of styles patients may use, it is clear that at times it is beneficial for the interviewer to begin to reframe the patient's problem in behavioral terms. The interviewer must remain flexible regarding the direction of the interview and flexible regarding the level of information gained in any single interview. Without this flexibility, the interviewer will become frustrated, which will begin to erode the rapport that is necessary for an effective interview.

All clinicians will, at some time during their career, interview difficult or challenging patients. Of course, the type of patient that is difficult to interview differs from interviewer to interviewer, but some reliably difficult patient characteristics include hostility, social inappropriateness, guardedness, and defensiveness. Most of these ways of presenting result from two sources: The patient dislikes the situation he is in, and/or the patient is presenting a behavioral style that is somewhat representative of his behavior outside the session. Thus, the behavioral interviewer's task is still to understand the contingencies that govern the patient's behavior.

One key to gathering as much information as possible about a difficult patient's behavior is for the interviewer to limit his or her own overt emotional responses, thus not reciprocating strong negative affect. This can be aided by the interviewer's developing a sense of what in-session problematic behaviors are truly consequential. At one extreme of this continuum, a patient can be physically threatening or actually violent; at the other extreme, a patient could be mildly insulting or rude. Where the interviewer draws the line in between these extremes will determine to what extent the patient's behavior and associated affect can be explored in the session, as opposed to limited. Does the interviewer need to respond to a patient's putting her feet on the coffee table in his office? Does it really matter if the patient takes books off the interviewer's shelf when entering the office? A limit may be a polite request to cease a behavior ("I would appreciate it if you would put your feet on the floor rather than on my desk") or an indication that the session would be stopped if the behavior does not change ("You will have to stop yelling and take a seat or we will have to stop for now").

Patients who are hostile or upset at an interviewer generally prompt the least effective behavior from the clinician. We do not intend to upset our patients, so when this happens we often respond defensively (e.g., "The behavioral approach *happens* to be the most effective way of conceptualizing and treating patients with anxiety problems"), argumentatively (e.g., "But that's really not what I meant"), or with an interpretation (e.g., "Maybe you are generalizing to me the things your husband has said to you"). There is no harm, and usually great long-term benefit, to simply acknowledging the error and demonstrating acceptance of the patient's feelings through accurate empathy. This requires practice because the interviewer's first response is usually highly emotional and very difficult to retrain.

Another way for the interviewer to limit his or her own destructive responses is to concentrate on remaining curious about what is precipitating and maintaining the patient's negative responses to the situation. As suggested earlier, it is important first to acknowledge and empathize with the patient's negative response. Then questions such as the following can elicit useful information without indicting the patient's reasoning or feelings: "I'm glad you told me about being so angry about the question that was insulting to you. Now I'd like to understand what you didn't like about it so that I can avoid doing that in the future. Can you tell me what about it made the question hit you so hard? And were there other things that I did or even someone else did that really made it all worse?"

## SUMMARY

Behavioral interviewing is a crucial aspect of behavioral assessment and treatment. It is a complex process that requires the interviewer to assess the patient's difficulties, abilities, and resources while at the same time developing a supportive working relationship. The behavioral interviewer uses the framework of learning principles in order to understand what precipitates and maintains problematic behavior. Although existing research provides some support for the usefulness of the behavioral interview, only a general consensus has been developed about the specific elements necessary in this type of assessment. A great deal of additional research is needed to support the reliability and validity of the selection of target behaviors as well as the functional analysis that behavioral interviews yield.

A skillful behavioral interview involves assessing a number of specific details about the topology of the presenting problem. In most instances the interviewer finds that the interview will flow better with some structure, which can be provided by suggesting to the patient the general sequence of the interview. During the discussion of the patient's complaints, the interviewer helps the patient provide detailed information about the frequency of difficulties, the antecedents and consequences of the patient's behavior occurring in problem situations, and the interpersonal context in which the problem occurs. Several difficulties may be examined in this way until the primary difficulties of the patient are understood. The patient's history is also examined to the extent that it may be relevant to the patient's difficulties. The interviewer closes the session with a summary of the information covered, some comment on the next step, and general support and encouragement for his or her desire for treatment.

It should be recognized that both the patient's and the therapist's characteristics influence the course of the interview. The interviewer should keep in mind the general goals of the discussion but remain flexible to account for the needs of the patient. Successful interviewers develop good listening skills, such as eye contact and appropriate posture. Rapport between the patient and interviewer is built through using accurate empathy, especially when empathic reflections are focused on the patient's emotions. In addition, interviewers will tend to use open-ended questions in the beginning of the interview but to use more close-ended questions in order to get more specific information as the interview progresses. Although the use of humor and self-disclosure has been seen as taboo in the past, judicious use by the interviewer can actually help build rapport.

Patients' goals and expectations of the evaluation and treatment process are the result of their respective cultures and life experiences. However, interviewers should be careful not to make assumptions about patients based on superficial demographic information—detailed inquiry is usually needed to understand fully how patients perceive their problems and the treatment setting. Patients sometimes present difficulties for the interviewer by being hostile, defensive, or inappropriate. Interviewers should make clear for themselves what specific behaviors are unacceptable in the office, versus actions that are unpleasant but may be valuable samples of the patients' behavior outside the session. When confronted by hostile patients, many clinicians fail to be appropriately empathic and do not sufficiently examine the reasons for the patients' criticism. Despite the discomfort associated with the negative affect directed toward the interviewer, it is still important that the interviewer try to understand the precipitants of the conflict situation as well as the factors maintaining it.

## REFERENCES

Bakeman, R., & Gottman, J. M. (1997). *Observing interaction: An introduction to sequential analysis*. New York: Cambridge University Press.

Bardone, A. M., Krahn, D. D., Goodman, B. M., & Searles, J. S. (2000). Using interactive voice response technology and timeline follow-back methodology in studying binge eating and drinking behavior: Different answers to different forms of the same question? *Addictive Behaviors, 25,* 1–11.

Beck, J. (1995). *Cognitive therapy: Basics and Beyond.* New York: Guilford Press.

Craig, R. J. (1989). The clinical process of interviewing. In R. J. Craig (Ed.), *Clinical and diagnostic interviewing* (pp. 3–34). Northvale, NJ: Jason Aronson.

Deffenbacher, J. L. (1992). A little more about behavioral assessment. *Journal of Counseling & Development, 70,* 632.

Foa, E. B., & Emmelkamp, P. M. G. (1983). *Failures in behavior therapy.* New York: John Wiley & Sons.

Ford, K., & Norris, A. E. (1997). Effects of interviewer age on reporting of sexual and reproductive behavior of Hispanic and African American youth. *Hispanic Journal of Behavioral Sciences, 19,* 369–376.

Galassi, J. P., & Perot, A. R. (1992). What you should know about behavioral assessment. *Journal of Counseling & Development, 70,* 624.

Harper, R. G. (2004). Behavioral medicine theory and medical disease. In R. G. Harper (Ed.), *Personality-guided therapy in behavioral medicine* (pp. 19–45). Washington, DC: American Psychological Association.

Hay, W. M., Hay, L. R., Angle, H.V., & Nelson, R. O. (1979). The reliability of problem identification in the behavioral interview. *Behavioral Assessment, 1,* 107–118.

Hodgins, D. C., & Makarchuk, K. (2003). Trusting problem gamblers: Reliability and validity of self-reported gambling behavior. *Psychology of Addictive Behaviors, 17,* 244–248.

Iwata, B. A., Wong, S. E., Riordan, M. M., Dorsey, M. F., & Lau, M. M. (1982). Assessment and training of clinical interviewing skills: analogue analysis and field replication. *Journal of Applied Behavior Analysis, 15,* 191–203.

Keane, T., Black, J. L., Collins, F. L., & Vinson, M. C. (1982). A skills training program for teaching the behavioral interview. *Behavioral Assessment, 4,* 53–62.

Kanfer, F. H., & Grimm, L. G. (1977). Behavioral analysis: Selecting target behaviors in the interview. *Behavior Modification, 4,* 419–444.

Kazdin, A. E. (1979). Situational specificity: The two-edged sword of behavioral assessment. *Behavioral Assessment, 1,* 57–75.

Lazarus, A. A. (1971). Notes on behavior therapy, the problem of relapse and some tentative solutions. *Psychotherapy, 8,* 192–196.

Lazarus, A. A. (1973) Multimodal behavior therapy: Treating the "BASIC ID." *Journal of Nervous and Mental Disease, 156,* 404–111.

Miltenberger, R. G., & Fuqua, R. W. (1985). Evaluation of a training manual for the acquisition of behavioral assessment interviewing skills. *Journal of Applied Behavior Analysis, 18,* 323–328.

Miltenberger, R. G., & Veltum, L. G. (1988). Evaluation of an instructions and modeling procedure for training behavioral assessment interviewing. *Journal of Behavioral and Experimental Psychiatry, 19,* 31–41.

Morganstern, K. P. (1976). Behavioral interviewing: The initial stages of development. In M. Hersen & A. S. Bellack (Eds.), *Behavioral Assessment: A practical handbook.* New York: Pergamon Press.

Morrison, R. L., & Bellack, A. S. (1987). *Medical factors and psychological disorders: A handbook for psychologists.* New York: Plenum Press.

Mueser, K. T., & Glynn, S. M. (1995). *Behavioral family therapy for psychiatric disorders.* New York: Allyn & Bacon.

Mullinix, S. D., & Galassi, J. P. (1981). Deriving the content of social skills training with a verbal response components approach. *Behavioral Assessment, 3,* 55–66.

Murphy, G. C., Hudson, A. M., King, N. J., & Remenyi, A. (1985). An interview schedule for use in the behavioural assessment of children's problems. *Behaviour Change, 2,* 6–12.

O'Boyle, M., & Concirpini, P. (1993). Medical complications with adults. In A. S. Bellack & M. Hersen (Eds.), *Handbook of behavior therapy in the psychiatric setting* (pp. 165–175). New York: Plenum Press.

O'Brien, W. H., & Haynes, S. N. (1993). Behavioral assessment in the psychiatric setting. In A. S. Bellack & M. Hersen (Eds.), *Handbook of behavior therapy in the psychiatric setting* (pp. 39–71). New York: Plenum Press.

O'Leary, K. D., & Wilson, G. T. (1975). *Behavior therapy: Application and outcome.* Englewood Cliffs, NJ: Prentice Hall.

O'Neill, R. E., Horner, R. H., Albin, R. W., Storey, K., & Sprague, J. R. (1990). *Functional analysis of problem behavior: A practical guide.* Sycamore, IL: Sycamore.

Riso, L. P., du Toit, P. L., Blandino, J. A., Penna, S., Dacey, S., Duin, J. S., et al. (2003). Cognitive aspects of chronic depression. *Journal of Abnormal Psychology, 112,* 72–80.

Rogers, C. R. (1961). *On becoming a person.* Boston: Houghton Mifflin.

Sobell, L. C., Sobell, M. B., Riley, D. M., Schuller, R., Pavan, D. S., Cancilla, A., et al. (1988). The reliability of alcohol abusers' self-reports of drinking and life events that occurred in the distant past. *Journal of Studies on Alcohol, 49,* 225–232.

Spitzer, R. L., Williams, J. B. W., Gibbon, M., & First, M. B. (1990). *User's guide for the structured clinical interview for DSM-III-R: SCID.* Washington, DC: American Psychiatric Press.

Sprague, J. R., & Horner, R. H. (1995). Functional assessment and intervention in community settings. *Mental Retardation & Developmental Disabilities Research Reviews, 1,* 89–93.

Swan, G. E., & MacDonald, M. L. (1978). Behavior therapy in practice: A national survey of behavior therapists. *Behavior Therapy, 9,* 799–807.

Turner, S. M., Hersen, M., & Heiser, N. (2003). The Interviewing Process. In M. Hersen & S. M. Turner (Eds.), *Diagnostic interviewing* (3rd ed., pp. 1–20). New York: Kluwer Academic/ Plenum.

Voeltz, L. M., & Evans, I. M. (1982). The assessment of behavioral interrelationships in child behavior therapy. *Behavioral Assessment, 4,* 131–165.

Weinhardt, L. S., Carey, M. P., Maisto, S. A., Carey, K. B., Cohen, M. M., & Wickramasinghe, S. M. (1998). Reliability of the Timeline Follow-Back sexual behavior interview. *Annals of Behavioral Medicine, 20,* 25–30.

Wilson, F. E., & Evans, I. M. (1983). The reliability of target-behavior selection in behavioral assessment. *Behavioral Assessment, 5,* 15–32.

Wilson, P. H., Spence, S. H., & Kavanagh, D. J. (1989). *Cognitive-behavioral interviewing for adult disorders: A practical handbook.* Baltimore: The Johns Hopkins University Press.

# 5

# ACTIVITY MEASUREMENT

WARREN W. TRYON

*Department of Psychology*
*Fordham University*
*Bronx, New York*

## INTRODUCTION

*Actigraphy* refers to the use of instruments to objectively measure and record activity level, especially in the natural environment over extended time periods. This chapter* is organized around the following questions: (a) Why is there interest in activity level? (b) Why measure what you can rate, and, alternatively, why rate what you can measure? (c) What does actigraphy contribute to the behavioral assessment of adults? (d) What case conceptualization and treatment planning issues are involved? (e) What methodological issues are involved? (d) What developmental issues and trends have been noted? (e) What instruments are available, and are they reliable and valid? This is a comprehensive textbook of behavioral assessment and accordingly I have endeavored to include all aspects of actigraphy pertinent to adults. Chapter 6 in *Clinician's Handbook of Child Behavioral Assessment*, entitled "Activity Measurement," is where the remaining applications should appear. The greatly expanded research base, in combination with space limitations, restricts coverage. Little more than citation, therefore, occurs in several places.

---

* This chapter is based on a variety of chapters and a book I have authored. It has become impossible to find different ways to effectively word some portions of the same material. Placing quotation marks around these passages and attributing authorship to myself serves no useful purpose and detracts from readability.

## WHY IS THERE INTEREST IN
## ACTIVITY LEVEL?

Why on Earth would anyone, especially a psychologist, be interested in measuring activity level? It just does not seem to be psychologically relevant or interesting. The answer is simple, straightforward, and practical. Behavior is the final common pathway for the cumulative effects of heredity and environment, including cognitive, affective, and behavioral processes. What one chooses to do in the next moment is the cumulative result of complex life span developmental events that encompass the broad spectrum of psychological processes. Whatever your choice, it involves measurable activity, ranging from zero to some maximum value. There is no choice one can make that is not characterized by some degree of movement, including zero. Everything that one does or does not do is reflected in activity level. Personal decisions span a large activity range, from low levels associated with choices to watch TV, read, and sleep through moderate choices such as walking and gardening to high levels associated with competitive sports and aerobic exercise. Personality concerns stable individual differences. Activity level is a highly heritable characteristic that emerges during gestation and is universally recognized as a major dimension of infant temperament (Thomas & Chess, 1977; Thomas, Chess, & Birch, 1968; Goldsmith et al., 1987) and characterizes the personality of children and adults into old age. Activity level is important during geriatric years (Tryon, 1998b) because it predicts the ability to live on one's own. That activity level pertains so widely to normal behavior means that it also applies broadly to psychological disorders. Table 5.1 documents that activity level is part of the inclusion or exclusion criteria of 48 *DSM-IV* disorders (Tryon, 2002), including sleep and its disruption (Tryon, 1996b, 2004a). No other psychological test or assessment procedure is so broadly applicable.

Actigraphy is also informative to psychologists, psychiatrists, and general physicians concerned with a wide variety of general medical and health-related matters. Increased activity level is associated with decreased all-cause mortality (Andersen, Schnohr, Schroll, & Hein, 2000; Slattery, Jacobs, & Nichaman, 1989). Literature reviewed later documents the following effects: (a) Actigraphy is responsive to and tracks changes in a variety of major medical matters. (b) Obesity is associated with reduced activity level. (c) Heart disease reduces activity level. (d) Actigraphy can track recovery from major surgery. (e) Fatigue is a common medical complaint. Chronic Fatigue Syndrome reduces activity level. (f) Infection, AIDS, and cancer tend to decrease activity level. Anyone who has ever had the flu can testify that activity level is lower while sick than otherwise. The following behavioral health and medicine applications are addressed: (a) anesthesia response, (b) surgery recovery, (c) essential hypertension, (d) heart disease, (e) cancer, (f) diabetes, (g) chronic obstructive pulmonary disease (COPD), (h) dementia, (i) arthritis, (j) response to infection and AIDS, (k) Chronic Fatigue Syndrome, (l) multiple sclerosis, (m) fibromyalgia, (n) osteoporosis, (o) total joint replacement survival, (p) chronic pain, (q) sickle cell crises, (r) cirrhosis, (s) traumatic brain injury, (t) smoking, and (u) menopause.

TABLE 5.1 Summary of *DSM-IV* for Which Activity Level Is Part of Inclusion or Exclusion Criteria

| Number | *DSM-IV* Code | *DSM-IV* Diagnosis | Inclusion Criterion (pages) | Exclusion Criterion Differential Diagnosis (pages) |
|---|---|---|---|---|
| 1 | 314.01 | Attention-Deficit/Hyperactivity Disorder, Combined Type | 80, 83–85 | |
| 2 | 314.00 | Attention-Deficit/Hyperactivity Disorder, Predominantly Inattentive Type | 80, 83–85 | |
| 3 | 314.01 | Attention-Deficit/Hyperactivity Disorder, Predominantly Hyperactive-Impulsive Type | 80, 83–85 | |
| 4 | 312.8 | Conduct Disorder | | ADHD (89), Manic Episode (89) |
| 5 | 313.81 | Oppositional Defiant Disorder | | ADHD (93), Conduct Disorder (93) |
| 6 | 293.89 | Catatonic Disorder | 170–171 | |
| 7 | 291.8 | Alcohol Withdrawal | 198 | |
| 8 | 292.89 | Amphetamine Intoxication | 207–208 | |
| 9 | 292.0 | Amphetamine Withdrawal | 209 | |
| 10 | 305.90 | Caffeine Intoxication | 213 | |
| 11 | 292.89 | Cocaine Intoxication | 224 | |
| 12 | 292.0 | Cocaine Withdrawal | 225–226 | |
| 13 | 292.89 | Inhalant Intoxication | 239 | |
| 14 | 292.0 | Nicotine Withdrawal | 244–245 | |
| 15 | 292.0 | Opioid Withdrawal | 251 | |
| 16 | 292.0 | Sedative, Hypnotic, or Anxiolytic Withdrawal | 266 | |
| 17 | 295.20 | Schizophrenia, Catatonic Type | 289 | |
| 18 | 295.70 | Schizoaffective Disorder | 295–296 | |
| 19 | 298.8 | Brief Psychotic Disorder | 304 | |
| 20 | 296.2 or 3 | Major Depressive Disorder | 320–325 | |
| 21 | 296.0 or 4 | Manic Episode | 328–331 | |
| 22 | 300.4 | Dysthymic Disorder | 345 | |
| 23 | 311 | Depressive Disorder Not Otherwise Specified | 350 | |
| 24 | 296. | Bipolar I Disorder | 350–358 | |
| 25 | 296.89 | Bipolar II Disorder | 359–363 | |
| 26 | 301.13 | Cyclothymic Disorder | 363–366 | |
| 27 | 296.80 | Bipolar Disorder Not Otherwise Specified | 366 | |
| 28 | 293.83 | Mood Disorder Due to a General Medical Condition | 366–370 | |
| 29 | 296.90 | Mood Disorder Not Otherwise Specified | 375 | |
| 30 | 309.81 | Post-Traumatic Stress Disorder | 427–429 | |

*(continues)*

TABLE 5.1   (*continued*)

| Number | DSM-IV Code | DSM-IV Diagnosis | Inclusion Criterion (pages) | Exclusion Criterion Differential Diagnosis (pages) |
|--------|-------------|------------------|-----------------------------|----------------------------------------------------|
| 31 | 308.3 | Acute Stress Disorder | 431–432 | PTSD (435), Mood Disorders (435) |
| 32 | 300.02 | Generalized Anxiety Disorder | 435–436 | |
| 33 | 307.1 | Anorexia Nervosa[a] | 540 | Major Depressive Disorder (544) |
| 34 | 307.51 | Bulimia Nervosa | 549 | Major Depressive Disorder (549) |
| 35 | 307.42 | Primary Insomnia | 557 | |
| 36 | 307.44 | Primary Hypersomnia | 557, 562 | |
| 37 | 347 | Narcolepsy | 562, 567 | |
| 38 | 780.59 | Breathing-Related Sleep Disorder | 567, 573 | |
| 39 | 307.45 | Circadian Rhythm Sleep Disorder | 573, 578 | |
| 40 | 307.47 | Dyssomnia Not Otherwise Specified | 579 | |
| 41 | 307.47 | Nightmare Disorder | 583 | |
| 42 | 307.46 | Sleep Terror Disorder | 583, 587 | |
| 43 | 307.46 | Sleepwalking Disorder | 587, 591 | |
| 44 | 307.42 | Insomnia Related to Another Mental Disorder | 592, 596 | |
| 45 | 307.44 | Hypersomnia Related to Another Mental Disorder | 592, 597 | |
| 46 | 780. | Sleep Disorder Due to a General Medical Condition | 597–601 | |
| 47 | 309.0 | Adjustment Disorder With Depressed Mood | | PTSD (626) |
| 48 | 333.99 | Neuroleptic-Induced Acute Akathesia | 679 | |

Reprinted with permission from Tryon (2002).

In sum, the answer to the question "Why on Earth would anyone, especially a psychologist, be interested in measuring activity level?" is that actigraphy informs six areas of personality development, 48 *Diagnostic and Statistical Manual* (*DSM*) diagnoses with as many as seven subtypes (see Table 5.1), and at least 21 areas of general medical and health applications, for a total of 75 applications. No other assessment procedure used by psychologists or physicians (a) has such a large range of application, (b) is as objective, reliable, and valid, and (c) results in such substantial samples of behavior from the natural environment as actigraphy. These features make actigraphy the Swiss army knife of behavioral assessment.

## WHY RATE WHAT YOU CAN MEASURE?

Why would one want to rate what he can measure? Is it better to affix postage after hefting an envelope or package or to weigh it on a scale? Is it better to estimate a patient's temperature after placing a hand on her forehead or to use a thermometer? Is it better to estimate what time it is or how long some process or event took or to use a clock or stopwatch? These seem like simple, perhaps even ridiculous choices, but social scientists continue to rate rather than measure activity level. *Actigraphy* refers to the instrumented measurement of activity level. While some methods of measuring activity level require that participants be confined to a laboratory, actigraphy connotes ambulatory monitoring under naturalistic conditions. Pedometers were introduced into this country by Thomas Jefferson between 1785 and 1789, at least 215 years ago, yet few investigators and clinicians use them to measure behavior. The history of science is a history of measurement advances. The quality of an investigation cannot exceed the quality of the measurements on which it is based. Tryon (1996a) discussed instrument-driven theory, how instruments and their development have fostered the development of scientific theory and medical practice.

Clinical psychologists prefer to rate rather than measure behavior. Cost is sometimes cited as a reason for preferring ratings over measurements. It is undeniably cheaper to have a parent or teacher rate a child's behavior than it is to purchase a $25 pedometer. However, it is also well known that cross-informant (e.g., parent–teacher) agreement ranges from .30 to .50 for all aspects of behavior (Achenbach, McConaughy, & Howell, 1987), much lower than the high rate of the combined form of ADHD, suggesting a diagnostic validity problem (R. A. Barkley, 2003). Actigraphy provides a common objective metric across situations. Convenience is another factor. Ratings involve simple questions that can be quickly answered in person, over the phone, or via the mail. Pedometers must be worn over some period of time; a behavioral sample must be taken. This requires minimal but some degree of cooperation, which may be inconvenient to request.

## SIGNS VERSUS SYMPTOMS

*Symptoms* are subjective self-reports. Pain, fatigue, blurred vision, nausea, and dizziness are examples. Symptoms are psychological states that include the full spectrum of thoughts, feelings, and behaviors that people present to practitioners. While many symptoms have one or more behavioral correlates that could be measured, common practice is to have patients rate their symptoms. Rating scales and psychophysical scaling procedures may standardize self-report methodology, but they are not objective measurements in the same way that instrumented measurements are. So-called "objective" psychological tests are based entirely on self-reported ratings. Personality tests like the MMPI require people to indicate whether thoughts, feelings, or behaviors are absent or present, whether they are true or false of them. Other psychological tests require people to rate, using a

Likert-type scale, the extent to which thoughts, feelings, and/or behaviors characterize them. Psychologists sometimes reject the medical model as a basis for clinical science and practice but continue to base their assessments, conclusions, and recommendations entirely on symptoms.

*Signs* are directly observable by clinicians and others (Teicher, 1995). Signs of disease include fever, rash, swelling, tremor, and irregular pulse. Signs also include measurements made with instruments such as the sphygmomanometer. Hypertension and hypotension are disease categories that are defined entirely by sphygmomanometer measurements. Signs also include physical and chemical analyses of blood, urine, and other specimens. For example, hypoglycemia and hyperglycemia are defined in terms of milligrams of sugar per deciliter of blood. Medical textbooks such as *Todd–Sanford–Davidsohn: Clinical Diagnosis and Management by Laboratory Methods* by Henry, Davidsohn, and Sanford (1984) contains hundreds of signs of disease derived from physical and chemical measurements of urine, blood, and other specimens. Medicine has made great strides through the diagnosis and management of disease based on signs. Actigraphy quantifies behavior in ways that are broadly relevant to psychology and medicine.

## WHY MEASURE WHAT YOU CAN RATE?

I was once told by a psychologist working in a prestigious hospital/medical center that actigraphy may have a place in research, where investigators require high-quality data, but activity ratings by parents and teachers are sufficient for clinical practice. I was also told that I could not trust clinical diagnoses but would have to redo them at a research-grade level. It seems that high-quality data are reserved for research and low-quality data are fine for clinical practice. Isn't this backwards? Clinical services directly impact the lives of people in need. Research results may get published and then may be read by some academicians and a few practitioners, but most research findings do not impact clinical practice. Arguably, clinicians require the best information possible.

## WHAT DOES ACTIGRAPHY CONTRIBUTE TO THE BEHAVIORAL ASSESSMENT OF ADULTS?

Actigraphy pertains to the inclusion and/or exclusion criteria of 48 *DSM-IV* disorders (cf. Table 5.1; Tryon, 2002) which make it the most widely applicable method of behavioral assessment available. Diagnostic relevance implies that longitudinal evaluation is pertinent to outcome assessment. If a variable is sufficiently important to constitute an inclusion criterion for a diagnostic category, then it is, by definition, an important outcome variable that should be monitored in order to evaluate the effectiveness of therapeutic interventions. An obvious intervention goal is to reduce the measured variable to where it no longer supports a positive diagnosis.

The headings in this section have been chosen to maximize relevance to other chapters in this volume. An additional subsection on behavioral health is included because actigraphy has multiple behavioral medicine applications. The reader should be aware that in addition to Chapter 6 in *Clinician's Handbook of Child Behavioral Assessment* (on measuring activity level in children), actigraphy is relevant to these other chapters in that book: Chapter 12 (on depression), Chapter 17 (on eating disorders), Chapter 19 (on conduct disorders), and Chapter 23 (on classroom assessment). Such breadth of application is unprecedented. We begin with temperament and personality assessment because of its relevance to normal development.

## TEMPERAMENT/PERSONALITY ASSESSMENT

Tryon (2002) reviewed the evidence supporting activity level as a dimension of temperament and personality trait. Activity level is arguably the first stable individual difference (personality factor) to develop. Eaton and Saudino (1992) reviewed 14 studies validating maternal fetal counts recorded during gestational weeks 27–43 and reported additional data that stable interfetal differences in activity level emerge by gestational week 34. Activity level is therefore the first personality characteristic to develop and does so prior to birth. This fact reflects strong genetic influence. DeFries, Gervais, and Thomas (1978) conclusively demonstrated the heritability of activity level across 30 generations of selective breading of high- and low-active mice that diverged from control animals to where their activity level distributions did not overlap.

The evidence that activity level is a primary dimension of infant temperament (e.g., Goldsmith et al., 1987; Thomas & Chess, 1977; Thomas et al., 1968) is essentially conclusive; no debate remains. A review of the temperament and personality literature reveals that activity level is a well-established personality dimension of middle childhood (Shiner, 1998), adult personality (Comrey, 1994; Guilford, Zimmerman, & Guilford, 1976), and adult temperament (Buss, 1989; Buss & Plomin, 1984; Lerner, Palermo, Sprio, & Nessleroade, 1982; Lerner et al., 1986; Waddington, 1998; Windle & Lerner, 1986).

## AFFECTIVE DISORDERS

Chapter 10 in this book concerns the behavioral assessment of depression. Tryon (2002) provided a detailed discussion of this topic that can only be treated in summary form here (cf. Table 5.1). The *DSM-IV* (American Psychiatric Association, 1994) definition of a Major Depressive Episode (MDE) lists nine characteristics, of which five must be present for a positive diagnosis. Three of these criteria concern activity. Item 4 specifies "insomnia or hypersomnia nearly every day" (p. 327). Wrist actigraphy supplemented by the Sleep Switch Device (Hauri, 1999) can document the presence of insomnia and hypersomnia. Item 5 specifies "psychomotor agitation or retardation nearly every day (observable by others, not merely subjective feelings of restlessness or being slowed down)" (p. 327). Most of this research has been conducted under controlled inpatient settings. Futterman and Tryon (1994) reported evidence of psychomotor retardation when comparing depressed and control outpatient women. T. J. Barkley and Tryon (1995) demonstrated psychomotor retardation within a college sample. Item 6 specifies "fatigue or loss of energy nearly every day." Unless occupational or other necessity forces the person to remain active, fatigue should be reflected in a less active lifestyle that can be tracked by activity measurement. People who elect to watch TV rather than take a walk or elect to stay home rather than shop will be less active. It is especially important to use fully proportional actigraphy when attempting to measure fatigue, to separate small or weak movements from normally energetic ones.

*DSM-IV* (American Psychiatric Association, 1994) requires that three of seven inclusion criteria be met if mood is expansive and four of seven if mood is only irritable. Two of these seven criteria entail activity. Item 2 specifies, "decreased need for sleep (e.g., feels rested after only three hours of sleep)" (p. 332). Wrist actigraphy supplemented by Sleep Switch Device (Hauri, 1999) measurements can document total sleep time and thereby determine if the patient is sleeping as little as three hours. Item 6 specifies, "increase in goal-directed activity (either socially, at work or school, or sexually) or psychomotor agitation" (p. 332). Both sources increase total activity. Actigraphy cannot distinguish between goal-directed activity and psychomotor agitation, but fortunately item 6 does not require this discrimination to be made. Having one or more Manic or Mixed Episodes is the essential defining feature of Bipolar I Disorder. Patients may have had previous MDEs or Substance-Induced Mood Disorders. Exclusion criteria include not being better accounted for by Schizoaffective Disorder or Delusional Disorder. The transition from depression to mania in bipolar patients typically occurs when the person remains active throughout their normal sleep period.

Affective Disorder comes in all gradations, from profoundly depressed through normal to manic frenzy. Modern actigraphs are capable of quantifying and tracking the fine gradations in activity level changes that correspond to the fine gradations in Affective Disorder. Depression typically disturbs sleep. We therefore turn to the role of actigraphy in sleep assessment.

## SLEEP DYSFUNCTION

This section summarizes some of the more important issues associated with actigraphic sleep assessment. Its content is also relevant to Chapter 18 concerning the behavioral assessment of sleep dysfunction.

Actigraphy has been used to study sleep for at least the past 30 years, since Kupfer, Detre, Foster, Tucker, and Delgado (1972) reported significant and substantial correlations between wrist activity and EEG-measured movement and wakefulness. Sufficient supportive data existed by 1995 to enable the Standards of Practice Committee (1995) of the American Sleep Disorders Association to support the use of actigraphy in evaluating certain aspects of sleep disorder. Littner et al. (2003) reinforced these recommendations on the basis of more current evidence.

Tryon (2004) discussed issues of validity in actigraphic sleep assessment at greater length than can be repeated here, but most of the main points are as follows. Although it is not generally accepted to say that intelligence is what the Wechsler Intelligence Scales measure, it is widely accepted to say that sleep is what polysomnography (PSG) measures; PSG is the gold standard of sleep. However, just as the concept of intelligence is not coextensive with and fully assessed by the Wechsler Scales, the concept of sleep is not coextensive with and fully assed by polysomnography.

Standard PSG sleep-scoring criteria recognize wake and several stages of sleep, thereby implying that sleep onset is a discrete event (Rechtschaffen & Kales, 1968). Tryon (2004) presented evidence that sleep onset entails a spectrum of changes comprising three broad phases. Phase 1 involves quiescence and immobility. Phase 2 entails decreased muscle tone (Chase & Morales, 1994; Perry & Goldwater, 1987). The behavioral gold standard against which alpha EEG changes were validated as a marker of sleep onset was the dropping of a hand-held object, an empty thread spool held between the thumb and forefinger (cf. Blake, Gerard, & Kleitman, 1939). Ogilvie, Wilkinson, and Allison (1989) used a handheld "deadman" switch requiring 90 grams of pressure to maintain closure to measure the "drop point." Franklin (1981) and Viens, De Koninck, Van den Bergen, Audet, and Christ (1988) described a similar apparatus suitable for home use. Hauri (1999) evaluated an inexpensive commercially available Sleep Switch Device (RMP, Inc., 716 Sunset Road, Boynton Beach, FL 33435) that correlated $r(23) = .98$, $p < .001$ with PSG measured sleep onset in a sample of 19 insomnia patients and 6 normal sleepers. Phase 3 involves a rise in auditory threshold and perceived sleep onset. Auditory threshold rises rapidly within 1 minute of the first EEG sleep spindle (Bonnet & Moore, 1982). Auditory threshold increases take place mainly during EEG stage 2 sleep (Bonato & Ogilvie, 1989). Subjects no longer respond to their name when it is spoken softly, to a light touch, or to normal external stimuli (Lindsley, 1957; Ogilvie & Wilkinson, 1984). Self-reported sleep onset, perceived sleep onset, occurs after the auditory threshold rises (Birrell, 1983; Bonato & Ogilvie; Lichstein, Hoelscher, Eakin, & Nickel, 1983). Espie, Lindsay, and Espie (1989) found that self-reported sleep onset occurred concurrent with auditory threshold increase. Lichstein et al. (1983) may be the only study indicating that self-reported sleep onset happens before auditory threshold increases occur.

Actigraphy keys on phase 1, whereas PSG keys on phase 2, which results in the systematic sleep-onset differences summarized by Tryon (1996b, 2004). Good sleepers rapidly move through these sleep stages, resulting in close correspondence between actigraphic and PSG sleep-onset times. Poor sleepers can take a long time to pass from phase 1 through phase 2 by lying quietly awake for long periods of time, resulting in substantial differences in actigraphic and PSG sleep-onset times. Hauri's (1999) Sleep Switch gives sleep-onset times that are close to PSG measurements.

Actigraphy cannot be expected to agree with PSG to a greater extent than PSG agrees with itself. In other words, the correlation between actigraph and PSG sleep measures cannot consistently exceed the reliability of PSG measures. Actigraph sleep scoring is always done by computer, and therefore reanalyzing the same data always gives the same results. Automatic PSG sleep stagers are available but are not yet as good as hand scoring (Carskadon & Rechtschaffen, 1994). Human scoring in general is subject to error. Interrater PSG sleep-scoring agreement values range from 80% to 98% (Ogilvie & Wilkinson, 1988). Whereas the reliability of scoring stage 2 sleep is approximately 90% (Spiegel, 1981, p. 62), the reliability of scoring stage 1 sleep can be as low as 60%. Hence, up to 40% of EEG stage 1 scoring, and therefore sleep–wake scoring, and consequently PSG vs. actigraphy differences, can be attributed to the unreliability of stage 1 sleep scoring. This 40% difference frequently equals or exceeds all of the sleep-onset differences between actigraphy and PSG.

Tryon (1996b) summarized 14 studies that validated wrist actigraphy against PSG and reported validity coefficients that ranged from .72 to .98 for total sleep time, .82 to .96 for percent sleep, from .56 to .91 for sleep efficiency, and from .49 to .87 for wake after sleep onset. Tryon (1996b) reported percent agreement statistics that ranged from 78.8% to 99.7% for sleep and from 48.5% to 79.8% for wake. Pollak, Tryon, Nagaraja, and Dzwonczyk (2001) also reported results within this range. Their percent agreement results were 82.0% for nights, 98.6% for days, and 76.9% for 24-hour periods, using logistic regression in a cross-validation sample of 10 participants, leaving 18.0%, 1.4%, and 23.1% agreement unaccounted for, respectively. This range of 2% to 23% error falls within the acceptable errors associated with accepted medical tests and the best intelligence and personality tests (Meyer et al., 2001). It therefore follows that actigraphy is as valid a sleep–wake indicator as common medical tests are valid indicators of pathology and the best psychological tests are indicators of intelligence and personality.

The relationship between inactivity and sleep and the ability to infer sleep from inactivity is threatened by at least the following measurement artifacts: (1) sleeping with an active bed partner; (2) sleeping in a waterbed or a rocking or vibrating bed; (3) sleeping with one's wrist on their chest or abdomen; (4) a concurrent movement disorder that does not consistently wake the person; (5) medications that produce movement but do not wake the person; (6) lying very still while awake for extended periods of time. Minimizing or eliminating these artifacts increases the probability of a correct inference. These artifacts impair inference more than the fact that systematic actigraphy–PSG differences vary across sleep disorders.

## EATING DISORDERS

**Anorexia Nervosa**

Chapter 12 concerns the behavioral assessment of eating disorders. An extraordinary body of evidence summarized at article length by Pierce and Epling (1994) and at book length by Epling and Pierce (1996) indicates that increased activity in combination with dietary restriction can result in *activity anorexia*, a disorder that is quite parallel with, and may frequently be misdiagnosed as, the *DSM-IV* disorder known as *anorexia nervosa*. The primary observation is that when food availability is restricted to one meal per day and access is given to an activity wheel, adolescent male and female rats begin to decrease their food intake and increase their activity level until they run and starve themselves to death! Running can increase to 15 km per day, which is considerable for humans and enormous for the much smaller rat. The essential absence of cognitive, self-image, and family conflict factors in rats, combined with the fact that such behavior change can be produced whenever the experimenter chooses to restrict food and provide access to a running wheel, excludes most of the etiological factors commonly cited regarding anorexia nervosa. The authors hypothesized that restricting food intake to one meal per day simulates famine conditions. Evolution has apparently favored continuous migration, reducing appetite to motivate migration until a more plentiful food supply is located. Hence, food restriction can set the occasion for sustained activity and heightened anorexia to facilitate migration. Because rats cannot get anywhere in their activity wheel and because the experimenter does not increase the frequency of food presentation, the animals never arrive at a more plentiful food supply and so continue running and migrating until death. Self-imposed food restriction and exercise opportunity appear to result in equally futile conditions for humans. Epling and Pierce discuss behavioral treatment of Activity Anorexia.

Activity measurements are conspicuously absent from the anorexia nervosa literature, despite the central role activity is thought to play in the maintenance of weight loss. No published outpatient activity measurements have been located to date. Some inpatient evidence indicates that persons diagnosed with anorexia nervosa are more active than normal. Blinder, Freeman, and Stunkard (1970) used pedometers to evaluate three consecutively admitted patients with anorexia nervosa on an inpatient psychiatric unit of a university hospital as part of a larger study. The ages of the three patients were 22, 15, and 20 years, respectively. Their pretreatment weights were 89.5, 91.0, and 63.5 lbs, respectively, with a mean of 81.3 lb. Their percent weight loss was 31, 29, and 63, respectively, with a mean of 41%. Unlimited passes were available during the first portion of hospitalization. The result was that all three subjects walked an average of 6.8 miles per day. Patient 1 was reported to have walked 8.5 miles per day. Stunkard (1960) reported that normal-weight women living in the nearby community walked an average of 4.9 miles per day.

Other inpatient evidence indicates that activity is predictive of therapeutic gains. Falk, Halmi, and Tryon (1985) obtained 24-hour wrist and ankle activity measurements, using Timex Model 108 Motion Recorders, from 20 hospitalized female anorectics during the first two weeks (14 consecutive days) of hospitalization. Their ages ranged from 13 to 32 years, with an average of 21.1 years ($S$ = 5.6 years). Their average weight at day 1 was 75.38% of their target weight. Activity level decreases when body weight becomes critically low. Scrimshaw and Pollitt (1984) noted that "it has long been recognized that malnourished children are apathetic and less active than well-nourished children" (p. ix). Falk et al. reported significant negative correlations between Hamilton Depression Ratings and wrist activity on days 2 ($r(18) = -.535$, $p < .05$) and 5 ($r(18) = -.513$, $p < .05$). Body weight steadily increased over the two-week study period, as indicated by a significant correlation ($r(12) = .991$, $p < .01$) between body weight and time. Wrist activity ($r(12) = .808$, $p < .01$) and ankle activity ($r(12) = .747$, $p < .01$) also consistently increased with time. This pattern led to significant correlations between wrist ($r(12) = .811$, $p < .01$) and ankle ($r(12) = .760$, $p < .01$) activity and percent target weight. Participants became more active as they became better nourished. Administration of cyproheptadine hydrochloride to seven participants on days 8–14 significantly reduced activity, as reflected by the correlation between a drug vs. no-drug code and wrist activity controlling for percent of target weight and time of $r(12) = -.878$, $p < .01$. The negative sign reflects coding no drug = 0 and drug = 1. Ankle activity was also suppressed by cyproheptadine hydrochloride ($r(12) = -.527$, $p < .06$). Amitriptyline hydrochloride suppressed neither wrist ($r(12) = -.342$, N.S.) nor ankle ($r(12) = -.016$, N.S.) activity.

Foster and Kupfer (1975) obtained nocturnal (2100–0700 hr) wrist activity counts from a 17-year-old female during her 122-day hospitalization. They reported a significant correlation between activity and weight during an 85-day no-medication baseline ($r(83) = .77$, $p < .001$). Greater activity was predictive of weight gain. Administration of 200–800 mg/day of chlorpromazine hydrochloride changed the aforementioned positive correlation into a significant negative one ($r(33) = -.76$, $p < .001$). Greater activity was then predictive of weight loss. The extent to which this drug effect was mediated through appetite disturbance is unclear.

**Obesity**

The definition of obesity for adults is a body mass index (BMI) of more than 30 kg/m$^2$ (Mokdad, Serdula, & Dietz, 1999). The prevalence of obesity increased from 12.0% in 1991 to 17.9% in 1998 to 19.8% in 2000 and has now reached epidemic proportions in the United States (Mokdad et al.; Mokdad & Bowman, 2001). Overweight is defined as a BMI between 25 and 30 kg/m$^2$ and is associated with a variety of disabilities and chronic illnesses, including diabetes and cardiovascular diseases. Overweight is associated with approximately 300,000 deaths annually (Allison, Fontaine, Manson, Stevens, & VanItallie, 1999). A sedentary lifestyle is one factor that contributes to the obesity epidemic. A reduction in work-related physical activity demands and improved transportation has contributed to a more sedentary lifestyle. Public health recommendations (Pate et al., 1995; U.S. Department of Health and Human Services, 1996) recommend 30 minutes or more of moderately intense activity, such as brisk walking on most if not all days. The report of the President's Council on Physical Fitness (2002) explored ways to use pedometers to measure how active people are and to motivate them to be more active.

Pedometers can be used to track daily activity level, providing feedback that can set the occasion for new behavior and to reward current behavior. These activities can be combined in the form of progressive goal setting. The following studies have used pedometers to track and/or motivate physical activity: Bassey, Patrick, Irving, Blecher, and Fentem, 1983; Fogelholm, Kukkonen-Harjula, and Oja, 1998; Iwane et al., 2000; Speck and Looney, 2001; Toda et al., 1998; Yamanouchi et al., 1995.

A device by the name of *Caltrac* estimates calories expended due to exercise, based on measured vertical acceleration at the waist and the wearer's sex, age, and weight. The wearer can also enter calories consumed. Every 3,500 calories burned more than consumed equates to 1 pound of fat loss. A search of the National Library of Medicine, Pub Med (http://www.ncbi.nlm.nih.gov/) using the keyword "caltrac" on 6/1/04 returned 72 articles, far more than can be summarized here. A Google search on the same day using the same keyword returned 878 hits, including several vendors who display pictures of and sell this device. The clinical objective is to increase calories burned by at least 100 per day and to reduce calories eaten by at least 100 per day, for a net savings of at least 200 calories per day, resulting in 1 pound lost every 17.5 days, or just over 20 pounds per year. Doubling this plan projects to a loss of about 1 pound every 9 days, or approximately 40 pounds per year.

## HEALTH BENEFITS OF INCREASED ACTIVITY

Slattery et al. (1989) reported that modest exercise significantly reduced mortality from *all* causes. When activity was divided into quintiles (five levels), escaping the most sedentary (1st quintile) category substantially reduced mortality risk. Paffenbarger, Hyde, Wing, and Steinmetz (1984) reported that the rate of all-cause mortality per 10,000 man-years of observation among 16,936 Harvard alumni between 1962 and 1978 was 84.8 for those expending less than 500 calories through exercise per week, 66.0 for those expending 500–1,999 calories per week, and 52.1 for those expending 2,000 or more calories per week ($p < .001$). Paffenbarger, Hyde, Wing, and Hsieh (1986) further reported on the 16,936 Harvard alumni sample and revealed that walking 9 or more versus 3 miles per week reduced the risk of death by 21%. Persons expending 3,500 calories per week had an all-cause mortality rate half that of those expending less than 500 calories per week. Expending 2,000 calories or more per week reduced all-cause death risk 28% below those expending less than 500 calories per week. Andersen et al. (2000) conducted a 14.5-year prospective study of 13,375 women and 17,265 men ages 20–93 years to assess the relationship between physical activity and all-cause mortality. Leisure time physical activity, including moderate activity, was found to be inversely associated with all-cause mortality in both men and women in all age groups. Bicycling as transportation conferred additional benefits. The 1996 Surgeon General's report (U.S. Department of Health and Human Services, 1996, pp. 85–87) provides additional evidence of an inverse dose–response relationship between activity level and all-cause mortality.

Activity has beneficial effects against coronary artery disease (Oberman, 1985; Paffenbarger & Hyde, 1984; Powell, Thompson, Caspersen, & Kendrick, 1987; Salonen, Puska, & Tuomilehto, 1982), obesity (Colvin & Olson, 1983; Hoiberg, Bernard, Watten, & Caine, 1984; Marston & Criss, 1984; Westover & Lanyon, 1990), colon cancer (Slattery, Schumacher, Smith, West, & Abd-Elghany, 1988), and all-cause mortality in both young (Blair et al., 1989; Bouchard, Shepard, Stephens, Sutton, & McPherson, 1990; Fox, Naughton, & Haskell, 1971), middle-aged (Leon, Connett, Jacobs, & Rauramaa, 1987; Morris et al., 1973; Morris, Everitt, Pollard, Chave, & Semmence, 1980), and older adults (Blumenthal et al., 1989; Cunningham, Rechnitzer, Howard, & Donner, 1987; King, Taylor, Haskell, & DeBusk, 1989). Blair et al. reported that the decline in death rates with increased levels of fitness is most pronounced in older persons. The 1996 Surgeon General's report (U.S. Department of Health and Human Services, 1996, pp. 87–110) provides additional evidence of an inverse relationship between activity level and heart disease.

## COMPUTER ASSESSMENT

Chapter 20 concerns the role of computers in behavioral assessment. Actigraphy is at the forefront of computer assessment. Modern actigraphs are computerized instruments that require a personal computer to interact with them. Actigraphs have an onboard clock that should be set to a time standard, the atomic clock in Colorado, using software such as Pawclock (http://www.sharewareorder.com/Pawclock-download-16182.htm). Software available from actigraph vendors is used to program when activity recording begins by specifying an hour, minute, and second of a month, day, and year. The actigraph waits until then to begin collecting data. The user can specify the recording epoch. Recording data at 1-minute intervals is fairly standard practice, except for sleep, where the standard recording epoch is 30 seconds. The data are downloaded from the actigraph to the personal computer using commercially available software. Data manipulation is done by computer, due to the many data points collected; 1,440 per 24 hours using a 1-minute recording epoch.

## EVALUATING OLDER ADULTS

Chapter 21 in this volume concerns behavioral assessment with older adults. Tryon (1998b) summarized the research literature on geriatric activity level. Some of the more important points are recapped here. Kraus and Raab (1961) coined the term *hypokinetic disease* to describe a spectrum of physical and mental disorder induced by inactivity. Disabilities normally associated with aging can be partially produced in young, healthy persons by protracted inactivity. Bortz (1982) discovered important parallels between normal aging and inactivity regarding the cardiovascular system, blood components, body composition, metabolic and regulatory functions, and the nervous system. Women tend to outlive their male counterparts but often spend years with chronic illnesses and disabilities (O'Brien & Vertinsky, 1991). These authors indicate that "evidence is rapidly accumulating that physical mobility is a critical survival need for the elderly" (p. 348). "Indeed, about 50% of what we currently accept as aging is now understood to be *hypokinesia* [emphasis added], a disease of 'disuse,' the degeneration and functional loss of muscle and bone tissue" (p. 348). The long-term benefits of exercise on health are both broad and substantial. Active life expectancy (ALE) refers to the years before disability alters one's functional status (cf. Manton, Stallard, & Liu, 1993). ALE is an important determinant of the health and service needs of persons over 65 years of age. Mobility is recognized as an essential component of self-care.

Elderly people evaluate their own health and the health of others in terms of activity (Burnside, 1978; Gueldner & Spradley, 1988), with more active persons perceived as healthier. Disease and depression reduce activity, and actigraphy can be used to quantify these changes.

## WORK-RELATED ISSUES

Chapter 24 in this volume concerns the role of behavioral assessment regarding work-related issues. Periodic changes in shift schedules from day to night or night to day can disrupt sleep (Monk, 1994). Actigraphy has been well validated against polysomnography regarding several indices of sleep (Littner et al., 2003; Standards of Practice Committee, 1995; Tryon, 1996b, 2004a). Hence, actigraphy is pertinent to the assessment of sleep-related work issues. Actigraphy can also track circadian rhythm changes caused by shift work.

## BEHAVIORAL HEALTH AND MEDICINE

A topic not included in this volume is the role of behavioral assessment in health psychology and behavioral medicine. This section briefly reviews some examples of health-related applications of activity assessment. Much more information can be found in the 1996 Surgeon General's report (U.S. Department of Health and Human Services, 1996).

## Anesthesia Response

Weinbroum, Ben Abraham, Ezri, and Zomer (2001) reported that real-time actigraphy during surgery is more sensitive and responsive to patient changes than are anesthesiologists' subjective observations.

## Surgery Recovery

Bisgaard, Klarskov, Kehlet, and Rosenberg (2002) used actigraphy to track recovery after uncomplicated laparoscopic cholecystectomy. The authors concluded there is no medical basis for prescribing more than 2 or 3 days of convalescence in otherwise young, healthy persons undergoing this type of surgery. Redeker and Wykpisz (1999) used actigraphy to evaluate the outcome of coronary artery bypass surgery. They reported stronger circadian rest–activity rhythms after vs. before surgery. Fielden et al. (2003) used actigraphy to assess sleep disturbance in 48 patients before and after total hip arthroplasty and found more efficient and less fragmented sleep after surgery.

## Essential Hypertension

Table 4-4 of the 1996 Surgeon General's report (U.S. Department of Health and Human Services, 1996, pp. 108–109) cited six studies supporting an inverse relationship between activity level and hypertension. Iwane et al. (2000) monitored the activity level of 730 employees in a manufacturing plant for 12 weeks. Thirty-two of them were hypertensive. Walking more than 10,000 steps per day significantly reduced blood pressure and increased exercise capacity. Moreau et al. (2001) divided 24 postmenopausal women with borderline-to-stage-1 hypertension into two groups. The 15 women in the experimental group walked 3 km per day more than their daily lifestyle activity level, measured with a pedometer, while the 9 women in the control group did not alter their lifestyle. Blood pressure dropped an average of 6 mm Hg after 12 weeks and 11 mm Hg after 24 weeks; both changes are statistically significant. Percent body fat, fasting plasma insulin, and dietary intake remained unchanged. Leary, Donnan, MacDonald, and Murphy (2000) simultaneously monitored blood pressure and activity level in 434 participants and found activity level to be an independent predictor of diurnal variation in blood pressure.

## Heart Disease

This important topic was addressed generally earlier in this chapter. More specifically, Walsh, Charlesworth, Andrews, Hawkins, and Cowley (1997) used pedometers to measure the daily activity level of 84 patients with chronic heart failure for an average of 710 days and found that reduced weekly activity was a strong predictor of death. Walsh, Andrews, Evans, and Cowley (1995) used pedometers to demonstrate that although exercise capacity and corridor walk tests demonstrated that the results of 12 weeks of vasodilator drug therapy was "successful, patients were not more active after vs. before treatment. Gottlieb et al.

(1999) used the Caltrac device and the doubly labeled water technique and found that while exercise training increased peak performance in patients with congestive heart failure, it did not increase their daily activity level. Teicher et al. (1986) used 48 hours of left wrist actigraphy in a 74-year-old male undergoing rehabilitation 6 weeks after his second stroke to demonstrate that stroke alters the circadian rhythm of activity in comparison to a 65-year-old recently retired normal control participant.

## Cancer

Table 4-5 of the 1996 Surgeon General's report (U.S. Department of Health and Human Services, 1996, pp. 114–117) reviewed 11 studies, of which seven supported an inverse relationship between activity level and colon cancer. Table 4-6 (U.S. Department of Health and Human Services, pp. 118–121) reviewed 14 studies, of which eight supported an inverse relationship between activity level and hormone-dependent cancers in women. Table 4-7 (U.S. Department of Health and Human Services, pp. 122–123) reviewed eight studies reporting either a small or inconsistent relationship between activity level and prostate cancer. Teicher et al. (1986) used wrist actigraphy to find both a 6- and an 11-cycles-per-day circadian component in addition to a 0.84-cycles-per-day cycle in an 80-year-old woman with a well-calcified 3-cm-diameter parasagittal meningioma to the right of the midline.

## Diabetes

Table 4-8 (U.S. Department of Health and Human Services, 1996, pp. 126–127) reviewed three studies, of which two supported an inverse dose-response relationship between activity level and non-insulin-dependent diabetes mellitus. The First Step Program (Tudor-Locke, Myers, Bell, Harris, & Wilson-Rodger, 2002; Tudor-Locke, Myers, & Rodger, 2000; Tudor-Locke & Ainsworth, 2001) is an 8-week, two-phase program based on social cognitive theory, self-efficacy, and social support (Bandura, 1986, 1997) that is designed to incrementally increase and sustain habitual physical activity levels in sedentary individuals with Type 2 diabetes. The adoption phase consists of four weekly group-based education and counseling meetings, combined with individual goal setting and self-monitoring using a pedometer for feedback. The adherence phase occurs over a subsequent 4-week period with continued individual goal setting and self-monitoring and limited telephone and/or postcard contact. Tudor-Locke et al. (2000, 2002) and Tudor-Locke and Ainsworth (2001) provide additional details of this successful program.

### Chronic Obstructive Pulmonary Disease (COPD)

Johnson, Woodcock, and Geddes (1983) reported a 16.8% activity level increase in 18 patients with severe breathlessness due to COPD while participating in a randomized placebo-controlled double-blind crossover trial regarding the effects of dihydrocodeine. Lilker, Karnick, and Lerner (1975) used pedometers to evaluate the effects of portable oxygen treatment on ambulation in nine men with COPD using a double-blind crossover study. Participants walked an average of 1.10 miles per day (SD = 0.94) during the 3-week baseline and only 1.35 miles per day (SD = 0.83) during a 5-week liquid air treatment. This difference was not statistically significant.

## Dementia

Disrupted activity/rest cycles constitute a principal reason why demented patients are institutionalized. Hatfield, Herbert, Van Someren, Hodges, and Hastings (2004) used actigraphy to confirm that deterioration in activity/rest cycles is a common, early, and progressive feature of home-dwelling patients with Alzheimer's disease. Ancoli-Israel, Clopton, Klauber, Fell, and Mason (1997) used wrist actigraphy to monitor the sleep/wake cycles in demented nursing home patients and found fragmented sleep/wake cycles in many patients. Teicher et al. (1986) reported six-cycles-per-day ultradian activity cycles in a 58-year-old demented alcoholic man that was nearly as prominent as his 0.94 activity level cycles per day, demonstrating clear circadian disruption. Lawrence, Teicher, and Finklestein (1989) used actigraphy with 17 severely demented patients with Alzheimer's disease to find increased levels of nocturnal activity, in both absolute and percentage terms. They also found a consistent phase delay, with acrophase, time of peak circadian activity, occurring approximately 1.75 hours later than nine normal control subjects. A subgroup of 6 "pacers" evidenced a 56% daytime activity increase and a 174% nighttime activity increase.

## Arthritis

Henderson, Lovell, Specker, and Campaigne (1995) used activity diaries and the Caltrac accelerometer to measure activity level over a 3-day period in 23 prepubertal children with mild-to-moderate juvenile rheumatoid arthritis (JRA) and 23 healthy control children. The children with JRA reported significantly less activity than controls, but the Caltrac scores were similar for both groups. This finding underscores the need to verify self-reports with instrumented measurements. Talbot, Gaines, Huynh, and Metter (2003) reported that a pedometer-driven walking program successfully increased physical activity in 34 older adults with osteoarthritis of the knee.

## Response to Infection and AIDS

The fact that people do not automatically know when they become HIV positive suggests that their activity level is probably unchanged from premorbid levels at that moment. The fact that death brings about the cessation of activity level provides a common endpoint. Infection-related fatigue may compromise lifestyle, thereby reducing diurnal activity level and disturbing sleep. Sheehan and Macallan (2000) monitored energy intake and expenditure, DC4 count, and clinical status in 33 HIV-positive men at 105 time points over a 3-year period prior to the era of highly active antiretroviral therapy. They reported that activity level decreased as infection increased. Lee, Portillo, and Miramontes (2001) used actigraphy to track sleep and activity patterns with fatigue in 100 women with HIV/AIDS. Persons with greater fatigue had significantly more difficulty falling asleep and had more nighttime awakenings than did persons with less fatigue. CD4 cell counts were unrelated to sleep and fatigue measures. Activity level may increase after acute episodes subside, but disease progression will eventually reduce activity level to zero at the time of death. It is suggested that waist activity level serves as a clinically useful measure of functional status, including wrist actigraphy to track sleep changes.

## Chronic Fatigue Syndrome

Jason, Tryon, Frankenberry, and King (1997) measured activity level with actigraphs and reported that activity level was related to predictors of fatigue but not to fatigue ratings. Vercoulen et al. (1997) used actigraphy to evaluate 51 patients with Chronic Fatigue Syndrome (CFS), 50 patients with the fatigued form of multiple sclerosis (MS), and 53 healthy controls for 12 days using actigraphy and found that the patients with CFS were less active than controls. The activity level of the patients with CFS was the same as for the patients with the fatigued form of MS. Tryon, Jason, Frankenberry, and Torres-Harding (2004) used actigraphs to measure activity level 24-hours per day in eight patients with CFS for 2–7 days and 10 matched controls for 5–7 days. They reported lower daytime activity and less regular activity–rest cycles in persons with CFS than controls.

## Multiple Sclerosis

The Vercoulen et al. (1997) study reported in the preceding paragraph reported that the patients with MS were less active than controls. The activity level of the patients with MS was the same as for the patients with CFS. Ng and Kent-Braun (1997) measured activity level in 17 patients with multiple sclerosis and 15 healthy sedentary controls using a three-dimensional accelerometer for 7 days. Participants also rated their activity level with an activity questionnaire. The results showed that the persons with MS were measurably less active than controls and rated themselves as such. However, the accelerometer was more sensitive than the questionnaire for detecting activity level differences in these sedentary groups.

## Fibromyalgia

Korszun et al. (2002) used actigraphy to monitor the activity level of 16 patients with uncomplicated fibromyalgia and 28 healthy controls. They reported normal daytime activity levels but disturbed sleep, i.e., higher-than-normal nocturnal activity.

## Osteoporosis

The 1996 Surgeon General's report (U.S. Department of Health and Human Services, 1996, pp. 130–132) documented the well-established role activity level plays in maintaining normal bone health throughout the life span and hypothe-sizes a positive developmental role in youth. Kitagawa, Omasu, and Nakahara (2003) reported that walking up to 12,000 steps per day improved ultrasound parameters of the calcaneus (heal bone) in elderly Japanese women. Further research is needed to determine if this translates into less bone loss.

### Total Joint Replacement Survival

Schmalzried et al. (1998) used pedometers to measure the activity level of 111 patients undergoing one complete hip or knee replacement. Patients took an average of 4,988 steps per day, ranging from 395 to 17,718 steps per day. The average extrapolates to approximately 0.9 million joint cycles per year. Activity level is a significant wear factor. Higher activity level was associated with shorter joint replacement survival.

### Chronic Pain

Wilson, Watson, and Currie (1998) used actigraphy and a daily diary to monitor wrist activity and sleep for two nights in 40 patients with chronic musculoskeletal pain and found that patients who gave high pain ratings also gave greater sleep impairment ratings. The actigraphy data did not confirm this relationship.

### Sickle Cell Crises

Dinges et al. (1990) used wrist actigraphy to document increased nocturnal activity in response to vaso-occlusive crises and prolonged (11 hours) of low-mobility sleep following pain offset in a 14-year-old boy.

### Cirrhosis

Cordoba et al. (1998) used wrist actigraphy to confirm sleep disturbance in cirrhotic patients.

### Traumatic Brain Injury

Quinto, Gellido, Chokroverty, and Masdeu (2000) used wrist actigraphy to detect circadian rhythm sleep disorder (Delayed Sleep Phase Syndrome) in a 48-year-old man who presented with sleep-onset insomnia and cognitive dysfunc-tion after a car accident.

### Smoking

Gardner, Sieminski, and Killewich (1997) had 34 smokers and 43 nonsmok-ers wear a Caltrac accelerometer and a pedometer for 2 days and reported that the smokers were significantly less active than the nonsmokers.

### Menopause

Baker, Simpson, and Dawson (2003) used actigraphy to document that peri-menopausal women experience longer and more numerous nocturnal arousals, resulting in less sleep.

## BEHAVIORAL NEUROPSYCHOLOGY

Chapter 22 concerns the role of behavioral assessment in behavioral neuropsychology. The sensitivity of actigraphy to mood disorders and health issues, reviewed earlier, makes it a valuable behavioral neuropsychology tool. Neuropsychological assessments are typically administered under artificial laboratory assessment conditions. This includes the use of actigraphy while tests are administered. Clinical interest concerns how people function during their everyday lives. Assessments made under standardized conditions must therefore be generalized to the natural environment. Actigraphy enables investigators to directly measure activity level in the natural environment and thereby track health-related status. The applications described earlier regarding dementia and AIDS illustrate two applications of actigraphy to behavioral neuropsychology, as discussed in this book.

## CASE CONCEPTUALIZATION AND TREATMENT PLANNING ISSUES

### WHAT DOES ACTIVITY LEVEL MEAN?

Activity level is not a single entity, nor are all activity monitors equivalent. Activity level implicitly refers to a site of attachment (see later). Different body parts have different activity levels. For example, the waist is consistently inactive and the wrist is periodically active when seated and reading a newspaper.

Some activity monitors count suprathreshold movements or time above threshold, while others measure the magnitude of movement. For example, pedometers count the number of times that vertical acceleration exceeds threshold. Hence, all steps taken that are associated with vertical movements in excess of the threshold value are counted the same way. The time-above-threshold mode of actigraphs sold by Ambulatory Monitoring, Inc., report activity units that reflect the number of seconds that activity in excess of a threshold was detected during the user-selected recording epoch. Other actigraphs sold by this and other vendors are fully proportional, in that they measure the magnitude of movement. Hence, one must consider the site of attachment that is most relevant to their inquiry and select a suitable device to attach there.

### ARTIFACT

Activity monitors respond only to their own movement. When firmly attached to a person, we presume that if the activity monitor is moving, then the person must also be moving. Loose attachment compromises this assumption to some degree. Holding onto a vibrating device such as a lawn mower will artifactually increase activity level readings even though these devices contain filters to minimize such artifacts. Vertical movements associated with riding in a car, bus, or other conveyance will also register as activity counts and may be attributed to movements made by the person. Tryon (2004) discussed the relationship between activity level and sleep. Cosleeping with an active partner and/or sleeping in a waterbed, where movements by the sleeper or cosleeper can reverberate, sleeping in a vibrating or rocking bed, and/or sleeping with one's wrist on the chest or abdomen can artifactually register as being awake when the person is asleep.

## WHEN TO USE ACTIGRAPHY?

Actigraphy is appropriately used before, during, and after treatment. Pretreatment diagnostic questions such as whether or not a person displays psychomotor retardation or early-morning awaking as part of a Major Depression assessment can be informed using actigraphy. Treatment issues such as titrating medication to where activity levels approximate normal values can be directly guided by continuous actigraphy. Outcome issues such as sleep normalization in depressed patients can be addressed using actigraphy.

## WHAT METHODOLOGICAL ISSUES ARE INVOLVED WITH ACTIGRAPHY?

### SITE OF ATTACHMENT

Activity monitors sense only their own movement and consequently only the movement at the site where they are attached. Activity level is specific to the site of attachment, and that differs across body sites. The wrist is the preferred site for sleep studies because the wrist is the site that most frequently shows movement when people are awake. The waist is associated with the center of gravity. Vertical movements of the waist are energy expensive because they entail moving one's entire body mass. This site is preferred when assessing energy expenditure and when monitoring movements that are likely to be detected by observers. The ankle is the preferred site of attachment for infants, in that it is a safer site since there is no risk that the child will accidentally strike his or her face with the device. Infants typically move their legs and arms together. The leg is stronger than the arm and can better support the actigraph. An actigraph placed over the abdomen can detect some breathing abnormalities, such as apneas. Multiple recording sites provide more information than single sites do. Monitoring both the wrist and the waist is desirable when possible.

### DURATION OF MEASUREMENT

The question of how long to measure can be answered in two ways. The first answer is provided by *DSM-IV* diagnostic requirements. The second answer concerns how large the behavioral sample needs to be to answer the question at hand. Presumably these answers should be the same. The absence of empirical data demonstrating the minimum measurement periods necessary to draw correct inferences and make correct diagnoses makes this a fruitful area for future research.

## *DSM-IV* Diagnostic Criteria

*DSM-IV* criteria for a Hypomanic Episode must last for at least 4 days (American Psychiatric Association, 1994, p. 338). *DSM-IV* criteria for a Manic Episode must be met nearly every day for at least 1 week (American Psychiatric Association, p. 332). *DSM-IV* criteria for a Major Depressive Episode must be met continuously for a 2-week period (American Psychiatric Association, p. 327). Hyperactivity must persist for at least 6 months in order for a diagnosis of Attention-Deficit/Hyperactivity Disorder, Predominantly Hyperactive Type or Combined Type, to be reached (American Psychiatric Association, p. 83). Criterion C for the Seasonal Pattern Specifier (American Psychiatric Association, p. 390) that can be applied to Major Depressive Episodes in Bipolar I Disorder, Bipolar II Disorder, or Major Depressive Disorder refers to a 2-year period. These diagnostic time frames determine the minimum duration of measurement necessary for each diagnosis to be reached. No reports could be found regarding adults that measured activity for these durations.

## Other Bases for Recommendation

Behavioral samples are content valid to the extent that they are representative of the behavior being assessed, just like psychometric tests are content valid if they adequately survey the domain being measured (Anastasi, 1988, p. 140; Linehan, 1980; Silva, 1993; Tryon 1998b, 2002). Behavioral observations made under office or laboratory conditions may or may not validly represent behavior displayed at other times. Test developers and behavioral assessors bear the burden of proof regarding content validity. Generalization must be demonstrated rather than assumed. Content validity depends on the duration of assessment as well as the conditions under which assessment occurs.

Refinetti (1993) recommended, based on common research practice, collecting data for 10 24-hr periods to assess circadian rhythms, on the basis that 10 replications is sufficient to estimate circadian parameters. General experimental design considerations suggest collecting data for 2 weeks. People tend to behave differently on the weekends than they do during the week. People sometimes have different schedules during the workweek. A 2-week behavioral sample allows for one replication of each day of the week and is a minimal behavioral sample in this regard. Measurement duration should be directly proportional to behavioral variability. It takes more time to adequately characterize more variable behavior.

## WHEN TO BEGIN?

Actigraphs enable one to begin collecting data at any hour, minute, second of any day of the year, so users have great flexibility with regard to when data collection begins. By convention, each day starts at midnight: 00 hours, 00 minutes, and 00 seconds. This is a good time to start data collection because it allows the person to wear the actigraph for several hours before data collection begins. It is good experimental procedure always to use the same start-up time. It remains uncertain as to whether there is any advantage of initiating data recording on the same day of the week.

## NEED FOR ACCURATE TIME

Actigraphs contain computers with programmable clocks. It is important that the user's PC clock be set to the correct time. I use Pawclock freeware from http://www.pawsoft.com/?p=products to synchronize my PC clock with the National Institute of Standards and Technology (NIST) atomic clock in Colorado, which is extraordinarily accurate. The NIST Web site (http://physics.nist.gov/cuu/Constants/Table/allascii.txt) lists its uncertainty as 0.000 000 0086e-21 seconds.

## ACTIVITY LOG

It is recommended that the wearer keep an activity log in order to facilitate data interpretation. Sometimes a qualitative record of what the person was doing helps clarify the meaning of actigraph data.

## ACTIVITY NORMS

Norms provide a context for interpreting test results, and the same is true for actigraphy data. No activity level norms currently exist. It is therefore not possible to say what constitutes normal activity level and therefore what constitutes hyperactivity or hypoactivity. The best that can be done is to collect data on a comparison person of the same sex, age, and occupation. A mail carrier is likely to take more steps per day than an accountant is. Nocturnal activity is an exception, in that wrist, and especially waist, activity should be near zero most of the time. The person's waking activity provides a context for evaluating nocturnal activity. Nocturnal activity should be small in comparison to diurnal values.

People can serve as their own controls when actigraphy is used to track treatment effects. For example, depressed persons should increase their daily activity level after successful treatment. Nocturnal activity should decrease as the person sleeps better (cf. Coffield & Tryon, 2004).

## DEVELOPMENTAL ISSUES AND TRENDS

Activity level is arguably the first stable individual difference (personality factor) to develop, and it does so during gestation. Eaton and Saudino (1992) reviewed 14 studies showing that mothers can reliably and validly detect fetal activity beginning with the 28th week of gestation. Fetal activity appears to increase and peak at around week 34. Stable individual differences were found at this time. Prenatal activity then decreases through week 39, creating a curvilinear prenatal developmental trend in activity level.

Existing evidence points to a curvilinear developmental path for activity level after birth as well. Eaton, McKeen, and Campbell (2001) compiled data from 12 different studies that objectively measured activity levels of 840 subjects ranging in age from 0.1 to 24.6 years. Their graphic presentation of these data indicate that activity level increases from the time the child can walk until around 8 years of age and then declines through age 16. It is curious that activity level peaks in normal children at approximately the same time as hyperactivity is typically reported in conjunction with the Primarily Hyperactive and Combined Types of Attention-Deficit/Hyperactivity Disorder. Tryon (1991, pp. 93–101) presents more detailed developmental evidence regarding activity level from birth (days 1–4) through age 12 that supports Eaton, McKeen and Campbell's curvilinear findings.

## AVAILABLE INSTRUMENTS

### INSTRUMENT SELECTION

**Pedometers**

Leonardo da Vinci (1452–1519) designed the first pedometer during the 15th century (Gibbs-Smith, 1978). Thomas Jefferson introduced the pedometer to America somewhere between 1785 and 1789 while he served as the American ambassador to France. Hence, American investigators have had access to pedometers for at least the past 215 years. Pedometers are commercially available through many vendors. A Google search on 5/29/04 using the term *pedometer vendors* yielded 1,230 hits. The small research literature regarding the reliability and validity of pedometers reviewed later indicates that pedometers are substantially more reliable and valid than the best psychological tests. Only one study (Bassett et al., 1996) could be located that compared several brands of pedometers.

**Step Counters**

Step counters are digital pedometers that record the number of steps taken. This information is used to calculate distance on the basis of a stride-length estimate. Inaccuracy introduced by such estimates can be avoided by reporting steps taken.

## Actigraph Counters

Some actigraphs, such as the basic Ambulatory Monitoring, Inc., model, can be set to one of two counting modes. The activity sensor is a small beam with a weight at one end that vibrates when the device is moved. These vibrations are converted to sinusoidal voltage changes that alternately become positive and negative. The zero-crossing-mode (ZCM) counts the number of times this voltage crosses zero. While this is a sensitive indicator that movement exists, all suprathreshold movement is treated the same way. More vigorous movements do not yield higher activity counts than less vigorous movements do. These actigraphs also have a time above threshold (TAT) mode. A timer is activated as long as movement exceeds a very low threshold. If the user has selected a 1-minute recording epoch, then the units of measure are seconds of suprathreshold activity per minute (visit http://www.ambulatory-monitoring.com/modes.html for details).

## Fully Proportional Actigraphs

Ambulatory Monitoring, Inc. (http://www.ambulatory-monitoring.com/), Manufacturing Technology, Inc. (formerly Computer Science Associates, Inc.) (http://www.mtiactigraph.com/), Mini Mitter (http://www.minimitter.com/), and Individual Monitoring Systems, Inc. (IM Systems), (http://www.imsystems.net/) all make actigraphs whose activity units are directly proportional to the intensity of activity level.

## INSTRUMENT RELIABILITY

Reliability sets the upper bound on validity, in that a test or instrument cannot consistently be more valid than it is reliable. It has been known for more than half a century that validity coefficients cannot consistently exceed the square root of reliability coefficients (Gulliksen, 1950, p. 97). Test–retest reliability is the most relevant to evaluating instruments. This form of reliability assessment evaluates the extent to which repeated measurements of the *same phenomenon* results in the same values. It is critical that the same phenomenon be measured, that it not change between the test and retest conditions. Evaluation of instrument reliability is best assessed under laboratory conditions, where the instrument can be repeatedly put through the same motions. People are not pendulums and cannot be expected to behave as consistently as mechanical devices from one trial to another. Placing activity monitors on people and asking them to repeat behaviors confounds instrument variation with participant variation and can thereby seriously underestimate instrument reliability. Tryon and Williams (1996) used two laboratory devices to standardize movement: a large pendulum and a spinner device. Three pendulum runs of 50 10-second epochs with three CSA (now sold by Manufacturing Technology Inc.) actigraphs were conducted. The largest discrepancy among the actigraphs constituted a 2.5% error, whereas the average error was approximately 0.6%; reliability was 97.5% to 99.4%. Tryon (2004b) used a 0.71-m-high precision pendulum with a 0.43-m-long movable arm and an initial angle of displacement of 15° (0.26 radians) to evaluate the reliability of four Ambulatory Monitoring, Inc., MotionLogger™ actigraphs and four BuzzBee™ actigraphs. Each actigraph was tested on the pendulum 10 times. The results yielded reliability coefficients of .98 for both models. Stricter coefficient of variation methods yielded reliability coefficients of 93% for the MotionLogger™ model and 97% for the BuzzBee™ model. Validity coefficients of at least .99 were obtained for both models.

## CLINICAL REPEATABILITY

The motive to repeatedly test people in standard situations is to determine how repeatable clinical measurements can be. Tryon (1991, pp. 9–14) distinguished clinical repeatability from instrument reliability. Clinical repeatability concerns the extent to which people return the same activity level measurements when assessed at two different times. Longer assessment times are needed to get reproducible results from more variable participants. Clinical repeatability estimates combine instrument unreliability with participant variation. This information is needed to accurately determine what degree of change is important and what is not.

Aggregation can reduce measurement error. Classical test theory understands that each measurement is composed of a true score plus error. Measurement errors are presumed to be random and normally distributed about zero. Summing scores over time results in the systematic accumulation of true score components and allows measurement errors to cancel each other. More repeated measurements (a larger behavioral sample) results in more cancellations and lower measurement errors. For example, the average bowling score over 20 games is a more repeatable number than is the average over five games than is the score of any one game. Similarly, the average over 1 or 2 weeks of activity level measurements is a more repeatable, stable number than is an average based on a day or a few hours of one day.

## VALIDITY

Behavioral assessment of activity level is frequently limited to a laboratory setting. The primary justification for this decision is that laboratories provide a controlled environment that is the same for all participants. However, investigators wish to generalize their findings to other settings. They aim to measure a property of participants' behavior that carries implication for their natural behavior. This means that measurements of naturally occurring behavior must be made to evaluate the validity of laboratory assessments. The ease and economy with which *in situ* behavioral measurements can be obtained questions the utility of estimating these data with abbreviated laboratory tests. Actigraphy enables investigators to measure activity level changes within and between naturally occurring settings and therefore yields a direct measure of the phenomenon of interest. Investigators who wish to substitute a laboratory-based estimate of this criterion measure must demonstrate, rather than assume, adequate predictability.

### PHANTOM MEASUREMENT

The reliability coefficients of most psychological tests are considerably greater than their validity coefficients, which means that these tests reliably measure something more than what they have been designed to measure. For example, a test–retest reliability coefficient of .9 means that 81% of second test variation can be explained in terms of first test variation. If the same test has a validity coefficient of .3, then test variation explains 9% of criterion variance. The remaining 72% of reliable variance concerns one or more variables that the test was not intended to measure and has been termed *phantom measurement* (Tryon & Bernstein, 2002). The main problem here is that changes in these phantom variables can be mistaken for therapeutic changes. Uncontrolled variation of phantom sources can inflate error variance and make it difficult to detect real change. It is therefore noteworthy that where studied, reliability and validity coefficients of pedometers and actigraphs are essentially the same (Tryon, 2004b). This means that these devices measure activity level and only activity level. Actigraphy may be the only behavioral assessment tool for which phantom measurement is essentially zero.

### CONCLUSIONS

Behavior is the final common pathway for the cumulative effects of heredity and environment, including cognitive, affective, and behavioral processes. Activity level reflects all of these sources of variation and therefore varies due to a broad set of psychologically relevant factors. Actigraphy provides objective instrumented activity level measurements while participants behave in their natural environment. Actigraphy is the Swiss army knife of behavioral assessment, in that it has numerous uses of interest to both clinicians and investigators in psychology and medicine. No other behavioral assessment technology has so many diagnostic and outcome assessment applications.

Modern actigraphs are simple to use and interface readily with personal computers. User-friendly software facilitates the processes of initializing actigraphs, downloading data, and reviewing results. While the cost of actigraphs has decreased over the years, inexpensive pedometers (step counters) are readily available for investigators and practitioners of more modest means. There is no longer any acceptable reason for depending entirely on ratings of activity level in research or clinical practice. The consequences of inaccurate assessment are much more immediate and certain in clinical practice than in research. Hence, the need to embrace actigraphy is more urgent for clinicians than for scientists.

## REFERENCES

Achenbach, T. M., McConaughy, S. H., & Howell, C. T. (1987). Child/adolescent behavioral and emotional problems: Implications of cross-informant correlations for situational specificity. *Psychological Bulletin, 101,* 213–232.

Allison, D. B., Fontaine, K. R., Manson, J. E., Stevens, J., & VanItallie, T. B. (1999). Annual deaths attributable to obesity in the United States. *Journal of the American Medical Association, 282,* 1530–1538.

American Psychiatric Association. (1994). *Diagnostic and statistical manual of mental disorders* (4th ed.). Washington, DC: Author.

Anastasi, A. (1988). Psychological testing. (6th ed.) New York: MacMillan.

Ancoli-Israel, S., Clopton, P., Klauber, M. R., Fell, R., & Mason, W. (1997). Use of wrist activity for monitoring sleep/wake in demented nursing-home patients. *Sleep, 20,* 24–27.

Andersen, L. B., Schnohr, P., Schroll, M., & Hein, H. O. (2000). All-cause mortality associated with physical activity during leisure time, work, sports, and cycling to work. *Archives of Internal Medicine, 160,* 1621–1628.

Baker, A., Simpson, S., & Dawson, D. (2003). Sleep disruption and mood changes associated with menopause. *Journal of Psychosomatic Research, 43,* 359–369.

Bandura, A. (1986). *Social Foundations of Thought and Action: A Social Cognitive Theory.* Englewood Cliffs, NJ, Prentice-Hall.

Bandura, A. (1997). *Self-efficacy: The exercise of control.* San Francisco: W. H. Freeman.

Barkley, R. A. (2003). Issues in the diagnosis of attention-deficit/hyperactivity disorder in children. *Brain & Development, 25,* 77–83.

Barkley, T. J., & Tryon, W. W. (1995). Psychomotor retardation found in college students seeking counseling. *Behaviour Research and Therapy, 33,* 977–984.

Bassett, D. R., Ainsworth, B. E., Leggett, S. R., Mathien, C. A., Main, J. A., Hunter, D. C., et al. (1996). Accuracy of five electronic pedometers for measuring distance walked. *Medicine and Science in Sports and Exercise, 28,* 1071–1077.

Bassey, E. J., Patrick, J. M., Irving, J. M., Blecher, A., & Fentem, P. H. (1983). An unsupervised aerobics physical training programme in middle-aged factory workers: Feasibility, validation, and response. *European Journal of Applied Physiology, 52,* 120–125.

Birrell, P. C. (1983). Behavioral, subjective, and electroencephalographic indices of sleep-onset latency and sleep duration. *Journal of Behavioral Assessment. 5,* 179–190.

Bisgaard, T., Klarskov, B., Kehlet, H., & Rosenberg, J. (2002). Recovery after uncomplicated laparoscopic cholecystectomy. *Surgery, 132,* 817–825.

Blair, S. N., Kohl, H. W., Paffenbarger, R. S., Jr., Clark, D. G., Cooper, K. H., & Gibbons, L. W. (1989). Physical fitness and all-cause mortality: A prospective study of healthy men and women. *Journal of the American Medical Association, 262,* 2395–2401.

Blake, H., Gerard, R. W., & Kleitman, N. (1939). Factors influencing brain potentials during sleep. *Journal of Neurophysiology, 2,* 48–60.

Blinder, B. J., Freeman, D. M. A., & Stunkard, A. J. (1970). Behavior therapy of anorexia nervosa: Effectiveness of activity as a reinforcer of weight gain. *American Journal of Psychiatry, 126,* 1093–1098.

Blumenthal, J. A., Emery, C. F., Madden, D. J., George, L. K., Coleman, R. E., Riddle, M. W., et al. (1989). Cardiovascular and behavioral effects of aerobic exercise training in healthy older men and women. *Journal of Gerontology: Medical Sciences, 44,* M147–M157.

Bonato, R. A., & Ogilvie, R. D. (1989). A home evaluation of a behavioral response measure of sleep/wakefulness. *Perceptual and Motor Skills, 68,* 87–96.

Bonnet, M. H., & Moore, S. E. (1982). The threshold of sleep: Perception of sleep as a function of time asleep and auditory threshold. *Sleep, 5,* 267–276.

Bortz II, W. M. (1982). Disuse and aging. *Journal of the American Medical Association, 248,* 1203–1208.

Bouchard, C., Shepard, R. J., Stephens, T., Sutton, J. R., & McPherson, B. D. (1990). *Exercise, fitness and health.* Champaign, IL: Human Kinetics.

Burnside, I. M. (1978). *Working with the elderly.* North Scituate, MA: Duxbury Press.

Buss, A. H. (1989). Temperaments as personality traits. In G. A. Kohnstamm, J. E. Bates, and M. K. Rothbart (Eds.), *Temperament in childhood* (pp. 49–58). New York: John Wiley & Sons.

Buss, A. H., & Plomin, R. (1975). *A temperament theory of personality development.* New York: John Wiley & Sons.

Buss, A. H., & Plomin, R. (1984). *Temperament: Early-developing personality traits.* Hillsdale, NJ: Erlbaum.

Carskadon, M. A., & Rechtschaffen, A. (1994). Monitoring and staging human sleep. In M. H. Kryger, T. Roth, & W. C. Dement (Eds.), *Principles and practice of sleep medicine* (2nd ed., pp. 943–960). London: W. B. Saunders.

Chase, M. H., & Morales, F. R. (1994). The control of motor neurons during sleep. In M. H. Kryger, T. Roth, & W. C. Dement (Eds.), *Principles and practice of sleep medicine* (2nd ed., pp. 163–175). London: W. B. Saunders.

Coffield, T. G., & Tryon, W. W. (2004). Construct validation of actigraphic sleep measures in hospitalized depressed patients. *Behavioral Sleep Medicine, 2,* 24–40.

Colvin, R. H., & Olson, S. B. (1983). A descriptive analysis of men and women who have lost significant weight and are highly successful at maintaining the loss. *Addictive Behaviors, 8,* 287–295.

Comrey, A. L. (1994). *Manual and handbook of interpretations for the Comrey Personality Scales.* San Diego, CA: EDITs.

Cordoba J., Cabrera, J., Lataif, L., Penev, P., Zee, P., & Blei, A. T. (1998). High prevalence of sleep disturbance in cirrhosis. *Hepatology, 27,* 339–345.

Costa, Jr., P. T., & McCrae, R. R. (1992). *Revised NEO Personality Inventory (NEO PI-R) and NEO Five-Factor Inventory (NEO-FFI): Professional manual.* Odessa, FL: Psychological Assessment Resources.

Costa, Jr., P. T., & McCrae, R. R. (1994). Stability and change in personality from adolescence through adulthood. In C. F. Halverson, Jr., G. A. Kohnstamm, & R. P. Martin (Eds.), *The developing structure of temperament and personality from infancy to adulthood* (pp. 139–150). Hillsdale, NJ: Erlbaum.

Costa, Jr., P. T., & Widiger, T. A. (Eds.). (1994). *Personality disorders and the five-factor model of personality.* Washington, DC: American Psychological Association.

Cunningham, D. A., Rechnitzer, P. A., Howard, J. H., & Donner, A. P. (1987). Exercise training of men at retirement: A clinical trial. *Journal of Gerontology, 42,* 17–23.

DeFries, J. C., Gervais, M. C., & Thomas, E. A. (1978). Response to 30 generations of selection for open-field activity in laboratory mice. *Behavior Genetics, 8,* 3–13.

Digman, J. M. (1990). Personality structure: Emergence of the five-factor model. *Annual Review of Psychology, 41,* 417–440.

Digman, J. M. (1994). Child personality and temperament: Does the five-factor model embrace both domains? In C. F. Halverson, Jr., G. A. Kohnstamm, and R. P. Martin (Eds.), *The developing structure of temperament and personality from infancy to adulthood* (pp. 323–338). Hillsdale, NJ: Erlbaum.

Dinges, D. F., Shapiro, B. S., Reilly, L. B., Orne, E. C., Ohene-Frempong, K., & Orne, M. T. (1990). Sleep/wake dysfunction in children with sickle cell crisis pain. *Sleep Research, 19,* 323.

Drachman, D. B., & Sokoloff, L. (1966). The role of movement in embryonic joint development. *Developmental Biology, 14,* 401–420.

Eaton, W. O., McKeen, N. A., & Campbell, D. W. (2001). The waxing and waning of movement: Implications for psychological development. *Developmental Review, 21,* 205–223.

Eaton, W. O., & Saudino, K. J. (1992). Prenatal activity level as a temperament dimension? Individual differences and developmental functions in fetal movement. *Infant Behavior and Development, 15,* 57–70.

Epling, W. F., & Pierce, W. D. (Eds.). (1996). *Activity anorexia: Theory, research, and treatment.* Mahwah, NJ: Earlbaum.

Espie, C. A., Lindsay, W. R., & Espie, L. C. (1989). Use of the sleep assessment device (Kelley and Lichstein, 1980) to validate insomniacs' self-report of sleep pattern. *Journal of Psychopathology and Behavioral Assessment, 11,* 71–79.

Falk, J. R., Halmi, K. A., & Tryon, W. W. (1985). Activity measures in anorexia nervosa. *Archives on General Psychiatry, 42,* 811–814.

Fielden, J. M., Gander, P. H., Horne, J. G., Lewer, B. M., Green, R. M., & Devane, P. A. (2003). An assessment of sleep disturbance in patients before and after total hip arthroplasty. *Journal of Arthroplasty, 18,* 371–376.

Fogelholm, M., Kukkonen-Harjula, K., & Oja, P. (1998). Eating control and physical activity as determinants of short-term weight maintenance after a very-low-calorie diet among obese women. *International Journal of Obesity and Related Metabolic Disorders, 23,* 203–210.

Foster, F. G., & Kupfer, D. J. (1975). Anorexia nervosa: Telemetric assessment of family interaction and hospital events. *Journal of Psychiatric Research, 12,* 19–35.

Fox III, S. M., Naughton, J. P., & Haskell, W. L. (1971). Physical activity and the prevention of coronary heart disease. *Annals of Clinical Research, 3,* 404–432.

Franklin, J. (1981). The measurement of sleep-onset latency in insomnia. *Behaviour Research and Therapy, 19,* 547–549.

Futterman, C. S., & Tryon, W. W. (1994). Psychomotor retardation found in depressed outpatient women. *Journal of Behavior Therapy and Experimental Psychiatry, 25,* 41–48.

Gardner, A. W., Sieminski, D. J., & Killewich, L. A. (1997). The effect of cigarette smoking on free-living daily physical activity in older claudication patients. *Angiology, 48,* 947–955.

Gibbs-Smith, C. (1978). *The inventions of Leonardo da Vinci.* London: Phaidon Press.

Goldsmith, H. H., Buss, A. H., Plomin, R., Rothbart, M. K., Thomas, A., Chess, S., et al. (1987). Roundtable: What is temperament? Four approaches. *Child Development, 58,* 505–529.

Gottlieb, S. S., Fisher, M. L., Freudenberger, R., Robinson, S., Zietowski, G., Alves, L., et al. (1999). Effects of exercise training on peak performance and quality of life in congestive heart failure patients. *Journal of Cardiac Failure, 5,* 188–194.

Gueldner, S. H., & Spradley, J. (1988). Outdoor walking lowers fatigue. *Journal of Gerontological Nursing, 14,* 6–12.

Guilford, J. S., Zimmerman, W. S., & Guilford, J. P. (1976). *The Guilford–Zimmerman Temperament Survey handbook: Twenty-five years of research and application.* San Diego, CA: Educational and Industrial Testing Service.

Gulliksen, H. (1950). *Theory of mental tests.* New York: John Wiley & Sons.

Hatfield, C. F., Herbert, J., Van Someren, E. J., Hodges, J. R., & Hastings, M. H. (2004). Disrupted daily activity/rest cycles in relation to daily cortisol rhythms of home-dwelling patients with early Alzheimer's dementia. *Brain, 127,* 1061–1074.

Hauri, P. (1999). Evaluation of a sleep switch device. *Sleep, 22,* 1110–1117.

Henderson, C. J., Lovell, D. J., Specker, B. L., & Campaigne, B. N. (1995). Physical activity in children with juvenile rheumatoid arthritis: quantification and evaluation. *Arthritis Care Research, 8,* 114–119.

Henry, J. B., Davidsohn, I., & Sanford, A. H. (1984). *Todd–Sanford–Davidsohn: Clinical diagnosis and management by laboratory methods* (17th ed.). Philadelphia: W. B. Saunders.

Hoiberg, A., Bernard, S., Watten, R. H., & Caine, C. (1984). Correlates of weight loss in treatment and at follow-up. *International Journal of Obesity, 8,* 457–465.

Iwane, M., Arita, M., Tomimoto, S., Satani, O., Matsumoto, M., Miyashita, K., et al. (2000). Walking 10,000 steps/day or more reduces blood pressure and sympathetic nerve activity in mild essential hypertension. *Hypertension Research, 23,* 573–580.

Jason, L. A., Tryon, W. W., Frankenberry, E., & King, C. (1997). Chronic fatigue syndrome: Relationships of self-ratings and actigraphy. *Psychological Reports, 81,* 1223–1226.

Johnson, M. A., Woodcock, A. A., & Geddes, D. M. (1983). Dihydrocodeine for breathlessness in "pink puffers." *British Medical Journal, 286,* 675–677.

King, A. C., Taylor, C. B., Haskell, W. L., & DeBusk, R. F. (1989). Influence of regular aerobic exercise on psychological health: A randomized, controlled trial of healthy middle-aged adults. *Health Psychology, 8,* 305–324.

Kitagawa, J., Omasu, F., & Nakahara, Y. (2003). Effect of daily walking steps on ultrasound parameters of the calcaneus in elderly Japanese women. *Osteoporosis International, 14,* 219–224.

Korszun, A., Young, E. A., Engleberg, N. C., Brucksch, C. B., Greden, J. F., & Crofford, L. A. (2002). Use of actigraphy for monitoring sleep and activity levels in patients with fibromyalgia and depression. *Journal of Psychosomatic Research, 52,* 439–443.

Kraus, H., & Raab, W. (1961). *Hypokinetic disease.* Springfield, Ill.: Charles C. Thomas.

Kupfer, D. J., Detre, T. P., Foster, F. G., Tucker, G. J., & Delgado, J. (1972). The application of Delgado's telemetric mobility recorder for human studies. *Behavioral Biology, 7,* 585–590.

Lawrence, J. M., Teicher, M. H., & Finklestein, S. P. (1989). Quantitative assessment of locomotor activity in psychiatry and neurology. In A. B. Joseph & R. Young (Eds.), *Disorders of movement in psychiatry and neurology* (pp. 449–462). Cambridge, MA: Blackwell Scientific Publications.

Leary, A. C., Donnan, P. T., MacDonald, T. M., & Murphy, M. B. (2000). Physical activity level is an independent predictor of the diurnal variation in blood pressure. *Journal of Hypertension, 18,* 405–410.

Lee, K. A., Portillo, C. J., & Miramontes, H. (2001). The influence of sleep and activity patterns on fatigue in women with HIV/AIDS. *Journal of the Association of Nurses in AIDS Care, 12, Suppl,* 19–27.

Leon, A. S., Connett, J., Jacobs, D. R., Jr., & Rauramaa, R. (1987). Leisure-time physical activity levels and risk of coronary heart disease and death. *Journal of the American Medical Association, 258,* 2388–2395.

Lerner, R. M., Palermo, M., Sprio, A., & Nessleroade, J. (1982). Assessing the dimensions of temperamental individuality across the life span: The Dimensions of Temperament Survey (DOTS). *Child Development, 53,* 149–160.

Lerner, R. M., Lerner, J. V., Windle, M., Hooker, K., Lenerz, K., & East, P. L. (1986). In R. Plomin & J. Dunn (Eds.), *The structure of temperament: Changes, continuities and challenges* (pp. 99–114). Hillsdale, NJ: Erlbaum.

Lichstein, K. L., Hoelscher, T. J., Eakin, T. L., Nickel, R. (1983). Empirical sleep assessment in the home: A convenient, inexpensive approach. *Journal of Behavioral Assessment, 5,* 111–118.

Lilker, E. S., Karnick, A., & Lerner, L. (1975). Portable oxygen in chronic obstructive lung disease with hypoxemia and corpulmonale. *Chest, 68,* 236–241.

Lindsley, O. R. (1957). Operant behavior during sleep: A measure of depth of sleep. *Science, 126,* 1290–1291.

Linehan, M. M. (1980). Content validity: Its relevance to behavioral assessment. *Behavioral Assessment, 2,* 147–159.

Littner M., Kushida, C. A., Anderson, W. M., Bailey, D., Berry, R. B., Davila, D. G., et al. Standards of Practice Committee of the American Academy of Sleep Medicine. (2003). Practice parameters for the role of actigraphy in the study of sleep and circadian rhythms: An update for 2002. *Sleep, 26,* 337–341.

Marston, A. R., & Criss, J. (1984). Maintenance of successful weight loss: Incidence and prediction. *International Journal of Obesity, 8,* 435–439.

Manton, K. G., Stallard, E., & Liu, K. (1993). Forecasts of active life expectancy: Policy and fiscal implications. *The Journals of Gerontology, 48,* 11–26.

Meyer, G. J., Finn, S. E., Eyde, L. D., Kay, G. G., Moreland, K. L., Dies, R. R., et al. (2001). Psychological testing and psychological assessment: A review of evidence and issues. *American Psychologist, 56,* 128–165.

Moessinger, A. C. (1988). Morphological consequences of depressed or impaired fetal activity. In W. P. Smotherman & S. R. Robinson (Eds.), *Behavior of the fetus.* Caldwell, NJ: Telford Press.

Mokdad, A. H., & Bowman, B. A. (2001). The continuing epidemics of obesity and diabetes in the United States. *Journal of the American Medical Association, 286,* 1195–1200.

Mokdad, A. H., Serdula, M. K., & Dietz, W. A. (1999). Spread of the obesity epidemic in the United States, 1991–1998. *Journal of the American Medical Association, 282,* 1530–1538.

Monk, T. H. (1994). Shift work. In M. H. Kryger, T. Roth, & W. C. Dement (Eds.), *Principles and practice of sleep medicine* (2nd ed., pp. 471–476). London: W. B. Saunders.

Moreau, K. L., Degarmo, R., Langley, J., McMahon, C., Howley, E. T., Bassett Jr., D. R., et al. (2001). Increasing daily walking lowers blood pressure in postmenopausal women. *Medicine and Science in Sports and Exercise, 33,* 1825–1831.

Morris, J. N., Chave, S. P. W., Adam, C., Sirey, C., Epstein, L., & Sheehan, D. J. (1973). Vigorous exercise in leisure time and the incidence of coronary heart disease. *The Lancet, 1,* 333–339.

Morris, J. N., Everitt, M. G., Pollard, R., Chave, S. P. W., & Semmence, A. M. (1980). Vigorous exercise in leisure time: Protection against coronary heart disease. *The Lancet, 2,* 1207–1210.

Ng, A. V., & Kent-Braun, J. A. (1997). Quantitation of lower physical activity in persons with multiple sclerosis. *Medicine and Science in Sports and Exercise, 29,* 517–523.

O'Brien, S. J., & Vertinsky, P. A. (1991). Unfit survivors: Exercise as a resource for aging women. *The Gerontologist, 31,* 347–357.

Oberman, A. (1985). Exercise and the primary prevention of cardiovascular disease. *American Journal of Cardiology, 55,* 10D–20D.

Ogilvie, R. D., & Wilkinson, R. T. (1984). The detection of sleep onset: Behavioral and physiological convergence. *Psychophysiology, 21,* 510–520.

Ogilvie, R. D., & Wilkinson, R. T. (1988). Behavioral versus EEG-based monitoring of all-night sleep/wake patterns. *Sleep, 11,* 139–155.

Ogilvie, R. D., Wilkinson, R. T., & Allison, S. (1989). The detection of sleep onset: Behavioral, physiological, and subjective convergence. *Sleep, 12,* 458–474.

Paffenbarger, Jr., R. S., & Hyde, R. T. (1984). Exercise in the prevention of coronary heart disease. *Preventive Medicine, 13,* 3–22.

Paffenbarger, Jr., R. S., Hyde, R. T., Wing, A. L., & Hsieh, C. C. (1986). Physical activity, all-cause mortality, and longevity of college alumni. *New England Journal of Medicine, 314,* 605–613.

Paffenbarger, Jr., R. S., Hyde, R. T., Wing, A. L., & Steinmetz, C. H. (1984). A natural history of athleticism and cardiovascular health. *Journal of the American Medical Association, 252,* 491–495.

Pate, R. R., Pratt, M., Blair, S. N., Haskell, W. L., Macera, C. A., Bouchard, C., et al. (1995). Physical activity and public health: A recommendation from the Centers for Disease Control and Prevention and the American College of Sports Medicine. *Journal of the American Medical Association, 273,* 402–407.

Perry, T. J., & Goldwater, B. C. (1987). A passive behavioral measure of sleep onset in high-alpha and low-alpha subjects. *Psychophysiology, 24,* 657–665.

Pierce, W. D., & Epling, W. F. (1994). Activity anorexia: An interplay between basic and applied behavior analysis. *Behavior Analyst, 17,* 7–23.

Pollak, C. P., Tryon, W. W., Nagaraja, H., & Dzwonczyk, R. (2001). How well does wrist actigraphy identify states of sleep and wakefulness? *Sleep Research, 24,* 957–965.

Powell, K. E., Thompson, P. D., Caspersen, C. J., & Kendrick, J. S. (1987). Physical activity and the incidence of coronary heart disease. *Annual Review of Public Health, 8,* 253–287.

President's Council on Physical Fitness and Sports. (2002, June). Taking steps toward increased physical activity. In *Research Digest* (Series 3, No. 17) (Pedometer). Retrieved from http://www.fitness.gov/Reading_Room/Digests/pcpfsdigestjune2002.pdf

Quinto, C., Gellido, C., Chokroverty, S., & Masdeu, J. (2000). Post-traumatic delayed sleep phase syndrome. *Neurology, 55,* 902–903.

Rechtschaffen, A., & Kales, A. (1968). *A manual of standard terminology, techniques and scoring system for sleep states of human subjects.* Washington, DC: Superintendent of Documents, Book 1–62.

Redeker, N. S., & Wykpisz, E. (1999). Effects of age on activity patterns after coronary artery bypass surgery. *Heart & Lung, 28,* 5–14.

Refinetti, R. (1993). Laboratory instrumentation and computing: Comparison of six methods for the determination of the period of circadian rhythms. *Physiology and Behavior, 54,* 869–875.

Robertson, S. S. (1985). Cyclic motor activity in the human fetus after midgestation. *Developmental Psychobiology, 18,* 411–419.

Robertson, S. S., & Dierker, L. J. (1986). The development of cyclic motility in fetuses of diabetic mothers. *Developmental Psychobiology, 19,* 223–234.

Sadeh, A., Hauri, P. J., Kripke, D. F., & Lavie, P. (1995). The role of actigraphy in the evaluation of sleep disorders. *Sleep, 18,* 288–302.

Salonen, J. T., Puska, P., & Tuomilehto, J. (1982). Physical activity and risk of myocardial infarction, cerebral stroke and death: A longitudinal study in eastern Finland. *American Journal of Epidemiology, 115,* 526–537.

Schmalzried, T. P., Szuszczewicz, E. S., Northfield, M. R., Akizuki, K. H., Frankel, R. E., Belcher, G., et al. (1998). Quantitative assessment of walking activity after total hip or knee replacement. *Journal of Bone and Joint Surgery American Volume, 80,* 54–59.

Scrimshaw, N. S., & Pollitt, E. (1984). Preface. In E. Pollitt and P. Amante (Eds.), *Energy intake and activity* (pp. ix–xii). New York: Alan R. Liss.

Sheehan, L. A., & Macallan, D. C. (2000). Determinants of energy intake and energy expenditure in HIV and AIDS. *Nutrition, 16,* 101–106.

Shiner, R. L. (1998). How shall we speak of children's personalities in middle childhood? A preliminary taxonomy. *Psychological Bulletin, 124,* 308–332.

Silva, F. (1993). *Psychometric foundations and behavioral assessment.* Thousand Oaks, CA: Sage Publications.

Slattery, M. L., Jacobs, Jr., D. R., & Nichaman, M. A. (1989). Leisure-time physical activity and coronary heart disease death: The U.S. Railroad Study. *Circulation, 79,* 304–311.

Slattery, M. L., Schumacher, M. C., Smith, K. R., West, D. W., & Abd-Elghany, N. (1988). Physical activity, diet, and risk of colon cancer in Utah. *American Journal of Epidemiology, 128,* 989–999.

Speck, B. J., & Looney, S. (2001). Effects of a minimal intervention to increase physical activity in women: Daily activity records. *Nursing Research, 50,* 374–378.

Spiegel R. (1981). *Sleep and sleeplessness in advanced age.* New York: SP Medical & Scientific Books.

Standards of Practice Committee. (1995). Practice parameters for the use of actigraphy in the clinical assessment of sleep disorders. *Sleep, 18,* 285–287.

Stunkard, A. J. (1960). A method of studying physical activity in man. *American Journal of Clinical Nutrition, 8,* 595–601.

Talbot, L. A., Gaines, J. M., Huynh, T. N., & Metter, E. J. (2003). A home-based pedometer-driven walking program to increase physical activity in older adults with osteoarthritis of the knee: A preliminary study. *Journal of the American Geriatric Society, 51,* 387–392.

Teicher, M. H. (1995). Actigraphy and motion analysis: New tools for psychiatry. *Harvard Review of Psychiatry, 3,* 18–35.

Teicher, M. H., Lawrence, J. M., Barber, N. I., Finklestein, S. P., Lieberman, H., & Baldessarini, R. J. (1986). Altered locomotor activity in neuropsychiatric patients. *Progress in Neuro-Psychopharmacology and Biological Psychiatry, 10,* 755–761.

Thomas, A., & Chess, S. (1977). *Temperament and development.* New York: Brunner/Mazel.

Thomas, A., Chess, S., & Birch, H. (1968). *Temperament and behavior: Disorders in children.* New York: New York University Press.

Toda, Y., Toda, T., Takemura, S., Wada, T., Morimoto, T., & Ogawa, R. (1998). Change in body fat, but not body weight or metabolic correlates of obesity, is related to symptomatic relief of obese patients with knee osteoarthritis after a weight control program. *Journal of Rheumatology, 25,* 2181–2186.

Tryon, W. W. (1991). *Activity measurement in psychology and medicine.* New York: Plenum Press.

Tryon, W. W. (1996a). Instrument-driven theory. *Journal of Mind and Behavior, 17,* 21–30.

Tryon, W. W. (1996b). Nocturnal activity and sleep assessment. *Clinical Psychology Review, 16,* 197–213.

Tryon, W. W. (1998a). Behavioral observation. In M. Hersen & A. S. Bellack (Eds.), *Behavioral assessment: A practical handbook* (4th ed., pp. 79–103). Boston: Allyn & Bacon.

Tryon, W. W. (1998b). Physical activity. In M. Hersen & B. B. Van Hasselt (Eds.), *Handbook of clinical geropsychology* (pp. 523–556). New York: Plenum Press.

Tryon, W. W. (2002). Activity level and *DSM-IV.* In S. Turner & M. Hersen (Eds.), *Adult psychopathology and diagnosis* (4th. ed., pp. 547–577). New York: John Wiley & Sons.

Tryon, W. W. (2004). Issues of validity in actigraphic sleep assessment. *Sleep, 27,* 158–165.

Tryon, W. W. (2005). The reliability and validity of two ambulatory monitoring actigraphs. *Behavior Research Methods, Instruments, and Computers,* in press.

Tryon, W. W., & Bernstein, D. (2002). Understanding measurement. In J. C. Thomas & M. Hersen (Eds.), *Understanding research in clinical and counseling psychology: A textbook* (pp. 27–68). Mahwah, NJ: Earlbaum.

Tryon, W. W., Jason, L., Frankenberry, E., & Torres-Harding, S. (2004). *Chronic fatigue syndrome impairs circadian rhythm of activity level.* Manuscript submitted for publication.

Tryon, W. W., & Williams, R. (1996). Fully proportional actigraphy: A new instrument. *Behavior Research Methods Instruments & Computers, 28,* 392–403.

Tudor-Locke, C., & Ainsworth, C. (2001). The relationship between pedometer-determined ambulatory activity and body composition variables. *International Journal of Obesity, 25,* 1571–1578.

Tudor-Locke, C., Myers, A. M., Bell, R. C., Harris, S., & Wilson-Rodger, N. (2002). Preliminary outcome evaluation of The First Step Program: A daily physical activity intervention for individuals with Type 2 diabetes. *Patient Education and Counseling, 47,* 23–28.

Tudor-Locke, C., Myers, A. M., & Rodger, N. (2000). Formative evaluation of The First Step Program: A practical intervention to increase daily physical activity. *Canadian Journal of Diabetes Care, 24,* 34–38.

U.S. Department of Health and Human Services. (1996). *Physical activity and health: A report of the Surgeon General.* Atlanta, GA: U.S. Department of Health and Human Services, Centers for Disease Control and Prevention, National Center for Chronic Disease Prevention and Promotion.

Vercoulen, J. H., Bazelmans, E., Swanink, C. M., Fennis, J. F., Galama, J. M., Jongen, P. J., et al. (1997). Physical activity in chronic fatigue syndrome: Assessment and its role in fatigue. *Journal of Psychiatric Research, 31,* 661–673.

Viens, M., De Koninck, J., Van den Bergen, R., Audet, R., & Christ, G. (1988). A refined switch-activated time monitor for the measurement of sleep-onset latency. *Behaviour Research and Therapy, 26,* 271–273.

Waddington, S. (1998). *Factor structure of the Revised Dimensions of Temperament Survey: College-aged and middle-aged adults.* Unpublished doctoral dissertation, Fordham University.

Walsh, J. T., Andrews, R., Evans, A., & Cowley, A. J. (1995). Failure of "effective" treatment for heart failure to improve normal customary activity. *British Heart Journal, 74,* 373–376.

Walsh, J. T., Charlesworth, A., Andrews, R., Hawkins, M., & Cowley, A. J. (1997). Relation of daily activity levels in patients with chronic heart failure to long-term prognosis. *American Journal of Cardiology, 79,* 1364–1369.

Weinbroum, A. A., Ben Abraham, R., Ezri, T., & Zomer, J. (2001). Wrist actigraphy in anesthesia. *Journal of Clinical Anesthesiology, 13,* 455–460.

Westover, S. A., & Lanyon, R. I. (1990). The maintenance of weight loss after behavioral treatment. *Behavior Modification, 14,* 123–137.

Wilson, K. G., Watson, S. T., & Currie, S. R. (1998). Daily diary and ambulatory activity monitoring of sleep in patients with insomnia associated with chronic musculoskeletal pain. *Pain, 75,* 75–84.

Windle, M., & Lerner, R. M. (1986). Reassessing the dimensions of temperamental individuality across the life span: The Revised Dimensions of Temperament Survey (DOTS-R). *Journal of Adolescent Research, 1,* 213–229.

Yamanouchi, K., Takashi, T., Chikada, K., Nishikawa, T., Ito, K., Shimizu, S., et al. (1995). Daily walking combined with diet therapy is a useful means for obese NIDDM patients not only to reduce body weight but also to improve insulin sensitivity. *Diabetes Care, 18,* 775–778.

# 6

# STRUCTURED AND
# SEMISTRUCTURED
# INTERVIEWS

DANIEL L. SEGAL
FREDERICK L. COOLIDGE
ALISA O'RILEY
BENJAMIN A. HEINZ

*Department of Psychology*
*University of Colorado at Colorado Springs*
*Colorado Springs, Colorado*

## INTRODUCTION

The architects of the original *Diagnostic and Statistic Manual* (American Psychiatric Association, 1952) were more or less doomed from the start. The definition of mental illness and criteria for the specific disorders were vague at best, and the reliability of diagnosis (even for the major and common disorders) was so poor that it called into serious question the validity of the entire classification system itself. The problem of nebulous and inadequately specified criteria was largely addressed in subsequent revisions of the *DSM*, of which the *DSM-IV-TR* (American Psychiatric Association, 2000) is the current incarnation. Another major contributor to poor reliability of diagnosis was the lack of uniformity of diagnostic questions to evaluate psychiatric symptoms and arrive at a formal diagnosis. This problem has been addressed by the development of structured interviews. Undeniably, since the 1970s the ability of clinicians and researchers to accurately diagnose psychiatric disorders has improved in quantum leaps, and structured interviews have contributed significantly to the advancement in diagnostic clarity and precision. In this chapter, we provide an overview of the major features and advantages of structured interviews, followed by a discussion of the most popular multidisorder structured interviews. We conclude with a review of

*Clinician's Handbook of Adult Behavioral*
*Assessment*

121

more specialized structured interviews to provide the reader with an appreciation for the diversity of clinical information that structured interviews can provide.

## BASIC ISSUES REGARDING STRUCTURED INTERVIEWS

Traditional assessment methods have relied on the unstructured, or "clinical," interview, behavioral and observational assessment, and psychometric testing. Regarding the interview component, there are important differences between an unstructured interview and a structured one. For starters, unstructured clinical interviews are heavily influenced by the individual client's needs, the client's responses, and the clinician's intuitions. With unstructured interviews, clinicians are entirely responsible for asking whatever questions they decide are necessary for them to reach a diagnostic conclusion. In fact, any type of question (relevant or not) can be asked in any way that fits the mood, preferences, training, and philosophy of the clinician. The amount and specific kind of information gathered during an interview are largely determined by the clinician's theoretical model (e.g., psychoanalytic, behavioral), view of psychopathology, training, knowledge base, and interpersonal style. As a consequence, one can imagine the kind of inconsistency and variability in an interview from one clinician to another.

Structured interviews, on the other hand, conform to a standardized list of questions, including follow-up questions, a standardized sequence of questioning, and, finally, systematized ratings of the client's responses. In fact, the impetus for the development of structured interviews was generated by the need to standardize questions and provide explicit guidelines for categorizing or coding responses. Adoption of such procedures serves to: (1) increase coverage of many disorders that otherwise might be overlooked, (2) enhance the diagnostician's ability to accurately determine if a particular symptom is present or absent, and (3) reduce variability among interviewers (i.e., reduce unreliability). These features of structured diagnostic interviews add much to developing clinical psychology into a true science (i.e., structured interviews are subject to evaluation and statistical analysis, and they are modified and improved based on the emerging database of the field).

It is also important to emphasize that the term *structured interview* is a broad one and that the actual amount of "structure" provided by an interview varies considerably. Basically, structured interviews can be divided into one of two types: fully structured and semistructured. In a fully structured interview, questions are asked verbatim to the respondent, the wording of probes used to follow up on initial questions is specified, and interviewers are trained not to deviate from this very specific format. In a semistructured interview, although the initial questions for each symptom are specified and are typically asked verbatim to the respondent, the interviewer has substantial latitude to follow up on responses. For example, the interviewer can modify existing questions and probes in any way and even devise completely new, innovative questions to more accurately rate specific symptoms. The amount of structure provided in a structured interview clearly impacts the extent of clinical experience and judgment needed to administer the interview appropriately: Semistructured interviews require clinically experienced examiners to administer the interview and to make diagnoses, whereas fully structured interviews can be administered by nonclinicians who receive training on the specific instrument, thus making fully structured interviews economical to use, especially in large studies.

Structured interviews are used in many different venues and for many different purposes. Application of structured interviews falls into three broad areas: research, clinical, and training use. The research domain is probably the most common for structured interviews, in which the interview is used to diagnose participants accurately so that etiology, comorbidity, and treatment approaches (among other topics) can be studied for a particular diagnosis or group of diagnoses. Certainly, good research requires that individuals assigned a diagnosis truly meet full criteria for that diagnosis. In clinical settings, structured interviews may be used as part of a comprehensive and standardized intake evaluation. A variation on this theme is that a structured interview may be used to clarify and confirm diagnoses based on an initial unstructured interview. Use of structured interviews for training in the mental health field is an ideal application because interviewers have the opportunity to learn (through repeated administrations) specific questions and follow-up probes used to elicit information and evaluate specific diagnostic criteria provided by the *DSM* system. Modeling one's own questions and flow of the interview from a well-developed structured interview can be an invaluable source of training for the clinician.

Over the past several decades, proliferation of structured interviews has been steady. Structured interviews have been created to assist with the differential diagnosis of all major Axis I (clinical) and all standard Axis II (personality) disorders. These structured interviews used for diagnosis are typically aligned with the *DSM* system and therefore assess the formal diagnostic criteria specified in the manual. But structured interviews for differential diagnosis are not the only kind of structured interviews; other structured interviews are more narrow in focus, for example, to assess a specific problem or form of psychopathology (e.g., eating disorders, borderline personality features) in great depth.

In the last two decades, evidence-based practice has become the cornerstone of clinical psychology. With the field's increasing emphasis on establishing psychotherapy as an empirically supported method of treating mental illness, the reliability and validity of our methods of diagnosis have become all-important components of treatment and clinical research. In order to justify the use of psychotherapy, we must justify the methods by which we classify and ascertain diagnoses. This becomes blatantly problematic when two different clinicians, interviewing the same client, furnish two different diagnoses, because they chose to ask completely different sets of questions. As noted earlier, one solution to this quandary was the development of structured interviews.

## ADVANTAGES AND DISADVANTAGES OF STRUCTURED AND SEMISTRUCTURED INTERVIEWS

Structured interviews were developed to improve our ability to accurately diagnose individuals, in both clinical and research settings. By systemizing the questions clinicians ask and the way answers to those questions are recorded and interpreted, structured interviews minimize needless variability in diagnostic evaluations (Morrison, 1988; Rogers, 2001; Rubinson & Asnis, 1989; Segal & Coolidge, 2003). Thus, by increasing reliability, structured interviews also increase validity of diagnosis, assuming the criteria on which diagnosis is based are also valid. In addition, structured interviews can be invaluable training tools for laypersons and clinicians-in-training (Morrison).

Despite the advantages of structured interviews, their use is not without controversy. Critics of structured interviews maintain that utilizing such interviews can severely damage rapport and, thus, the therapeutic relationship essential to psychotherapy (Rogers, 2001; Rubinson & Asnis, 1989). Some critics also argue that the validity of structured interviews is questionable, because such interviews are based on diagnostic criteria that have not been established as valid in all cases (Rogers; Rubinson & Asnis). Finally, structured interviews may be limited because they sacrifice either the breadth or the depth of information attained (Rogers; Rubinson & Asnis). Next, we examine each of the arguments in more detail. A brief summary of advantages and disadvantages is presented in Table 6.1.

### ADVANTAGES OF STRUCTURED AND SEMISTRUCTURED INTERVIEWS

#### Increased Reliability

Perhaps the most important advantage of structured interviews centers on increased reliability. By systemizing and standardizing the questions interviewers ask and the way those questions are presented, structured interviews improve reliability in a variety of ways. First, structured interviews decrease the amount of information variance in interviews (Segal & Coolidge, 2003). That is, structured interviews decrease the chances that two different interviewers will elicit different information from the same client, which may result in different diagnoses. Interviewers may arrive at different information from clients for a variety of reasons. For example, they may ask different questions, they may cover different criteria for specific disorders, they may ask questions in different sequences, they may rate the intensity of client's reported symptoms in different ways, or they may record the information clients give them differently (Rogers, 2001). Structured interviews help eliminate this variability by standardizing all of these aspects of a diagnostic evaluation. Thus, interrater reliability, or the like-

TABLE 6.1    Advantages and Disadvantages of Structured Interviews

| Advantages of Structured Interviews | Disadvantages of Structured Interviews |
| --- | --- |
| **Increased Reliability:** Because questions are standardized, structured interviews result in decreased variability among interviewers, which enhances interrater reliability. Structured interviews also increase the reliability of assessment for a client's symptoms across time as well as the reliability between client report and collateral information. | **May Hinder Rapport:** Use of structured interviews may damage rapport because they are problem centered, not person centered, and poorly trained interviewers may neglect to use their basic clinical skills during the assessment. |
| **Increased Validity:** Structured interviews ensure that diagnostic criteria are covered systematically and completely. This is important because it serves to increase the validity of diagnosis. | **Limited by the Validity of the Classification System Itself:** Structured interviews used for diagnosis are inherently tied to diagnostic systems. Thus, they are only as valid as the systems on which they are based. Furthermore, it is difficult to establish the validity of particular structured interviews because there is no gold standard in psychiatric diagnosis. |
| **Utility as Training Tools:** Nonclinicians can easily be trained to administer fully structured interviews, which can be cost effective in both research and clinical settings. In addition, structured interviews are excellent training tools for clinicians-in-training because structured interviews promote the learning of specific diagnostic questions and probes used by experienced clinical interviewers. | **Breadth versus Depth:** Structured interviews are limited because they cannot cover all disorders or topic areas. When choosing a structured interview, one must think carefully about the trade-offs of breadth versus depth of assessment. |

lihood that two different interviewers examining the same individual will arrive at the same diagnosis, is greatly increased.

Increased interrater reliability has broad implications in both clinical and research settings. Because many methods of psychological treatment are intimately tied to diagnoses, it is imperative that diagnoses be accurate (Segal & Coolidge, 2001). Thus, if different clinicians interviewing the same client arrive at different diagnostic conclusions, it would be challenging at best to make a definitive decision about treatment. Similarly, accurate diagnosis is also essential for some types of clinical research, for example, that addressing the causes and treatments of specific forms of psychopathology (Segal & Coolidge). Imagine a study examining different treatments for Major Depressive Disorder. In such a study, it would be imperative to be certain that those in the treatment groups actually suffer from depression. Indeed, we must be able to diagnose participants with depression accurately and definitively before we can even begin to examine effectiveness of treatment for the disorder or theories of etiology.

In addition to increasing interrater reliability, structured interviews increase the likelihood that the diagnosis is reliable across time and across different sources of information (Rogers, 2001). In many clinical and research settings, clients or participants are in fact assessed on different occasions. The danger in making multiple assessments is that if an interviewer evaluates a client in a different manner with different questions on different occasions, the client's presentation may be completely different, not because the client's symptoms or diagnosis has changed but rather because the way the client is asked about those symptoms has changed. Utilizing a standardized interview for multiple assessments helps ensure that if a client's presentation has changed, it is because his or her symptoms are actually different, not because of variance in interviews (Rogers). Likewise, in many settings, clinicians conduct collateral interviews with important people in the client's life to get a broader picture of the client's symptoms, problems, and experiences. Using a structured interview for both a client and a collateral source may greatly increase the chances that discrepancies between client and collateral interviews are real, rather than just by-products of interviewing styles (Rogers).

### Increased Validity

Validity of diagnosis has to do with the meaningfulness or usefulness of the diagnosis, and reliability is a required prerequisite for validity. Thus, by virtue of the fact that structured interviews greatly increase reliability of diagnosis, they also increase the likelihood that a diagnosis is valid. Structured interviews also improve the validity of diagnoses in other ways. The systematic construction of structured interviews lends a methodological validity to these types of assessments, compared to unstructured approaches. Because structured interviews are designed to assess well-defined diagnostic criteria thoroughly and accurately, they are often better assessments of those criteria than are unstructured interviews (Rogers, 2001; Segal & Coolidge, 2003). According to Rogers, clinicians who use unstructured interviews sometimes diagnose too quickly and may miss comorbid diagnoses. Thus, because structured interviews "force" clinicians to assess all of the specified criteria for a broad range of diagnoses, they offer a more thorough and valid assessment of many disorders, compared to unstructured interviews.

To elaborate, some unstructured interviews may provide information about the presence or absence of only a few common mental disorders. Coverage of other disorders may be neglected during an unstructured interview if, for example, the interviewer is unfamiliar with the specific criteria of some disorders. Some unstructured interviews may also provide limited information about whether comorbid psychopathology exists as well as inconsistent information about the severity of the psychopathology. Structured interviews, because they incorporate systematic ratings, easily provide information that allows for the determination of the level of severity and the level of impairment associated with a particular diagnosis, and structured interviews provide the same information about any comorbid conditions.

## Utility as Training Tools

Structured interviews can be invaluable training tools for both laypersons working in the field and clinicians-in-training (Morrison, 1988; Segal & Coolidge, 2003). Structured interviews can be a useful means of ensuring that laypersons who are making preliminary mental health assessments, for example, intake staff at hospitals, are evaluating individuals thoroughly and accurately. In the case of nonclinician interviewers, fully structured interviews are advisable because they minimize the amount of clinical judgment needed for accurate administration. Structured interviews can be invaluable tools in the training of mental health professionals as well. Becoming familiar with structured interviews may help inexperienced clinicians develop an understanding of the flow, format, and questions inherent in a good diagnostic interview.

## DISADVANTAGES OF STRUCTURED AND SEMISTRUCTURED INTERVIEWS

## May Hinder Rapport

The most common criticism of structured interviews is that their use may significantly damage rapport (Rogers, 2001; Rubinson & Asnis, 1989; Segal & Coolidge, 2003). Critics of structured interviews argue that reliable and accurate diagnosis of a client is useless if it comes at the cost of the development of the therapeutic alliance, which is the basis of psychotherapy. Structured interviews may damage rapport because they are problem centered rather than person centered. There is a danger that interviewers may get so wrapped up in the protocol of their interview that they fail to demonstrate the warmth and genuine regard necessary to form an alliance. In addition, interviewers who are overly focused on the questions they must "get through" in an interview may miss important behavioral cues or other information that could prove essential to the case (Rogers; Segal & Coolidge).

Proponents of structured interviews point out that the problem of rapport building during a structured interview can be overcome with training and experience (Rogers, 2001). Structured interviews can be conducted in such a way that they help to establish rapport and understanding of the client, especially if interviewers make an effort to utilize their basic clinical skills. In order to ensure that this is the case, however, interviewers must be aware of the potential negative effects of structured interviews on rapport building and make building a therapeutic alliance a prominent goal during an interview, even when they are also focused on following protocol. It behooves those who use structured interviews to engage their respondents in a meaningful way during the interview and to avoid a rotelike interviewing style that may serve to alienate. On the other hand, some clients actually like the structured interview approach to assessment because it is perceived as thorough and detailed; in these cases, rapport is easily attained.

### Limited by the Validity of the Classification System Itself

Earlier, we noted that structured interviews frequently offer a more valid assessment of diagnostic criteria than unstructured interviews. Thus, proponents of structured interviews claim, structured interviews are more valid in general. The assumption inherent in this argument is that our diagnostic criteria are valid. Some would argue, however, that this assumption is a false one (Morrison, 1988; Rogers, 2001). Diagnostic criteria, in particular the criteria of the *DSM*, have often been criticized for lack of validity. Although each successive edition of the *DSM* has been better grounded in scientific research, critics have maintained that the criteria for some diagnoses are not well examined enough to constitute any sort of validity (Segal & Coolidge, 2003). This point is evidenced by the fact that the criteria for many disorders have changed significantly from one edition to another in the evolution of the *DSM*. Furthermore, research suggests that the criteria in the *DSM* are often severely limited by culture (Rogers). Thus, the criteria may only be valid for a particular group of individuals at a particular point in time. All in all, the way we conceptualize diagnoses, while improving, is far from perfect. And, because structured interviews are intimately tied to diagnostic criteria, they are, by definition, limited by the same inadequacies inherent in those criteria.

In addition to this problem with diagnostic criteria, structured interviews have other problems with validity. Specifically, it is difficult to establish the validity of any particular structured interview (Morrison, 1988). Our best means of establishing validity of a structured interview is to compare diagnoses obtained from such interviews to diagnoses obtained by expert clinicians or by other structured interviews. This is inherently problematic because we cannot be certain that diagnoses by experts or other structured interviews are themselves valid (Morrison; Rogers, 2001; Segal & Coolidge, 2003).

### Breadth versus Depth

A final criticism of structured interviews centers on the fact that no one structured interview can be all things in all situations. A particular structured interview cannot cover all disorders and eventualities (Morrison, 1988; Rogers, 2001; Segal & Coolidge, 2003). For example, if a structured interview has been designed to cover an entire diagnostic system (like the *DSM*, which identifies over several hundred specific disorders), then the inquiries about each disorder must be limited to a few inclusion criteria. Thus, the fidelity of the official diagnostic criteria has been compromised for the sake of a comprehensive interview. If the fidelity of the criteria is not compromised, then the structured interview becomes unwieldy, in terms of time and effort, on the part of both the interviewer and interviewee. Most structured interviews attempt some kind of compromise between these two approaches.

Thus, as for breadth versus depth of approach, users of structured interviews are forced to make a choice about what is most useful in a given situation. Both choices have their limitations. If a clinician or researcher decides to utilize an interview that provides great breadth of information, it is ensured that a wide range of disorders and a great many different areas of a respondent's life are assessed. However, one may not have the depth of information needed to fully conceptualize a case. On the other hand, deciding to utilize an interview focused on one or two specific areas will provide clinicians and researchers with a wealth of information about those specific areas, but it may result in missing information that could lead to an additional diagnosis or a different case conceptualization. Thus, it is essential to understand that when choosing a particular structured interview, there are often trade-offs regarding breadth and depth of information.

### WEIGHING BOTH ADVANTAGES AND DISADVANTAGES

Our examination of the arguments for and against the use of structured interviews highlights the importance of carefully contemplating what is needed in a particular clinical or research situation before choosing to utilize a structured interview. Structured interviews can be invaluable tools in both clinical and research work; however, it is essential that one not employ such tools without accounting for some of the problems inherent in their use. Another perspective voiced by Rogers (2001) is that it would be unwise to view the interviewing process as an either/or proposition (i.e., unstructured vs. structured interview). In certain situations, unstructured interviews may meet the objectives of a particular clinical inquiry more efficiently than a structured interview. For example, in a crisis situation, flexibility on the part of the clinician is needed to meet the pressing demands of this fluid and potentially volatile interaction. However, structured interviewing allows for the assessment of the reliability of the interviewing process itself, which speaks to the validity of psychiatric diagnoses as well as of the entire classification system.

In summary, it is apparent that introduction of operationalized, specified, empirically derived, and standardized criteria for mental disorders in conjunction with introduction of standardized structured diagnostic interviews has revolutionized the diagnostic process and vastly improved reliability and validity. A conclusion that one can draw about the specific impact of structured interviews is that they have greatly improved clinical and research endeavors by providing a more standardized, scientific, and quantitative approach to the evaluation of mental disorders and clinical problems. Specific interviews are discussed next.

## STRUCTURED AND SEMISTRUCTURED
## INTERVIEWS FOR DIFFERENTIAL DIAGNOSIS

Interviews discussed in this section are the Diagnostic Interview Schedule for *DSM-IV*, the Schedule for Affective Disorders and Schizophrenia, the Structured Clinical Interview for *DSM-IV* Axis I Disorders, and the Structured Clinical Interview for *DSM-IV* Axis II Personality Disorders. All assess a variety of disorders and therefore can assist in the important task of differential diagnosis (i.e., discriminating which disorder(s) among similar ones the respondent meets criteria for) while also providing for a full assessment of comorbid psychopathology.

### THE DIAGNOSTIC INTERVIEW SCHEDULE FOR *DSM-IV*

The Diagnostic Interview Schedule for *DSM-IV* (DIS-IV; Robins et al., 2000) is designed to ascertain the presence or absence of major psychiatric disorders of the *DSM-IV* (American Psychiatric Association, 1994). It is unique among the multidisorder diagnostic interviews in that it is a *fully structured* interview specifically designed for use by nonclinician interviewers, whereas the other interviews are semistructured. By definition, a fully structured interview clearly specifies all questions and probes and does not permit deviations. Thus, the DIS-IV, by virtue of its structure, minimizes the amount of clinical judgment and experience required to administer it.

To ensure standardized administration of the DIS, the paper-and-pencil version of the instrument is no longer recommended, due to the complicated format. Instead, a computerized version of the DIS-IV (C-DIS) is recommended. Computerized administration may be interviewer administered or self-administered. In both formats, the exact wording of all questions and probes are presented to the respondent in a fixed order on a computer screen, and rephrasing of questions is discouraged, although DIS interviewers can repeat questions as necessary to ensure that they are understood by the respondent. All questions are written to be closed-ended, and replies are coded with a forced choice "yes" or "no" format, which eliminates the need for clinical judgment to rate responses. The DIS gathers all necessary information about the subject from the subject, and collateral sources of information are not used. The DIS is self-contained and covers all necessary symptoms to make many *DSM-IV* diagnoses. The coded responses are entered directly into a database during the interview, and the diagnosis is made according to the explicit rules of the *DSM-IV* diagnostic system.

In 1978, development of the original DIS was begun by researchers at the Washington University Department of Psychiatry in St. Louis at the request of the National Institutes of Mental Health (NIMH). At that time, the NIMH Division of Biometry and Epidemiology was planning a set of large-scale, multicenter epidemiological investigations of mental illness in the general adult population in the United States as part of its Epidemiological Catchment Area Program. Variables under study included incidence and prevalence of many psychiatric disorders and utilization profiles of health and mental health services. With this impressive purpose in mind, development of a structured interview that could be administered by nonclinicians was imperative, due to the prohibitive cost of using professional clinicians as interviewers. As a result, the DIS was designed as a fully structured diagnostic interview, and it was explicitly crafted so that it can be administered and scored by nonclinician interviewers.

The DIS has undergone several major revisions since its inception. For example, the original DIS (Robins, Helzer, Croughan, & Ratcliff, 1981) covered criteria for *DSM-III* (American Psychiatric Association, 1980) disorders. DIS questions and diagnostic algorithms were revamped to establish compatibility with *DSM-III-R* (American Psychiatric Association, 1987); this is called Version DIS-III-R (Robins, Helzer, Cottler, & Goldring, 1989). The current version of the DIS (Version IV; Robins et al., 2000) is closely tied to the *DSM-IV* system; to this end, *DSM* diagnostic criteria for the disorders have been faithfully turned into specific questions on the DIS.

Because the DIS was designed for epidemiological research with normative samples, interviewers do not elicit a presenting problem from the respondent, as would be typical in unstructured clinical interviews. Rather, DIS interviews begin by asking questions about symptoms in a standardized order. Like other structured interviews, the DIS has sections that cover different disorders. Each diagnostic section is independent, except where one diagnosis preempts another. Once a symptom is reported to be present, further closed-ended questions are asked about diagnostically relevant information, such as severity, frequency, time frame, and possibility of organic etiology of the symptom. The DIS includes a set of core questions that are asked of each respondent. Core questions are followed by contingent questions that are administered only if the preceding core question is endorsed. DIS interviewers utilize a "probe flowchart" that indicates which probes to use in which circumstances.

For each symptom, the respondent is asked to state whether it has ever been present and how recently. All data about the presence or absence of symptoms and time frames of occurrence are coded and entered into the computer. Consistent with its use of nonclinician interviewers who may not be overly familiar with the *DSM-IV* or psychiatric diagnosis, the diagnostic output of the DIS is generated by a computer program that analyzes data from the completed interview. The output provides estimates of prevalence for two time periods: current and lifetime.

Due to its highly structured format, full administration of the DIS-IV typically requires between 90 and 150 minutes. To shorten administration time, the modular format makes it possible to drop evaluation of disorders that are not of interest in a particular study. Another option is to drop further questioning for a particular disorder once it is clear that the threshold number of symptoms needed for diagnosis will not be met. Although designed for use by nonclinician administrators, training for competent administration of the DIS is necessary. Trainees typically attend a 1-week training program at Washington University, during which they review the DIS manual, listen to didactic presentations about the structure and conventions of the DIS, view videotaped vignettes, complete workbook exercises, and conduct several practice interviews, followed by feedback and review. Additional supervised practice is also recommended.

The psychometric properties of the original DIS and its revisions are excellent, and such data have been documented in an impressive array of studies. The interested reader is referred to Compton and Cottler (2004) for an excellent summary of the psychometric characteristics of the DIS. Overall, the DIS has proven to be a popular and useful diagnostic assessment tool, especially for large-scale epidemiological research. The DIS has been translated into over a dozen languages. It is used in countries across the globe for epidemiological research and served as the basis for the Composite International Diagnostic Interview used by the World Health Organization. Presently, the DIS-IV is the only well-validated case-finding strategy that can make *DSM-IV* diagnoses in large-scale epidemiological research. Like earlier versions, the DIS-IV can be expected to enjoy widespread application in psychiatric research, service, and training. For information on DIS materials, training, and developments, the interested reader may consult the DIS Web site, http://epi.wustl.edu.

## THE SCHEDULE FOR AFFECTIVE DISORDERS AND SCHIZOPHRENIA

The Schedule for Affective Disorders and Schizophrenia (SADS; Endicott & Spitzer, 1978) is a semistructured diagnostic interview designed to evaluate a range of Axis I clinical disorders, with a focus on mood and psychotic disorders. Ancillary coverage is provided for anxiety symptoms, substance abuse, psychosocial treatment history, and antisocial personality features. The SADS provides in-depth but focused coverage of the mood and psychotic disorders and also supplies meaningful distinctions of impairment in the clinical range for these disorders.

The original SADS focused on psychiatric symptoms as specified by the Research Diagnostic Criteria (RDC; Spitzer, Endicott, & Robins, 1978), which made available specific inclusion and exclusion criteria for many psychiatric disorders. The RDC predated publication of the *DSM-III* (American Psychiatric Association, 1980) and was a significant predecessor of that system. Many of the specified criteria described in the RDC were adopted for inclusion in *DSM-III*. As such, much information derived from SADS interviews can be applied to make *DSM*-based diagnoses.

The SADS is intended to be used with adult respondents and to be administered by trained mental health professionals. It focuses heavily on the differential diagnosis of mood and psychotic disorders, with great depth of assessment in these areas. In the beginning of the interview, a brief overview of the respondent's background and psychiatric problems is elicited in an open-ended inquiry. The SADS is then divided into two parts, each focusing on a different time period.

Part I provides for a thorough evaluation of current psychiatric problems and concomitant functional impairment. A unique feature of the SADS is that for the current episode, symptoms are rated when they were at their worst levels, to increase diagnostic sensitivity and validity. In contrast, Part II provides a broad overview of past episodes of psychopathology and treatment. Overall, the SADS covers over 20 diagnoses in a systematic and comprehensive fashion and provides for diagnosis of both current and lifetime psychiatric disorders. Some examples include Schizophrenia (with six subtypes), Schizoaffective Disorder, Manic Disorder, Hypomanic Disorder, Major Depressive Disorder (with 11 subtypes), Minor Depressive Disorder, Panic Disorder, Obsessive-Compulsive Disorder, Phobic Disorder, alcoholism, and Antisocial Personality Disorder (Endicott & Spitzer, 1978).

In the SADS, questions are clustered according to specific diagnoses, which improves the flow of the interview. For each disorder, standard questions are specified to evaluate specific symptoms of that disorder. Questions are either dichotomous or rated on a Likert scale, which allows for uniform documentation of levels of severity, persistence, and functional impairment associated with each symptom. To supplement patient self-report and obtain the most accurate symptom picture, the SADS allows for consideration of all available sources of information (i.e., chart records, input from relatives). In addition to the standard questions asked of each respondent, optional probes may be selectively used to clarify responses, and unstructured questions may be generated by the interviewer to augment answers to the optional probes. Thus, considerable clinical experience and judgment are needed to administer the SADS. To reduce the length of administration and evaluation of symptoms that are not diagnostically significant, many diagnostic sections begin with screening questions that provide for "skip-outs" to the next section if the respondent shows no evidence of having the disorder. Administration of the SADS typically takes between $1\frac{1}{2}$ and $2\frac{1}{2}$ hours. Formal diagnostic appraisals are made by the interviewer after the interview is completed. At present, no computer scoring applications have been designed, due to the complex nature of the diagnostic process and the strong reliance on clinical judgment.

As noted earlier, the SADS was designed for use by trained clinicians. Considerable clinical judgment, interviewing skills, and familiarity with diagnostic criteria and psychiatric symptoms are requisite for competent administration. As such, it is recommended that the SADS be administered only by professionals with graduate degrees and clinical experience, such as clinical psychologists, psychiatrists, and psychiatric social workers (Endicott & Spitzer, 1978). Training in the SADS is intensive and can encompass several weeks. The process includes reviewing the most recent SADS manual and practice in rating written case vignettes and videotaped SADS interviews. Additionally, trainees typically watch and score live interviews as if participating in a reliability study with a simultaneous-rating design. Throughout, discussion and clarification with expert interviewers regarding diagnostic disagreements or difficulties add to the experience.

Finally, trainees conduct their own SADS interviews, which are observed and critiqued by the expert trainers.

Numerous additional versions of the SADS have been devised, each with a distinct focus and purpose. Perhaps the most common is the SADS-L (Lifetime version), which can be used to make both current and lifetime diagnoses but has significantly fewer details about current psychopathology than the full SADS and results in a quicker administration time. The SADS-L generally is used with nonpsychiatric samples in which there is no assumption of a significant current psychiatric problem. The SADS—Change Version is also popular and consists of 45 key symptoms from the SADS Part 1. Extensive study of the SADS suggests that it possesses excellent psychometric characteristics, and the interested reader is referred to Rogers, Jackson, and Cashel (2004) for a comprehensive review of these data.

The SADS has been translated into several languages, but its primary use has been in North America. The SADS has been widely used in clinical research over the past three decades and consequently has a large body of empirical data associated with it. As such, it is often the instrument of choice for clinical researchers desiring in-depth assessment of depression and schizophrenia. The extensive subtyping of disorders provided by the SADS is also highly valued by clinical researchers. However, due to its length and complexity, the SADS is less often chosen for use in typical clinical settings.

## THE STRUCTURED CLINICAL INTERVIEW FOR *DSM-IV* AXIS I DISORDERS

The Structured Clinical Interview for *DSM-IV* Axis I Disorders (SCID-I) is a flexible, semistructured diagnostic interview designed for use by trained clinicians to diagnose many adult *DSM-IV* Axis I mental disorders. The current version is the product of many prior editions, which were updated and modified over time. With each revision, the SCID has been reworked to enhance accuracy and ease of use, culminating in the February 2001 revision, when the SCID was updated to match the *DSM-IV-TR* (American Psychiatric Association, 2000). The SCID-I has widespread popularity as an instrument to obtain reliable and valid psychiatric diagnoses for clinical, research, and training purposes, and it has been used in more than 1,000 studies.

The original SCID was designed for application in both research and clinical settings. Recently, the SCID has been split into two distinct versions: the Research Version and the Clinician Version. The Research Version covers more disorders, subtypes, and course specifiers than the Clinician Version and therefore takes longer to complete. The benefit, however, is that it provides a wealth of diagnostic data that are particularly valued by clinical researchers. The research version is distributed by the Biometrics Research Department of the New York State Psychiatric Institute.

The Clinician Version of the SCID (SCID-CV; First, Spitzer, Gibbon, & Williams, 1997a) is designed for use in clinical settings. It has been trimmed down to encompass only those *DSM-IV* disorders that are most typically seen in clinical practice and can further be abbreviated on a module-by-module basis. The SCID-CV contains six self-contained modules of major diagnostic categories (Mood Episodes, Psychotic Symptoms, Psychotic Disorders, Mood Disorders, Substance Use Disorders, and Anxiety and Other Disorders). Table 6.2 provides a list of specific *DSM-IV* diagnoses covered by the SCID-CV.

TABLE 6.2    Diagnostic Coverage of the SCID—Clinician Version

Mood Disorders
   Bipolar I Disorder
   Bipolar II Disorder
   Bipolar Disorder NOS
   Cyclothymic Disorder
   Dysthymic Disorder
   Major Depressive Disorder
   Depressive Disorder NOS[a]
   Mood Disorder Due to a GMC[a]
   Substance-Induced Mood Disorder
Psychotic Disorders
   Schizophrenia (with five subtypes)
   Schizophreniform Disorder
   Schizoaffective Disorder
   Delusional Disorder
   Brief Psychotic Disorder
   Psychotic Disorder Due to a GMC[a]
   Substance-Induced Psychotic Disorder
   Psychotic Disorder NOS[a]
Substance Use Disorders
   Alcohol Abuse/Alcohol Dependence
   Amphetamine Abuse/Amphetamine Dependence
   Cannabis Abuse/Cannabis Dependence
   Cocaine Abuse/Cocaine Dependence
   Hallucinogen Abuse/Hallucinogen Dependence
   Opioid Abuse/Opioid Dependence
   Phencyclidine Abuse/Phencyclidine Dependence
   Sedative, Hypnotic, or Anxiolytic Abuse/Sedative, Hypnotic, or Anxiolytic Dependence
   Other (or Unknown) Substance Abuse/Other (or Unknown) Substance
Anxiety Disorders
   Panic Disorder with Agoraphobia
   Panic Disorder without Agoraphobia
   Obsessive-Compulsive Disorder
   Post-traumatic Stress Disorder
   Anxiety Disorder Due to a GMC[a]
   Substance-Induced Anxiety Disorder
   Anxiety Disorder NOS[a]

*(continues)*

TABLE 6.2 *(continued)*

Adjustment Disorders
  Adjustment Disorder with Depressed Mood
  Adjustment Disorder with Anxiety
  Adjustment Disorder with Mixed Anxiety and Depressed Mood
  Adjustment Disorder with Disturbance of Conduct
  Adjustment Disorder with Mixed Disturbance of Emotions and Conduct
  Unspecified Adjustment Disorder
Disorders Covered in Summarized Fashion (without specific diagnostic criteria)
  Agoraphobia without History of Panic Disorder
  Social Phobia
  Specific Phobia
  Generalized Anxiety Disorder
  Somatization Disorder
  Undifferentiated Somatoform Disorder
  Hypochondriasis
  Body Dysmorphic Disorder
  Anorexia Nervosa
  Bulimia Nervosa

*a*NOS = Not Otherwise Specified; GMC = General Medical Condition.

The modular design of the SCID is a major strength of the instrument because administration can be customized easily to meet the unique needs of the user. For example, the SCID can be shortened or lengthened to include only those categories of interest, and the order of modules can be altered. The format and sequence of the SCID were designed to approximate the flowchart and decision trees followed by experienced diagnostic interviewers. The SCID begins with an open-ended overview portion, during which the development and history of the present psychological disturbance are elicited and tentative diagnostic hypotheses are generated. Then the SCID systematically presents modules that allow for assessment of specific disorders and symptoms. Most disorders are evaluated for two time periods: current (meets criteria for the past month) and lifetime (ever met criteria).

Consistent with its linkage with *DSM-IV*, formal diagnostic criteria are included in the SCID booklet, thus permitting interviewers to see the exact criteria to which the SCID questions pertain. This unique feature makes the SCID an excellent training device for clinicians because it facilitates the learning of diagnostic criteria and good questions to assess the criteria. The SCID has many open-ended prompts that encourage respondents to elaborate freely about their symptoms. At times, open-ended prompts are followed by closed-ended questions to fully clarify a particular symptom. Although the SCID provides structure to cover criteria for each disorder, its semistructured format provides significant latitude for interviewers to restate questions, ask for further clarification, probe, and challenge if the initial prompt was misunderstood by the interviewee or clarification is needed to fully rate a symptom. SCID interviewers are encouraged to use all sources of information about a respondent, and gentle challenging of the respondent is encouraged if discrepant information is suspected.

During administration, each symptom is rated as either absent (or below threshold) or present (and clinically significant). A question mark (?) denotes that inadequate information was obtained to code the symptom. The SCID flowchart instructs interviewers to "skip out" of a particular diagnostic section when essential symptoms are judged to be below threshold or absent. These skip-outs result in decreased time of administration as well as the skipping of items with no diagnostic significance. Administration of the SCID is usually completed in one session and typically takes from 45 to 90 minutes. Once administration is completed, all current and past disorders for which criteria are met are listed on a Diagnostic Summary sheet.

The SCID is optimally administered by trained clinicians who have knowledge about psychopathology, *DSM-IV* criteria, and diagnostic interviewing. Due to the semistructured format of the SCID, proper administration often requires that interviewers restate or clarify questions in ways that are sometimes not clearly outlined in the manual in order to judge accurately if a particular diagnostic criterion has been met. The task requires that SCID assessors have a working knowledge of psychopathology and *DSM-IV* as well as basic interviewing skills. Standard procedures for training to use the SCID include carefully reading the SCID Users Guide (First, Spitzer, Gibbon, & Williams, 1997b), reviewing the SCID administration booklet and score sheet, viewing SCID videotape training materials that are available from the SCID authors, and conducting role-played practice administrations with extensive feedback discussions. Next, trainees may administer the SCID to representative participants who are jointly rated so that a discussion about sources of disagreements can ensue. In research settings, a formal reliability study is advantageous. The reliability and validity of the SCID in adult populations with diverse disorders have been evaluated in a number of investigations, with generally excellent results among widely varied participant samples and experimental designs (see First & Gibbon, 2004; also Segal, Hersen & Van Hasselt, 1994).

Overall, the SCID is a widely used and respected assessment tool. It has been translated into 12 languages and has been applied successfully in research studies and clinical practice in many countries. Computer-assisted clinician-administered versions of the SCID-CV and SCID Research Version are available. A self-administered computerized screening version of the SCID, called the SCID-Screen-PQ, is also available, but it does not produce final diagnoses. Rather, likely diagnoses are further evaluated by a full SCID interview or a clinical evaluation. For more information on the SCID, the interested reader may visit the SCID Web site, www.scid4.org.

## THE STRUCTURED CLINICAL INTERVIEW FOR *DSM-IV*
## AXIS II PERSONALITY DISORDERS

To complement the Axis I version of the SCID, a version focusing on Axis II personality disorders according to *DSM-IV* has been developed, called the Structured Clinical Interview for *DSM-IV* Axis II Personality Disorders (SCID-II; First, Gibbon, Spitzer, Williams, & Benjamin, 1997). Instruments such as the SCID-II are particularly important because clinicians and researchers alike have struggled with their ability to accurately diagnose personality disorders and distinguish one personality disorder from another (Coolidge & Segal, 1998; Westen & Shedler, 2000). The SCID-II has a semistructured format similar to that of the SCID Axis I version, but it covers the 10 standard *DSM-IV* Axis II personality disorders as well as Depressive Personality Disorder and Passive-Aggressive Personality Disorder (which are listed as disorders to be studied further in an appendix of the *DSM-IV*).

For comprehensive assessment, the SCID-II may be easily used in conjunction with the Axis I SCID, which would be administered prior to personality disorder assessment. This is encouraged so that the respondent's present mental state can be considered when judging the accuracy of self-reported personality traits. The basic structure and conventions of the SCID-II closely resemble those of the SCID-I. One unique feature of the SCID-II is that it includes a self-report Personality Questionnaire, which is a 119-item screening component that can be administered prior to the interview portion and takes about 20 minutes. The purpose of the Personality Questionnaire is to reduce overall administration time, because only those items that are scored in the pathological direction are further evaluated during the structured interview portion.

During the structured interview component, the pathologically endorsed screening responses are further pursued to ascertain whether the symptoms are actually experienced at clinically significant levels. Here, the respondent is asked to elaborate about each suspected personality disorder criterion, and specified prompts are provided. Like the Axis I SCID, the *DSM-IV* diagnostic criteria are printed on the interview page for easy review, and responses are coded as follows: ? = inadequate information, 1 = absent or false, 2 = subthreshold, and 3 = threshold or true. Each personality disorder is assessed completely, and diagnoses are made before proceeding to the next disorder. The modular format permits researchers and clinicians to tailor the SCID-II to their specific needs and reduce administration time. Clinicians who administer the SCID-II are expected to use their clinical judgment to clarify responses, gently challenge inconsistencies, and ask for additional information as required to rate accurately each criterion. Collection of diagnostic information from ancillary sources is permitted. Complete administration of the SCID-II typically takes less than 1 hour.

Training requirements and interviewer qualifications are similar to that of the Axis I SCID. There is no clinician version of the SCID-II. The psychometric properties of the SCID-II are strong, and the interested reader is referred to First and Gibbon (2004) for a comprehensive review. Given the extensive coverage of the personality disorders, modular approach, and strong operating characteristics, the SCID-II should remain a popular and effective tool for personality disorder assessment. The SCID-II Web site is the same as for the SCID Axis I version, www.scid4.org.

## SPECIALIZED STRUCTURED AND SEMISTRUCTURED INTERVIEWS

In this section, we describe briefly a host of specialized interviews that are commonly used in clinical or research arenas.

### STRUCTURED INTERVIEW OF REPORTED SYMPTOMS

The Structured Interview of Reported Symptoms (SIRS; Rogers, 1992) is a fully structured interview designed specifically for the assessment of feigning of mental disorders and related response styles. The SIRS by itself is an effective measure of feigning, although it is commonly paired with the Minnesota Multiphasic Personality Inventory (MMPI-2; Butcher, Dahlstrom, Graham, Tellegen, & Kaemmer, 1989) as a supplement. The SIRS may also be used when a suspected malingerer has declined to complete the MMPI or other psychological testing (Rogers, 2001). The SIRS has 172 items, and the output includes eight primary and five supplementary scales. Three primary scales examine very unusual symptom presentation in terms of rare symptoms, preposterous content, and atypical symptom pairs. Four primary scales look at the range and severity of symptom endorsements, including blatant symptoms of a major mental disorder, subtle symptoms more likely to be associated with minor psychological problems, indiscriminant reporting of symptoms, and overendorsement of symptoms with extreme severity. The final primary scale evaluates differences between self-report and observation during the interview (Rogers, 2001). The primary purpose of the SIRS is to precisely classify feigning and nonfeigning respondents, and it has its strongest application in forensic settings. Rogers (2001) recommends that the SIRS be used whenever the feigning of mental disorders is suspected.

### EVALUATION OF COMPETENCY TO STAND TRIAL—REVISED

The Evaluation of Competency to Stand Trial—Revised (ECST-R; Rogers, Tillbrook, & Sewell, 2004) is a semistructured interview for assessing the underlying dimensions of competency to stand trial. It is also designed to screen systematically for malingering and feigned incompetence. The ECST-R contains three competency scales that correspond to standards in the field: Consult with Counsel, Factual Understanding of Courtroom Proceedings, and Rational Understanding of Courtroom Proceedings. The interview was developed as a tool for the growing number of psychologists who work with the legal system. The ECST-R contains scales called the Atypical Presentation (ATP) scales, which are used to screen for malingering. There are five subscales of the ATP: ATP-P (psychotic subscale), ATP-N (nonpsychotic subscale), ATP-B (both the ATP-P and ATP-N subscales), ATP-I (impairment subscale), and ATP-R (realistic subscale). The ATP scales were found to be useful in the screening of malingering, and they provide ancillary data about feigned incompetence in cases where malingering has been established (Rogers et al., 2004).

## STRUCTURED INTERVIEW FOR THE FIVE-FACTOR MODEL OF PERSONALITY

The Structured Interview for the Five-Factor Model of Personality (SIFFM; Trull et al., 1998) is a semistructured interview used to gauge the major dimensions of the famous Five-Factor Model (FFM) of personality: neuroticism, extraversion, openness, agreeableness, and conscientiousness. The SIFFM also provides assessment of the facets for each major dimension that are particularly important regarding differentiation among personality disorders. The SIFFM was modeled after the self-report NEO Personality Inventory Revised (NEO-PI-R) and comprises 120 items related to the FFM. The SIFFM is considered to be of use to clinical researchers whose interests are in assessing personality and personality disorders (Trull et al.).

## DIAGNOSTIC INTERVIEW FOR BORDERLINES—REVISED

The Diagnostic Interview for Borderlines—Revised (DIB-R; Zanarini, Gunderson, Frankenburg, & Chauncey, 1989) is a semistructured interview used for evaluating and diagnosing Borderline Personality Disorder. Notably, the DIB-R was designed to enhance discrimination between clinically diagnosed borderline patients and the other personality disorders. The DIB-R has four distinct sections, each evaluating a core aspect of borderline personality: affect, cognition, impulse action patterns, and interpersonal relationships. In total, the interview includes 186 questions that make inquiries into 108 scored areas. In the DIB-R, all questions are geared to the preceding two years of the respondent's life. The measure has been found successful in discriminating those with Borderline Personality Disorder from those without (Zanarini et al.) and is a popular measure for in-depth assessment of the borderline construct.

## DIAGNOSTIC INTERVIEW SCHEDULE—HAMILTON RATING SCALE FOR DEPRESSION

The Diagnostic Interview Schedule—Hamilton Rating Scale for Depression (DIS-HRSD; Whisman et al., 1989) is a fully structured interview designed to measure depression severity and is used primarily in research settings. As the name implies, the DIS-HRSD is based on the widely used Hamilton Rating Scale for Depression (Hamilton, 1960), which is a clinician-administered rating scale for depressive symptoms. A drawback to the original Hamilton Rating Scale, however, is that Hamilton provided only general guidelines for administration and scoring, which can negatively impact the reliability of the instrument. In contrast, the fully structured DIS-HRSD clearly specifies administration and scoring and has the further advantage that it does not need to be administered by an experienced clinician.

## ACUTE STRESS DISORDER INTERVIEW

The Acute Stress Disorder Interview (ASDI; Bryant, Harvey, Dang, & Sackville, 1998) is a structured interview designed to diagnose Acute Stress Disorder. The ASDI contains 19 items that are dichotomously scored based on criteria from the *DSM-IV*. The dichotomous scoring system is used for the following three reasons: to formally identify cases of Acute Stress Disorder, to allow the ASDI to be given after a disaster, and to allow nonclinicians to administer the ASDI. The ASDI appears to be a useful tool to identify those individuals who suffer from Acute Stress Disorder and who are at risk for long-term Post-Traumatic Stress Disorder. The measure is successful at discriminating those diagnosed with Acute Stress Disorder from those who do not meet the criteria for the disorder (Bryant et al.).

## INTERVIEW FOR THE DIAGNOSIS OF EATING DISORDERS—IV

The Interview for the Diagnosis of Eating Disorders—IV (IDED-IV; Kutlesic, Williamson, Gleaves, Barbin, & Murphy-Eberenz, 1998). The IDED-IV is a semistructured interview developed to adhere strictly to *DSM-IV* diagnostic criteria for anorexia nervosa, bulimia nervosa, binge eating disorder, and eating disorder not otherwise specified. Compared to earlier versions of the interview, the IDED-IV includes more inquiries about demographic information and eating disorder history, expanded instructions for administration of the interview, and condensed ratings from a seven- to a five-point rating scale (Kutlesic et al.).

## EATING DISORDER EXAMINATION

The Eating Disorder Examination (EDE; Cooper & Fairburn, 1987) is a semistructured interview constructed to evaluate the broad range of eating disorder psychopathology, including assessment of people who have concerns about their body shape and weight. The interview consists of 62 items and requires brief training for administration. The EDE has been widely used in studies of eating disorder psychopathology as well in outcome studies in the area (Cooper & Fairburn).

## ANXIETY DISORDERS INTERVIEW
## SCHEDULE FOR *DSM-IV*

The Anxiety Disorders Interview Schedule for *DSM-IV* (ADIS-IV; Brown, Di Nardo, & Barlow, 1994) is a semistructured interview that focuses primarily on the anxiety disorders but also provides assessment of some mood, substance, and somatoform disorders. The ADIS-IV focuses on current diagnoses only. A modification called the ADIS-IV Lifetime version (Di Nardo, Brown, & Barlow, 1994) provides assessment of current and lifetime disorders as well as a diagnostic timeline that promotes accurate determination of the onset, remission, and temporal sequence of the disorders. A strength of the ADIS-IV is that it provides both dimensional and binary evaluation of the disorders. Major segments of the ADIS-IV and ADIS-IV-L consist of demographics, inquiries about the presenting complaint and stressors, diagnostic sections for *DSM-IV* anxiety disorders, mood disorders, somatoform disorders, substance-related disorders, a section of screening questions for other major disorders, questions regarding family history of psychological disorders, medical history, and psychosocial treatment history, the Hamilton rating scales, and a diagnostic timeline (in the ADIS-IV-L only).

## SUMMARY AND CONCLUSIONS

This chapter highlights the fact that structured and semistructured interviews have greatly facilitated the task of differential diagnosis and problem clarification in diverse clinical and research settings. The reliability of diagnosis is much improved with the use of structured interviews, compared to the unstandardized approach common in clinical practice, and improved reliability provides the foundation for enhanced validity or meaningfulness of diagnosis. Given the field's recent emphasis on empirically supported psychotherapeutic interventions and processes (Beutler & Castonguay, in press; Kendall, 1998), we hope that a concomitant focus on clinically relevant, standardized, and validated assessment procedures will be realized as well. Structured and semistructured interviews can and should play an important role in the advancement of the science of clinical psychology.

## REFERENCES

American Psychiatric Association. (1952). *Diagnostic and statistical manual of mental disorders.* Washington, DC: Author.

American Psychiatric Association. (1980). *Diagnostic and statistical manual of mental disorders* (3rd ed.). Washington, DC: Author.

American Psychiatric Association. (1987). *Diagnostic and statistical manual of mental disorders* (3rd ed., revised). Washington, DC: Author.

American Psychiatric Association. (1994). *Diagnostic and statistical manual of mental disorders* (4th ed.). Washington, DC: Author.

American Psychiatric Association. (2000). *Diagnostic and statistical manual of mental disorders* (4th ed., text revision). Washington, DC: Author.

Beutler, L. E., & Castonguay, L. G. (in press). *Empirically supported principles of therapy change.* New York: Oxford University Press.

Brown, T. A., Di Nardo, P. A., & Barlow, D. H. (1994). *Anxiety Disorders Interview Schedule for DSM-IV (ADIS-IV).* San Antonio, TX: Psychological Corporation.

Bryant, R. A., Harvey, A. G., Dang, S. T., & Sackville, T. (1998). Assessing Acute Stress Disorder: Psychometric properties of a structured clinical interview. *Psychological Assessment, 10,* 215–220.

Butcher, J. N., Dahlstrom, W. G., Graham, J. R., Tellegen, A., & Kaemmer, B. (1989). *Minnesota Multiphasic Personality Inventory—2 (MMPI-2): Manual for administration and scoring.* Minneapolis: University of Minnesota Press.

Compton, W. M., & Cottler, L. B. (2004). The Diagnostic Interview Schedule (DIS). In M. Hilsenroth & D. L. Segal (Eds.), *Personality assessment.* Volume 2 in M. Hersen (Ed.-in-Chief), *Comprehensive handbook of psychological assessment* (pp. 153–162). New York: John Wiley & Sons.

Coolidge, F. L., & Segal, D. L. (1998). Evolution of the personality disorder diagnosis in the *Diagnostic and Statistical Manual of Mental Disorders. Clinical Psychology Review, 18,* 585–599.

Cooper, Z., & Fairburn, C. (1987). The Eating Disorder Examination: A semistructured interview for the assessment of the specific psychopathology of eating disorders. *International Journal of Eating Disorders, 6,* 1–8.

Di Nardo, P. A., Brown, T. A., & Barlow, D. H. (1994). *Anxiety Disorders Interview Schedule for DSM-IV: Lifetime version (ADIS-IV-L).* San Antonio, TX: Psychological Corporation.

Endicott, J., & Spitzer, R. L. (1978). A diagnostic interview: The Schedule for Affective Disorders and Schizophrenia. *Archives of General Psychiatry, 35,* 837–844.

First, M. B., & Gibbon, M. (2004). The Structured Clinical Interview for DSM-IV Axis I Disorders (SCID-I) and the Structured Clinical Interview for DSM-IV Axis II Disorders (SCID-II). In M. Hilsenroth & D. L. Segal (Eds.), *Personality assessment.* Volume 2 in M. Hersen (Ed.-in-Chief), *Comprehensive handbook of psychological assessment* (pp. 134–143). New York: John Wiley & Sons.

First, M. B., Spitzer, R. L., Gibbon, M., & Williams, J. B. W. (1997a). *Structured Clinical Interview for DSM-IV Axis I Disorders—Clinician Version (SCID-CV).* Washington, DC: American Psychiatric Press.

First, M. B., Spitzer, R. L., Gibbon, M., & Williams, J. B. W. (1997b). *User's guide to the Structured Clinical Interview for DSM-IV Axis I Disorders—Clinician Version (SCID-CV).* Washington, DC: American Psychiatric Press.

First, M. B., Gibbon, M., Spitzer, R. L., Williams, J. B. W., & Benjamin, L. S. (1997). *Structured Clinical Interview for DSM-IV Axis II Personality Disorders (SCID-II).* Washington, DC: American Psychiatric Press.

Hamilton, M. (1960). A rating scale for depression. *Journal of Neurology, Neurosurgery, and Psychiatry, 23,* 56–62.

Kendall, P. C. (1998). Empirically supported psychological therapies. *Journal of Consulting and Clinical Psychology, 66,* 3–6.

Kutlesic, V., Williamson, D. A., Gleaves, D. H., Barbin, J. M., & Murphy-Eberenz, K. P. (1998). The Interview for the Diagnosis of Eating Disorders—IV: Application to DSM-IV diagnostic criteria. *Psychological Assessment, 10,* 41–48.

Morrison, R. L. (1988). Structured interviews and rating scales. In A. S. Bellack & M. Hersen (Eds.), *Behavioral assessment: A practical handbook* (3rd ed., pp. 252–277). New York: Pergamon Press.

Robins, L. N., Helzer, J. E., Cottler, L. B., & Goldring, E. (1989). *The Diagnostic Interview Schedule, Version III-R.* St. Louis, MO: Washington University School of Medicine.

Robins, L. N., Helzer, J. E., Croughan, J., & Ratcliff, K. S. (1981). National Institute of Mental Health Diagnostic Interview Schedule: Its history, characteristics, and validity. *Archives of General Psychiatry, 38,* 381–389.

Robins, L. N., Cottler, L. B., Bucholz, K. K., Compton, W. M., North, C. S., & Rourke, K. (2000). *The Diagnostic Interview Schedule for DSM-IV (DIS-IV).* St. Louis, MO: Washington University School of Medicine. Last revision, 1–2000.

Rogers, R. (1992). *Structured Interview of Reported Symptoms.* Tampa, FL: Psychological Assessment Resources.

Rogers, R. (2001). *Handbook of diagnostic and structured interviewing.* New York: Guilford Press.

Rogers, R., Jackson, R. L., & Cashel, M. (2004). The Schedule for Affective Disorders and Schizophrenia (SADS). In M. Hilsenroth & D. L. Segal (Eds.), *Personality assessment.* Volume 2 in M. Hersen (Ed.-in-Chief), *Comprehensive handbook of psychological assessment* (pp. 144–152). New York: John Wiley & Sons.

Rogers, R., Tillbrook, C. E., & Sewell, K. W. (2004). *Evaluation of Competency to Stand Trial—Revised (ECST-R).* Odessa, FL: Psychological Assessment Resources.

Rubinson, E. P., & Asnis, G. M. (1989). Use of structured interviews for diagnosis. In S. Wetzler (Ed.), *Measuring mental illness: Psychometric assessment for clinicians* (pp. 43–66). Washington, DC: American Psychiatric Press.

Segal, D. L., & Coolidge, F. L. (2001). Diagnosis and classification. In M. Hersen & V. B. Van Hasselt (Eds.), *Advanced abnormal psychology* (2nd ed., pp. 5–22). New York: Kluwer Academic/Plenum Press.

Segal, D. L., & Coolidge, F. L. (2003). Structured interviewing and *DSM* classification. In M. Hersen & S. Turner (Eds.), *Adult psychopathology and diagnosis* (4th ed., pp. 72–103). New York: John Wiley & Sons.

Segal, D. L., Hersen, M., & Van Hasselt, V. B. (1994). Reliability of the Structured Clinical Interview for *DSM-III-R*: An evaluative review. *Comprehensive Psychiatry, 35,* 316–327.

Spitzer, R. L., Endicott, J., & Robins, E. (1978). Research diagnostic criteria. *Archives of General Psychiatry, 35,* 773–782.

Trull, T. J., Widiger, T. A., Useda, J. D., Holcomb, J., Doan, B., Axelrod, S. R., et al. (1998). A structured interview for the assessment of the five-factor model of personality. *Psychological Assessment, 10,* 229–240.

Westen, D., & Shedler, J. (2000). A prototype matching approach to diagnosing personality disorders: Toward *DSM-V. Journal of Personality Disorders, 14,* 109–126.

Whisman, M. A., Strosahl, K., Fruzzetti, A. E., Schmaling, K. B., Jacobson, N. S., & Miller, D. M. (1989). A structured interview version of the Hamilton Rating Scale for Depression: Reliability and validity. *Psychological Assessment: A Journal of Consulting and Clinical Psychology, 11,* 238–241.

Zanarini, M. C., Gunderson, J. G., Frankenburg, F. R., & Chauncey, D. L. (1989). The Revised Diagnostic Interview for Borderlines: Discriminating BPD from other Axis II disorders. *Journal of Personality Disorders, 3,* 10–18.

# 7

# SELF-ASSESSMENT

SANDRA T. SIGMON
STEPHANIE M. LAMATTINA

*Department of Psychology*
*University of Maine*
*Orono, Maine*

## INTRODUCTION

It has been around 20 years since the last comprehensive chapter was written that focused exclusively on self-monitoring (Bornstein, Hamilton, & Bornstein, 1986). Since that chapter was published in 1986, there have been many new applications and technological developments about this behavioral assessment procedure. Over the years, numerous terms have been used to describe the process of systematically observing and recording one's own ongoing behavior (i.e., self-assessment, self-monitoring, self-observation, self-recording). Some authors have suggested that the term *self-monitoring* be replaced with the term self-observation in order to distinguish it from the personality construct of self-monitoring (Cone, 1999; Jackson, 1999). For historical continuity, however, the terms *self-monitoring* and *self-assessment* will be used interchangeably in this chapter.

Self-assessment continues to be one of the most commonly used assessment methods in clinical research and practice. Since the early 1960s, research has provided considerable empirical support for the continued utilization of this assessment method. Self-assessment has been used to help individuals monitor the frequency, antecedents, and consequences of problematic behaviors (i.e., behaviors that need to decrease or increase). This type of information greatly contributes to the understanding and formulation of the functional analysis approach to problematic behaviors (Haynes, 2000). In some of the earlier studies that focused on this assessment technique, researchers found an added benefit as well as a potential problem with the self-monitoring process; individuals reacted to the process by decreasing the baseline frequency of behaviors just by observing their own behavior (e.g., Ciminero, Nelson, & Lipinski, 1977). Since this finding, self-monitoring has become an integral component of most empirically supported treatments, with the explicit purpose of increasing sensitivity to behavior occurrence, increasing awareness of the frequency of the behavior, and then providing techniques to decrease/increase target behaviors even further (Korotitsch & Nelson-Gray, 1999).

An increase in self-assessment research and use coincided with the ascent of the behavior therapy movement in the 1960s and 1970s. Because of behavior therapy's commitment to objective assessment, research began focusing on assessment techniques that relied less on inference. It is interesting to note that this quest for more objective assessment procedures paralleled early attempts in psychology to teach individuals how to be better introspectionists (Kazdin, 1974). Early research on behavioral assessment reflected its roots in behavior therapy; examining behavior change in the client's environment, focusing on self-control in addition to external control, and an increasing interest in assessing private events (e.g., thoughts, urges, images, fantasies; Ciminero et al., 1977). Innovative techniques were devised with an emphasis on an idiographic approach to assessment that did not appear to be subject to evaluation by classic psychometric methods.

Because of behavior therapy's focus on the situational specificity of behavior and less reliance on indirect and inferential methods of assessment, behavioral assessment techniques were not evaluated with regard to classic psychometric principles (Goldstein & Hersen, 1990). Goldstein and Hersen remarked that such lack of attention to psychometrics in the past resulted in the "baby thrown out with the bath water" (p. 11) but noted that more recently the "baby is being returned from the discarded bath water" (p. 12). In contrast to early researchers, who proposed that behavioral assessment techniques should only be evaluated functionally (e.g., Nelson, 1983), recent articles have revisited the applicability of psychometrics to self-monitoring (Cone, 1999; Jackson, 1999).

Several authors have conceptualized self-monitoring, in addition to other behavioral assessment measures, as falling along continuums of directedness (Cone, 1999) and convenience (Korotitsch & Nelson-Gray, 1999). When compared to methods of self-report (e.g., questionnaires, interviews) that fall toward the indirect end of the directness continuum, self-monitoring falls closer to the direct end (Cone). For example, in self-monitoring, an individual observes and records a target behavior in a certain place within close proximity in time to its occurrence. In contrast, on self-report measures, an individual reports behaviors that occurred at another time and another place. Korotitsch and Nelson-Gray also note that behavioral assessment measures can be placed along a continuum of convenience. In terms of convenience, the foregoing behavioral assessment methods appear to switch places along the continuum. Indirect measures (e.g., self-report on questionnaires and interviews) are found at the most convenient end of the spectrum because they are easy to administer and can be completed relatively quickly. On the other hand, self-monitoring methods can fall at different points of the convenience spectrum, depending on the complexity and expense of the method utilized.

In order to self-monitor, an individual engages in a multicomponent process (e.g., Cone, 1999; Korotitsch & Nelson-Gray, 1999). First, the individual must be aware that the behavior occurred (i.e., the client discriminates whether or not a response has occurred; Bornstein et al., 1986). For example, if an individual will be monitoring the frequency of binge-eating episodes, then he or she should be clear about what constitutes a binge-eating episode (i.e., objective versus subjective binge). In the second part of the process, the individual records occurrences of the behavior, which could also include other relevant information (e.g., antecedents, consequences, contextual variables). Korotitsch and Nelson-Gray propose that both aspects of the process are needed for accurate data collection. In some contexts, it may also be helpful for the individual to analyze the collected data and display the results (Cone).

## POTENTIAL USES OF SELF-ASSESSMENT

Several reasons contribute to the widespread use of self-assessment in clinical research and practice. First, self-monitoring represents a relatively inexpensive and efficient way to gather information on target behaviors (Korotitsch & Nelson-Gray, 1999). In its simplest form, self-monitoring may only require paper and pencil, making it one of the most portable, practical, and cost efficient means of assessment (e.g., Baird & Nelson-Gray, 1999; Bornstein et al., 1986). Because of the nature of some target behaviors, it may be impractical (e.g., target behavior may be obsessions, sexual fantasies) or too costly to employ direct observation methods by independent observers. Although self-monitoring can have reactive effects (discussed in a later section), it eliminates external observer bias. In addition, some target behaviors may be observable only by the client (e.g., thoughts, images).

Second, self-monitoring can be used for clients with a wide range of psychological and medical issues, such as eating disorders (e.g., Latner & Wilson, 2002; Wilson & Vitousek, 1999), HIV-related sexual behavior (Weinhardt, Forsyth, Carey, Jaworski, & Durant, 1998), frontal lobe dysfunction (Alderman, Fry, & Youngson, 1995), chronic pain (e.g., Kerns, Finn, & Haythornthwaite, 1988), insomnia (e.g., Savard & Morin, 2002), anxiety disorders (e.g., Campbell & Brown, 2002; Craske & Tsao, 1999; Rapee, Craske, & Barlow, 1990), and substance use (e.g., Tucker, Vuchinich, & Murphy, 2002). In fact, Korotitsch and Nelson-Gray (1999) assert that "currently, self-monitoring procedures are described and recommended within most empirically supported treatments" (p. 415).

Third, self-monitoring allows clients to become more aware of their behaviors (e.g., Haynes, 1978; Wilson & Vitousek, 1999). Through the self-monitoring process, a client can receive continuous and immediate feedback about target behaviors that occur outside of the therapeutic setting. Similarly, such data can reveal behavioral patterns that may not be readily apparent to therapists and clients. For example, an individual with binge-eating disorder may not be aware of the antecedents that precede a binge-eating episode. However, after continuously monitoring food intake for several weeks, the client and therapist can review the monitoring forms to recognize common patterns (e.g., the client always binge-eats after work on days when she does not eat breakfast).

Fourth, self-monitoring represents the only way to access private events (e.g., thoughts, emotions, perceptions) and behaviors that do not typically occur in observable conditions (e.g., drug use, sexual activity) and that are inaccessible to outside observers (Baird & Nelson-Gray, 1999; Foster, Laverty-Finch, Gizzo, & Osantowski, 1999). For example, one component of cognitive-behavioral therapy for depression involves having a client record antecedents (e.g., employer does not speak to the client) and consequences of a problematic situation (e.g., negative mood, fails to get a task done on time) in which negative, automatic thoughts are occurring (e.g., "my boss must hate me," "I am such a loser"). The recording of these types of situations and thoughts can help the client and therapist focus on recurring cognitive schemas that can be challenged during treatment.

Finally, in an age when managed care requires accountability, self-monitoring provides a valuable method for keeping track of client progress (Korotitsch & Nelson-Gray, 1999; Strosahl & Robinson, 2004). Surveys have estimated that self-monitoring is used between 38% (Bornstein, Bridgwater, Hickey, & Sweeney, 1980) and 44% of the time (Elliott, Miltenberger, Kaster-Bundgaard, & Lumley, 1996) in clinical research. It is not known, however, how often self-monitoring methods are used by practitioners to gather assessment data. Although use of self-assessment methods continues to proliferate, research on psychometric applicability and its clinical utility have not experienced a paralled increase (Cone, 1999).

## FUNCTIONS OF SELF-ASSESSMENT

Self-assessment can fulfill several functions related to assessment and intervention efforts: education/description (Haynes, 1978), diagnostic clarification (Cone, 1998; Korotitsch & Nelson-Gray, 1999), pretreatment assessment, ongoing treatment evaluation, and as a behavior change agent itself (Ciminero et al., 1977).

### EDUCATION/DESCRIPTION

Because of its diverse applicability and ease of use, self-monitoring has been used to gain a better understanding of target behaviors, antecedents, and consequences (e.g., Cone, 1998; Haynes, 1978; Jackson, 1999). For example, 97 patients diagnosed with Panic Disorder with Agoraphobia (PDA) self-monitored their panic attacks for a period of 6–12 weeks in order to gain detailed information about precipitating circumstances and attack symptomatology (Garssen, de Beurs, Buikhuisen, van Balkom, Lange, & van Dyck, 1996). Using self-monitoring techniques, the researchers were able to learn more about the variety and frequency of symptoms that individuals diagnosed with PDA experience both before and during panic attacks. This type of information contributes to a better understanding of the impact that behaviors may have across settings, behavior frequency and disruption, and intensity of the responses.

## DIAGNOSTIC CLARIFICATION

Self-monitoring can be used to clarify that a diagnosis is warranted for a particular individual (Korotitsch & Nelson-Gray, 1999). In the *Diagnostic and Statistical Manual of Mental Disorders* (*DSM-IV-TR*, American Psychiatric Association [APA], 2000) psychological disorders (e.g., Bipolar II Disorder, Generalized Anxiety Disorder, Premenstrual Dysphoric Disorder) have specific criteria that must be present (or absent) for a diagnosis to be made. Making an accurate diagnosis can be difficult for numerous reasons (e.g., the client may have little awareness of problematic behaviors, it is unclear whether or not the presenting symptoms occur for a medical condition or another Axis I disorder). In such cases, self-monitoring may be useful to help determine the most accurate diagnosis. For example, to diagnose an individual with Premenstrual Dysphoric Disorder (PMDD), the *DSM-IV* requires that the presenting symptoms not be an exacerbation of symptoms for another disorder and also that the cyclical pattern of symptoms occur for two consecutive months (APA). More importantly, the *DSM-IV* requires that the presence of symptoms be confirmed by daily self-monitoring for two consecutive months (APA).

Because panic attacks can occur in the context of other anxiety disorders (e.g., Social Phobia, Specific Phobia), it is important to clarify the context in which the attacks occur. Verifying the functional reason for the panic attacks by self-monitoring could be useful in clarifying the relations between the panic attacks and the context in which they occur in order to make a more accurate diagnosis. For example, after the client self-monitors for a certain period of time, the therapist and client may discover that the client only experiences panic attacks when he or she speaks in public. In this situation, a diagnosis of Social Phobia would be more accurate and might lead to a more effective treatment. Self-monitoring data may also be helpful when clients present with vague symptoms or goals (e.g., Korotitsch & Nelson-Gray, 1999). In general, self-monitoring appears to be a useful technique for clarifying diagnoses.

## PRETREATMENT ASSESSMENT

Overall, self-assessment can be useful in identifying target behaviors, their antecedents, and their controlling variables. Self-monitoring is often used in behavioral assessment to obtain baseline information about target behaviors prior to an intervention (Ciminero et al., 1977; Korotitsch & Nelson-Gray, 1999). Clinicians utilize self-monitoring as part of a thorough functional analysis, with the aim of determining the frequency and intensity of identified target behaviors (Haynes, 1978). In addition, self-monitoring helps identify antecedents and consequences that functionally relate to the target behaviors (Ciminero et al., 1977). For example, an individual with trichotillimania might be asked to monitor frequency of hair pulling and also indicate the situation, time, and mood state when hair pulling occurs. The purpose of the self-assessment would be to determine which events are functionally related to hair pulling. In this example, it may be that the client engages in more frequent hair pulling when she is watching television and reports feeling bored.

Information gained through self-monitoring represents a valuable addition to information that might be obtained through clinical interviews or self-report questionnaires. Instead of relying solely on the client's ability to accurately remember and retrospectively report how often behaviors took place and the relevant contextual variables, self-monitoring allows the clinician and client to recognize the severity and impact of the client's problems as they take place in real time (Cone, 1999). In addition, self-monitoring may help determine which behaviors covary and their controlling variables in order to test out hypotheses about their relations (Haynes, Leisen, & Blaine, 1997). During preintervention assessment, self-monitoring illustrates the pragmatic principles grounded in behavioral assessment; the behaviors and controlling variables identified help guide the formulation of a treatment plan (Korotitsch & Nelson-Gray, 1999).

## TREATMENT EVALUATION

Self-monitoring is used in behavioral assessment to monitor the effects of ongoing treatment (Ciminero et al., 1977). In particular, a client will continue to self-monitor throughout treatment so that the information collected during the treatment phase can be compared to the client's baseline data. Thus, self-monitoring provides an opportunity for the therapist and client to continuously assess the client's progress instead of waiting until the end of therapy to assess whether or not the treatment was effective (Korotitsch & Nelson-Gray, 1999). The therapist (along with the client) can use the information collected to guide decisions regarding the utility of the treatment strategies that are selected.

For example, if the client appears to be making progress, the therapist can continue with the existing treatment (e.g., cognitive behavioral treatments [CBT] for bulimia nervosa). If the client is making few, if any, gains, then the therapist might decide to modify the current treatment (e.g., rely more on the behavioral components of CBT). However, if the client's symptoms appear to be worsening or if the treatment appears to have no effect, then the therapist might decide to discontinue the current treatment and implement a new treatment approach (e.g., stop CBT and begin interpersonal psychotherapy).

The information collected during self-monitoring can also guide the focus of individual treatment sessions. In a review of self-monitoring and eating disorders, Wilson and Vitousek (1999) acknowledge that self-monitoring represents the most important component of CBT when treating individuals diagnosed with an eating disorder. The authors mention that "each session begins with a review of the patient's self-monitoring records. The agenda for each session is based on each patient's response to the previous therapy session" (p. 484). Taken as a whole, continuous self-monitoring during the treatment phase provides essential information to monitor and evaluate the effects of ongoing treatment.

## SELF-ASSESSMENT AS AN INTERVENTION

Self-monitoring can be used to facilitate changes in an individual's behavior (Haynes, 1978). A change in a target behavior's frequency, after an individual begins self-monitoring, is defined as the *reactive effects* of self-monitoring (Baird & Nelson-Gray, 1999). In general, the change in behavior frequency usually occurs in a therapeutically beneficial direction (i.e., there is a decrease in problematic behaviors and/or an increase in more appropriate behaviors; Haynes). This phenomenon has been found in numerous studies looking at clinically relevant behaviors, such as cigarette smoking (Frederiksen, Epstein, & Kosevsky, 1975), suicidal ideation (Clum & Curtin, 1993), and tics (Thomas, Abrams, & Johnson, 1971). For example, 30 women diagnosed with either bulimia nervosa or Binge Eating Disorder self-monitored their daily food intake for a period of 6–18 days. Results indicated a statistically significant reduction in the frequency of binge-eating episodes over the self-assessment period (Latner & Wilson, 2002). In fact, results indicated that the frequency of binge-eating episodes recorded during the self-monitoring phase decreased by more than half (44%) as compared to those reported during the initial interview (Latner & Wilson).

Despite initial benefits in treatment, some clinicians and researchers have found reactive effects in self-monitoring to be short-lived (e.g., Critchfield & Vargas, 1991; Febbraro & Clum, 1998). Self-monitoring may, however, represent a useful strategy to implement at the beginning of treatment to facilitate early change in the client's behavior. This information could increase the probability that a client will continue treatment; however, additional treatment approaches should be implemented throughout therapy so that the client can continue to improve (Korotitsch & Nelson-Gray, 1999). For example, individuals who consistently self-monitored food consumption during a long-term weight-loss program (People at Risk) lost more weight than individuals who did not continue to self-monitor (Baker & Kirschenbaum, 1993). This type of finding has led weight-loss researchers to conclude that successful weight-loss programs must have consistent and continuous self-monitoring as a central component (e.g., Wadden et al., 1997).

Although the potential reactive side effects of self-monitoring are typically advantageous for treatment purposes, these effects may pose a problem for assessment of pretreatment target behaviors (Jackson, 1999). Researchers interested in obtaining data for descriptive purposes (e.g., comparing the number of negative automatic thoughts between individuals diagnosed with depression and a comparison group) may have individuals self-monitor the targeted behavior in an attempt to make comparisons between groups. However, self-monitoring, due to its reactive effects, may actually minimize the differences found between the groups. Similarly, reactive effects of self-monitoring may decrease the differences found when comparing an individual's baseline data with post-treatment data. Due to reactivity effects, information collected at baseline may not accurately reflect the frequency of the client's behavior before self-monitoring began. In summary, self-monitoring can sometimes facilitate behavior changes in an individual's behavior, and, depending on the clinician's or researcher's goals, the changes may be considered favorable.

## METHODOLOGICAL CONSIDERATIONS

When deciding to use self-assessment methods, a number of issues needs to be considered before choosing a particular technique. In general, the therapist or researcher needs to determine the purpose for self-monitoring, the nature of the target behavior, the method that will be used to gather information, and the type of monitoring device to be used. The following sections will describe various methodological components involved in self-monitoring.

### ASPECTS OF THE TARGET BEHAVIOR

**Frequency Counts**

Frequency counts are commonly used when a therapist or researcher is interested in the rate of a target behavior and asks the client to record each occurrence of the behavior (Ciminero et al., 1977). For example, a client may be asked to record the number of cigarettes that he or she smokes each day. Frequency counts are useful when the self-monitored behavior occurs at a low-to-medium frequency, when the behavior is a distinct event, and when it is important to understand the number of times the individual engages in the behavior (Foster et al., 1999).

When self-monitoring frequency counts, it is also important for the behavior to have a clear beginning and end so that separate instances of the behavior can be recorded (Foster et al., 1999). Similarly, it would be difficult (and potentially misleading) to monitor frequency counts for ongoing behaviors such as talking and smiling. For example, if a client with social skills deficits engages in a conversation for 30 seconds with one individual and then with another individual for 20 minutes, these occurrences would only be counted as two instances of social interaction. However, each conversation lasted for a different duration, so important information would be lost if the clinician or researcher relied solely on frequency counts. In addition, the client may become frustrated with the amount of time spent trying to self-monitor high-frequency behaviors (e.g., recording the number of negative thoughts in one day).

There are several advantages for self-monitoring frequency counts. First, frequency counts are relatively simple to record and instructions for the process are typically easy to understand (Foster et al., 1999). Second, frequency conveys a direct measure regarding the amount of times a behavior occurs, and many behavioral treatment goals attempt to increase (or decrease) certain behaviors (e.g., Bellack & Schwartz, 1976). Third, frequency measures reflect changes over time, providing an opportunity for the clinician and client to have continuous, ongoing feedback regarding the client's progress.

### Duration

Duration represents another dimension of a target behavior that an individual can self-monitor (Baird & Nelson-Gray, 1999). Duration methods require an individual to self-monitor the amount of time a target behavior occurs (Foster et al., 1999). For example, an individual who engages in compulsive behaviors can self-monitor the amount of time spent cleaning his or her house. Duration is a particularly useful method for measuring continuous, ongoing responses that can vary in length (Ciminero et al., 1977). Therefore, it is important to clearly define the start point and endpoint of a response. Duration is also beneficial when the length of time spent engaging in a behavior is more important than the number of times the behavior takes place (Foster et al.).

For example, an individual diagnosed with Obsessive-Compulsive Disorder may engage in excessive, lengthy hand-washing rituals that limit his or her ability to engage in other activities. Therapeutically, the amount of time this individual spends hand washing (e.g., five hours per day) is more of a concern than the rate of hand washing (e.g., three times a day). In a similar vein, researchers compared the amount of time individuals diagnosed with Generalized Anxiety Disorder (GAD) and non-GAD controls spent worrying (Dupuy, Beaudoin, Rhéaume, Ladouceur, & Dugas, 2001). Each participant recorded the number of minutes spent worrying daily, for two weeks, in a self-monitoring notebook. The researchers concluded that self-monitoring the duration of time spent worrying was a valid and helpful measure of worry, especially given that the results significantly correlated with the current gold standard measure for worry, the *Penn State Worry Questionnaire* (Dupuy et al.).

### Latency

Latency, the amount of time it takes an individual to begin the target behavior, represents a third aspect of behavior commonly recorded with self-monitoring methods (Foster et al., 1999). Latency can be conceptualized as the amount of time elapsed between some beginning point or antecedent and the target behavior (Foster et al.). For example, latency would be very relevant for an individual who is self-monitoring aspects of his or her insomnia. The beginning point would be when the client lays down in bed, and the endpoint or target behavior would be when the client falls asleep. Similar to duration, latency needs to have a clearly defined beginning point and endpoint.

### Intensity

A fourth dimension of behavior recorded with self-monitoring methods is intensity (Cone, 1999). Measures of intensity require the individual to record the magnitude or strength of a behavior, often using a global subjective rating (Foster et al., 1999). For example, an individual could self-monitor the intensity of his or her depressed mood using a 10-point Likert scale ranging from 1 ("not at all") to 10 ("extremely depressed"). Foster and colleagues suggest that it is important to work with the client to develop unambiguous anchors (e.g., past experiences) for each point on the scale to maintain client consistency over time. In another example, it may be useful to monitor the intensity of an anger outburst; one very intense anger outburst (e.g., screaming, hitting others, and breaking things) could have more impact on an individual's social and occupational relations (e.g., friends, relatives, coworkers) than more relatively minor outbursts (e.g., slamming a door, walking off). In this situation, the magnitude of the target behavior may be more important than the number of times the behavior takes place.

## SELF-ASSESSMENT RECORDING FORMATS

After determining which dimension of the target behavior will be the focus of self-assessment, the next step involves a decision regarding the best way to record the information. Various recording formats have been used to obtain data for self-monitoring and are presented next.

### Event Sampling

Event sampling represents a procedure used to capture each time the behavior occurs throughout a specified time period (e.g., five hours, one day, two weeks). This format is typically helpful when an individual needs to monitor only one low-frequency behavior (Foster et al., 1999). For example, an individual records each instance of self-abuse (e.g., cutting) for a period of one week.

### Interval Recording

Interval recording represents another format used to capture data for self-monitoring (Cone, 1999). With this strategy, an individual self-monitors his or her target behaviors for a single block of that is further divided into a series of smaller intervals (Foster et al., 1999). During each interval, the individual records whether or not the target behavior occurred. It is important to note that the individual only records whether or not the behavior has occurred; if there are multiple instances of the target behavior within the same interval, they are not recorded separately. Chronic mood states, anxiety symptoms, muscle tension ratings, and intrusive thoughts are examples of behaviors that may be recorded by intervals.

## Momentary Time Sampling

Self-monitoring of target behaviors can also be recorded with a format known as momentary time sampling (Cone, 1999). Momentary time sampling involves having an individual record a behavior each time he or she receives a signal or cue (e.g., tone, vibration; Foster et al., 1999). For example, electronic signals are periodically sent to a client on a handheld computer as a cue to record his or her level of social anxiety at that moment in time. Time-sampling formats have the benefit of varying different aspects of the procedure, such as frequency of signals, duration of the time frame, and signal patterns (Foster et al.).

Overall, multiple formats (e.g., event sampling, interval recording, time sampling) can be used to gather self-monitoring information. The clinician or researcher interested in using self-monitoring should take into consideration the same issues involved in determining the aspect of the target behavior being monitored.

### SELF-ASSESSMENT DEVICES

The final methodological consideration involves the selection of a self-monitoring device. According to Ciminero and colleagues (1977), clinicians and researchers should consider the following device characteristics before making a final decision: portability (i.e., manageable, handy), simplicity (i.e., user-friendly), cost (i.e., economical), and obtrusiveness (i.e., noticeable to individual, not others). Ideally, the authors also state, the target behavior should be recorded in real time (Ciminero et al.). The following devices are routinely used for self-monitoring of target behaviors.

## Paper and Pencil

Paper-and-pencil techniques allow an individual to record information about target behavior rates and relevant controlling variables (Ciminero et al., 1977). For example, an individual diagnosed with Binge Eating Disorder can record the number of binge-eating episodes in addition to the situations that preceded the binge and the consequences that occurred following the binge episode. Diaries are commonly used paper-and-pencil devices that allow individuals to provide more detailed information regarding the target behavior and its controlling variables (Baird & Nelson-Gray, 1999). In general, paper-and-pencil devices are cost effective and manageable (Foster et al., 1999).

## Mechanical Devices

Mechanical devices have also been used to gather information regarding frequency of the target behavior (Ciminero et al., 1977). Golf-stroke counters and belt/wrist counters are examples of mechanical devices. An individual diagnosed with agoraphobia might self-monitor the number of panic attacks experienced in a particular situation (e.g., a mall) using a mechanical device. In this situation, the individual would only click the counter each time he or she experienced a panic attack. Typically, mechanical counters are user-friendly, inexpensive, and suitably noticeable to only the individual self-monitoring (Foster et al., 1999).

Timing devices are often used in self-monitoring to collect information about the duration of a single target behavior (Ciminero et al., 1977). For example, an individual can use a stopwatch or kitchen timer to measure the amount of time spent worrying. However, this method does not allow for information to be recorded about potential controlling variables (Foster et al., 1999). Despite this limitation, timing devices are generally cost effective, simple to use, and unobtrusive (Haynes, 1978).

**Electronic Devices**

Electronic devices are becoming a popular method for self-monitoring. Tape recorders, video cameras, cellular phones, and pagers (e.g., Johnson & Larson, 1982) have been used for self-monitoring purposes. Johnson and Larson used the experience-sampling method (ESM) to compare 15 normal-weight individuals diagnosed with bulimia nervosa to 24 controls. In this study, participants carried a pager for one week and completed self-monitoring forms when they were signaled by a pager at least once within a 2-hour period between 8:00 AM and 10:00 PM throughout the day. Individuals from both groups completed a total 2789 forms (bulimia nervosa group: 627 total, 44.8 per person; control group: 2117 total, 46.5 per person). Results from the study indicate that individuals diagnosed with bulimia nervosa experienced more negative moods, spent greater time alone, and were more preoccupied with thinking about, preparing, or eating food. The researchers concluded that ESM was a useful procedure for obtaining information about the binge–purge cycle and also the behaviors, thoughts, and feelings experienced by individuals diagnosed with bulimia nervosa.

Over the past 15 years, other instruments have expanded the scope of behaviors that can be used in self-assessment. Pedometers are often used to assess how many steps have been taken. Actigraphs have been utilized to look at activity patterns during wake-and-sleep cycles. In behavioral medicine, ambulatory monitoring of physiological activity, blood pressure monitoring, blood glucose monitoring, and peak air flow and respiration monitoring have greatly increased the awareness of the relation between environmental events and internal responses (Haynes, 1998).

**Computers**

Recently, the use of computers in behavioral assessment has greatly increased. As a result, more opportunities for self-assessment are available. Computer-assisted data collection is only as limited as the individual's expertise and creativity in devising a method. These methods can be cost effective if individuals self-monitor behaviors on personal digital assistants (PDAs) (e.g., Norton,

Wonderlich, Myers, Mitchell, & Crosby, 2003) or handheld computers. Such computers can be programmed to cue an individual when it is time to record (e.g., time sampling), or frequency counts can be recorded. These types of data can be downloaded and summarized for the therapist and client. Another advantage of handheld computers is that they will likely reduce the error variance associated with other self-monitoring devices (e.g., Haynes, 1998).

Prospective data can be recorded and a more accurate sample of behavioral events in real time can be captured with computer recordings. For example, Taylor, Fried, and Kenardy (1990) had individuals with Panic Disorder record the frequency of panic attacks, the setting, and the thoughts they experienced surrounding the attacks. Similarly, Agras, Taylor, Feldman, Losch, and Burnett (1990) had obese clients monitor the amount of food intake, their weight, and the goals and amount of exercise. These devices are portable and appear to be less obtrusive in the client's environment (e.g., high numbers of individuals currently carry cell phones and pagers). Receiving a beep on a device to record may be less noticeable now than it might have been 20 years ago.

In summary, numerous devices are available for recording self-monitoring information. Although written almost 30 years ago, suggestions for choosing self-monitoring devices are still relevant (Ciminero et al., 1977). First, the device needs to be relatively manageable. Second, the device needs to be simple to use. Third, the device needs to be relatively cost effective. Fourth, the device should be sufficiently noticeable to the individual engaging in the self-monitoring, however barely discernible to surrounding individuals.

## REACTIVITY

When self-monitoring is used for assessment purposes, therapists and researchers may want to minimize reactivity in order to get more accurate baseline information (Bornstein et al., 1986). When self-monitoring is used as an intervention, the researcher and clinician may want to maximize the reactive effects. In order to gain a better understanding of what effects occur under what circumstances for which subjects and with what type of self-monitoring methods, more research needs to be conducted (e.g., Korotitsch & Nelson-Gray, 1999). The following variables have been identified that can contribute to reactivity in self-monitoring: salience and cue value of the discriminative stimulus for recording; awareness of checks on accuracy of self-monitoring; training to conduct self-monitoring; frequency and timing of self-monitoring; motivation and expectations of the client; the nature of the target behavior (positive and nonverbal behaviors may be more reactive); valence of the target behavior; concurrent demands on the client in addition to self-monitoring; consequences for compliance with self-monitoring; and maintenance of reactive effects (Korotitsch & Nelson-Gray). Thus, maximizing or minimizing reactivity effects will be guided by the specific assessment and intervention goals of self-monitoring.

## PSYCHOMETRIC CONSIDERATIONS

Whether or not classic psychometric principles can and should be used to evaluate behavioral assessment remains a debated issue (e.g., Cone, 1998; Jackson, 1999; Nelson, 1983). Haynes (1990) proposed that behavioral assessment procedures be evaluated on "applicability and utility, reliability, validity, and sources of error variance" (p. 442). However, the author also notes that there are difficulties with evaluating behavioral assessment with the principles underlying psychometric theory. Behavioral assessment is based on the notion that behaviors are not stable; they are situation specific. Historically these methods, in particular self-monitoring, have only been evaluated with regard to face validity and accuracy.

Jackson (1999) presents a number of issues that should be considered if psychometrics are applied to behavioral assessment procedures. According to the author, assessment procedures should be evaluated with regard to whether or not the procedure fulfills its intended purpose. In the case of self-monitoring, a decision must first be made about what is being measured. For example, it is important to distinguish conceptually what is being assessed. Are clients self-monitoring behaviors or response classes (whether observable or private) in real time? Or are clients being asked about hypothetical constructs or abilities/skills that are less likely to be affected by time (e.g., trait anxiety, coping skills, problem-solving skills)?

The concepts of accuracy and content validity may be more applicable to the evaluation of information obtained by self-monitoring of behaviors and response classes in real time. For hypothetical constructs or ability/skill monitoring, the psychometric concepts of reliability (e.g., stability over time), content validity, discriminant validity, convergent validity, concurrent validity, and predictive validity are more relevant for evaluation (Jackson, 1999). However, it is difficult to evaluate the accuracy of self-monitored private events when these events are not accessible to independent observers or to external means of recording these behaviors. For a more in-depth discussion of the applicability of psychometric principles to self-monitoring, readers are encouraged to consult the following excellent resources: Cone, 1995, 1998, 1999; Haynes, 1998; and Jackson. The following section focuses on behaviors that are observable by independent means with regard to accuracy.

### ACCURACY

Principles of behavioral assessment are guided by a functional approach (i.e., how well the measure guides decision-making processes and treatment goals). Thus, the role of self-monitoring is not just to describe behavior but also to provide a means to assess the functions of the behavior and its maintaining variables. In addition, like other measures used in behavioral assessment, self-monitoring methods need to be supported by empirically validated data to ensure that what it intends to measure approximates the real behavior (Jackson, 1999). Therefore accuracy (i.e., the extent to which data reflect the true properties of the behavior) is an important psychometric concept for evaluating self-monitoring procedures (Baird & Nelson-Gray, 1999; Ciminero et al., 1977).

According to Korotitsch and Nelson-Gray (1999), three methods are commonly used to assess accuracy in self-monitoring. First, agreement comparisons can be made between the individual who is self-monitoring and an independent external observer. For example, high agreement was obtained between external observers and individuals self-monitoring of swimming laps (e.g., McKenzie & Rushall, 1974), number of cigarettes smoked (e.g., Frederiksen et al., 1975), and face-touching episodes (Nelson, Lipinski, & Black, 1976). However, in some studies, external observers may also contribute to self-monitoring reactivity. For example, Green (1978) compared temporal monitoring patterns (e.g., conducting monitoring before or after eating) of obese women to external observers. Results indicated that although temporal monitoring patterns did not lead to significant weight reduction alone, reactivity to an observer did contribute significantly to weight loss. In general, to achieve maximum accuracy, an observer should use the same recording procedure to record the identical target behavior (i.e., same operational definition) that the individual is self-monitoring. In addition, an independent observer should be recording information while the individual is self-monitoring (Jackson, 1999).

Second, data collected with self-monitoring can be compared to data collected by mechanical devices. In this situation, a mechanical device would be used to independently record each behavior occurrence, and the information obtained would be compared to the data collected from the individual's self-monitoring. For example, individuals with insomnia were asked to keep sleep logs (e.g., self-record sleep latency, sleep time, number of wakening episodes during the night), while polysomnography recordings were obtained in a laboratory setting (Coates, Killen, George et al., 1982). Results indicated that the self-recorded sleep log information positively correlated (although not perfectly) with the objective measures of total sleep time and latency to sleep obtained by polysomnography. Although self-assessment methods may not always be as accurate as more objective measures (e.g., mechanical devices), therapists and researchers often cite cost effectiveness, ease of use, and convenience as primary reasons for the continued use of self-monitoring methods (e.g., Barton, Blanchard, & Veazey, 1999).

Third, self-monitoring data can be compared to naturally occurring consequences of the behavior. For example, an individual who is self-monitoring alcohol consumption can take a blood test to compare the number of self-reported drinks consumed with blood alcohol levels. However, it should be noted that the natural by-products are not considered "ideal" incontrovertible indices (i.e., one-to-one correspondence between measure and behavior) because a third factor (e.g., confounding variables, measurement limitations) may be causing the results (Jackson, 1999). Unfortunately, none of the foregoing techniques can be used to assess accuracy when self-monitoring private events or covert behaviors given these behaviors are only accessible to the individual who is self-monitoring (e.g., Ciminero et al., 1977; Korotitsch & Nelson-Gray, 1999).

Researchers have identified numerous variables that appear to have an effect on the accuracy of self-monitored data (Ciminero et al., 1977; Jackson, 1999; Korotitsch & Nelson-Gray, 1999). For example, providing training in self-monitoring has been shown to increase accuracy (Foster et al., 1999). According to Foster and colleagues, some training is better than no training; the training should include clear descriptions of the behavior being targeted and explicit directions regarding when to monitor and how to use the device. During training, it may be beneficial to have the individual repeat back all information and model correct ways to self-monitor.

Accuracy in self-monitoring also appears to increase when the individual is told that he or she is being checked for accuracy (Korotitsch & Nelson-Gray, 1999; Ciminero et al., 1977). In addition, research has shown that individuals tend to self-monitor more accurately when they are provided reinforcement for accurate monitoring (Baird & Nelson-Gray, 1999). Conversely, researchers have shown that accuracy decreases when an individual self-monitors while simultaneously engaging in other tasks (Korotitsch & Nelson-Gray). Hence, individuals should only monitor one behavior until they become comfortable, at which time additional target behaviors could be monitored.

Taken together, it is important to consider accuracy when using self-monitoring in behavioral assessment. The following methods are used to assess accuracy in self-monitoring: comparison to an external observer, comparison to a mechanical device, and comparison to natural by-products. Accuracy appears to be influenced by several factors, such as the type of target behavior, the number of target behaviors being recorded at the same time, awareness of accuracy checks, and whether or not reinforcement is included. Numerous researchers assert that training an individual on how and what to self-monitor increases accuracy (Ciminero et al., 1977; Foster et al., 1999; Jackson, 1999).

## CONTENT VALIDITY

Content validity represents another psychometric concept that may be useful in evaluating the meaning and usefulness of data collected from self-monitoring procedures (Haynes, Richard, & Kubany, 1995; Jackson, 1999). Self-monitoring involves an assumption that multiple samples of the target behavior need to be sampled across time and situations. Thus, one potential value of using self-monitoring methods is greater access to many samples of behavior. In some cases, a therapist or researcher may access the literature and ascertain how many samples might be sufficient in order to have enough information for assessment purposes. In general, more stable behaviors of interest may need fewer samples for sufficient representation (Jackson).

Explicit behavioral definitions may be useful in ensuring that the monitored behavior adequately reflects and represents the conceptualized or intended target.

For example, an individual who smokes is asked to monitor each time and to specify the conditions under which he or she smokes a cigarette. The definition of smoking, however, must specify exactly what constitutes smoking—from one puff only to smoking the entire cigarette. In evaluating the content validity of self-monitoring, Jackson (1999) suggests that therapists and researchers carefully consider the purpose and meaning of the data.

## ISSUES FOR THE 21ST CENTURY

With the advent of managed care and its concern with documenting outcomes, indirect methods of assessment have proliferated. Given that indirect methods of assessment (e.g., self-report questionnaires, interviews) are quick and easy to administer, research on these methods has risen dramatically, whereas research on self-monitoring has declined (Korotitsch & Nelson-Gray, 1999). Clinicians, however, continue to value the more direct method of self-monitoring and find it useful in their practice (e.g., Elliott et al., 1996). Korotitsch and Nelson-Gray (1999) note that the "climate of managed care also demands high-quality assessment that can enhance formulation of effective intervention as well as sensitive measures that can detect changes in the behaviors of interest" (p. 416). This type of climate may be particularly conducive to research on self-monitoring methods that can effectively evaluate treatment effectiveness.

## FUTURE RESEARCH

Many questions remain unanswered regarding the validity and utility of data collected from self-monitoring procedures. Given that a lot of the earlier work on reactivity focused on nonclinical populations, this research needs to be replicated with clinical samples. Sensitivity of self-monitoring compared to other assessment methods also needs to be investigated. Potential biases associated with self-monitoring, the impact of self-monitoring on the quality of treatment, potential negative effects of self-monitoring (e.g., increased rumination or self-focus), and psychometric principles should be examined in order to evaluate the validity and utility of self-monitoring procedures.

## SUMMARY

Self-monitoring is a commonly used technique in behavioral assessment that involves having an individual monitor and record his or her own behaviors. Behavioral assessors value self-monitoring because it is a practical method that emphasizes the situational specificity of target behaviors as they occur in the environment. In addition, self-monitoring is considered one of the only means for assessing covert behaviors. Within behavioral assessment, self-monitoring has five primary purposes: education/description, diagnostic clarification, pretreatment assessment, treatment evaluation, and facilitation of behavior change. Self-monitoring represents a flexible technique that can capture different dimensions of behavior (e.g., frequency, intensity), using various recording formats (e.g., momentary time sampling, interval recording) and devices (e.g., paper-and-pencil, PDAs). Given current demands for competent and quality assessment (Cone, 1997), self-monitoring data need to be continuously and rigorously evaluated to ensure they are useful and meaningful for their intended purpose (Jackson, 1999).

## REFERENCES

Agras, W. S., Taylor, C. B., Feldman, D. E., Losch, M., & Burnett, K. F. (1990). Developing computer-assisted therapy for the treatment of obesity. *Behavior Therapy, 21*, 99–109.

Alderman, N., Fry, R. K., & Youngson, H. A. (1995). Improvement of self-monitoring skills, reduction of behaviour disturbance and the dysexecutive syndrome: Comparison of response cost and a new programme of self-monitoring training. *Neuropsychological Rehabilitation, 5*, 193–221.

American Psychiatric Association. (2000). *Diagnostic and statistical manual of mental disorders* (4th ed., revised). Washington, DC: Author.

Baird, S., & Nelson-Gray, R. O. (1999). Direct observation and self-monitoring. In S. C. Hayes, D. H. Barlow, & R. O. Nelson-Gray (Eds.), *The scientist practitioner: Research and accountability in the age of managed care* (2nd ed., pp. 353–386). Boston: Allyn & Bacon.

Baker, R. C., & Kirschenbaum, D. S. (1993). Self-monitoring may be necessary for successful weight control. *Behavior Therapy, 24*, 377–394.

Barton, K. A., Blanchard, E. B., & Veazey, C. (1999). Self-monitoring as an assessment strategy in behavioral medicine. *Psychological Assessment, 11*, 490–497.

Bellack, A. S., & Schwartz, J. S. (1976). Assessment for self-control programs. In M. Hersen & A. S. Bellack (Eds.), *Behavioral assessment: A practical handbook* (pp. 111–142). Elmsford, NY: Pergamon Press.

Bornstein, P. H., Bridgwater, C. A., Hickey, J. C., & Sweeney, T. M. (1980). Characteristics and trends in behavioral assessment: An archival analysis. *Behavioral Assessment, 2*, 125–133.

Bornstein, P. H., Hamilton, S. B., & Bornstein, M. T. (1986). Self-monitoring procedures. In A. R. Ciminero, K. S. Calhoun, & H. E. Adams (Eds.), *Handbook of behavioral assessment* (pp. 176–222). New York: John Wiley & Sons.

Campbell, L. A., & Brown, T. A. (2002). Generalized anxiety disorder. In M. M. Antony & Barlow, D. H. (Eds.), *Handbook of assessment and treatment planning for psychological disorders* (pp. 147–177). New York: Guilford Press.

Ciminero, A. R., Nelson, R. O., & Lipinski, D. P. (1977). Self-monitoring procedures. In A. R. Ciminero, K. S. Calhoun, & H. E. Adams (Eds.), *Handbook of behavioral assessment* (pp. 195–232). New York: John Wiley & Sons.

Clum, G. A., & Curtin, L. (1993). Validity and reactivity of a system of self-monitoring suicide ideation. *Journal of Psychopathology & Behavioral Assessment, 15*, 375–385.

Coates, T. J., Killen, J. D., George, J., Marchini, E., Silverman, S., & Thoresen, C. (1982). Estimating sleep parameters: A multitrait-multimethod analysis. *Journal of Consulting and Clinical Psychology, 50*, 345–352.

Cone, J. D. (1995). Assessment practice standards. In S. C. Hayes, V. M. Follette, R. M. Dawes, & K. Grady (Eds.), *Scientific standards for psychological practice: Issues and recommendations* (pp. 201–224). Reno, NV: Context Press.

Cone, J. D. (1997). Issues in functional analysis in behavioral assessment. *Behaviour Research and Therapy, 35,* 259–275.

Cone, J. D. (1998). Psychometric considerations: Concepts, contents, and methods. In A. S. Bellack & M. Hersen (Eds.), *Behavioral assessment: A practical handbook* (4th ed., pp. 22–46). Boston: Allyn & Bacon.

Cone, J. D. (1999). Introduction to the special section on self-monitoring: A major assessment method in clinical psychology. *Psychological Assessment, 11,* 411–414.

Craske, M. G., & Tsao, J. C. I. (1999). Self-monitoring with panic and anxiety disorders. *Psychological Assessment, 11,* 466–479.

Critchfield, T. S., & Vargas, E. A. (1991). Self-recording, instructions, and public self-graphing: Effects on swimming in the absence of coach verbal interaction. *Behavior Modification, 15,* 95–112.

Dupuy, J. B., Beaudoin, S., Rhéaume, J., Ladouceur, R., & Dugas, M. J. (2001). Worry: Daily self-report in clinical and nonclinical populations. *Behaviour Research and Therapy, 39,* 1249–1255.

Elliott, A. J., Miltenberger, R. G., Kaster-Bundgaard, J., & Lumley, V. (1996). A national survey of assessment and therapy used by behavior therapists. *Cognitive and Behavioral Practice, 3,* 107–125.

Febbraro, G. A. R., & Clum, G. A. (1998). Meta-analytic investigation of the effectiveness of self-regulatory components in the treatment of adult problem behaviors. *Clinical Psychology Review, 18,* 143–161.

Foster, S. L., Laverty-Finch, C., Gizzo, D. P., & Osantowski, J. (1999). Practical issues in self-observation. *Psychological Assessment, 11,* 426–438.

Frederiksen, L. W., Epstein, L. H., & Kosevsky, B. P. (1975). Reliability and controlling effects of three procedures for self-monitoring smoking. *Psychological Record, 25,* 255–263.

Garssen, B., de Beurs, E., Buikhuisen, M., van Balkom, A., Lange, A., & van Dyck, R. (1996). On distinguishing types of panic. *Journal of Anxiety Disorders, 10,* 173–184.

Goldstein, G., & Hersen, M. (1990). Historical perspectives. In G. Goldstein & M. Hersen (Eds.), *Handbook of psychological assessment* (pp. 3–17). New York: Pergamon Press.

Green, L. (1978). Temporal and stimulus factors in self-monitoring by obese persons. *Behavior Therapy, 9,* 328–341.

Haynes, S. N. (1978). Self-monitoring. In S. N. Haynes (Ed.), *Principles of behavioral assessment* (pp. 292–311). New York: Gardner Press.

Haynes, S. N. (1990). Behavioral assessment of adults. In G. Goldstein & M. Hersen (Eds.), *Handbook of psychological assessment* (2nd ed., pp. 423–462). New York: Pergamon Press.

Haynes, S. N. (1998). The changing nature of behavioral assessment. In A. S. Bellack & M. Hersen (Eds.), *Behavioral assessment: A practical handbook* (4th ed., pp. 1–21). Boston: Allyn & Bacon.

Haynes, S. N. (2000). Behavioral assessment of adults. In G. Goldstein & M. Hersen (Eds.), *Handbook of psychological assessment* (3rd ed., pp. 471–502). New York: Pergamon Press.

Haynes, S. N., Leisen, M. B., & Blaine, D. D. (1997). Design of individualized behavioral treatment programs using functional analytic clinical case models. *Psychological Assessment, 9,* 334–348.

Haynes, S. N., Richard, D. C. S., & Kubany, E. S. (1995). Content validity in psychological assessment: A functional approach to concepts and methods. *Psychological Assessment, 7,* 238–247.

Jackson, J. L. (1999). Psychometric considerations in self-monitoring assessment. *Psychological Assessment, 11,* 439–447.

Johnson, C., & Larson, R. (1982). Bulimia: An analysis of moods and behavior. *Psychosomatic Medicine, 44,* 341–351.

Kazdin, A. E. (1974). Self-monitoring and behavior change. In M. J. Mahoney & C. E. Thorsen (Eds.), *Self-control: Power to the person* (pp. 218–246). Monterey, CA: Brooks-Cole.

Kerns, R. D., Finn, P., & Haythornthwaite, J. (1988). Self-monitored pain intensity: Psychometric properties and clinical utility. *Journal of Behavioral Medicine, 11,* 71–82.

Korotitsch, W. J., & Nelson-Gray, R. O. (1999). An overview of self-monitoring research in assessment and treatment. *Psychological Assessment, 11,* 415–425.

Latner, J. D., & Wilson, G. T. (2002). Self-monitoring and the assessment of binge eating. *Behavior Therapy, 33,* 465–477.

McKenzie, T. L., & Rushall, B. S. (1974). Effects of self-recording on attendance and performance in a competitive swimming training environment. *Journal of Applied Behavior Analysis, 7,* 199–206.

Nelson, R. O. (1983). Behavioral assessment: Past, present, and future. *Behavioral Assessment, 5,* 195–206.

Nelson, R. O., Lipinski, D. P., & Black, J. L. (1976). The relative reactivity of external observations and self-monitoring. *Behavior Therapy, 7,* 314–321.

Norton, M., Wonderlich, S. A., Myers, T., Mitchell, J. E., & Crosby, R. D. (2003). The use of palmtop computers in the treatment of bulimia nervosa. *European Eating Disorders Review, 11,* 231–242.

Rapee, R. M., Craske, M. G., & Barlow, D. H. (1990). Subject-described features of panic attacks using self-monitoring. *Journal of Anxiety Disorders, 4,* 171–181.

Savard, J., & Morin, C. M. (2002). Insomnia. In M. M. Antony & D. H. Barlow (Eds.), *Handbook of assessment and treatment planning for psychological disorders* (pp. 523–555). New York: Guilford Press.

Strosahl, K. D., & Robinson, P. J. (2004). Behavioral assessment in the era of managed care: Understanding the present, preparing for the future. In S. N. Haynes, E. M. Heiby, & M. Hersen (Eds.), *Comprehensive handbook of psychological assessment: Vol. 3. Behavioral assessment* (pp. 427–449). New York: John Wiley & Sons.

Taylor, C. B., Fried, L., & Kenardy, J. (1990). The use of real-time computer diary for data acquisition and processing. *Behaviour Research and Therapy, 28,* 93–97.

Thomas, E. J., Abrams, K. S., & Johnson, J. B. (1971). Self-monitoring and reciprocal inhibition in the modification of multiple tics of Gilles de la Tourette's syndrome. *Journal of Behavior Therapy and Experimental Psychiatry, 2,* 159–171.

Tucker, J. A., Vuchinich, R. E., & Murphy, J. G. (2002). Substance use disorders. In M. M. Antony & D. H. Barlow (Eds.), *Handbook of assessment and treatment planning for psychological disorders* (pp. 415–452). New York: Guilford Press.

Wadden, T. A., Berkowitz, R. I., Vogt, R. A., Steen, S. N., Stunkard, A. J., & Foster, G. D. (1997). Lifestyle modification in the pharmacologic treatment for obesity: A pilot investigation of a potential primary care approach. *Obesity Research, 5,* 218–226.

Weinhardt, L. S., Forsyth, A. D., Carey, M. P., Jaworski, B. C., & Durant, L. E. (1998). Reliability and validity of self-report measures of HIV-related sexual behavior: Progress since 1990 and recommendations for research and practice. *Archives of Sexual Behavior, 27,* 155–180.

Wilson, G. T., & Vitousek, K. M. (1999). Self-monitoring in the assessment of eating disorders. *Psychological Assessment, 11,* 480–489.

# 8

---

# PSYCHOPHYSIOLOGICAL

# ASSESSMENT

KEVIN T. LARKIN

*Department of Psychology*
*West Virginia University*
*Morgantown, West Virginia*

## INTRODUCTION

Comprehensive assessment of patients with psychological problems requires gathering information across multiple domains, including information that can be self-reported as well as directly or indirectly observed. This fundamental approach to assessment has long been advocated by behavioral assessment authorities, including the classic tripartite assessment of anxiety (i.e., behavioral, self-reported, physiological) established by Lang (1968) and the extension of this approach into the behavioral assessment grid described by Cone (1978). Although this chapter focuses on psychophysiological assessment, the reader is reminded that a comprehensive assessment of any psychological problem involves obtaining observational data as well as documentation of self-reported phenomena.

In contrast to other assessment strategies, psychophysiological measurement involves neither subjective appraisals of functioning nor direct observation of easily detectable responses. Rather, psychophysiological assessment employs sophisticated electronic monitoring and recording of physiological parameters that can provide information regarding a particular patient's presenting problem or response to treatment. Although countless physiological parameters can be measured, psychophysiological assessment typically focuses on parameters known to be affected by nervous system activity, including both components of the central nervous system as well as both branches of the peripheral nervous system (i.e., the somatic nervous system and the autonomic nervous system). Recording apparatuses have become more sophisticated, so psychophysiological assessment now includes measures of nervous system functioning that could have only been dreamt about a decade ago (e.g., cortical activation via brain imaging).

Not surprisingly, early efforts to employ psychophysiological methods of assessment focused on gross changes in fairly easily detectible physiological phenomena such as heart rate and sweat gland activity. For example, Carl Jung (1910) employed a measure of skin resistance, which he termed the *psychogalvanic response*, on patients in his therapeutic practice. By simply noting words that elicited the most substantial skin resistance responses during word association tasks, he was able to quickly identify unconscious conflicts to target in analysis. Instrumentation in these early applications, however, was very crude and not sensitive enough to measure the minute physiological alterations (e.g., micromhos) that occur in response to presentation of mentally challenging or threatening stimuli. With the development of the polygraph, additional physiological parameters could be detected and measured systematically and were found to reflect changes in nervous system activity, including the brain (electroencephalography), muscles (electromyography), the heart (electrocardiography), eye movements (electrooculography), and the digestive system (electrogastrography). These devices also enabled signal amplification so that previously undetectable physiological changes could be easily observed and recorded. Over the decades, computerized signal acquisition systems were developed that permitted even further refinements in psychophysiological measurement. For example, the electrical activity of the heart measured via computerized electrocardiography yielded direct measures of important components of the signal itself, such as systolic time intervals, T-wave amplitude, and indices of contractile force, all measures that could not easily be determined using the paper record of the polygraph. Most recently, these computerized systems have been rebuilt as microprocessors, enabling development of tiny data-acquisition systems that can be worn by patients as they encounter activities that occur during normal daily life.

When employing psychophysiological assessment for almost any physiological parameter, an important distinction is made between *tonic* and *phasic* measures. Tonic measures of psychophysiology refer to physiological measures obtained during periods of time in which no specific stimulus has been presented to the individual (e.g., resting or baseline psychophysiological measures). For example, measures of elevated blood pressure observed among patients with essential hypertension and elevated electrical activity in the frontalis muscles of patients with tension muscle headaches represent measures of tonic physiological states.

In contrast, phasic psychophysiological measures reflect the magnitude of alterations that occur in response to known environmental stimuli. For example, heart rate is known to increase during speaking conditions, and the magnitude of this reaction is much greater among socially anxious patients in comparison to low socially anxious controls. Phasic psychophysiological measures are often expressed in terms of simple change scores, in which resting values are subtracted from values obtained during presentation of a particular stimulus context.

Although the distinction between tonic and phasic measures is important in basic psychophysiological research, it becomes less obvious in applications of

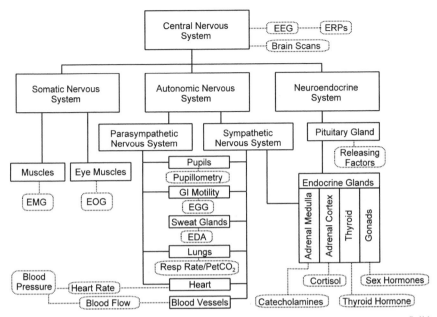

FIGURE 8.1  Organ systems and associated psychophysiological measurement parameters. Solid lines depict primary neural connections; dotted lines depict physiological parameters commonly measured in psychophysiological studies. *Key*: EEG = electroencephalography; ERPs = event related potentials; EMG = electromyography; EOG = electrooculography; GI = gastrointestinal; EGG = electrogastrography; EDA = electrodermal activity; Resp = respiration; PetCO$_2$ = pulmonary end tidal carbon dioxide.

psychophysiological assessment methods when employed with clinical populations, where threatening stimuli of internal origin are often present. When assessing a phobic patient, for example, obtaining presumably tonic psychophysiological measures may be influenced unknowingly by a failure to account for the patient's internal anticipation of exposure to a phobic stimuli. In other words, "true" rest periods may be difficult to achieve among certain psychiatric conditions.

The primary purpose of this chapter is to summarize briefly the vast quantity of empirical work pertaining to the various parameters examined in psychophysiological investigations. Although a great deal of psychophysiological investigation has been conducted aimed at examining normal, adaptive responses to various stimulus presentations, the focus of this chapter is on using psychophysiological assessment with populations exhibiting various psychiatric disorders, specifically studies on experimental psychopathology. For additional information regarding the effect of human behavior on psychophysiological measures, the reader is referred to Stern, Ray, and Quigley (2001).

Figure 8.1 illustrates the organization of various psychophysiological parameters that have been examined with respect to a wide range of psychiatric disorders. Parameters include those that largely reflect central nervous system functioning as well as those that reflect somatic and autonomic nervous system functioning. In order to provide a clear organization of the various measures of psychophysiological functioning, this schematic diagram grossly oversimplifies the complexity of relations among organ systems and their associated measurement parameters. In fact, all interrelations between organ systems and the negative feedback systems involved in regulating these organ systems have been omitted from this figure, for purposes of clarity.

## CENTRAL NERVOUS SYSTEM FUNCTIONING

Although the central nervous system (CNS) comprises both the brain and the spinal cord, psychophysiological measurement of CNS activity has focused primarily on cortical functioning. Obviously, direct measures of neural activity of the brain are not possible in patients for whom the cortex is not typically exposed. Rather, psychophysiological parameters, which necessarily rely on surface electrodes or various imaging strategies for detection, can only provide indirect estimates of cortical activity. As depicted in Figure 8.1, electrical neural functioning occurring in the CNS can be detected using electroencephalography and associated measures of event-related electrical potentials. Measures of cortical functioning have also more recently been conducted using various brain-imaging strategies.

### ELECTROENCEPHALOGRAPHY (EEG)

Electrical signals that emanate from neural activity in the brain can be detected using surface electrodes located on the scalp. In particular, measurement of these signals has been quite important in assessing general levels of cortical alertness and sleepiness. During states of alert wakefulness and mental or physical activation, the brain typically elicits a high-frequency, low-amplitude electrical activity called *beta* activity. During periods of relaxed wakefulness with eyes closed, however, the frequency of these electrical waves decreases and their amplitude increases slightly, resulting in recognizable *alpha* activity. Brain waves of even lower-frequency, *theta* and *delta* electrical brain wave activity, characterize various stages of deep sleep. Interestingly, as an individual enters paradoxical, or rapid-eye-movement (REM), sleep, the low-frequency electrical activity associated with deep sleep gives way to brain waves that are indistinguishable from *beta* wave activity. Therefore, the brain is just as awake during episodes of dreaming as it is during everyday problem solving.

Although measurement of EEG using early recording devices required the simultaneous detection and plotting of dozens of electrode configurations as well as a technician with a trained eye, computerized quantification of EEG signals has permitted more immediate and sophisticated analyses. For example, spectral analyses of the EEG signal has enabled technicians very quickly to ascertain the predominant electrical wave form associated with a given time period. Based on the connection between cortical arousal and various psychopathologic disorders, EEG has been examined in several studies of experimental psychopathology. For example, studies have shown that alpha activity is decreased among patients with both anxiety disorders (e.g., Sachs, Anderer, Dantendorfer, & Saletu, 2004) and Attention-Deficit Hyperactivity Disorder (e.g., Barry, Clarke, & Johnstone, 2003). Additionally, patients with depressive disorders have been shown to display an EEG asymmetry characterized by increased alpha activity in the left frontal cortical regions (Gotlib, Ranganath, & Rosenfeld, 1998).

Although measures of EEG have provided important information regarding tonic levels of cortical arousal, they have not proven as useful in measuring phasic changes in cortical activity in response to specific stimuli. No doubt, this is a result of the fact that EEG represents a gross measure of the total electrical activity of the millions of neurons in the cortex. Alterations in the electrical activity of a single neural pathway in response to a specific stimuli would hardly impact a measure of total cortical arousal. However, surface electrodes employed to measure EEG can be used to provide reliable indices of phasic cortical response through the assessment of what have been termed *event-related potentials*.

## EVENT-RELATED POTENTIALS (ERPS)

Electrical cortical responses to a specific stimulus can be measured as long as the stimulus can be presented repeatedly during data acquisition. Using multiple stimulus presentations, a computer averages measures of electrical activity in a designated area of the brain; through this averaging process, random electrical activity of the cortex fades into the background, leaving an observable waveform associated with the presentation of the stimulus. Within milliseconds (ms) following presentation of a stimulus, a series of characteristic waveforms can be detected that are tied to hypothesized components of information processing. A positive wave that occurs approximately 300 ms following stimulus presentation (known as the P300 wave) is associated with cognitive processing of the stimulus, including attention, stimulus discrimination, and decision making. The P300 is most notably detected using what has been called the "oddball" paradigm; using this paradigm, one stimulus is repeatedly presented, followed by a different stimulus (i.e., the "oddball"). The magnitude of the P300 wave is clearly enhanced following presentation of the "oddball," lending support to the hypothesis that this component of the ERP wave is associated with awareness that a different stimulus has just been detected.

Because information processing is significantly disrupted in patients with thought disorders, patients with schizophrenia have been examined for decades using ERP research, including the "oddball" paradigm. Results of these studies have shown that P300 waves are noticeably smaller among patients with schizophrenia (e.g., Steinhauer & Zubin, 1982). Interestingly, the magnitude of the P300 wave returns to normal following treatment with neuroleptic medication, suggesting that the disruption in information processing detected among patients with schizophrenia is unique to their condition during a psychotic state.

ERP research has also been conducted on patients with other psychiatric disorders known to be associated with problems in information processing. For example, diminished P300 waves have been observed among children diagnosed with Attention-Deficit Disorder (Jonkman et al., 2000) and elderly patients diagnosed with dementia (Frodl et al., 2002). Recently, Pollak and Tolley-Schell (2003) reported enhanced P300 waves among physically abused children exposed to angry faces, indicating that increased attentional engagement was detected using this paradigm. In brief, the P300 component of the ERP waveform can be reliably used to ascertain both enhanced and reduced attentional processing associated with a number of diagnostic conditions.

Additional components of cortical electrical activity have been observed using ERP research methods. Slow potentials, such as the contingent negative variation (CNV), reflect gradual shifts in electrical potential that occur over several hundred milliseconds. CNV, for example, is observed when a participant is provided a warning stimulus before stimulus delivery. During this brief period when the participant is presumably waiting and anticipating stimulus delivery, a negative potential gradually emerges. CNV, therefore, has been hypothesized to correspond to expectancy. Like the more rapid responses of the ERP, slow potentials have been shown to exhibit characteristic dampened profiles among various types of psychopathology, including schizophrenia (McNeely, West, Christensen, & Alain, 2003), depression, and anxiety disorders (Tecce & Cattanach, 1987).

## BRAIN IMAGING

With the advent of radiographic imaging strategies (e.g., positron emission tomography [PET]) and the more recent functional magnetic resonance imaging (MRI) technologies, research on experimental psychopathology has been able to examine more closely brain regions associated with various diagnostic groups. In general, these functional brain-imaging methods estimate cortical function in various regions of the brain by detecting the use of oxygen and/or glucose. Presumably, increased localized use of oxygen or glucose translates into increased neural activity in that brain region. Both tonic and phasic measures of cortical functioning obtained through brain-imaging methods can be useful to experimental psychopathologists.

Functional brain-imaging strategies have been conducted using patients with a wide array of psychiatric conditions. For example, prefrontal cortical activation that normally occurs during inhibition of a learned task has been shown to be impaired among patients with schizophrenia (MacDonald & Carter, 2003), lending support to hypotheses that schizophrenia is associated with frontal lobe dysfunction. In another functional neuroimaging study, limbic system activation was shown to be higher among patients diagnosed with Major Depression when exposed to negative feedback during a cognitive task (Tucker, Luu, Frishkoff, Quiring, & Poulsen, 2003), indicating that hypersensitivity of the limbic system functioning plays a role in affective disorders. Brain-imaging research has also elucidated the importance of limbic system activation in Post-Traumatic Stress Disorder (Bremner et al., 1999) and enhanced activation of the orbitofrontal regions of the cortex in Obsessive-Compulsive Disorder (Anderson & Savage, 2004).

Brain-imaging strategies have also proven useful in detecting changes in cortical functioning that occur in response to treatment. For example, reductions in brain activity in the caudate nucleus, detected via PET scan, have been observed following treatment for Obsessive-Compulsive Disorder with either pharmacotherapy or behavior therapy (Baxter et al., 1992). In a recent intervention study, changes in brain activity were shown to differ between pharmacologic and cognitive-behavioral treatments for Major Depression (Goldapple et al., 2004); pharmacologic treatment was associated with increased prefrontal activation and hippocampal hypoactivity, whereas cognitive-behavioral treatment was associated with the opposite physiological pattern. Clearly, by using brain-imaging technology, we are learning a great deal about how various successful treatment strategies work.

## SOMATIC NERVOUS SYSTEM FUNCTIONING

The somatic nervous system refers to components of the central and peripheral nervous systems that regulate sensorimotor activity. Although many neural fibers of the somatic nervous system lie outside the CNS, several regions of the CNS are also involved in sensorimotor functioning, including the spinal cord and several cranial nerves that regulate motor activity of the muscles on the face and head. For example, three cranial nerves, the oculomotor (III), the trochlear (IV), and the abducens (VI) nerves, are responsible for eye movements. Signals for muscle activity for the rest of the body are transmitted from the brain to peripheral regions via the spinal cord.

## EYE MOVEMENTS

Eye movements can be detected through gross visual observations or through movement sensors placed adjacent to the eyes, instrumentation referred to as electrooculography (EOG). Sleep researchers rely heavily on these measures of eye movements to depict onset and cessation of REM sleep. Although there are a variety of recognizable types of eye movements during the awakened state, considerable amount of research has focused on smooth-pursuit eye movements, a relatively slow eye movement used to track moving objects in the environment. These studies have confirmed that patients with schizophrenia exhibit notable dysfunctions of smooth-pursuit eye movement (Sponheim, Iacono, Thuras, Nugent, & Beiser, 2003). Interestingly, first-degree relatives of patients with schizophrenia also exhibit identical dysfunctional smooth-pursuit eye movements, suggesting that this physiological phenomenon represents a marker for vulnerability for schizophrenia.

One type of eye movement that has received recent attention in experimental psychopathology is the magnitude of the eye blink response that occurs as a part of the startle response. Very simply, when an individual is exposed to an unpredictable burst of white noise, a startle reflex occurs, accompanied by an eye blink. Lang (1995) demonstrated that the magnitude of the eye blink startle response was enhanced under conditions of arousal of negative emotions, such as anger, fear, and sadness. Interestingly, the magnitude of the eye blink startle response can be attenuated if a prepulse stimulus (i.e., warning stimulus) is delivered beforehand, a phenomenon termed *prepulse inhibition*. The magnitude of this prepulse inhibition effect has been shown to be influenced by the valence of the emotion experienced among anxious or fearful individuals, so startle responses are attenuated during pleasant emotions but enhanced during unpleasant emotions (Cook, 1999). The distinction between the magnitudes of prepulse inhibition effects for pleasant and unpleasant emotions is not observed among patients with antisocial traits, individuals who presumably do not exhibit normal fear-based learning (Levenston, Patrick, Bradley, & Lang, 2000). Prepulse inhibition has been investigated in several patient samples; for example, patients with a variety of anxiety disorders, including Panic Disorder (e.g., Ludewig, Ludewig, Geyer, Hell, & Vollenweider, 2002) and Obsessive-Compulsive Disorder (e.g., Swerdlow, Benbow, Zisook, Geyer, & Braff, 1993), exhibit attenuated prepulse inhibition effects.

## MUSCLE ACTIVITY

Electrical muscular activity, detected via electromyography (EMG), is measured using sets of electrodes similar to those used for measuring EEG or EOG. Increased electrical activity occurs in a particular muscle group during muscle tension, and reductions in electrical activity in the muscle group occur under relaxed states. Although EMG can be measured from any muscle group in the body, the resulting signal tends to represent a global measure of bodily muscle tension, because muscle groups quite distal from the electrode site can influence the signal. Certainly, movements affect EMG, but so does underlying muscle tension. In fact, EMG has served as a very helpful indicator of muscle tension in assessing and evaluating treatments for patients with muscle tension headaches (e.g., Ong, Nicholson, & Gramling, 2003). Furthermore, measures of EMG have been useful in assessing psychophysiological responses among patients with Post-Traumatic Stress Disorder (e.g., Carlson, Singelis, & Chemtob, 1997), Generalized Anxiety Disorder (e.g., Hazlett, McLeod, & Hoehn-Saric, 1994), and Panic Disorder (e.g., Beck & Scott, 1987).

## AUTONOMIC NERVOUS SYSTEM
## FUNCTIONING

The autonomic nervous system comprises two branches: the sympathetic nervous system, which is responsible for the fight–flight activation system affecting peripheral organ systems, and the parasympathetic nervous system, which is responsible for the relaxation response affecting many of the same organ systems. In brief, the fight–flight response, which is commonly triggered by the presence of a threatening stimulus, involves a redistribution of blood flow and energy resources from the body's primary organs to fuel the muscle and brain activity needed to confront or escape from the source of threat. In contrast, the relaxation response returns blood flow to homeostatic life support systems (e.g., the gastrointestinal system). Although initially thought to operate reciprocally, the sympathetic and parasympathetic branches of the autonomic nervous system have been shown to operate independently (Berntson, Cacioppo, & Quigley, 1991). In fact, both sympathetic and parasympathetic activity can be enhanced in response to a given stimulus. As depicted in Figure 8.1, many psychophysiological measures can be used to assess autonomic nervous system activity.

### PUPILLOMETRY

Pupillary dilation and constriction represent easily observable physiological responses that reflect sympathetic and parasympathetic nervous system activation, respectively. In contrast to the electrodes used to measure several other psychophysiological parameters, pupillometry involves measurement of pupil diameter via a video recording camera. Although pupil diameter seems fairly easy to measure, measurement is complicated by numerous extraneous factors, including eye movement, a number of eye reflexes, and the amount of light present in the environment. When psychophysiologists have controlled these sources of variability, they have learned a great deal about the relation between pupil diameter and CNS activity; in brief, the magnitude of pupillary responses to specific stimuli has been shown to be associated with cognitive processing occurring in the CNS (Granholm & Steinhauer, 2004). As such, pupillary responses to selected stimuli can be used to examine indirect parameters of cognitive processing among various pathological conditions. For example, the magnitude of the pupillary response to a given stimulus has been shown to be significantly reduced among patients with schizophrenia (Steinhauer & Zubin, 1982) and Alzheimer's dementia (Fotiou, Fountoulakis, Tsolaki, Goulas, & Palakaris, 2000), conditions both hypothesized to be associated with dysfunctional cognitive processing. Additionally, because psychoactive drugs are known to alter pupillometric responses, this psychophysiological assessment strategy has proven useful in detecting external drug use among patients in substance abuse treatment programs (Murillo, Crucilla, Schmittner, Hotchkiss, & Pickworth, 2004).

## GASTROINTESTINAL MOTILITY

The gastrointestinal system is influenced by both sympathetic and parasympathetic nervous systems; sympathetic activation results in decreased blood flow to the gastrointestinal system, while parasympathetic activity results in increased blood flow for purposes of digestion and motility. The electrogastrogram (EGG) is a device that employs electrodes positioned over the abdomen that monitor the electrical activity and contractility of the gastrointestinal system. Because stress is associated with increased gastric dysrhythmia (Stern, Vasey, Hu, & Koch, 1991), investigators have turned to examining EGG recordings among patients with disorders that affect the gastrointestinal system. In these studies, abnormal EGG responses have been observed in patients with gastroesophageal reflux disease (Leahy, Besherdas, Clayman, Mason, & Epstein, 2001), functional dyspepsia, and irritable bowel syndrome (Leahy, Besherdas, Clayman, Mason, & Epstein, 1999). In an interesting application of EGG technology, Gianaros, Stern, Morrow, and Hickok (2001) demonstrated that pretreatment episodes of gastric tachyarrhythmia predicted incidence of chemotherapy-induced nausea among cancer patients.

## ELECTRODERMAL ACTIVITY

Electrodermal activity (EDA) stands out as a measure of autonomic nervous system functioning that is solely mediated by sympathetic nervous system without parasympathetic influence. Unusually, this tract of the autonomic nervous system employs acetylcholine as a neurotransmitter, rather than the more commonly observed noradrenergic sympathetic nervous system neurotransmission. In contrast to other sweat glands of the body, the eccrine glands on the palms of the hands and the soles of the feet are responsive to mental activation and emotion, and the degree of sweat gland activity can be measured easily using surface electrodes attached to the hand or fingers. Several measures of EDA can be obtained, the most common being skin conductance level (SCL) and skin conductance response (SCR). In both cases a low-current electrical charge is transmitted across the surface of the skin. Because sweat is an excellent conductor, the charge is conducted more quickly when sweat activity increases and more slowly when sweat activity decreases. SCL represents a tonic measure of EDA, and SCR represents a phasic measure of EDA in response to a given stimulus. Some authors have reported EDA findings using the terms *skin resistance level* and *skin resistance response*; these values are simply inverse measures of SCL and SCR, respectively. Because the skin possesses its own intrinsic electrical activity, this can also be measured without exposing the skin to an external electrical source, a measure termed *skin potential*. Most experimental work on EDA, however, reports findings in terms of SCL or SCR.

During exposure to stressful stimuli, sweat glands exhibit increased rates of secretion that result in increased SCR; when the stressful stimuli are removed, measures of skin conductance gradually return to prestress levels. Therefore, both measures of magnitude of SCR and recovery rate can be examined. Numerous investigations of SCR and recovery rate have been conducted on patient populations. In general, patients with anxiety disorders exhibit higher SCLs (e.g., Bond, James, & Lader, 1974) and greater SCRs during exposure to feared stimuli and slower recovery rates than nonanxious controls (e.g., Wessel & Merckelbach, 1998), and patients with antisocial personality characteristics or disturbances of conduct exhibit lower SCLs and smaller SCRs to stress than controls (Lorber, 2004). Therefore, studies employing measures of EDA have confirmed that patients with anxiety disorders are overaroused, while patients with antisocial traits are more commonly underaroused.

EDA has been examined in patient populations other than those with anxiety or antisocial/conduct disorders. For example, SCRs of depressed patients are typically dampened, in contrast to nondepressed controls (e.g., Iacano, 1984). In contrast, patients with schizophrenia typically exhibit increased SCL as well as frequent nonspecific SCRs (Dawson & Schell, 2002), and patients with binge-eating disorders exhibit heightened SCRs during exposure to their favorite binge food (Vögele & Florin, 1997).

EDA has been particularly valuable in assessing physiological components of the anxiety response of patients undergoing treatment. In his classic study on systematic desensitization, Paul (1966) demonstrated the superiority of the desensitization procedure for treating phobia by using SCR as an outcome measure. Boulougoulis, Marks, and Marset (1971) demonstrated that significantly greater reductions in SCR occurred among participants receiving exposure therapy, in contrast to those being treated with desensitization. Based on the importance of assessing EDA in these early-intervention studies, monitoring of sympathetic arousal via EDA continues to be employed as an indicator of treatment progress in many clinic settings.

## RESPIRATION

Respiration is another easily detectable psychophysiological measure. Although it can be thought of as a measure of autonomic nervous system activity, it is also regulated from brain stem mechanisms in the CNS as well as through somatic diaphragm muscle activity. Although many sophisticated measures of respiratory parameters can be obtained (e.g., end tidal volume, peak inspiratory flow), researchers have typically focused on a simple measure of respiratory rate or amplitude. It is well known, for example, that rate of respiration increases under conditions of anxiety and stress but decreases under conditions of relaxation. Despite its ease of measurement, it is not used frequently in studies on experimental psychopathology, except among relatively recent studies examining the role of hyperventilation in the etiology of Panic Disorder (see Wilhelm & Roth, 2001). In brief, due to the significance of respiratory symptoms among many patients diagnosed with Panic Disorder, researchers have examined whether the report of these symptoms was based on actual differences in respiratory functioning among patients with Panic Disorder. Indeed, Hegel and Ferguson (1997) reported that patients with Panic Disorder exhibited lower pulmonary end-tidal $CO_2$ levels than Generalized Anxiety Disorder patients or nonanxious controls. These findings support clinical observations that chronic hyperventilation is involved in the etiology of panic disorder.

## CARDIOVASCULAR ACTIVITY

Measures of cardiovascular functioning represent the most widely used psychophysiological measures of autonomic functioning, due to the relative ease with which heart rate (HR) signals and blood pressure (BP) determinations can be made. Although there is a relation between HR and BP, it is not a simple or direct one. BP in the circulatory system is influenced by both cardiac and vascular factors. Both increases in HR and amount of blood ejected from the heart during each beat (i.e., stroke volume) represent cardiac influences that lead to increased BP through increased cardiac output. The degree of vasoconstriction and vasodilation in various segments of the circulatory system represent vascular influences on BP by altering peripheral resistance to blood flow. Because systolic blood pressure reflects BP during cardiac pump action, it is commonly assumed to represent a better index of the cardiac influence on BP than vascular influences; in contrast, diastolic blood pressure is often assumed to be a better index of vascular influences on BP. Although these assumptions tend to be true, more accurate measures of cardiac and vascular influences on BP can be obtained using impedance cardiography (see Sherwood et al., 1990).

Cardiac parameters, such as HR, reflect the joint innervation of the sympathetic and parasympathetic nervous systems, while vascular parameters, such as forearm blood flow, reflect sympathetic nervous system activation; firing of the β-adrenergic branch results in vasodilation in the forearm, and firing of the α-adrenergic branch results in vasoconstriction. Although HR is one of the more commonly used psychophysiological parameters, it is often difficult to interpret due to its dual innervation by sympathetic and parasympathetic systems. Increases in HR in response to a given stimulus could represent increased sympathetic arousal, decreased parasympathetic activation, or some combination of the two. Some additional cardiovascular measures have proven useful in assisting researchers in determining which neural system is responsible for the observed cardiac effects. Pre-ejection period (PEP) is a systolic time interval of the cardiac cycle that has been shown to reflect primarily β-adrenergic activation. Heart rate variability (HRV) and respiratory sinus arrhythmia (RSA), the degree to which HR is influenced by the respiratory cycle, have been shown to reflect vagal parasympathetic influences on the heart. Thus, shortening of the PEP accompanying a faster HR suggests that the increased cardiac arousal is mediated by the sympathetic nervous system, and decreased HRV or RSA accompanying a faster HR suggests that the increased cardiac arousal is mediated by the reduced parasympathetic nervous system tone.

Similar to EDA, both tonic and phasic measures of HR are commonly elevated among patients with anxiety disorders, in contrast to nonanxious individuals (e.g., Bond et al., 1974), and persons with antisocial traits exhibit lower HR and HR responses to stress than controls (Lorber, 2004). To examine whether these observed differences in HR can be attributed to sympathetic or parasympathetic influences, some investigators have measured PEP or HRV in patient groups. Both Generalized Anxiety Disorder and Panic Disorder, for example, are associated with decreased HRV (Friedman & Thayer, 1998; Thayer, Friedman, & Borkovec, 1996), indicating a parasympathetic nervous system dysfunction in these anxiety disorders. Comparable parasympathetic dysfunction has been observed among depressed patients (e.g., Gorman & Sloan, 2000). In contrast, reduced PEP response has been observed among male adolescents with conduct disorders (Beauchaine, Katkin, Strassberg, & Snarr, 2001), suggesting that sympathetic nervous system dysfunction may be responsible for the commonly observed lower HR among persons with antisocial traits. Comparable findings have been reported among patients with other impulse control problems, such as bulimia nervosa (Koo-Loeb, Pedersen, & Girdler, 1998).

Measures of BP and forearm blood flow have also been shown to distinguish patients with anxiety disorders from controls. Increased BP responses (e.g., Buckley & Kaloupek, 2001) and increased forearm blood flow (i.e., vasodilation; e.g., Kelly & Walter, 1969) have been observed among patients with a variety of anxiety disorders. Reductions in blood flow to the extremities (i.e., vasoconstriction) among anxious patients have also been reported (e.g., Ackner, 1956), indicating that the distribution of blood flow in the circulation in patients with anxiety disorders mimics blood flow observed during the classic fight–flight response. Finally, measures of blood volume in genital regions have proven instrumental in assessing patients with sexual disorders or sexual dysfunctions (Geer, O'Donohue, & Schorman, 1986).

## NEUROENDOCRINE SYSTEM FUNCTIONING

Measures of neuroendocrine system activity typically involve blood draws or urine screens, although recent assays have been developed to assess various elements of the neuroendocrine system from salivary samples. Some investigators do not consider measures of neuroendocrine activity as psychophysiological parameters, for they typically require invasive assessment methods. However, for the purposes of this chapter and because of the ease with which blood, urine, and salivary samples can be obtained, they can be considered here. Additionally, because the neuroendocrine system is quite responsive to stress, both tonic and phasic measures can be obtained from patient samples exposed to clinically relevant stimuli. The neuroendocrine system operates much like the nervous system, except it employs the bloodstream, rather than neural pathways, for signal transmission. For example, the pituitary gland, in response to a brain signal, emits chemical-releasing or -stimulating factors into the bloodstream that travel through the circulatory system and trigger various endocrine glands to release hormones. Catecholamines (norepinephrine and epinephrine) and cortisol are released from the adrenal gland, thyroid hormone is released from the thyroid glands, and various sex hormones (e.g., estrogen, testosterone) are released from the gonads. Obviously, blood concentrations of all of these hormones and releasing/stimulating factors can be measured through a simple blood draw.

## HYPOTHALAMIC-PITUITARY–RELEASING FACTORS

Although several pituitary-releasing or -stimulating factors have been identified and measured, only a few have been systematically examined with respect to various psychiatric disorders. For example, corticotropin-releasing factor (CRF), the hormone released by the pituitary that triggers the release of cortisol by the adrenal cortex, has been shown to be elevated among persons with both anxiety and mood disorders (Ströhle & Holsboer, 2003). Thyroid-stimulating hormone (TSH), which similarly leads to the release of thyroid hormone by the thyroid glands, has been reported to be decreased among patients with anxiety or mood disorders (Rao, Vartzopoulos, & Fels, 1989). Because mood and anxiety disorders are both hypothesized to be associated with altered hypothalamic-pituitary function, it is not surprising that several studies have explored hormone levels associated with altered releasing- or stimulating-factor levels among a variety of psychopathological conditions.

## STRESS HORMONES

Although many hormones can be measured, most experimental psychopathologists have concentrated on the so-called stress hormones: cortisol, epinephrine, and norepinephrine. Cortisol is released into circulation from the adrenal cortex and has been shown to be elevated in a number of patient samples, including patients with anxiety disorders, such as Panic Disorder (Bandelow et al., 2000) and Obsessive-Compulsive Disorder (Monteleone, Catapano, Tortorella, & Maj, 1997), and mood disorders (Ströhle & Holsboer, 2003). Comparable to psychophysiological parameters of the autonomic nervous system, cortisol levels have been shown to be lower among patients with antisocial personality characteristics (Bergman & Brismar, 1994).

Catecholamines are released from the adrenal medulla and have direct excitatory effects on the cardiovascular system as well as the autonomic nervous system. In particular, norepinephrine has been shown to be elevated in patients with anxiety and mood disorders (e.g., Sevy, Papadimitriou, Surmont, Goldman, & Mendlewicz, 1989) but reduced among patients with antisocial personality traits (e.g., Lidberg, Levander, Schalling, & Lidberg, 1978).

Levels of thyroid hormone have also been investigated among various patient groups. Rao et al. (1989), for example, reported lower levels of thyroid hormones among both anxious and depressed women. Interestingly, recent reports have indicated that elevated thyroid hormone levels are associated with antisocial behaviors (Soderstrom & Forsman, 2004).

In summary, distinct neuroendocrine profiles have emerged among anxiety/ mood disorders and antisocial/conduct disorders. In general, these profiles are consistent with findings derived from studies of the autonomic nervous system that support Gray's (1975) hypothesis that anxiety disorders are associated with hyperresponsive behavioral inhibition systems and that antisocial behavior disorders are associated with hyporesponsive systems.

## FACETS OF PSYCHOPHYSIOLOGICAL ASSESSMENT

It is apparent that researchers have numerous physiological parameters to consider when electing to employ psychophysiological assessment in studies on experimental psychopathology. Foremost among these considerations is selecting the appropriate measurement parameter(s). Although one certainly needs to consider the availability of recording instrumentation, that should not represent the primary consideration in making this decision. Of utmost importance in selecting the measurement parameter is considering the appropriateness of specific parameters and their conceptual relevance to the experimental question being asked. For example, studies examining the efficacy of progressive muscle relaxation training certainly should employ EMG for purposes of evaluating treatment outcome. Many researchers have fallen prey to a tendency to select psychophysiological assessment measures that are relatively easy to assess (e.g., HR) when other parameters may have been more appropriate. Although changes in HR, for example, may reflect sympathetic nervous system activation, they may also reflect alterations in parasympathetic influence, rendering interpretations of the neural systems involved in changes in HR difficult to make.

In general, it is a good rule of thumb to employ multiple psychophysiological measures whenever possible. According to Fowles (1986), HR is a better index of the behavioral activation system and EDA is a better measure of the behavioral inhibition system. Based on this premise, HR would be more appropriate for measuring interventions for impulse control disorders and EDA would be more appropriate for measuring interventions for anxiety disorders. Obviously, if both parameters were assessed, stronger conclusions could be drawn regarding the specific neural systems affected by the intervention.

Once appropriate parameters have been selected, researchers should carefully consider their selection of stimuli used during assessment and the mode of stimulus presentation. It is well known that both type of task selected and the mode of presentation will influence the psychophysiological response profile, a phenomenon termed *stimulus response specificity*. For example, tasks involving processes of sensory intake (e.g., watching a film segment) will elicit quite distinct physiological responses, in comparison with tasks involving sensory rejection (e.g., recalling a fearful incident; Lacey, Kagan, Lacey, & Moss, 1963). In this regard, it is essential to include a nonpatient comparison group to elucidate the expected physiological response profile for the specific task chosen. Like selecting physiological responses to measure, multiple stimuli are optimal, including standardized "control" stimuli to evaluate overall physiological responsiveness. Additionally, with the advent of ambulatory recording technology, exposure to real-life threatening stimuli can be considered, rather than relying entirely on contrived laboratory situations or standardized laboratory stressors, which both have limited generalizability to real-life settings.

Although the appropriateness of selected stimuli is important, it is also essential to obtain measures of physiological functioning proximal to stimulus presentation to serve as resting or baseline levels. Of considerable importance is allowing the patient to accommodate to the novel surroundings of the experimental environment, a process termed *adaptation*. Depending on the nature of the experimental procedure, the duration of this adaptation phase may differ. For example, in studies employing cannula placement for purposes of neuroendocrine or arterial pressure assessment, patients often need a much longer adaptation period to "calm down" after insertion of the cannula. In many cases (e.g., highly anxious patients), it may be more difficult to obtain reliable tonic measures of physiological functioning during these resting periods than to obtain the phasic response levels during stimulus presentation. It is also important to obtain resting levels that are proximal to the stimulus presentations, for many factors (e.g., time of day, temperature, substance use, menstrual phase) are known to alter resting physiological state and could make findings difficult to interpret if the patient is instructed to return at a different day or time for completion of the assessment.

Physiological responses to repeated presentations of the same stimuli tend to decrease over time, a process called *habituation*. In some patient samples, however, habituation may be delayed. For example, SCRs among phobic patients exposed to feared stimuli may not habituate as quickly as SCRs of nonphobic controls, possibly due to the typically abbreviated exposure times that phobic patients can endure. Habituation rates among patients normalize following interventions aimed at increasing the duration of exposure to feared stimuli (e.g., exposure therapy, implosive therapy). However, because habituation is a universal phenomenon, experimental psychopathologists are obligated to employ appropriate control conditions in order to interpret physiological responses to repeated stimulus presentations.

Once data have been collected, the experimenter needs to consider how such psychophysiological data will be reduced and analyzed. Although raw scores of physiological functioning can be simply recorded and analyzed, psychophysiologists are frequently interested in analyzing the difference between the resting state and during stimulus presentation. As stated earlier, one strategy for handling psychophysiological data is through calculation of change scores, by simply subtracting average values of a rest period from those obtained during presentation of a designated stimulus (e.g., phobic object). Although this strategy is widely used, it can be criticized because there is often an association between resting levels and the magnitude of the physiological response, a phenomenon called the *law of initial values*. Elevated resting levels of a given parameter may be associated with reductions in the magnitude of physiological responding due to a ceiling effect or with increased physiological responding due to a priming effect. In order to control for the association between resting and stress-induced physiological levels, psychophysiological researchers have employed analyses of covariance or residualized change scores to remove the portion of "reactive" variance that is explained by resting levels of that parameter.

Psychophysiological parameters, of course, should not represent sole dependent variables in studies of experimental psychopathology; rather, they should be combined with measures of affect, cognition, and behavior obtained via self-report and direct behavioral observations. However, inclusion of several measurement domains can be problematic for researchers, because correlations among these various response channels are typically quite low. Wilhelm and Roth (2001) argue convincingly that concordance among physiological and self-reported measurement parameters can be improved if more attention is paid to making sure assessment domains are measuring a common construct. For example, physiological respiratory parameters are more likely to be associated with self-reported ratings of shortness of breath than with overall anxiety symptoms. Thus, experimental psychopathologists need to select the nonphysiological parameters of interest as carefully as the physiological parameters.

## SUMMARY

Psychophysiological assessment provides researchers and clinicians important clues about cognitive and emotional functioning that are not easily observed with the naked eye. Through the careful selection of response parameters and application of recording apparatuses, these tiny physiological responses can be detected and used to explore underlying physiological pathologies of psychological disorders as well as effective strategies for monitoring treatment progress and outcome. Given the careful attention to the selection of physiological parameters and eliciting stimuli, important knowledge regarding the physiological foundations for a variety of psychological disorders has been acquired. For example, based on sound psychophysiological research, distinct autonomic nervous system and neuroendocrine profiles have been observed among patients with anxiety/ mood disorders and those with disorders of conduct. In addition, certain psychophysiological measures have become useful markers for psychopathology, such as smooth-pursuit eye movement dysfunctions among persons at risk for developing schizophrenia. As distinct physiological systems at the root of various psychiatric disorders are identified, interventions aimed specifically at those underlying physiological disturbances can be developed and tested both in the laboratory and during daily life. With continued collaboration between psychophysiologists and experimental psychopathologists, the role of psychophysiological assessment holds much promise in assessing and treating numerous psychological disorders.

## REFERENCES

Ackner, B. (1956). The relationship between anxiety and level of peripheral vasomotor activity. *Journal of Psychosomatic Research, 1,* 21–48.

Anderson, K. E., & Savage, C. R. (2004). Cognitive and neurobiological findings in obsessive-compulsive disorder. *Psychiatric Clinics of North America, 27,* 37–47.

Bandelow, B., Wedekind, D., Sandvoss, V., Broocks, A., Hajak, G., Pauls, J., et al. (2000). Diurnal variation of cortisol in panic disorder. *Psychiatry Research, 95,* 245–250.

Barry, R. J., Clarke, A. R., & Johnstone, S. J. (2003). A review of electrophysiology in attention-deficit/hyperactivity disorder: I. Qualitative and quantitative electroencephalography. *Clinical Neurophysiology, 114,* 171–183.

Baxter, L. R., Schwartz, J. M., Bergman, K. S., Szuba, M. P., Guze, B. H., Mazziotta, J. C., et al. (1992). Caudate glucose metabolic rate changes with both drug and behavior therapy for obsessive-compulsive disorder. *Archives of General Psychiatry, 49,* 681–689.

Beauchaine, T. P., Katkin, E. S., Strassberg, Z., & Snarr, J. (2001). Disinhibitory psychopathology in male adolescents: Discriminating conduct disorder from attention-deficit/hyperactivity disorder through concurrent assessment of multiple autonomic states. *Journal of Abnormal Psychology, 110,* 610–624.

Beck, J. G., & Scott, S. K. (1987). Frequent and infrequent panic: A comparison of cognitive and autonomic reactivity. *Journal of Anxiety Disorders, 1,* 47–58.

Bergman, B., & Brismar, B. (1994). Hormone levels and personality traits in abusive and suicidal male alcoholics. *Alcoholism, Clinical and Experimental Research, 18,* 311–316.

Berntson, G. G., Cacioppo, J. T., & Quigley, K. S. (1991). Autonomic determinism: The modes of autonomic control, the doctrine of autonomic space, and the laws of autonomic constraint. *Psychological Review, 98,* 459–487.

Bond, A. J., James, D. C., & Lader, M. H. (1974). Physiological and psychological measures in anxious patients. *Psychological Medicine, 4,* 364–373.

Boulougouris, J. C., Marks, I. M., & Marset, P. (1971). Superiority of flooding (implosion) to desensitization for reducing pathological fear. *Behavior Research and Therapy, 9,* 7–16.

Bremner, J. D., Staib, L. H., Kaloupek, D., Southwick, S. M., Soufer, R., & Charney, D. S. (1999). Neural correlates of exposure to traumatic pictures and sound in combat veterans with and without posttraumatic stress disorder: A positron emission tomography study. *Biological Psychiatry, 45,* 806–816.

Buckley, T. C., & Kaloupek, D. G. (2001). A meta-analytic examination of basal cardiovascular activity in posttraumatic stress disorder. *Psychosomatic Medicine, 63,* 585–594.

Carlson, J. G., Singelis, T. M., & Chemtob, C. M. (1997). Facial EMG responses to combat-related visual stimuli in veterans with and without posttraumatic stress disorder. *Applied Psychophysiology and Biofeedback, 22,* 247–259.

Cone, J. D. (1978). The Behavioral Assessment Grid (BAG): A conceptual framework and a taxonomy. *Behavior Therapy, 9,* 882–888.

Cook, E. W. (1999). Affective individual differences, psychopathology, and startle reflex modification. In M. E. Dawson, A. M. Schell, & A. H. Bohmelt (Eds.), *Startle modification: Implications for neuroscience, cognitive science, and clinical science* (pp. 187–208). New York: Cambridge University Press.

Dawson, M. E., & Schell, A. M. (2002). What does electrodermal activity tell us about prognosis in the schizophrenia spectrum? *Schizophrenia Research, 54,* 87–93.

Fotiou, F., Fountoulakis, K. N., Tsolaki, M., Goulas, A., & Palikaras, A. (2000). Changes in pupil reaction to light in Alzheimer's disease patients: A preliminary report. *International Journal of Psychophysiology, 37,* 111–120.

Fowles, D. C. (1986). The psychophysiology of anxiety and hedonic affect: Motivational specificity. In B. F. Shaw, Z. V. Segal, T. M. Vallis, & F. E. Cashman (Eds.), *Anxiety disorders: Psychological and biological perspectives* (pp. 51–66). New York: Plenum Press.

Friedman, B. H., & Thayer, J. F. (1998). Anxiety and automatic flexibility: A cardiovascular approach. *Biological Psychology, 47,* 243–263.

Frodl, T., Hampel, H., Juckel, G., Bürger, K., Padberg, F., Engel, R., et al. (2002). Value of event-related P300 subcomponents in the clinical diagnosis of mild cognitive impairment and Alzheimer's disease. *Psychophysiology, 39,* 175–181.

Geer, J. H., O'Donohue, W. T., & Schorman, R. H. (1986). Sexuality. In M. G. H. Coles, E. Donchin, & S. W. Porges (Eds.), *Psychophysiology: Systems, processes, and applications* (pp. 407–430). New York: Guilford Press.

Gianaros, P. J., Stern, R. M., Morrow, G. R., & Hickok, J. T. (2001). Relationship of gastric myoelectrical and cardiac parasympathetic activity to chemotherapy-induced nausea. *Journal of Psychosomatic Research, 50,* 263–266.

Goldapple, K., Segal, Z., Garson, C., Lau, M., Beiling, P., Kennedy, S., et al. (2004). Modulation of cortical-limbic pathways in major depression: Treatment-specific effects of cognitive behavior therapy. *Archives of General Psychiatry, 61,* 34–41.

Gorman, J. M., & Sloan, R. P. (2000). Heart rate variability in depressive and anxiety disorders. *American Heart Journal, 140*(Suppl. 4), 77–83.

Gotlib, I. H., Ranganath, C., & Rosenfeld, P. (1998). Frontal EEG alpha asymmetry, depression, and cognitive functioning. *Cognition and Emotion, 12,* 449–478.

Granholm, E., & Steinhauer, S. R. (Eds.). (2004). Pupillometric measures of cognitive and emotional processes. *International Journal of Psychophysiology, 52,* 1–6.

Gray, J. A. (1975). *Elements of a two-process theory of learning.* New York: Academic Press.

Hazlett, R. L., McLeod, D. R., & Hoehn-Saric, R. (1994). Muscle tension in generalized anxiety disorder: Elevated muscle tonus or agitated movement? *Psychophysiology, 31,* 189–195.

Hegel, M. T., & Ferguson, R. J. (1997). Psychophysiological assessment of respiratory function in panic disorder: Evidence for a hyperventilation subtype. *Psychosomatic Medicine, 59,* 224–230.

Iacano, W. G. (1984). Electrodermal activity in euthymic patients with affective disorders: One-year retest stability and the effects of stimulus intensity and significance. *Journal of Abnormal Psychology, 93,* 304–311.

Jonkman, L. M., Kemner, C., Verbaten, M. N., Van Engeland, H., Camfferman, G., Buitelaar, J. K., et al. (2000). Attentional capacity, a probe ERP study: Differences between children with attention-deficit hyperactivity disorder and normal control children and effects of methylphenidate. *Psychophysiology, 37,* 334–346.

Jung, C. G. (1910). The association method. *American Journal of Psychology, 21,* 219–269.

Kelly, D., & Walter, C. J. (1969). A clinical and physiological relationship between anxiety and depression. *British Journal of Psychiatry, 115,* 401–406.

Koo-Loeb, J. H., Pedersen, C., & Girdler, S. S. (1998). Blunted cardiovascular and catecholamine stress reactivity in women with bulimia nervosa. *Psychiatry Research, 80,* 13–27.

Lacey, J. I., Kagan, J., Lacey, B. C., & Moss, H. A. (1963). The visceral level: Situational determinants and behavioral correlates of autonomic response patterns. In P. H. Knapp (Ed.), *Expression of the emotions in man* (pp. 161–196). New York: International Universities Press.

Lang, P. J. (1968). Fear reduction and fear behavior: Problems in treating a construct. In J. M. Shlien (Ed.), *Research in psychotherapy* (pp. 90–102). Washington, DC: American Psychological Association.

Lang, P. J. (1995). The emotion probe: Studies of motivation and attention. *American Psychologist, 50,* 372–385.

Leahy, A., Besherdas, K., Clayman, C., Mason, I., & Epstein, O. (1999). Abnormalities of the electrogastrogram in functional gastrointestinal disorders. *American Journal of Gastroenterology, 94,* 1023–1028.

Leahy, A., Besherdas, K., Clayman, C., Mason, I., & Epstein, O. (2001). Gastric dysrhythmias occur in gastro-oesophageal reflux disease complicated by food regurgitation but not in uncomplicated reflux. *Gut, 48,* 212–215.

Levenston, G. K., Patrick, C. J., Bradley, M. M., & Lang, P. J. (2000). The psychopath as observer: Emotion and attention in picture processing. *Journal of Abnormal Psychology, 109,* 373–385.

Lidberg, L., Levander, S., Schalling, D., & Lidberg, Y. (1978). Urinary catecholamines, stress, and psychopathy: A study of arrested men awaiting trial. *Psychosomatic Medicine, 40,* 116–125.

Lorber, M. F. (2004). Psychophysiology of aggression, psychopathy, and conduct problems: A meta-analysis. *Psychological Bulletin, 130,* 531–552.

Ludewig, S., Ludewig, K., Geyer, M. A., Hell, D., & Vollenweider, F. X. (2002). Prepulse inhibition deficits in patients with panic disorder. *Depression and Anxiety, 15,* 55–60.

MacDonald, A. W., & Carter, C. S. (2003). Event-related fMRI study of context processing in dorsolateral prefrontal cortex of patients with schizophrenia. *Journal of Abnormal Psychology, 112,* 689–697.

McNeely, H. E., West, R., Christensen, B. K., & Alain, C. (2003). Neurophysiological evidence for disturbances of conflict processing in patients with schizophrenia. *Journal of Abnormal Psychology, 112,* 679–688.

Monteleone, P., Catapano, F., Tortorella, A., & Maj, M. (1997). Cortisol response to d-fenfluramine in patients with Obsessive-Compulsive Disorder and in healthy subjects: Evidence for a gender-related effect. *Neuropsychobiology, 36,* 8–12.

Murillo, R., Crucilla, C., Schmittner, J., Hotchkiss, E., & Pickworth, W. B. (2004). Pupillometry in the detection of concomitant drug use in opioid-maintained patients. *Methods and Findings in Experimental and Clinical Pharmacology, 26,* 271–275.

Ong, J. C., Nicholson, R. A., & Gramling, S. E. (2003). EMG reactivity and oral habits among young adult headache sufferers and painfree controls in a scheduled-waiting task. *Applied Psychophysiology and Biofeedback, 28,* 255–265.

Paul, G. L. (1966). *Insight versus desensitization in psychotherapy: An experiment in anxiety reduction.* Palo Alto, CA: Stanford University Press.

Pollak, S. D., & Tolley-Schell, S. A. (2003). Selective attention to facial emotion in physically abused children. *Journal of Abnormal Psychology, 112,* 323–338.

Rao, M. L., Vartzopoulos, D., & Fels, K. (1989). Thyroid function in anxious and depressed patients. *Pharmacopsychiatry, 22,* 66–70.

Sachs, G., Anderer, P., Dantendorfer, K., & Saletu, B. (2004). EEG mapping in patients with social phobia. *Psychiatry Research, 131,* 237–247.

Sevy, S., Papadimitriou, G. N., Surmont, D. W., Goldman, S., & Mendlewicz, J. (1989). Noradrenergic function in generalized anxiety disorder, major depressive disorder, and healthy subjects. *Biological Psychiatry, 25,* 141–152.

Sherwood, A., Allen, M. T., Fahrenberg, J., Kelsey, R. M., Lovallo, W. R., & van Doornen, L. J. (1990). Methodological guidelines for impedance cardiography. *Psychophysiology, 27,* 1–23.

Soderstrom, H., & Forsman, A. (2004). Elevated triiodothyronine in psychopathy—possible physiological mechanisms. *Journal of Neural Transmission, 111,* 739–744.

Sponheim, S. R., Iacono, W. G., Thuras, P. D., Nugent, S. M., & Beiser, M. (2003). Sensitivity and specificity of select biological indices in characterizing psychotic patients and their relatives. *Schizophrenia Research, 63,* 27–38.

Steinhauer, S., & Zubin, J. (1982). Vulnerability to schizophrenia: Information processing in the pupil and event-related potential. In E. Usdin and I. Hanin (Eds.), *Biological markers in psychiatry and neurology* (pp. 371–385). New York: Pergamon Press.

Stern, R. M., Ray, W. J., & Quigley, K. S. (2001). *Psychophysiological recording* (2nd ed.). New York: Oxford University Press.

Stern, R. M., Vasey, M. W., Hu, S., & Koch, K. L. (1991). Effects of cold stress on gastric myoelectric activity. *Journal of Gastrointestinal Motility, 3,* 225–228.

Ströhle, A., & Holsboer, F. (2003). Stress responsive neurohormones in depression and anxiety. *Pharmacopsychiatry, 36*(Suppl. 3), S207–S214.

Swerdlow, N. R., Benbow, C. H., Zisook, S., Geyer, M. A., & Braff, D. L. (1993). A preliminary assessment of sensorimotor gating in patients with Obsessive-Compulsive Disorder. *Biological Psychiatry, 33,* 298–301.

Tecce, J. J., & Cattanach, L. (1987). Contingent negative variation (CNV). In E. Niedermeyer & F. Lopes da Silva (Eds.), *Electroencephalography: Basic principles, clinical applications and related fields* (2nd ed., pp. 657–679). Baltimore: Urban & Schwarzenberg.

Thayer, J. F., Friedman, B. H., & Borkovec, T. D. (1996). Autonomic characteristics of Generalized Anxiety Disorder and worry. *Biological Psychiatry, 39,* 255–266.

Tucker, D. M., Luu, P., Frishkoff, G., Quiring, J., & Poulsen, C. (2003). Frontolimbic response to negative feedback in clinical depression. *Journal of Abnormal Psychology, 112,* 667–678.

Vögele, C., & Florin, I. (1997). Psychophysiological responses to food exposure: An experimental study in binge eaters. *International Journal of Eating Disorders, 21,* 147–157.

Wessel, I., & Merckelbach, H. (1998). Memory for threat-relevant and threat-irrelevant cues in spider phobics. *Cognition and Emotion, 12,* 93–104.

Wilhelm, F. H., & Roth, W. T. (2001). The somatic symptom paradox in *DSM-IV* anxiety disorders: Suggestions for a clinical focus in psychophysiology. *Biological Psychology, 57,* 105–140.

# PART II

## EVALUATION OF SPECIFIC DISORDERS AND PROBLEMS

# 9

# ANXIETY AND FEAR

F. DUDLEY MCGLYNN
TODD A. SMITHERMAN
AMANDA M. M. MULFINGER

*Department of Psychology*
*Auburn University*
*Auburn University, Alabama*

## INTRODUCTION

This chapter provides an overview of some recent developments in the conceptualization of anxiety and anxiety disorders, along with a summary characterization of assessment in the context of cognitive behavior therapy. The chapter also includes a case study that shows some of the desiderata of anxiety assessment from our point of view. The procedural details of assessment vary substantially across different diagnostic categories. However, the various procedures are anchored in common assessment strategies. The focus here is on common strategies. We can provide only a cursory sample of material from a massive literature. Detailed and comprehensive narratives about anxiety disorders and assessment of anxiety and anxiety-related phenomena are available elsewhere (Antony & Barlow, 2002; Antony, Orsillo, & Roemer, 2001; Barlow, 2002), as is a more in-depth integrative review (McGlynn & Rose, 1998).

## HISTORICAL CHANGES TO THE ASSESSMENT OF ANXIETY DISORDERS

The past several decades have witnessed important changes in at least three arenas that are integral to a discussion of cognitive behavioral approaches to assessing anxiety disorders. We begin the narrative by overviewing those changes.

## THE CHANGING ANXIETY CONSTRUCT

In the early days of the behavior therapy movement, the anxiety construct was per se not discussed frequently. Eysenck (1960) argued that anxiety was a set of respondent behaviors that obeyed the laws of Pavlovian conditioning. Wolpe (e.g., 1958) insisted that anxiety was fundamentally a matter of sympathetic activation. These representations were accepted more or less uncritically. Somewhat later came the realization that a simple Pavlovian account of anxiety does not accord with major facts. Theorists such as Eysenck (1976) and Rachman (1976) attempted to preserve a place for Pavlovian conditioning by styling it as one of several "pathways" via which anxiety can be acquired and by broadening its explanatory scope, for example, by expanding the category of aversive unconditional respondents to include frustration (see Delprato & McGlynn, 1984). Similarly there were attempts to improve the cogency of a Pavlovian account of anxiety by arguing that interoceptive events can participate as cue-stimuli (Hallam, 1978) and by arguing that evolutionarily salient aversive events participate in respondent conditioning more readily than do other events (Seligman, 1971).

The notion that anxiety amounts to sympathetic activation was challenged by the finding of low intercorrelations between psychophysiological measures of anxiety and measures taken from the self-report and behavioral domains (Rachman & Hodgson, 1974). The account of anxiety as a conditioned emotional respondent was replaced by the "three-channel" construct; anxiety became a multireferential construct that served to organize thinking about events at the self-report, behavioral, and psychophysiological levels of measurement (Lang, 1968).

More recently the literature shows interest in cognitive and information-processing explanations of anxiety-related phenomena. There are "complete" cognitive theories of anxiety (e.g., Carr, 1979; Reiss, 1980), there are important new explanatory constructs such as anxiety sensitivity (Reiss, Peterson, Gursky, & McNally, 1986), and there is a rapidly growing literature about biased processing of threat-related information among anxious persons (e.g., Ehlers, 1993; Mathews & MacLeod, 1985; McNally, Foa, & O'Donnell, 1989).

Interest in how we should conceptualize anxiety has been paralleled by interest in how we should think about relations between anxiety, panic, and fear. The prevailing viewpoint seems to be that panic and fear are much the same (Craske, 1991) but that anxiety is different (Barlow, 1988, 2002). Panic and fear prepare the organism to escape from imminent danger; they differ only with respect to intensity and stimulus control. Anxiety, on the other hand, is related to vigilance/scanning and to appraisals of threat and of the adequacy of personal coping.

Developments such as those noted earlier have culminated in the appearance of multidimensional models of various anxiety disorders, models in which behavioral, cognitive, and biological concepts are integrated (e.g., Ehlers & Margraf, 1989; Rapee, 1987). One illustrative example is provided by Barlow's (1988, 2002) model of Panic Disorder with Agoraphobia, or PDA. Development of PDA begins when biological and/or psychological diatheses combine with life stress to produce unusual bodily sensations that are benign but detectable. Bodily sensations, in turn, become cues for fearful catastrophizing. Next the fearful catastrophizing prompts increased attention to such sensations, attention that leads to further catastrophizing and to behavioral avoidance of situations wherein the sensations are expected to occur. Much work remains in refining and validating contemporary multidimensional models of the various anxiety disorders (cf. McNally, 1994). However, they do focus attention on the need to take into account the multiple aspects of complex anxiety displays.

## THE CHANGING FACE OF "BEHAVIORAL" ASSESSMENT

All forms of psychological assessment involve presenting stimuli and recording responses. The stimuli that are presented and the responses that are recorded vary widely across assessors, owing to differences in the goals of assessment, in psychometric assumptions, and in the theoretical mechanisms that connect responses to stimuli.

In traditional forms of psychological assessment, the focus is on intrapersonal constructs that are related to personality and psychopathology. The stimuli used for traditional assessment usually are statements about behavioral dispositions that are organized into questionnaires; the responses of interest are ratings that reflect the respondent's degree of agreement with each of the statements. Historically prominent in traditional assessment is the assumption that important controls over behavior reside within the individual in the form of personality traits or psychopathological conditions.

In behavioral assessment the focus is on behavior-in-environment. The stimuli used for behavioral assessment are subsets and/or analogues of real-life stimuli that are clinically germane; the responses of interest are subsets and/or analogues of adaptively significant naturalistic performances. Inherent in behavioral assessment is the idea that important controls over behavior reside in the environment.

Assessment that occurs before and during cognitive behavioral treatment of anxiety disorders mirrors the practices of both traditional and behavioral assessment. Some behavior therapists have recognized that important conflicts exist between traditional and behavioral assessment and have worked toward an explicit and practical reconciliation (e.g., Collins & Thompson, 1993; Haynes & Uchigakiuchi, 1993). More generally, there is tacit recognition that important individual difference variables, such as trait anxiety (Spielberger, Gorsuch, & Lushene, 1970), anxiety sensitivity (Reiss et al., 1986), and somatic attentional focus (Chambless, Caputo, Bright, & Gallagher, 1984), can only be assessed with traditional methods and recognition that "mental contents" such as meta-worry (Borkovec, Hazlett-Stevens, & Diaz, 1999) and anxious self-talk (Martzke, Andersen, & Cacioppo, 1987) are best assessed with self-reports.

## CONTEMPORARY COGNITIVE BEHAVIORAL
## TREATMENT

Early on there were three separate and competing treatments for anxiety-related problems: systematic desensitization (Wolpe, 1958), participant modeling (Bandura, 1976), and flooding (Malleson, 1959). During the 1970s, Marks (1973, 1975) popularized the notion that the various competing behavioral treatments for anxiety enjoyed success for the same basic reason: They all promoted exposure to anxiety-cue stimuli. Since that time, "exposure" has been a central theme of anxiety treatment. Coupled with the broadened conception of potential anxiety-cue stimuli (see earlier), the procedural centrality of exposure has eventuated in modern "exposure technology": in one way or another exposing anxious clients for prolonged periods to exteroceptive and/or interoceptive cue-stimuli for anxiety.

The 1980s witnessed the growth of interest in cognitive aspects of anxiety and its treatment. One aspect of that evolution was the work of therapists such as Ellis (1962) and Meichenbaum (1974), who emphasized that maladaptive thinking lies at the heart of anxiety and, therefore, that the focus of therapy should be cognitive alteration. Another aspect of the evolution was new theories of anxiety that stressed catastrophic expectations concerning the likelihood, aversiveness, and untoward consequences of encounters with feared stimuli (Carr, 1979; Reiss, 1980). As a result of these influences and others, cognitive alteration came to be a basic goal of psychological treatment.

It is fair to say that cognitive behavior therapy for anxiety usually entails some combination of exposing clients to anxiety cues and helping them learn to think differently about anxiety-related events and their ability to cope with such events. Most recently, cognitive behavior therapy packages exist in manualized versions (Craske, Barlow, & Meadows, 2000).

## ASSESSMENT STRATEGIES

### SELF-REPORT METHODS

In general the methods used for assessing anxiety and fear can be divided into three categories: obtaining self-reports, observing behavior, and recording physiological events. Behavior therapists have, from time to time, voiced serious objections to assessment based on self-reports, objections related to "deficiencies in reliability and validity, contamination by faking and bias, low correlations with concurrent behavioral and physiological measures, and error associated with acquiescence, social desirability, and other response sets" (Nietzel, Bernstein, & Russell, 1988, p. 297). Nonetheless, self-reporting remains the most common source of data for anxiety assessment (Lawyer & Smitherman, 2004). Self-report methods serve two functions: (a) They provide inexact but convenient data about motor acts and physiological events, and (b) they provide criterional information about subjective states of affairs (e.g., the content of catastrophic thinking, the themes of worry, the intensity of fear experience). In the following narrative, self-report assessment is divided into interviews, questionnaires, self-monitoring, and situational ratings.

## Interviews

Clinical interviews can be categorized as implicitly structured, semistructured, or structured. Clinical interviewing is structured implicitly by three interview functions: (a) Interviewing fosters a therapeutic partnership, (b) it guides the selection of additional assessment techniques, and (c) it furnishes the behavioral details that flesh out initial and ongoing case conceptualization. Semistructured and structured interviews both contain specific questions that are asked in specific orders; they differ in the extent to which the interviewer is free to deviate from the protocol. When assessing for any anxiety disorder, the semistructured interview of choice is the Anxiety Disorders Interview Schedule for *DSM-IV* (ADIS-IV; Brown, Di Nardo, & Barlow, 1994). The ADIS-IV was developed progressively as a tool to parallel the revisions of the anxiety disorder classifications in the psychiatric nomenclature. The ADIS-IV allows for gathering demographic information and identifying presenting problems. Then various anxiety disorders are explored hierarchically and in detail, along with mood and somatoform disorders, mixed anxiety and depression, substance use, psychotic symptoms, and medical disorders. A Lifetime Version also exists of the ADIS-IV, or ADIS-IV-L (Di Nardo, Brown, & Barlow, 1994). The main addition in the ADIS-IV-L is a history of previous episodes that affords a more thorough picture of the individual's problems.

## Questionnaires

Questionnaires enjoy the primary advantages of being easy to administer and score. Many questionnaires provide information on the presence and severity of common specific fears, such as fears of snakes, thunderstorms, and public speaking (see Nietzel et al., 1988). Other questionnaires prompt the individual to rate various symptoms associated with targeted anxiety disorders. For example, the Social Phobia and Anxiety Inventory (Turner, Beidel, Dancu, & Stanley, 1989) prompts ratings about subjective, behavioral, and physiological events in settings related to social phobia and agoraphobia. The validity of questionnaires has been questioned, primarily due to the obtrusive and self-report nature of the format. However, questionnaires are arguably the best way to obtain a clear picture of the individual's interpretation of his or her own anxiety symptoms.

Some important questionnaires are not about anxiety symptoms per se, but rather are about theoretical mechanisms that assist in understanding those symptoms as they occur in targeted anxiety disorders. One prominent example is the Anxiety Sensitivity Index (Reiss et al., 1986). As mentioned earlier, one view of panic attacks emphasizes the role of catastrophic thinking about normally benign bodily sensations (Clark, 1986). The Anxiety Sensitivity Index is a 16-item questionnaire that quantifies habitually fearful preoccupation with the potentially adverse consequences of such sensations. Another prominent example is the Penn State Worry Questionnaire (Meyer, Miller, Metzger, & Borkovec, 1990). The accepted view of Generalized Anxiety Disorder emphasizes the causal significance of chronic worry. The Penn State Worry Questionnaire has 16 items that combine to quantify the respondent's tendency to worry.

## Self-Monitoring

In self-monitoring, the client monitors and records some aspect of the behavior of interest (e.g., frequency, intensity, duration). Usually a standard form for record keeping is provided; often there is an instruction to turn in the record forms on some regular basis (e.g., at each visit).

Self-monitoring was not common in the early anxiety assessment literature. More recently, however, self-monitoring has become increasingly prominent. Probably this reflects the modern construction of panic as a discrete response as well as influence on assessment practices from protocols for self-management of anxiety (i.e., Marks, 1978).

Self-monitoring shares the weaknesses of all methods of self-report and has unique disadvantages, including reactivity. Because self-monitors are asked to attend to and record a behavior before or after it occurs, the behavior is inevitably influenced. Early research recognized this potential problem and attempted to evaluate the accuracy of self-monitored data by comparing it with other-monitored data, with mechanically transduced data, and with measured by-products of self-monitored behavior (Nelson, 1977). Nelson demonstrated that accuracy of self-monitored data is best when the recorder is aware of being checked, when he or she receives accuracy-based incentives, and when instructions and descriptions of target behaviors are clear and distractions limited. In general, self-recorders are likely to underreport negatively valenced target behaviors and to overreport positively valenced target behaviors.

Problems such as reactivity notwithstanding, self-monitoring has proven to be an effective means of assessing behavior in clinical practice (see *Psychological Assessment*, Vol. 11, Issue 4, 1999). Furthermore, assessment via self-monitoring plays an important role in contemporary treatment of Panic Disorder, Generalized Anxiety Disorder, and Obsessive-Compulsive Disorder, among other conditions. Panic Disorder clients are often asked to fill out Step-by-Step Analysis of Panic Attacks forms, Daily Mood Records, and other forms (Craske et al., 2000) to track the frequency and severity of panic attacks. Generalized Anxiety Disorder clients often use Relaxation Records, Worry Records, and Daily Mood Records to track the antecedents of worry and the frequencies with which untoward outcomes are realized (Zinbarg, Craske, & Barlow, 1992). Obsessive-compulsive clients are sometimes asked to complete Self-Monitoring of Rituals forms (Kozak & Foa, 1997) to monitor which thoughts or situations trigger which rituals, how long the rituals last, and how much distress they cause.

Handheld or palmtop computers have emerged as valuable research tools for self-monitoring in the context of assessing anxiety disorders. C. B. Taylor, Fried, and Kenardy (1990), for example, provided 20 Panic Disorder patients with handheld computers. The computers prompted and recorded answers to questions about panic experiences and symptoms.

**Situational Ratings**

When questionnaires and interviews are used to prompt reports of fear intensity, the functional stimuli are written or oral statements. Of course, one can use actual stimuli to prompt reports of fear intensity. One can also instruct clients to visualize "stimuli" and then prompt reports about the fear intensities associated with imaging. Wolpe's (1973) Subjective Units of Discomfort Scale (SUDS) is commonly used. In using the SUDS, the client is told, " 'Think of the worst anxiety you have ever experienced or can imagine experiencing, and assign to this the number 100. Now think of the state of being absolutely calm and call this zero' " (p. 120). These instructions provide anchor points for subsequent fear ratings before and after exposure to fear cues and/or to fear-imagery instructions.

Visual analogue scales can also be used to prompt ratings of fear intensity before and after real and visualized encounters with feared stimuli. Clients are instructed simply to mark somewhere along a line that has anchors, such as "absolute calm" to "terror." Ratings of fear intensity have also been recorded continuously for research purposes. For example, McGlynn, Rose, and Lazarte (1994) used a system composed of a manual-input dial, a skin-conductance module, software for analogue-to-digital conversion, and a computer. Participants were instructed to monitor their fear levels continuously by adjusting the dial.

Self-rating of fear can be extended beyond the domain of intensity by incorporating semantic-differential methods. In one example of this approach, objects, events, and words are rated on the factor analytically derived affective dimensions of valence, arousal, and dominance (Mehrabian & Russell, 1974). The original self-assessment manikin (SAM) is an interactive computer program on which respondents adjust emotion-relevant features of a computer-generated figure to describe their own affect; real-time records of the adjustments are made (Lang, 1980). More recently, a paper-and-pencil version of the SAM has been reported (Bradley & Lang, 1994).

## BEHAVIORAL METHODS

Assessment of motor behavior has been a prominent feature of behavior therapy since the 1960s, when Lang and his colleagues (e.g., Lang & Lazovik, 1963) measured fear of snakes with a behavioral avoidance test. The early popularity of behavioral tests probably derived from their apparent objectivity (i.e., by their contrast with self-report measures). The continuing popularity of assessing actual behavior mirrors the centrality of motor acts in disorders such as Specific Phobia, Agoraphobia, and Obsessive-Compulsive Disorder. The following narrative describes behavioral avoidance tests, interpersonal performance tests, biological challenge tests, and symptom induction tests.

**Behavioral Avoidance Tests**

Measuring behavior in the presence of a feared stimulus (i.e., an object or a situation) allows assessors to obtain data that are less subject to bias than are data from self-report measures. A behavioral avoidance test (BAT) can occur in either a contrived or naturalistic setting and involves having the client confront a feared stimulus in order to measure his or her response. Contrived BATs generally take place in a laboratory setting and include the stimulus, the client, a means of measurement, and, perhaps, various response induction aids, such as pointers and gloves. In the case of snake phobia, for example, a caged snake is placed at the end of a measured walkway; the fearful person is asked to walk as far as possible toward the snake and engage in a series of progressively more difficult tasks that culminate with handling the snake. An assessment of the individual's fear level is based on how far he or she is able to get through the series of tasks; these scores can be compared with other individuals' performances or with the individual's previous scores. Naturalistic BATs occur in real-world settings but include the same components as contrived BATs. In general, the client is instructed to confront a clinically focal setting (a tall building for an acrophobic, a shopping mall for an agoraphobic, etc.). Sometimes the client is encouraged to work through a previously created hierarchy of tasks, culminating with the most feared (and difficult) activity (Mathews, Gelder, & Johnston, 1981). Research-oriented clinicians and treatment centers have often standardized some of their naturalistic BATs (see Barlow, 2002). Standardization of naturalistic BATs affords comparisons between individuals and across occasions. The decision to use a contrived or naturalistic BAT is made based on practicality, the availability of settings, and the priority assigned to external validity. Naturalistic BATs provide the best potential for external validity.

**Interpersonal Performance Tests**

Assessing behavior in social and public arenas began with socially fearful individuals engaging in public speaking under the observation of trained assessors (Paul, 1966). What began as a measure of onstage anxiety has progressed into measurement associated with carefully tailored, individual, interpersonal situations. The most common form of interpersonal performance test involves heterosocial interactions between a socially anxious individual and an attractive confederate of the opposite sex. Assessors often set up situations in which conversation is requested of the shy individual as he or she is confronted with another individual (e.g., Borkovec, Stone, O'Brien, & Kaloupek, 1974). Researchers have begun recording such conversations and coding them for categorized anxiety behaviors (Haemmerlie, 1983), and role-play protocols have been developed to standardize the study of interpersonal performances. In the Behavioral Situations Test (Barrios, 1983), for example, socially insecure young men hear a description of an anxiety-invoking situation, receive 30 seconds to prepare, and then act out the situation with a young, previously unknown woman. The entire interaction is recorded and coded, and individuals provide self-report and physiological data.

## Biological Challenge Tests and Symptom Induction Tests

Biological challenge tests and symptom induction tests are designed to produce somatic symptoms of panic in the service of assessment. Both sets of procedures allow for evaluation of panic-related symptoms and of the client's responses to the symptoms (cognitive catastrophizing, avoidance behaviors, safety signal utilization, etc.). Biological challenge tests induce the physiological and/or subjective phenomena of panic through administration of a chemical agent such as yohimbine, caffeine, sodium lactate, cholecystokinin, or epinephrine. By far the most commonly used agent in biological challenge tests is carbon dioxide ($CO_2$). Carbon dioxide inhalation produces a valid clinical analogue of naturally occurring panic (Sanderson & Wetzler, 1990) and can be conducted without medical oversight (Forsyth & Karekla, 2001). In contrast to the pharmacological provocation of biological challenge tests, symptom induction tests engage the client in a variety of exercises designed to produce the feared sensations. Commonly used exercises include running in place for 1 minute, voluntary hyperventilation for 1 minute, and breathing through a coffee straw for 2 minutes (Barlow, 2002). The panicogenic effects of symptom induction tests such as voluntary hyperventilation are typically weaker than those of $CO_2$ inhalation (Rapee, Brown, Antony, & Barlow, 1992). Symptom induction tests, however, are easier to implement in a clinical setting, do not require the purchase of expensive equipment, and may be combined with BATs in order to mimic panic symptoms in naturalistic contexts (Antony & Swinson, 2000).

With both biological challenge tests and symptom induction tests, clients rate their level of anxiety before, during, and after the test as well as the degree of similarity between the symptoms experienced and those experienced during a "real-life" panic attack. As is true of other methods of behavioral assessment, biological challenge tests and symptom induction tests can be used in exposure treatment and as tools for monitoring progress in treatment. Because they help identify and prioritize the specific sensations that are feared by the client, biological challenge tests and symptom induction tests lay the foundation for interoceptive exposure treatment. They are contraindicated, however, in clients with histories of chronic respiratory conditions, cardiovascular disorders, renal disease, seizure-related disorders, stroke, and head injury.

## PSYCHOPHYSIOLOGICAL METHODS

Psychophysiological methods have been used for 40 years in research settings to capture anxiety phenomena (see Papillo, Murphy, & Gorman, 1988). Ambulatory psychophysiological monitoring of anxious clients with portable bioelectric signal recorders emerged during the 1980s (e.g., Freedman, Ianni, Ettedgui, & Puthezhath, 1985; C. B. Taylor et al., 1986). Subsequent work has revealed unexpected complexities, such as panic without biological signatures and biological markers without panic. For that reason and others, ambulatory psychophysiological monitoring has not yet become a standard or frequent aspect of clinical assessment (but see Hofmann & Barlow, 1996).

## RESEARCH BASIS

Empiricism has been a prominent feature of behavior therapy since the beginning of the behavior therapy movement in the 1960s. For the most part, that allegiance to empirically guided practice remained intact as behavior therapy evolved into cognitive behavior therapy. In the arena of anxiety disorders, there is a vast array of assessment instruments and tactics built on firm empirical foundations (see Antony & Barlow, 2002; Antony et al., 2001). A few prominent examples are overviewed next.

The ADIS series of semistructured interviews has always reflected concern with fundamentals, such as interrater reliabilities of *Diagnostic and Statistical Manual of Mental Disorders* (*DSM*) diagnoses. Early on, a conservative evaluation of the interrater reliabilities of *DSM-III* (American Psychiatric Association, 1980) diagnoses among raters who used the ADIS was undertaken with 125 consecutive admissions to an anxiety disorders clinic (Barlow, 1987). The reliabilities were impressive, especially for disorders with clear behavioral referents, such as Obsessive-Compulsive Disorder and Specific Phobia. Continuing evaluation of interrater reliabilities for *DSM* diagnoses based on ADIS-R (Di Nardo & Barlow, 1988) and ADIS-IV interviews also produced impressive results and showed, by and large, that *DSM-IV* (American Psychiatric Association, 1994) diagnoses were more reliable than were *DSM-III-R* (American Psychiatric Association, 1987) diagnoses.

There also is a large research literature on the psychometric properties of specialized interview structures that focus on specific diagnostic entities. The PTSD module of the Structured Clinical Interview for *DSM-IV* (SCID-IV; Spitzer, Williams, Gibbon, & First, 1994) and the Yale–Brown Obsessive-Compulsive Scale (Goodman et al., 1989) are two prominent examples.

The numerous questionnaires used in contemporary assessment of anxiety, fear, and related processes have, for the most part, been subject to careful psychometric evaluation (see especially Antony et al., 2001). For one important example, the Penn State Worry Questionnaire has been shown to have excellent psychometric properties (see Molina & Borkovec, 1994). It is now a fundamental tool for assessing Generalized Anxiety Disorder. For another prominent example, the Anxiety Sensitivity Index has been shown to have excellent psychometric properties as well as sensitivity to treatment influence (see S. Taylor, 1999). It is now central in the assessment of Panic Disorder. For a third example, the Social Phobia and Anxiety Inventory has received extensive psychometric characterization (see Antony et al.) and figures prominently in the evaluation of Social Phobia.

Behavioral avoidance has been used since the early 1960s as an index related to fear and has itself been subject to research, mostly during the early 1970s. Research has demonstrated that avoidance is not a direct or straightforward index of fear but, rather, is influenced by a variety of factors embedded in the contextual and procedural details of avoidance assessment (see Bernstein, 1973). Hence, avoidance is part of the three-channel construct (Lang, 1968); it is "loosely coupled" with fear experience and fear-related physiology.

There is surprisingly little psychometric research on data derived from $CO_2$ challenges and symptom induction exercises. Such research is needed insofar as the data produced by biological and behavioral challenges clearly are influenced by contextual as well as biological factors (see McNally, 1994).

## CLINICAL UTILITY

In the early years of clinical psychology, there was little connection between the activities of assessment and those of psychotherapy. Standard batteries of tests and projective techniques served mainly to inform a *DSM-I* (American Psychiatric Association, 1952) diagnosis and to determine a client's intellectual suitability for psychological treatment. That state of affairs began to change when the behavior therapy movement emerged. The empirical posture of behavior therapy mandated meaningful measurement of treatment outcomes. Behavioral assessment arrived on the scene and remained a prominent interest as behavior therapy expanded into behavioral medicine and evolved into cognitive behavior therapy. The net result is that relatively careful and specialized assessment is now integral to planning and monitoring the effects of cognitive behavioral treatment.

Clinical interviewing serves to guide assessment and to solicit reports of idiographic details. Skilled interviewing early on fosters hope and points toward to-be-used interview structures and supplemental assessment. As planning progresses and treatment begins, interviewing pinpoints problematic anxiety behaviors, identifies the antecedents and consequences of anxiety behaviors, and affords conceptualization of the cognitive schemata that often bind anxiety behaviors to their environmental contexts.

Interview guides such as the ADIS series have become increasingly prominent. The ADIS is a major tool for differential diagnosis within the anxiety disorders. Very similar behaviors sometimes merit different diagnoses. Fear of disease can instantiate Specific Phobia or participate in Obsessive-Compulsive Disorder; fear of enclosed places might merit a diagnosis of Specific Phobia or Panic Disorder, and so forth. Correct diagnosis is important because, as in these examples, different diagnoses call for different treatments.

The ADIS interview also calls attention to comorbid conditions. The anxiety disorders commonly occur together and in concert with depression, substance-use disorders, and personality disorders. Various comorbid conditions call for additional assessment and treatment, and have implications for the success of treatment for the anxiety disorders (see Antony & Barlow, 2002).

Questionnaires are ubiquitous in contemporary cognitive behavioral practice. Some uses of questionnaires were noted earlier. In general, questionnaires provide relatively reliable and quantitative information that supplements data from interviews and from specialized assessments.

Space does not permit additional narrative about specialized assessment strategies such as situational ratings, self-monitoring, symptom induction tests, and the like. Suffice it to say that the specialized assessment strategies evolved in the explicitly empirical zeitgeist of behavior therapy and cognitive behavior therapy. They function to supplement and validate interview impressions, to guide the details of treatment planning, and to provide relatively objective indices of the effects of treatment on targeted conditions.

## ASSESSMENT, CONCEPTUALIZATION, AND TREATMENT PLANNING

Clinicians who treat anxiety disorders are fortunate that multifaceted theoretical models are available that can be used to provide conceptual superstructures for clinical activities (see especially Barlow, 1988, 2002). In common these models point to potential assessment arenas, such as predisposing factors, stressful life events, anxiety-cue stimuli, attentional and cognitive responses to anxiety-cue stimuli, and anxiety behaviors and experiences.

Clinicians who treat anxiety disorders are also fortunate that a large empirical literature is available to guide disorder-specific nuances in assessment activities. In the assessment of Generalized Anxiety Disorder, for one example, the clinician might assess the strength of a client's motive to avoid emotion, because worry-contingent avoidance of emotion is theorized to strengthen worry (Borkovec & Roemer, 1995). The clinician might also assess a client's beliefs about the functions of worry, because some beliefs might perpetuate it (Borkovec et al., 1999). In assessing Obsessive-Compulsive Disorder, for a second example, the clinician might assess a client's belief in thought-action fusion, or belief that thinking about an unwanted event renders that event probable (Shafran, Thordarson, & Rachman, 1996). Obviously a strongly held belief in thought-action fusion might hinder assessment by inhibiting disclosure of obsessional thinking.

Ordinarily an initial diagnosis points to several treatment options. Considerations related to those options then guide further assessment. Results of that assessment guide the choice of treatment, some of the details of treatment, and further assessment as needed. The iterative flow between treatment planning and continuing assessment eventuates in a relatively detailed plan for beginning treatment and for monitoring the effects of treatment. For example, ADIS-structured and related interviewing might point to PDA. Ignoring diagnostic implications about comorbid conditions and the like, the diagnosis of PDA indicates that treatment might focus on panic attacks, agoraphobia, or both, depending on their adaptive salience. Further interviewing might, in turn, point to severe panic and mild agoraphobia, indicating that panic per se should be the focus of treatment, at least initially. Once panic is targeted for treatment, assessment might continue with $CO_2$ challenge or symptom induction exercises (Barlow & Craske, 2000) to identify likely somatic triggers for panic, and with administration of the Agoraphobic Cognitions Questionnaire (Chambless et al., 1984) to identify themes of panic-related cognition. When supplemented with further interviews, those assessments should provide information for the tailoring of interoceptive exposure protocols and cognitive restructuring. (At some point, self-monitoring would also be introduced to provide ongoing assessment of treatment effects.)

The case described in the next section illustrates how assessment guides the focus of treatment.

## CASE STUDY

An apparent fear of enclosed spaces (claustrophobia) is relatively common in the general population (Fredrikson, Annas, Fischer, & Wik, 1996). According to the current conceptualization, claustrophobia entails fear of being restricted and/or fear of suffocating (e.g., Rachman & Taylor, 1993). While claustrophobia is classified as a Specific Phobia, it has significant parallels with Panic Disorder (Craske, Zarate, Burton, & Barlow, 1993), and it sometimes shows overlap with the themes of Social Phobia. Claustrophobia thus subsumes several of the issues inherent in assessment of anxiety and fear. A case of claustrophobia is described here.

### IDENTIFICATION

The client, Lara, was a 26-year-old Caucasian female. She was a graduate student in English who attended a local university.

### PRESENTING COMPLAINTS

When asked why she was seeking services, Lara stated that since childhood she had fearfully avoided places such as elevators, airplanes, and subways. Now her classes were located on the upper floors of a main campus building, and her avoidance of elevators occurred at the expense of conversing with fellow students and professors who frequently rode together. She was concerned also about her habit of misrepresenting her reason for not riding the elevators. She sought treatment to overcome her fear of elevators.

## HISTORY

Lara indicated that, as a toddler, she frequently cried when she rode elevators. Her developing claustrophobia was compounded by her two brothers, who, on several occasions, wrapped a sheet around her and locked her in a closet. Ultimately, she began avoiding other places in which she was afraid she might become trapped. When Lara was in the fifth grade, her parents required that she ride in an elevator with them. Lara recalled the episode as very traumatic, stating that she "huddled in the corner and cried." Since that time, Lara had not ridden an elevator.

When she was in her early 20s, Lara's car stalled on the interstate late one night. She became terrified that a passerby might realize she was vulnerable and attempt to harm her; she crouched on the floor of the car until assistance arrived 3 hours later. Apparently, Lara experienced a panic attack at that time. She described the symptoms of shallow breathing, racing heartbeat, disorientation, and depersonalization. By and large, however, her "panic attacks" had been confined to claustrophobia-related situations in which she feared being unable to escape.

## PEER AND WORK ISSUES

Lara served as a graduate teaching assistant for undergraduate English classes and as a result interacted with many other graduate students and professors. Her refusal to ride elevators with them to and from class resulted in her feeling like an "outcast" among her colleagues and being reluctant to socialize with them in other contexts.

## FAMILY ISSUES

Lara's fiancé was aware of her fear of enclosed places but discounted her fear as insignificant or even humorous. As a result, he was not supportive as Lara sought treatment, and she engaged in out-of-session homework exercises without his support.

## BEHAVIORAL ASSESSMENT RESULTS

Assessment occurred over four meetings with Lara, all in an outpatient psychology clinic. The initial meeting consisted of an intake interview, mental status exam, and administration of the Beck Depression Inventory–II (BDI-II; Beck, 1996). Lara's responses to the initial intake interview highlighted her fear of enclosed places and of having a panic attack. They also made apparent the history of her difficulties as well as the accompanying work and family issues described earlier. Lara's score on the BDI-II was a 2, indicative of a minimal level of depressive symptomatology that did not warrant clinical attention. The ADIS-IV was administered during the second session. Her responses indicated that she met diagnostic criteria only for Specific Phobia, confirming that her anxiety and panic were attributable primarily to being in small, enclosed spaces.

During the last two assessment sessions, Lara was administered three questionnaires germane to her claustrophobic fear and engaged in two behavioral tests. The questionnaires administered were the Claustrophobia Questionnaire (CLQ; Radomsky, Rachman, Thordarson, McIsaac, & Teachman, 2001), the Agoraphobic Cognitions Questionnaire (ACQ; Chambless et al., 1984), and the Anxiety Sensitivity Index—Revised (ASI-R; S. Taylor & Cox, 1998).

The CLQ is commonly used to assess claustrophobic fear. It provides a total score as well as subscale scores for fear of restriction and fear of suffocation. Lara's score of 49 on the CLQ approximated the mean score of a group of claustrophobic students ($M = 51.8$) reported by Radomsky et al. (2001). Her subscale scores indicated that her claustrophobia related to fear of restriction and confinement, not to fear of suffocation.

Paniclike fear of somatic events has consistently been associated with claustrophobia (e.g., Craske & Sipsas, 1992). Therefore, the ACQ and ASI-R were administered to assess Lara's fear of panic-related bodily sensations. Her total score on the ACQ (2.14) was slightly below the mean of 2.32 reported for outpatients with agoraphobia (Chambless et al., 1984). As with her subscale scores on the CLQ (see earlier), her responses to the ASI-R suggested that a minimal portion of her anxious thinking was allocated to respiratory fears (e.g., suffocation, shortness of breath). There was some fear that others would notice her anxiety.

Two types of behavioral avoidance tests were used to assess Lara's fear of restriction. In the first, Lara was encouraged to enter one of the target elevators on campus and to remain inside for as long as possible. The therapist noted her behavior over several attempts and obtained SUDS ratings of situational fear. Lara was able to step into the elevator and to remain inside until the doors began closing. Her SUDS ratings ranged from 70 to 80 (out of 100). The second behavioral avoidance task involved exposure to a mock MRI device (Wood & McGlynn, 2000). A mock MRI device was chosen because it afforded precise quantification of fear behavior and was known to measure fear of restriction specifically (McGlynn, Karg, & Lawyer, 2003). Lara was given a controller that operated the device and asked to insert herself fully for as long as possible. She was able to insert herself head-first only 24 in. into the 90-in. tube and then immediately withdrew. She reported a fear rating of 50 on a 100-point scale. Her behavior confirmed the dominance of restriction fear in her claustrophobia.

## ETHICAL AND LEGAL ISSUES OR COMPLICATIONS

We were aware of no ethical or legal issues of note. Scheduling was complicated by the unexpected illness and hospitalization of Lara's mother. Lara demurred from discussing her mother's illness.

## CONCEPTUALIZATION AND TREATMENT
## RECOMMENDATIONS

Our working model of Lara's claustrophobia was relatively straightforward. Thinking about riding one of the clinically focal elevators occasioned catastrophic thinking about potential panic and about being unable to escape (restriction). The catastrophic thinking occasioned anticipatory fear, which, in turn, was followed by avoidance of the focal elevator. Avoidance of the elevator(s) was negatively reinforced by the termination of anticipatory fear and, unfortunately, functioned to forestall corrective exposure experiences. The problem had origins in the horseplay of Lara's brothers and in the panic experience beside the interstate highway.

For treatment we recommended (and used) an interesting variant of *in vivo* exposure. Ordinarily, exposure therapy is guided empirically; fearsome objects and events are identified as clinically focal, and clients are exposed to them for long durations so that fear subsides. In the case of Lara, exposure therapy was guided psychometrically; Lara was to be exposed initially to our mock MRI apparatus because mock MRI exposure involved extreme restriction. After learning to tolerate mock MRI exposure, she was to be exposed to elevator experiences of various durations, with various numbers of passengers, and so forth. Had fear of suffocation also been prominent, we would have recommended exposure to breath-holding exercises, masks, and the like before or along with elevator experiences.

## SUMMARY

Our concepts of fear- and anxiety-related disorders take the form of multielement models with biological, behavioral, and cognitive features. Our assessment of these disorders entails both behavioral and traditional methods. Treatment, in general, involves exposing clients to anxiety cues and helping clients learn to think differently about them.

Some of our major assessment strategies are based on clients' self-reports: interviews, questionnaires, self-monitoring, and situational ratings. Other important assessment strategies involve samples of behavior: behavioral avoidance tests, interpersonal performance tests, biological challenge tests, and symptom induction exercises. (Psychophysiological assessment is not used routinely and was omitted here.)

Many of our assessment methods enjoy substantial research support; this is especially true of questionnaires. Semistructured interviewing and questionnaires provide information that is integral to initial diagnosis and preliminary treatment planning. Continued interviewing and behavior-based assessment guide the choice of treatment and shape its details. A case of claustrophobia illustrates one way in which assessment results can guide treatment.

# REFERENCES

American Psychiatric Association. (1952). *Diagnostic and statistical manual of mental disorders* (1st ed.). Washington, DC. Author.

American Psychiatric Association. (1980). *Diagnostic and statistical manual of mental disorders* (3rd ed.). Washington, DC. Author.

American Psychiatric Association. (1987). *Diagnostic and statistical manual of mental disorders* (3rd ed., rev.). Washington, DC. Author.

American Psychiatric Association. (1994). *Diagnostic and statistical manual of mental disorders* (4th ed.). Washington, DC. Author.

Antony, M. M., & Barlow, D. H. (Eds.). (2002). *Handbook of assessment and treatment planning for psychological disorders.* New York: Guilford Press.

Antony, M. M., Orsillo, S. M., & Roemer, L. (2001). *Practitioner's guide to empirically based measures of anxiety.* New York: Kluwer/Plenum Press.

Antony, M. M., & Swinson, R. P. (2000). *Phobic disorders and panic in adults: A guide to assessment and treatment.* Washington, DC: American Psychological Association.

Bandura, A. (1976). Effecting change through participant modeling. In J. D. Krumboltz & C. E. Thoresen (Eds.), *Counseling methods* (pp. 248–265). New York: Holt, Rinehart, & Winston.

Barlow, D. H. (1987). The classification of anxiety disorders. In G. L. Tischler (Ed.), *Diagnosis and classification in psychiatry: A critical appraisal of the DSM-III* (pp. 223–242). Cambridge, MA: Cambridge University Press.

Barlow, D. H. (1988). *Anxiety and its disorders: The nature and treatment of anxiety and panic* (1st ed.). New York: Guilford Press.

Barlow, D. H. (2002). *Anxiety and its disorders: The nature and treatment of anxiety and panic* (2nd ed.). New York: Guilford Press.

Barlow, D. H., & Craske, M. G. (2000). *Mastery of your anxiety and panic (MAP-3).* San Antonio, TX: Psychological Corporation/Graywind.

Barrios, B. A. (1983). The role of cognitive mediators in heterosocial anxiety: A test of self-efficacy theory. *Cognitive Therapy and Research, 7,* 543–554.

Beck, A. T. (1996). *Beck Depression Inventory* (2nd ed.). San Antonio, TX: Psychological Corporation.

Bernstein, D. A. (1973). Situational factors in behavioral fear assessment: A progress report. *Behavior Therapy, 4,* 41–48.

Borkovec, T. D., Hazlett-Stevens, H., & Diaz, M. L. (1999). The role of positive beliefs about worry in Generalized Anxiety Disorder and its treatment. *Clinical Psychology and Psychotherapy, 6,* 126–138.

Borkovec, T. D., & Roemer, L. (1995). Perceived functions of worry among Generalized Anxiety Disorder subjects: Distraction from more emotionally stressing topics? *Journal of Behavior Therapy and Experimental Psychiatry, 26,* 25–30.

Borkovec, T. D., Stone, N. M., O'Brien, G. T., & Kaloupek, D. G. (1974). Evaluation of a clinically relevant target behavior for analogue outcome research. *Behavior Therapy, 5,* 504–514.

Bradley, M. M., & Lang, P. J. (1994). Measuring emotion: The self-assessment manikin and the semantic differential. *Journal of Behavior Therapy and Experimental Psychiatry, 25,* 49–59.

Brown, T. A., Di Nardo, P. A., & Barlow, D. H. (1994). *Anxiety Disorders Interview Schedule for DSM-IV (ADIS-IV).* Albany, NY: Graywind.

Carr, A. T. (1979). The psychopathology of fear. In W. Sluckin (Ed.), *Fear in animals and man* (pp. 199–235). New York: Van Nostrand Rheinhold.

Chambless, D. L., Caputo, G. C., Bright, P., & Gallagher, R. (1984). Assessment of fear in agoraphobics: The Body Sensations Questionnaire and the Agoraphobic Cognitions Questionnaire. *Journal of Consulting and Clinical Psychology, 52,* 1090–1097.

Clark, D. M. (1986). A cognitive approach to panic. *Behaviour Research and Therapy, 24,* 461–470.

Collins, F. L., & Thompson, K. J. (1993). The integration of empirically derived personality assessment data into a behavioral conceptualization and treatment plan: Rationale, guidelines, and caveats. *Behavior Modification, 17,* 58–71.

Craske, M. G. (1991). Phobic fear and panic attacks: The same emotional states triggered by different cues? *Clinical Psychology Review, 11,* 599–620.

Craske, M. G., Barlow, D. H., & Meadows, E. A. (2000). *Mastery of your anxiety and panic: Therapist guide for anxiety, panic, and agoraphobia (MAP-3).* San Antonio, TX: Psychological Corporation/Graywind.

Craske, M. G., & Sipsas, A. (1992). Animal phobias versus claustrophobias: Exteroceptive versus interoceptive cues. *Behaviour Research and Therapy, 30,* 569–581.

Craske, M. G., Zarate, R., Burton, T., & Barlow, D. H. (1993). Specific fears and panic attacks: A survey of clinical and nonclinical samples. *Journal of Anxiety Disorders, 7,* 1–19.

Delprato, D. J., & McGlynn, F. D. (1984). Behavioral theories of anxiety disorders. In S. M. Turner (Ed.), *Behavioral theories and treatment of anxiety* (pp. 1–49). New York: Plenum Press.

Di Nardo, P. A., & Barlow, D. H. (1988). *Anxiety Disorders Interview Schedule—Revised (ADIS-R).* Albany, NY: Phobia and Anxiety Disorders Clinic.

Di Nardo, P. A., Brown, T. A., & Barlow, D. H. (1994). *Anxiety Disorders Interview Schedule for DSM-IV: Lifetime Version (ADIS-IV-L).* San Antonio, TX: Psychological Corporation/Graywind.

Ehlers, A. (1993). Interoception and panic disorder. *Advances in Behavior Research and Therapy, 15,* 3–21.

Ehlers, A., & Margraf, J. (1989). The psychophysiological model of panic attacks. In P. M. G. Emmelkamp, W. T. A. M. Everaerd, F. W. Kraaimaat, & M. J. M. van Son (Eds.), *Fresh perspectives on anxiety disorders* (pp. 1–30). Amsterdam: Swets & Zeitlinger.

Ellis, A. (1962). *Reason and emotion in psychotherapy.* New York: Lyle Stuart.

Eysenck, H. J. (Ed.). (1960). *Behaviour therapy and the neuroses.* Oxford, UK: Pergamon Press.

Eysenck, H. J. (1976). The learning theory model of neurosis—A new approach. *Behaviour Research and Therapy, 14,* 251–267.

Forsyth, J. P., & Karekla, M. (2001). Biological challenge in the assessment of anxiety disorders. In M. M. Antony, S. M. Orsillo, & L. Roemer (Eds.), *Practitioner's guide to empirically based measures of anxiety* (pp. 31–36). New York: Kluwer/Plenum Press.

Fredrikson, M., Annas, P., Fischer, H., & Wik, G. (1996). Gender and age differences in the prevalence of specific fears and phobias. *Behaviour Research and Therapy, 34,* 33–39.

Freedman, R. R., Ianni, P., Ettedgui, E., & Puthezhath, N. (1985). Ambulatory monitoring of panic disorder. *Archives of General Psychiatry, 42,* 244–250.

Goodman, W. K., Price, L. H., Rasmussen, S. A., Mazure, C., Fleischman, R. L., Hill, C. L., et al. (1989). The Yale–Brown Obsessive Compulsive Scale: I. Development, use, and reliability. *Archives of General Psychiatry, 46,* 1006–1011.

Haemmerlie, F. M. (1983). Heterosocial anxiety in college females. A biased interactions treatment. *Behavior Modification, 7,* 611–623.

Hallam, R. S. (1978). Agoraphobia: A critical review of the concept. *British Journal of Psychiatry, 133,* 314–319.

Haynes, S. N., & Uchigakiuchi, P. (1993). Incorporating personality trait measures in behavioral assessment: Nuts in a fruitcake or raisins in a mai tai? *Behavior Modification, 17,* 72–92.

Hofmann, S. G., & Barlow, D. H. (1996). Ambulatory psychophysiological monitoring: A potentially useful tool when treating panic relapse. *Cognitive and Behavioral Practice, 3,* 53–61.

Kozak, M. J., & Foa, E. B. (1997). *Mastery of Obsessive-Compulsive Disorder: A cognitive approach.* San Antonio, TX: Psychological Corporation/Graywind.

Lang, P. J. (1968). Fear reduction and fear behavior: Problems in treating a construct. In J. M. Shlien (Ed.), *Research in psychotherapy: Vol. 3* (pp. 90–102). Washington, DC: American Psychological Association.

Lang, P. J. (1980). Behavioral treatment and biobehavioral assessment: Computer applications. In J. B. Sidowski, J. H. Johnson, & T. A. Williams (Eds.), *Technology and mental health care delivery systems* (pp. 119–137). Norwood, NJ: Ablex.

Lang, P. J., & Lazovik, A. D. (1963). Experimental desensitization of a phobia. *Journal of Abnormal and Social Psychology, 66,* 519–525.

Lawyer, S. R., & Smitherman, T. A. (2004). Trends in anxiety assessment. *Journal of Psychopathology and Behavioral Assessment, 26,* 101–106.

Malleson, N. (1959). Panic and phobia. *Lancet, 1,* 225–227.

Marks, I. M. (1973). The reduction of fear: Towards a unifying theory. *Canadian Psychiatry Association, 18,* 9–12.

Marks, I. M. (1975). Behavioral treatments of phobic and obsessive-compulsive disorders: A critical appraisal. In M. Hersen, R. M. Eisler, & P. M. Miller (Eds.), *Progress in behavior modification: Vol 1.* (pp. 66–143). New York: McGraw-Hill.

Marks, I. M. (1978). *Living with fear.* New York: McGraw-Hill.

Martzke, J. S., Andersen, B. L., & Cacioppo, J. T. (1987). Cognitive assessment of anxiety disorders. In L. Michelson & L. Ascher (Eds.), *Anxiety and stress disorders: Cognitive-behavioral assessment and treatment* (pp. 62–88). New York: Guilford Press.

Mathews, A. M., Gelder, M. G., & Johnston, D. W. (1981). *Agoraphobia: Nature and treatment.* New York: Guilford Press.

Mathews, A., & MacLeod, C. (1985). Selective processing of threat cues in anxiety states. *Behaviour Research and Therapy, 23,* 563–569.

McGlynn, F. D., Karg, R., & Lawyer, S. R. (2003). Fear responses to mock magnetic resonance imaging among college students: Toward a prototype experiment. *Journal of Anxiety Disorders, 17,* 335–347.

McGlynn, F. D., & Rose, M. P. (1998). Assessment of anxiety and fear. In A. S. Bellack & M. Hersen (Eds.), *Behavioral assessment: A practical handbook* (4th ed., pp. 179–209). Needham Heights, MA: Allyn & Bacon.

McGlynn, F. D., Rose, M. P., & Lazarte, A. (1994). Control and attention during exposure influence arousal and fear among insect phobics. *Behavior Modification, 18,* 371–388.

McNally, R. J. (1994). *Panic Disorder: A critical analysis.* New York: Guilford Press.

McNally, R. J., Foa, E. B., & O'Donnell, C. D. (1989). Memory bias for anxiety information in patients with Panic Disorder. *Cognition and Emotion, 3,* 27–44.

Mehrabian, A., & Russell, J. A. (1974). *An approach to environmental psychology.* Cambridge, MA: MIT Press.

Meichenbaum, D. H. (1974). *Cognitive behavior modification.* Morristown, NJ: General Learning Press.

Meyer, T. J., Miller, M. L., Metzger, R. L., & Borkovec, T. D. (1990). Development and validation of the Penn State Worry Questionnaire. *Behaviour Research and Therapy, 28,* 487–495.

Molina, S., & Borkovec, T. D. (1994). The Penn State Worry Questionnaire: Psychometric properties and associated characteristics. In G. C. L. Davey & F. Tallis (Eds.), *Worrying: Perspectives on theory, assessment, and treatment* (pp. 265–283). New York: John Wiley & Sons.

Nelson, R. O. (1977). Methodological issues in assessment via self-monitoring. In J. D. Cone & R. P. Hawkins (Eds.), *Behavioral assessment: New directions in clinical psychology* (pp. 217–240). New York: Brunner/Mazel.

Nietzel, M. T., Bernstein, D. A., & Russell, R. L. (1988). Assessment of anxiety and fear. In A. S. Bellack & M. Hersen (Eds.), *Behavioral assessment: A practical handbook* (3rd ed., pp. 280–312). New York: Pergamon Press.

Papillo, J. F., Murphy, P. M., & Gorman, J. M. (1988). Psychophysiology. In C. G. Last & M. Hersen (Eds.), *Handbook of anxiety disorders* (pp. 217–250). New York: Pergamon Press.

Paul, G. L. (1966). *Insight vs. desensitization: An experiment in anxiety reduction.* Stanford, CA: Stanford University Press.

Rachman, S. (1976). The passing of the two-stage theory of fear and avoidance: Fresh possibilities. *Behaviour Research and Therapy, 14,* 125–131.

Rachman, S., & Hodgson, R. S. (1974). Synchrony and desynchrony in fear and avoidance. *Behaviour Research and Therapy, 12,* 311–318.

Rachman, S., & Taylor, S. (1993). Analyses of claustrophobia. *Journal of Anxiety Disorders, 7,* 281–291.

Radomsky, A. S., Rachman, S., Thordarson, D. S., McIsaac, H. K., & Teachman, B. A. (2001). The Claustrophobia Questionnaire. *Journal of Anxiety Disorders, 15,* 287–297.

Rapee, R. (1987). The psychological treatment of panic attacks: Theoretical conceptualization and review of evidence. *Clinical Psychology Review, 7,* 427–438.

Rapee, R. M., Brown, T. A., Antony, M. M., & Barlow, D. H. (1992). Response to hyperventilation and inhalation of 5.5% carbon dioxide–enriched air across the *DSM-III-R* anxiety disorders. *Journal of Abnormal Psychology, 101,* 538–552.

Reiss, S. (1980). Pavlovian conditioning in human fear: An expectancy model. *Behavior Therapy, 11,* 380–396.

Reiss, S., Peterson, R. A., Gursky, D. M., & McNally, R. J. (1986). Anxiety sensitivity, anxiety frequency, and the prediction of fearfulness. *Behaviour Research and Therapy, 24,* 1–8.

Sanderson, W. C., & Wetzler, S. (1990). Five percent carbon dioxide challenge: Valid analogue and marker of panic disorder? *Biological Psychiatry, 27,* 689–701.

Seligman, M. E. P. (1971). Phobias and preparedness. *Behavior Therapy, 2,* 307–320.

Shafran, R., Thordarson, D., & Rachman, S. (1996). Thought action fusion in Obsessive-Compulsive Disorder. *Journal of Anxiety Disorders, 5,* 379–391.

Spielberger, C. D., Gorsuch, R. L., & Lushene, R. E. (1970). *Manual for the State–Trait Anxiety Inventory.* Palo Alto, CA: Consulting Psychologists Press.

Spitzer, R. L., Williams, J. B. W., Gibbon, M., & First, M. B. (1994). *Structured Clinical Interview for DSM-IV (SCID-IV).* New York: Biometric Research Department, New York State Psychiatric Institute.

Taylor, C. B., Fried, L., & Kenardy, J. (1990). The use of a real-time computer diary for data acquisition and processing. *Behaviour Research and Therapy, 28,* 93–97.

Taylor, C. B., Sheikh, J., Agras, W. S., Roth, W. T., Margraf, J., Ehlers, A., et al. (1986). Self-report of panic attacks: Agreement with heart rate changes. *American Journal of Psychiatry, 143,* 478–482.

Taylor, S. (Ed.). (1999). *Anxiety sensitivity: Theory, research, and treatment of the fear of anxiety.* Mahwah, NJ: Erlbaum.

Taylor, S., & Cox, B. J. (1998). An expanded Anxiety Sensitivity Index: Evidence for a hierarchic structure in a clinical sample. *Journal of Anxiety Disorders, 12,* 463–483.

Turner, S. M., Beidel, D. C., Dancu, C. V., & Stanley, M. A. (1989). An empirically derived inventory to measure social fears and anxiety: The Social Phobia and Anxiety Inventory. *Psychological Assessment, 1,* 35–40.

Wolpe, J. (1958). *Psychotherapy by reciprocal inhibition.* Stanford, CA: Stanford University Press.

Wolpe, J. (1973). *The practice of behavior therapy* (2nd ed.). New York: Pergamon Press.

Wood, B. S., & McGlynn, F. D. (2000). Research on posttreatment return of claustrophobic fear, arousal, and avoidance using mock diagnostic imaging. *Behavior Modification, 24,* 379–394.

Zinbarg, R. E., Craske, M. G., & Barlow, D. H. (1992). *Mastery of your anxiety and panic: Therapist guide.* San Antonio, TX: Psychological Corporation/Graywind.

# 10

## DEPRESSION

PAULA TRUAX
AARON TRITCH
BARB CARVER

*Counseling Psychology Program*
*Pacific University*
*Portland, Oregon*

### INTRODUCTION

Depression is one of the most frequently experienced and diagnosed mental disorders in the United Stated today. It is estimated that as many as 12–25% of the population will experience a significant depression within their lifetime, and at any given time up to 5% of men and 9% of women have an active Major Depressive Disorder (MDD; American Psychiatric Association, 2000). Because disorders within this spectrum are composed of a number of emotional, cognitive, behavioral, and physical symptoms, thorough assessment and monitoring are necessary to adequately treat such unique constellations of symptoms. Behavioral assessment approaches incorporate a variety of procedures to collect and review information for the purposes of conceptualization, diagnosis, treatment planning, and monitoring of treatment progress.

The primary goal of this chapter is to introduce concepts and techniques common to the behavioral assessment of depression. Of great importance are assessment strategies that incorporate the use of diagnostic interviewing and standardized measures of depression. In order for mental health practitioners to successfully implement these approaches, a firm understanding is needed of the various instruments available, their research bases, and their practical utility. Moreover, it is important to recognize the direct application of these assessment tools to conceptualization and treatment planning for individual clients. What follows is a description of interview strategies and standardized self-report instruments for use in the behavioral assessment of depression. These approaches are incorporated into a general discussion of behavioral case conceptualization and treatment planning and are then further illustrated through use of a clinical case study.

## ASSESSMENT STRATEGIES

### INTERVIEW METHODS

An interview is an essential part of a multimethod, multidimensional assessment of depression. Diagnostic interviews can produce a wide variety of information, depending on their structure and format. Three common interview formats for depression will be reviewed: unstructured, semistructured, and structured formats.

### Unstructured Clinical Interview

An unstructured clinical interview has a flexible format in which clinicians ask a variety of open-ended questions. This approach allows the client to respond in his/her own words and to collaborate in clarifying the answers as needed. However, the information gathered might be more difficult to categorize and possibly less accurate than a more structured assessment. Truax (2002a) indicated that in order to increase the reliability of unstructured interviews, the clinician must have knowledge about depressive diagnostic categories and differential diagnoses. In addition, the clinician must be able to apply the knowledge through inquiring specifically about each depressive symptom, time frame, and severity while also inquiring about the main symptoms of other possible diagnoses. Differential diagnosis can be difficult, especially between depression diagnoses. Here, developing a timeline of the mood episodes can be helpful in differentiating diagnoses such as recurrent MDD without interepisode recovery from MDD in partial remission superimposed on Dysthymic Disorder.

### Semistructured Interviews

Semistructured interviews are another option for assessing depression. Semistructured and unstructured interviews are similar, in that both use open-ended questions and allow for clarifying questions; however, a semistructured interview is guided by a predetermined set of probes that are asked verbatim. The Structured Clinical Interview for the *DSM-IV* (SCID-CV; First, Spitzer, Gibbons, & Williams, 1996), the Schedule for Affective Disorders and Schizophrenia (SADS; Endicott & Spitzer, 1978), the Inventory of Depressive Symptomology: Clinician Rated (IDS-C; Rush, Gullion, Basco, Jarrett, & Trivedi, 1996), the Manual for the Diagnosis of Major Depression (MDMD; Huyser, De Jonghe, Jinkers, & Schalken, 1996), and the Hamilton Rating Scale for Depression (HRSD; Hamilton, 1960) are commonly used semistructured interviews for the diagnostic assessment of depression.

### Structured Clinical Interview for the DSM-IV—Clinician Version

The SCID-CV is a semistructured interview that focuses on *Diagnostic and Statistical Manual of Mental Disorders* (*DSM-IV*) diagnoses rather than symptom severity (Rogers, 2001). The SCID-CV covers a breadth of Axis I disorders commonly seen in clinical practice and was designed to aid clinicians in differential diagnosis (Nezu, Ronan, Meadows, & McClure, 2000). The SCID-CV begins with an unstructured overview section that includes current problem, symptoms, and treatment history. The SCID-CV is organized into six modules (Mood Episodes, Psychotic Symptoms, Psychotic Disorders, Mood Disorders, Substance Use Disorders, and Anxiety/Other Disorders; First et al., 1996) and is administered in a sequential manner, beginning with the most current behavior and moving toward lifetime occurrence. This hierarchical design is useful because it creates a framework that allows the clinician systematically to go through each *DSM-IV* criterion and create a specific and clear diagnostic distinction between disorders. The modules may be used independently or together; thus, clinicians may focus solely on depression (unipolar or bipolar) if it is clear that is the presenting concern.

### Schedule for Affective Disorders and Schizophrenia

The SADS (Endicott & Spitzer, 1978) is semistructured interview that focuses primarily on mood and psychotic disorders, with a lesser emphasis on anxiety and substance use disorders. The SADS was developed to assess 23 psychiatric disorders as specified by the Research Diagnostic Criteria (RDC; Spitzer, Endicott, & Robins, 1975, 1978), with subcategories for schizophrenia, Schizoaffective Disorder, and MDD. The SADS is divided into two sections: (1) the current severity of psychopathology within the past week and (2) the intensity, frequency, and duration of previous episodes of psychopathology. The SADS also includes the Global Assessment Scale (GAS), which provides an overall 1-to-100 rating of the client's level of current functioning. Additionally, the SADS has been updated to incorporate the *DSM-IV* criteria (Fryer, Endicott, Mannuzza, & Klein, 1995).

### Inventory of Depressive Symptomology: Clinician Rated

The IDS-C is a semistructured interview designed to measure overall depressive symptom severity and symptom change (Rush et al., 1996). It can be used in inpatient or outpatient populations and discriminates between depressed and euthymic states while also being sensitive to symptom change (Nezu et al., 2000). The IDS-C consists of 30 items that measure ascending levels of frequency, duration, intensity, and severity of depressive symptoms. It uses a three-factor model (cognitive/mood, anxiety/arousal, and sleep regulation) assessed with scripted questions about the preceding 7 days. Each item represents a depressive symptom, such as sadness, rated on a 4-point scale (Rush et al.).

### Hamilton Rating Scale for Depression

The HRSD is a 21-item clinician-rated assessment followed by an in-depth clinical interview. Each MDD symptom is rated for severity over the past few days or the past week. There are no specific probes, and clinicians are advised to keep direct questions to a minimum (Hamilton, 1960).

### Manual for the Diagnosis of Major Depression

The MDMD is a semistructured interview based on the diagnostic criteria of the *DSM-III-R* (American Psychiatric Association, 1993) for MDD and its subtypes, excluding the subtype of "with psychotic features." It also assesses the severity of depressive symptoms "during the worst period of the current episode." The interview results in categorical information about the presence or absence of MDD as well as its possible subcategories (Rush et al., 1996).

## Structured Clinical Interviews

Structured clinical interviews have a predetermined set of standardized questions, with optional probes, that are all asked verbatim. They also have a more rigorous standardization process and therefore tend to greater interrater reliability than semistructured or unstructured interviews. Due to the rigidity of structured interviews, however, answers cannot be clarified with additional unscripted questions; therefore, some valuable information might be missed. Structured interviews are useful because they can be administered by a wide variety of people with various skill levels. One of the most commonly used structured interviews for MDD is the Diagnostic Interview Schedule (DIS; Robins, Helzer, Croughan, & Ratcliff, 1981).

### Diagnostic Interview Schedule

The DIS is a commonly used structured interview for current and lifetime diagnoses of mental disorders, including depression and other mood disorders. It was originally developed for the NIMH's Epidemiological Catchment Area Program, where a fully structured format was necessary because it was being administered by nonprofessionals (Reiger et al., 1984). The DIS used the *DSM-III* (American Psychiatric Association, 1980), the Research Diagnostic Criteria (RDC; Spitzer et al., 1978), and the Feighner criteria (Feighner et al., 1972). Updated versions were published in 1995 (DIS-IV; Robins, Cotter, Bucholz, & Compton, 1995) and again in 2001, making it compatible with the *DSM-IV* (Rogers, 2001). Except for a few introductory questions, all questions in the DIS are closed-ended and asked verbatim. The interviewee replies using a forced-choice format, and the responses are coded as a yes or a no. Most of the sections begin with screening questions that permit skipping sections in which there is no evidence of symptoms. However, due to the rigid structure of the interview, sections should not be omitted.

## SELF-REPORT METHODS

Self-report methods may be used to augment the clinical interview or to screen for depression. These instruments may target depression directly or assess secondary symptoms, such as hopelessness (Beck & Steer, 1988), suicidality (Reynolds, 1991), beliefs (Kendall, Howard, & Hays, 1989), and behaviors (MacPhillamy & Lewinsohn, 1982). Traditionally, self-report measures have been used to monitor the severity of a depressive episode for those already diagnosed with a depressive disorder; however, they may also be employed as case-finding instruments to screen for the presence or absence of MDD (Montano, 1994). Self-report instruments are completed by the client and consist of a number of questions that require a forced choice (e.g., Likert scale, true/false, multiple choice), as opposed to open-ended questions. Three of the most common self-report measures are the Beck Depression Inventory—II (BDI-II; Beck, Steer, & Brown, 1996), a self-report version of the HRSD entitled the Hamilton Depression Inventory (HDI; Reynolds & Kobak, 1995a); the Centers for Epidemiological Studies Depression Scale (CES-D; Radloff, 1977), and the Patient Health Questionnaire—9 (PHQ-9; Spitzer, Kroenke, & Williams, 1999).

### Beck Depression Inventory—2nd Edition

The BDI-II is a commonly used 21-item self-report paper-and-pencil measure of depressive severity scored on a 4-point, 0–3 scale, with total scores ranging from 0 to 63. Participants are instructed to rate each depressive symptom by circling the statement that is most descriptive of their experiences over the past two weeks. The BDI-II was constructed to reflect the diagnostic criteria for MDD as described in the *DSM-IV*. Completion of the BDI-II typically takes 5–10 minutes, and it can be scored easily by clinicians or clinical staff (Beck et al., 1996). Scores are derived and interpreted by totaling all of the endorsed statements and comparing the total to severity cutoff scores based on the standardization sample provided in the manual (Beck et al.). The following severity levels were derived to achieve a balance between sensitivity and specificity in classifying adults diagnosed as depressed with the SCID: 0–13 = minimal; 14–19 = mild; 20–28 = moderate; 29–63 = severe.

### Hamilton Depression Inventory

The HDI is a 23-item paper-and-pencil self-report measure of depressive severity created to evaluate multiple elements of individual depressive symptoms in an attempt to reflect the process of a clinical interview (Reynolds and Kobak, 1995b). Consistent with *DSM-IV* criteria, questions on the HDI were designed to assess the severity of depressive symptoms over a two-week period. Each of the 23 items were derived from the original HRSD, which is delivered as a clinical interview and may contain two to four "probes" or questions, for a total of 38 probes. These probes act as follow-up questions for items already endorsed. Items on the instrument vary, with score ranges of 0–2 and 0–4. This measure was designed for individuals age 18 and older and takes approximately 10 minutes to complete (Reynolds & Kobak, 1995b). A 17-item, 31-probe version and a 9-item, 15-probe version are also available. The HDI is considered a continuous measure of depression, with higher scores indicating greater depressive severity; however, when used as a case-finding instrument, a cutoff score of 19 is recommended (Reynolds & Kobak, 1995b).

## Center for Epidemiological Studies—Depression Scale

The CES-D is a 20-item paper-and-pencil self-report measure initially created for epidemiology research on depression to identify the presence or absence of a likely depressive disorder (Radloff, 1977). This instrument may be used to evaluate severity or as a case-finding instrument. The CES-D focuses heavily on the affective symptoms of depression during the preceding week and was designed for ease of administration, with items rated on a 0–3 scale [i.e., 0 = "Rarely or none of the time (less than 1 day)," 1 = "Some or little of the time (1–2 days)," 2 = "Occasionally or a moderate amount of time (3–4 days)," and 3 = "Most or all of the time (5–7 days)"] and a range of total scores from 0 to 60. Items vary from "I thought my life had been a failure" to "I had crying spells," and four of the items are reverse-scored. For use as a case-finding instrument, an original cutoff score of 16 was proposed by Radloff, which, despite its high sensitivity, has been criticized for low specificity (Santor, Zuroff, Ramsay, Cervantes, & Palacios, 1995). A cutoff score of 27 has been proposed by Schulberg and colleagues (1985) and supported by Zich, Attkisson, and Greenfield (1990) to provide the best balance of sensitivity and specificity in the identification of cases of depression in medical patients.

## Patient Health Questionnaire—9

The PHQ-9 is the nine-item depression submeasure of the Patient Health Questionnaire, a self-report version of the Primary Care Evaluation of Mental Disorders (Kroenke & Spitzer, 2002; Kroenke, Spitzer, & Williams, 2001; Spitzer et al., 1999; Whooley, Avins, Miranda, & Browner, 1997). This self-report instrument can be used for either monitoring depressive severity or as a case-finding instrument for detecting depression. Items on the measure were selected to represent the diagnostic criteria for MDD as described in the *DSM-IV* and are ranked on a 0–3 scale (i.e., 0 = "not at all," 1 = "several days," 2 = "more than half the days," and 3 = "nearly everyday") for the previous two weeks, with a possible total range of 0–27. The level of depressive severity is determined by totaling all of the items and comparing this to scores of none (0–4), mild (5–9), moderate (10–14), moderately severe (15–19), and severe (20–27). For use as a case-finding instrument, individuals who endorse either depressed mood or anhedonia and five other items at "more than half the days," are considered likely to be clinically depressed (Kroenke et al., 2001). For screening purposes, Kroenke and Spitzer (2002) recommend a score of 10, for it provides the best balance of sensitivity and specificity in detecting depression.

## Self-Report Measures Associated with Depression

In addition to assessing the severity of depression, measures of secondary depression features such as hopelessness, suicidality, beliefs, and behaviors may facilitate case conceptualization, treatment planning, and mode-specific outcome assessment. Examples of such instruments include: the Beck Hopelessness Scale (BHS; Beck & Steer, 1988), a 20-item true/false self-report measure to investigate negative attitudes regarding the future; and the Suicide Probability Scale (SPS; Cull & Gill, 1988), a 36-item measure designed to monitor and predict suicidal behavior. Although these measures do not replace a thorough and methodical clinical interview, they can be helpful in case conceptualization as well as the monitoring of specific symptoms and related constructs. Other self-report measures may focus on associated theory-specific features of depression, such as the Automatic Thought Questionnaire—Revised (ATQ-R; Kendall et al., 1989), the Cognitive Triad Inventory (CTI; Beckham, Leber, Watkins, Boyer, & Cook, 1986), and the Pleasant Events Schedule (PES; MacPhillamy & Lewinsohn, 1982). These instruments focus on specific features of cognitive and behavioral conceptualizations of depression.

## RESEARCH BASIS

All of the depression interview and self-report instruments presented earlier have been evaluated for reliability and validity; each has advantages and disadvantages.

## INTERVIEW METHODS

For interviews, one of the most important psychometric issues is interrater reliability. Interrater reliability varies across different types of interviews. The interrater reliability of an unstructured clinical interview, for example, tends to be low; however, reliability is higher for semistructured and structured interviews. Overall, all of the semistructured interviews noted earlier have moderate-to-high interrater reliability and good validity, with each of the interviews having specific strengths (Nezu et al., 2000). The SCID has good-to-excellent interrater reliability for identifying depressive symptoms and the presence/absence of a current episode; however, it is less reliable for symptom severity. Another strength of the SCID is that it maintains its high level of reliability for depression diagnosis across diverse cultures and translations (Rogers, 2001). The SADS, HRSD, and IDS-C are more sensitive to symptom change and severity than the SCID, and they have high interrater reliability, good internal consistency, and good validity (Nezu et al.). The SADS has the greatest interrater reliability for presence vs. absence of current episodes; however, it takes longer to administer than the HRSD or the IDS-C (Nezu et al.; Rogers). Structured interviews tend to have the highest interrater reliability. The DIS has excellent interrater reliability (.95) and similar levels of reliability between the English and Spanish versions (Rogers; Nezu et al.).

Diagnostic interview validity is somewhat more difficult to assess than interrater reliability because there is no clear "gold standard" for depression diagnosis. Further, when gold standards are identified, they are often the very interviews being reviewed here; thus, the process becomes tautological. One alternative diagnostic validity method is a comparison between expert clinician or consensus diagnoses and more structured interview diagnoses. Although, a number of validity studies have found lower levels of agreement between structured interviews and expert clinicians than interrater reliability (Fennig, Craig, Tanenberg-Karant, & Bromet, 1994; Steiner, Tebes, Sledge, & Walker, 1995), other research has found very good convergent validity (85.7% agreement) between the SCID-CV and the consensus diagnoses of expert clinicians (Miller, Dasher, Collins, Griffiths, & Brown, 2001). Further, for MDD specifically, graduate student–administered DIS interviews demonstrated good convergent validity (intraclass correlation of .85, $p < .001$) with the less structured, expert-administered HRSD interviews (Whisman et al., 1989). Taken together, these psychometric findings suggest that semistructured and structured interviews have adequate interrater reliability and convergent validity with experts. Thus, these interviews may provide more standardized and reliable assessments of depression than the more commonly used unstructured clinical interview.

## SELF-REPORT METHODS

Numerous studies have investigated the psychometric quality of the various self-reports for depression. In general, all four of the previously described measures of depression demonstrate strong internal consistency. Similar alpha coefficients have been observed for the BDI-II and HDI ($\alpha = .93$ and $\alpha = .94$, respectively; Beck et al., 1996; Reynolds & Kobak, 1995a). Although slightly lower, strong alpha coefficients were also noted for the PHQ-9 and CES-D ($\alpha = .89$ and $\alpha = .90$, respectively; Kroenke et al., 2001; Radloff, 1977). Of the four, the BDI-II ($r = .93$) and HDI ($r = .96$) demonstrated superior test–retest reliabilities after a one-week delay (Beck et al.; Reynolds and Kobak, respectively). Thus, whereas all reviewed measures were internally consistent, the BDI-II and HDI appear the most stable over time.

Validity assessment provides an estimate of a measure's accuracy and includes concepts such as *convergent validity* (extent to which the target measure correlates with another measure of the same contruct), *divergent* or *discriminant validity* (the extent to which the target measure differentially correlates with discrepant constructs), and *criterion validity* (the extent to which an instrument predicts crossing a criterion, such as presence of MDD). First, convergent validity for the BDI-II, HDI, and CES-D with the HRSD has been found to be significant for all of these measures, with the HDI showing the strongest association ($r = .94$;

Reynolds & Kobak, 1995a) and the CES-D the weakest ($r = .44$; Radloff, 1977). Amongst the self-report measures, the BDI-II and the HDI have demonstrated a high degree of agreement, with correlations ranging from .84 to .93 (Dozois, 2003; Reynolds & Kobak). Further, it has been reported that the CES-D and PHQ-9 are highly positively related to measures of overall distress, such as the Symptom Checklist—90 (SCL-90; Derogatis, 1977, 1994) and the Symptom Checklist—20 (SCL-20; Katon et al., 1996). Second, for divergent or discriminant validity, one of the most important issues for depression assessment is differentiating between depression and anxiety severity. While all measures reviewed demonstrate some ability to discriminate between depression and anxiety, the correlations are often statistically significant for both constructs, and the differences between the correlations are often not substantial. For example, when compared to SCL-90 subscales, the BDI-II correlates significantly with the depression subscale ($r = .89$, $p < .001$) and the anxiety subscale ($r = .71$, $p < .001$; Steer, Ball, Ranieri, & Beck, 1997). Similarly, in a study of nonclinical undergraduate students, the HDI demonstrated significant correlations ($p < .001$) with depression measures (.82–.84) and with the Beck Anxiety Inventory (.76; BAI; Beck & Steer, 1993). Finally, *criterion validity*, or the extent to which a measure predicts the presence or absence of MDD, is typically determined by establishing a self-report cutoff score that maximizes sensitivity and specificity as compared to a "gold-standard" interview such as the SCID. Most measures reviewed demonstrated good sensitivity and specificity in outpatient populations (e.g., BDI-II, 84% and 82%; PHQ-9, 98% and 80%; Sprinkle et al., 2002; Löwe et al., 2004, respectively). Among nonclinical populations, the CES-D has been most commonly used and validated in diverse groups and translations, including elderly patients (Beekman et al., 1997; Haringsma, Engels, Beekman, Spinhoven, 2004); Arab women (Ghubash, Daradkeh, Al Naseri, Al Bloushi, & Al Daheri, 2000), Spanish-speaking rural Mexican women (Salgado-de Snyder & Maldanado, 1994), and Native Americans (Somervell et al., 1993). Although specificities tended to be lower (57–83%), sensitivities remained high (82–100%). Taken together, these findings suggest that these self-report instruments have good convergent validity and marginal discriminant validity for anxiety; and when used as case-finding instruments, the PHQ-9 has the best balance between sensitivity and specificity; however, the CES-D has been validated with the greatest variety of populations.

## CLINICAL UTILITY

### INTERVIEW METHODS

Unstructured clinical interviews are, by far, the most commonly used clinical assessment methods for depression. These interviews allow the clinician to gain a variety of information from the client while establishing a therapeutic relationship. Given that a significant body of literature supports the role of the therapeutic alliance in a positive therapy outcome (Horvath & Symonds, 1991; Martin, Garske, & Davis, 2000), a clinical interview may be a good method for balancing the needs of therapy with data collection.

Semistructured clinical interviews also have good clinical utility, but they require specific training and can be time consuming and expensive. Semistructured interviews offer a breadth of information, but often at the expense of gaining in-depth information about specific aspects of the depression. The SCID, for example, covers a breadth of Axis I disorders in order to identify and rule out initial diagnoses; however, it is not sensitive to changes in mood and should not be used to assess treatment changes. In contrast, the SADS is better for measuring depression treatment progress and outcome (Rogers, 2001). Because it is based on the RDC, however, and not the *DSM-IV*, additional assessment may be needed. One alternative is the IDS-C, which may be used to evaluate depression severity and is based in *DSM-IV* criteria.

Structured depression interviews, in contrast, may be administered by non-professionals and may require less training. However, these structured interviews typically result in less breadth and a greater probability that some information will be missed. The DIS is useful when the goal of the interview is depression diagnosis rather than symptom severity (Rogers, 2001). An additional advantage is that the DIS is the only structured interview adequately validated in Spanish with a Hispanic population (Alcázar et al., 1992). However, for the trained professional, such structured interviews may be cumbersome and inhibit the development of the therapeutic relationship.

## SELF-REPORT MEASURES

Self-report measures of depression are widely used in a number of clinical settings due to the quality of information provided, ease of administration, and relatively low cost. The information obtained varies, depending on the instrument, and may include areas such as diagnostic criteria of the *DSM-IV* for MDD (e.g., BDI-II and PHQ-9), specific symptoms of depression (e.g., BHS), or information that would be similar to that gathered in a clinical interview (e.g., HDI). Further, specific instruments regarding certain theoretical views of depression etiology and maintenance may be used. The ATQ-R, for example, is used to assess the relationship between thinking patterns and beliefs in accordance with the cognitive theory of depression. Combined, these self-report instruments may augment treatment planning and outcome assessment.

Modern self-report depression measures have good clinical utility because they provide important clinical information, are easy to administer and score, and are relatively inexpensive. Most instruments reviewed take 10 minutes or less to complete and can be scored by summing items and comparing totals to norms in the test manual. The 21-item BDI-II, for example, takes 5–10 minutes to complete and 1–2 minutes to score and interpret; this makes it an excellent clinical tool to be administered just prior to scheduled sessions (Beck et al., 1996). More-over, these measures do not require a professional for administration or scoring; therefore, these tasks can be delegated to clerical staff, lessening the impact on clinician and session time (Spitzer et al., 1999). Specific score ranges for depres-sive severity can be obtained with testing materials, and several were described earlier. Although self-report instruments should not be used alone for depression diagnosis, they may aid busy clinicians in screening for possible depression symptoms (Montano, 1994; Muñoz, Le, & Ippen, 2000). Most instruments described earlier have cutoff scores to identify those with probable depression so that they can be targeted for diagnostic interviews. Financially, these measures remain relatively cost effective for regular clinical use. Cost to obtain these instru-ments varies, from measures such as the CES-D, available in the public domain free of charge, to the BDI-II, available for purchase through the Psychological Corporation® as a pay-per-administration instrument. In sum, interview and self-report assessment are essential to gathering information, forming hypotheses about depression cause, maintenance, and treatment, and evaluating therapeutic outcome.

## ASSESSMENT, CONCEPTUALIZATION, AND TREATMENT PLANNING

With careful observation and assessment at its core, the goals of behavioral case conceptualization are to create a meaningful story about who the client is (observation), why the client might be depressed (hypotheses about cause), main-tenance factors for staying depressed (hypotheses about maintenance), and pos-sible helpful treatments (hypotheses about treatment). Consistent with the underlying principles of behavior theory, behavioral case conceptualization is based in the foundational concept that all behaviors (maladaptive and adaptive) are acquired, maintained, and changed through the events that precede and follow them—the antecedents and consequences, respectively. Specifically, antecedent and consequential events are functionally related to target behaviors when they influence whether those behaviors will occur or reoccur. Thus, behavioral case conceptualization ultimately will involve identifying and developing a plan for modifying functional antecedents or consequences for a target behavior. The four stages in a behavioral conceptualization are (1) observation/data gathering, (2) developing hypotheses, (3) testing hypotheses, and (4) revising hypotheses (Truax, 2002b). The stages will be reviewed in detail next and then directly applied to a clinical case example.

### STAGE 1: OBSERVATION/DATA GATHERING

Within a behavioral context, information gathering consists of two parts. The first is identification and operational definition of observable treatment targets.

The second is assessment of the behavioral context of depressive symptoms. The most common way of gaining this information is through a clinical interview, which focuses on historical context, client presentation, presenting problem, and diagnosis. Other supplemental assessment methods include direct and natural observations, self-report questionnaires, and self-monitoring.

## Identifying and Operationally Defining Target and Diagnosis

Behavioral theorists identify observable behavioral targets (e.g., crying) as well as internal experiences (e.g., feeling blue) and develop operational definitions of these targets. These operational definitions involve observable, measurable, specific descriptions of the target behaviors. For example, instead of using traits to define internal experiences (e.g., unmotivated, resistant), the frequency, intensity, and duration of specific behaviors associated with internal experience are identified and quantified (e.g., verbal description of depressed mood at an intensity level of 8 on a 0–10 scale). Further, collaboratively developing a life-span timeline of symptoms can clarify the course of the disorder and symptoms, thereby aiding in diagnosis and treatment planning.

Although most empirically supported treatments are based in diagnostic categories, there is significant controversy among behavioral theorists about the utility of traditional diagnosis. Some argue that because diagnoses are only descriptions of symptoms and fail to consider the function of target behavior (e.g., negative reinforcement; Follette & Houts, 1996), they may blur essential variables responsible for target behavior maintenance. However, because diagnosis remains at the center of case conceptualization and is required for third-party payment and clinical practice in most agencies, it is included here. Some methods to improve the accuracy and clinical utility of diagnoses include involving the client in the processes, using structured or semistructured interviews, and considering important cultural influences on symptoms.

## Assessment of Behavioral Context

The final stage in the observation/data-gathering stage involves *functional assessment*. The most important goal of functional assessment is to increase knowledge about the context in which target behaviors occur. Effective behavioral case conceptualization requires identification of current internal (e.g., cognitive, emotional, and physical) and external events (e.g., situational and behavioral) that precede and follow target behavior (e.g., depressed mood at a 9 on a 0–10 scale, with higher scores indicating more severe depression) and increase the probability the behavior will occur or reoccur.

### Historical Context

Although behavioral theorists focus more on current maintenance factors than past causal factors, information about the historical context, or *setting events*, gained through a thorough *biopsychosocial assessment* can illuminate possible current maintenance factors. Six areas that should be addressed in identifying possible setting events are learning and modeling, significant life events, genetic factors, physical factors, and sociocultural factors (Truax, 2002b).

### Present Context

The primary goal in functional assessment is to identify current functional internal and external events that precede and follow treatment target behaviors and affect their occurrence or reoccurrence. Functional antecedents immediately precede the target behavior and increase the probability that the target behavior will occur. Antecedents may be identified by inquiring about events just prior to the target behavior, with specific attention given to location, people present, the situation, and the client's behavior. It is also important to inquire about the client's physical, emotional, and cognitive states. Functional consequences immediately follow target behavior and directly increase or decrease the probability that the behavior will reoccur. Reinforcers are consequences that increase reoccurrence of target behavior; these can be positive (e.g., adding positive stimuli) or negative (i.e., removing aversive stimuli), while punishers are those that reduce future occurrences of target behavior. A functional analytic assessment with noncognitively impaired adults may involve interviews, self-report questionnaires, self-observation, and/or direct observation of factors that improve or worsen target behavior, such as depressed mood.

### STAGE 2: DEVELOPING HYPOTHESES

After depression has been observed and assessed, testable hypotheses are formed regarding the cause, maintenance, and treatment options. Causal hypotheses are formulated from the biopsychosocial assessment; maintenance hypotheses are developed from the functional assessment; and treatment hypotheses are derived from primary client concerns, the case conceptualization, and appropriately generalized empirical literature (Truax, 2002b).

### Treatment Plan

A treatment plan is a natural next step to the development of hypotheses about cause, maintenance, and treatment; it turns speculative hypotheses about treatment into testable hypotheses. The testing of treatment hypotheses requires a specific treatment plan consisting of specific measurable goals, interventions, and measurements of each goal. The treatment plan should be a collaborative process between therapist and client, with specific, measurable, realistic goals consistent with the presenting concerns and treatment hypotheses. Each goal should also have a target completion date. Interventions should be grounded in empirical literature and target hypothesized functional relationships. Standardized (e.g., BDI-II) and idiographic (e.g., subjective units of distress 0–100; SUDs) measurements should be used to monitor and track progress.

### STAGES 3 AND 4: TESTING AND REVISING HYPOTHESES

The hypotheses are tested through conducting treatment according to the treatment plan and accurately measuring progress. When data from standardized and idiographic outcome measurements suggest that treatment hypotheses are incorrect, the clinician returns to the observation phase and collects additional data to form revised hypotheses. The new treatment plan is implemented and new hypotheses are tested. As the client progresses through treatment and depressive symptoms change, treatment hypotheses should be regularly reviewed to ensure continued appropriateness. Throughout treatment, behavioral clinicians should be responsive to client outcome assessment. If a client makes clinically significant change (Jacobson & Truax, 1991), for example, treatment may be discontinued early. If, on the other hand, a client fails to make expected changes, the treatment and conceptualization may need minor or major changes to produce better outcomes.

## CASE STUDY

This case exemplifies the assessment and case conceptualization principles presented earlier.

### IDENTIFICATION

Jason is a 53-year-old married, white male and a father of two adult children from a previous marriage. Jason said that he has been married to his current wife for the last five years. He reported that until six months prior to the initial assessment he owned and operated a small software subcontracting and distribution company, which, due to reported "poor business decisions," was forced to cease operations and sell off all assets. Jason said the loss of his business had created a significant financial burden for him and his wife and forced the use of money the couple had set aside for retirement. Prior to the loss of his business, Jason also reported that he was completing coursework for his MBA at a local university. He noted that the precipitating event for seeking therapy at this time was an "ever-increasing sense of hopelessness."

### PRESENTING COMPLAINTS

An unstructured clinical intake interview was used to assess Jason's emotional, physical, cognitive, and behavioral concerns. Emotionally, Jason reported that he is often sad, explaining he is "undeserving of feeling happy" because his "poor business sense" bankrupted his dreams for a comfortable and enjoyable retirement. He stated that he often feels overwhelmed by "uncontrollable bouts of hopelessness and guilt" regarding the loss of his company and the perceived negative effect on his wife and family. Jason described these feelings as "unremitting" and "ever-present" since the decline of his business.

Jason reported several physical and behavioral symptoms he attributed to his current mood. He noted he has had difficulty with sleep onset and maintenance, averaging 1–3 hours of sleep each night. Further, Jason described a dramatic reduction in appetite, with the unintentional loss of nearly 30 pounds since closing his company. In addition to losing interest in eating, Jason reported a loss of interest in a number of previously pleasurable activities, such as hiking, golfing, and reading. He said he has experienced a considerable decrease in energy, feels incapable of completing such activities, and doubts he would derive enjoyment from them should his energy return. Jason reported that he no longer participates in any social activities, again preferring to remain at home, where he sits quietly in front of the television. Further, he noted considerable difficulty concentrating and stated that his wife has taken over the majority of personal and business responsibilities. Jason reported that his troubles with concentration have also made it difficult for him to do his schoolwork, resulting in several failed classes since the loss of his business.

Cognitively, Jason described a negative outlook for himself, others, and his future, including a number of thoughts about his marriage, his children, his competence, and a need to be perfect. Jason's beliefs about his marriage were that he is undeserving of his wife's love and would soon lose her because he is no longer successful. Similarly, he believed he was no longer deserving of respect or love from his two adult children and that they would no longer wish to associate with him. He further described that he "has to be flawless" to be deserving of the attention or affection of others. Overall, Jason noted feeling anxious and depressed regarding these beliefs. Jason also noted some passive suicidal ideation involving occasional thoughts that "things would be better if I wasn't around." He reported having these thoughts once or twice weekly, but he denied any plan, intent, or previous suicidal behavior.

## HISTORY

Jason denied any history of mania or hypomania and related only one experience of depressed mood similar to his current state. At the time of his divorce from his first wife, at age 45, he underwent what he described as a "significant depression." Jason noted feelings of worthlessness and guilt related to his exwife's affair that led to her leaving the relationship. He reported a similar pattern of decreased eating, sleeping, and activity that continued for approximately three months after his exwife moved out of the house. When questioned about what he did to relieve the depression, he stated that "I just snapped out of it one day." A more formal depression timeline corroborated Jason's initial report of the number of episodes and the course of the mood disturbances. He also reported he believed his father suffered from undiagnosed depression on and off throughout his life. Jason said this was especially true during periods of stress or hardship within the family.

## PEER AND WORK ISSUES

Jason reported that he has not actively sought employment since the loss of his company because his concentration difficulties and negative self-talk preclude him from successfully reviewing the classified advertisements. At home, Jason reported that he has relinquished the majority of decisions to his wife and his attorney. Jason reported that he avoids contact with his peers, for fear he will be viewed as a "failure." He also avoids his MBA classes because he fears he will be unable to complete the necessary work and will be a failure. This has led Jason to spend almost no time with any members of his social circle.

## FAMILY ISSUES

Jason reported a number of family issues currently affecting him. He stated that his wife has grown distant and angry because he no longer is "willing to make a decision." He reported that she feels burdened that she is now the "primary breadwinner," in charge of both the business and family finances. He said that his wife has been spending increasing amounts of time socializing with friends away from home, and he fears she will soon ask for a divorce. Jason also reported that his two children, who have both professional and financial connections to his business, have also been adversely affected by the recent closure. He said his two children have expressed frustration about his lack of leadership in helping meet the demands of creditors. Jason noted that both of his children have been forced to leave the state in search of work and are unable to help with the lingering business affairs. He said that these events have left him feeling isolated from those he loves. Jason reported that he was an only child and that both of his parents died several years previously; he described the fact that his parents have died as a "relief" because they would be "greatly disappointed" by his current situation.

## BEHAVIORAL ASSESSMENT RESULTS

A functional assessment was conducted to explore Jason's mood and behavioral disturbance. The goal of functional assessment is to identify and explore the function of specific, mutable target behaviors believed to be exacerbating or maintaining the frequency, intensity, and duration of a client's negative affect (Haynes & O'Brien, 1990; Iwata, Kahng, Wallace, & Lindberg, 2000). Haynes, Nelson, Thacher, and Kaholokula (2002) noted that target behaviors considered in the functional assessment (FA) should be "controllable, functional" (p. 54) and related to the client's presenting complaints. For Jason, the primary target concern was depressed mood and the accompanying inactivity. These concerns were further defined with a structured interview assessment to clarify diagnosis, a standardized self-report assessment to evaluate the severity of his depressed mood, and an unstructured clinical interview to evaluate the frequency, intensity, and duration of Jason's target concerns.

## Identifying and Operationally Defining Target and Diagnosis

### Structured-Interview Assessment

Use of the SCID-CV indicated that Jason met *DSM-IV* criteria for a Major Depressive Episode. Further, his symptoms were consistent with an Axis I diagnosis of MDD, Recurrent, Moderate. Dysthymic Disorder was ruled out because Jason had more than two consecutive months of normal mood during the preceding two years. Adjustment Disorder with Depressed Mood was also ruled out because Jason's symptoms met the full criteria for depression.

### Self-Report Assessment

Jason was administered a BDI-II at intake, resulting in a score of 28, indicating moderate depression. Individual items with maximum scores were sadness, pessimism, past failure, loss of pleasure, guilty feelings, self-dislike, loss of energy, and concentration difficulties. Jason endorsed a score of 1 (0–3 rating scale) for suicidal thoughts or wishes; this supports his report of passive suicidal ideation without intent or plan.

### Unstructured Clinical Interview

An unstructured clinical interview was used to further evaluate the frequency, intensity, and duration of Jason's depressed mood. Jason stated that his depression has lasted approximately six months (duration). He rated his average negative affect as a 7 on an idiographic scale of depression, where 0 is the absence of depression and 10 is extreme depression (intensity). He said that although his depressed mood was unremitting, the intensity varied from as low as a 3 to as high as a 9. He reported an average of three times weekly when his depression exceeded a 9 on the same idiographic scale (frequency).

## Functional Assessment

The primary goals of functional assessment were to identify internal and external antecedents and consequences functionally related to Jason's more severe depressed mood. Although this assessment may be conducted through direct observation, self-observation, functional experiments, and clinical interviews, the most common methods for functional assessment in noncognitively impaired adults are the clinical interview and self-monitoring. For Jason, the clinical interview and self-monitoring were combined. The clinical interview involved specific questions about events before and after more severe depression. The self-monitoring assessment was implemented between sessions 2 and 4. Jason was asked to monitor his mood three times daily on the 0–10 scale. If his mood reached or exceeded a 9, Jason was asked to write down internal (cognitive, emotional, and physical) and external (situational and behavioral) events immediately before and after he noticed an increase in depression.

## ETHICAL AND LEGAL ISSUES OR COMPLICATIONS

Ethical issues that should be considered in every case are the competence of the clinician to effectively address the presenting problem(s), informed consent to treatment, competence, confidentiality, and avoidance of multiple roles. In the present case, Jason has come to therapy alone and has been fully informed of the risks and benefits of treating his depressed mood. Jason's therapist has been trained and supervised in empirically supported treatments for a variety of affective disorders, including depression, and Jason's personal information has been handled confidentially. Further, the guiding ethical principles of beneficence (the obligation to do good) and nonmaleficence (the obligation to do no harm) are central to client care and treatment.

Legal issues specific to the practice of psychology vary among states; however, several legal issues are universal across states and should be considered. These include basic handling of risk issues such as suicide, homicide, abuse, and domestic violence. In the present case, the only identified risk issue is Jason's passive suicidal ideation. A formal suicide assessment suggested no previous suicidal history, good current and past impulse control, and no current or past plans or intent. Further, although he endorsed significant levels of hopelessness, he also reported that his family and his religious beliefs were significant deterrents to self-harm. Jason also readily contracted not to hurt himself. Taken together, it appears that Jason is at mild risk for suicidal behavior; thus, suicidality will be regularly assessed. Jason denied any homicidal ideation as well as any domestic violence. At this time, his level of functioning is not suggestive of the need for hospitalization; however, should Jason become a risk to himself or others, hospitalization will be considered, along with less restrictive options such as increased treatment, day treatment, and family monitoring. Further, all legal, ethical, and risk issues should be monitored throughout treatment.

## CASE CONCEPTUALIZATION AND
## TREATMENT RECOMMENDATIONS

Behavioral case conceptualization involves developing hypotheses about the cause and maintenance of presenting concerns as well as hypotheses about what treatment is likely to be effective. Hypotheses about cause are developed through biopsychosocial assessment; and hypotheses about maintenance are a direct by-product of functional assessment. Hypotheses about effective treatments should reflect the hypotheses about cause and maintenance as well as existing internally and externally valid research supporting their use.

## Hypotheses About Cause

As already noted, several biopsychosocial issues should be considered as possible causal factors: learning and modeling, life events, genetics, physical factors, drugs and substances, and sociocultural factors. First, regarding learning and modeling, Jason reported that his family of origin gave him a good deal of positive attention when he felt sad (e.g., hugging, releasing from chores, asking if "OK"). Jason may also have observed his father modeling these behaviors as reactions to stressful or unpleasant situations. Second, and perhaps more salient, however, is the recent life event of Jason's business loss. This loss has shaped his experience of himself, others, and his future. Jason's history of only one other depressive episode, at the time of his previous divorce, suggests that significant stressors have a considerable effect on his mood. Third, the fact that Jason's father suffered from an apparent undiagnosed recurrent depression suggests a genetic factor could be at least partly responsible for Jason's current depression. However, given that there is no specific genetic marker for a propensity toward depressive disorders, it is not possible to disentangle potential genetic and environmental factors and their influence on Jason. Fourth, Jason's denial of significant current or past medical problems, as well as the use of any prescription or nonprescription medications or substances, suggests that neither physical factors nor substance use are significant causes for his depression. Finally, regarding sociocultural factors, Jason is a university-educated, middle-aged, upper-middle-class white male of German descent. Jason's culture is one that emphasizes family, education, industriousness, and financial success; he reported such values were reflected in his family and friends. Jason's recent loss of his business stands in direct conflict with his cultural and social values and likely contributes to his depressed mood. Further, his inactivity and reported inability to competently participate in personal and business affairs, as well as the current familial discord, similarly violate the expectations of his cultural background.

## Hypotheses About Maintenance

Through the clinical interview and self-monitoring, several potential functional variables were identified. The target behavior was identified as depressed mood of 9 or greater (on a 0–10 scale, with 10 being the most intense depression). Antecedents to the more intense depressed mood included thoughts of being a failure (cognitive), feelings of hopelessness (emotional), overwhelming fatigue (physical), family conversations about the business (situational), staying in bed all morning, and watching television for more than two hours (behavioral). See Figure 10.1.

Jason reported several consequences of severe depressed mood that may increase the probability of reoccurrence. Although Jason did not directly identify any positive consequences of his depressed mood, responses to other interview

| Antecedents | Target Behavior | Consequences |
|---|---|---|
| **Situational**<br>• Conversations with his wife about nonparticipation in business affairs and marital relationship<br>**Behavioral**<br>• Staying in bed beyond 9 AM<br>• Being alone<br>• Sitting on the couch and watching television<br>**Cognitive**<br>• Thoughts of being a failure and undeserving of love and support<br>**Emotional**<br>• Hopelessness<br>**Physical**<br>• Fatigue | **Depressed mood at a 9** (0- to 10-pt scale, with 0 = no depression, 10 = extreme depression) | **Positive reinforcement** (consequences that involve the addition of stimuli that increase the probability the behavior will reoccur)<br>• Wife and children state concern about his mood<br>• Positive feelings while watching favorite TV shows<br>**Negative reinforcement** (consequences that involve the removal of aversive stimuli, thus increasing probability behavior will occur again)<br>• Escape from anxiety involved in making daily decisions<br>• Escape from wife's unhappy statements about marriage<br>**Setups** (consequences that become antecedents for more depression)<br>• Feelings of failure and hopelessness<br>• Sleep disturbance<br>• Arguments with wife and kids<br>• Ever-worsening business affairs |

FIGURE 10.1    Jason's functional assessment.

questions suggested that his wife and children's expressions of concern for him as well as his general enjoyment of television might have a positive reinforcing effect. Jason was somewhat aware, however, that his depression and inactivity allowed escape from several anxiety-provoking situations, including daily business decisions and his wife's unhappy statements about him (negative reinforcement). Perhaps most clear to Jason were the negative consequences (setups) that acted as antecedents for future severe depression; these included feelings of failure, sleep disturbance, family arguments, and continued business failures.

## TREATMENT RECOMMENDATIONS

Cognitive behavioral therapy (CBT) for depression has more research supporting its effectiveness than any other psychotherapy (Craighead, Hart, Craighead, & Ilardi, 2002). Further, CBT performs similarly to psychotropic medication immediately following treatment and outperforms medication in the long term (Friedman et al., 2004). In addition, the assessment of causal and maintenance factors for Jason's depression suggest that behavioral and cognitive variables are frequent antecedents and consequences for exacerbations in Jason's depression. Thus, CBT appears to be a logical choice for Jason's treatment. Additionally, Jason's inactivity would be likely to benefit from the first treatment intervention in CBT: behavioral activation. First, an activity baseline should be employed as a means to understand exactly what activities Jason participates in throughout the day and how much pleasure he derives from them. After this baseline has been established, activity scheduling should be completed. Collaboratively, Jason and therapist should brainstorm activities that Jason can do throughout the week that are anticipated by Jason to be pleasurable. These activities may be graded, with the easier activities completed earlier in therapy and more difficult tasks completed as therapy progresses. To increase the probability that task achievement will be repeated, these behaviors should be reinforced through self-reward. Initially, a list of rewards should be created collaboratively between Jason and his therapist, and a brief discussion regarding reinforcement principals should be included. Rewards can include virtually anything experienced as reinforcing for Jason (e.g., self-praise, dinner at a favorite restaurant); this will, of course, vary from client to client and depend heavily on their interests.

In addition to inactivity, Jason's depression is often preceded or followed by self-defeating beliefs about himself, others, and/or the future. According to Young, Weinberger, and Beck (2001), this is a hallmark of depression and an important focus of CBT for depression. When maladaptive automatic thoughts are identified and effectively challenged, depressed mood is often reduced (Young et al.). This identification and challenging of alarming thoughts is typically completed through the use of an automatic-thought record. Such forms ask the client to identify activating events, beliefs, and automatic thoughts regarding themselves, others, and the situation as well as the physical, emotional, and behavioral consequences of those beliefs. Clients are further instructed in the classification of maladaptive thoughts, the disputation of these automatic thoughts, and documentation of the effects of replacing disputed thoughts with less alarming cognitions. After clients master the identification and challenging of automatic thoughts, core beliefs may be identified (e.g., "I am unlovable") and challenged through interventions such as the positive-thought log (i.e., identifying evidence for and against an alternative to the maladaptive core belief, such as "I am basically a lovable person"). Given that Jason's depression appears to be maintained by self-defeating automatic and core beliefs, cognitive interventions are recommended in addition to behavioral interventions. These interventions should be introduced after Jason has begun to reduce his depression through the behavioral interventions discussed earlier.

Put more simply, the primary hypothesis about treatment is that CBT for depression will reduce Jason's depression. Further, behavioral interventions will increase his activity level, and cognitive interventions will reduce his self-defeating beliefs. To test these hypotheses, the following variables will be assessed. At pretest and posttest, overall depression, behavioral activity, and dysfunctional cognitions will be assessed with the BDI-II, PES, and ATQ-R, respectively. At weekly intervals, depression will be assessed with the PHQ-9, because of its brevity and to avoid the test–retest effects of the BDI-II (Longwell & Truax, in press). At monthly intervals, the PES and ATQ-R will be administered to evaluate mode-specific treatment effects. If the depression scores are steadily declining and result in eventual clinically significant change (Jacobson & Truax, 1991), no further intervention would be needed. If Jason's scores are not substantially improved by six to eight sessions and/or he remains in the clinically distressed range after a full course of CBT (12–20 sessions), further assessment may be needed to guide treatment. It may become apparent, for example, in a follow-up functional assessment that Jason's interpersonal functioning is a primary causal or maintenance factor. In such a case, another empirically supported therapy, such as interpersonal therapy (Cascalenda, Perry, & Looper, 2002), may be the treatment of choice.

## SUMMARY

As has been demonstrated, behavioral assessment of depression is an efficient means for conceptualization, diagnosis, and treatment planning. With functional assessment at the core, standardized depression measures, idiographic assessment, and both structured and unstructured interview assessment illuminate the important contextual maintenance factors for an individual's depressed mood. Further, this distinct understanding directly informs treatment planning and monitoring strategies for use in therapy. This approach may be even more attractive in the current managed care climate, for managed care organizations often require the use of empirically supported assessment and treatment approaches. Behavioral assessments allow for clear and measurable treatment goals and lend themselves well to evidence-based treatment strategies. Overall, behavioral assessment is a centerpiece to effective depression conceptualization and interventions.

## REFERENCES

Alcázar, F. D. P., Albacete Belmonte, A., Meroño Méndez, A., Artiz Martínez, M., et al. (1992). Validez de la versión española del Diagnostic Interview Schedule. Tercera versión revisada (DIS-III–R). *Actas Luso-Espanolas de Neurologia, Psiquiatria y Ciencias Afines, 20,* 257–262.

American Psychiatric Association. (1980). *Diagnostic and statistical manual of mental disorders: DSM-III* (3rd ed.). Washington, DC: Author.

American Psychiatric Association. (1993). *Diagnostic and statistical manual of mental disorders: DSM-III-R* (3rd ed., rev.). Washington, DC: Author.

American Psychiatric Association. (2000). *Diagnostic and statistical manual of mental disorders* (4th ed., text revision). Washington, DC: Author.

Beck, A. T., & Steer, R. A. (1988). *Beck Hopelessness Scale manual.* San Antonio: Psychological Corporation.

Beck, A. T., & Steer, R. A. (1993). *The Beck Anxiety Inventory manual.* San Antonio, TX: Psychological Corporation.

Beck, A. T., Steer, R. A., & Brown, G. K. (1996). *Beck Depression Inventory* (2nd ed.). San Antonio, TX: Psychological Corporation.

Beckham, E. E., Leber, W. R., Watkins, J. T., Boyer, J. L., & Cook, J. B. (1986). Development of an instrument to develop Beck's cognitive triad: The Cognitive Triad Inventory. *Journal of Consulting and Clinical Psychology, 54,* 566–567.

Beekman, A. T. F., Deeg, D. J. H., Van Limbeek, J., Braam, A. W., De Vries, M. Z., & Van Tilburg, W. (1997). Criterion validity of the Center for Epidemiologic Studies Depression scale (CES-D): Results from a community-based sample of older subjects in the Netherlands. *Psychological Medicine, 27,* 231–235.

Casacalenda, N., Perry, J. C., & Looper, K. (2002). Remission in Major Depressive Disorder: A comparison of pharmacotherapy, psychotherapy, and control conditions. *American Journal of Psychiatry, 159,* 1354–1360.

Craighead, W. E., Hart, A. B., Craighead, L. W., & Ilardi, S. S. (2002). Psychosocial treatments for Major Depressive Disorder. In P. E. Nathan & J. M. Gordon (Eds.), *A guide to treatments that work* (2nd ed., pp. 245–261). London: Oxford University Press.

Cull, J. G., & Gill, W. S. (1988). *Suicide Probability Scale (SPS) manual.* Los Angeles, CA: Western Psychological Services.

Derogatis, L. R. (1977). *The SCL-90-R: Scoring administration and procedures manual.* Baltimore: Johns Hopkins University, School of Medicine.

Derogatis, L. R. (1994). *The SCL-90-R: Scoring administration and procedures manual* (3rd ed.). Minneapolis, MN: National Computer Systems.

Dozois, D. J. (2003). The psychometric characteristics of the Hamilton Depression Inventory. *Journal of Personality Assessment, 80,* 31–40.

Endicott, J., & Spitzer, R. L. (1978). A diagnostic interview: The Schedule for Affective Disorders and Schizophrenia. *Archives of General Psychiatry, 35,* 837–844.

Feighner, J. P., Robins, E., Guze, S. B., Woodruff, R. A., Jr., Winokur, G., & Munoz, R. (1972). Diagnostic criteria for use in psychiatric research. *Archives of General Psychiatry, 26,* 57–63.

Fennig, S., Craig, T. J., Tanenberg-Karant, M., & Bromet, E. J. (1994). Comparison of facility and research diagnoses in first-admission psychotic patients. *American Journal of Psychiatry, 151,* 1423–1429.

First, M. B., Spitzer, R. L., Gibbon, M., & Williams, J. B. W. (1996). *Structured Clinical Interview for DSM-IV Axis I disorders, Clinician Version (SCID-CV).* Washington, DC: American Psychiatric Press.

Follette, W. C., & Houts, A. C. (1996). Models of scientific progress and the role of theory in taxonomy development: A case study of the *DSM. Journal of Consulting & Clinical Psychology, 64,* 1120–1132.

Friedman, M. A., Detweiler-Bedell, J. B., Leventhal, H. E., Horne, R., Keitner, G. I., & Miller, I. W. (2004). Combined psychotherapy and pharmacotherapy for the treatment of Major Depressive Disorder. *Clinical Psychology: Science & Practice, 11,* 47–68.

Fryer, A. J., Endicott, J., Mannuzza, S., & Klein, D. F. (1995). *Schedule for Affective Disorders and Schizophrenia—Lifetime Version, modified for the study of anxiety disorders, updated for DSM-IV (SADS-LA-IV).* Unpublished measure, Anxiety Genetics Unit, New York State Psychiatric Institute, New York.

Ghubash, R., Daradkeh, T. K., Al Naseri, K. S., Al Bloushi, N. B. A., & Al Daheri, A. M. (2000). The performance of the Center for Epidemiologic Study Depression Scales (CES-D) in an Arab female community. *International Journal of Social Psychiatry, 46,* 241–249.

Hamilton, M. (1960). A rating scale for depression. *Journal of Neurology, Neurosurgery and Psychiatry, 23,* 56–62.

Haringsma, R., Engels, G. I., Beekman, A. T. F., & Spinhoven, P. (2004). The criterion validity of the Center for Epidemiological Studies Depression Scale (CES-D) in a sample of self-referred elders with depressive symptomatology. *International Journal of Geriatric Psychiatry, 19,* 558–563.

Haynes, S. N., & O'Brien, W. H. (1990). Functional analysis in behavior therapy. *Clinical Psychology Review, 10,* 649–668.

Haynes, S. N., Nelson, K. G., Thacher, I., & Kaholokula, J. K. (2002). Outpatient behavioral assessment and treatment target selection. In M. Hersen & L. K. Porselius (Eds.), *Diagnosis, conceptualization, and treatment planning for adults: A step-by-step guide* (pp. 35–70). Mahwah, NJ: Erlbaum.

Horvath, A. O., & Symonds, B. D. (1991). Relation between working alliance and outcome in psychotherapy: A meta-analysis. *Journal of Counseling Psychology, 38,* 139–149.

Huyser, J., De Jonghe, F., Jinkers, F., & Schalken, H. F. A. (1996). The manual for the Diagnosis of Major Depression (MDMD): Description and reliability. *International Journal of Methods in Psychiatric Research, 6,* 1–4.

Iwata, B. A., Kahng, S. W., Wallace, M. D., & Lindberg, J. S. (2000). The functional analysis model of behavioral assessment. In J. Austin & J. Carr (Eds.), *Handbook of applied behavior analysis* (pp. 61–89). Reno, NV: Context Press.

Jacobson, N. S., & Truax, P. (1991). Clinical significance: A statistical approach to defining meaningful change in psychotherapy research. *Journal of Consulting and Clinical Psychology, 59,* 12–19.

Katon, W., Robinson, P., Von Korff, M., Lin, E., Bush, T., Ludman, E., et al. (1996). A multifaceted intervention to improve treatment of depression in primary care. *Archives of General Psychiatry, 53,* 924–932.

Kendall, P. C., Howard, B. L., & Hays, R. C. (1989). Self-referent speech and psychopathology: The balance of positive and negative thinking. *Cognitive Therapy and Research, 13,* 583–598.

Kroenke, K., & Spitzer, R. L. (2002). The PHQ-9: A new depression diagnostic severity measure. *Psychiatric Annals, 32,* 509–515.

Kroenke, K., Spitzer, R. L., & Williams, J. B. W. (2001). The PHQ-9: Validity of a brief depression severity measure. *Journal of General Internal Medicine, 16,* 606–613.

Longwell, B. T., & Truax, P. (2005). The effects of weekly, monthly, and bimonthly administrations of the Beck Depression Inventory—II: Psychometric properties and clinical implications. *Behavior Therapy, 36,* 265–275.

Löwe, B., Spitzer, R. L., Gräfe, K., Kroenke, K., Quenter, A., Zipfel, S., et al. (2004). Comparative validity of three screening questionnaires for *DSM-IV* depressive disorders and physicians' diagnoses. *Journal of Affective Disorders, 78,* 131–140.

MacPhillamy, D. J., & Lewinsohn, P. M. (1982). The Pleasant Events Schedule: Studies on the reliability, validity, and scale intercorrelation. *Journal of Consulting and Clinical Psychology, 50,* 363–380.

Martin, D. J., Garske, J. P., & Davis, M. K. (2000). Relation of the therapeutic alliance with outcome and other variables: A meta-analytic review. *Journal of Consulting & Clinical Psychology, 68,* 438–450.

Miller, P. R., Dasher, R., Collins, R., Griffiths, P., & Brown, F. (2001). Inpatient diagnostic assessments: 1. Accuracy of structured vs. unstructured interviews. *Psychiatry Research, 105,* 255–264.

Montano, C. B. (1994). Recognition and treatment of depression in a primary care setting. *Journal of Clinical Psychiatry, 55,* 18–34.

Muñoz, R. F., Le, H., & Ippen, C. G. (2000). We should screen for major depression. *Applied and Preventive Psychology, 9,* 123–133.

Nezu, A. M., Ronan, G. F., Meadows, E. A., & McClure, K. S. (2000). *Practitioner's guide to empirically based measures of depression.* New York: Kluwer Academic/Plenum Press.

Radloff, L. S. (1977). The CES-D Scale: A self-report depression scale for research in the general population. *Applied Psychological Measurement, 1,* 385–401.

Reiger, D. A., Myers, J. K., Kramer, M., Robins, L. N., Blazer, D. G., Hough, R. L., et al. (1984). The NIMH Epidemiologic Catchment Area Program: Historical context, major objectives and study population characteristics. *Archives of General Psychiatry, 41,* 934–941.

Reynolds, W. M. (1991). Psychometric characteristics of the Adult Suicidal Ideation with college students. *Journal of Personality Assessment, 56,* 289–307.

Reynolds, W. M., & Kobak, K. A. (1995a). Reliability and validity of the Hamilton Depression Inventory: A paper-and-pencil version of the Hamilton Depression Rating Scale Clinical Interview. *Psychological Assessment, 7,* 472–483.

Reynolds, W. M., & Kobak, K. A. (1995b). *Hamilton Depression Inventory (HDI): Professional manual.* Odessa, FL: Psychological Assessment Resources.

Robins, L. N., Cotter, L., Bucholz, K., & Compton, W. (1995). *Diagnostic Interview Schedule, Version IV.* St. Louis, MO: Washington School of Medicine.

Robins, L. N., Helzer, J. E., Croughan, J., & Ratcliff, K. S. (1981). National Institute of Mental Health Diagnostic Interview Schedule: Its history, characteristics, and validity. *Archives of General Psychiatry, 38,* 381–389.

Rogers, R. (2001). *Handbook of diagnostic and structured interviewing.* New York: Guilford Press.

Rush, A. J., Gullion, C. M., Basco, M. R., Jarrett, R. B., & Trivedi, M. H. (1996). The Inventory of Depressive Symptomology (IDS): Psychometric properties. *Psychological Medicine, 26,* 477–486.

Salgado-de Snyder, V. N., & Maldonado, M. (1994). The psychometric characteristics of the Depression Scale of the Centro de Estudios Epidemiologicos in adult Mexican women from rural areas. *Salud Publica Mexicana, 36,* 200–209.

Santor, D. A., Zuroff, D. C., Ramsay, J. O., Cervantes, P., & Palacios, J. (1995). Examining scale discriminability in the BDI and the CES-D as a function of depressive severity. *Psychological Assessment, 7,* 131–139.

Schulberg, H. C., Saul, M., McClelland, M., Ganguli, M., Christy, W., & Frank, R. (1985). Assessing depression in primary medical and psychiatric practice. *Archives of General Psychiatry, 42,* 1164–1170.

Somervell, P. D., Beals, J., Kinzie, J. D., Boehnlein, J., Lueng, P., & Manson, S. M. (1993). Criterion validity of the Center for Epidemiologic Studies Depression Scale in a population sample from an American Indian village. *Psychiatry Research, 47,* 255–266.

Spitzer, R. L., Endicott, J., & Robins, E. (1975). *Research diagnostic criteria.* New York: New York State Psychiatry Institute, Biometrics Research.

Spitzer, R. L., Endicott, J., & Robins, E. (1978). Research diagnostic criteria for use in psychiatric research. *Archives of General Psychiatry, 35,* 773–782.

Spitzer, R. L., Kroenke, K., & Williams, J. B. W. (1999). Validation and utility of a self-report version of the PRIME-MD: The PHQ-9 primary care study. *The Journal of the American Medical Association, 282,* 1737–1744.

Sprinkle, S. D., Lurie, D., Insko, S. L., Atkinson, G., Jones, G. L., Logan, A. R., et al. (2002). Criterion validity, severity cut scores, and test–retest reliability of the Beck Depression Inventory—II in a university counseling center sample. *Journal of Counseling Psychology, 49,* 381–385.

Steer, R. A., Ball, R., Ranieri, W. F., & Beck, A. T. (1997). Further evidence for the construct validity of the Beck Depression Inventory—II with psychiatric outpatients. *Psychological Reports, 80,* 443–446.

Steiner, J. L., Tebes, J. K., Sledge, W. H., & Walker, M. L. (1995). A comparison of the Structured Clinical Interview for *DSM-III-R* and clinical diagnoses. *Journal of Nervous & Mental Disease, 183,* 365–369.

Truax, P. (2002a). Major Depressive Disorder. In M. Hersen & L. K. Porzelius (Eds.), *Diagnosis, conceptualization, and treatment planning: A textbook.* Mahway, NJ: Erlbaum.

Truax, P. (2002b). Behavioral case conceptualization for adults. In M. Hersen (Ed.), *Clinical behavior therapy: Adults and children* (pp. 3–36). New York: John Wiley & Sons.

Whisman, M. A., Strosahl, K., Fruzzetti, A. E., Schmaling, K. B., Jacobson, N. S., & Miller, D. M. (1989). A structured interview version of the Hamilton Rating Scale for Depression: Reliability and validity. *Psychological Assessment, 1,* 238–241.

Whooley, M. A., Avins, A. L., Miranda, J., & Browner, W. S. (1997). Case-finding instruments for depression: Two questions are as good as many. *Journal of General Internal Medicine, 12,* 439–445.

Young, J. E.,Weinberger, A. D., & Beck, A. T. (2001). Cognitive therapy for depression. In David H. Barlow (Ed.), *Clinical handbook of psychological disorders: A step-by-step treatment manual* (3rd ed., pp. 264–308). New York: Guilford Press.

Zich, J. M., Attkisson, C. C., & Greenfield, I. K. (1990). Screening for depression in primary care clinics: The CES-D and the BDI. *International Journal of Psychiatry in Medicine, 20,* 259–277.

# 11

## SOCIAL SKILLS DEFICITS

NINA HEINRICHS

*Department of Clinical Psychology, Psychotherapy, and Assessment*
*TU Braunschweig*
*Braunschweig, Germany*

ALEXANDER L. GERLACH

*Psychological Institute I*
*Muenster, Germany*

STEFAN G. HOFMANN

*Center for Anxiety and Related Disorders at Boston University*
*Boston, Massachusetts*

### INTRODUCTION

Zigler and Philips (1960) were the first to implicate that a lack of social skills (they used the term *social effectiveness*) may partially be responsible for the onset and exacerbation of a number of psychiatric disorders. Hersen and Bellack (1976a, 1976b) realized the clinical implications of this finding and tested whether treatment targeting social skills improved the outcome of treatment in chronic mental health patients. Over the years, the issue of social skills has attracted many researchers, resulting in an expansive and burgeoning literature. A computerized search in November 2004 using the Social Sciences Citation Index indicated that 2648 publications contained the term *social skills*. This is probably an underestimate of the number of actual publications dealing with the topic of social skills because many other terms (e.g., interpersonal skills, interpersonal competence, social competence, and communication competence) have been used interchangeably. Despite the fact that there is no official category (*DSM-IV* or ICD-10) involving social skills deficits as a primary problem in patients, a large amount of empirical data has been amassed.

Over the years, studies appeared examining a wide variety of mental disorders with social skills deficits (e.g., depression, social phobia, schizophrenia,

*Clinician's Handbook of Adult Behavioral*
*Assessment*

bipolar disorder, alcoholism; Conger & Conger, 1986). Consequently, some authors began questioning the credibility of the social skills deficit hypothesis and its ability to explain the mechanisms responsible for the development of psychiatric disorders (e.g., McFall, 1982). At the same time, the role of social perception or social sensitivity in the research of social skills was highlighted instead (e.g., Morrison & Bellack, 1981). Whereas before, most research had focused on the behavioral response components, studies emerged that looked at the ability of individuals to "read" social situations and the expression of emotions.

## DEFINITION OF SOCIAL SKILLS

There are several definitions of social skills. The common element of these definitions is the emphasis on goal orientation. For example, Morgan (1980) defined social skills as an ability to achieve the objectives that a person has for interacting with others. Other prominent definitions (e.g., Libet & Lewinsohn, 1973) refer to the consequences of one's social behaviors, with the aim to minimize negative outcomes and maximize positive outcomes in social situations. Most definitions are rather abstract and do not pinpoint concrete behaviors. Typical socially skilled behaviors are, among others, assertive behaviors, smiling and being friendly, terminating unwished-for interpersonal contacts, and appropriately reacting to criticism (e.g., Gambrill, 1995). However, classification of these behaviors as socially skilled strongly depends on the context in which they occur. The definition must, therefore, be expanded to include behavioral adaptation to the situational requirements. Classification of behavior as socially skilled is probably not possible without considering the situational context (Becker & Heimberg, 1988).

Going beyond a pure behavioral definition of social skills, Bellack (1979) suggested that social skills include four aspects: verbal elements (e.g., empathic communication style), nonverbal elements (e.g., eye contact), situational elements, and knowledge about these situational requirements. Therefore, social competence includes more than social performance. It refers not only to *objectively observable behavior* but also to *perception* and *evaluation* of social situations.

## SOCIAL COMPETENCE VERSUS SOCIAL PERFORMANCE

The concept of social skills is closely related to social performance (e.g., Goldfried & D'Zurilla, 1969) and social competence (e.g., Ford, 1985). An individual can be socially competent even if the person does not act socially skilled in a given situation. This is consistent with Stravynski and Amado's (2001) distinction between the *intrapersonal* and *interpersonal* view of social skills. The *intrapersonal view* reflects a trait approach to social skills. For example, the authors state that "being socially skilled . . . is not an observable performance, but rather an underlying quality that manifests itself in, or may be inferred from, actual behavior" (p. 110). In contrast, the *interpersonal view* assumes that social skills are a function of the specific situation and not of the person. These different views have specific implications for the assessment of social skills because multiple assessment methods of social behaviors in a variety of social situations would be necessary to measure social skills from an interpersonal view. In contrast, one assessment of social behavior would be sufficient when measuring social skills from an intrapersonal view (Kanning, 2003).

In summary, a satisfactory definition of social skills is still lacking, despite (a) numerous attempts to conceptualize the term throughout the years (Adams, 1987; Curran, 1979; Libet & Lewinsohn, 1973; O'Connor, 1989; Trower, Bryant, & Argyle, 1978) and (b) a wide dissemination of the term in clinical research and practice. There are many different forms of social skills, and not all social skills are equally relevant in each situation. There may be general social skills, which are less dependent on the situation, such as perspective-taking and listening skills, and more specific social skills, which depend more on the situation. Despite the necessity of a multidimensional approach to social skills, an evidence-based taxonomy of social skills is lacking.

## PERCEPTION AND PROCESSING OF SOCIAL INFORMATION

McFall (1982) argued that encoding skills, decision skills, and enactment skills are all necessary to act socially competent. Furthermore, Morrison and Bellack (1981) pointed out that social perception or social sensitivity is an important aspect of social skills. The authors distinguished between skills of assessment ("social perception") and response skills ("social skills"). However, social perception can be even further divided into a number of different skills, such as the perception of emotion and the perception of intention of a person.

Various studies have examined the association of mental disorders and the ability to accurately appraise emotional expressions. A number of different mental disorders have been associated with impaired appraisal of emotional expressions, including schizophrenia (Corrigan, 1997), bipolar disorder (McClure, Pople, Hoberman, Pine, & Leibenluft, 2003), alcoholism (Kornreich et al., 2002), and social phobia (Melfsen & Florin, 2003). Studies further suggest a link between social adjustment and the ability to correctly recognize facial expressions (e.g., Carton, Kellser, & Pape, 1999; Denham, McKinley, Couchoud, & Holt, 1990).

A number of authors have used film or video vignettes of social situations to test the ability of an individual to correctly interpret more complex social events (e.g., Burns & Beier, 1973; Costanzo & Archer, 1989; Rosenthal, Archer, Koivumaki, DiMatteo, & Rogers, 1979). Although these measures have been criticized because of their poor convergent validity (Feldman & Thayer, 1980), a number of studies have shown that scores on such tests are meaningfully correlated with measures of psychological disturbance. For example, measures of social anxiety are negatively correlated with interpersonal perception (Schroeder & Ketrow, 1997). Furthermore, relatives of patients with schizophrenia show worse performance in social perception tests than controls (Toomey, Seidman, Lyons, Faraone, & Tsuang, 1999). The remainder of this chapter will provide an overview of the presently available methods to assess social skills.

## ASSESSMENT STRATEGIES AND THEIR RESEARCH BASIS

### COGNITIVE SKILLS TESTS

As mentioned earlier, different assessment strategy may be implicated, depending on the definition used for social skills. Some definitions include cognitive aspects of social skills, such as perception or knowledge of social situations (e.g., Bellack, 1979; McFall, 1982). One possible strategy to assess such cognitive/perceptual social skills is to administer traditional social intelligence tests. Typical tasks in these tests include the assignment of names to faces and knowledge questions about social norms. A classic example of such a test is the Six-Factor Test of Social Intelligence (O'Sullivan & Guilford, 1966). This test consists of six subtests: cartoon prediction, expression grouping, missing picture, missing cartoon, picture exchange, and social translation. However, the various attempts to assess social competence via social cognitive intelligence tests has not been very fruitful, because the performance in these tasks did not predict socially skilled behavior in social interactions and it overlapped significantly with general intelligence (Marlowe, 1985; Riggio, Messamer, & Throckmorton, 1991). Other indicators of social skills, such as self-report, pencil-and-paper tests, and behavioral observations, seem to be better indicators of social skills.

### SELF-REPORT INSTRUMENTS

Measuring social skills with self-report instruments has a number of distinct advantages. Self-report measures are easy to apply and relatively inexpensive, and it is possible to assess social skills with self-report measures over a wide range of social behaviors and situations (Segrin, 2000). However, self-report measures also have a number of disadvantages. Most importantly, measures of social skills are often correlated with measures of psychiatric disorders, such as social anxiety (e.g., Wallander, Conger, Mariotto, Curran, & Farrell, 1980) or depression (e.g., Segrin). Therefore, it is unclear whether these self-report instruments measure psychiatric status per se or, as intended, social skills. As mentioned earlier, a similar problem exists for measures of social intelligence, which is also a component of social competence. Self-report measures of social intelligence are highly correlated with verbal intelligence. In other words, it is quite difficult to establish social intelligence as an independent construct (Bastians & Runde, 2002).

When considering the use of self-report measures of social skills, it is important to realize that these instruments do not measure behavior per se. Instead, they measure the individual's perception of his/her abilities in social situations. Social phobic patients, for example, often underestimate their social skills considerably. Therefore, the often-reported mismatch between self-report and behavioral assessment of social skills does not necessarily suggest a lack of validity of the instruments assessing social skills.

A large number of questionnaires have been developed for assessment of social skills since the introduction of the first questionnaire to measure social skills by Wolpe and Lazarus (Wolpe-Lazarus Assertiveness Questionnaire, 1966). General measures of social skills assess basic components such as "emotional expressivity," "emotional sensitivity," "emotional control," "social expressivity," "social sensitivity," and "social control" (Riggio, 1986) or such as "social assertiveness," "directiveness," "defense of rights," "confidence," and "empathy" (Lorr, Youniss, & Stefic, 1991). More specific questionnaires assess more specific social behavior, such as dating skills (e.g., the survey of heterosexual interactions; Twentyman & McFall, 1975) and interpersonal assertiveness (e.g., Gambrill & Richey, 1975).

## CLINICIAN-RATED INSTRUMENTS

To our knowledge, no clinician-rated instrument has been published to directly measure social skills. However, Becker and Heimberg (1988) recommend the following interview procedure for a thorough assessment of social skills: The interviewer prepares a matrix in which the columns are labeled with different types of social behaviors (e.g., public speaking, initiating a conversation, assertion). The rows represent different persons with whom the interviewee may interact (e.g., partner, parents, friends, work colleagues, authority figures). Becker and Heimberg recommend that patients rate the discomfort they experience when performing a specific task in the various situation–person combinations on a scale from 0 to 100.

## BEHAVIORAL ASSESSMENTS

In contrast to cognitive performance tests, social skills are not assessed directly with behavioral assessments. The clinician usually has to infer the patient's social skills based on the performance shown in the behavioral assessment. These observational methods vary in the degree of standardization and include self-observation and clinician observation. Self-observations have the advantage of being easily conducted in the natural environment of the patient, for example, through daily diaries. This method is especially helpful for behaviors that are otherwise not accessible, such as observing the behavior of a patient at home after discharge from the hospital for several subsequent days. Clinician observation often occurs in an artificial setting, usually the laboratory. This is not necessarily a disadvantage, because the observational situation and the daily situation outside the laboratory do not need to match in all aspects. The most important point to consider is to include those aspects of the natural situation that play a decisive role in the interpersonal behavior displayed in everyday life. The most frequently used tasks and methods in an observational setting in a laboratory are role-plays, presentation tasks (either presenting a topic to another person or disclosing information about oneself to another person), spontaneous speech, and group discussions. Although each of these tasks may be administered by itself, it is often preferred to combine these tasks into one test of social skills. This approach is often referred to as the *behavioral assessment test* (BAT).

Despite the name, BATs are not limited to assessment of behaviors. In a typical BAT, patients are asked to perform a particular task, such as giving a speech (e.g., Gerlach, Wilhelm, Gruber, & Roth, 2001; Hofmann, Gerlach, Wender, & Roth, 1997) or interacting with others (Dykman, Abramson, Horowitz, & Usher, 1991). Subsequent to performing the task, the patient is typically asked about his or her level of distress on a 0- to 100-point Likert scale. Table 11.1 shows several vari-

TABLE 11.1    Behavioral Assessment Tests: Potential Variations

| Variable | Examples |
|---|---|
| Modus of instructional presentation | Live |
|  | Recorded on audiotape |
|  | Written on a sheet of paper |
| Timing of instruction | Only once, prior to BAT |
|  | Repeatedly, prior to BAT |
|  | Also during BAT |
| Content of instruction | "Do as well as possible." |
|  | "Behave in a way that it is still comforting to you." |
|  | "You may talk about any topic you wish." |
|  | "Please talk about the death sentence." |
| Criterion behavior | Molecular: |
|  |     Distance to interacting partner |
|  |     Fluency of words |
|  |     Length of speech and speech pauses |
|  |     Number of filled pauses |
|  |     Frequency and length of eye contact |
|  | Molar: |
|  |     Assertion |
|  |     Interpersonal affection |
| Behavior of instructor | Instructor is present/absent |
|  | Instructor is modeling behavior or not |
| Setting of BAT | In a laboratory or in a real-life situation |
|  | In a virtual reality |
| Data scoring | Directly in situation |
|  | From videotape |
|  | From audiotape |
| Features of evaluator | Same person as instructor/clinician |
|  | Independent person |

Source: Adapted from Nietzel, Bernstein, & Russell (1988).

ables to consider when planning a BAT. All tasks need to be adapted to the particular diagnostic group and clinical or research question.

A disadvantage of BATs is their uncertain psychometric properties. The few studies that reported good psychometric data were limited to very specific and highly standardized performance tests, such as public speaking (Beidel, Turner, Jacob, & Cooley, 1989). The decision to use a BAT as an assessment tool for social skills will have to be based on a variety of factors, some of which are outlined in Table 11.1. Molecular behaviors, such as the length of the speech and the frequency or length of eye contact are only assessed quantitatively. However, there is no linear relationship between the construct and the observed behavior. For example, more or longer eye contact does not necessarily imply a more socially skilled behavior, because staring is usually not rated as socially competent (Trower, 1980). Therefore, a second approach focuses on more global behaviors (the *molar* level).

A number of rating systems for social competence have been developed for analyzing behavioral data. These systems usually focus on either the molecular level or the molar level. Although they are not mutually exclusive, it has been noted that their results may not be directly comparable (Stravynski & Amado, 2001).

Curran (1982) developed a popular role-play test that uses a molar rating system, the Simulated Social Interaction Test (SSIT). Participants undergo eight different social situations in the context of role-plays. The contents are "being criticized," "being the focus of attention," "anger," "meeting someone of the opposite sex," "expression of warmth," "receive compliments," "conflict with a close relative," and "interpersonal loss." A confederate is present and initiates the situation. The interactions are videotaped and subsequently rated by independent evaluators on two global dimensions of social competence: *anxiety* (1 "extremely anxious" to 11 "not at all anxious") and *performance* (1 "not at all skillful" to 11 "extremely skillful"). This rating system shows high inter- and intrarater reliability, good discriminant validity, but somewhat poor convergent validity (Curran, 1982; Curran et al., 1982; Mersch, Breukers, & Emmelkamp, 1992). Among the disadvantages of assessing social skills with global constructs is the correlation of the ratings with other personal features of the participants, such as outer appearance (Hope & Mindell, 1994).

Another BAT-based rating system of social performance was developed by Fydrich, Chambless, Perry, Bürgener, and Beazley (1998). The rating system focuses primarily on nonverbal indicators of social competence. The behavioral task consists of initiating and maintaining a conversation with a person from the opposite sex for three minutes. The rating system includes five behavioral categories, and each category is specified further: "eye contact," "voice and language" (pitch, intonation, clarity of speech, volume), "speech length" (monosyllabic, short answers, prolonged answers that impede a conversation), "physical restlessness and nervousness" (arm or leg movement, self-manipulation, facial expression, body gesture), and "conversation fluency." The raters evaluate the performance during the role-play according to these categories on a Likert scale from (1) "very good" to (5) "very bad." The system is characterized by good reliability (e.g., high interrater agreements for the categories: .75–.95) and satisfactory validity (e.g., construct validity and discriminant validity). Although developed primarily for individuals with social phobia, the rating system measures central elements of social behavior that are associated with social skills across different mental disorders (Monti et al., 1984). The disadvantage of the rating system is the large amount of time required for preparing and scoring.

## CLINICAL UTILITY

As stated earlier, social skills deficits are often associated with poor performance in social situations (Trower et al., 1978), which are both closely linked to the individual's social developmental background (Hopko, McNeil, Zvolensky, & Eifert, 2001). Whereas some emotional disorders, such as social phobia, are seen as being caused by social skills deficits, other disorders, such as depression (e.g., Tse & Bond, 2004) are believed to cause these skills deficits. Although it remains uncertain whether social skills are the cause or the consequence of mental disorders, a variety of studies have shown that social skills training is beneficial to individuals with mental disorders (e.g., Bellack, Buchanan, & Gold, 2001; Mersch, Emmelkamp, Bögels, & van der Sleen, 1989; Wallace, 1998; Wlazlo, Schröder-Hartwig, Hand, Kaiser, & Münchau, 1990). Subsequently, we briefly review the significance of social skills to several selected emotional disorders.

### SOCIAL PHOBIA

A number of publications in the 1970s and '80s indicated that a lack of social skills cause and maintain social anxiety (McFall, 1982; Trower et al., 1978). Specifically, it was assumed that an individual fears to fail social norms or expectations because of the skills deficit. It is controversial if individuals with social phobia are less socially skilled than others because they are lacking the skills (lack of the potential) or because their anxiety inhibits access to their skills (lack of the performance despite presence of the potential). Some researchers attempted to bypass the term *social skills* in social phobia, due to its connotation of lack of ability, by using more general terms, such as *performance quality* (Cohn & Hope, 2001).

Recently, the assumption of social skills deficit as a cause or by-product of social anxiety has been challenged (Stravynski & Amado, 2001). In reviewing evidence for the role of social skills in social phobia, Stravynski and Amado come to the following conclusion: "No evidence has emerged to link social phobia consistently with deficits of social skills, let alone to suggest that they play a causal role of any kind" (p. 124). Given the initial enthusiasm for the social skills deficit hypothesis, this assessment may be disappointing. Nevertheless, many individuals with social phobia benefit from social skills training when it is combined with other treatment strategies (Cohn & Hope, 2001).

## DEPRESSION

As in the case of social phobia, social skills deficits are common among individuals with depression (e.g., Ellgring, 1986; Segrin, 2000). In fact, depression and social skills seem to share a high proportion of variance in self-report measures (>70%; Cole, Lazarik, & Howard, 1987). The lack of social skills is central to multifactor models of depression. It is suggested that social skills deficits play a role as triggers and maintaining factors in depression (Segrin & Abramson, 1994). Some earlier studies have reported that social skills deficits did not significantly influence depression but that depression significantly impacted social skills (e.g., Cole & Mistead, 1989). In a recent review on the impact of depression on social skills, Tse and Bond (2004) concluded that social skills deficits are manifestations of depression. On the other hand, depressed patients appear to benefit from social skills training, and social skills training is a regular component of cognitive-behavioral treatment approaches (e.g., Segrin, 2000), suggesting that improving interpersonal skills may help to reduce mood disturbances.

## SCHIZOPHRENIA

Schizophrenia strongly interferes with the individual's social functioning (e.g., Bellack, 2004). Therefore, social skills trainings are a common element in the psychological treatment of schizophrenia. In contrast to the case with other disorders, social skills deficits are not seen as a causal factor of schizophrenia. Instead, it has been noted that schizophrenia is associated with cognitive impairments, positive and negative symptoms that limit the individual in social performance. Because a substantial proportion of patients continue to show residual symptoms after acute symptoms have subsided, social skills training is particularly important for the rehabilitation of patients (Wallace, 1998). One aspect of schizophrenia is impaired affect recognition. In fact, negative affect recognition is more greatly impaired in schizophrenia than in other disorders, such as substance abuse (Bell, Bryson, & Lysaker, 1997). Correct affect recognition is a necessary precondition for appropriate interpersonal behavior (see p. 237). Thus, schizophrenic patients may benefit from social skills training. Reviews of the evidence for social skills trainings in schizophrenia demonstrate that it produces significant and stable improvements in social functioning (Wallace). Therefore, social skills trainings are included in practice guidelines for schizophrenia (Bellack et al., 2001). However, there are two shortcomings: (1) Assessment of social skills in schizophrenia lacks preciseness (Wallace), and (2) despite the promising data on its efficacy, data are insufficient on the effectiveness (clinical utility) of social skills training in schizophrenia (Bellack et al.).

## ALCOHOL ABUSE OR DEPENDENCE

It has been suggested that individuals with poor social skills may drink alcohol to relieve social stress in the absence of more adaptive responses (e.g., Monti, Gulliver, & Myers, 1994). Several studies provide support for this notion and show that prealcoholic heavy-drinking teenagers are less socially skilled than their light- or nondrinking peers (O'Leary, O'Leary, & Donovan, 1976). Furthermore, it is established that alcoholic patients have lower interpersonal and social skills than healthy controls and experience more discomfort in situations that require assertiveness (for an overview, see Monti et al.). For example, alcoholic patients have more difficulties correctly identifying emotional facial expressions, and these difficulties are related to interpersonal problems (Kornreich et al., 2002). Also, general social skills trainings are an effective treatment for alcohol-use disorders (Miller & Wilbourne, 2002). Unfortunately, the mechanism responsible for the treatment effect is unclear, because there is no firm empirical support for the association between treatment success and social skills (Morgenstern & Longabaugh, 2000).

Alcohol- or drug-refusal skills, a special form of social skills, has received much attention in the research focusing on reasons for alcohol abuse and relapse after treatment (e.g., Scheier, Botvin, Diaz, & Griffin, 1999). Rist and Davies-Osterkamp (1977) were among the first to develop a behavior program to teach patients alcohol-refusal skills. This early study showed that refusal skills improved substantially as a result of the intervention. Furthermore, drug and alcohol prevention programs often focused on refusal skills (e.g., Cuijpers, 2002). Generally, interactive drug and alcohol prevention programs focusing either on general social skills or specifically on refusal skills seem to be more effective than noninteractive programs (e.g., Tobler et al., 2004). Thus, social skills training is an important component in most treatment programs for alcoholism and drug abuse.

## BORDERLINE PERSONALITY DISORDER

Borderline Personality Disorder (BPD) is characterized by significant interpersonal problems. The main treatment approach (dialectical behavioral therapy [DBT]; Linehan, 1993) is competency based and includes a number of strategies to improve social skills. However, in light of the relevance of interpersonal skills to this disorder, it is surprising there are only very few studies on the observed social competence of BPD patients. Clinicians usually describe a waxing and waning of socially skilled behaviors in BPD patients that has been entitled "pretended social competence" (Linehan). Studies suggest that the perception of emotional expressions of faces seems unimpaired in BPD (Wagner & Linehan, 1999). However, BPD patients may be more at risk of showing poor social skills when they feel rejected or abandoned (Renneberg, Mücke, Wallis, Fydrich, Thomas, 2003). In a recent study on socially competent behavior in BPD patients, Renneberg and colleagues found lower social competence in both BPD patients and depressed patients. In addition, both groups evaluated their own behavior more negatively than a group of nonclinical control participants. However, only BPD patients were rated as less competent in nonverbal aspects of social behavior after a negative mood induction, compared to their performance after a positive mood induction. They differed significantly from both other groups in their perception of the interaction partner after the negative mood induction.

## DISFIGUREMENT

People with visible disfigurement experience more difficulties when trying to contact others and receive more negative feedback (e.g., being stared or cursed at) than people without such disfigurement (Thompson & Kent, 2001). First-time encounters are particularly problematic (Porter, Beuf, Lerner, & Norlund, 1990). Consequently, most psychological treatment programs focus on ways to ameliorate the social impact of visible differences. Important components of such treatments include practical strategies to deal with social encounters. This is especially important because social avoidance and loneliness are more closely related to the psychological distress experienced by the patients than is the degree of disfigurement (Root, Kent, & Alabie, 1994). Similarly, lack of social interaction skills are more relevant for predicting distress in patients than, for example, is the location of a disfigurement (Robinson, 1997). Cognitive behavioral treatment involving social skills training reduces social avoidance behavior, increases life satisfaction, and reduces anxiety and depression (e.g., Kleve, Rumsey, Wyn-Williams, & White, 2002). Interestingly, this effect was independent of the degree of social anxiety due to the disfigurement. Psychosocial treatment is also effective if it consists exclusively of social skills training (Robinson, Rumsey, & Partridge, 1996).

In sum, the social skills concept remains an elusive clinical entity. Whereas the clinical utility of social skills training has been widely supported, many questions remain concerning the definition and assessment of social skills deficits.

## TREATMENT PLANNING

Several issues are important to consider when including social skills training in the treatment process. First, behaviors and skills that are potentially important for the practical social context of the patient should be identified. It is important to consider norms and demands of behaviors in the patient's environment. Different situations demand different behaviors. Next, the ability of the patient, in terms of skills and behaviors, should be assessed and quantified (if possible). It is advisable to employ role-play situations that closely represent the target behavior and situation.

The literature provides few guidelines on how the assessment of social skills should relate to treatment planning and delivery. Therefore, we subsequently take a first step at outlining the potential problem-specific implications derived from the assessment of social skills for training purposes. However, in light of the scant evidence and research on this link, the illustration is preliminary in nature.


## CASE STUDY

### IDENTIFICATION, PRESENTING COMPLAINTS, AND HISTORY

The patient we describe for our illustration was a 26-year-old single male who lived with his parents in the family's home in a small suburban town. He identified social anxiety as his primary problem and reported that he would avoid almost all social situations in his daily life. He requested treatment because of his parents' deteriorating health and stated he would simply be unable to live by himself without the support of his parents because of his social anxiety.

The patient underwent a structured diagnostic interview, the Anxiety Disorders Interview Schedule for *DSM-III-R* (ADIS; DiNardo & Barlow, 1988). The ADIS screens for all Axis I mood and anxiety disorders and assigns a clinical severity rating (CSR) on a scale from 0 (no distress/interference) to 8 (extreme distress/interference). A CSR rating of 4 or higher marks the clinical threshold.

The present patient met criteria for the following Axis I diagnoses: Social Phobia, generalized subtype (clinical severity rating, CSR: 7) and Obsessive-Compulsive Disorder (CSR: 6). Furthermore, he met criteria for Avoidant Personality Disorder (CSR: 6) on Axis II and Tinnitus on Axis III. The raters coded problems related to the social environment and occupational problems on Axis IV and assigned a Global Assessment of Functioning score of 58 (current) on Axis V (serious symptoms or any serious impairment in social, occupational, or school functions).


### BEHAVIORAL ASSESSMENT OF SOCIAL SKILLS

A multimodal and multimethod assessment was conducted that also included a role-play to assess social skills and/or performance deficits. Two distinct areas were assessed: (1) the perception of social situations (knowledge about social norms and appropriate responses) and (2) the ability to behave in appropriate ways in certain social situations (self- and clinician rated).

In order to measure social ability, a BAT was constructed. Specifically, the clinician asked the patient to maintain and initiate a five-minute conversation with a female confederate. The clinician observed this interaction through a one-way mirror and estimated the number of eye contacts and their length, recorded observable behaviors of anxiety (such as hand tremor), and recorded the conversation strategies the patient used.

The patient reported intense anxiety before and during the interaction and displayed clear signs of anxious behaviors. Specifically, the patient showed visible trembling as an overt expression of his anxiety. The behavioral observation further demonstrated that he looked at the other person only three times and he was able to maintain eye contact for only a few seconds. During the BAT, he asked no questions and gave only brief answers. After two and a half minutes, he terminated the task.

In order to measure the patient's perception of social norms, he was asked to read a list of vignettes in which a social situation and a behavioral response is described (for a complete version of this instrument, please contact the first author). For example, one of the vignettes read:

> A wife tells her husband that she would like to complete her studies to get a final degree. He however disapproves of this idea and is saying: "Why do you want to do this all? You know that you are unable to cope with the extra distress this will cause."

The patient was asked to classify the given response as assertive, aggressive, or socially insecure. He demonstrated good skills in perceiving social situations, and he appropriately classified the responses to these situations as assertive, aggressive, or socially insecure. In fact, he showed good insight and sensitivity for the possible emotional responses of the other person(s) described in the social vignettes. This suggests that he was sufficiently skilled to discriminate social situations and their requirements.

In order to assess self-perceived ability to show a certain behavioral response, a second questionnaire, consisting of different vignettes, was administered. The patient was asked to indicate on a scale from 0 (easy) to 100 (very difficult) how difficult he believed it would be for him to show a particular behavior in response to the situation. It became clear that the patient had problems with being assertive (all situations independent of the context rated 85% or higher). The social context and relationship to the person was an important dimension that influenced his ratings. For situations that involved disclosing emotions, he reported moderate (50–70%) difficulties if the other person was a significant other.

## CONCEPTUALIZATION AND TREATMENT RECOMMENDATIONS

The patient showed severe performance deficits due to his social anxiety. Interestingly, social judgment was unaffected, because he was able to identify the appropriate social behaviors in a given situation. He also clearly demonstrated a lack of skills in initiating and maintaining a conversation with a stranger and was deficient in assertiveness skills. Therefore, treatment focused primarily on assertiveness skills combined with exposure and cognitive intervention techniques.

## SUMMARY

The construct of social skills is poorly defined. Nevertheless, it appears to be an important treatment component for some disorders. Social skills have been assessed via different methods. Social intelligence tests are not recommended because of their overlap with general intelligence. Self-report measures seem to be a reliable and valid way to assess social skills. However, clinicians need to remember that the results of these instruments should be interpreted in the context of the particular mental disorder. Finally, behavioral assessment tests may constitute a reliable approach to assess social skills. The drawback, however, is the difficulty to distinguish potential suppression effects on social performance caused by the presence of mental disorders from the ability to show certain behaviors. In addition, there are no clear guidelines on whether one should assess molar or molecular behaviors of social performances, and the decision will, again, depend on the psychopathology.

Another neglected aspect is the link between assessment results and treatment planning. In many cases, social skills training is administered as one of the many treatment components, but it remains uncertain whether social skills trainings have any specific treatment effects above and beyond exposure strategies and cognitive interventions.

## REFERENCES

Adams, J. A. (1987). Historical review and appraisal of research on the learning retention and transfer of human motor skills. *Psychological Bulletin, 101,* 41–74.

Bastians, F., & Runde, B. (2002). Measurement of social competencies. *Zeitschrift für Psychologie, 210,* 186–196.

Becker, R. E., & Heimberg, R. G. (1988). Assessment of social skills. In A. Bellack & M. Hersen (Eds.), *Behavioral assessment* (pp. 365–395). Oxford, UK: Pergamon Press.

Beidel, D. C., Turner, S. M., Jacob, R. G., & Cooley, M. R. (1989). Assessment of social phobia: Reliability of an impromptu speech task. *Journal of Anxiety Disorders, 3,* 149–158.

Bell, M., Bryson, G., & Lysaker, P. (1997). Positive and negative affect recognition in schizophrenia: A comparison with substance-abuse and normal control subjects. *Psychiatry Research, 73,* 73–82.

Bellack, A. S. (1979). A critical appraisal of strategies for assessing social skill. *Behavioral Assessment, 1,* 157–176.

Bellack, A. S. (2004). Skills training for people with severe mental illness. *Psychiatric Rehabilitation Journal, 27,* 375–391.

Bellack, A. S., Buchanan, R. W., & Gold, J. M. (2001). The American Psychiatric practice guidelines for schizophrenia: Scientific base and relevance for behavior therapy. *Behavior Therapy, 32,* 283–308.

Burns, K. L., & Beier, E. G. (1973). Significance of vocal and visual channels in decoding of emotional meaning. *Journal of Communication, 23,* 118–130.

Carton, J. S., Kessler, E. A., & Pape, C. L. (1999). Nonverbal decoding skills and relationship well-being in adults. *Journal of Nonverbal Behavior, 23,* 91–100.

Cohn, L. G., & Hope, D. A. (2001). Treatment of social phobia: A treatments-by-dimensions review. In S. G. Hofmann & P. M. DiBartolo (Eds.), *From social anxiety to social phobia: Multiple perspectives* (pp. 354–378). Needham Heights, MA: Allyn & Bacon.

Cole, D. A., Lazarick, D. L., & Howard, G. S. (1987). Construct validity and the relation between depression and social skill. *Journal of Counseling Psychology, 34,* 315–321.

Cole, D. A., & Milstead, M. (1989). Behavioral correlates of depression: Antecedents or consequences? *Journal of Counseling Psychology, 36,* 408–416.

Conger, A. J., & Conger, J. C. (1986). Assessment of social skills. In A. R. Ciminero, K. S. Calhoun, & H. E. Adams (Eds.), *Handbook of behavioral assessment* (pp. 526–560). New York: John Wiley & Sons.

Corrigan, P. W. (1997). The social perceptual deficits of schizophrenia. *Psychiatry—Interpersonal and Biological Processes, 60,* 309–326.

Costanzo, M., & Archer, D. (1989). Interpreting the Expressive Behavior of Others—the Interpersonal Perception Task. *Journal of Nonverbal Behavior, 13,* 225–245.

Cuijpers, P. (2002). Effective ingredients of school-based drug prevention programs—A systematic review. *Addictive Behaviors, 27,* 1009–1023.

Curran, J. P. (1979). Social skills: Methodological issues and future directions. In A. S. Bellack & M. Hersen (Eds.), *Research and practice in social skills training* (pp. 319–354). New York: Plenum Press.

Curran, J. P. (1982). A procedure for the assessment of social skills: The Simulated Social Interaction Test. In J. P. Curran & P. M. Monti (Eds.), *Social skills training: A practical handbook for assessment and treatment* (pp. 348–373). New York: Guilford Press.

Curran, J. P., Wessberg, H. W., Farell, A. D., Monti, P. M., Corriveau, D. P., & Coyne, N. A. (1982). Social skills and social anxiety: Are different laboratories measuring the same construct? *Journal of Consulting and Clinical Psychology, 50,* 396–406.

Denham, S. A., Mckinley, M., Couchoud, E. A., & Holt, R. (1990). Emotional and behavioral predictors of preschool peer ratings. *Child Development, 61,* 1145–1152.

DiNardo, P. A., & Barlow, D. H. (1988). *Anxiety Disorders Interview Schedule-Revised (ADIS-R).* Graywind Allications Inc./The Psychological Corporation: San Antonio, TX.

Dykman, B. M., Abramson, L. Y., Horowitz, L. M., & Usher, M. (1991). Schematic and situational determinants of depressed and nondepressed students' interpretation of feedback. *Journal of Abnormal Psychology, 100,* 45–55.

Ellgring, H. (1986). Nonverbal expression of psychological states in psychiatric patients. *European Archives of Psychiatry, Neurology Sciences, 236,* 30–34.

Feldman, M., & Thayer, S. (1980). A comparison of three measures of nonverbal decoding ability. *Journal of Social Psychology, 112,* 91–97.

Ford, M. E. (1985). The concept of competence: Themes and variations. In H. A. Marlowe & R. B. Weinberg (Eds.), *Competence development* (pp. 3–49). Springfield, IL: Charles C Thomas.

Fydrich, T., Chambless, D. L., Perry, K. J., Bürgener, F., & Beazley, M. B. (1998). Behavioral assessment of social performance: A rating system for social phobia. *Behaviour Research and Therapy, 36,* 995–1010.

Gambrill, E. (1995). Assertion skills training. In W. O'Donohue & L. Krasner (Eds.), *Handbook of social skills training* (pp. 81–118). Boston: Allyn & Bacon.

Gambrill, E. D., & Richey, C. A. (1975). Assertion inventory for use in assessment and research. *Behavior Therapy, 6,* 550–561.

Gerlach, A. L., Wilhelm, F. H., Gruber, K., & Roth, W. T. (2001). Blushing and physiological arousability in social phobia. *Journal of Abnormal Psychology, 110,* 247–258.

Goldfried, M. R., & D'Zurilla, T. J. (1969). A behavioral analytic model for assessing competence. In C. D. Spielberger (Ed.), *Current topics in clinical and community psychology* (pp. 151–196). New York: Academic Press.

Hersen, M., & Bellack, A. S. (1976a). Multiple baseline analysis of social skills training in chronic schizophrenics. *Journal of Applied Behavior Analysis, 9,* 239–245.

Hersen, M., & Bellack, A. S. (1976b). Social skills training for chronic psychiatric patients—Rationale, research findings, and future directions. *Comprehensive Psychiatry, 17,* 559–580.

Hofmann, S. G., Gerlach, A. L., Wender, A., & Roth, W. T. (1997). Speech disturbances and gaze behavior during public speaking in subtypes of social phobia. *Journal of Anxiety Disorders, 11,* 573–585.

Hope, D. A., & Mindell, J. A. (1994). Global social skills rating: Measures of social behaviour or physical attractiveness. *Behaviour Research and Therapy, 32,* 463–469.

Hopko, D. R., McNeil, D. W., Zvolensky, M. J., & Eifert, G. H. (2001). The relation between anxiety and skill performance–based anxiety disorders. A behavioral formulation of social phobia. *Behavior Therapy, 32,* 185–207.

Kanning, U. P. (2003). *Diagnostik Sozialer Kompetenzen* [Assessment of social competencies]. Göttingen, Germany: Hogrefe.

Kleve, L., Rumsey, N., Wyn-Williams, M., & White, P. (2002). The effectiveness of cognitive-behavioral interventions provided at "Outlook", a disfigurement support unit. *Journal of Evaluation in Clinical Practice, 8,* 387–394.

Kornreich, C., Philippot, P., Foisy, M. L., Blairy, S., Raynaud, E., Dan, B., et al. (2002). Impaired emotional facial expression recognition is associated with interpersonal problems in alcoholism. *Alcohol and Alcoholism, 37,* 394–400.

Libet, J. M., & Lewinsohn, P. M. (1973). Concept of social skill with special reference to the behavior of depressed persons. *Journal of Consulting and Clinical Psychology, 40,* 304–312.

Linehan, M. M. (1993). Cognitive-behavioral treatment of borderline personality disorder. New York: Guilford Press.

Lorr, M., Youniss, R. P., & Stefic, E. C. (1991). An Inventory of Social Skills. *Journal of Personality Assessment, 57,* 506–520.

Marlowe, H. A. (1985). Competence: A social intelligence perspective. In H. A. Marlowe & R. B. Weinberg (Eds.), *Competence development* (pp. 50–82). Springfield, IL: Charles C Thomas.

McClure, E. B., Pope, K., Hoberman, A. J., Pine, D. S., & Leibenluft, E. (2003). Facial expression recognition in adolescents with mood and anxiety disorders. *American Journal of Psychiatry, 160,* 1172–1174.

McFall, R. M. (1982). A review and reformulation of the concept of social skills. *Behavioral Assessment, 4,* 1–33.

Melfsen, S., & Florin, I. (2003). Aspects of emotional competence in socially anxious children. *Zeitschrift für Klinische Psychologie und Psychotherapie, 32,* 307–314.

Mersch, P. P., Breukers, P., & Emmelkamp, P. M. G. (1992). The Simulated Social Interaction Test: A psychometric evaluation with Dutch social phobic patients. *Behavioral Assessment, 14,* 133–151.

Mersch, P. P., Emmelkamp, P. M. G., Bögels, S. M., & van der Sleen, J. (1989). Social phobia: Individual response patterns and the effects of behavioral and cognitive interventions. *Behaviour Research and Therapy, 27,* 421–434.

Miller, W. R., & Wilbourne, P. L. (2002). Mesa Grande: A methodological analysis of clinical trials of treatments for alcohol use disorders. *Addiction, 97,* 265–277.

Monti, P. M., Gulliver, S. B., & Myers, M. G. (1994). Social skills training for alcoholics: Assessment and treatment. *Alcohol and Alcoholism, 29,* 627–637.

Monti, P. M., Boice, R., Fingeret, A. L., Zwickend, R., Kolko, D., Munroe, S., et al. (1984). Midlevel measurement of social anxiety in psychiatric and nonpsychiatric samples. *Behaviour Research and Therapy, 22,* 651–660.

Morgan, R. G. T. (1980). Analysis of social skills: The behavior analysis approach. In W. T. Singleton, P. Spurgeon, & R. B. Stammers (Eds.), *The analysis of social skill* (pp. 103–130). New York: Plenum Press.

Morgenstern, J., & Longabaugh, R. (2000). Cognitive-behavioral treatment for alcohol dependence: A review of evidence for its hypothesized mechanisms of action. *Addiction, 95,* 1475–1490.

Morrison, R. L., & Bellack, A. S. (1981). The role of social perception in social skill. *Behavior Therapy, 12,* 69–79.

Nietzel, M. T., Bernstein, D. A., & Russell, R. L. (1988). Assessment of anxiety and fear. In A. S. Bellack & M. Hersen (Eds.), *Behavioral assessment. A practical handbook* (pp. 280–312). New York: Pergamon Press.

O'Connor, K. (1989). Psychophysiology and skilled behavior: A theoretical revision. *Journal of Psychophysiology, 3,* 219–223.

O'Leary, D. E., O'Leary, M. R., & Donovan, D. M. (1976). Social skill acquisition and psychosocial development of alcoholics: A review. *Addictive Behaviors, 1,* 111–120.

O'Sullivan, M., & Guilford, J. P. (1966). *Six-Factor Test of Social Intelligence.* Beverly Hills, CA: Sheridian Psychological Services.

Porter, J. R., Beuf, A. H., Lerner, A. B., & Nordlund, J. J. (1990). The effect of vitiligo on sexual relationships. *Journal of the American Academy of Dermatology, 22,* 221–222.

Renneberg, B., Mücke, M., Wallis, H., Fydrich, T., & Thomas, C. (2003). Wie sozial kompetent sind Patientinnen mit Borderline Persönlichkeitsstörungen [Social competence in Borderline Personality Disorder]. *Verhaltenstherapie und Verhaltensmedizin, 24,* 329–345.

Riggio, R. E. (1986). Assessment of basic social skills. *Journal of Personality and Social Psychology, 51,* 649–660.

Riggio, R. E., Messamer, J., & Throckmortin, B. (1991). Social and academic intelligence: Conceptually distinct but overlapping constructs. *Personality and Individual Differences, 12,* 695–702.

Rist, F., & Davies-Osterkamp, S. (1977). An alcohol contact program: Training for increased security of alcoholics in trial situations. *Drug & Alcohol Dependence, 2,* 163–173.

Robinson, E. (1997). Psychological research on visible differences in adults. In R. Lansdown, N. Rumsey, A. Bradbury, A. Carr, & J. Partridge (Eds.), *Visibly different: Coping with disfigurement* (pp. 102–111). London: Butterworth Heinemann.

Robinson, E., Rumsey, N., & Partridge, J. (1996). An evaluation of the impact of social interaction skills training for facially disfigured people. *British Journal of Plastic Surgery, 49,* 281–289.

Root, S., Kent, G., & Abadie, M. S. (1994). The relationship between disease severity, disability, and psychological distress in patients undergoing PUVA treatment for psoriasis. *Dermatology, 189,* 234–237.

Rosenthal, R., Archer, D., Koivumaki, J., DiMatteo, R., & Rogers, P. (1979). Assessing sensitivity to nonverbal communication: The PONS test. *Division 8 Newsletter, APA.*

Scheier, L. M., Botvin, G. J., Diaz, T., & Griffin, K. W. (1999). Social skills, competence, and drug refusal efficacy as predictors of adolescent alcohol use. *Journal of Drug Education, 29,* 251–278.

Schroeder, J. E., & Ketrow, S. M. (1997). Social anxiety and performance in an interpersonal perception task. *Psychological Reports, 81,* 991–996.

Segrin, C. (2000). Social skills deficits associated with depression. *Clinical Psychology Review, 20,* 379–403.

Segrin, C., & Abramson, L. Y. (1994). Negative reactions to depressive behaviors: A communication theories analysis. *Journal of Abnormal Psychology, 103,* 655–668.

Stravynski, A., & Amado, D. (2001). Social phobia as a deficit in social skills. In S. G. Hofmann & P. M. DiBartolo (Eds.), *From social anxiety to social phobia: Multiple perspectives* (pp. 107–129). Needham Heights, MA: Allyn & Bacon.

Thompson, A., & Kent, G. (2001). Adjusting to disfigurement: Processes involved in dealing with being visibly different. *Clinical Psychology Review, 21,* 663–682.

Tobler, N. S., Roona, M. R., Ochshorn, P., Marshall, D. G., Streke, A. V., & Stackpole, K. M. (2004). School-based adolescent drug prevention programs: 1998 meta-analysis. *Journal of Primary Prevention, 20,* 275–336.

Toomey, R., Seidman, L. J., Lyons, M. J., Faraone, S. V., & Tsuang, M. T. (1999). Poor perception of nonverbal social-emotional cues in relatives of schizophrenic patients. *Schizophrenia Research, 40,* 121–130.

Trower, P. (1980). Situational analysis of the components and processes of behavior of socially skilled and unskilled patients. *Journal of Consulting and Clinical Psychology, 48,* 327–339.

Trower, P., Bryant, B., & Argyle, M. (1978). *Social skills and mental health.* Pittsburgh, PA: University of Pittsburgh Press.

Tse, W. S., & Bond, A. J. (2004). The impact of depression on social skills. *Journal of Nervous and Mental Disease, 192,* 260–268.

Twentyman, C. T., & McFall, R. M. (1975). Behavioral training of social skills in shy males. *Journal of Consulting and Clinical Psychology, 43,* 384–395.

Wagner, A. W., & Linehan, M. M. (1999). Facial expression recognition ability among women with borderline personality disorder: Implications for emotional regulation? *Journal of Personality Disorders, 13,* 329–344.

Wallace, C. J. (1998). Social skills training in psychiatric rehabilitation: Recent findings. *International Review of Psychiatry, 10,* 9–19.

Wallander, J. L., Conger, A. J., Mariotto, M. J., Curran, J. P., & Farrell, A. D. (1980). Comparability of selection instruments in studies of heterosexual-social problem behaviors. *Behavior Therapy, 11,* 548–560.

Wlazlo, Z., Schröder-Hartwig, K., Hand, I., Kaiser, G., & Münchau, N. (1990). Exposure *in vivo* versus social skills training in social phobia. Long-term outcome and differential effects. *Behaviour Research and Therapy, 28,* 181–193.

Wolpe, J., & Lazarus, A. (1966). *Behavior therapy techniques.* New York: Pergamon Press.

Zigler, E., & Phillips, L. (1960). Social effectiveness and symptomatic behaviors. *Journal of Abnormal and Social Psychology, 61,* 231–238.

# 12

## EATING DISORDERS

### TIFFANY M. STEWART
### DONALD A. WILLIAMSON

*Pennington Biomedical Research Center*
*Baton Rouge, Louisiana*

### INTRODUCTION

Selection of appropriate assessment measures for eating disorders should be based on the construct or assessment question of interest. For example, different assessment measures will probably be required for screening, diagnosis, and assessment of treatment outcome. Eating disorders, as defined by the *DSM-IV* (American Psychiatric Association, 1994), may be conceptualized as having multiple symptom domains that are important to assess. Thus, eating disorders are best assessed in a multidimensional fashion, including six very important features of eating disorders: body size, restrictive eating, binge eating, compensatory behavior (e.g. purging), body image, and general psychopathology. It is important to utilize reliable and valid measures to assess the construct of interest at all time points, including screening, diagnosis, and treatment outcome. To establish an eating disorder diagnosis, *DSM-IV* diagnostic criteria, summarized in Table 12.1, should be used.

This chapter provides an "at a glance" reference for assessment of eating disorders, including anorexia nervosa (AN), bulimia nervosa (BN), Binge Eating Disorder (BED), and Eating Disorder Not Otherwise Specified (EDNOS), in a multidimensional fashion. First, selected methods that can be utilized for assessment of eating disorders are described, including screening measures, diagnostic interviews, and multisymptom measures. Measures that assess pathological eating, body image, and body weight are also described. Suggestions for the examination of physical/medical issues, comorbid psychopathology, and special problems are presented. Information on the research basis of the assessment measures is presented. Recommendations for the clinical use of these measures are provided. Table 12.2 presents a summary of the methods, reliability and valid-

TABLE 12.1    Summary of *DSM-IV* Diagnostic Criteria for Anorexia and Bulimia Nervosa

### *DSM-IV* Criteria for Anorexia Nervosa

A. Refusal to maintain body weight at or above a minimally normal weight for age and height.

B. Despite being underweight, the person has an intense fear of gaining weight or becoming fat.

C. Body image disturbance. Denial of seriousness of low weight status.

D. The absence of at least three consecutive menstrual cycles (in females who have past puberty).

*Types*

*Restricting type:* The person has not regularly engaged in binge eating or compensatory (i.e., purging) behavior.

*Binge-eating/purging type:* The person has regularly engaged in binge eating or compensatory behavior.

### *DSM-IV* Criteria for Bulimia Nervosa

A. Episodes of binge eating that are recurrent. An episode of binge eating has both of the following characteristics:

    (1) Eating in a discrete period of time, an objectively large amount of food

    (2) A sense of lack of control over eating during the episode

B. Recurrent compensatory behavior in order to prevent weight gain (e.g., self-induced vomiting; misuse of laxatives, diuretics, enemas, other medications; fasting; or excessive exercise).

C. The binge-eating and compensatory behaviors both occur at least twice a week for 3 months.

D. Self-evaluation is strongly influenced by body shape and weight.

E. The disturbance does not occur exclusively during episodes of anorexia nervosa.

*Types*

*Purging type:* The person has regularly engaged in self-induced vomiting or the misuse of laxatives, diuretics, or enemas.

*Nonpurging type:* The person has used other compensatory behaviors, such as fasting and excessive exercise, but has not regularly engaged in self-induced vomiting or misuse of laxatives, diuretics, or enemas.

---

These criteria are derived from the criteria specified by the American Psychiatric Association (1994).

ity information, and preferred environment utility (clinical or research) reviewed in this chapter. Table 12.2 is broken down by category of the measures. On each of the measures, information on assessment domains (e.g., body size, binge eating, body image), psychometric properties (i.e., reliability and validity), and information on clinical utility (e.g., research or clinical setting) is provided. Next, assessment is discussed in the context of case conceptualization and treatment planning. A case study is presented. Finally, conclusions are summarized.

## ASSESSMENT STRATEGIES

### SCREENING MEASURES FOR EATING DISORDERS

Some of the measures that have been established as useful, reliable, and valid for screening the presence of eating disorders are described here. A summary of these measures may be found in Table 12.2.

TABLE 12.2 Summary of Eating Disorder Assessment Methods, Domains Measured by Each Method, and Psychometric Properties

| | Body Size | Binge Eating | Compensatory Behavior | Restrictive Eating | Body Image | General Psychopathology | Reliability | Validity | Clinical Utility |
|---|---|---|---|---|---|---|---|---|---|
| **Screening** | | | | | | | | | |
| Eating Attitudes Test | | X | X | X | | | TR, IC | CC, CT, CR | R |
| Eating Disorder Diagnostic Scale | | X | X | X | | | TR, IC | CT, CR, CC | R, C |
| Eating Disorder Examination Questionnaire | | X | X | X | X | | TR, IC | CT, CR, CC | R, C |
| **Diagnosis** | | | | | | | | | |
| Eating Disorder Examination | | X | X | X | X | | IR, TR, IC | CO, CT, CR, CC, D | R |
| Interview for the Diagnosis of Eating Disorders—IV | | X | X | X | X | | IR, TR | CO, CR, CT | R, C |
| **Multiscale Measures** | | | | | | | | | |
| Eating Disorder Inventory—2 | | X | X | X | X | X | TR, IC | CO, CT, CR | R, C |
| Multidimensional Assessment of Eating Disorder Symptoms | | X | X | X | X | X | TR, IC | CC, CR | R, C |
| **Pathological Eating Habits** | | | | | | | | | |
| Bulimia Test Revised | | X | X | | X | | TR, IC | CO, CC, CT, CR, D, P | R |
| Self-Monitoring | | X | X | X | X | | | | C |
| Eating Inventory | | X | | X | | | TR | CC, D | R, C |
| Binge Eating Scale | | X | | | | | IC | CC | R, C |

*(continues)*

TABLE 12.2 *(continued)*

| | Body Size | Binge Eating | Compensatory Behavior | Restrictive Eating | Body Image | General Psychopathology | Reliability | Validity | Clinical Utility |
|---|---|---|---|---|---|---|---|---|---|
| **Body Image** | | | | | | | | | |
| Body Image Assessment | | | | | X | | TR | CO, CC, D | R, C |
| Body Morph Assessment | | | | | X | | TR | CO, CC, CT, D | R, C |
| Body Shape Questionnaire | | | | | X | | TR | CR, CC, D | R, C |
| **Body Mass/Weight** | | | | | | | | | |
| Body Mass Index | X | | | | | | | | R, C |
| **Comorbid Diagnosis** | | | | | | | | | |
| Structural Clinical Interview *DSM-IV-I* | | | | | | X | TR, IR | | R |
| Structural Clinical Interview *DSM-IV-II* | | | | | | X | TR, IR | | R |
| **Special Problems** | | | | | | | | | |
| Food Craving Inventory | | X | | | | | TR, IC | CC, CO, CT, D | R, C |
| Body Checking Questionnaire | | | | | X | | TR, IC | CC, D | R, C |
| Muscle Appearance Satisfaction Scale | | | | | X | | TR, IC | CO, D | R, C |

Reliability is denoted by the following abbreviations: test–retest (TR), internal consistency (IC), and interrater (IR). Validity is denoted by the following abbreviations: construct (CO), content (CT), concurrent (CC), divergent (D), predictive (P), and criterion validity (CR). Clinical utility is designed to differentiate between primary use in research settings (R) or clinical settings (C).

## Eating Attitudes Test

The Eating Attitudes Test (EAT; Garner & Garfinkel, 1979) is a 40-item self-report inventory that measures the symptoms of anorexia nervosa. A modified version, the EAT-26, was developed in response to factor analysis of the original EAT (Garner, Olmstead, Bohr, & Garfinkel, 1982) and has been found to be highly correlated with the EAT ($r = .98$; Garner et al.). It can differentiate persons diagnosed with AN and BN from controls and from persons diagnosed with BED (Williamson, Prather, McKenzie, & Blouin, 1990). The EAT and EAT-26 are two of the most commonly used self-report inventories in eating disorder treatment studies (Williamson, Anderson, & Gleaves, 1996).

## Eating Disorder Diagnostic Scale

The Eating Disorder Diagnostic Scale (EDDS; Stice, Telch, & Rizvi, 2000) is a brief self-report (22 items) measure that utilizes content from the *DSM-IV* diagnostic criteria to form its questions. This measure is designed to diagnose AN, BN, and BED in accordance with *DSM-IV* criteria (American Psychiatric Association, 1994). The EDDS has not been as widely utilized in the literature as the EAT and EAT-26.

## Eating Disorder Examination—Questionnaire

The Eating Disorder Examination—Questionnaire (EDE-Q; Fairburn & Beglin, 1994) follows the content of the questions used in the interview called the Eating Disorders Examination (described shortly) to assess the central features of AN and BN. It can also be adapted for use with BED.

### DIAGNOSTIC INTERVIEWS FOR EATING DISORDERS

Diagnostic interviews are the most thorough, reliable, and valid methods for establishing clinical diagnoses. Two interviews (semistructured) for eating disorders that have been developed and tested are described in the following section. Properties of these measures are presented in Table 12.2.

## Eating Disorder Examination

The Eating Disorder Examination (EDE; Cooper & Fairburn, 1987; Fairburn & Cooper, 1993), currently in its 12th edition, is a semistructured interview designed to assess psychopathology associated with AN and BN. The EDE measures two behaviors: methods of extreme weight control and overeating. It has four subscales (restraint, eating concern, shape concern, weight concern). The interviewer rates the severity of symptoms. This feature of the EDE is important for measuring episodes of binge eating, because it removes some of the subjectivity of what defines a "binge," as the term *binge* is often defined differently by the patient and the professional. The EDE can be used to differentiate eating disorder patients from controls (Cooper, Cooper, & Fairburn, 1989). It can also differentiate between people who restrict their eating and individuals who have BN (Cooper et al.; Rosen, Vara, Wendt, & Leitenberg, 1990). The EDE is considered to be one of the best methods for assessing the core symptoms of eating disorders.

### Interview for Diagnosis of Eating Disorders—IV

The Interview for Diagnosis of Eating Disorders, fourth version (IDED-IV; Kutlesic, Williamson, Gleaves, Barbin, & Murphy-Eberenz, 1998), was developed specifically for the purpose of establishing differential diagnoses of AN, BN, BED, and EDNOS using the diagnostic criteria established by the American Psychiatric Association (1994). Factor analysis of the IDED-IV has found that it has three subscales: binge eating, compensatory behavior/fear of fatness, and drive for thinness. It has also been used to reliably differentiate obesity from Binge Eating Disorder (Kutlesic et al.).

## MULTISCALE QUESTIONNAIRES FOR EATING DISORDERS

Two of the most well-developed multiscale questionnaires for eating disorders are described next. For a quick summary, these measures may be found in Table 12.2.

### Eating Disorder Inventory—2

The EDI-2 was developed for use with AN and BN (Garner, 1991). The EDI-2 is a 91-item self-report measure that assesses symptom domains associated with eating disorders. The EDI-2 was developed from an earlier version of the measure (EDI; Garner, Olmstead, & Polivy, 1983). The EDI-2 retained the original scales from the EDI and added several additional scales. These scales on the EDI-2 include asceticism, impulse regulation, social insecurity, drive for thinness, bulimia, body dissatisfaction, ineffectiveness, perfectionism, interpersonal distrust, interoceptive awareness, and maturity fears.

### Multidimensional Assessment for Eating Disorder Symptoms

The Multidimensional Assessment of Eating Disorder Symptoms (MAEDS; Anderson, Williamson, Duchmann, Gleaves, & Barbin, 1999) is designed to measure treatment outcome with eating disorders. The MAEDS has six scales, which include binge eating, restrictive eating, purgative behavior, fear of fatness, avoidance of forbidden foods, and depression. The MAEDS measures the core symptoms of eating disorders and has 56 questions.

## METHODS FOR ASSESSING PATHOLOGICAL
## EATING HABITS

A variety of methods, including the EAT, have been developed to measure unhealthy or pathological eating habits. Other useful and widely used measures of eating habits are described in this section and summarized in Table 12.2.

### Bulimia Test—Revised

The Bulimia Test—Revised (BULIT-R; Thelen, Farmer, Wonderlich, & Smith, 1991) is designed to measure the symptoms of bulimia, as defined by *DSM-III-R* (American Psychiatric Association, 1987). The BULIT-R has 28 items. Much of the psychometric research on the BULIT was conducted on an earlier version (BULIT; M. C. Smith & Thelen, 1984). The BULIT and BULIT-R have been found to be highly correlated, however ($r = .99$; Thelen et al.). Recently, multisymptom scale questionnaires such as the MAEDS have replaced the BULIT-R because of the BULIT-R's specificity for BN.

### Self-Monitoring

Self-monitoring of food intake is a useful method for obtaining information about eating behavior and for conducting a functional analysis of pathological eating behavior (Williamson, 1990). Information collected via self-monitoring includes type and amounts of food eaten, eating patterns, frequency and topography of binge episodes and purgative behavior, and mood before and after the meal (Crowther & Sherwood, 1997). Self-monitoring is recommended as a clinical tool but should be interpreted with caution, given the limitations of low reliability and validity.

### Eating Inventory

Stunkard and Messick (1985) developed the Three-Factor Eating Questionnaire, which has been renamed the Eating Inventory (EI; Stunkard & Messick, 1988). The Eating Inventory has three scales: dietary (cognitive) restraint, disinhibition, and perceived hunger. Research has demonstrated that the dietary restraint and disinhibition scales are not correlated, which supports the conclusion that intention to diet and overeating may not be causally linked (Williamson, Lawson, et al., 1995). However, the perceived hunger and disinhibition scales have been found to be positively correlated (Williamson, Lawson, et al.). A series of studies (Westenhoefer, 1991; Williamson, Lawson, et al.; C. F. Smith, Williamson, Bray, & Ryan, 1999) has reported that rigid approaches to dieting are associated with overeating, whereas flexible approaches to dieting are not associated with overeating. This line of research led to development of a revision of the dietary restraint scale that consists of two dimensions: rigid dieting and flexible dieting. In a recent study reported by Stewart, Williamson, and White (2002), it was found that the flexible dieting scale was not associated with the symptoms of AN and BN, whereas the rigid dieting scale was associated with the presence of eating disorder symptoms.

### Binge Eating Scale

The Binge Eating Scale (BES) is a 16-item questionnaire that measures the severity of binge eating (Gormally, Black, Daston, & Rardin, 1982).

## BODY IMAGE ASSESSMENT METHODS

The methods described here were selected based on their satisfactory psychometric properties (validity and reliability) and their clinical utility. For a more comprehensive view on body image assessment, please refer to Stewart and Williamson (2004a). For a summary of these measures, including reliability and validity information, refer to Table 12.2.

### Body Image Assessment

The Body Image Assessment (BIA) is a figural stimulus test for measuring body image (Williamson, Davis, Bennett, Goreczny, & Gleaves, 1989). The original BIA was later extended (addition of nine silhouettes) to accommodate obese individuals and men and was renamed the Body Image Assessment for Obesity (BIA-O) (Williamson, Womble, et al., 2000). The BIA-O measures estimates of current (CBS), ideal (IBS), and reasonable body size (RBS), using pictures of body silhouettes that vary from very thin to very obese. The discrepancy between CBS and IBS has been validated as a measure of body dissatisfaction (Williamson, Gleaves, Watkins, & Schlundt, 1993). Norms for different genders and races with different body sizes have also been developed for the BIA-O (Williamson, Womble, et al., 2000).

### Body Morph Assessment

Stewart, Williamson, Smeets, and Greenway (2001) developed and validated a computerized body image assessment procedure called the Body Morph Assessment (BMA). Like the BIA-O, the BMA measures estimates of current, ideal, and reasonable body size, and these estimates were validated against the BIA-O. However, unlike the BIA-O, it is computer based and self-administered. In the last few years, a revised version called the BMA 2.0 has been developed and tested (Stewart, Williamson, & Allen, 2002). The BMA 2.0 can be utilized with men and women as well as with Caucasians and African Americans. The BMA 2.0 measures very small increments of changes in body size estimation. There are 100 total increments, from the extremely thin endpoint on the measure to the obese endpoint. The BMA 2.0 is a more sophisticated, automated body image assessment method than traditional silhouette methods (e.g., BIA-O). The graphic representation of the stimuli utilizes realistic human images as opposed to silhouettes. The BMA 2.0 is recommended for clinicians who specialize in eating disorders and can be used to track changes in body image over time.

## Body Shape Questionnaire

The Body Shape Questionnaire (BSQ) is a 34-item self-report questionnaire that measures excessive concern about one's body size and shape (Cooper, Taylor, Cooper, & Fairburn, 1987). The BSQ measures body dissatisfaction and intention to diet, and it has been validated as a measure for defining overconcern about body size and shape in normal-weight women (Williamson, Lawson, et al., 1995). Short forms of the BSQ have been developed (Evans & Dolan, 1993). This includes one form developed for use specifically with anorexia nervosa (Dowson & Henderson, 2001).

## MEASUREMENT OF BODY WEIGHT

### Body Mass Index

Height and weight are very useful measures when tracking treatment progress in eating disorders. Height and weight can be converted into body mass index (BMI), which is given in kilograms per square meter. Body mass index has become the standard method for expressing a relationship between height and weight and is important when reporting progress during treatment. Normal weight is usually defined as BMI between 18.5 and 24.9; overweight is between 25 and 29.9; and a BMI greater than 30 is often used to define obesity (World Health Organization [WHO], 1998). The World Health Organization guidelines (ICD-10) recommend a BMI equal to or less than 17.5 as a guideline for AN (WHO, 1992). A somewhat less strict guideline has been adapted by some methods of assessment, e.g., IDED-IV, BMI = 18.0. As a suggested guideline, *DSM-IV* recommends less than 85% of expected weight. However, it is recommended that this guideline not be strictly held. Thus, it is recommended that a reasonable range of BMI for the diagnosis of AN be between 17.5 and 18.5. Further, it is important to note that in children, BMI is not a stable factor, as it is in adults. In children, BMI increases with age until the age of 18.

## PHYSICAL FACTORS AND MEDICAL STATUS

Physicians and psychologists must be attentive to the medical complications of eating disorders. These medical symptoms are often the only external signs of the presence of an eating disorder. Most eating disorder patients are very secretive about eating and weight management habits. Therefore, a thorough medical and physical examination is recommended for individuals suspected of having an eating disorder. A comprehensive assessment may include medical history, physical examination, and laboratory evaluation. Physical examination may consist of weight (computed into BMI status), body composition, state of hydration, dental/oral evaluation, standard organ system examination (skin, cardiac, abdominal, musculoskeletal, neurological evaluation), assessment of mental status and affect, and gynecological examination for women.

TABLE 12.3　Summary of Medical/Physical Assessment of AN, BN, and BED

|  | Anorexia Nervosa | Bulimia Nervosa | Binge Eating Disorder |
|---|---|---|---|
| **Common physical signs** | • Inanition<br>• Bradycardia<br>• Hypotension<br>• Hair loss<br>• Low body temperature<br>• Dry skin<br>• Lanugo<br>• Brittle hair<br>• Brittle nails<br>• Peripheral edema<br>• Loss of menses<br>• Irregular menses | • Erosion of dental enamel<br>• Peripheral edema<br>• Salivary gland enlargement<br>• Abrasions on fingers or back of hand from self-induced vomiting | • Overweight status<br>• Complications of obesity |
| **Common medical and/or psychological histories** | • Denial of significance of weight loss<br>• Body image disturbance<br>• Excessive exercise<br>• Anxiety<br>• Depression<br>• Fatigue<br>• Headaches<br>• Constipation<br>• Cold intolerance | • Denial of binge/purge behaviors<br>• Body image disturbance<br>• Anxiety<br>• Depression<br>• Fatigue<br>• Headaches<br>• Constipation<br>• Abdominal bloating<br>• Irregular menses | • Shame regarding binge eating<br>• Concern about overweight status<br>• Request for diet advice<br>• Eating binges<br>• Anxiety<br>• Depression<br>• Social isolation |

For a more comprehensive description of medical status and physical factors associated with eating disorders, refer to Pomeroy (2004).

Table 12.3 summarizes physical signs and common medical/psychological histories of AN, BN, and BED. Common physical signs of AN are inanition, bradycardia, hypotension, hair loss, low body temperature, dry skin, formation of fine hair on the body (Lanugo), brittle hair and nails, peripheral edema, and loss of menstrual cycle or irregular menses (Pomery, 2004). Common medical and psychological histories are denial of significance of weight loss, body image disturbance, excessive exercise, anxiety, depression, fatigue, headaches, constipation, and cold intolerance. Physical symptoms specifically associated with BN are erosion of dental enamel, peripheral edema, salivary gland enlargement, and irregular menses. It is important to note that most BN cases are normal weight and may appear healthy on presentation. Physical symptoms of BED may consist of overweight status and complications of obesity. Medical and psychological histories may include shame regarding binge eating, concern about overweight status, request for diet advice, eating binges, anxiety, and depression. For a comprehensive review of the assessment of physical factors and medical status, refer to Pomery.

## DIAGNOSIS AND ASSESSMENT OF COMORBID PSYCHIATRIC DISORDERS

This section describes several methods that have been successfully utilized to assess for other psychiatric problems that accompany eating disorders. A significant percentage of eating disorder cases seen in clinical practice (as much as 50%) have additional psychiatric problems that require treatment (Williamson, 1990). Properties of these measures are also summarized in Table 12.2.

### Structural Clinical Interview for the Diagnosis of *DSM-IV* Axis I Disorders

The Structured Clinical Interview for *DSM-IV* Axis I Disorders (SCID; First, Gibbon, Spitzer, & Williams, 1995) is considered the "gold standard" for the valid diagnosis of comorbid psychiatric disorders. The SCID-I is a semistructured interview that queries all of the disorders in the DSM-IV. Because of its comprehensive format, it is time consuming. This format is recommended primarily for use in research studies. For other methods of assessment of comorbid psychopathology, please refer to chapters in this book on depression, anxiety, and Axis II disorders.

### Structural Clinical Interview for the Diagnosis of *DSM-IV* Axis II Disorders

The Structured Clinical Interview for *DSM-IV* Axis II Disorders (SCID-II; First, Spitzer, Gibbon, et al., 1994) consists of a self-report screening personality questionnaire and a structured interview process. The screening questionnaire is followed by a structured interview to assess potential comorbid personality diagnoses that may accompany eating disorders.

## ASSESSMENT OF SPECIAL PROBLEMS

Symptom-specific measures related to special concerns accompanying eating disorders are described in this section. These special concerns are often unique to concerns about eating and body size and shape in eating disorders. Relevant aspects of these measures are presented in Table 12.2.

### Food Craving Inventory

The Food Craving Inventory (FCI; White, Whisenhunt, Williamson, Greenway, & Netemeyer, 2002) was developed to measure general and specific food cravings, i.e., cravings for starches, sweets, and fats.

### Body Checking Questionnaire

Body checking is a behavioral symptom associated with eating disorders that consists of compulsive checking of various body areas, e.g., stomach, buttocks, hips. Examples of body checking include compulsive weighing, obsessive observation in the mirror, and measuring the body. The Body Checking Questionnaire (BCQ; Reas, Whisenhunt, Netemeyer, & Williamson, 2002) was developed to measure the severity of this set of behavioral symptoms.

### Muscle Appearance Satisfaction Scale

Mayville, Williamson, White, Netemeyer, and Drab (2002) developed the Muscle Appearance Satisfaction Scale (MASS) to measure excessive concern with the appearance of muscularity, in men. This obsession is often associated with compulsive weight lifting and use of steroids.

## RESEARCH BASIS

Psychometric properties taken into account when choosing an appropriate assessment include reliability (test–retest, interrater, and internal consistency) and validity (content, criterion, construct). For a description of these indices, please see Anderson and Paulosky (2004). Many of the aforementioned eating disorder measures have been established through research to be valid and reliable. This information can be found "at a glance" in Table 12.2.

## SCREENING MEASURES

Screening measures that have been established to be reliable and valid include the EAT, EDDS, EDE-Q, EDE, and IDED-IV. Test–retest reliability (Carter & Moss, 1984) and internal consistency (Garner & Garfinkle, 1979) of the EAT are satisfactory. The EAT has been found to have good concurrent validity. Tests of the reliability and validity of the EDDS found strong support for its use as a brief screening device (Stice et al., 2000). Reliability and validity of the EDE-Q has been established.

## DIAGNOSIS

Diagnostic measures that have been found to be reliable and valid include the EDE and the IDED-IV. Interrater reliability for individual items and the subscales of the EDE has been found to be satisfactory (Cooper & Fairburn, 1987; Wilson & Smith, 1989). Furthermore, test–retest reliability (Rizvi, Peterson, Crow, & Agras, 2000) and internal consistency of the EDE (Cooper et al., 1989) are satisfactory. The reliability and validity of the IDED-IV has been established in a number of studies of anorexia and bulimia nervosa, and it has been used to reliably differentiate BED from simple obesity (Kutlesic et al., 1998). The IDED-IV has good reliability and validity, and it reliably differentiates the different eating disorder diagnoses (Kutlesic et al.).

## MULTISCALE MEASURES

Multiscale questionnaires of eating disorders that have been found to have good psychometric properties include the EDI-2 and the MAEDS. Test-retest reliability of the EDI subscales has been found to be satisfactory (Crowther, Lilly, Crawford, & Shepard, 1992; Wear & Pratz, 1987). The internal consistency estimates of the original scales of the EDI-2 are higher than those for the new scales (Eberenz & Gleaves, 1994). The EDI subscales discriminate patients diagnosed with eating disorders from nonclinical controls (Garner et al., 1983; Schoemaker, Verbraak, Breteler, & van der Staak, 1997). The test–retest reliability, internal consistency, concurrent validity, and criterion validity of the six scales of the MAEDS have been tested and found to be satisfactory (Anderson et al., 1999; Martin, Williamson, & Thaw, 2000). The MAEDS has been successfully used in one prevention study (Varnado-Sullivan et al., 2001) and one treatment-outcome study (Williamson, Thaw, & Varnado, 2001). These studies found that the scales of the MAEDS were sensitive to changes in eating disorder symptoms and that the total score of the MAEDS can be used as an index of treatment outcome (Varnado-Sullivan et al.).

## PATHOLOGICAL EATING HABITS

Methods for assessing pathological eating habits that have been found to be valid and reliable include the BULIT-R, EI, and BES. The BULIT has been found reliable and valid as a measure of bulimic symptoms (Thelen et al., 1991), and it discriminates individuals diagnosed with BN from those diagnosed with AN and from nonclinical controls (Welch, Thompson, & Hall, 1993; Williamson et al., 1990). However, there is some controversy over the reliability and validity of self-monitoring, e.g., self-reported binge/purge episodes and food intake (Anderson & Maloney, 2001). Many studies have reported that errors in the estimation of food portion sizes are common. Also, some people deliberately deny eating pathology on self-report forms or minimize quantities of food consumed (Crowther & Sherwood, 1997). A final concern with self-monitoring is that there is no standard method for self-monitoring. Despite these limitations, self-monitoring can be a useful clinical tool, and it is highly recommended during assessment and treatment for eating disorders. The reliability and validity of the BES have been established, and it has been used in many studies of binge eating and Binge Eating Disorder (Williamson & Martin, 1999). Recent studies have found that the BES tends to overestimate the presence of BED (Williamson & Martin; Varnado et al., 1998). The EDE and IDED-IV, described earlier, are semi-structured interviews that provide a more accurate method for measuring binge eating. Therefore, the primary use of the BES is for quick measurement of binge-eating severity. It is recommended that it not be used for diagnostic or screening purposes.

## BODY IMAGE

Some of the most reliable and valid body image measures are the BIA, BIA-O, BMA, BMA-2, and the BSQ. The reliability and validity of the BIA has been established in a series of studies (Williamson, Barker, Bertman, & Gleaves, 1995; Williamson, Cubic, & Gleaves, 1993; Williamson, Davis, et al., 1989; Williamson, Womble, et al., 2000). The BIA-O has been validated for use with Caucasian men and women and African American men and women. The reliability and the validity of the BMA and the BMA 2.0 have been supported (Stewart et al., 2001, 2002). The BSQ has been shown to have good reliability and validity and has been shown to discriminate between persons with BN and nonclinical controls (Cooper et al., 1987; Rosen, Jones, Ramirez, & Waxman, 1996). In a longitudinal study of high school females, Womble, Williamson, Netemeyer, and Netemeyer (1998) found the BSQ to be a very good predictor of the development of bulimic symptoms one year later.

## COMORBID DIAGNOSIS

The SCID has been found to be a reliable and valid measure for the diagnosis and assessment of comorbid psychiatric disorders (First et al., 1995; First, Spitzer, Williams, & Gibbon, 1996). The SCID's semistructured interview format has been found to be a reliable and valid method for establishing psychiatric diagnoses based on the diagnostic criteria established by the American Psychiatric Association (1994).

## SPECIAL PROBLEMS

The reliability and validity of the FCI, BCQ, and MASS have been established for the assessment of special features of eating disorders. The reliability and validity of the FCI have been established (White et al., 2002), and four subscales were developed: cravings for sweets, for starches, for fats, and for forbidden foods. Also, the FCI yields a total score that can be used as a general index of the severity of food craving (Reas et al., 2002). Internal consistency, test–retest reliability, construct validity, and divergent validity were established for the MASS. A five-factor structure was confirmed for the MASS, including bodybuilding dependence, muscle checking, substance use, injury, and muscle satisfaction (Mayville et al., 2002).

## CLINICAL UTILITY

Many of the aforementioned measures have clinical utility for the assessment of eating disorders. However, due to the multidimensional nature of eating disorders, all of these categories of measurement play a significant role in the comprehensive assessment process.

## SCREENING

To screen for the presence of an eating disorder, the EAT may be best conceptualized as a measure of general eating disorder pathology, whereas the EDDS is primarily used to screen for the presence of AN, BN, and BED. The EDE-Q can be used to screen for the presence of binge eating, purging, and extreme concerns related to body size/shape and eating. Thus, the most appropriate measure may be chosen based on the specific construct of interest.

## DIAGNOSIS

To diagnose an eating disorder, the EDE is an interview method utilized for the measurement of the severity of eating disorders. It was developed as a measure of treatment outcome. While the EDE has been found to be reliable and valid, it is less suitable for some purposes, such as screening and frequent use in clinical settings, due to the lengthy time required for its completion (over an hour). Also, special training is required for proper administration. Unlike the EDE, the primary use for IDED-IV in clinical settings is the differential diagnosis of AN, BN, BED, and EDNOS.

## MULTISCALE MEASURES

In clinical practice, it is often helpful to use a single questionnaire to measure a range of problem areas. The EDI may be utilized to discriminate eating disorders from normal controls and also as a measure of treatment outcome. To date, the EDI has been the most widely used multiscale self-report questionnaire for eating disorders. However, the MAEDS was designed specifically for use as a treatment-outcome measure. The multiple scales of the MAEDS allow for a precise analysis of the profile of eating disorder symptoms (Martin et al., 2000). The MAEDS is brief and easily administered and is the best alternative to the EDI-2 as a multiscale measure of eating disorder symptoms as well as the best alternative to the EDE as a measure of treatment outcome.

## PATHOLOGICAL EATING HABITS

Measures such as the BULIT-R, EI, BES, as well as the aforementioned EAT have been established as methods for the assessment of pathological eating habits. Self-monitoring of food intake may also be included in this category. In this sense, the BULIT-R is utilized primarily as a measure of bulimic symptoms. The EI is most useful for measuring the severity of intent to restrict eating and to overeat, whereas the BES is most utilized for a quick measurement of actual binge-eating severity. Further, self-monitoring of food intake in eating disorders may serve as a treatment-outcome measure, with particular regard to self-reported binge/purge episodes. While self-monitoring is an essential component of cognitive behavior therapy for eating disorders, there is concern about method standardization as well as reliability and validity. Despite these limitations, it is useful to use self-monitoring for the report of food intake, binge/purge episodes, as well as cognitions related to eating, mood, and body image.

## BODY IMAGE

Over the past three decades, the number of methods for the assessment of body image concerns has grown significantly. These measures range from cumbersome and time consuming to efficient and requiring minimal effort to administer and complete. The BIA-O and the BMA 2.0 are both applicable to a wide range of people, including different genders, sizes, and races. They both measure estimates of current, ideal, and acceptable/reasonable body size as well as indices of body dissatisfaction and body size overestimation. Unlike the BIA-O and the BMA 2.0, the BSQ is a more specific way to measure excessive concern about body size and shape. It is also easy to complete and quickly administered.

## COMORBID DIAGNOSIS

The SCID and SCID-II, as well as other, more specific measures (please refer to additional chapters in this book), may be utilized as methods for the diagnosis and assessment of comorbid psychiatric disorders. The SCID and SCID-II are used primarily in research studies, since their administration is time consuming and requires special training.

## SPECIAL PROBLEMS

Symptom-specific measures for eating disorders that are efficient and user friendly include the FCI, BCQ, and MASS. All of the measures may be used to assess a particular symptom domain, which may be of special concern for particular individuals. The FCI objectively evaluates the severity of food craving. The BCQ evaluates the severity of body-checking behaviors. The MASS measures excessive concern with the appearance of muscularity, and it may be used with individuals who express concern about being too thin or those who engage in compulsive weight lifting to increase body size.

## ASSESSMENT, CONCEPTUALIZATION, AND TREATMENT PLANNING

Due to the complexity of the assessment of eating disorders, it is particularly challenging to make simple recommendations for this process. It is suggested that the selection of assessment methods be based on careful consideration of the referral questions and the psychometric properties of the assessment methods chosen. Within this context, we make the following recommendations for a standard assessment battery to adequately assess the multiple dimensions of eating disorders.

### STANDARD ASSESSMENT BATTERY

The EAT is recommended for the purpose of screening for the presence of eating disorder symptoms, because it has very well-established validity and reliability. The IDED-IV is recommended as the diagnostic interview of choice. The IDED-IV is the only method validated specifically as a diagnostic test for anorexia nervosa, bulimia nervosa, Binge Eating Disorder, and Eating Disorder Not Otherwise Specified (American Psychiatric Association, 1994). The SCID is recommended as a method for establishing comorbid psychiatric diagnoses on Axis-I. The SCID-II is recommended as a method for establishing comorbid diagnoses on Axis-II. The MAEDS is recommended as a multiscale questionnaire to obtain an objective profile of the severity of eating disorder symptoms. The BIA or BIA-O is recommended for the efficient, reliable, and valid assessment of body image; for clinicians seeking a more sophisticated, self-administered computer measure of body image, the BMA 2.0 is recommended. For all cases, it is important that a complete physical exam and medical history be assessed. It is recommended that height and weight be measured and converted into BMI. Body weight (and height in children) needs to be monitored throughout treatment. We recommend that weight be measured without providing direct feedback to the eating disorder patients by weighing them with their back facing the scale, because exposure to this information can often complicate the treatment process. For further description of these procedures, refer to Stewart and Williamson (2004b).

### ASSESSMENT OF TREATMENT OUTCOME

To evaluate changes in eating behavior, we recommend use of self-monitoring and the MAEDS as a standard feature of treatment. The MAEDS may be administered on a regular basis, e.g., weekly or monthly, to track changes in key symptom domains. It is important that BMI be assessed and recorded at regular intervals throughout treatment. We recommend that body weight be taken daily with patients engaging in inpatient and partial hospitalization treatment. For outpatients, it is recommended that weight be recorded at every visit. Finally, for a thorough assessment of outcome, the EDE may be administered at the beginning and end of treatment.

## CASE STUDY

### IDENTIFICATION AND PRESENTING COMPLAINTS

Lily, a white female, was 19 at the time of presentation for treatment. She had just begun her sophomore year in college. Height (5'4"), weight (95 lb), and weight assessment revealed a BMI of 16.3. Physical/medical interview and examination revealed abdominal pain, difficulties with gastric reflux, constipation, and fatigue. Lily was accompanied by her parents for the initial assessment session, due to her reservations and fear about treatment. Lily reported eating as little as possible every day, particularly a diet that did not exceed 300–500 calories a day. She reported no exercise, due to fatigue. She reported symptoms of depression, body image disturbance, and social isolation. Table 12.4 summarizes aspects of the presented case study, including identification, presenting complaints, history, peer and school issues, family issues, behavioral assessment results, ethical issues and complications, conceptualization, and treatment recommendations.

### HISTORY

The historical information that Lily provided regarding her eating disorder behaviors was corroborated by her parents. She indicated that throughout her freshman year of college (approximately one year before entering treatment) young men in her class began to make playful comments about her body, particularly about her buttocks and thighs. Although these comments were, for the most part, compliments, this commentary drew Lily's attention to these parts of her body, and she began to seek out information on dieting to lose a "few" pounds and reduce the size of these body parts. She reported entering into a period of what she believed to be healthy eating (low-fat diet not exceeding 1200 calories per day). This period lasted a few months, after which Lily reported gradually decreasing fat and calories per day until she became engaged in a rigid eating plan of 300–500 calories per day. She reported that her fear of fat became more severe over time and that many of her favorite foods became "forbidden" due to their high level of fat content (e.g., ice cream and peanut butter). Over the course of approximately 8 months' time, Lily's BMI decreased from 20.3 to 16.3 (weight reduced from 118 to 95 lb). She reported that her menstrual period had become irregular, and, for the prior two months, she had not had a period at all. She reported that she gradually lost the energy and motivation to exercise and engage in activities with her friends. She indicated that she felt worthless and never felt good about her body or herself as a person. Although a good student, Lily's schoolwork began to suffer and her grades began to decline.

TABLE 12.4 Summary of Case Study

| Identification | Presenting Complaints | History | Peer and School Issues | Family Issues | Behavioral Assessment Results | Ethical Issues and Complications | Conceptualization | Treatment Recommendations |
|---|---|---|---|---|---|---|---|---|
| Female | Abdominal pain | Teasing | Decline in grades | Overprotective and rigid parents | IDED-IV: Diagnosis: AN, restricting type | Over the age of 18, therefore had to consent to inpatient treatment | Slow restriction of caloric intake due to concerns about weight and fear of fat | Inpatient stay for stabilization of eating and weight |
| Caucasian | Gastric reflux | Intention to restrict intake | Decreased social activity with friends | Enmeshed family | MAEDS: depression, fear of fatness, restrictive eating, avoidance of forbidden foods | | Reduction of calories | Goal of 85% of ideal body weight to reduce level of care |
| Age: 19 | Constipation | Restriction of caloric intake | | Rigid religious orientation—morality based | | | Weight loss success reinforced calorie restriction and provided temporary relief of fears of fatness | Individual therapy |
| 5'4" | Fatigue | Establish forbidden foods | | | BIA-O: over-estimation of body size, dissatisfaction with body size | | | Group therapy |
| 95 lb | Daily intake: 300–500 cal | Decreased body weight | | | Therapeutic meals—anxiety | | Intensified restriction of calories | Therapeutic meals |
| BMI = 16.3 | No exercise | Absence of menstrual period | | | Mild motivation for treatment | | Emaciated body weight | MAEDS assessment for treatment outcome |
| | Depression | | | | | | Loss of energy and fatigue | BMI for treatment outcome |
| | Body image disturbance | | | | | | Depression and social isolation | |
| | Social isolation | | | | | | Feelings of loss of control around food | |
| | | | | | | | Increased avoidance of eating | |
| | | | | | | | Time periods with an empty stomach, which reinforced feeling "thin" | |
| | | | | | | | Chronic feelings of fullness and anxiety due to constipation | |
| | | | | | | | Further avoidance of eating | |
| | | | | | | | Poor nutrition and physical/medical issues | |

## FAMILY AND SCHOOL ISSUES

Clinical interview yielded family variables of relevance. Lily's parents were overprotective and rigid. Even though Lily was attending college away from home, Lily's mother was very involved with her life and stayed at the dorm with her on occasion to help her with laundry, schoolwork, decision making, etc. This increased after Lily began to show signs of illness. Therefore, Lily rarely made independent life decisions and felt incapable of doing so. Her family was of a rigid religious orientation that stressed stringent morality. Lily felt as if she never lived up to these standards, even though she was a good student, did not drink alcohol or use tobacco or drugs, and did not engage in premarital sexual activity.

## BEHAVIORAL ASSESSMENT RESULTS

Clinical and behavioral assessment revealed that Lily was an AN case, restricting type. The assessment battery utilized to assess Lily consisted of the IDED-IV, MAEDS, BIA-O, and the SCID-II. The IDED-IV was utilized to clarify diagnosis. The MAEDS was utilized to establish a baseline measure of symptoms for future treatment progress and outcome measurements. Upon initial assessment, Lily scored above the mean on depression, fear of fatness, restrictive eating, and avoidance of forbidden foods, with scores of fear of fatness and restrictive eating exceeding two standard deviations above the mean. Lily was evaluated for Axis II disorders with the SCID-II, indicating absence of a comorbid personality disorder. Body image disturbance was assessed with the BIA-O. Results of the BIA-O indicated that Lily overestimated her current body size and experienced severe body dissatisfaction at the time of assessment. Lily was also behaviorally observed during therapeutic meals. This behavioral observation indicated that Lily experienced substantial anxiety during meals, especially if the meal included any of her forbidden foods, particularly sweet foods. Lily reported mild motivation to improve her health and recover from her eating disorder, but this motivation for treatment was muffled by her fear of gaining weight.

## CONCEPTUALIZATION AND TREATMENT PLANNING

Lily's case can best be viewed as the "slippery slope" phenomenon, in which an individual begins slowly to restrict caloric intake in relation to concerns about weight or becoming fat and then continues to lower the goal weight as well as intake to accommodate anxiety and concerns about fatness. Lily began with a gradual process of caloric restriction and continued in the process until she reduced her caloric intake to dangerous levels of intake and an emaciated body weight. She felt she no longer had control over the process of eating and experienced significant fear when she approached food; thus, she began to avoid eating as much as possible. This avoidance promoted long intervals of experiencing an empty stomach, which was less aversive than a full stomach. Constipation, when present, fueled her feelings of fullness, which often further promoted avoidance of eating.

The treatment recommendations for Lily included an inpatient stay to stabilize eating and weight, with a goal of 85% of her ideal body weight to be achieved in order to move to a lower level of care (e.g., partial hospitalization). Individual therapy, group therapy, and therapeutic meals were recommended and were included in the hospital program. Please see Stewart and Williamson (2004b) for further information on levels of care and treatment recommendations for eating disorder patients. Body weight and body composition were assessed on a daily basis, and the MAEDS was administered on a weekly basis to assess treatment progress and outcome. A summary of this case study may be seen in Table 12.4.

## SUMMARY

There are a vast number of assessment measures that have been developed for the purpose of the assessment of eating disorder pathology. A significant percentage of these measures have been shown to be valid and reliable. We believe it is important that eating disorders be assessed as thoroughly as possible, capturing all important domains mentioned in this chapter, including proper diagnosis, adequate assessment of multiple symptom domains, adequate assessment of pathological eating habits, including self-monitoring, proper assessment of the multiple dimensions of body image, valid assessment of BMI and body composition, assessment of physical/medical abnormalities, assessment of comorbid psychiatric disorders, and assessment of special problems that individual cases may present. However, few treatment studies actually incorporate a thorough multidimensional assessment into their protocols (Anderson & Paulosky, 2004). Additionally, because there is no "standard" assessment battery of measures for the assessment of eating disorders, assessment batteries are vastly different across research studies, which creates difficulty when interpreting and comparing outcome results of different treatments. Readers may refer to the assessment, conceptualization and treatment section of this chapter for a recommended standard battery. Furthermore, in clinical practice, due to time constraints and low rates of reimbursement for assessment of eating disorders, corners are often cut to make the most efficient diagnosis and treatment decisions possible. In sum, eating disorders are multifaceted disorders with many specialized domains to be assessed before adequate conceptualization and treatment can be recommended. When considering assessment tools, it is important that measures that will adequately address the assessment question and measure the construct of interest be selected, measures with strong psychometric properties be utilized, and measures be utilized, to the best of the clinician or researcher's ability, that are efficient and user friendly for the professional as well as the patient.

## REFERENCES

American Psychiatric Association. (1987). *Diagnostic and statistical manual of mental disorders* (3rd ed. Rev.). Washington, DC: Author.

American Psychiatric Association. (1994). *Diagnostic and statistical manual of mental disorders* (4th ed.). Washington, DC: Author.

Anderson, D. A., & Maloney, K. C. (2001). The efficacy of cognitive-behavioral therapy on the core symptoms of bulimia nervosa. *Clinical Psychology Review, 21,* 971–988.

Anderson, D. A., & Paulosky, C. A. (2004). Psychological assessment of eating disorders and related features. In J. K. Thompson (Ed.), *Handbook of eating disorders and obesity* (pp. 112–129). New York: John Wiley & Sons.

Anderson, D. A., Williamson, D. A., Duchmann, E. G., Gleaves, D. G., & Barbin, J. M. (1999). Development and validation of a multifactorial treatment outcome measure for eating disorders. *Assessment, 6,* 7–20.

Butcher, J. N. (1990). *MMPI-2 in psychological treatment.* New York: Oxford University Press.

Carter, P. I., & Moss, R. A. (1984). Screening for anorexia and bulimia nervosa in a college population: Problems and limitations. *Addictive Behaviors, 9,* 417–419.

Cooper, Z., Cooper, P. J., & Fairburn, C. G. (1989). The validity of the Eating Disorder Examination and its subscales. *British Journal of Psychiatry, 154,* 807–812.

Cooper, Z., & Fairburn, C. G. (1987). The Eating Disorder Examination: A semistructured interview for the assessment of the specific psychopathology of eating disorders. *International Journal of Eating Disorders, 6,* 1–8.

Cooper, P. J., Taylor, M. J., Cooper, Z., & Fairburn, C. G. (1987). The development and validation of the Body Shape Questionnaire. *International Journal of Eating Disorders, 6,* 485–494.

Crowther, J. H., & Sherwood, N. E. (1997). Assessment. In D. M. Garner & P. E. Garfinkel (Eds.), *Handbook of treatment for eating disorders* (2nd ed., pp. 34–49). New York: Guilford Press.

Dowson, J., & Henderson, L. (2001). The validity of a short version of the Body Shape Questionnaire. *Psychiatry Research, 102,* 263–271.

Eberenz, K. P., & Gleaves, D. H. (1994). An examination of the internal consistency and factor structure of the Eating Disorders Inventory—2 in a clinical sample. *International Journal of Eating Disorders, 16,* 371–379.

Evans, C., & Dolan, B. (1993). Body Shape Questionnaire: Derivation of shortened "alternative forms." *International Journal of Eating Disorders, 13,* 315–321.

Fairburn, C., & Beglin, S. J. (1994). Assessment of eating disorders: Interview or self-report questionnaires? *International Journal of Eating Disorders, 16,* 363–370.

Fairburn, C. G., & Cooper, Z. (1993). The Eating Disorder Examination (12th ed.). In C. G. Fairburn & G. T. Wilson (Eds.), *Binge eating: Nature, assessment, and treatment* (pp. 317–360). New York: Guilford Press.

First, M. B., Gibbon, M., Spitzer, R. L., & Williams, J. B. W. (1995). User's guide for the Structural Clinical Interview for *DSM-IV* Axis I disorders (SCID-I, Version 2.0). Washington, DC: American Psychiatric Press.

First, M. B., Spitzer, R. L., Gibbon, M. et al. (1994). Structured Clinical Interview for *DSM-IV* Axis II personality disorders (SCID-II, version 2.0). Biometrics Research Department, New York State Psychiatric Institute.

First, M. B., Spitzer, R. L., Williams, J. B. W., & Gibbon, M. (1996). Structured clinical interview for *DSM-IV.* New York: New York State Psychiatric Institute, Biometrics Research.

Garner, D. M. (1991). *Eating Disorder Inventory—2 manual.* Odessa, FL: Psychological Assessment Resources.

Garner, D. M., & Garfinkel, P. E. (1979). The Eating Attitudes Test: An index of the symptoms of anorexia nervosa. *Psychological Medicine, 9,* 273–279.

Garner, D. M., & Garfinkel, P. E. (1979). The Eating Attitudes Test: An index of the symptoms of anorexia nervosa. *Psychological Medicine, 9,* 273–279.

Garner, D. M., Bohr, Y., & Garfinkel, P. E. (1982). The Eating Attitude Test: Psychometric features and clinical correlates. *Psychological Medicine, 12,* 871–878.

Garner, D. M., Olmstead, M. P., & Polivy, J. (1983). Development and validation of a multidimensional eating disorder inventory for anorexia nervosa and bulimia. *International Journal of Eating Disorders, 2,* 15–34.

Gormally, J., Black, S., Daston, S., & Rardin, D. (1982). The assessment of binge eating severity among obese persons. *Addictive Behaviors, 7,* 47–55.

Graham, J. R. (1987). *The MMPI: A Practical Guide*, 2nd ed. New York: Oxford University Press.

Hurley, J. B., Palmer, R. L., & Stretch, D. (1990). The specificity of the Eating Disorders Inventory: A reappraisal. *International Journal of Eating Disorders, 9,* 419–424.

Kelly, C., Ricciardelli, L. A., & Clarke, J. D. (1999). Problem eating attitudes and behaviors in young children. *International Journal of Eating Disorders, 25,* 281–286.

Kutlesic, V., Williamson, D. A., Gleaves, D. H., Barbin, J. M., & Murphy-Eberenz, K. P. (1998). The Interview for the Diagnosis of Eating Disorders—IV: Application to *DSM-IV* diagnostic criteria. *Psychological Assessment, 10,* 41–48.

Martin, K. C., Williamson, D. A., & Thaw, J. M. (2000). Criterion validity of the Multiaxial Assessment of Eating Disorders Symptoms. *International Journal of Eating Disorders, 28,* 303–310.

Mayville, S. B., Williamson, D. A., White, M. A., Netemeyer, R., & Drab, D. L. (2002). Development of the Muscle Appearance Satisfaction Scale: A self-report measure for the assessment of muscle dysmorphia symptoms. *Assessment, 9,* 351–360.

Mond, J. M., Hay, P. J., Rodgers, B., Owen, C., & Beumont, P. J. V. (2004). Temporal stability of the Eating Disorders Questionnaire. *International Journal of Eating Disorders, 36,* 195–203.

Pomeroy, C. (2004). Assessment of medical status physical factors. In J. K. Thompson (Ed.), *Handbook of eating disorders and obesity* (pp. 81–111). New York: John Wiley & Sons.

Reas, D. L., Whisenhunt, B. L., Netemeyer, R., & Williamson, D. A. (2002). Development of the Body Checking Questionnaire: A self-report measure of body checking behavior. *International Journal of Eating Disorders, 31,* 324–333.

Rizvi, S. L., Peterson, C. B., Crow, J. C., & Agras, W. S. (2000). Test–retest reliability of the Eating Disorder Examination. *International Journal of Eating Disorders, 28,* 311–316.

Rosen, J. C., Jones, A., Ramirez, E., & Waxman, S. (1996). Body Shape Questionnaire: Studies of validity and reliability. *International Journal of Eating Disorders, 20,* 315–319.

Rosen, J. C., Vara, L., Wendt, S., & Leitenberg, H. (1990). Validity studies of the Eating Disorder Examination. *International Journal of Eating Disorders, 9,* 519–528.

Schoemaker, C., Verbraak, M., Breteler, R., & van der Staak, C. (1997). The discriminant validity of the Eating Disorder Inventory—2. *British Journal of Clinical Psychology, 36,* 627–629.

Smith, M. C., & Thelen, M. H. (1984). Development and validation of a test for bulimia. *Journal of Consulting and Clinical Psychology, 52,* 863–872.

Smith, C. F., Williamson, D. A., Bray, G. A., & Ryan, D. H. (1999). Flexible vs. rigid dieting strategies: Relationship with adverse behavioral outcomes. *Appetite, 32,* 295–305.

Stewart, T. M., & Williamson, D. A. (2004a). Assessment of body image disturbances. In J. Kevin Thompson (Ed.). *Handbook of eating disorders and obesity* (pp. 495–514). New York: John Wiley & Sons.

Stewart, T. M., & Williamson, D. A. (2004b). Multidisciplinary treatment of eating disorders. I: Structure and costs of treatment. *Behavior Modification, 28,* 812–830.

Stewart, T. M., Williamson, D. A., & Allen, R. (2002). *The Body Morph Assessment 2.0 (BMA 2.0): A psychometric study.* Paper presented at the meeting of the Association for the Advancement of Behavior Therapy, Reno, NV.

Stewart, T. M., Williamson, D. A., Smeets, M. A. M., & Greenway, F. L. (2001). The Body Morph Assessment: Development of a computerized measure of body image. *Obesity Research, 9,* 43–50.

Stewart, T. M., Williamson, D. A., & White, M. A. (2002). Rigid vs. flexible dieting: Association with eating disorder symptoms in nonobese women. *Appetite, 38,* 39–44.

Stice, E., Telch, C. F., & Rizvi, S. L. (2000). Development and validation of the Eating Disorder Diagnostic Scale: A brief self-report measure of anorexia, bulimia, and binge eating disorder. *Psychological Assessment, 12,* 123–131.

Stunkard, A. J., & Messick, S. (1985). The three-factor eating questionnaire to measure dietary restraint, disinhibition, and hunger. *Journal of Psychosomatic Research, 29,* 71–83.

Stunkard, A. J., & Messick, S. (1988). *The Eating Inventory.* San Antonio, TX: Psychological Corporation.

Thelen, M. H., Farmer, J., Wonderlich, S., & Smith, M. (1991). A revision of the Bulimia Test: The BULIT-R. *Psychological Assessment, 3,* 119–124.

Varnado, P. J., Williamson, D. A., Bentz, B. G., Ryan, D. H., Rhodes, S. K., O'Neil, P. M., et al. (1998). Prevalence of Binge Eating Disorder in obese adults seeking weight loss treatment. *Eating and Weight Disorders, 2,* 117–124.

Varnado-Sullivan, P. J., Zucker, N., Williamson, D. A., Reas, D., Thaw, J., & Netemeyer, S. B. (2001). Development and implementation of the Body Logic Program for adolescents: A two-stage prevention program for eating disorders. *Cognitive and Behavioral Practice, 8,* 248–259.

Wear, R. W., & Pratz, O. (1987). Test–retest reliability for the Eating Disorder Inventory. *International Journal of Eating Disorders, 6,* 767–769.

Welch, G., Thompson, L., & Hall, A. (1993). The BULIT-R: Its reliability and clinical validity as a screening tool for *DSM-III-R* bulimia nervosa in a female tertiary education population. *International Journal of Eating Disorders, 14,* 95–105.

Westenhoefer, J. (1991). Dietary restraint and disinhibition: Is restraint a homogeneous construct? *Appetite, 16,* 45–55.

White, M. A., Whisenhunt, B. L., Williamson, D. A., Greenway, F. L., & Netemeyer, R. G. (2002). Development and validation of the Food Craving Inventory. *Obesity Research, 10,* 107–114.

Wiggins, J. S. (1966). Substantive dimensions of self-report in the MMPI item pool. *Psychological Monographs, 80,* 22 (whole no. 630).

Williamson, D. A. (1990). Assessment of eating disorders: Obesity, anorexia, and bulimia nervosa. Elmsford, NY: Pergamon Press.

Williamson, D. A., Anderson, D. A., & Gleaves, D. G. (1996). Anorexia and bulimia: Structured interview methodologies and psychological assessment. In K. Thompson (Ed.), *Body image, eating disorders, and obesity: An integrative guide for assessment and treatment* (pp. 205–223). Washington, DC: American Psychological Association.

Williamson, D. A., Barker, S. E., Bertman, L. J., & Gleaves, D. H. (1995). Body image, body dysphoria, and dietary restraint: Factor structure in nonclinical subjects. *Behavior Research Therapy, 33,* 85–93.

Williamson, D. A., Cubic, B. A., & Gleaves, D. H. (1993). Equivalence of body image disturbances in anorexia and bulimia nervosa. *Journal of Abnormal Psychology, 102,* 177–180.

Williamson, D. A., Davis, C. J., Bennett, S. M., Goreczny, A. J., & Gleaves, D. H. (1989). Development of a simple procedure for assessing body image disturbances. *Behavioral Assessment, 11,* 433–446.

Williamson, D. A., DeLany, J. P., Bentz, B. G., Bray, G. A., Champagne, C. M., & Harsha, D. W. (1997). Gender and racial differences in dieting and social pressures to gain weight among children. *Journal of Gender, Culture, & Health, 2,* 231–234.

Williamson, D. A., Gleaves, D. H., Watkins, P. C., & Schlundt, D. G. (1993). Validation of self-ideal body size discrepancy as a measure of body dissatisfaction. *Journal of Psychopathology and Behavioral Assessment, 15,* 57–68.

Williamson, D. A., Kelley, M. L., Davis, C. J., Ruggiero, L., & Blouin, D. (1985). Psychopathology of eating disorders: A controlled comparison of bulimic, obese, and normal subjects. *Journal of Clinical and Consulting Psychology, 53,* 161–166.

Williamson, D. A., Lawson, O. J., Brooks, E. R., Wozniak, P. J., Ryan, D. H., Bray, G. A., et al. (1995). Association of body mass with dietary restraint and disinhibition. *Appetite, 25,* 31–41.

Williamson, D. A., & Martin, C. K. (1999). Binge Eating Disorder: A review of the literature after publication of *DSM-IV. Eating and Weight Disorders, 4,* 103–114.

Williamson, D. A., & O'Neil, P. M. (2004). Obesity and Quality of Life (2004). In G. Bray & C. Bouchard (Eds.), *Handbook of obesity* (2nd ed). Marcel Dekker.

Williamson, D. A., Prather, R. C., McKenzie, S. J., & Blouin, D. C. (1990). Behavioral assessment procedures can differentiate bulimia nervosa, compulsive overeater, obese, and normal subjects. *Behavioral Assessment, 12,* 239–252.

Williamson, D. A., Thaw, J. M., & Varnado, P. J. (2001). Cost-effectiveness analysis of a hospital-based cognitive-behavioral treatment program for eating disorders. *Behavior Therapy, 32,* 459–477.

Williamson, D. A., Womble, L. G., Zucker, N. L., Reas, D. L., White, M. A., Blouin, D. C., et al. (2000). Body Image Assessment for Obesity (BIA-O): Development of a new procedure. *International Journal of Obesity, 24,* 1326–1332.

Wilson, G. T., & Smith, D. (1989). Assessment of bulimia nervosa: An evaluation of the Eating Disorder Examination. *International Journal of Eating Disorders, 8,* 173–179.

Womble, L. G., Williamson, D. A., Netemeyer, S. B., & Netemeyer, R. G. (1998). Risk factors for the development of bulimic symptoms in high school girls: A one-year longitudinal study. *Journal of Gender, Culture, & Health, 3,* 227–241.

World Health Organization. (1992). The ICD-10 classification of mental and behavioral disorders: Clinical descriptions and diagnostic guidelines. Geneva, Switzerland: Author.

World Health Organization. (1998). *Obesity: Preventing and managing the global epidemic.* Report of a WHO Consultation on Obesity, Geneva, Switzerland, June 3–5, 1997 (Publication No. WHO/NUT/NCD/98.1).

# 13

## ALCOHOL AND DRUG ABUSE

PETER M. MILLER

*Center for Drug and Alcohol Programs*
*Department of Psychiatry and Behavioral Sciences*
*Medical University of South Carolina*
*Charleston, South Carolina*

### INTRODUCTION

Thorough and accurate individual assessment is fundamental to treatment and research related to substance abuse. There are basically three stages of a comprehensive assessment plan for substance abusing patients (Carroll, 1995).

Stage 1, *screening assessment*, is often brief and designed to detect either harmful substance use that may lead to addiction or full-blown abuse and dependence. The aim is to discover those who require prevention or brief intervention or those needing a more extensive evaluation by a substance abuse specialist.

Stage 2, *problem assessment*, is basically diagnostic in nature, focusing on the formal identification of a substance use disorder as well as psychiatric comorbidities. This stage also includes an assessment of severity of the addiction and cravings associated with dependence.

Stage 3, *personal assessment*, provides more individual information helpful in treatment planning. This stage includes the assessment of consumption patterns, readiness to change, reasons for substance use, and social support.

Substance abuse assessment is important for several reasons. It provides an accurate diagnosis and a detailed picture of the clinical problem. Assessment provides valuable data required for treatment planning and serves as a baseline against which follow-up evaluations can be compared. As discussed by Donovan (1988), comprehensive substance abuse assessment is required by a number of accrediting bodies, such as the Joint Commission on Accreditation of Healthcare Organizations and the Commission on Accreditation of Rehabilitation Facilities.

A number of substance abuse assessment instruments are targeted toward both alcohol and drugs (primarily, but not limited to, opiates and cocaine). Since a variety of instruments are available, focus will be placed on those demonstrating sufficient reliability and validity for recommended use and those that are used most frequently by clinicians and researchers.

## ASSESSMENT STRATEGIES

### SCREENING ASSESSMENTS

*Screening* refers to the use of evidence-based procedures for detecting individuals with substance-related problems or those who are at risk for those problems. Screening assessments are brief and conducted in settings in which the prevalence of substance use problems is high, such as emergency departments, trauma centers, and primary care clinics.

A number of self-report screening tools are available, specifically for identifying at-risk drinking. One of the earliest alcohol screening tools was the Michigan Alcohol Screening Test (MAST) (Selzer, 1971), a 24-item screening tool. Several shorter versions with as few as nine items have since been developed (Connors & Volk, 2003). Some of the most widely used alcohol screening tools are those that are very brief, such as the CAGE, consisting of four items and requiring only a minute or less to administer (Ewing, 1984). CAGE is an acronym for cut down, annoyed, guilty, and eye opener, words from each of the four items.

The Alcohol Use Disorders Identification Test (AUDIT) is a longer (10 items) questionnaire developed by the World Health Organization specifically for use by general practitioners (Saunders, Aasland, Babor, de la Fuente, & Grant, 1993). The AUDIT is useful in a variety of settings, including outpatient medical clinics, hospitals, emergency departments, and the workplace. A shorter version of the AUDIT, the AUDIT-C, consists of only three quantity/frequency questions (Piccinelli, Tessari, & Bortolomasi, 1997). More recently, brief alcohol screening instruments, such as the TWEAK (Russell et al., 1994) for pregnant women, have been developed specifically for use with specialized populations.

Compared to the number of alcohol screening instruments available, few brief screening tools to assess drug use in workplace or medical settings have been developed. One notable exception is the Drug Abuse Screening Test (DAST) (Skinner, 1982). The original DAST consisted of 28 items, focusing on drug abuse and its consequences. The DAST-20 (available from the Centre for Addiction and Mental Health in Toronto) is a more recent edition that correlates .99 with the original screening test.

### DIAGNOSIS AND PROBLEM ASSESSMENT

Once individuals are initially screened for alcohol or drug use in Stage 1, the need exists for a more thorough diagnostic assessment. This includes an assessment of specific diagnosis of abuse or dependence as well as assessment of comorbid psychiatric diagnoses, such as depression and anxiety disorders frequently associated with substance abuse. In addition, information on the frequency, nature, and severity of craving is essential, since cravings constitute an integral part of the dependence syndrome.

The Addiction Severity Index (ASI) is a semistructured diagnostic interview designed to address potential problem areas with alcohol/substance abusers (McLellan, Luborsky, O'Brien, & Woody, 1980). A skilled interviewer can gather information on recent and lifetime problems in about an hour. A computer-administered version, the ASI-MV, is also available (Butler et al., 2001).

To make a formal diagnosis of alcohol or drug abuse or dependence, the Structured Clinical Interview for *DSM-IV* (SCID) is useful. This semistructured interview is designed for making *DSM-IV* diagnoses, either Axis I disorders (SCID-I) or Axis II disorders (SCID-II). The instrument is designed to be administered by a clinician or a trained mental health professional, and the administration takes about one hour.

In addition to the diagnosis of alcohol and drug dependence, a universal characteristic of dependence that is often assessed is the presence of cravings. *Cravings* refers to the desire or urge to experience the effects of a previously experienced psychoactive substance (United Nations International Drug Control Program and World Health Organization, 1992).

Since cravings for substances are often experienced as continuous rather than discrete (i.e., mild, moderate, severe) phenomena, a visual analogue scale (VAS) can be used to assess their strength. The VAS is an instrument that measures a characteristic, such as a craving, believed to range across a continuum of values and that cannot be directly measured easily (Wewers & Lowe, 1990). The VAS is typically a horizontal line, 100 millimeters in length, anchored by word descriptors, "not at all" at one end and "extremely" at the other end. The patient marks the point on the line that represents his/her current state of craving. The score is determined by measuring in millimeters from the left hand end of the line to the point the patient marked.

A variety of self-report craving assessments are also available. The Yale–Brown Obsessive-Compulsive Scale for Heavy Drinking (Y-BOCS-hd) is a 10-item questionnaire that measures (1) the frequency and intrusive nature of thoughts about drinking (i.e., obsessions) and (2) loss of control over drinking (i.e., compulsions). Developed by Modell, Glaser, Mountz, Schmaltz, and Cyr (1992), this was the first multi-item test developed for measuring alcohol cravings.

Probably the best-known and most frequently used measure of alcohol craving is the Obsessive-Compulsive Drinking Scale (OCDS). By modifying the Y-BOCS-hd, Anton, Moak, and Latham (1996) developed this 14-item, self-administered test that can be completed in five minutes. Patients respond to each item by selecting one of five statements that range from minimal to maximal endorsement of the item. Patients are asked to rate their cravings over a one- or two-week period. A key item measured is a person's ability to resist urges to drink.

The Alcohol Craving Questionnaire (ACQ) is a self-administered instrument containing 47 items, with each being scored on a 7-point Likert scale, ranging from "strongly disagree" to "strongly agree" (Singleton, Tiffany, & Henningfield, 1995). It measures five separate domains of alcohol craving: (1) desire to drink alcohol, (2) intension to drink alcohol, (3) lack of control over alcohol, (4) positive outcome expectancies, and (5) expectancy of relief from withdrawal or alcohol's negative effects. The ACQ is designed to measure cravings as the individual is experiencing them in the present, i.e., as he/she is completing the test. The questionnaire shows high internal consistency (.91) and high test–retest reliability (.82) and correlates highly with the OCDS.

To assess craving for drugs, Weiss, Griffin, Hufford, and colleagues (1997) developed the Cocaine Craving Scale, a three-item questionnaire with good internal consistency (ranging from .85 to .90). Franken, Hendriks, and van den Brink (2002) developed a drug-related version of the alcohol-related Obsessive-Compulsive Drinking Scale (OCDS) (Anton et al., 1996) known as the Obsessive Compulsive Drug Use Scale (OCDUS). Three factors explain 68% of the common factor variance. These factors include heroin thoughts and interference, desire and control, and resistance to thoughts and intention. All scales have good reliability and concurrent validity for clinical or research use.

## PERSONAL ASSESSMENT

The final stage of assessment consists of a more individual evaluation of the nature and scope of the client's substance abuse problems. This assessment of consumption patterns, reasons for use and abuse, readiness to change, and social support provides a basis on which treatment goals are specified and therapeutic strategies outlined.

The timeline follow-back procedure can provide a reliable functional analysis of drinking behavior when administered by interview, paper-and-pencil, telephone, or computer (Sobell, Brown, Leo, & Sobell, 1996). Respondents are asked to provide retrospective estimates of their daily drinking over a specified period of time, which can vary up to 12 months from the interview date. A calendar format is used to provide memory anchors and to enhance recall. The assessment takes about 10–15 minutes to complete a 90-day recall.

In searching for a less time-consuming method, O'Farrell, Fals-Stewart, and Murphy (2003) developed the drug use frequency (DUF) measure, which provides much less detail than the TLFB but can be administered in significantly less time. The DUF asks respondents about their frequency of use in the past 6 months of sedatives, hypnotics, tranquilizers, cannabis, stimulants, heroin, cocaine, phencyclidine (PCP), and hallucinogens. This method shows high correlations with the TLFB as well as with collateral reports.

In addition to self-reports of consumption, direct observation of consummatory behavior in laboratory settings has been reported (Davidson, Palfai, Bird, & Swift, 1999). These assessment protocols involve either direct consumption (e.g., drinking alcoholic beverages) or cue exposure, whereby the individual is exposed to the sight or smell of the substance (e.g., looking at cocaine or pictures of someone taking cocaine) and asked to rate cravings.

A widely used method to assess reasons for drinking alcohol is the Inventory of Drinking Situations (IDS), a 100-item self-report questionnaire developed by Annis (1982). Respondents are asked to rate their frequency of heavy drinking in each of 100 situations during the past year. Ratings are made on a 4-point Likert scale, ranging from "never" to "almost always." The Substance Abuse Relapse Assessment (SARA) helps to identify events that typically precede substance use as well as consequences that follow it (Shoenfeld, Peters, & Dolente, 1993). It is especially helpful in developing relapse-prevention goals for clients who use multiple substances and in monitoring those goals as treatment proceeds.

Motivation is typically assessed via the concept of "readiness to change," based on the transtheoretical model, an integrative model of behavior change upon which therapeutic interventions can be matched to the client's motivational stage (Prochaska & Velicer, 1997). The Readiness to Change Questionnaire (RTCQ) is a 12-item instrument designed to assign individuals to a particular stage of change (Heather, Gold, & Rollnick, 1991). It can be used to assess motivational stage with any type of substance abuser. The RTCQ has very high internal consistency and test–retest reliability. The University of Rhode Island Change Assessment (URICA) is a 32-item questionnaire widely used in assessing motivation in individuals with alcohol problems (DiClemente & Hughes, 1990) and drug abuse disorders (Abellanas & McLellan, 1993).

Finally, the Stages of Change Readiness and Treatment Eagerness Scale (SOCRATES) is another popular instrument for assessing motivation (Miller & Tonigan, 1996). The SOCRATES differs from the URICA in that it asks questions specifically about alcohol and other drug use, whereas the URICA asks more generally about the client's "problem." The most recent form is a 19-item scale that has high validity and test–retest reliability.

The Situational Confidence Questionnaire—39 (SCQ-39) provides an assessment of a client's confidence in resisting the urge to use drugs or alcohol excessively across 39 hypothetical situations (Annis & Graham, 1988). The SCQ is useful in assessing self-efficacy in situations involving alcohol and a variety of drugs (Ross, Filstead, Parrella, & Rossi, 1994). The SCQ-39 is often used in conjunction with the Inventory of Drinking (Drug) Situations (IDS) to assess both reasons for substance use and confidence in resisting urges triggered by those reasons. A similar instrument for alcohol use but one that puts more emphasis on total abstinence rather than the avoidance of heavy use is the Alcohol Abstinence Self-Efficacy (AASE) scale (DiClemente, Carbonari, Montgomery, & Hughes, 1994).

Positive social and family support has long been considered a significant factor in a client's successful treatment outcome (DiClemente, 2003). The Significant-Other Behavior Questionnaire (SBQ) is a 24-item assessment that rates the likelihood that a significant other will respond in specific positive or negative ways to the client (Love, Longabaugh, Clifford, Beattie, & Peaslee, 1993). Two forms are available, allowing either the client to rate the significant other or the significant other to rate himself/herself.

The Important People and Activities (IPA) questionnaire assesses alcohol or drug-specific social support obtained from friends and family (Clifford, Longabaugh, & Beattie, 1992). This is an interviewer-administered instrument that measures attitudinal and behavioral support for substance use, lack of sanctions against substance use, and attitudinal and behavioral support for substance use.

## RESEARCH BASIS

### SCREENING

From a psychometric standpoint, the ultimate value of a screening instrument is related to its sensitivity and specificity. *Sensitivity* refers to the accuracy with which the test detects individuals who have a substance use or abuse problem ("true positives"). *Specificity* refers to the test's effectiveness, through a "negative" score, in detecting people who do *not* have a substance use or abuse problem ("true negatives"). Both factors are important in detecting as many substance users as possible and in avoiding false negatives.

The MAST has demonstrated high sensitivity (80%) and specificity (70%), although, with the development of more recent brief screening instruments, its use has declined. The CAGE has shown sensitivities ranging from 43% to 94% in detecting alcohol abuse and alcoholism, although it may fail to identify excessive drinkers who are high risk but nondependent (Fiellin, Reid, & O'Connor, 1989).

The AUDIT has shown more consistent results than the CAGE with women, the elderly, and differing cultural groups (Reinert & Allen, 2002). It is better than the CAGE in detecting high-risk drinking but not as good at identifying alcohol abuse and dependence. The shorter AUDIT-C is 99.7% as sensitive as the full AUDIT (Gordon et al., 2001). An even shorter version, the AUDIT-3, made up of the third question of the AUDIT-C, shows a 98.3% sensitivity when compared to the full AUDIT (Gordon et al.).

The TWEAK is one of the few screening instruments that has been validated among women and among African American women. Having two or more indications of problem drinking on this test for pregnant women is associated with their infant's lower birth weight, lower APGAR scores, and smaller head circumference (Russell & Skinner, 1988).

The DAST provides a total quantitative score, indicating severity of drug use. It has shown high sensitivity (96%) and specificity (80%) (Maly, 1993).

## DIAGNOSIS AND PROBLEM ASSESSMENT

The two most widely used diagnostic instruments for alcohol and drug abuse, the ASI and the SCID, have good internal consistency and test–retest reliability as well as established content, construct, and predictive validity (Leonhard, Mulvey, Gastfriend, & Shwartz, 2000) in relation to the *DSM-IV*. The ASI has also been widely used for treatment planning and outcome evaluation.

Severity of craving, as measured by the OCDS as well as cue reactivity measures, has been found to be predictive of relapse and continued substance use with both alcohol (Anton et al., 1996) and cocaine (Rohsenow, Martin, & Monti, 1998). Rohsenow and colleagues (1994) found that cravings as measured by reactivity to alcohol cues during detoxification predicted greater frequency of drinking during a 3-month follow-up period. Behavioral and cue reactivity laboratory assessment have also been used to evaluate the efficacy of new pharmacotherapies for substance abuse. Davidson and colleagues (1999) demonstrated that treatment with naltrexone for one week diminished alcohol consumption and drinking speed in a laboratory session among young heavy drinkers.

In the National Institute on Drug Abuse Collaborative Cocaine Treatment Study, a comparative study of psychosocial treatments, the Cocaine Craving Scale was administered weekly to all subjects (Weiss, Griffin, Mazurick, et al., 2003). The scale not only predicted substance use during the subsequent week but also showed variation by treatment condition, suggesting that some treatments may have reduced the link between craving and subsequent use.

The timeline follow-back (TLFB) method is one of the most widely used and well-validated clinical measures of self-reported alcohol use (Sobell & Sobell, 1992). It provides a reliable and valid assessment for a functional analysis of alcohol and drug use. Fals-Stewart, O'Farrell, Rutigliano, Freitas, and McFarlin (2000) conducted TLFB assessments with drug-abusing adult patients in treatment at baseline, post-treatment, and quarterly for a year. Patients' reports about their drug use using this method had high test–retest reliability, convergent and discriminant validity with other measures, agreement with collateral informants' reports, and agreement with patient urine assays.

The Readiness to Change Questionnaire is a well-established measure that has been used to detect clinically meaningful motivational stages related to treatment outcome (Carbonari & DiClemente, 2000). Donovan (2003) notes that this instrument can be used not only to identify readiness to change but also to predict subsequent substance use, direct the selection of interventions, and serve as an outcome measure to evaluate brief interventions. Since the RTCQ was originally developed for individuals being screened in medical settings, Heather, Luce, Peck, Dunbar, and James (1999) developed the Readiness to Change Questionnaire Treatment Version (RTCQ-TV), for use with clients already in treatment for substance abuse. More advanced stages of change on the RTCQ-TV (e.g., action stage compared to precontemplation stage) are correlated with better treatment outcomes in alcoholism programs (Heather et al.).

The Situational Confidence Questionnaire (SCQ-39) provides a problem index score that can be calculated for each of eight situational categories, although, more recently, Annis and Graham (1995) compressed these categories into four: high negative profile, high positive profile, low physical discomfort profile, and low testing personal control profile. These investigators found that high-negative-profile individuals (compared to those with high positive profiles) were more likely to be alcohol dependent, to drink alone, and to be women.

As a frequently used clinical measure of social support, the Important People and Activities (IPA) questionnaire provides one of the best indicators of abstinence social support (Zywiak, Longabaugh, & Wirtz, 2002). Longabaugh, Wirtz, Beattie, Noel, and Stout (1995) also have found this measure useful in matching clients to treatments. For example, they found that patients with a stronger and more positive social support network had better therapeutic outcomes when exposed to certain treatment modalities (e.g., 12-step facilitation therapy).

## CLINICAL UTILITY

All of these basic assessment instruments can prove to be invaluable to a clinician in initial evaluation and diagnosis, treatment planning, treatment monitoring, and follow-up assessment. In addition to providing diagnostic information, assessment instruments such as the ASI provide scores for specific problem areas, including medical status, employment and support, drug use, alcohol use, legal status, family and social status, and psychiatric status. Such information allows the clinician to formulate a broad picture of the client's current problems related to addiction.

In addition to diagnosis, it is clinically helpful to assess cravings, since most clients report that cravings are a frequent and troublesome aspect of their problem. Assessment of cravings helps the clinician evaluate the strength of the client's addiction and monitor progress throughout the treatment process. For example, an objective measure of decreased cravings can be used as feedback to bolster the concept that the client is "getting better." Increases in measured level of cravings can serve as a danger signal indicating that relapse may be imminent, especially if the client is experiencing high-risk situations (e.g., increased family or job stress).

Assessment of motivation or readiness to change is based on the model that people change by going through a series of stages over time (precontemplation, preparation, action, and maintenance). Therapeutic interventions matched to each stage will coincide with the client's readiness to change in such a way that clinical outcome will be more positive (Velicer, Prochaska, Rossi, & DiClemente, 1996). For example, interventions designed for a heavy drinker in the precontemplation stage would focus on increasing motivation rather than on developing coping skills, as would be the case in the action stage.

Another important aspect of clinical assessment is the identification of emotional, cognitive, environmental, and social factors precipitating substance use. Individuals vary widely in their reasons for substance use. Triggering events might range from social anxiety to the presence of drinking companions to physiological withdrawal symptoms. The preponderance of some reasons over others leads to the selection of significantly different treatment goals and treatment modalities. Assessment instruments such as the timeline follow-back procedure and the Inventory of Drinking Situations can be invaluable in this regard.

## ASSESSMENT, CONCEPTUALIZATION, AND TREATMENT PLANNING

The major goal of assessment in the treatment of alcohol and drug abuse is to gather enough detailed information about each client's condition and his/her related problems to set appropriate treatment goals, choose relevant therapeutic strategies, and, basically, to maximize the chances that treatment will be successful. Since each individual's problem situation is unique, assessment provides the most efficient way to conceptualize the specific psychological, social, and biological issues involved in each case. Assessment gives the clinician each client's personal profile on which to understand the alcohol-drug-related issues of each case.

Conceptualization and treatment planning involve integration of assessment information to establish short- and long-term therapeutic goals, select appropriate, evidence-based interventions, prepare for obstacles to behavior change, and monitor treatment progress. Assessment of problem areas, antecedents and consequences of alcohol and drug abuse, cravings, motivation, and social support provides the necessary elements for the treatment plan. In this way, treatment is individualized, with clients being matched to therapeutic strategies most appropriate to their problems.

## CASE STUDY

### IDENTIFICATION

Elaine Kavanaugh is a 49-year-old woman who has been a practicing attorney for 20 years. She was referred to the university's Department of Psychiatry by the Emergency Department for evaluation of a possible alcohol abuse problem.

## PRESENTING COMPLAINTS

Elaine reported that she has been "all stressed out" lately and has not been sleeping well. She was superficially cooperative during the intake interview but seemed vague, uncomfortable, and embarrassed. She responded to questions but gave only minimal information about herself and did not elaborate on her responses. She had been to the emergency room two weeks previously for treatment of a broken clavicle, but she was not sure why the physician referred her to psychiatry.

## HISTORY

A month previously, Elaine "walked into a door" at home late one evening and sustained a black eye and a laceration over her left eyebrow. She had trouble stopping the bleeding, so she went to the hospital's emergency department. More recently, she tripped over a stool in her living room and sustained a broken clavicle.

Elaine denied any previous history of psychological problems. She denied using illicit or prescription drugs at the present time. She experimented with marijuana a few times in college but has not tried it again since. During law school, she drank quite a lot on weekends (five to six beers a night) and often became intoxicated when celebrating after an exam. At the present time, she reported drinking a glass of wine or two with dinner and one or two more glasses prior to bedtime on most evenings.

Elaine describes her early home life as "very dysfunctional." Her father was a district sales manager who drank heavily every night and was emotionally and physically abusive to her mother. Her mother was very passive and suffered from bouts of depression. Her younger brother, a dentist, has been hospitalized for alcoholism twice in the past three years.

## PEER AND WORK ISSUES

Elaine is a partner in a busy law practice and specializes in estate planning. In recent weeks, she has been continually behind in her work and is wondering if she should cut back on her practice. She feels there are not enough hours in the day to get things done. On a social level, she does not associate with her partners outside of work. Other than work and family, she has few close friends and few outside interests.

## FAMILY ISSUES

Elaine is married to a surgeon, Steve, and they have two children, Lisa, age 8, and Tim, age 14. Her husband has an extremely busy practice and is called to the hospital several evenings a week. When he is home, he retreats to his study, spending little time with either Elaine or the children. Elaine feels frustrated and lonely.

## BEHAVIORAL ASSESSMENT RESULTS

During Elaine's previous visit to the emergency department, a routine alcohol screening was conducted by the nurse, using the Alcohol Use Disorders Identification Test-C (AUDIT-C). This instrument revealed a score of 8, which placed her in a high-risk drinking category (scores of 4 or more lead to further assessment). Screening revealed that she was drinking 28 drinks a week and on some evenings as many as 5 or 6 drinks. A screening score of this magnitude typically leads to a more thorough evaluation for possible alcohol abuse and/or dependence. This is the reason she was referred for a more complete assessment.

During a two-session evaluation, Elaine was administered the following assessment instruments: timeline follow-back (TLFB), Structured Clinical Interview I, Obsessive Compulsive Drinking Scale (OCDS), Readiness to Change Questionnaire (RTCQ), and the Significant-Other Behavior Questionnaire (SBQ). On the TLFB, it was apparent that Elaine was a daily drinker, consuming an average of at least a bottle of wine per evening (about five 5-ounce drinks). Her heavy drinking was limited to the evenings at home and she never drank during the day or at work. When she was feeling particularly stressed or "down in the dumps," she often drank more alcohol and, on six occasions in the past month, had consumed nearly two bottles of wine in the evening.

The SCID-1 was administered not only to determine the presence of alcohol abuse and/or dependence but also to assess for a mood or anxiety disorder, either of which is a common comorbid condition of alcohol use disorders. Depression was suspected from the clinical interview, during which Elaine complained about lack of energy, sleep difficulties (i.e., early-morning awakening), and an inability to concentrate on her work. The SCID-1 revealed a diagnosis of alcohol abuse but not alcohol dependence. Although Elaine was experiencing episodes of personal injury because of her drinking, she did not show enough *DSM-IV* signs of physical dependence (e.g., tolerance, loss of control, withdrawal) to be diagnosed as alcohol dependent.

The SCID also indicated the presence of a major depressive disorder. Elaine showed five of the *DSM-IV* criteria for a depressive episode, including depressed mood most of the day, diminished interest in activities, insomnia, loss of energy, and feelings of worthlessness. Although Elaine showed mild anxiety, her SCID assessment did not indicate the presence of an anxiety disorder.

Since Elaine complained of alcohol cravings, the OCDS was administered to provide an assessment of their nature and severity. Elaine scored very high on the compulsive subscale, indicating loss of control over drinking. When questioned about this, she indicated that she often promises herself to drink only one or two glasses of wine but always ends up drinking much more. Elaine's score on the obsessive subscale of the OCDS was low, indicating that she was not experiencing intrusive thoughts about alcohol. However, such thoughts are typically experienced during a period of reduced drinking or abstinence, and Elaine had not recently attempted to discontinue her alcohol consumption. These craving measures, especially the obsessive subscale, would serve as a useful baseline to evaluate Elaine's progress during treatment.

The Readiness to Change Questionnaire (RTCQ) indicated that Elaine was in the contemplation stage of readiness to change. This indicates that while she did not feel immediately ready to reduce or stop her drinking, she was at least thinking about her drinking as a problem, with the intention of doing something about it at some point in the near future.

Finally, Elaine was asked to complete the Significant-Other Behavior Questionnaire (SBQ) in relation to her husband's typical responses to her drinking. Results showed that her husband withdraws from her when she is drinking. This typically resulted in more drinking on her part.

## ETHICAL AND LEGAL ISSUES OR COMPLICATIONS

While there were no readily apparent ethical or legal issues in the assessment of this case, a potential issue that arises in substance abuse assessment should be noted. For example, an ethical and possible legal issue might arise if, during initial screening or full evaluation, Elaine had refused to cooperate or denied excessive drinking when there was evidence to the contrary. This would have been particularly problematic in this case since Elaine's drinking was affecting her physical well-being. The clinician would then be faced with the issue of whether or not Elaine was a danger to herself (by falling or driving under the influence) or to her children.

## CONCEPTUALIZATION AND TREATMENT
## RECOMMENDATIONS

Based on this evaluation, Elaine was diagnosed with Alcohol Abuse and Major Depressive Disorder. Since these comorbid conditions typically exacerbate each other, treatment becomes more complex. In Elaine's case, it was difficult to determine which condition preceded the other, even though there was no past history of major depression. As a young adult, though, she did exhibit a pattern of episodic binge drinking. Alcohol may have been aggravating her feelings of depression and leading to even more drinking. On the other hand, her symptoms of depression were triggering excessive drinking. For example, the functional analysis from the TLFB indicated that she often drank to quell her feelings of worthlessness and to help induce sleep. Both conditions would require simultaneous treatment.

The evaluation also indicated that Elaine was drinking more than was previously apparent and, by her admission, more than she realized. It also showed that excessive drinking was often triggered by loneliness, depression, and feelings of worthlessness. Both the severity of her cravings and the extent of her drinking had been increasing over the last three months.

Support from her husband for sobriety was lacking. Basically, he ignores her drinking, and the couple has been living separate lives for several months. Apparently, Elaine and her husband spend little time together, even when she is not drinking (e.g., during the days on weekends).

Based on this evaluation, recommendations for intervention include simultaneous treatment of Elaine's depression and alcohol abuse using cognitive-behavioral therapy for both conditions, with the addition of pharmacotherapy for her depression. Focus of treatment would be on developing better coping strategies, managing cravings, and developing better awareness and management of negative thinking patterns.

Since Elaine's excessive drinking pattern was leading to self-injury and showed signs of worsening, an initial goal of total abstinence should be established. Her past binge-drinking behavior and her hereditary predisposition to alcohol abuse (i.e., her father and brother were abusive drinkers) do not bode well for her to establish and maintain a moderate drinking pattern.

Behavioral marital therapy is recommended, since she and her husband seem to have a poor, almost nonexistent relationship. Goals would include not only strengthening the relationship but also teaching her spouse to become more active in reinforcing new, nondrinking behavior patterns.

In addition, Elaine needs assistance in better lifestyle balancing. She seems overwhelmed with her professional work and is involved in few, if any, reinforcing activities by herself or with her family.

## SUMMARY

Valid and reliable assessment is critical for the overall clinical care of substance-abusing individuals. In addition, research protocols rely on accurate assessment for valid scientific conclusions.

Fortunately, there is a variety of assessment instruments available for use in the substance abuse field, ranging from simple screening tools to more comprehensive diagnostic inventories and instruments to guide treatment planning. The plethora of instruments developed and validated over the past 20 years provides both the clinician and the researcher a vast array of choices.

From a clinical standpoint, not only do these assessment methods provide valuable information on treatment planning and implementation, but they also help to monitor a client's progress throughout treatment and at follow-up. Assessment has become increasingly more important in the clinical arena due to greater emphasis on accountability for the effectiveness of therapeutic interventions.

Assessment should be included as a routine and essential part of the treatment process for substance abuse treatment. Valid and reliable tools are available; most are brief, easy to administer, and easily scored. In addition, specialized instruments exist for a wide variety of substance-abusing patient populations.

## REFERENCES

Abellanas, L., & McLellan, A. T. (1993). "Stages of change" by drug problem in concurrent opioid, cocaine, and cigarette users. *Journal of Psychoactive Drugs, 25,* 307–313.

Annis, H. M. (1982). *Inventory of drinking situations.* Toronto, Ontario, Canada: Addiction Research Foundation.

Annis, H. M., & Graham, J. M. (1988). *Situational confidence questionnaire: User's guide.* Toronto, Ontario, Canada: Addiction Research Foundation.

Annis, H. M., & Graham, J. M. (1995). Profile types on the Inventory of Drinking Situations: Implications for relapse prevention counseling. *Psychology of Addictive Behaviors, 9,* 176–182.

Anton, R. F., Moak, D. H., & Latham, P. K. (1996). The Obsessive-Compulsive Drinking Scale: A new method of assessing outcome in alcoholism treatment studies. *Archives of General Psychiatry, 53,* 225–231.

Bandura, A. (1997). *Self-efficacy: The exercise of control.* New York: W.H. Freeman.

Butler, S. F., Budman, S. H., Goldman, R. J., Newman, F. L., Beckley, K. E., Trottier, D., et al. (2001). Initial validation of a computer-administered Addiction Severity Index: The ASI-MV. *Psychology of Addictive Behaviors, 15,* 4–12.

Carbonari, J. P., & DiClemente, C. C. (2000). Using transtheoretical model profiles to differentiate levels of alcohol abstinence success. *Journal of Consulting and Clinical Psychology, 68,* 810–817.

Carroll, K. M. (1995). Methodological issues and problems in the assessment of substance use. *Psychological Assessment, 7,* 349–358.

Clifford, P. R., Longabaugh, R., & Beattie, M. (1992). Social support and patient drinking: A validation study. *Alcoholism: Clinical and Experimental Research, 16,* 403.

Connors, G. J., & Volk, R. J. (2003). Self-report screening for alcohol problems among adults. In J. P. Allen & V. B. Wilson (Eds.), *Assessing alcohol problems* (pp. 21–35). Washington, DC: National Institute on Alcohol Abuse and Alcoholism.

Cox, L. S., Tiffany, S. T., & Christen, A. G. (2001). Evaluation of the Brief Questionnaire of Smoking Urges (QSU-brief) in laboratory and clinical settings. *Nicotine & Tobacco Research, 3,* 7–16.

Davidson, D., Palfai, T., Bird, D., & Swift, R. (1999). Effects of naltrexone on alcohol self-administration in heavy drinkers. *Alcoholism: Clinical and Experimental Research, 23,* 195–203.

DiClemente, C. C. (2003). *Addiction and change.* New York: Guilford Press.

DiClemente, C. C., Carbonari, J. P., Montgomery, R. P. G., & Hughes, S. O. (1994). The Alcohol Abstinence Self-Efficacy Scale. *Journal of Studies on Alcohol, 55,* 141–148.

DiClemente, C. C., & Hughes, S. O. (1990). Stages of change profiles in outpatient alcoholism treatment. *Journal of Substance Abuse, 2,* 217–235.

DiClemente, C. C., Prochaska, J. O., Fairhurst, S. K., Velicer, W. F., Velasquez, M. M., & Rossi, J. S. (1991). The process of smoking cessation: An analysis of precontemplation, contemplation, and preparation stages of change. *Journal of Consulting and Clinical Psychology, 59,* 295–304.

Donovan, D. M. (1988). Assessment of addictive behaviors: Implications of an emerging biopsychosocial model. In D. M. Donovan & G. A. Marlatt (Eds.), *Assessment of addictive behaviors* (pp. 3–48). New York: Guilford Press.

Donovan, D. M. (2003). Assessment to aid in the treatment planning process. In J. Allen & V. B. Wilson (Eds.), *Assessing alcohol problems.* Washington, DC: National Institute on Alcohol Abuse and Alcoholism.

Ewing, J. A. (1984). Detecting alcoholism: The CAGE questionnaire. *Journal of the American Medical Association, 252,* 1905–1907.

Fagerstrom, K. O. (1978). Measuring degree of physical dependence to tobacco smoking with reference to individualization of treatment. *Addictive Behaviors, 3,* 235–241.

Fagerstrom, K. O., & Schneider, N. G. (1989). Measuring nicotine dependence: A review of the Fagerstrom Tolerance Questionnaire. *Journal of Behavioral Medicine, 12,* 159–182.

Fals-Stewart, W., O'Farrell, T. J., Rutigliano, P., Freitas, T., & McFarlin, S. K. (2000). The Timeline Followback reports of psychoactive substance use: Psychometric properties. *Journal of Consulting and Clinical Psychology, 68,* 134–144.

Fiellin, D. A., Reid, M. C., & O'Connor, P. G. (1989). Screening for alcohol problems in primary care: A systematic review. *Archives of Internal Medicine, 160,* 1977–1989.

Franken, I. H. A., Hendriks, V. M., & van den Brink, W. (2002). Initial validation of two opiate craving questionnaires: The Obsessive Compulsive Drug Use Scale and the Desires for Drug Questionnaire. *Addictive Behaviors, 27,* 675–685.

Gordon, A. J., Maisto, S. A., McNeil, M., Kraemer, K. L., Conigliaro, R. L., Kelley, M. E., et al. (2001). Three questions can detect hazardous drinking. *Journal of Family Practice, 50,* 313–320.

Heather, N., & Bradley, B. P. (1990). Cue exposure as a practical treatment for addictive disorders: Why are we waiting? *Addictive Behaviors, 15,* 335–337.

Heather, N., Gold, R., & Rollnick, S. (1991). *Readiness to Change Questionnaire: User's manual.* Kensington: University of New South Wales.

Heather, N., Luce, A., Peck, D., Dunbar, B., & James, I. (1999). Development of a treatment version of the Readiness to Change Questionnaire. *Addiction Research, 7,* 63–83.

Heishman, S. J., Singleton, E. G., & Moolchan, E. T. (2003). Tobacco Craving Questionnaire: Reliability and validity of a new multifactorial instrument. *Nicotine & Tobacco Research, 5,* 645–654.

Hughes, J. R., Gust, S. W., & Pechacek, T. F. (1987). Prevalence of tobacco dependence and withdrawal. *Americal Journal of Psychiatry, 144,* 205–208.

Kawakami, N., Takatsuka, N., Inaba, S., & Shimizu, H. (1999). Development of a screening questionnaire for tobacco/nicotine dependence according to ICD-10, *DSM-III-R,* and *DSM-IV. Addictive Behaviors, 24,* 155–166.

Killen, J. D., Fortmann, S. P., Newman, B., & Varady, A. (1991). Prospective study of factors influencing the development of craving associated with smoking cessation. *Psychopharmacology, 105,* 191–196.

Leonhard, C., Mulvey, K., Gastfriend, D. R., & Shwartz, M. (2000). Addiction Severity Index: A field study of internal consistency and validity. *Journal of Substance Abuse Treatment, 18,* 129–135.

Longabaugh, R., Wirtz, P. W., Beattie, M. C., Noel, N., & Stout, R. (1995). Matching treatment focus to patient social investment and support: 18-month follow-up results. *Journal of Consulting and Clinical Psychology, 63,* 296–307.

Love, C. T., Longabaugh, R., Clifford, P. R., Beattie, M., & Peaslee, C. F. (1993). The Significant-Other Behavior Questionnaire (SBQ): An instrument for measuring the behavior of significant others toward a person's drinking and abstinence. *Addiction, 88,* 1267–1279.

Maly, R. C. (1993). Early recognition of chemical dependences. *Primary Care, 20,* 33–50.

Marlatt, G. A. (1990). Cue exposure and relapse prevention in the treatment of addictive behaviors. *Addictive Behaviors, 15,* 395–399.

McLellan, A. T., Luborsky, L., O'Brien, C. P., & Woody, G. E. (1980). An improved diagnostic instrument for substance abuse patients: The Addiction Severity Index. *Journal of Nervous and Mental Diseases, 168,* 26–33.

Miller, W. R., & Tonigan, J. S. (1996). Assessing drinkers' motivation for change: The Stages of Change Readiness and Treatment Eagerness Scale (SOCRATES). *Psychology of Addictive Behaviors, 10,* 81–89.

Modell, J., Glaser, F., Mountz, J., Schmaltz, S., & Cyr, L. (1992). Obsessive and compulsive characteristics of alcohol abuse and dependence: Quantification by a newly developed questionnaire. *Alcoholism: Clinical and Experimental Research, 16,* 266–271.

O'Farrell, T. J., Fals-Stewart, W., & Murphy, M. (2003). Concurrent validity of a brief self-report drug use frequency measure. *Addictive Behaviors, 28,* 327–337.

Piccinelli, M., Tessari, E., & Bortolomasi, M. (1997). Efficacy of the Alcohol Use Disorders Identification Test as a screening tool for hazardous alcohol intake and related disorders in primary care: A validity study. *British Medical Journal, 314,* 420–424.

Piper, M. E., Piasecki, T. M., Federman, E. B., Bolt, D. M., Smith, S. S., Fiore, M. C., et al. (2004). A multiple motives approach to tobacco dependence: The Wisconsin Inventory of Smoking Dependence Motives (WISDM-68). *Journal of Consulting and Clinical Psychology, 72,* 139–154.

Prochaska, J. O., & Velicer, W. F. (1997). The transtheoretical model of health behavior change. *Journal of Health Promotion, 12,* 38–48.

Reinert, D. F., & Allen, J. P. (2002). The Alcohol Use Disorders Identification Test (AUDIT): A review of recent research. *Alcoholism: Clinical and Experimental Research, 26,* 272–279.

Rohsenow, D. J., Martin, R., & Monti, P. M. (1998). Predicting cocaine use outcomes from craving in simulated high-risk situations: Preliminary results. *Proceedings of the 60th Annual Scientific Meeting of the National Institute on Drug Abuse, 179,* 165.

Rohsenow, D. J., Monti, P. M., Rubonis, A. V., Sirota, A. D., Niaura, R. S., Colby, S., et al. (1994). Cue reactivity as a predictor of drinking among male alcoholics. *Journal of Consulting and Clinical Psychology, 62,* 620–626.

Ross, A. A., Filstead, W. J., Parrella, D. P., & Rossi, J. J. (1994). A comparison of high-risk situations for alcohol and other drugs. *American Journal of Addiction, 3,* 241–253.

Russell, M., & Skinner, J. B. (1988). Early measures of maternal alcohol misuse as predictors of adverse pregnancy outcomes. *Alcoholism: Clinical and Experimental Research, 12,* 824–830.

Russell, M., Martier, S. S., Sokol, R. J., Mudar, P., Bottoms, S., Jacobson, S., et al. (1994). Screening for pregnancy risk-drinking. *Alcoholism: Clinical and Experimental Research, 18,* 1156–1161.

Saunders, J. B., Aasland, O. G., Babor, T. F., de la Fuente, J. R., & Grant, M. (1993). Development of the Alcohol Use Disorders Identification Test (AUDIT): WHO collaborative project on early detection of persons with harmful alcohol consumption—II. *Addiction, 88,* 791–804.

Selzer, M. L. (1971). The Michigan Alcoholism Screening Test: The quest for a new diagnostic instrument. *American Journal of Psychiatry, 127,* 1653–1656.

Shadel, W. G., Niaura, R., & Abrams, D. B. (2001). Does completing a craving questionnaire promote increased smoking cravings? An experimental investigation. *Psychology of Addictive Behaviors, 15,* 265–267.

Shoenfeld, L., Peters, R., & Dolente, A. (1993). *SARA, Substance Abuse Relapse Assessment: Professional manual.* Odessa, FL: Psychological Assessment Resources.

Singleton, E. G., Tiffany, S. T., & Henningfield, J. E. (1995). Development and validation of a new questionnaire to assess craving for alcohol. In L. S. Harris (Ed.), *Problems of drug dependence, 1994: Proceedings of the 56th Annual Scientific Meeting, the College on Problems of Drug Dependence* (Vol. 153, p. 289). Rockville, MD: National Institute on Drug Abuse.

Skinner, H. A. (1982). The Drug Abuse Screening Test. *Addictive Behaviors, 7,* 363–371.

Sobell, L. C., Brown, J., Leo, G. I., & Sobell, M. B. (1996). The reliability of the Alcohol Timeline Followback when administered by telephone and computer. *Drug and Alcohol Dependence, 42,* 49–54.

Sobell, L. C., & Sobell, M. B. (1992). Timeline Follow-back: A technique for assessing self-reported alcohol consumption. In R. Z. Litten & J. Allen (Eds.), *Measuring alcohol consumption: Psychosocial and biological methods* (pp. 41–71). Totowa, NJ: Humana Press.

Tiffany, S. T., & Drobes, D. J. (1991). The development and initial validation of a questionnaire on smoking urges. *British Journal of the Addictions, 86,* 1467–1476.

United Nations International Drug Control Program and World Health Organization. (1992). *Informal expert committee on the craving mechanism* (Vol. 92-54439T).

Velicer, W. F., DiClemente, C. C., Rossi, J. S., & Prochaska, J. O. (1990). Relapse situations and self-efficacy: An integrative model. *Addictive Behaviors, 15,* 271–283.

Velicer, W. F., Prochaska, J. O., Rossi, J., & DiClemente, C. C. (1996). A criterion measurement model for addictive behaviors. *Addictive Behaviors, 21,* 555–584.

Weiss, R. D., Griffin, M. I., Hufford, C., Muenz, L. R., Najavits, L. M., Jansson, S. B., et al. (1997). Early prediction of initiation of abstinence from cocaine: Use of a craving questionnaire. *American Journal of Addiction, 6,* 224–231.

Weiss, R. D., Griffin, M. I., Mazurick, M. S., Berkman, B., Gastfriend, D. R., Frank, A., et al. (2003). The relationship between craving, psychosocial treatment, and subsequent cocaine use. *American Journal of Psychiatry, 160,* 1320–1325.

Wewers, M. E., & Lowe, N. K. (1990). A critical review of visual analogue scales in the measurement of clinical phenomena. *Research in Nursing and Health, 13,* 227–236.

World Health Organization. (1992). *The ICD-10 classification of mental and behavioral disorders: Clinical descriptions and diagnostic guidelines.* Geneva, Switzerland: Author.

Zywiak, W. H., Connors, G. J., Maisto, S. A., & Westerberg, V. S. (1996). Relapse research and the Reasons for Drinking Questionnaire: A factor analysis of Marlatt's relapse taxonomy. *Addiction, 91,* S121–130.

Zywiak, W. H., Longabaugh, R., & Wirtz, P. W. (2002). Decomposing the relationships between pre-treatment social network characteristics and alcohol treatment outcome. *Journal of Studies on Alcohol, 63,* 114–121.

# 14

# MARITAL DYSFUNCTION

GARY R. BIRCHLER

*Department of Psychiatry*
*School of Medicine*
*University of California*
*San Diego, California*

WILLIAM FALS-STEWART

*Research Triangle Institute*
*Research Triangle Park,*
*North Carolina*

## INTRODUCTION

The pessimistic view about marriage in the United States is that the institution is in a serious decline. A prevailing divorce rate of approximately 45–50% has led exponentially to millions of children of divorce, many of whom, as adults, understandably have problems committing to long-term intimate relationships. These individuals tend to marry later and later, if at all; and once married, they experience a higher risk for divorce as compared to children raised in intact biological families (Amato & DeBoer, 2001). Moreover, in general, the health consequences of separation and divorce are not good; many partners and their children suffer a number of psychological and physical maladies for a year or two after divorce—and, unfortunately, some people experience long-lasting residual effects (Amato & Booth, 1997; Schmid, 2004).

That said, the optimistic view about marriage, compared to its predominant alternative lifestyles (i.e., remaining single, being divorced, or cohabitating) is that when a marriage relationship is satisfying and healthy, it constitutes the best social institution for having and raising healthy children, for keeping adult partners mentally and physically healthy, and for sustaining people throughout their lives when they are faced with various developmental stressors and challenging life events (Schmid, 2004; Waite & Gallagher, 2000). Moreover, more attention is being devoted to (1) helping partners become educated about healthy marital relationships, (2) trying to prevent divorce and nuclear family breakup, and (3) developing more sophisticated assessment and intervention models to conceptualize marital dysfunction and to offer preventative (Markman, Stanley, & Blumberg, 2001) and remedial treatments that are empirically valid (Baucom, Shoham, Mueser, Daiuto, & Stickle, 1998). This chapter presents a basic model for how to conceptualize couple problems and outline methods to assess both problems and strengths inherent in distressed relationships as they present for professional evaluation and therapy.

## ASSESSMENT STRATEGIES

Basically, four assessment strategies can be employed to evaluate the strengths and vulnerabilities in a couple's relationship: (1) dyadic and individual interviewing, (2) administration of self-report inventories, (3) behavioral observation of couple communication and problem solving, and (4) self/spouse observation in the couple's natural environment.

### INTERVIEWING

Most contemporary behavioral approaches to evaluating couples include a semistructured interview process. That is, the clinician is interested in finding out certain information that can be precategorized and is appropriate for couple intake and follow-up evaluation sessions. Naturally, all therapists will want to hear about the partners' presenting complaints. Most therapists also inquire about their goals for therapy and information about the development of the relationship and the course of events leading to the presenting problems. Beyond that, the domains of interest tend to be associated with the therapeutic approaches employed. For example, we ask a variety of questions related to the 7 C's framework of individual and couple functioning: character features, cultural and ethnic factors, contract, commitment, caring, communication, and conflict resolution (Birchler, Doumas, & Fals-Stewart, 1999; see later definitions). Sampling other prominent cognitive-behavioral approaches, we note that Gottman (1999) claims to be investigating seven questions related to his model of a sound marital house: (1) Where is each partner in the marriage? (2) What is the nature of their marital friendship? (3) Is their sentiment override positive or negative? (*Sentiment override* refers to the partners' prevailing emotional sentiments and the extent to which these overriding sentiments cast a positive or negative shadow over their ongoing cognitions and interactions within the relationship.) (4) Are the partners capable of soothing self and other? (5) What is the nature of conflict and its regulation? (6) Can they honor each other's life dreams and create shared meaning? (7) Do potential sources of resistance exist?

Halford (2001) and Epstein and Baucom (2002) present very comprehensive conceptual models of what types of information can be gathered during interview assessment sessions. Their labels for domains of interest are similar, and these domains can be compared favorably to the 7 C's framework presented in more detail in this chapter. Areas of inquiry include (1) the environmental and psychological contexts from which the partners come and in which they currently operate (i.e., cultural and ethnic factors, current community, friend and family influences), (2) individual characteristics (i.e., personality styles, temperament, physical and mental health issues, personal goals and agendas for couple therapy, etc.), (3) external influences (e.g., life events, resources, and stressors), and (4) individual and couple adaptive processes (e.g., communication and conflict resolution skills, support and understanding between the partners, use of community, friend, and family resources, management of any existing enduring vulnerabilities (i.e., challenging character features affecting the partners). These important domains of influences and individual and couple functioning result in the current and prospective status (i.e., outcomes) that describe the couple.

Finally, to briefly describe a model of assessing couple dysfunction that derives, in part, from traditional cognitive-behavioral roots yet departs from that model to emphasize acceptance strategies over behavior change techniques, we mention the integrative behavioral couple therapy (IBCT) approach developed by Jacobson and Christensen (1996) and colleagues. This approach suggests that not even the majority of couples' presenting problems are amenable to traditional behavioral interventions. Accordingly, the assessment process is less problem oriented and more designed to answer the following six questions. (1) How distressed is this couple? (2) How committed are the partners to the relationship? (3) What are the irreconcilable differences and potentially resolvable issues that cause conflict? (4) Why are these issues such a problem for the couple? (5) What are the couple's strengths that are keeping them together? (6) What can treatment do for them? The answers to these questions provide the basis for a formulation of the couple's conflict themes, the extent of partners' polarized perspectives, and emphasis on implementing acceptance strategies vs. behavior change interventions. Essentially, in this approach, relatively speaking, those couples who are found to be severely distressed, have low commitment to the relationship, have certain incompatible goals, hold rigid and polarized positions, and do not demonstrate the present ability to collaborate, accommodate, and compromise with one another are more likely candidates, at least initially in the treatment process, for acceptance-based interventions (cf. Jacobson & Christensen). In the IBCT conceptualization, couples found to be at the other ends of the continua noted earlier may well be better candidates for a cognitive-behavioral (i.e., change-oriented) approach at the outset.

As represented in all five prominent approaches mentioned earlier, the couple assessment process typically features one or more conjoint interviews of the partners, combined with at least one separate interview of each partner. In a final evaluation session with the couple, the therapist offers a basic formulation of the relationship's strengths and problems. If couple therapy is appropriate, the couple is invited to collaborate in defining ongoing treatment goals, including methods to be employed, the time frame for treatment, etc. Similarly, all of these contemporary approaches have described a number of basic objectives, questions, and related tasks for the intake meeting, for a second conjoint session, for the individualized interviews, and for the feedback session [additional detail describing our particular approach is presented elsewhere (Birchler, Magana, & Fals-Stewart, 2003)].

## THE INITIAL SESSION AND THE COUPLE RELATIONSHIP ASSESSMENT BATTERY

It is strongly encouraged that the first meeting include both partners, despite any requests that may be made for separate first meetings. This procedure helps to establish that it is the couple relationship that constitutes the "client" vs. taking the side of either partner. Client–therapist introductions and clinic registration procedures (and perhaps a discussion of fees and insurance coverage) normally start off the meeting. Next, before getting into a discussion of presenting complaints, we prefer to address important issues of confidentiality and any verbal and/or written consent for treatment that may be appropriate. For example, we have discussions and written consent forms that inform the couple about state laws and situations that may force us to break confidentiality (e.g., threat of harm to self or others, child abuse, elder abuse, direct evidence of domestic violence, court-ordered litigation, and inquiries from insurance companies). Additionally, in our setting we solicit permission for one-way mirror observation and/or video-taping of the sessions; both methods are used for supervision, case management, and client observation and feedback purposes.

Once the business-related items are covered, we state that the remainder of the session will be devoted to hearing about each partner's concerns and that we all will make a decision at the end of the session whether it makes sense to continue and what the continuing assessment process will entail. Then we invite each partner, respectively, to share: "What brings you to the clinic today?" We make sure that each partner has an opportunity to explain what his or her current concerns are, how these problems may have developed over time, why they are seeking help at this point in time, and what related goals and expectations each partner might have for couple therapy. As time allows, some analysis and detail about major concerns are discussed and identification of other problems experienced by the partners and the couple may be elicited. Over 45–50 minutes we find that this intake process typically provides enough information for participants to decide whether or not to commit to completing the evaluation.

If the couple continues, what follows is (1) a second conjoint meeting, featuring an observed communication sample of couple problem solving, (2) individual history-taking session(s), and (3) the final summary and treatment-planning session. We then hand each what we call the Couple Relationship

Assessment Battery (see details later), and partners are asked to take theirs home, complete the inventory on their own, and to bring them back the following session so that the questionnaires can be scored and a summary report prepared in time for discussion at the final evaluation session. Partners are allowed to discuss the questionnaires at home after they fully complete them, but only if both of them agree to discuss the results.

## THE SECOND CONJOINT INTERVIEW SESSION AND THE COMMUNICATION SAMPLE

When the couple returns for the second conjoint session, we like to debrief them regarding two issues: What were their reactions to having made and participated in the initial session? What was it like filling out the Couple Relationship Assessment Battery? The answers to these questions vary widely among couples, and we believe that their responses tell us something important about the quality and nature of their relationship. Partners who have a positive and hopeful attitude about initiating couple therapy, who may have had a good follow-up discussion about these issues on their own, who seemed impressed with the therapist and the description of the program, and who not only completed the 1–2 hours of inventories but also had a constructive attitude and interaction about what may have been learned definitely seem to demonstrate a better collaborative approach and to achieve a better outcome from participating in couple therapy. In contrast, partners who do not say a word to one another about the first session or who left angry and disappointed in their partner or the therapist or the program and who either do not complete the questionnaires or do not believe in their relative value and did not discuss them do seem, in our considerable experience, to have a more closed, conflicted, or disengaged relationship, and these couples seem to have a poorer prognosis for therapy.

The debriefing may take 5–10 minutes. Then we prepare the couple to provide what we call a "communication sample" (CS) of couple conflict problem solving. Based on the presenting problems and the just-collected inventories, it is relatively easy to help the couple identify an issue about which they have a moderate disagreement. The couple is asked to demonstrate how they attempt to solve the problem while the therapist observes (from within the room or from behind a one-way mirror or by live observation via video monitoring). This procedure is a classic behavioral assessment tool that has been used reliably for over three decades to assess couples' optimal abilities to solve problems effectively. We do ask partners about the representativeness of the sample and find that if their own patterns differ at home, they are usually described as less effective than what is observed *in vivo* in the clinic. For example, at home couples may not discuss such issues at all, or they may quickly escalate to verbal abuse and disrespectful interchanges that may lead to angry withdrawal or extended fights.

The communication sample usually gives the therapist a good idea of whether basic problem-solving communication skills exist and, relatively speaking, which of four basic types of conflict resolution patterns prevail [e.g., an affirming, validating pattern of communication, an escalating sequence leading to verbal abuse and perhaps, in some circumstances, to physical violence, a conflict-avoiding, disengaged pattern of withdrawal by both partners, or a mixed demand–withdraw pattern that has been shown to characterize many dysfunctional relationships (Christensen & Heavey, 1990; Notarius & Markman, 1993)]. After the sample is provided, we thank the couple for their willingness to participate and do whatever is necessary to help them calm down (if necessary) and make the transition to the other tasks of session 2.

Accordingly, during the second half of the second conjoint session, we invite the couple to provide a narrative of their relationship developmental history. This is a near-universal domain of inquiry in couple assessment. The general purposes of taking this history are threefold. (1) Foremost, we want to gain an understanding of the circumstances of the couple's meeting: What attracted the partners to one another? Were there initial difficulties? What led to their mutual decision to marry (or establish a monogamous intimate relationship)? (2) Hopefully, by inquiring about the initial features of mutual attraction, we can access with the couple information of a positive nature (in part to offer a positive contrast to the current distress reports and/or perhaps a negative experience during the just-concluded problem-solving discussion, and (3) to determine whether, in fact, one or both partners can access and express warmth and positive affect while describing some part of their history together. The demonstration of positive affect when retelling their acquaintanceship and dating history has been shown to predict a better outcome for the relationship than when the therapist elicits a narrative dominated by negative affect, resentments, and disappointments (Gottman, 1994). As needed, the remaining time may be used to make further inquiries into aspects of the presenting problems, relationship-conflict themes, and/or functioning status of the 7 C's (Birchler, Doumas, & Fals-Stewart, 1999).

## INDIVIDUAL INTERVIEWS

As mentioned earlier, it is commonplace to conduct separate interviews with each partner. These sessions may be conducted simultaneously during a third meeting, overall in circumstances where there are cotherapists; a single therapist also can split the third session, devoting 20–25 minutes to each partner sequentially, or, usually better, the solo therapist may offer two separate full sessions, one to each partner on the same or on different days. The determining factors for these options are the amount of individualized assessment information the therapist anticipates needing to obtain (e.g., more time is recommended for interviewing older people, perhaps with multiple marriages, with complex co-occurring mental or physical health problems, and given any suspected motivational problems and/or suspected hidden agendas, a risk for domestic violence, or harboring secrets, etc.). Although, some groups have slightly different objectives in carrying out these individual meetings, our objectives are fairly typical. Note that at this point in the process, the therapist has conducted two conjoint interviews and has received the completed inventories from both partners. S/he should have a pretty clear understanding of the presenting complaints and hopefully s/he has had an opportunity to review the questionnaires to prompt further areas of inquiry or clarification. Accordingly, we typically spend about 60% of the time available in the personal interview learning about the partner's developmental history, up until s/he met the current partner (that is, the onset and course of the couple's history was discussed previously). Obviously, only the highlights of people's lives can be reviewed in this brief biosketch; essentially, the therapist fast-forwards through normal/typical life experiences and slows down to explore in appropriate detail any negative, traumatic, or abnormal developments while also observing the client's particularly positive life experiences and his or her developmental opportunities and assets. We cover childhood and adolescent contexts and experiences while exposed to the family of origin and to any alternative family constellations. We review social and academic progress and experiences and military, occupational, and intimate relationship histories as well as any problems with the law or mental or physical maladies.

With the remaining 40% of the individual session time, we explore the partner's personal views about present relationship problems (noted from the conjoint interviews and/or the relationship assessment inventories), including such topics as commitment to the relationship and to therapy, any hidden agendas (e.g., unannounced plans to separate or divorce, participation in any relationship-denigrating activities, such as affairs, substance abuse, sexual addictions, gambling), and any topics the partner wishes to bring up while in the one-to-one interview situation. We may also explore the partner's current views and expectations regarding possible therapeutic interventions and possible outcomes. For example, Are you willing to change according to the wishes of your mate? Do you think your partner can or will be able to change according to your goals? What might happen if certain goals are or are not reached as a function of couple therapy? Finally, note again that although we are quite willing to keep certain private information private, with the exception of domestic violence risk, we also maintain a basic "no secrets" policy for all contacts with the partners throughout couple assessment and therapy. That is, if we learn of something that is contrary to the legal, moral, ethical, or otherwise agreed-on therapeutic contract that is either explicit or implied with the couple, we will encourage, help with, and/or require disclosure of such information to the mate. If we determine that such disclosure is appropriate and necessary for couple therapy to progress and the person declines to do so, we will unilaterally terminate the process without much explanation to the other partner. This latter circumstance is very rare in practice. But due to potentially serious consequences for all involved, it must be anticipated in advance of any possible occurrence.

## THE COUPLE RELATIONSHIP ASSESSMENT
## BATTERY (CRAB)

In addition to the semistructured clinical interview process and the communication/problem-solving information obtained from the communication sample, most cognitive-behavioral approaches administer a number of inventories to the couples. Of course, the practitioners of the various groups choose the specific inventories included in any given battery. However, it is common to include measures of couple relationship satisfaction and related areas of agreement and disagreement, couple communication and conflict patterns, and various screening measures for the existence and extent of verbal or physical abuse, depression and other psychological problems, and substance abuse.

Our battery takes about 1.5–2 hours to complete; we inform couples that these inventories provide important and extensive information about couple and individual function that serves to complement our interviews and that this important information would otherwise take about 10 hours to gather through personal interviews. Although, there is some delay for some partners and couples in completing this battery, we consider compliance a fair measure of clients' motivation, or we realize that some people may need certain assistance to complete these forms. In any case, we encourage them to get the information completed before we can conduct the round table so that we have a complete picture of their relationship. Rarely, but possibly, the administration of the CRAB may be postponed or cancelled due to clinical imperatives: couple in crisis, inability to complete the forms due to factors related to language, vision, associated stress, unusual type or length or relationship, etc.

Here we will list the measures we employ currently; some are common and well known, others are perhaps unique to our clinics. The following measures are representative of the kinds of information sought during couple assessment by the use of generally reliable and validated paper-and-pencil self-report measures.

1. *Demographic form.* The CRAB includes a rather standard demographics form that provides information about age, status and length of relationship, income, race/ethnicity, religion, education, and employment status.

2. *Dyadic Adjustment Scale* (DAS; Spanier, 1976). This is a 32-item test that has been given to thousands of happy and unhappy couples. It gives four summary scores *for each person* that can be added together to indicate his or her global satisfaction with the relationship. Subscales relate to consensus, cohesion, satisfaction, and affection. Due to some known reliability problems with the subscores, we usually are interested in the partners' relative total DAS scores. A total score of 100 is the borderline. Individual or couple averaged scores above 100 are in the direction of satisfaction (total possible = 151), while scores below 100 indicate relative dissatisfaction. Previous groups of happy couples averaged 115. Couples seeking marital therapy in our clinics have averaged 71.

3. *Relationship Closeness Inventory* (RCI; Doss, 2004). Similar to the Dyadic Adjustment Scale, this measures partners' feelings about their relationship. However, this scale specifically measures how close the two partners report feeling toward each other. For example, one item asks them how much they agree with statements like "My partner is my best friend," "I can tell my partner anything," and "I can rely on my partner for anything." A total score of 15 indicates that partners feel relatively neutral about these statements—neither agreeing nor disagreeing. Scores lower than 15 indicate that they tend to feel somewhat distant from their partners; scores over 15 (up to a possible maximum of 30) indicate that they feel somewhat to extremely close to their partners. Comparing partners' scores offers a relative sense of their feelings of closeness to one another.

4. *Frequency and Acceptability of Partner Behavior Inventory* (FAPBI; Christensen & Jacobson, 1997). On this measure, subjects report how often their partner is doing certain behaviors. Results are compared to "happy" couples in four areas: affection/intimacy (e.g., physical, verbal, sexual intimacy), support/caring (e.g., help with housework, time together, help with finances, child care), demand/critical (e.g., critical of me, verbal abuse, controlling), and betrayal (dishonest, inappropriate with opposite sex, uses substances). Scores above zero indicate that partners report one another doing more of those behaviors than happy couples; scores below zero indicate reports of partners doing less of those behaviors than happy couples. On this measure, partners also report how much change they would like in one another's behaviors in the indicated areas. Since these four areas are often implicated in couple distress, specific information regarding relative frequency and desired changes can appropriately be incorporated into treatment plans.

5. *Response to Conflict Scale* (RTC; Birchler & Fals-Stewart, 1994). This 12-item scale attempts to assess what potentially unhelpful responses partners make, if any, when engaged in couple conflicts. Generally, these behavioral responses are ineffective, if not destructive, ways of handling disputes. Each partner is asked to indicate the proportion of times self (and partner) responds to conflict in the indicated way, e.g., with "yelling or screaming," "nagging," "ignoring," "leaving the scene" on a 9-point scale, from "never" to "always." Patterns of active and/or passive maladaptive responding to conflict can be identified for modification using this 5-minute measure.

6. *Inventory of Rewarding Activities* (IRA; Birchler, 1983). We believe that couple satisfaction is often reflected in how individuals choose to spend their time. Our impression is that some couples do not work hard enough to ensure having quality activities together. In other relationships, one or both partners may be too dependent on the other or one another. For various reasons, partners may spend too much time together, thus neglecting personally stimulating outside interests. This inventory estimates how partners are typically allocating their weekly time among work, sleep, neutral or nonrewarding activities, and rewarding activities, and it also estimates the relative proportion of elective rewarding activities each partner engages in according to certain social formats [i.e., alone,

with partner only, with partner and other adults, with family (with or without partner), and with others (not including partner)]. Excessive time or too little time spent in various rewarding activities could be a potential danger sign. The final section on the 100-item Inventory of Rewarding Activities asks which activities on the questionnaire each partner would like to do more of with his or her partner.

7. *Marital Status Inventory* (MSI; Weiss & Cerreto, 1980). This 14-item questionnaire asks each partner to answer true or false to questions that indicate whether any and which steps toward separation or divorce may have been taken. The steps range from "thoughts about divorce" to "we are divorced." Previous research has indicated that a score of 4 or greater tends to predict separation, divorce, or deterioration in relationship satisfaction over time.

8. *Brief Symptom Inventory* (BSI; Derogatis, 1993). This 53-item inventory queries about a comprehensive variety of physical and mental symptoms that a person may have experienced during the previous week. The degree of distress ranges, on a 5-point scale, from "not at all" to "extremely." This questionnaire serves as a screen regarding each partner's perceived level of personal physical and/or psychological distress.

9. *Relationship and Individual Strengths and Problems.* At the end of the battery partners are asked to provide in their own words a list of their top four relationship and personal strengths and problems. This list serves as another opportunity for partners to identify their own perceived strengths and areas for improvement in self and in the relationship. Having been sensitized by completing the previous inventories, this list may confirm known and/or offer new information.

Taken together, these questionnaires provide a fairly comprehensive survey of partners' individual and relationship functioning, including strengths, problem areas, general closeness, conflict management, and relationship satisfaction.

Alternative measures of marital function that we recommend include the *Marital Satisfaction Inventory* (MSI; Snyder, 1979, 1997), the *Areas of Change Questionnaire* (AC; Weiss & Birchler, 1975), the *Locke–Wallace Marital Adjustment Test* (LWMAT; Locke & Wallace, 1959), the revised *Conflict Tactics Scale* (CTS2; Straus, Hamby, Boney-McCoy, & Sugarman, 1996), and the *Relationship Belief Inventory* (RBI; Eidelson & Epstein, 1982).

### SELF/SPOUSE OBSERVATION

In addition to interviews, self-report measures, and behavioral observation of communication and problem solving, the fourth potential assessment method is the use of self/spouse observation in the natural environment. Accordingly, as a unique information-gathering strategy, one or both partners may be asked to observe their own and/or their spouse's behaviors between sessions. For example, if during the intake session partners offer different statements about the existence or frequency of a certain behavior (arguments, husband coming home late, amount of time spent on the computer, etc.), partners could be asked to observe and keep track of these behaviors during the next week. These can be assigned as needed to clarify just what is going on at home. Weiss (1975) even developed an extensive 400-item checklist of pleasing and displeasing behaviors that spouses might engage in at home. Spouses note the frequency and pleasure factor associated with exhibited behaviors. In more recent practice, self/spouse observation assignments typically have been reserved for the intervention phase of couple therapy. Indeed, it is known that assignments to clients to observe behaviors exhibited by self or spouse may actually alter the frequency and nature of the behaviors under observation, thus potentially compromising the so-called baseline "assessment" purpose of using this method.

## THE ROUND TABLE

The final conjoint assessment session where the case formulation is presented and where intervention planning occurs is called the "round table." In most cases the therapist has prepared a concise yet comprehensive presentation of the various assessment findings and s/he seeks understanding, "buy in," and the couple's commitment to ongoing treatment for their problems. Occasionally, when couple therapy is neither the initial, the primary, nor a concurrent treatment of choice (or when one or both partners lack the motivation or schedule availability to continue), the meeting is used to summarize the findings of the evaluation, to make whatever referrals are appropriate for alternative therapies or activities, and to terminate the process. Options include no treatment of any kind, individual or group psychotherapy for one or both partners, Group-Anonymous participation, bibliotherapy or other self-help activities. Occasionally, a referral for couple therapy to some other provider is appropriate, one who may offer an alternative skill set or alternative logistical arrangement (e.g., sex therapy, behavioral couples therapy for substance abuse, emotion-focused or psychodynamically oriented couple therapy, community-based location, or evening hours, etc.).

## RESEARCH BASIS AND CLINICAL UTILITY

In general, the four assessment methods just described have been evolving since the operant interpersonal treatment of marital discord and subsequent field of behavioral marital therapy were first developed (Stuart, 1969; Weiss, Hops, & Patterson, 1973). A typical feature of behavior therapy is to observe the nature and frequency of targeted behaviors and, if possible, to understand their function before designing interventions to alter them. Accordingly, since the late 1960s behavioral marital therapists, before developing a treatment plan, have been developing self-report measures to determine what behaviors are being exchanged between partners. Self-report measures have been a very important part of the assessment of marital dysfunction, although they are likely insufficient when used as the sole basis for evaluating the effectiveness of couple therapy. Apart from general marital satisfaction, most of the early measures in this field were developed to count behaviors as a basis for pre- to post-treatment comparisons and for describing, collectively across couples and clinics, the basic nature of marital discord. Over time, as the behaviorally oriented social learning therapists began to incorporate the investigation of cognitions, attitudes, and, more recently, emotions into their work, related measures have been developed (cf. Epstein & Baucom, 2002).

Similarly, some of the earliest investigations into the nature of marital distress employed what we call the Communication Sample to observe *in vivo* how happy, compared to unhappy, couples actually communicated when attempting to solve a marital conflict (Birchler, Weiss, & Vincent, 1975; Gottman, Markman, & Notarius, 1977; Jacobson & Margolin, 1979; Vincent, Weiss, & Birchler, 1975). Over the past three and one-half decades, several comprehensive and complicated interactional scoring systems have been developed in order to interpret and reduce couple problem-solving communication to reliable, valid, and quantifiable information that has both empirical and clinical utility. Examples include the Marital Interaction Coding System (Heyman, Weiss, & Eddy, 1995; Hops, Wills, Patterson, & Weiss, 1972), the Couple Interactional Scoring System (Gottman, 1979; Markman & Notarius, 1987), and the Kategoriensystem fur Partnerschaftliche Interaktion (Hahlweg et al., 1984).

Many of these coding systems are designed to account not only for the relative frequency of certain positive and negative behaviors but also for the sequencing or patterns of behaviors displayed. For example, Gottman (1994) has described the *four horsemen of the apocalypse*, which were discovered by observing the communication exchanges among hundreds of couples in his research. They are (1) persistent criticism, (2) persistent defensiveness, (3) expressions of contempt or disgust, and (4) withdrawal, or so-called stonewalling. When couples were observed exchanging these types of behaviors, over time their marriages were found to be more at risk for separation, divorce, and/or significant deterioration in relationship dissatisfaction. A prominent example of a problematic pattern of communication observed in many distressed couples has been called the demand–withdraw (Christensen & Heavey, 1990) or pursuit–distancer (Notarius & Markman, 1993) dynamic. As one partner makes a demand for action, the other fails to respond or withdraws. In turn each behavior tends to increase the frequency and intensity of the other and the couple ends up in a self-perpetuating negative communication pattern.

In summary, despite the information that may be learned during clinical interviews and gleaned from self-report measures, there is really no substitute for actually observing the couple demonstrating their skills and motivation or lack of them via the communication sample. These samples can be videotaped and subsequently used for therapist study and treatment planning, for feedback (narrative and video) to the couple, and for pre- to post-treatment comparison and related research purposes.

## ASSESSMENT, CONCEPTUALIZATION, AND TREATMENT PLANNING

The multimethod approach to assessment in couple therapy comprises the four methods described earlier: clinical interviews, self-report inventories, the communication sample, and possibly self/spouse observation in the natural environment. Collectively these diverse methods provide both confirming information and method-based unique information about the functional level of the couple's relationship. Based on the comprehensive information gathered, we then apply the 7 C's framework to complete an initial conceptualization of the case and commence with treatment planning. At this point, let us define the 7 C's and mention some of the sources of information inherent in our approach for understanding them. Here we will present the 7 C's in common language we might use when explaining these domains of intimate function to the couple during the round table. For more detail please refer to Birchler et al. (1999).

### CHARACTER FEATURES

Character features refers to the basic type of person and personality one brings to the relationship. For example, if one has a sense of humor, personal integrity, honesty, loyalty, and a positive upbringing and outlook on life and is free of significant mental or physical health problems, then one would be rated more favorably on character features. On the other hand, more challenging character features for being in an intimate relationship may include a negative attitude about life, substance abuse, significant mental or physical health problems, dishonesty, and untrustworthiness. In addition, some otherwise-OK character features simply may not be compatible or constitute a good mix for a given couple: One wants to go out and socialize constantly, the other is more solitary and wants to stay at home. Similarly, relatively negative character features, if compatible, may not constitute a problem for a given couple (e.g., Bonny and Clyde). Character features information comes from the conjoint interviews, personal histories, collateral information, the BSI, and, in many settings, the examination of partners' medical records.

### CONTRACT

Contract refers to the difference between what each partner wants and what each one gets in the relationship. How close does our experience match our expectations? Contract features may be explicit and openly understood: We are going to have a baby and you will stay at home while I work. Or contract features may be implicit and sometimes misunderstood: I expect that you will help me care for the baby and we will accomplish the housework as equals. Couple contracts change naturally over the relationship life cycle; many couples need to revise or renegotiate their contracts to maintain growth and satisfaction. Contract information comes from the conjoint interviews, relationship history, and the various paper-and-pencil instruments noted earlier (e.g., AC, IRA, FAPBI, RBI).

## CULTURAL AND ETHNIC FACTORS

This domain refers to the developmental and contextual environments in which each partner was raised and the traditions and preferences s/he has for living life. Partners can either benefit from or be in conflict about one or many of the following factors: cultural, ethnic, racial, and religious differences; male and female gender roles and responsibilities; how to appreciate and handle working, the importance of and management of money; how to handle and express anger; how to discipline children; how to celebrate birthdays and holidays. Similarities reduce adjustments, but too much sameness can be boring. Differences add diversity and excitement, but differences also can make compromise and adjustment difficult. Information for cultural and ethnic factors comes from the conjoint interviews, personal histories, and behavioral observation of the couple interacting and describing their styles and preferences.

## COMMITMENT

There are two relationship and one therapy-related aspects of commitment to consider. The first important aspect is *stability*. Relationships last longer when partners are loyal and committed to the relationship for the long run—through thick and thin—and they have little or no desire to separate, despite any problems. The second important relationship aspect of commitment is the commitment to *quality*. That is, partners are willing to invest effort in the relationship, to do the work required to make it healthy and personally satisfying for both participants. Some couples have a commitment to stability but not to quality. They can experience long, unhappy marriages. Others are committed to quality and personal happiness, but they run away at the first signs of difficulty, giving little effort to work through the inevitable problems. Couples who are committed to stability *and* quality have the best chance for a long-term intimate relationship. Thirdly, in order to have success in couple therapy, both partners also have to be *committed to the therapy* process itself, to believe in and work toward the goals outlined for therapy. Otherwise the couple therapy may fail and the quality of the relationship may be threatened. Commitment information comes from the conjoint interviews, relationship history, and paper-and-pencil instruments: DAS, MSI, IRA.

## CARING

Caring is a broad term that incorporates several important aspects of an intimate relationship. Couples rated high in caring actively demonstrate support, understanding, and validation of their mates; they have and show appreciation for who they are as people. In addition, there is sufficient activity and compatibility in the ways in which partners demonstrate affection. Greetings, touching, intimate talking, companionship activities—all are desired and expressed in mutually satisfying ways. Individual and mutually rewarding activities are in balance, as opposed to partners' feeling trapped, possessed, or abandoned. Finally, the couple's sex life is enjoyable, healthy, trustworthy, and active at a level satisfactory to both partners. Couples rated lower on caring have problems and need improvement in one or more of the foregoing areas of function. Caring information comes from the conjoint interviews, behavioral observation of the couple, and various inventories: DAS, IRA, RCI.

## COMMUNICATION

Communication is the basic interactional skill that makes a relationship work. Couples who develop and maintain effective communication are much more likely to be able to address all the other concerns suggested by the 7 C's analysis. Effective communication occurs when both partners have the competence and the motivation to share important information with one another about their thoughts, feelings, and actions. When messages truly intended and sent by speakers are the same exact messages that are fully understood by the listener, good communication results (intent = impact: Gottman, Notarius, Gonso, and Markman, 1976). Communication information comes from the conjoint interviews, communication sample, and paper-and-pencil instruments: DAS, RCI.

## CONFLICT RESOLUTION

In addition to general basic conversation and communication skills, couples have to be able to work together effectively to make decisions, to solve daily problems in living, and to manage the inevitable relationship conflicts that arise. Elements of accommodation, assertiveness, negotiation and compromise, emotional expression and regulation, and anger management come into play. Some couples get into trouble by being too conflict avoidant, and issues do not get addressed; others tend to escalate conflicts into verbal and sometimes physical abuse. Both styles in the extreme can do certain damage to the relationship. Couples need to be able to resolve disagreements, or agree to disagree, without becoming disconnected or abusive. Information about conflict resolution comes from the conjoint interviews, communication sample, and various paper-and-pencil instruments: DAS, RTC, FAPBI, AC, CTS2. Finally, the reader may note that the Marital Satisfaction Inventory (Snyder, 1979, 1997) includes 280 items constituting 11 scales, and it attempts, in one comprehensive inventory, to assess many of the areas covered by the 7 C's framework and couples' common areas of concern.

## CASE STUDY

An actual case description may help to illustrate the assessment process just described.

### IDENTIFICATION

Jake (35) and Jenny (32) dated for 10 months before marrying, and at the time of the intake they had been married for almost 3 years. They had a 20-month-old toddler who was cared for during the week by a nanny, since both partners worked. However, since they worked in different aspects of the real estate business, neither kept regular hours. Unpredictably, either one might be called on to serve clients any of seven days or nights per week; alternatively, either might be at home, depending on business and family obligations. Finally, although the couple was fairly affluent and enjoyed their respective jobs, they felt stress from actively planning to build a new house.

### PRESENTING COMPLAINTS

After the therapist discussed clinic policies and procedures, insurance matters, and confidentiality issues, the couple was asked what brought them to the clinic. Jake spoke first and said that they had been fighting so frequently of late that he was beginning to question whether he would stay in the marriage. He said that Jenny seemed to be unhappy with him, his work, and with what was going on around the house. She was "on him" constantly, and he was reacting with anger and rage at her persistent criticism. As he spoke, Jenny began to be tearful. She offered that it was true that they were fighting too much but that she was no longer going to respond to his "threats of divorce." She complained that he expected her to work 24/7 but also to be available to care for the child, to cook meals, to manage the nanny, to manage her clients like he thought they should be handled, and to be available to him sexually. If she complained about these activities, he would first "blow up," perhaps threaten her or throw things, and then stop the verbal abuse only after he threatened to divorce her. Jake countered that Jenny rarely cooked any meals at all, that she often gave her clients a higher priority than their daughter or him, and that she expected him to be available to babysit on a moment's notice, without regard to his work or personal schedule. Yes, he would get mad when she would clam up and refuse to discuss or resolve these ongoing issues. When queried, he admitted that some of their worst fights occurred before, during, or after they went out and had been drinking together. Both partners admitted to problematic drinking at times on the weekends. Jenny said that Jake had pushed and shoved her on two occasions during the past year during loud, angry arguing between them.

## HISTORY

Two aspects of history are gathered in this approach: developmental history of the couple and personal developmental histories of each partner (the latter are obtained in separate interviews). The couple met at a bar in Indiana through mutual friends. Jake was finishing his BA degree in financial management and Jenny was working as an accountant. Each was attracted to the other's physical appearance, and they shared a witty sense of humor. Both talked about liking the other's spirit of independence and abilities to take care of themselves both personally and financially. Jenny had been previously married but had currently been single for three years. Jake had never been married but had experienced two short-lived cohabitating relationships. Neither partner had any children previous to this relationship.

Their dating months were described as somewhat volatile. They worked hard, partied hard, traveled a fair amount, and had some very good times. However, they also had some significant instances of discord, marked by jealousy and mutual resentments about lack of attention to one another. Nevertheless, both said they were ready to get married and have a child before they got too much older. Jake proposed after about six months of dating, and they were married four months later. Jenny was not happy with her accounting job and she was not making enough money according to Jake, so after he graduated they decided to move to California. Jake began working for a mortgage firm, and Jenny studied for a real estate broker's license. Jenny got pregnant sooner than expected. Jake did not like his boss, so he quit and worked for another firm. Jenny not only got her broker's license, but within a year she was making very good money. Her schedule was unpredictable, and sometimes she worked long hours. After they had the baby, given her income, they hired virtually a full-time nanny and Jake quit his job to try work as a self-employed agent. It was in this nontraditional context that the arguing, verbal abuse, mild domestic violence, occasional big fights after drinking, and threats of divorce increased. Both stated that they might already be divorced were it not for their daughter, whom they both love and would not want to leave in a broken home.

Individual interviews were brief, but information gained enlightened the therapist about the character features expressed by these partners. Jake grew up in Texas. He was the second oldest of four children. His father was basically a functional alcoholic who went to work regularly and provided for the family, but there was frequent parental arguing and several instances that he could recall of physical altercations between his father and mother and between his father and older brother. He was not close to his older brother and, being five years older than his two younger sisters, he bossed them around considerably. His parents divorced when he was 14 years old. He did OK in school; apparently he was bright, but an underachiever who was somewhat rebellious after his dad was no longer active in disciplining him. He described his mother as passive and often depressed; he did not have much respect for her. He has never been in trouble with the law, he graduated high school with B's and C's, and after working at a bank for almost 10 years he was accepted into college at age 28. By then he had "matured" and sought a graduate degree in business administration. He lived with girlfriends on two occasions for 2- and 3-year periods, describing these relationships as "up and down." He has been drinking alcohol moderately since adolescence, but he has used few street drugs. When queried, he said that he really does not want to divorce Jenny, but he gets so angry and frustrated interacting with her that this threat just comes to his mind and since it gets her attention he persists in using it. On the other hand, he also realizes that the quality of the marriage is not sufficient for good health for either partner or for the baby.

Jenny grew up in Indiana, the youngest of three girls in her family. Her father was pretty strict, but since she was the baby he spoiled her. Her sisters complained that she had it so much easier than they did because her father treated her like a "princess." The family was middle class, not wanting for material goods but not affluent either. Her parents are still married and doing well. She did well in school and was able to get an accounting degree in a state school by working part time. She got married to a high school sweetheart during her first year in college, but the relationship lasted less than one year after they quickly "grew apart." She liked to have fun and to party, including some instances of alcohol abuse (i.e., getting drunk and embarrassing herself socially), but says such incidents have been infrequent. She has never been in trouble with the law. She finished college, dated several other men, and was yearning for a steady relationship when she met Jake.

## PEER AND WORK ISSUES

Currently, neither partner seems to have individual friends. They often work long hours at odd times, and they claim that being parents of a two-year-old leaves little time for socializing. However, they do attend a frequent number of one another's work-related "real estate" functions, and they try to go out together weekly, either to a function or to dinner "on the town." Occasionally, they state that, alcohol enhanced, one or the other might get a little inappropriate with opposite-sex adults, and this can lead to a fight after the party. As mentioned previously, the fact that Jake does not have a job out of the home and that Jenny is often working long hours and has neither the time nor motivation to be domestic (i.e., perform traditional wifely and motherly duties) causes almost daily conflict. Jenny says she currently is the primary breadwinner, but Jake wants her income and a wife and mother. Her position is that he can't have all three. On the other hand, she resents his having no real job, and he is resentful and/or unavailable when she needs support for her work. Finally, their real estate work sometimes requires them to share clients (i.e., selling, buying, and financing homes), and they often get into arguments about how to manage these clients. Overall, the couple is quite successful in their work; money is not the problem.

## FAMILY ISSUES

At the time of presentation, the couple had been married for about three years and had a young daughter. Although they said they might be divorced were it not for the daughter, they nevertheless have a number of arguments about who has to take care of her when the nanny is not available. An additional family factor was that Jake had almost no interest in seeing or visiting his siblings or parents (in Texas) and Jenny was interested in visiting her family in Indiana over the holidays, on vacations, and talking on the phone. This difference in family connection also caused periodic friction between Jake and Jenny.

## BEHAVIORAL ASSESSMENT RESULTS

In summary form, the sections immediately foregoing describe the information obtained from the conjoint and individual interviews. The communication sample was obtained at the beginning of the second conjoint session, as usual. The topic chosen was "conflict around asking Jake to babysit the daughter when Jenny unexpectedly had to meet with clients and for whatever reason the nanny was not available to cover the needed time." The therapist left the room and observed the 10-minute discussion through a one-way mirror. Jake began talking immediately when the therapist left the room. Basically, he complained that Jenny was too often unorganized or unassertive in her management of clients and that she just assumed that Jake could babysit, without regard to his activities. He also complained that she did a poor job arranging for the nanny to be available as needed for evening and weekend times. Before Jenny could respond, Jake went on to describe how her lack of client management and limit setting on her availability to clients also impacted their ability to have any cooked meals together or family time with the baby. The strong implication was that, although she was having an excellent year selling real estate, she was failing as a mother, wife, and supportive partner to Jake. As Jake talked, Jenny became more and more tearful and morose; Jake did not seem to respond to her sadness whatsoever.

After this long accusatory monologue, Jenny made an ineffective attempt to defend herself. She responded that, after all, Jake was the one who wanted her to be so active in selling real estate. Her success was not only labor intensive, it also allowed him to work independently at home. She apologized if she failed to give him enough notice about babysitting in the nanny's absence, but reminded him that clients did not give much notice to her either. She did feel the need to be generally available to them and meet their schedules to get the sales made. She claimed that 10- to 12-hour days left her little energy and motivation to cook or spend as much time with Jenny as she would like. As Jenny talked, Jake looked at her intently and seemed to be getting angrier. The therapist made the choice to return to the room after about eight minutes of observing the two monologues.

The couple was immediately asked if the observed discussion was representative of what might take place at home. Both nodded their heads in assent, but Jenny then said that more times than not, the argument would escalate as Jake became more angry and upset and she would withdraw to keep from worsening the fight. Jake said that Jenny would often refuse to talk rather than deal with the issue to his satisfaction. Jenny said that giving in to Jake was the best way to get the arguments to calm down; Jake shook his head in apparent disgust. On some occasions, after a relative blowup, the partners would persist in a cold war for a few days, slowly moving back to civility and cooperation but usually not solving the problem at hand.

This CS and debriefing were quite impressive to the therapist, who realized that, unfortunately, the "four horsemen" were alive and operating for this couple: criticism, defensiveness, displays of contempt, and withdrawal. Moreover, the couple admittedly had poor recovery and repairing skills. The atmosphere between them had become more tense and intimidating over the past few months.

Table 14.1 summarizes the scores obtained for the CRAB for Jake and Jenny. Detailed discussion of inventories and many items that we might engage the couple in during the round table is beyond the scope of this chapter; however, a brief summary of highlights will be presented. The "X" marks in the Problem Area column of the table indicate that a score for either partner was clinically different enough from accepted general norms that the area is highlighted for explanation and treatment planning. Obviously, based solely on the quantifiable inventories, this couple has a significant number of concerns. Foremost is a set of DAS scores that are in the moderately dissatisfied range. Jake's global satisfaction score appears significantly lower than does Jenny's. The partners' RCI scores reflect a similar pattern, with both scores below a typical distressed couple's score and Jake's score again lower than Jenny's. The scores on the FAPBI show additional partner differences. Although neither endorsed concerns about betrayal, Jake felt unusually unsupported and deprived of affection and intimacy from Jenny. Jenny also felt unsupported and was particularly sensitive to being criticized by Jake. Taken together, this couple is not very satisfied with their marriage, each feels distant and somewhat unloved by their partners, and Jenny perceives Jake as demanding and critical.

The RTC reflected a pattern of significant levels of maladaptive responding to conflict. Whereas happy couples average about 25% of the time engaging in ineffective behaviors, Jake endorsed 68% of the time for himself and Jenny indicated maladaptive behaviors on his part at 85% of the time they engage in conflict. Jenny's self- and spouse-rated overall scores were lower at 45% and 56%, respectively, but still well above happy couples' levels. Scale inspection showed that Jake was particularly "active" in conflict interactions, noted for occasionally "hitting, biting, and scratching," and he received higher scores for yelling and

TABLE 14.1 Summary of the Couple Relationship Assessment Battery

| Inventory[a] (Range) | Jake | Jenny | Cutoff Score | Problem Area |
|---|---|---|---|---|
| DAS (0–151) | 75 | 83 | 100 | X |
| RCI (0–30) | 8 | 11 | 15 | X |
| FAPBI Z-scores[b] | | | | |
| Affection/intimacy (−8–+8) | −3 | +2 | 0 | X |
| Support/caring (−8–+8) | −5 | −2 | 0 | X |
| Demanding/criticism (−8–+8) | 0 | −4 | 0 | X |
| Betrayal (−8–+8) | +1 | +3 | 0 | |
| RTC | | | | |
| Self (0–100%) | 68% | 45% | 25% | X |
| Partner (0–100%) | 56% | 85% | 25% | X |
| IRA | | | | |
| Alone (0–100%) | 20% | 16% | 26% | |
| Together (0–100%) | 48% | 54% | 34% | X |
| Social (0–100%) | 14% | 11% | 12% | |
| Family (0–100%) | 16% | 15% | 21% | X |
| Others (0–100%) | 2% | 4% | 7% | X |
| MSI (0–14) | 9 | 4 | 4 | X |
| BSI T-scores[c] | | | | |
| Global severity | 55 | 62 | 50 | X |
| Positive symptoms | 42 | 48 | 50 | |
| Severity endorsed items | 60 | 54 | 50 | X |

[a] DAS = Dyadic Adjustment Scale, RCI = Relationship Closeness Inventory, FAPBI = Frequency and Acceptability of Partner Behavior Inventory, RTC = Response to Conflict Scale, IRA = Inventory of Rewarding Activities, MSI = Marital Status Inventory, BSI = Brief Symptoms Inventory.

[b] A score of 0 on the FAPBI represents the average scores for happy couples.

[c] Global severity is the T-score of subject's overall severity of symptoms across the entire 53-item measure. Positive symptoms is the T-score of the total number of problems that subject endorsed (out of 53 total). Severity endorsed items is the T-score of the severity on the items that subject endorsed. Specific subscales include anxiety, depression, hostility, interpersonal sensitivity, phobic anxiety, obsessive-compulsive, somatization, paranoia, and psychosis.

criticizing. Jenny's pattern was marked by "passive" behaviors, such as sulking, leaving the scene, and crying. This couple has major problems concerning conflict resolution.

The IRA measures distribution of rewarding activities into five social formats over the previous month. Inspection of the data suggests that this couple depends on one another for approximately 50% of their rewarding activities, compared to 34% activities together for happy couples. Moreover, they both indicate too few activities with other adults, excluding partner (2%–4% vs. 7% for happy couples). The family proportion of activities is not far off the average for happy couples, but clinical interviewing determined that almost all of these activities included the couple with their baby; again, there is little social stimulation outside the nuclear family. The IRA results help to explain the relative isolation of this family from outsiders and thus increased pressure for meeting diverse needs through the immediate partner or child.

The MSI scores (where increased risk for separation and divorce exists for scores of 4 or higher) are 9 for Jake and 4 for Jenny. High MSI scores are reflective of low commitment to the relationship. Finally, the BSI, measuring individual psychological and physical symptoms, resulted in a relatively high global severity score for Jenny (62 vs. 50 as average $T$-score); for Jake, the severity of endorsed items was 60 vs. 50 as average $T$-score). BSI subscale inspection indicated high scores on anxiety, hostility, and interpersonal sensitivity for Jake and on anxiety and depression for Jenny.

Finally, we always like to look at the self-reported personal and relationship strengths and problem areas to determine the extent to which our clinical interviews, communication sample, and Couple Relationship Assessment Battery have captured (or missed) the partners' narrative lists of strengths and weakness. Abbreviated here, Jake listed his personal strengths as "smart, hard working, good father, and stays in good shape." Relationship strengths listed were "a priority on being a good parent for his daughter, tremendous partnership business potential and good sex life (when not fighting)"; he left the fourth space blank. His four personal problems were anger management, achieving modified career plan, impatient with incompetence in others, and smoking. Relationship problems mentioned were "fight too much, cannot work in the house together, meddling in each other's business deals, and Jenny assumes he will take care of the child as if he had nothing else to do." Jenny indicated her personal strengths as "care about people, devoted mother, works hard in business, and good sense of humor." Relationship strengths were "financial success, good parents, sexually attracted to one another, and enjoy outside activities as a couple." Her personal problems listed were "do not get enough exercise, occasionally drink too much, not enough time for the baby, and bitchy when tired." Relationship problems noted were "Jake's anger and intimidation when he does not get his way, their inability to discuss and solve problems, Jake's interfering in her business deals, and fighting over childcare responsibilities.

Taken together, the information obtained from the complete couple assessment process usually provides sufficient data to formulate an appropriate treatment plan.

## ETHICAL AND LEGAL ISSUES AND COMPLICATIONS

In this particular case, the main concern regarding ethical and legal issues was the safety issue that arises when this couple's arguing escalates into verbal abuse and occasionally has advanced to mild–moderate physical violence (i.e., Jake throwing things, slamming doors, occasionally pushing and shoving Jenny). At the time of the assessment period, there had been no reports or evidence of significant personal threat or physical harm. However, in these circumstances we recommend that the therapist carefully make three points: (1) no angry touching at any time by either partner, (2) review safety planning in the event that arguments get out of control (e.g., separations, time-outs, table and bring hot issues to therapy, call 911 if necessary), and (3) outline the consequences should physical violence occur (e.g., therapist's requirement to break confidentiality and inform the authorities about risk for harm, what the police do when called on a 911, and the increasingly serious legal and personal consequences of engaging in domestic violence). In most cases involving common couple violence, these preliminary safeguards help protect the couple while engaged in couple therapy.

## CONCEPTUALIZATION AND TREATMENT RECOMMENDATIONS

As already mentioned, following the individual and conjoint clinical interviews, the observed communication sample of communication and problem solving, and after an analysis of the CRAB results, we then turn to an analysis of the 7 C's as a framework for providing feedback to the couple and for treatment planning. We have devised a simple 7-point scale for each of the 7 C's, and the therapist, often in consultation with the marital treatment team, makes an informed estimate of the quality of function for the 7 C's. The 1–7 scale is anchored at "1" by "extraordinary vulnerability," at "4" by "mixed," and at "7" by "extraordinary strength." There is one number assigned for the couple relationship regardless of each particular partner's relative contribution to the domain of function. Generally speaking, any element of the 7 C's rated less than "4" becomes an important area for therapeutic intervention; areas rated "4" and "5" also are potential targets for relationship improvement. These rated domains of function, when combined with any additional content areas (i.e., specific presenting problems and goals of treatment brought by the couple), constitute the target areas for couple therapy.

Here are the therapist ratings and brief rationale for Jake and Jenny: The basis for any "1–4" ratings convert directly into treatment goals.

Character features = 4, based on Jake's anger management issues, the couple's propensity for violence-prone arguments, and a mixture of personal anxiety, depression, and emotional sensitivities within and between the partners.

Cultural and ethnic factors = 4, based on the fact that they come from totally opposite families as far as closeness-disengagement/intimacy-hostility goes, and these oppositional family relational styles cause the couple some conflict. They also have yet to work out an effective balance of traditional vs. egalitarian role expectations. Jake seems to expect Jenny to be a major income provider and also a traditional stay-at-home wife and mother. Jenny also seems frustrated with her inability to perform to expectations in all three roles. She wants Jake to be more traditional as an active career person; at the moment he is more of a reluctant stay-at-home father.

Contract = 3. Contract issues are a significant problem for this couple. As stated earlier, the partners' expectations for themselves, their partner, and their marriage do not currently meet their experiences. The explicit and implicit aspects of the relational contract need to be explored and explicated and an ongoing plan agreed on.

Commitment = 2. The therapist rated commitment 2 rather than 3 for "effect." That is, s/he wants to get the couple's attention here, using the lower rating for that purpose. Stability is threatened when Jake says that he will not stay married if Jenny's support of him is not improved; he also threatens divorce often when they get into heated arguments. The couple has stated in interview that they might be separated were it not for the baby. Commitment to quality is apparent thus far in the assessment process. They have attended sessions reliably, complied with the various evaluation tasks, and appear motivated to fix or end the marriage. More information about their commitment to quality and to therapy will emerge as the treatment phase is started.

Caring = 4. The partners demonstrate good aspects of caring in their role as parents; when they are getting along, they both enjoy their sex life. The downside comes from their apparent disrespect for one another when they argue and their frequent disengagement from positive emotional and phys- ical contact. It is an area that needs improvement, but it may function sec- ondary to the need for improvements in other areas (e.g., contract, communication, and conflict-resolution skills). Based on the IRA results, they also need to modify the source and structure of their personal support systems, rewarding activities, and overall exposure to one another. It will be recommended that one of them, at least, get an office outside the home where he or she goes to work most days and that they cultivate additional couple-based and separate personal friends to spend quality time with and get support from, and thereby get relief from too frequent contact with and dependence on one another.

Communication = 2. The rigid and disrespectful communication sample and the reported demand–withdraw pattern of interaction at home suggests major concern with the partner's motivation and abilities to communicate effectively. Their skill or performance deficits in this area must be addressed if they are to understand and improve other areas of their marriage.

Conflict resolution = 1. The score of "1" vs. "2" also is given for effect, to get the attention of this couple to work in this area. All four horsemen were evident in the CS; the couple is prone to verbal abuse, if not increasing potential for domestic violence. Moreover, alcohol use often contributes to the problem here and should be addressed and probably modified.

This case illustrates a couple that is in significant need of couple therapy. Without treatment, the risk is high for separation and divorce, if not for physical violence on the way to relationship deterioration. Many couples have more mod- erate 7 C's ratings and two to three areas to work on. This couple enjoys few resources for stability and quality in the marriage. However, their commitment to their daughter (or not having to split her time), their clear positive business potential and opportunity for an affluent lifestyle, and their emerging desire to be more effective in achieving a healthy intimate relationship can all hopefully provide the basis for committing to a 6- to 9-month process of therapy and some success in achieving their goals.

## SUMMARY

An assessment process for evaluating distressed or dysfunctional couple relationships was described. A state-of-the-art multimethod assessment process involves semistructured interviews of the couple and of each partner separately. An observed sample of couple communication and problem solving provides unique information about performance and skill deficits in these important areas of interaction. A variety of well-known paper-and-pencil self-report questionnaires offers complementary and additional information about couple (dys)function and goals for treatment. Finally, the 7 C's framework for analyzing and interpreting relationship domain treatment goals was applied to a case example of a distressed couple seeking evaluation for couple therapy.

## REFERENCES

Amato, P. R., & Booth, A. (1997). *A generation at risk.* Cambridge, MA: Harvard University Press.

Amato, P. R., & DeBoer, D. D. (2001). The transmission of marital instability across generations: Relationship skills or commitment to marriage? *Journal of Marriage & the Family, 63,* 1038–1051.

Baucom, D. H., Shoham, V., Mueser, K., Daiuto, A. D., & Stickle, T. R. (1998). Empirically supported couple and family interventions for marital distress and adult mental health problems. *Journal of Consulting and Clinical Psychology, 66,* 53–88.

Birchler, G. R. (1983). Marital dysfunction. In M. Hersen (Ed.), *Outpatient behavioral therapy: A clinical guide* (pp. 229–269). New York: Grune & Stratton.

Birchler, G. R., Doumas, D. M., & Fals-Stewart, W. S. (1999). The Seven Cs: A behavioral systems framework for evaluating marital distress. *The Family Journal, 7,* 253–264.

Birchler, G. R., & Fals-Stewart, W. (1994). The Response to Conflict Scale: Psychometric properties. *Assessment, 1,* 335–344.

Birchler, G. R., Magana, C., & Fals-Stewart, W. (2003). Marital dyads. In M. Hersen and S. M. Turner (Eds.), *Diagnostic interviewing* (3rd ed., pp. 365–391). New York: Kluwer Academic/Plenum Press.

Birchler, G. R., Weiss, R. L., & Vincent, J. P. (1975). Multimethod analysis of reinforcement exchange between maritally distressed and nondistressed spouse and stranger dyads. *Journal of Personality and Social Psychology, 31,* 349–360.

Christensen, A., & Heavey, C. L. (1990). Gender and social structure in the demand/withdraw pattern of marital conflict. *Journal of Personality and Social Psychology, 59,* 73–81.

Christensen, A., & Jacobson, N. S. (1997). *Frequency and Acceptability of Partner Behavior Inventory.* Unpublished manuscript, University of California, Los Angeles.

Derogatis, L. R. (1993). *Brief Symptom Inventory,* manual. Minneapolis, MN: National Computer Systems.

Doss, B. (2004). *Relationship Closeness Inventory.* Unpublished manuscript, Texas A&M University, College Station, TX.

Eidelson, R. J., & Epstein, N. (1982). Cognition and relationship maladjustment: Development of a measure of dysfunctional relationship beliefs. *Journal of Consulting and Clinical Psychology, 50,* 715–720.

Epstein, N. B., & Baucom, D. H. (2002). *Enhanced cognitive-behavioral therapy for couples.* Washington, DC: American Psychological Association.

Gottman, J. M. (1979). *Marital interaction: Experimental investigations.* New York: Academic Press.

Gottman, J. M. (1994). *What predicts divorce?* Hillsdale, NJ: Erlbaum.

Gottman, J. M. (1999). *The marriage clinic: A scientifically based marital therapy.* New York: W. W. Norton.

Gottman, J. M., Markman, H. J., & Notarius, C. I. (1977). The topography of marital conflict: A sequential analysis of verbal and nonverbal behavior. *Journal of Marriage and the Family, 39,* 461–477.

Gottman, J. M., Notarius, C., Gonso, J., & Markman, H. (1976). *A couple's guide to communication.* Champaign, IL: Research Press.

Hahlweg, K., Reisner, L., Kohli, G., Vollmer, M., Schindler, L., & Revenstorf, D. (1984). Development and validity of a new system to analyze interpersonal communication (KPI: Kategorien-system fur partnerschaftliche Interaktion). In K. Hahlweg & N. S. Jacobson (Eds.), *Marital interaction: Analysis and modification* (pp. 182–198). New York: Guilford Press.

Halford, W. K. (2001). *Brief therapy for couples.* New York: Guilford Press.

Heyman, R. E., Weiss, R. L., & Eddy, J. M. (1995). Marital Interaction Coding System: Revision and empirical evaluation. *Behaviour Research and Therapy, 33,* 737–746.

Hops, H., Wills, T. A., Patterson, G. R., & Weiss, R. L. (1972). *Marital Interaction Coding System.* Unpublished manuscript. University of Oregon and Oregon Research Institute, Eugene.

Jacobson, N. S., & Christensen, A. (1996). *Integrative couple therapy.* New York: W. W. Norton.

Jacobson, N. S., & Margolin, G. (1979). *Marital therapy: Strategies based on social learning and behavior-exchange principles.* New York: Brunner/Mazel.

Locke, H. J., & Wallace, K. M. (1959). Short marital adjustment prediction tests: Their reliability and validity. *Marriage and Family Living, 21,* 251–255.

Markman, H. J., & Notarius, C. I. (1987). Coding marital and family interaction: Current status. In T. Jacob (Ed.), *Family interaction and psychopathology: Theories, methods, and findings* (pp. 329–390). New York: Plenum Press.

Markman, H. J., Stanley, S. M., & Blumberg, S. L. (2001). *Fighting for your marriage.* San Francisco: Jossey-Bass.

Notarius, C. I., & Markman, H. (1993). *We can work it out: Making sense of marital conflict.* New York: Putnam's Sons.

Schmid, R. E. (2004, December 16). Married people healthier, study finds. *Boston Globe Associated Press.*

Snyder, D. K. (1979). Multidimensional assessment of marital satisfaction. *Journal of Marriage and the Family, 41,* 813–823.

Snyder, D. K. (1997). *Manual for the Marital Satisfaction Inventory.* Los Angeles: Western Psycho-logical Services.

Spanier, G. B. (1976). Measuring dyadic adjustment: New scales for assessing the quality of marriage and similar dyads. *Journal of Marriage and the Family, 38,* 15–28.

Straus, M. A., Hamby, S. L., Boney-McCoy, S., & Sugarman, D. B. (1996). The revised Conflict Tactics Scales (CTS2): Development and preliminary psychometric data. *Journal of Family Issues, 17,* 283–316.

Stuart, R. B. (1969). Operant interpersonal treatment for marital discord. *Journal of Consulting and Clinical Psychology, 33,* 675–682.

Vincent, J. P., Weiss, R. L., & Birchler, G. R. (1975). A behavioral analysis of problem solving in distressed and nondistressed married and stranger dyads. *Behavior Therapy, 6,* 475–487.

Waite, L. J., & Gallagher, M. (2000). *The case for marriage.* New York: Doubleday.

Weiss, R. L. (1975). *Spouse Observation Checklist.* Unpublished manuscript, University of Oregon at Eugene.

Weiss, R. L., & Birchler, G. R. (1975). *Areas of Change Questionnaire.* Unpublished manuscript, University of Oregon at Eugene.

Weiss, R. L., & Cerreto, M. (1980). The Marital Status Inventory: Development of a measure of dissolution potential. *American Journal of Family Therapy, 8,* 80–86.

Weiss, R. L., Hops, H., & Patterson, G. R. (1973). A framework for conceptualizing marital conflict, a technology for altering it, some data for evaluating it. In M. Hersen & A. S. Bellack (Eds.), *Behavior change: Methodology, concepts and practice* (pp. 309–342). Champaign, IL: Research Press.

# 15

# SEXUAL DEVIATION

## NATHANIEL MCCONAGHY

*School of Psychiatry*
*University of New South Wales*
*Paddington, New South Wales, Australia*

## INTRODUCTION

When behavioral assessment was introduced in the 1960s, under the influence of the current behaviorist theory, it was argued that such assessment should be based on observation of subjects' motor behaviors rather than on their self-reports. As research demonstrated the failure of behavior observed in laboratory situations to predict behavior in real life due to such factors as social desirability, there was a return by many behaviorally oriented theorists to an appreciation of cognitive processes, referred to as the *cognitive revolution* (Mahoney, 1977). It was acknowledged that self-report was necessary to explore these processes and that behaviors could be validly assessed by such reports. Bellack and Hersen (1988) concluded that the preeminence of behavioral observation was no longer accepted and that it was not reasonable to contrast behavioral and nonbehavioral assessment in an either/or, good/bad manner. The clinical interview was thus accepted as an important component of behavioral assessment. What became controversial was the degree to which such interviews should be structured. Most behavioral assessment of men and women with sexual deviations deal with the majority who come to the attention of researchers and clinicians, namely, sexual offenders, most of whom are men.

## ASSESSMENT STRATEGIES

### THE CLINICAL INTERVIEW

The reliance on the clinical interview as a major form of assessment of sexual offenders is apparent in the description of programs for their treatment. The assessment procedure of the Twin Rivers Program (Gordon & Hover, 1998) used extensive interviews and formal testing. Hudson, Wales, and Ward (1998), in the Kia Marama program for child molesters, had a 2-week period devoted to assessment that included a series of clinical interviews, beginning with the man's view of his offending and the factors and processes that led up to this and going on to cover issues of social competency. They covered details regarding the offender's general life management skills; his ability to use leisure effectively; his interpersonal goals and ability to form satisfying intimate relationships; his beliefs and attitudes about self; his ability to regulate his affect, particularly negative emotions; his capacity for empathy and perception of victim harm; his sense of responsibility for the offenses and the extent to which he still minimized some aspects of his offending; his views regarding sex, particularly his own entitlement and the appropriateness of sexual contact between adults and children, and what needs he considered were satisfied by his deviant and nondeviant sexual activity; and, finally, his use of both pornography and intoxicants. Worling (1998) stated that to gather information on sexual arousal (and other sensitive information) in the SAFE-T program for adolescent sexual offenders, reliance was placed on establishing a caring and supportive therapeutic relationship with the offender and then asking questions. Jenkins (1998) also emphasized the need for engagement in the treatment of his client group of males ages 13–20. From their descriptions, both clinicians seemed to rely entirely on the clinical interview to obtain information from their clients concerning their behavior.

Most clinicians conduct the interview in a form commonly described as *unstructured*. This term is misleading because the clinical interview does have a structure, in the sense that it investigates specified domains of the client's behavior, though not in a specific order. Marshall (1999) listed the appropriate domains for interviewing sex offenders as sexual behavior, social functioning, life history, cognitive processes, personality, substance abuse, physical problems, and relapse-related issues. Goldberg (1997) pointed out that the clinical interview, rather than systematically checking a symptom inventory, started with investigation of the clients' presenting condition. It proceeded to assess their mental state from their appearance and general behavior, talk, mood, attention, and thought content, evidence of abnormal beliefs or interpretations of experiences or bodily sensations, and cognitive status in terms of memory, orientation, and general knowledge. Students being trained to use a clinical interview are commonly encouraged to keep a list of such domains by them to ensure that all are investigated. The order in which this is done is varied in response to the client's behavior.

If the client has been referred in relation to a charge of a sexual offence, all the information related to the charge should be obtained and read before the initial interview. Otherwise the clinical interview is usually commenced by asking clients the nature of their problem or why they have sought help. This gives the client the opportunity to take charge of the interview, while the content of his or her response should provide much of the information required to establish the nature of the presenting complaint. Additional necessary information can be obtained after the clinician becomes directive in questioning. This information usually includes any past history of similar problems, other illnesses, previous treatment, childhood and adolescent relationships with parents and siblings, social and sexual relationships and practices including fantasies, unwanted sexual experiences, coercive acts experienced or carried out, and history of contraceptive use where appropriate. Educational and work history, current domestic, social, sexual, and occupational situations, including the nature and extent of recreational interests and activities, Internet use for sexual purposes, use of recreational drugs, including alcohol and tobacco as well as any medications, and any past criminal offenses also need to be determined. If the clients' presentations of their history, including their vocabulary, suggest the presence of memory or intellectual impairment, this will require specific investigation. Severity of depression requires assessment if there is evidence of reduced enjoyment of life events or of appetite or sleep disturbance. If the client has had previous treatment or been charged or convicted with criminal offences, records of such treatment or charges should be obtained. Determining the significance of deviant sexual fantasies needs to be done with caution. A significant percentage of normal men report sexual arousal to visual stimuli or fantasies of the infliction of pain or suffering on women or of sexual acts with juveniles (Crepault & Couture, 1980; Person, Terestman, Myers, Goldberg, & Salvadori, 1989). The likelihood that the person will act on these fantasies therefore needs to be determined. Investigation of some sexual experiences poses special difficulties. If the client indicates his problem is related to sexual interest in children, it is necessary to inform him that if he states that sexual activity with a child has taken place, the therapist has a mandatory obligation to provide this information to the relevant authorities. Reports of some clients with sexual deviations that they were victims of childhood sexual abuse have been accepted by many therapists as of importance in the etiology and treatment of their condition, though others have argued that these reports may be made in the hope of obtaining the sympathy of the therapist or of more lenient treatment (Freund, Watson, & Dickey, 1990; McConaghy, 1993). Wyatt and Peters (1986) recommended use of multiple probing questions about specific types of abusive sexual behaviors by interviewers given special training in ideologically correct attitudes, to identify women who had been sexually abused in childhood. Studies using this methodology found much higher prevalence rates than did studies not using them. At the same time it is necessary to avoid influencing the client by suggestion to develop false memories of coercion. Heavy damages have been levied against therapists on the basis that they implanted false memories of child sexual abuse in clients (Okami, 1999).

Jones, Winkler, Kacin, Salloway, and Weissman (1998) pointed out that with members of ethnic minorities, the breadth of assessment needed to be extended beyond that commonly investigated. Minority families could have strong links with religious institutions, and spirituality may be one of their most important sources of support. This should be assessed because such support could be integrated into the treatment program. The home and neighborhood environments and the schools of adolescent minority offenders may require investigation to identify possible barriers that if unaddressed could result in failure to attend or engage in treatment. Religious affiliation may of course need to be taken into account with some clients who are members of ethnic majorities.

Because it provides the client's final impression, the termination of the clinical interview is of major importance, and adequate time must be left for this. The client should not leave feeling he has been asked many questions but received no information. When a treatment plan is proposed, the clinician should ensure that clients are fully aware of what it entails and why it, rather than alternatives, has been selected.

## INTERVIEW OF SIGNIFICANT OTHERS

With the client's permission, interview of significant relatives or friends and his partner if he has one is advisable to obtain confirmatory evidence of his account and possible additional information. As well as interviewing them individually, interview of partners with the clients will provide information concerning the nature of their relationship from observation of their interaction in the interview, interpreted in the light of both partners' accounts of their present and previous relationships. In addition to verbal expressions indicative of affection or hostility, or indeed of both, the couple's body language, including supportive touching, usually gives the interviewer additional insights.

## THE STRUCTURED INTERVIEW

In response to evidence of the low reliability of diagnoses based on clinical interviews, discussed subsequently, researchers, particularly those involved in epidemiological studies, devoted considerable attention to attempts to improve it. Improved reliability of course does not guarantee improved validity, an issue that is only recently receiving adequate attention. The major issue for clinicians involved in client treatment is whether adopting procedures that focus on increasing reliability will improve client outcome. No attempts have been made to investigate what was termed by Nelson and Hayes (1981) the *treatment validity* of diagnoses reached by different clinicians or procedures. Treatment validity of a diagnosis measures the outcome with the treatment selected on the basis of that diagnosis. Clearly improvement of this aspect of diagnoses would be of value to clinicians. Increasing the reliability of diagnoses was accomplished in two ways. First, the criteria for making the diagnosis were standardized, as in the *Diagnostic and Statistical Manual of Mental Disorders*, 4th ed.: text revision (*DSM-IV-TR*) (American Psychiatric Association [APA], 2000), and attempts were made to operationalize the definitions of the criteria, to limit differences in their interpretation by different interviewers.

The second method to improve reliability was development of structured or semistructured interviews. With structured interviews the interviewers ask the same questions in the same order and manner, usually after training to ensure they do so. Provided the client answered the questions in the same way in interviews by two different interviewers, the diagnoses made by the two based on the clients' answers and interpreted by the same operationally defined diagnostic criteria should be the same. That is, their reliability would be perfect. Semistructured interviews allowed the interviewer, again usually following training, to depart to some extent from the structured set of questions. Unlike clinical interviews, most structured and semistructured interviews investigate only the clients' symptomatology, not other aspects of their life history. The most widely used structured and semistructured interviews used to provide *DSM* diagnoses have not included modules for diagnosing sexual disorders. Assessment in most sex offender treatment programs would appear to rely on clinical rather than structured interviews (Marshall, Fernandez, Hudson, & Ward, 1998).

Clinicians also experienced problems with the *DSM-IV-TR* diagnoses for sexual deviations, which are termed *paraphilias* in the *DSM*. Rape or sexual assault was not classified. Pedophilia was, but not the sexual offense of hebephilia, sexual activity of an adult with pubertal or immediately postpubertal subjects, though hebephiles and pedophiles with male victims share common features. Compared to hebephiles and pedophiles with female victims, they are more likely to commence their offenses in adolescence, and they usually have many more victims, against whom they offend less frequently. Their victims are more likely to be unknown to them. Also they are less likely to form close friendships with or be sexually attracted to adults of either sex (McConaghy, 1993). Many clinicians criticized the diagnostic criterion for paraphilias in earlier versions of the *DSM* that they should cause clinically significant distress or impairment in social, occupational, or other important areas of functioning. They pointed out that many sexually deviant behaviors that were indisputably unacceptable and illegal appeared to have caused no distress or impairment to the offender until they were detected (McConaghy, 1997). The *DSM-IV-TR* took the clinicians' criticism into account by changing this criterion for pedophilia, voyeurism, exhibitionism, and frotteurism, to enable the diagnosis to be made if the person has acted on the urges and, for sexual sadism, if the person has acted on the urges with a nonconsenting person. However, it retained the criterion that the condition should cause clinically significant distress or impairment for the remaining paraphilias. The common offensive behavior of obscene telephoning, which is seldom detected, would therefore not be diagnosed as a paraphilia, except in the unusual event that it caused the offender clinically significant distress or impairment in social, occupational, or other important areas of functioning.

The further criterion for diagnosis of a paraphilia, the experience over a period of at least six months of recurrent, intense sexually arousing fantasies, sexual urges or behaviors involving the particular deviant behavior, was also criticized. Marshall and Eccles (1991) pointed out that many rapists, incest offenders, exhibitionists, and a substantial number of nonfamilial child molesters do not display or report deviant sexual urges, yet they persistently engage in sexually offensive behaviors, so most clinicians tended to ignore *DSM* diagnoses. Subjects who carry out these behaviors are commonly called *sex offenders*, a term requiring legal rather than mental disorder criteria. Marshall and Kennedy (2003) considered a sexual act with a nonconsenting person, whether the act be heterosexual, homosexual, or sadistic, was best viewed as an illegal act rather than a symptom of a psychological disorder. Green (2002) suggested that pedophilia be treated similarly, not as a disorder but as an illegal act with a child, who, of course, is a nonconsenting person.

Knight and Prentky (1993) developed a structured interview, termed the Developmental Interview, which lasts 2–3 hours and was based on several interview schedules, to study incarcerated sex offenders. It consists of 541 questions and statements regarding the subject's family, developmental experiences, school experiences, and peer relations through childhood and a lengthy section containing self-descriptive statements. It is programmed for computer administration, permitting considerable flexibility in formatting and presenting questions, allowing response-based branching so that follow-up questions could gather more detailed information about specific responses. In addition, subjects complete an inventory administered in two 1- to 1.5-hour sessions, which was based on self-report inventories and focused especially on areas such as sexual fantasies. Empirically validated Likert scales derived from the inventory were shown to have good test–retest reliability and high internal consistency.

## QUESTIONNAIRES AND RATING SCALES

Marshall (1999), in his review of current North American treatment programs, considered that because most programs were on a limited budget, if a fully comprehensive assessment package were employed, there would be little time or resources left to do treatment. Under these conditions, interviews should provide most of the information, along with a limited set of self-report measures. Personality, self-esteem, intimacy, victim empathy, sexual behavior, sexual fantasies, hostility toward women, rape-myth acceptance, and impulsivity measures are among those more commonly used. Catania, Gibson, Chitwood, and Coates (1990a) concluded that with regard to data about which subjects have privacy concerns, current evidence suggested self-administered questionnaires reduced measurement error as compared to face-to-face interviews. Holland, Zolondek, Abel, Jordan, and Becker (2000) believed that use of such questionnaires had become an integral part of assessing sexual interest in sex offenders, and it was sometimes easier for offenders to admit deviant thoughts and behaviors on self-report questionnaires. They advanced evidence that the Sexual Interest Cardsort Questionnaire had high internal consistency and correlated well with clinical classification. They emphasized it should be used only as part of a broad assessment including clinical interview. Cultural differences need to be taken into account in considering the use of these measures to assess sexual offenders from different ethnic backgrounds. Cull and Wehner (1998) pointed out that use of true–false or multiple-choice questionnaires with Australian Aboriginal offenders could produce misleading answers and that psychometric instruments should be used sparingly and cautiously. Moro (1998) found psychological tests such as the Minnesota Multiphasic Personality Inventory and tools such as the Multiphasic Sex Inventory typically useless with Hispanic offenders, because there were language difficulties. Jones et al. (1998) commented that some minority clients have negative associations with the concept of pencil-and-paper testing, owing to prior failure in the education system, or have difficulty with the concept of there being no right or wrong answers. They recommended that only instruments that have been normed and validated cross-culturally should be used.

Behavioral inventories are particularly useful to researchers who wish to obtain data inexpensively from a number of subjects and in quantifiable form suitable for statistical analysis. Bancroft, Loftus and Scott Long (2003) considered that there were also advantages in telephone interviewing as compared to face-to-face interviewing, and evidence was increasing that computerized methods of inquiry were more effective in eliciting answers to sensitive questions. A significant percentage of subjects report socially disapproved behaviors or feelings with anonymous questionnaires when it is unlikely they would report them with nonanonymous questionnaires. About 15% of male and 2% of female university students in the United States and Australia anonymously reported some likelihood of having sexual activity with a prepubertal child if they could do so without risk (Malamuth, 1989; McConaghy, Zamir, & Manicavasagar, 1993).

Rating scales introduced to improve assessment of the risk that sex offenders would reoffend have proved increasingly popular. The Static 99 (Hanson & Thornton, 1999), as its name implies, provides a score based on static variables, such as the offender's age, prior sexual and nonsexual offenses, and relationship to the victim, and hence does not assess possible changes following treatment. The SONAR (Sex Offender Need Assessment Rating; Hanson & Harris, 2000) includes dynamic variables, such as intimacy deficits, social influences, attitudes to sexual offenses, and sexual self-regulation, to evaluate possible changes in risk.

## PENILE PLETHYSMOGRAPHY

Freund (1963) introduced the use of penile volume plethysmography to assess men's sexual arousal to pictures of men and women. Subsequent workers found penile circumference responses to be easier to measure and decided, despite evidence to the contrary (discussed subsequently), that they were equivalent to penile volume responses. The penile circumference responses of sexual offenders to depictions of males and females of various ages and to auditory descriptions of noncoercive, coercive, and aggressive sexual interactions with males and females of various ages were introduced to assess pedophiles and rapists. Early studies reported that as groups they could be distinguished from control subjects. Subsequent studies showed inconsistent results (McConaghy, 1993). Marshall (1996) suggested the wisest course of action may be to withdraw clinical use of penile circumference assessment of paraphilic interest until more adequate data were available, but he later considered that, despite its limitations, it could contribute, in combination with other measures, to determining which offenders displayed deviant arousal, and therefore needed treatment, and their response to treatment (Marshall & Fernandez, 2000). Worling (1998) stated that in the SAFE-T program for treating adolescent sexual offenders, phallometric assessment was not used, one reason being the possibility that exposing adolescents to visual or auditory images of deviant sexual activities could negatively affect their emerging sexual development. He also had doubts concerning the validity of the procedure with adolescents and believed that it took the focus off other core issues in sexual offending, such as self-esteem, intimacy deficits, and the thoughts and emotions that perpetuate offending. Kelly (1998) reported that plethysmography was not often used with sexually offending clergy, because stimulus material of a pornographic nature placed the offender in the "occasion of sin."

## TESTOSTERONE LEVELS

Testosterone-level assessment has been used to gauge the response of sex offenders to antiandrogen medication (McConaghy, Blaszczynski, & Kidson, 1988).

## RESEARCH BASIS

### CLINICAL AND STRUCTURED INTERVIEWS

The value of diagnoses based on clinical interviews is still commonly criticized on the basis of the low reliability (49% to 63%) found in studies in the 1970s and '80s (Matarazzo, 1983). These compared the diagnoses made on the same clients by different clinicians, using their personal interview procedures and diagnostic criteria. At that time little attention was given to development of consistent diagnostic criteria. Currently most clinicians largely accept standardized criteria, such as those of the *DSM-IV-TR*. It is likely that similar studies of diagnoses made in clinical interviews would now find higher reliability. This was the case for the only such study that has been conducted (Peters & Andrews, 1995). Research has largely been limited to investigating the reliability and validity of structured interviews. However, no studies have investigated their reliability using the methodology of the 1970s and '80s studies of clinical interviews. This would require comparison of diagnoses reached using different structured or semistructured interviews and also different accepted diagnostic criteria. Studies doing one of these two things have been carried out and found levels of reliability that were not superior to those found by Mararazzo with clinical interviews (Andrews, Peters, Guzman, & Bird, 1995; van den Brink et al., 1989).

In regard to the validity of diagnoses reached by structured as compared to clinical interviews, Peters and Andrews (1995) pointed out that to assess the validity of those based on structured interviews, they needed to be compared with diagnoses of established validity, yet such diagnoses are lacking. Because it was the lack of faith in the reliability and validity of the clinical interview that instigated the move to develop structured interviews, they concluded that a single clinical interview was not an appropriate "gold standard" against which to assess diagnoses reached by structured interviews and that in the absence of such a standard, Spitzer (1983) had suggested use of a clinical standard, which he termed a LEAD standard. This acronym referred to the three requirements for this standard diagnosis: (1) It should be based on longitudinal information, obtained not in one evaluation but at several points in time. (2) It should be a consensus diagnosis made by at least two experts after they independently evaluate the client. (3) All data available for the client, except that from the instrument being assessed, should be taken into account in reaching the diagnosis. This could include questionnaire data, previous clinical information, and information from contacts. The advantage of the LEAD procedure was considered to be that it emulated actual clinical practice.

Peters and Andrews (1995) found that it was not until the 1990s that studies examined the reliability and validity of LEAD diagnoses. They cited studies finding that these diagnoses were stable over a six-month period and that their interrater reliability was as good as that of diagnoses made using structured and semistructured interviews. Peters and Andrews concluded that the LEAD standard proved a useful and robust procedure against which to test other diagnostic procedures. They used it to assess the validity of the CIDI-Auto-structured interview, the World Health Organization–approved computerized version of the pencil-and-paper CIDI (WHO, 1993) and found agreement for particular diagnostic categories was poor, with only two diagnoses having a kappa greater than .4. The CIDI-Auto was unlikely to diagnose ill subjects as well but to diagnose many well subjects as ill. This evidence suggests there has been an unfortunate lack of balance in attempts to improve interviewing assessment. Extensive resources have been devoted to the development of structured interviews to be administered by trained laypersons for use in epidemiological research, with the expectation they would provide reliable and valid diagnoses. Meanwhile little attention has been given to evaluating and if necessary attempting to improve the reliability and treatment validity of the clinical interview, which appears to remain the most widely used procedure for making diagnoses for treatment purposes by clinicians.

An incidental finding of the study of Peters and Andrews (1995) indicated that the reliability of clinical interviews made by psychologists and psychiatrists working in the same treatment unit was high, as was their validity assessed against LEAD diagnoses. They found the agreement between the diagnoses made by two interviewers following independent initial routine clinical interviews was excellent (kappa = .93). When the initial diagnoses were compared with the LEAD diagnoses made after 2–10 months, they were identical for 86 of the 98 clients. This finding suggests that if resources were devoted in the professional education of clinicians to evaluating and improving their training in clinical interviewing, they should be able to make diagnoses using it that have levels of reliability and validity as high as those reported in the study of Peters and Andrews.

A number of studies have demonstrated the validity of self-reports for particular sexual behaviors. Degree of reduction in sex offenders' deviant sexual urges correlated with the medroxyprogesterone-produced reduction in their levels of testosterone, to which they were blind (McConaghy et al., 1988). Incidence of HIV seroconversion was predicted from risk indices based on self-reported sexual behaviors (Catania, Gibson, Marin, Coates, & Greenblatt, 1990b). A reported increase in safe-sex behaviors correlated with a fall in prevalence of sexually transmitted diseases (McConaghy, 1993). In regard to the validity of risk assessment procedures, using follow-up data of sex offenders assessed on the Static 99 when released from a number of institutions, Hanson and Thornton (1999) found that more than half of the 12% with scores of 6 or more reoffended sexually within 15 years, whereas only 10% of the 24% with scores of 0 or 1 did. Because it is a static score, many clinicians do not modify it if there is a need to assess the recidivism risk of sex offenders who have been released for a number of years without reoffending. It would seem that a long period without reoffending would reduce the level of risk indicated by the Static 99 score, for the graphs provided by Hanson and Thornton indicated that the likelihood that those with higher scores would reoffend is highest in the first few years after release and then gradually reduces. Hanson and Thornton suggested that inclusion of dynamic factors would be likely to increase the scale's predictive accuracy. Hanson and Harris (2000) attempted to validate the SONOR dynamic risk assessment scale by comparing the scores of sex offenders who had reoffended with those who had not. The SONOR items distinguished the two groups. Because the scorers were aware which subjects had reoffended and which had not, a retrospective study would seem necessary before significant weight is given this dynamic assessment. Evidence reported by Seto, Harris, Rice, and Barbaree (2004) suggested that the addition of psychopathy assessment may improve the prediction of recidivism obtained using a static assessment scale. There is clearly a need for valid actuarial assessments of recidivism risk, because that made by clinicians based on their clinical judgment has been found to be low or even inaccurate. In a follow-up of 193 treated inmates, more of those rated at release as showing a good response sexually reoffended than those rated as showing a poor response (Quinsey, Khanna, & Malcolm, 1998).

## PENILE PLETHYSMOGRAPHY

When penile circumference responses (PCRs) were introduced to assess sexual arousal, it was assumed they were equivalent to penile volume responses (PVRs). However, unlike PVRs, which can be measured within 10 seconds of exposure to the eliciting stimulus, PCRs require two minutes or more to develop (McConaghy, 1974). This time allows men so motivated to modify their responses to the stimuli presented by fantasizing alternative stimuli, for example, fantasizing aversive stimuli when shown pictures of children. Using brief presentations of visual stimuli of nude children and adults, few pedophiles requested to produce penile volume responses indicating a preference for adult women were able to do so (Freund, 1971). With 54-second presentations, 17 of 20 university students on request were able to produce responses indicating either a preference or equal interest in female children as in adults (Wilson, 1998). In addition, the ability of both assessment procedures to discriminate pedophiles and rapists from normal controls is limited by the fact that a significant percentage of controls show evidence of arousal to stimuli of children or acts of sexual aggression (Bernat, Calhoun, & Adams, 1999; Fedora et al., 1992; McConaghy, 1993). Meta-analysis of studies using penile circumference assessment demonstrated that it discriminated rapists from nonrapists, as groups (Lalumiere & Quinsey, 1994). The fact that it was necessary to combine the results of several studies by meta-analysis to obtain convincing statistical evidence that the assessment discriminated the two groups would seem evidence that it should be used only to investigate groups, not individuals. Nevertheless the authors concluded that the result supported its use to identify individual offenders' treatment needs and risk of recidivism.

Marshall and Eccles (1991) criticized Abel and Rouleau's (1990) recommendation that PCR assessments should include evaluation of all possible sexual deviations, based on their finding of a high incidence of multiple paraphilias among sex offenders. Marshall and Eccles pointed out that evaluation of the index offense could take up to 6 hours and that to assess all possible paraphilias, up to 21 in number, would increase the time required enormously. In their experience few exhibitionists and child molesters had additional paraphilias. Certainly offenders who are repeatedly charged are usually charged with the same offense.

## CLINICAL UTILITY

The utility of the clinical interview provided by its flexibility has maintained its use by most therapists, in preference to the rigidly structured interview. There are two major reasons for therapists' preference for the flexible interview. First, it enables establishment of a therapeutic relationship to be commenced while the information relevant for treatment is being collected. Particularly given the sensitivity of information concerning sexual deviations, the interviewer can vary the nature and order of their questions in the light of the client's responses and behavior. The interviewer can decide, possibly intuitively more than consciously, the persona to adopt that is most likely to elicit the client's trust and enable him or her to feel at ease. This requires taking into account the client's sex, age, appearance, dress, socioeconomic background, intelligence, vocabulary, level of education, ethnic origin, and moral, ethical, and sexual attitudes and values. If clients show signs of guilt, embarrassment, or reluctance to talk when particular topics are introduced, clinicians can respond with encouragement and support. They can thus elicit crucial information, which may not be obtained with the rigid format of a structured interview or questionnaire. Clients are unlikely to reveal such information unless the clinician establishes a relationship with them that makes them confident it will not be disclosed, deliberately or inadvertently, without their permission. Relevant information from clients who are developmentally delayed, brain damaged, severely depressed, markedly thought disordered, confused, or under the influence of substances can often only be obtained by the appropriate modification of questioning that is possible with the clinical interview, unlike more structured procedures. It is generally accepted that structured procedures are not suitable for clients who cannot give coherent responses to questions or maintain attention for periods of 30 minutes or more. In a validity study of the widely used structured Composite International Diagnostic Interview (CIDI) in clients with schizophrenia (Cooper, Peters, & Andrews, 1998), clients who could not do so were excluded. Some clients with severe depression, confusion, brain damage, or developmental delay or under the influence of substances also cannot meet these criteria. Establishing and maintaining a relationship with these clients in which adequate information can be obtained requires the more flexible approach of the clinical interview. Also, these clients are rarely able or motivated to complete self-rating scales or questionnaires. This is particularly relevant in the assessment of sex offenders, a percentage of whom are intellectually impaired, brain-damaged, or psychotic (McConaghy, 1993).

Second, the flexible interview allows the clinician to commence assessment of the client's personality. The importance of this assessment in influencing therapeutic management is being increasingly recognized. Coker and Widiger (2005) reviewed evidence that above 50 per cent of clients in clinical settings have some form of personality disorder, with antisocial personality disorder being diagnosed in up to 50 per cent of inmates within correctional settings. They pointed out that the course and treatment of most disorders are substantially altered by the presence of a comorbid personality disorder, yet the prevalence of personality disorder is generally underestimated in clinical practice. They suggested that this could be due to a lack of time to provide systematic or comprehensive evaluations of personality functioning. There are therefore obvious advantages in beginning this evaluation along with establishment of a therapeutic relationship while collecting information for diagnosis of sexual disorders. Personality assessment is also of importance in the clinician's assessment of the extent the client's self-report can be accepted without modification and the extent it should be regarded as distorted and in need of further confirmation. Clients who are attention seeking are likely to exaggerate their symptoms, those with antisocial personalities may lie concerning them, and those who are depressed or have the high ethical standards commonly associated with obsessional features may present them in a somewhat negative light.

Commonly the clinician commences the clinical interview nondirectively, adopting a listening approach and asking a minimum of questions, thus giving the client the opportunity to take charge. This allows assessment of such aspects of the client's personality as confidence, verbal ability, assertiveness, and dominance. If as the interview progresses in a nondirective mode, the client ceases to provide relevant information, the clinician can become more directive. The assumption of a more directive role needs to be done in a manner that does not threaten or antagonize assertive clients or allow obsessional or paranoid clients, who commonly provide excessive details, to consider that the clinician is dismissing information they consider highly relevant.

## ASSESSMENT, CONCEPTUALIZATION, AND TREATMENT PLANNING

Marshall and Serran (2004) consider that though many authorities recommend use of a highly structured manualized approach to treatment of offenders, an overly structured program approach limits the clinician's flexibility to modify treatment to fit the client's ability and learning style, which should be determined in a comprehensive assessment prior to treatment. They emphasized the importance of the therapeutic relationship in influencing the outcome of treatment of sexual offenders, citing evidence that 25% of the variance in treatment outcome is attributable to such factors as the therapist's style, client's perception, and the client–therapist alliance. In a series of studies of the influence of therapist behavior on treatment change in sexual offenders, they found that the four most important therapist behaviors were empathy, warmth, rewardingness, and directiveness. They cautioned that directiveness could be overdone when the therapist comes to control the decisions made by clients. In particular, harshly confrontational approaches recommended by some therapists correlated negatively with the behavioral changes sought. Enhancement of self-esteem was considered a major factor in giving sex offenders control over their offensive behaviors (Marshall, Champagne, Sturgeon, & Bryce, 1997). Marshall and Serran recommended establishment of effective training programs to instill effective therapist behaviors.

Some therapists consider that modification of pedophile or sexually assaultive urges of offenders is possible using such behavioral techniques as aversive procedures and orgasmic reconditioning. However, the evidence that modification of deviant urges occurred was change in the offenders' penile circumference

responses (PCRs) to stimuli eliciting such urges. As pointed out earlier, men motivated to do so are able to markedly influence these responses. Such motivation
is likely when their ability to produce PCRs indicating reduction of deviant urges
results, as is commonly the case, in cessation of unpleasant aversive treatments
and earlier release from incarceration. No evidence has been advanced that such
behavioral techniques can modify pedophile or rapist urges assessed by penile
volume responses, which are more difficult to modify (McConaghy, 2002a,
2002b). Marshall, Anderson, and Fernandez (1999) report evidence that deviant
sexual preference, as assessed by PCRs, was reduced to within the normal range
by cognitive behavioral approaches that did not involve attempts to change sexual
preference. They suggested that directly targeting sexual preferences in the treatment of sexual offenders may be unnecessary and that deviant sexual preferences
may be epiphenomenona. An alternative possibility is that the changes in PCRs
were due to the offenders' modifying them and that attempts to change deviant
sexual preferences are unnecessary, for such change is not possible. If so, the aim
of treatment should be to encourage offenders to control such urges, using cognitive behavioral methods in the context of an effective client–therapist alliance.

The possibility that sexual offending behavior can become compulsive,
increasing the offender's inability to control it, is commonly not accepted, on the
grounds that such a belief can encourage the offender not to accept full responsibility for his behavior. However, the effectiveness of treatments aimed at reducing such compulsivity suggests that they should be incorporated in treatment
when clinical evidence suggests such compulsivity is present. One such treatment, imaginal desensitization, was developed on the basis of a theory that
compulsive behaviors, sexual and nonsexual, were driven by behavior-
completion mechanisms established in the brain when behaviors were carried out
regularly. If the behavior was not carried out in the presence of cues for it, the
mechanisms produced increased arousal, experienced as anxiety or tension, which
was aversive enough to cause the subject to complete the behavior against his or
her will (McConaghy, 1993). With imaginal desensitization, subjects were trained
to relax and while relaxed to visualize being exposed to the cues for the compulsive behavior. They then visualized not completing the behavior, but carrying
out an alternative appropriate behavior while remaining relaxed. Imaginal desensitization was shown to be more effective in giving clients control over compulsive sexual behaviors than the still commonly employed aversive therapy, covert
sensitization (McConaghy & Armstrong, 1985). With sexual offenders experiencing difficulty in controlling deviant behaviors in the community, use of antiandrogen medication orally or intramuscularly to lower their testosterone level is
of value (McConaghy et al., 1988). As pointed out earlier, such reduction correlates with reduction in deviant urges. Low dosage of the medication sufficient to
reduce the client's testosterone level to 30% of the pretreatment level is effective
in giving him control over deviant urges while allowing him to maintain acceptable sexual activities. Where compulsivity is a factor, as the client learns to
control this, the medication can be gradually withdrawn. In clients such as men

with marked developmental delay who are not able to respond to cognitive behavioral approaches, prolonged use of such medication can allow them to behave appropriately in the community.

## CASE STUDY

### IDENTIFICATION

Mr. S. A. was a 35-year-old married man who worked as an excavator operator.

### PRESENTING COMPLAINTS

He reported he had been charged six months previously with having sexual relations with the daughter of his de facto wife, which commenced two years previously, when she was age 9.

### HISTORY

Because I had no prior notification that Mr. A. had been charged with an offense, I had no legal records at the time of the initial interview. Mr. A. presented as a fit, healthy man who, while able to present his account of his history in detail, showed a degree of naiveté in discussing his emotional relationships. In regard to his sexual history, he stated that since his teenage years he had been aware that he had a high sex drive. Throughout his adult life he would often masturbate up to 10 or 15 times per day. He said that after a few hours he would often feel that his penis was "getting too strong" and that he would have to masturbate to relieve the tension. He said that at times he would have to masturbate about five times each night, waking with an erection and needing to ejaculate in order to get back to sleep. He said that he felt that he was addicted to the "ejaculation part of sex" and therefore to masturbation and would like to minimize this addiction. He recounted two incidents that occurred when he was 11 or 12 that appeared to have strongly influenced his beliefs about sexual activity between children and adults. A female babysitter about 19 years old said to him, "Someone really loves you if they kiss you on the lips." She asked him to get into bed with her and she kissed him on the lips, and he thinks she may also have fondled him sexually. He didn't ask her to stop the behavior because it was the first time he felt loved. Shortly afterward, another female babysitter, also about 19, let him fondle her breasts and rubbed her body against his penis. He said "I didn't think it was abuse" and that he thought he said "I love you" to the babysitter, and if he didn't say it he certainly felt it. Since adolescence he had been aware of a sexual interest in pubescent girls, finding their physical development arousing. In his teenage years and 20s he chose girlfriends who were three to five years younger than he was. He had not had a significant long-term sexual relationship prior to meeting his de facto partner but had had a number of brief relationships and visited prostitutes on a regular basis. He met his partner seven years previously at a country music festival. She was the same age and was an Australian Aboriginal. Her daughter, then age 4, had been born to a Maori father. Initially they were together only intermittently, due to quarrels about her gambling and drinking. However, after he met her and following some months of separation and finding that she was 7 months pregnant, he lived with her more or less continuously. They had three children together, twin girls age 4 and a boy age 5 at the time of the interview. He believed his wife loves him, but they fight all the time because she always wants money to gamble on poker machines and can stay away from home drinking for some days. They lived in a Housing Commission accommodation in a Sydney suburb, and the entire family slept together in the same room. His wife mixed closely with her relatives, who put pressure on him to give them money. They spent money the day they received it, whereas he tried to save it until next payday to adequately support his children. Her relatives had very free attitudes regarding sexual talk, and girls age 11 smoked and were sexually active. The Department of Community Services had been notified when one of his twin daughters, then age 3, was found to be infected with gonorrhea when she was treated for a vaginal discharge. Both Mr. A. and his partner were found to be free of sexually transmitted diseases, and police were unable to identify the perpetrator. Both he and his wife were cleared of any impropriety. Mr. A. believed one on his wife's brothers committed the crime, but this was never proven. Her relatives believed that this brother raped his youngest daughter when she was 3. Mr. A. had to intervene at times to prevent his wife from leaving their daughter with this brother when she went on drinking sprees. Her father had been violent to her, and she could be violent with the children, so he needed to be with his family to prevent this.

In relation to the index offenses, he said that his de facto partner's daughter, M., had attempted to kiss and cuddle him from a very young age, even when his partner was around. He attributed this to his partner's never showing any love but being verbally abusive to her. He believed when M. cuddled him she would touch him sexually, which he attributed to evidence he had heard that she had been sexually interfered with prior to living together permanently with his partner. Sexual activity with his de facto partner, which had been waning over the past few years, was conducted in the family bedroom while they believed all other family members were asleep. When M.'s breasts began to develop at age 9, he became aware of sexual arousal to her, and sexual activity commenced that culminated in intercourse. He added, "She would come to my bed; I would never go to hers. I'd tell her no but give in." He denied that he ever threatened her in any way. He said that M. acted as a mother to his three children, whereas his partner commonly neglected them, and he often felt that he was falling in love with M. When M. was age 11, an older girl staying in their house saw M. and Mr. A. in bed together and informed her mother. A few weeks later, when the mother was drinking with Mr. A. and his partner and a number of neighbors, she revealed this information and the police were called. Mr. A. admitted his guilt. He denied sexual activity with any other pre-, peri-, or immediately postpubescent females in his adult life. At the time of the interview, Mr. A.'s partner was still living with him and their children and M. was living with her father's mother outside Sydney. Mr. A.'s sexual fantasies frequently included sexual activity with M. At my request, Mr. A.'s partner made three appointments to be interviewed, but on all occasions failed to attend.

In relation to the use of alcohol and other drugs, Mr. A. said he commenced drinking alcohol in his teenage years and that up until the time he was charged, he drank most days, sometimes up to 12 glasses of beer at a time. Subsequently he reduced this so that at the time of interview he never drank more than four glasses in a day and most days less than this or none. He smoked cannabis regularly until age 17, when after using it he became paranoid, feeling that everyone was laughing at him. He was so frightened and distressed he only used it occasionally since and last smoked it about four or five years ago. He had tried amphetamines once in the past but fell asleep and had used no other illicit psychoactive substances. He gave up smoking cigarettes at the age of 19.

He had not seen a psychiatrist prior to the interview with me and had had no serious illnesses.

## PEER AND WORK ISSUES

Mr. A. said that he left school at age 15 after successfully completing his School Certificate. He never enjoyed studying but was good at sports and mixed well and had a number of friends. He then completed three years of a carpentry apprenticeship but ceased this due to lack of work opportunities during a recession at the time. He then commenced work as an excavator operator but also would at times travel to work on fishing boats in the north of Australia. There he became attracted to what he termed the free and easy way of life of Aboriginals and for six months lived on an Aboriginal mission with the younger of his two sisters, who also became attracted to their way of life. Nevertheless he disapproved of the fact that they would try and obtain money from him whenever possible. He had worked in his current position as an excavator operator for over two years and said his employer would report positively about his reliability. About a year ago he obtained a helicopter license, hoping to use it mustering cattle at a station. He had always been able to make good money working shift work and long hours.

## FAMILY ISSUES

Mr. A. was adopted at birth and grew up on the Northern Beaches in Sydney with his adoptive parents and his two younger sisters, who were also adopted. His mother had always hated him and when he was age 4 told him he was adopted. After that she said he wouldn't cuddle her anymore. She loved the middle sister but did not like the younger sister, but he felt emotionally close to both sisters. He loved his father, who had an alcohol problem. His adoptive parents separated when he was about 10 years of age and he lived with his mother until he was age 16. He found his relationship with his mother emotionally abusive, because she would refer to him very negatively, resulting in his having very low self-esteem. Between the ages of 16 and 19 he lived with his father. Currently his father, now about 70 years of age, is in poor health, which Mr. A. attributed to his lifelong excess consumption of alcohol. He saw him infrequently. He said his mother was also an alcoholic and that they did not stay in touch because "I don't like her . . . we're always fighting." He keeps in touch with both of his adoptive sisters. He met his biological mother about four years ago. She was living in Queensland. She told him he was adopted at birth after she became pregnant out of wedlock. She was married with children, and he felt she did not wish to maintain a relationship with him.

## BEHAVIORAL ASSESSMENT RESULTS

Mr. A.'s score on the Static 99 was 2, based on his having received four sentencing dates for criminal nonsexual offenses plus a conviction for nonsexual violence. A score of 2 indicated a medium-low risk of reoffending sexually, with 16% of the offenders studied who obtained this score reoffending in 15 years (Hanson & Thornton, 1999).

## ETHICAL AND LEGAL ISSUES OR COMPLICATIONS

Mr. A. reported a number of convictions, including driving under the influence of alcohol, malicious damage, and assault of a police officer, which had resulted in fines but not incarceration. The last conviction was seven years ago. He had no previous charges in relation to sexual offending. He gave permission for his criminal record and for the files on his children to be obtained from the Department of Social Security.

## CONCEPTUALIZATION AND TREATMENT
## RECOMMENDATIONS

Following a rejecting relationship with his adoptive mother, between the ages of 10 and 12 Mr. A. experienced sexual contacts with two female babysitters age 19 to which he believed he reacted positively, experiencing them as expressions of the love he had always been denied. In the 1994 study by Laumann, Gagnon, Michael, and Michaels of the sexual behavior of a representative U.S. population sample, about 8% of males reported they were touched sexually before puberty or when they were 12 or 13 by a woman over age 14. The majority regarded the experience as positive rather than abusive. This belief would need to be explored, with emphasis that such experiences, like any form of sexual activity of adults with children, are seriously abusive, for children cannot understand the significance of such sexual behaviors and their possible consequences, when with increasing age they develop an understanding of this significance and how their trust was exploited. Mr. A. also would need to become aware of and acknowledge his tendency to minimize responsibility for his abusive behavior, evidenced in such statements as that M. would come to his bed and he would never go to hers. This would require pointing out the falsity of his belief that she was coming for sexual reasons rather than for the affection that she did not receive from her mother, a belief based on his own wishes to gratify the sexual attraction he was aware he felt for her. He also would need to accept that the irresponsible behavior of his wife in no way reduced his responsibility.

Changes in Mr. A.'s beliefs and attitudes could be monitored by asking him to write accounts of these throughout the counseling procedure. Though Mr. A. showed clear evidence of not accepting total responsibility, at no stage did he deny carrying out any of the abusive behaviors. He showed a strong sense of responsibility to provide appropriate affection for his biological children and to work consistently to provide financially for all the people in his care. These positive features of his behavior should be used to provide emotional support and positive regard while the therapist encouraged Mr. A. to accept the errors in his thinking. Mr. A.'s control over his sexual attraction to girls showing pubertal development needed to be reinforced both cognitively and with behavioral treatments, such as imaginal desensitization, to eliminate possible compulsive urges to act on this attraction. This treatment should also be used to address his compulsive urges to masturbate. It is probable that Mr. A.'s heavy use of alcohol contributed to reduced control of his sexual urges (Looman, Abracen, DiFazio, & Maillet, 2004). Prolonged monitoring of his behavior to see that he maintained his current low use would be indicated. Mr. A. would also need counseling to address his low self-esteem and unresolved feelings of not being loved by his mother, revealed in his history and suggested by his need to seek out his birth mother. This would be aided if he was in a loving relationship with his wife, but it would seem unlikely that their relationship could be improved by couples therapy, in view of her avoiding consultations.

Because there was a high likelihood that Mr. A. would receive a custodial sentence, the Department of Social Security would need to be alerted to arrange appropriate care for his children if the irresponsible treatment of them by his partner was confirmed. It would need to be established that M. was receiving appropriate counseling and that psychological assessment of the three children of Mr. A. and, if possible, his partner was arranged.

## SUMMARY

The clinical interview, the major form of assessment of sexual offenders, is described. The more limited use of structured interviews and problems with *DSM-*

*IV-TR* diagnoses of sexual deviations are discussed. Questionnaires and rating scales are commonly used to provide additional information. Research indicates that with appropriate training, clinicians can reach diagnoses based on clinical interviews that have high reliability and validity. Penile circumference response assessment can be misleading due to the ability of offenders to modify the responses. The flexibility of the clinical interview contributes significantly to its clinical utility, as does its ability to allow the interviewer to commence assessment of the client's personality and commence establishment of the therapeutic relationship. The value of attempts to modify deviant urges using behavioral strategies is questioned and the need to treat compulsive aspects of sexual offenses emphasized. A case study of a man who sexually abused his stepdaughter is provided.

## REFERENCES

Abel, G. G., & Rouleau, J. L. (1990). The nature and extent of sexual assault. In W. L. Marshall, D. R. Laws, & H. E. Barbaree (Eds.), *Handbook of sexual assault: Issues, theories, and treatment of the offender* (pp. 9–21). New York: Plenum Press.

American Psychiatric Association. (2000). *Diagnostic and statistical manual of mental disorders* (4th ed., text revision). Washington, DC: Author.

Andrews, G., Peters, L., Guzman, A-M., & Bird, K. (1995). A comparison of two structured diagnostic interviews: CIDI and SCAN. *Australian and New Zealand of Psychiatry, 29,* 124–132.

Bancroft, J., Loftus, J., & Scott Long, J. (2003). Reply to Rosen and Laumann. *Archives of Sexual Behavior, 32,* 213–216.

Bellack, A. S., & Hersen, M. (1988). Future directions of behavioral assessment. In A. S. Bellack & M. Hersen (Eds.), *Behavioral assessment: A practical handbook* (3rd ed., pp. 610–615). New York: Pergamon Press.

Bernat, J. A., Calhoun, K. S., & Adams, H. E. (1999). Sexually aggressive and nonaggressive men: Sexual arousal and judgments in response to acquaintance rape and consensual analogues. *Journal of Abnormal Psychology, 108,* 662–673.

Catania, J. A., Gibson, D. R., Chitwood, D. D., & Coates, T. J. (1990a). Methodological problems in AIDS behavioral research: Influences on measurement error and participation bias in studies of sexual behavior. *Psychological Bulletin, 108,* 339–362.

Catania, J. A., Gibson, D. R., Marin, B., Coates, T. J., & Greenblatt, R. M. (1990b). Response bias in assessing sexual behaviors relevant to HIV transmission. *Evaluation and Program Planning, 13,* 19–29.

Coker, L. A., & Widiger, T. A. (2005). Personality disorders. In J. E. Maddux & B. A. Winstead (Eds.), *Psychopathology: Foundations for a contemporary understanding* (pp. 201–227). Mahwah, NJ: Erlbaum.

Cooper, L., Peters, L., & Andrews, G. (1998). Validity of the Composite Diagnostic Interview (CIDI) psychosis module in a psychiatric setting. *Journal of Psychiatric Research, 32,* 361–368.

Crepault, C., & Couture, M. (1980). Men's erotic fantasies. *Archives of Sexual Behavior, 9,* 565–581.

Cull, D. M., & Wehner, D. M. (1998). Australian Aborigines: Cultural factors pertaining to the assessment and treatment of Australian Aboriginal Sexual Offenders. In W. L. Marshall, Y. M. Fernandez, S. M. Hudson, & T. Ward (Eds.), *Sourcebook of treatment programs for sexual offenders* (pp. 431–444). New York: Plenum Press.

Fedora, O., Reddon, J. R., Morrison, J. W., Fedora, S. K., Pascoe, H., & Yeudall, L. T. (1992). Sadism and other paraphilias in normal controls and nonaggressive sex offenders. *Archives of Sexual Behavior, 21,* 1–15.

Freund, K. (1963). A laboratory method of diagnosing predominance of homo- or heteroerotic interest in the male. *Behavior Research and Therapy, 1,* 85–93.

Freund, K. (1971). A note on the use of the phallometric method of measuring mild sexual arousal in the male. *Behavior Therapy, 2,* 223–228.

Freund, K., Watson, R., & Dickey, R. (1990). Does sexual abuse in childhood cause pedophilia? An exploratory study. *Archives of Sexual Behavior, 19,* 557–568.

Goldberg, D. (1997). *The Maudsley handbook of practical psychiatry.* Oxford, UK: Oxford University Press.

Gordon, A., & Hover, G. (1998). The Twin Rivers sex offender treatment program. In W. L. Marshall, Y. M. Fernandez, S. M. Hudson, & T. Ward (Eds.), *Sourcebook of treatment programs for sexual offenders* (pp. 3–15). New York: Plenum Press.

Green, R. (2002). Is pedophilia a mental disorder? *Archives of Sexual Behavior, 31,* 467–471.

Hanson, R. K., & Harris, A. (2000). *The Sex Offender Need Assessment Rating (SONAR): A method for measuring change in risk levels 2000–1.* http://www.sgc.gc.ca/EPub/Corr/e200001b/e200001b. htm

Hanson, R. K., & Thornton, D. (1999). *Static 99: Improving actuarial risk assessments for sex offenders.* http://www.sgc.gc.ca/epub/Corr/e199902/e199902.htm

Holland, L. A., Zolondek, S. C., Abel, G. G., Jordan, A. D., & Becker, J. V. (2000). Psychometric analysis of the sexual interest cardsort questionnaire. *Sexual Abuse: A Journal of Research and Treatment, 12,* 107–122.

Hudson, S. M., Wales, D. S., & Ward, T. (1998). Kia Marama: A treatment program for child molesters in New Zealand. In W. L. Marshall, Y. M. Fernandez, S. M. Hudson, & T. Ward (Eds.), *Sourcebook of treatment programs for sexual offenders* (pp. 17–28). New York: Plenum Press.

Jenkins, A. (1998). Invitations to responsibility: Engaging adolescents and young men who have been sexually abused. In W. L. Marshall, Y. M. Fernandez, S. M. Hudson, & T. Ward (Eds.), *Sourcebook of treatment programs for sexual offenders* (pp. 163–189). New York: Plenum Press.

Jones, R. L., Winkler, M. X., Kacin, E., Salloway, W. N., & Weismann, M. (1998). Community-based sexual offender treatment for inner-city African American and Latino youth. In W. L. Marshall, Y. M. Fernandez, S. M. Hudson, & T. Ward (Eds.), *Sourcebook of treatment programs for sexual offenders* (pp. 457–476). New York: Plenum Press.

Kelly, A. F. (1998). Clergy offenders. In W. L. Marshall, Y. M. Fernandez, S. M. Hudson, & T. Ward (Eds.), *Sourcebook of treatment programs for sexual offenders* (pp. 303–318). New York: Plenum Press.

Knight, R. A., & Prentky, R. A. (1993). Exploring characteristics for classifying juvenile sex offenders. In H. E. Barbaree, W. L. Marshall, & S. M. Hudson (Eds.), *The juvenile sex offender* (pp. 45–83). New York: Guilford Press.

Lalumiere, M. L., & Quinsey, V. L. (1994). The discriminability of rapists from non–sex offenders using phallometric measures: A meta-analysis. *Criminal Justice and Behavior, 21,* 150–175.

Laumann, E. O., Gagnon, J. H., Michael, R. T., & Michaels, S. (1994). *The social organization of sexuality.* Chicago: University of Chicago Press.

Looman, J., Abracen, J., DiFazio, R., & Maillet, G. (2004). Alcohol and drug abuse among sexual and nonsexual offenders: Relationship to intimacy deficits and coping strategies. *Sexual Abuse: A Journal of Research and Treatment, 16,* 177–189.

Mahoney, M. J. (1977). Reflections on the cognitive-learning trend in psychotherapy. *American Psychologist, 32,* 5–13.

Malamuth, N. M. (1989). The attraction to sexual aggression scale: Part two. *Journal of Sex Research, 26,* 324–354.

Marshall, W. L. (1996). Assessment, treatment and theorizing about sex offenders. *Criminal Justice and Behavior, 23,* 162–199.

Marshall, W. L. (1999). Current status of North American assessment and treatment programs for sexual offenders. *Journal of Interpersonal Violence, 14*, 221–239.

Marshall, W. L., Anderson, D., & Fernandez, Y. (1999). Cognitive behavioral treatment of sexual offenders. Chichester, UK: John Wiley & Sons.

Marshall, W. L., Champagne, F., Sturgeon, C., & Bryce, P. (1997). Increasing the self-esteem of child molesters. *Sexual Abuse: A Journal of Research and Treatment, 9*, 321–333.

Marshall, W. L., & Eccles, A. (1991). Issues in clinical practice with sex offenders. *Journal of Interpersonal Violence, 6*, 68–93.

Marshall, W. L., & Fernandez, Y. M. (2000). Phallometric testing with sexual offenders: Limits to its value. *Clinical Psychology Review, 20*, 807–822.

Marshall, W. L., Fernandez, Y. M., Hudson, S. M., & Ward, T. (1998). *Sourcebook of treatment programs for sexual offenders.* New York: Plenum Press.

Marshall, W. L., & Kennedy, P. (2003). Sexual sadism in sexual offenders: An elusive diagnosis. *Aggression and Violent Behavior, 8*, 1–22.

Marshall, W. L., & Serran, G. A. (2004). The role of the therapist in offender treatment. *Psychology, Crime, and Law, 10*, 309–320.

Matarazzo, J. D. (1983). The reliability of psychiatric and psychological diagnosis. *Clinical Psychology Review, 3*, 103–145.

McConaghy, N. (1974). Measurements of change in penile dimensions. *Archives of Sexual Behavior, 3*, 381–388.

McConaghy, N. (1993). *Sexual behavior: problems and management.* New York: Plenum Press.

McConaghy, N. (1997). Sexual and gender identity disorders. In S. M. Turner & M. Hersen (Eds.), *Adult psychopathology and diagnosis* (3rd ed., pp. 409–464). New York: John Wiley & Sons.

McConaghy, N. (2002a). Electrical aversion. In M. Hersen & W. Sledge (Eds.), *Encyclopedia of psychotherapy, vol. 1* (pp. 719–730). New York: Elsevier Science.

McConaghy, N. (2002b). Orgasmic reconditioning. In M. Hersen & W. Sledge (Eds.), *Encyclopedia of psychotherapy, vol. 2* (pp. 299–305). New York: Elsevier Science.

McConaghy, N., & Armstrong, M. S. (1985). Expectancy, covert sensitization, and imaginal desensitization in compulsive sexuality. *Acta Psychiatrica Scandanavica, 72*, 176–187.

McConaghy, N., Blaszczynski, A., & Kidson, W. (1988). Treatment of sex offenders with imaginal desensitization and/or medroxyprogesterone. *Acta Psychiatrica Scandanavica, 77*, 199–206.

McConaghy, N., Zamir, R., & Manicavasagar. (1993). Nonsexist sexual experiences survey and scale of attraction to sexual aggression. *Australian and New Zealand Journal of Psychiatry, 27*, 686–693.

Moro, P. E. (1998). Treatment for Hispanic sexual offenders. In W. L. Marshall, Y. M. Fernandez, S. M. Hudson, & T. Ward (Eds.), *Sourcebook of treatment programs for sexual offenders* (pp. 445–456). New York: Plenum Press.

Nelson, R. O., & Hayes, S. C. (1981). Nature of behavioral assessment. In A. S. Bellack & M. Hersen (Eds.), *Behavioral Assessment* (2nd ed., pp. 3–37). New York: Pergamon Press.

Okami, P. (1999). Review: Making monsters: false memories, psychotherapy, and sexual hysteria. *Archives of Sexual Behavior, 28*, 387–390.

Person, E. S., Terestman, N., Myers, W. A., Goldberg, E. L., & Salvadori, C. (1989). Gender differences in sexual behaviors and fantasies in a college population. *Journal of Sex and Marital Therapy, 15*, 187–198.

Peters, L., & Andrews, G. (1995). Procedural validity of the computerized version of the Composite International Diagnostic Interview (CIDI-Auto) in the anxiety disorders. *Psychological Medicine, 25*, 1269–1280.

Quinsey, V. L., Khanna, A., & Malcolm, P. B. (1998). A retrospective evaluation of the regional treatment center sex offender treatment program. *Journal of Interpersonal Violence, 13*, 621–644.

Seto, M. C., Harris, G. T., Rice, M. E., & Barbaree, H. E. (2004). The screening scale for pedophilic interests predicts recidivism among adult sex offenders with child victims. *Archives of Sexual Behavior, 33*, 455–466.

Spitzer, R. L. (1983). Psychiatric diagnosis: Are clinicians still necessary? *Comprehensive Psychiatry, 24,* 399–411.

van den Brink, W., Koeter, M. W. J., Ormel, J., Dijkstra, W., Giel, R., Slooff, C. J., et al. (1989). Psychiatric diagnosis in an outpatient population. *Archives of General Psychiatry, 46,* 369–372.

Wilson, R. J. (1998). Psychophysiological signs of faking in the phallometric test. *Sexual Abuse: A Journal of Research and Treatment, 10,* 113–126.

Worling, J. R. (1998). Adolescent sexual offender treatment at the SAFE-T program. In W. L. Marshall, Y. M. Fernandez, S. M. Hudson, & T. Ward (Eds.), *Sourcebook of treatment programs for sexual offenders.* New York: Plenum Press.

Wyatt, G. E., & Peters, S. D. (1986). Issues in the definition of child sexual abuse in prevalence research. *Child Abuse and Neglect, 10,* 231–240.

# 16

## PSYCHOTIC BEHAVIOR

### NIRBHAY N. SINGH

*ONE Research Institute*
*Chesterfield, Virginia*

### MOHAMED SABAAWI

*Department of Psychiatry*
*University of Kentucky*
*Lexington, Kentucky*

### INTRODUCTION

Psychotic behavior in individuals generally arises from a variety of disorders, of which schizophrenia is the most common and best studied. Significant impairment of reality testing is the main conceptual theme these disorders have in common. The disorders are delineated on the basis of different aspects of their phenomenology. Schizophrenia is marked by various characteristic dysfunctional patterns in the individual's thinking (e.g., delusions, derailment or incoherence of thought processes), perceptions (e.g., hallucinations), language (e.g., poverty of speech), emotions (e.g., anhedonia, apathy, flat or inappropriate affect), social behavior (e.g., bizarre behaviors, extreme social withdrawal, catatonia), and life functioning (e.g., poor self-care, inability to maintain valued personal or societal role functions). A diagnosis of schizophrenia involves a variety of subtypes that are characterized by the predominant symptomatology at the time of evaluation (American Psychiatric Association, 2000). These subtypes include paranoid, disorganized, catatonic, undifferentiated, and residual. In addition, individuals may be classified in terms of the longitudinal course of schizophrenia: episodic with interepisode residual symptoms; episodic with no interepisode residual symptoms; continuous; single episode in partial remission; single episode in full remission; and other or unspecified pattern.

Other psychotic disorders include Schizophreniform Disorder, Schizoaffective Disorder, Delusional Disorder, Brief Psychotic Disorder Due to a General

Medical Condition (e.g., brain tumor), Substance-Induced Psychotic Disorder, Shared Psychotic Disorder, and Psychotic Disorder Not Otherwise Specified. Individuals that suffer from other psychiatric disorders, including mood disorders, delirium, and dementia, may have a clinical presentation that includes significant psychotic symptoms. In addition, individuals with certain personality disorders (e.g., schizoid, schizotypal, or paranoid disorders) may share certain characteristics or symptoms with some individuals with schizophrenia. Some transient stress-related psychotic symptoms may also occur in individuals with borderline personality disorders.

There is no universally accepted definition of the term *psychotic*. In its narrowest operational definition, *psychotic* has been used to describe "delusions or prominent hallucinations, with the hallucinations occurring in the absence of insight into their pathological nature" (American Psychiatric Association, 2000, p. 297). When used in a somewhat broader sense, it has included (a) delusions and prominent hallucinations, with the individual retaining insight into the unreal nature of the experiences, and/or (b) the presence of symptoms not including delusions or hallucinations (e.g., disorganized thought process, bizarre behavior, and negative symptoms).

In the *DSM-IV-TR* (American Psychiatric Association, 2000), the term *psychotic* is used to refer to certain symptoms, but different aspects of these symptoms are emphasized because they vary across diagnostic categories. As noted in the diagnostic criteria of schizophrenia in *DSM-IV-TR*, the term *psychotic* refers to delusions, any prominent hallucinations, disorganized speech, disorganized or catatonic behavior, or negative symptoms as defined later. The term is used in the same sense when *DSM-IV-TR* outlines the diagnostic criteria for Schizophreniform Disorder, Schizoaffective Disorder, and Brief Psychotic Disorder. However, "in psychotic disorder due to a general medical condition and in substance-induced psychotic disorder, *psychotic* refers to delusions or only those hallucinations that are not accompanied by insight. Finally, in delusional disorder and shared psychotic disorder, *psychotic* is equivalent to delusional" (American Psychiatric Association, p. 298). Although delusions remain constant across diagnostic categories, they are not always required for the diagnosis of psychotic disorders and they may be associated with other positive symptoms, depending on the actual diagnosis. Positive symptoms are generally accepted as behavioral excesses, including delusions, hallucinations, positive formal thought disorder (e.g., disorganized speech), and bizarre behavior (e.g., abnormal appearance, social interaction, and motor function). Negative symptoms are generally viewed as behavioral deficits that include apathy, limited speech, anhedonia, flat affect, and inattentiveness.

Due to the overlapping of psychotic and other symptoms in a variety of conditions, differential diagnosis is necessary to define the nature of an individual's psychotic behavior. The differential diagnosis typically considers such factors as the individual's premorbid adjustment, onset, duration, and nature of the psychotic symptoms; concomitant disorders and other features of the same disorder;

and setting and context in which the symptoms occur. Other factors include the individual's medical condition and current level of functioning. An accurate diagnosis is important because the treatment and rehabilitation pathways may differ for psychotic behavior arising from different disorders. A careful phenomenological assessment is necessary for a meaningful formulation of the unique biological and psychosocial needs of each individual with psychotic behavior.

## ASSESSMENT STRATEGIES

Several standard or traditional assessment methods measure a broad range of psychopathology in individuals with psychotic disorders. Given that psychotic behaviors are manifested through a number of Axis I disorders, these methods help the clinician develop a rigorous diagnostic formulation and differential diagnosis. Furthermore, these methods enable the clinician to assess the individual's view and understanding of the nature of the disorder and the need for treatment as well as willingness to engage in and adhere to a valid treatment plan.

### ADMISSION ASSESSMENTS

In general, any new inpatient or outpatient admission will begin with an admission psychiatric and nursing evaluation within the first 24 hours, followed by a holistic or integrated interdisciplinary assessment of the individual within the first week of admission. These assessments should assist the individual's treatment team to develop a person-centered treatment plan that focuses on both symptom and functional recovery. The scope and depth of the assessments will vary, depending on the setting, the type and phase (i.e., acute, stabilization, stable) of the disorder, and the goals of the admission. The choice of additional assessments will depend on the results of the admission and integrated interdisciplinary assessments.

### ASSESSMENT OF PSYCHOPATHOLOGY

Many general measures can be used to assess the presence and intensity of psychopathology or disorder-specific symptoms. Probably the five most widely used instruments include the Brief Psychiatric Rating Scale (BPRS; Overall & Gorham, 1988); Positive and Negative Syndrome Scale (PANSS; Kay, Opler, & Fiszbein, 1994); Scale for the Assessment of Negative Symptoms (SANS; Andreasen, 1983); Scale for the Assessment of Positive Symptoms (SAPS; Andreasen, 1984), and Schedule for the Deficit Syndrome (SDS; Kirkpatrick, Buchanan, McKenney, Alphs, & Carpenter, 1989). The clinician will need to use supplemental assessment instruments to assess comorbid disorders that are common in individuals with schizophrenia and other psychotic disorders, such as major depressive and substance use disorders.

## ASSESSMENT OF INSIGHT AND TREATMENT ATTITUDES

Clinicians often report that they can develop a more focused, person-centered treatment plan if they can gain some knowledge of the individual's insight into his or her psychiatric disorder(s) and the individual's attitude toward treatment. In this context, insight means that the individual knows he or she has a psychiatric disorder, that the disorder requires treatment, and that he or she should engage in and adhere to the treatment. The Insight and Treatment Attitudes Questionnaire (ITAQ; McEvoy et al., 1989) is a brief, psychometrically robust 11-item scale that can be used to measure an individual's awareness of his or her schizophrenia and insight into the need for treatment. The scale is best used by skilled clinicians who have experience in evaluating and treating individuals with schizophrenia and other psychotic disorders.

Given the ubiquity of drugs in the treatment of schizophrenia and other psychotic disorders, it is useful to assess an individual's subjective response to medication. The Drug Attitude Inventory (DAI; Hogan & Awad, 1992) was designed as a self-reported measure of an individual's subjective perception of the effects of medication and his or her attitudes and beliefs about medication. Most individuals can complete the DAI, although those with low literacy skills may need some assistance in completing the inventory. Scores on the DAI correlate highly with antipsychotic medication compliance (96% accuracy) and noncompliance (83% accuracy). A more comprehensive assessment instrument, the Rating of Medication Influences (ROMI; Weiden et al., 1994), can be used for the same purpose, but it is lengthy and requires substantial training to administer.

## ASSESSMENT OF QUALITY OF LIFE

In the recovery model of mental health service provision, it is critical that assessments focus not only on symptom and functional recovery but also on quality of life (QOL) measures (Anthony, Cohen, Farkas, & Gagne, 2002). QOL is a multidimensional construct that includes physical, psychological, and social functioning and may include other dimensions, such as living conditions, job, and health-related attributes (Power, 2003). QOL measures are generally used to assess baseline and therapeutic effects of interventions from the subjective perspective of the individual to whom services are provided. Ideally, a person's quality of life is assessed through self-report measures, but it can also be obtained through clinical interview and clinician observations if the individual is unable or unwilling to complete the assessment.

There is no consensus on the best method for assessing QOL, but clinicians have an abundance of choice in terms of valid and reliable instruments designed to measure QOL in specific populations. Current research literature suggests that the following three instruments may provide the best measure of QOL in individuals with severe and persistent mental illness: the Quality of Life Interview (QOLI; Lehman, 1995); the Quality of Life Scale (QLS; Heinrichs, Hanlon, &

Carpenter, 1984); and the Wisconsin Quality of Life Index (W-QLI; Becker, Diamond, & Sainfort, 1993). In addition, the W-QLI is deemed the most appropriate instrument for assessing QOL in individuals with schizophrenia whose negative symptoms significantly impact their lives.

In terms of mental health, most of the relevant QOL measures are premised on this question: "Given the current state of your mental illness (or a specific psychotic disorder), how do you perceive your quality of life?" From a recovery perspective, clinicians may wish to assess an individual's life satisfaction notwithstanding the individual's mental illness. The following measures may be useful for this purpose: Quality of Life Enjoyment and Satisfaction Questionnaire (Q-LES-Q; Endicott, Nee, Harrison, & Blumenthal, 1993); Quality of Life Index (QLI; Ferrans & Powers, 1985); and the Quality of Life Inventory (QOLI; Frisch, 1994). The selection of an instrument will depend on the particular components of QOL that a clinician wishes to measure.

## ASSESSMENT OF READINESS FOR CHANGE

In a recovery model of mental health service delivery system, the concept of *readiness for change* is of paramount interest. An individual's psychotic behavior may be so serious in terms of severity, frequency, intensity, and duration that it interferes with his or her quality of life. The clinician may think the person needs to be in treatment. Whether the individual agrees with the clinician's assessment will depend on the individual's understanding of the disorder, the need for treatment, and agreement to engage in the treatment. To determine at what level the treatment should begin, clinicians often assess the individual's readiness for change; that is, they assess the individual's level of motivation for engaging in treatment and rehabilitation and the individual's perception of his or her ability to engage in the therapeutic process (Cohen, Anthony, & Farkas, 1997). Readiness for change does not assess the individual's capacity to change because that quality is a given in all individuals.

There are several methods for conceptualizing and assessing readiness for change, or the level at which mental health services should begin. For example, the American Association of Community Psychiatrists has developed the Level of Care and Utilization Scale (LOCUS; http://www.comm.psych.pitt.edu/finds/locus.html), which assesses the individual in the following domains: risk of harm, functional status, medical and psychiatric comorbidity, recovery environment, treatment and recovery history, and engagement.

The University of Rhode Island Change Assessment (URICA; McConnaughy, Prochaska, & Velicer, 1983) is probably the most widely used instrument for assessing an individual's readiness to change in terms of addictive behaviors. However, the instrument has gained increasing use in mental health generally as a clinical tool that enables clinicians to gain some insight into an individual's readiness for change in terms of stages of change. Although the URICA provides data on only four stages of change (precontemplation, contemplation, action, and maintenance), clinicians can extrapolate from the data and use their own clinical judgment to determine the stage not included in the URICA—preparation.

In terms of readiness for change, individuals at the precontemplation stage show no intention to change and indicate no awareness that a problem exists even in the face of substantial evidence to the contrary. Those at the contemplation stage are aware of the existence of a problem and have begun to think about making changes in their lives but have yet to make a commitment to actually act on their awareness. Individuals at the preparation stage have begun to prepare for change and have made some minimal changes, but their extant efforts have been inconsistent and largely unsuccessful. Those at the action stage have committed substantial amounts of time and energy to changing their behavior and over-coming the problem(s) and have been largely successful for a period of about six months. Finally, those at the maintenance level have committed substantial amounts of time and energy to consolidate the changes they have made in their lives, generalize their newly learned skills, lessen the risk factors and enhance protective factors for their psychiatric disorders, and engage in wellness activities.

In a variation on this theme, the Ohio Department of Mental Health's recovery process model uses the following stages in their community-based service delivery system: dependent/unaware, dependent/aware, independent/aware, and interdependent/aware (Townsend, Boyd, Griffin, & Hicks, 2000). Knowing where the individual falls along the continuum of recovery from dependent/unaware to interdependent/aware enables clinicians to collaboratively develop with the individual his or her recovery management plan.

## ASSESSMENT OF STRENGTHS

The current zeitgeist in psychology is developing individuals' strengths and managing their weaknesses. Indeed, the raison d'être of positive psychology was the development of a technology for identifying and enhancing people's personal, social, and environmental assets and, by increasing their strengths, relegating their weaknesses or problems to secondary status (Lopez & Snyder, 2003). In mental health, the individual's strengths provide the basis for developing clinical interventions and providing social supports (Rapp, 1998). In this context, what-ever the individual has or presents (including personal attributes, characteristics, skills, diseases, and disorders) can be used as strengths to achieve symptom and functional recovery and to enhance quality of life (Singh, Sabaawi, & Singh, 2004).

There are several ways of assessing an individual's strengths, depending on the context of the assessment (Lopez & Snyder, 2003). Rapp (1998), for example, has presented an assessment matrix that focuses on life domains (i.e., daily living situation, financial, social, and spiritual supports, health, leisure/recreational) and current status (i.e., What is going on today? What is available now?), the individual's desires and aspirations (i.e., What do I want?), and personal/social resources (i.e., What have I used in the past?). Another example is the Strengths-Based Assessment, a 45-item protocol that clinicians can use as a basis for holding a conversation with the individual (Singh, 1999). The aim of this conversation is to facilitate the mutual exploration of the individual's general strengths and the highlighting of specific strengths the individual wishes to enhance or use in recovering from mental illness. This assessment tool was recently used to explore the strengths an individual could use to develop a mindfulness-based intervention for Obsessive-Compulsive Disorder (Singh, Wahler, Winton, Adkins, and the Mindfulness Research Group, 2004). The strengths conversation highlights for the clinical areas the individual identifies as being important to him or her.

## FUNCTIONAL ASSESSMENTS

In the behavioral assessment literature, especially the applied behavior analytic literature, *functional assessment* refers to two general methods for identifying the functions a behavior may serve for an individual—interview and direct observation. The term *functional assessment* is often incorrectly used interchangeably with *functional analysis*. In functional assessment, the clinician undertakes a functional analysis interview or undertakes direct observations to determine if there is a possible correlation between the target behavior and specific antecedents and consequences. In functional analysis, the clinician systematically manipulates the environment to assess its impact on the target behavior. However, the clinician can use the data from either the functional assessment or the functional analysis to develop testable hypotheses about the functions of a target behavior of an individual.

### Interview

The Functional Assessment Interview (FAI; O'Neill et al., 1997) is the standard work in this area. Designed specifically as an interview-based functional assessment of individuals with developmental disabilities, a modified version of this structured interview has been used for a similar purpose with individuals with psychiatric disorders. Indeed, the interview works well because, unlike individuals with developmental disabilities, who may not be able to respond fully to the interview questions, this is typically not a problem with individuals with mental illness. Experienced behavior analysts can complete an FAI with an individual with psychotic behaviors in about an hour. In addition, clinicians can use the FAI to gather information from informants who know the individual well, such as nursing staff, other care providers, family members, and significant others. The FAI enables the clinician to determine the nature of the target behavior, the context in which it occurs, its antecedents and consequences, and the individual's likely motivation for engaging in the behavior.

If the FAI clearly indicates why an individual may engage in the target behavior, clinicians may continue to interview the individual to determine the functional equivalence of the target behavior. For example, if the individual being treated is able to verbalize why he or she engages in a behavior, such as aggression, the clinician may ask the person what purpose the aggression serves for him, i.e., what the individual receives or avoids by engaging in the behavior. Then the clinician can ask the individual to think of other more socially acceptable ways of meeting the same needs. Basically, the clinician tries to assist the individual in achieving need fulfillment by engaging in other behaviors that are functionally equivalent to but more socially acceptable than the target behavior.

**Direct Observations**

Observations in multiple contexts provide a useful method to assess the current status of the target behavior in terms of its frequency, intensity, latency, and duration. Observations can be undertaken continuously or on some specified schedule, such as time sampling. Direct observations can focus on just the target behavior or on the antecedents, behavior, and consequences of the behavior (i.e., ABC observations). The observations can be focused in terms of specific contexts (e.g., in the therapeutic milieu, during groups) or in all contexts. The data from direct observations can be presented in a scatter plot so that the frequency, patterns, and the context in which the target behavior occurs are visually evident (Touchette, MacDonald, & Langer, 1985). Thus, a scatter plot should indicate when and where the behavior will need intervention.

Direct observations of positive symptoms of schizophrenia may be achieved in a number of ways. Observations of formal thought disorder (i.e., disorganization of speech) and content of thought (i.e., delusions) can be made during an interview or regular interactions with the individual. Observations of hallucinations can be made with regard to certain behaviors of the individual, such as tilting of the head as if listening to someone and talking with someone who is not there. Direct observations can also be made of negative symptoms of schizophrenia. For example, individuals who have symptoms of avolition or apathy display poor personal grooming and hygiene—uncombed hair, dirty nails, unbrushed teeth, and disheveled clothes. Those with alogia, or limited speech, display poverty of utterances and content of speech, latency in responses, and blocking in stream of speech. Those with anhedonia lack interest in recreational activities, do not develop close relationships with others, and do not engage in other activities that they once found pleasurable. Those with flat or blunted affect show limited range in emotional expression, decreased spontaneous movements and gestures, and very little emotional arousal—stare vacantly with lifeless eyes and speak with flat and toneless voice. Even though direct observations are time consuming, they can provide a wealth of critical clinical information on the positive and negative symptoms displayed by an individual with schizophrenia or other psychotic disorders, if done systematically.

**Rating Scales and Questionnaires**

There are several rating scales and questionnaires that can be used to elicit further information on the nature and functions of the target behavior.

For example, the Contingency Analysis Questionnaire (Wieseler, Hanson, Chamberlain, & Thompson, 1985) and the Questions about Behavioral Function (QABF; Matson & Vollmer, 1995) are used extensively for this purpose in the field of developmental disabilities. Recently, the QABF was adapted for use with individuals with severe and persistent mental illness (QABF-MI; Matson, Vollmer, & Singh, 2003). The QABF-MI is a 25-item scale that measures the motivation of an individual's behavior in terms of five empirically derived factors: physical, attention, tangible, escape, and nonsocial. The scale has excellent psychometric properties, including interrater agreement (.96–.98 across factors), test–retest reliability (.86–.99 across factors), and coefficient alpha (.84–.92 across factors).

Ratings scales and questionnaires can be used as screening instruments to develop hypotheses of the functions the target behavior serves for the individual and establish a foundation for undertaking structural and functional analyses.

## Structural Analysis

A structural analysis is an important part of a comprehensive behavioral assessment. The clinician can use data gathered from functional assessments to determine the role of setting events or antecedents in the genesis and maintenance of the individual's target behavior. Specific setting events or antecedents are manipulated while the consequences of the behavior are held constant. For example, the physical environment (e.g., room size, type of room—dining room vs. group therapy room), activities (e.g., mall group vs. individual therapy vs. leisure or recreation time), demands (e.g., nature of task—easy vs. difficult, paid vs. unpaid), people (e.g., preferred vs. nonpreferred staff), and schedules (e.g., few breaks vs. many breaks) can all be manipulated to assess if any of these conditions are correlated to the occurrence of the target behavior.

## Functional Analysis

A functional analysis involves manipulating the consequences of the target behavior to determine the likely reinforcers that maintain it. As for a structural analysis, the clinician can use data gathered from functional assessments to set up tightly controlled conditions in which to manipulate consequences that may maintain the target behavior. For example, a typical analysis may include five different types of sessions presented in a random order: (1) attention in the absence of aggression (control condition); (2) attention immediately following aggression; (3) escape from demands (e.g., required attendance at a mall group) contingent on aggression; (4) absence of any overt stimulation (to test for self-stimulatory nature of the behavior); and (5) presentation of tangibles (e.g., desired objects, such as cigarettes, food, drinks) following aggression. Our own experience in undertaking this sort of functional analysis with individuals with schizophrenia and other psychotic disorders is that the data rarely favor one consequence a' all others and that the data are usually mixed and inconclusive. Furthermore, analyses provide only a hint of what may be occurring and rarely contribute directly to an intervention. For example, when a functional analysis suggests that attention is the maintaining or motivating variable, it would be foolhardy to develop a treatment plan based on just those data. The astute clinician would undertake further assessments to evaluate why and what kind of attention is responsible, because the attention could be caused by multiple factors, such as behavioral disinhibition, an inability to delay gratification, anxiety or social phobia, and intermittent reinforcement of the attention itself.

## ASSESSMENT VIA SELF-MONITORING

Individuals with schizophrenia and other psychotic disorders can be taught to systematically record specific behaviors in specific contexts. Typically, this approach is most effective when the behavior is of interest to the individual and is selected collaboratively by the clinician and the individual. The behavior is defined in behavioral, observable, or measurable terms, and the individual is taught how to collect the data immediately following each occurrence of the behavior. The data can be collected on data sheets or on handheld computers (Agras, Taylor, Feldman, Losch, & Burnett, 1990).

Self-monitoring has the usual problems associated with self-report measures, in that the data are thought to lack reliability and validity and may be biased. However, a recovery model of mental health services requires the individual to take as much control of recovery as his or her functional status allows and to rely on external assistance as little as possible. This assumes that the individual will learn to monitor his or her own behavior and to self-implement interventions. Thus, while self-monitoring may have certain drawbacks in terms of research data, it offers the most viable and useful method of self-empowerment for individuals in need of mental health services. Indeed, it is one of the most popular methods utilized by therapists in clinical practice because many behaviors of individuals needing mental health services cannot be externally monitored (e.g., specific thoughts, stressors, and triggers to delusions and hallucinations).

In summary, we agree with Haynes and O'Brien (2000) that behavioral assessment is much broader than is traditionally understood or used by applied behavior analysts and must include empirically supported multitechnique and multi-informant assessment strategies. Furthermore, in accord with the principles of recovery in mental health, clinicians should emphasize involving the individual in the assessment process.

## RESEARCH BASIS

The standard admissions psychiatric assessments are based on extensive *DSM-IV* field trials that clearly show that current diagnostic evaluations are far more reliable than those contained in the *DSM-III-R* (American Psychiatric Association, 1987, 1994). The admissions psychological assessments are derived from tests that have proven psychometric reliability and validity. Assessments from other disciplines are based more on clinical findings and history of use rather than on an extensive body of empirical research. The assessment instruments for measuring general psychopathology (e.g., BPRS, PANSS, SANS, SAPS, and SDS) are some of the most widely used because of their broad clinical applicability and proven reliability and validity (Perkins, Stroup, & Lieberman, 2000). Although there is less psychometric data on the measures used for assessing insight and treatment attitudes, the current data suggest that the instruments are psychometrically robust.

Quality of life is a concept that has come of age, and there are many good measures of it (Oliver, Huxley, Bridges, & Mohamad, 1996). These measures are particularly important because they offer the perspective of the individuals being treated, in terms of their perceptions of the value of mental health services. The concept is so broad that no one scale necessarily can cover all aspects of quality of life. Thus, the scales have inherent limitations dictated by the purpose and scope of the instruments. The reliability and validity of the scales are good to excellent, but there is somewhat low criterion validity because each scale is purported to measure something slightly different from extant scales. The scales included in this chapter (e.g., QOLI, QLS, W-QLI, Q-LES-Q, and QLI) have adequate reliability and validity and are some of the most frequently used rating scales in this area (Rabkin, Wagner, & Griffin, 2000).

Since Prochaska and DiClemente (1983) advanced the notion of stages of change in addictive behaviors, their transtheoretical stages of change model has been increasingly used in health and mental health to link treatment to an individual's stage of readiness for change. The URICA (McConnaughy et al., 1983) was developed to provide a tool for assessing the stages of change. Even though the transtheoretical model posits five stages of change (i.e., precontemplation, contemplation, preparation, action, and maintenance), factor analysis of the URICA resolved into only four factors, with no preparation factor. The scale has been used extensively in the field of addictions and has been found to be robust for that purpose. The scale provides data that can be used to determine where an individual is along the continuum from precontemplation to maintenance and enables the clinician to match the proposed treatment to the individual's stage of readiness.

Personal strength is a central concept in positive psychology as well as in the recovery model of service delivery in mental health. However, there is the unresolved issue as to the definition of strength. Strength has been narrowly defined as an individual's assets, with a focus on the positive aspects (see Lopez & Snyder, 2003), while others have defined it broadly as whatever the individual brings to the clinical situation (Singh, 2001). Thus, there is no consensus on what is to be measured. Furthermore, there are no standardized measures or methods for measuring an individual's strengths, either in the narrow or in the broad sense. Current measures use qualitative approaches for gathering and interpreting the data.

The research literature on functional assessments is vast, especially given that it forms the very foundation for much of behavioral interventions. Given space limitations, detailed exposition of the theoretical and research bases for functional assessments will not be covered here, but can be found in Haynes (1998) and Haynes and O'Brien (2000).


## CLINICAL UTILITY

Our assessment methodology emphasizes multiple methods of data collection from multiple sources of information to develop a holistic picture of an individual's strengths, treatment needs, and maintenance of wellness. Generally, past and current information about the individual is best obtained from the individual, family, significant others, and records from previous admissions to mental health facilities. Multiple assessment techniques (e.g., standardized tests, structured interviews, rating scales, direct observations) are used because any single methodology provides only limited information. For example, diagnostic interviews provide data that pertain to possible primary and comorbid diagnoses, but they do not inform the clinician about the severity of a disorder or how the individual's behavior compares with that of others with the same underlying disorder. Multiple sources of information are used because the individual's behavior may and often does vary by setting. In addition, the individual may view his or her own behavior quite differently than others, such as clinicians or family members, do. Thus, clinical utility of the assessments is enhanced by using multiple techniques to collect data from multiple sources.

Rating scales can be used with multiple informants to rate the individual's behavior across multiple contexts. In addition, many rating scales have a self-report version that can be used to gather similar information from the individual himself or herself. The self-report rating scales are particularly useful in collecting data on internalized signs and symptoms, such as delusions and hallucinations, anxiety, and depression. Given that a psychometrically robust rating scale is normed on a given population, clinicians can compare the findings with regard to the individual's peers or reference group to determine the clinical significance of the multiple ratings. Further, rating scales are time and cost efficient for the clinician.

The clinical utility of the assessments are greatly enhanced if the structured interviews and behavior rating scales are used in a complementary manner. Psychiatric diagnoses are categorical and require a clinician to gather data on the number of symptoms that are present and then to determine if these symptoms meet current diagnostic criteria for a specific disorder. Typically, behavior rating scales are designed to measure psychopathology as a continuous (rather than categorical) dimension in a normative population and do not have a cutoff point beyond which the individual is deemed to have pathology. When these two data sources are combined, they provide not only a psychiatric diagnosis of the individual but also a measure of the frequency and severity of the behavioral endpoints of the psychiatric diagnosis when compared to the individual's normative group.

Direct behavioral observation data can be used to complement the data obtained from interviews and behavior rating scales. Direct observations are far less susceptible to rater bias than behavioral ratings (Towns, Singh, & Beale, 1984) and enable the clinician to understand the individual's behavior in the context in which it occurs (e.g., residential unit, small groups, dental visit). When the observations are structured, as in structural or functional analogue settings, the environment can be systematically manipulated and the consequences of the individual's behavior held constant; or the consequences can be systematically manipulated and the environment in which the behavior occurs held constant. Direct observations in these two settings will inform the clinician of the nature of the antecedents and consequences that give rise to or maintain the behavior, respectively.

The psychiatrist can use the behavioral assessment data to determine which approach to pharmacotherapy to take for symptom recovery. In general, the assessment data are used to determine the psychosocial, psychoeducational, and environmental supports needed by the individual. By using the behavioral data, the psychiatrist can determine if a primary illness, target symptom, or behavioral-pharmacological hypothesis approach would be in the best interests of the individual. A primary illness approach is taken when the assessment data suggest that the target behavior (e.g., aggression) is an integral part of a psychiatric disorder (e.g., command hallucination) and that pharmacologically managing the hallucination will alleviate symptoms of the disorder, including aggression. However, if the behavioral assessment data show that the aggression occurs at a frequency or severity that poses a danger to self or others or if the aggression does not occur reliably in the context of the primary illness, the psychiatrist may use a target symptom approach to control the behavior. A behavioral-pharmacological hypothesis approach may be used if there is a hypothesized cause for the behavior and evidence shows that the behavior is amenable to pharmacological treatment. For example, there are two hypotheses regarding self-aggression in some individuals with developmental disabilities due to an endogenous opiate dysregulation. Empirical evidence suggests that self-aggression in these individuals can be substantially reduced and sometimes eliminated pharmacologically with use of naltrexone (Sandman & Touchette, 2002).

In sum, the assessment data can have much clinical utility, in terms of informing clinicians about the nature and course of the psychiatric disorder, behavioral endpoints of the disorder, and associated or collateral instrumental behavior.

## ASSESSMENT, CONCEPTUALIZATION, AND TREATMENT PLANNING

In inpatient treatment, an individual's treatment team (which includes the individual as an equal member) is the smallest unit responsible for the assessment, conceptualization, and treatment planning. The treatment team undertakes a comprehensive set of multitechnique and multi-informant assessments that will provide a holistic picture of the individual, in terms of his or her strengths, symptom status, and need for clinical intervention. The assessments include an evaluation of the individual's functional status across multiple domains. In addition, the assessments identify the individual's disabilities, problems, needs, barriers to fulfilling life goals, role functioning, and an enhanced quality of life.

Assessments inform the diagnosis, and the diagnosis alerts the treatment team members of the need for further assessments to clarify the clinical picture of the individual. One of the goals is to understand the individual's presenting psychiatric problems at the highest level of diagnostic sophistication that can be achieved based on a comprehensive interdisciplinary assessment (Singh et al., 2004). There are four levels of diagnostic sophistication: (a) symptomatic, which includes isolated symptoms (e.g., auditory hallucinations) that provide an indication of a possible diagnosis (e.g., Psychotic Disorder Not Otherwise Specified); (b) syndromic, which includes the constellation of signs and symptoms that have been present for a given time, to which standardized inclusionary and exclusionary criteria can be applied to derive a diagnosis (e.g., depression); (c) pathophysiologic, which includes structural or biochemical changes that indicate the diagnosis (e.g., an individual presenting with anxiety, depression or manic excitement, weakness, excessive sweating, tremors, and, in some cases, disturbances of thought and cognition may have elevated thyroid function tests that suggest a diagnosis of hyperthyroidism); and (d) etiologic, in which the diagnosis is based on known causative factors.

All assessment and diagnostic information about the individual is synthesized and conceptualized into a case formulation that provides the basis for making clinical predictions in a fairly scientific manner. Case formulation is the first step that leads to clinical hypotheses regarding the individual's current status, clinical course, and future treatments. Typically, all members of the treatment team contribute to the case formulation because it is an integration of their collective assessments and clinical judgments. Working together can help the team members resolve conflicting assessment data and reduce error and bias in interpreting the clinical findings.

Case formulation can be structured in several ways, depending on the theoretical orientation of the team members (Eells, 1997). However, there may be multiple approaches, even among clinicians using a single theoretical approach. For example, there are several approaches within behavior therapy, including problem solving (Nezu, Nezu, Friedman, & Haynes, 1997), cognitive-behavioral

(Persons, 1989), dialectical behavior therapy (Linehan, 1993), and functional analytic (Haynes & O'Brien, 1990).

Given the diversity of approaches, we have developed and found useful a phenomenological approach to case formulation, called the 6 P's (Singh et al., 2004). The 6 P's approach requires the systematic discussion of pertinent data in the following sequence:

1. *Pertinent history*—a brief sketch of who the individual is, including preferences and dislikes
2. *Predisposing factors*—biological (e.g., prenatal and genetic factors, complications during pregnancy or delivery, mother's use of substances during pregnancy, head trauma), psychiatric disorder and history, psychosocial (e.g., emotional, physical, or sexual abuse, parental divorce and separation), medical illnesses/risks, and functional deficits (e.g., self-care, community functioning, socialization, communications, vocational, cognition/language)
3. *Precipitating factors*—prescribed medications, medical conditions, major psychosocial stressors, and substance and alcohol abuse
4. *Perpetuating factors*—personality disorders, chronic medical conditions, substance and alcohol abuse, current status of psychiatric disorder(s), and nonadherence to treatment protocol, including medication regimen
5. *Previous treatments and the individual's responses to them*—treatments utilized during the course of the individual's psychiatric illness, response to previous treatments, adverse effects of psychotropic and other medications, and culture-based treatments
6. *Present status*—current signs and symptoms of psychiatric disorder(s), current interventions, functional strengths, wellness concerns, current forensic issues, and areas in need of further intervention

When stated in this sequence, the case formulation leads directly to the delineation of the individual's needs, the goals and objectives of the current admission or hospitalization, and therapy and wellness interventions. Given the basic premise that rehabilitation is done *with* and not *to* an individual, the individual is involved in the assessment process to the fullest extent possible, given his or her current functional status and desired level of involvement in the change process. Such collaboration enhances clinicians' understanding of the individual's interests, hopes, motivation, optimism, and confidence in recovery from his or her disabilities and other personal and social challenges. Furthermore, this process often provides clinicians with insight relative to the individual's overt lack of motivation for change; for example, it could be due to low environmental awareness, incomplete knowledge of real choices, lack of knowledge about alternative ways of achieving the same ends, or fear of change. Such insights provide the basis for treatment planning.

As a part of the integrated assessments, clinicians assess the individual's motivation for engaging in treatment, because treatment progress is related to pretreatment readiness for change. Research and practice-based evidence suggests that positive outcomes are more likely when the interventions and techniques used to deliver the interventions match the individual's level of readiness or stage of change (Prochaska, DiClemente, & Norcross, 1992). The treatment objectives are written in behavioral, observable, or measurable terms, with the first objective written at the readiness level of the individual. Successive treatment objectives are developed to match successive levels of readiness until the individual reaches the maintenance phase of change. The treatment objectives are written in terms of what the individual will do to achieve symptom and functional recovery. The interventions that correspond to these objectives are written in terms of what the clinical staff will do to assist the individual to achieve these objectives. Furthermore, for each intervention, the clinical staff attempts to utilize one or more of the individual's strengths so that the individual can learn to take control of his or her recovery with the least amount of professional assistance needed.

## CASE STUDY

Individuals with paranoid schizophrenia have prominent delusions or auditory hallucinations, but, in general, their cognitive functioning and affect are relatively intact. Their delusions are typically persecutory, grandiose, or both, and their hallucinations revolve around the content of their delusional theme. Furthermore, the persecutory and grandiose delusions may predispose the individual to suicidal behavior and/or violence due to anxiety, anger, aloofness, and argumentativeness. We describe the case of an individual with Schizophrenia, Paranoid Type.

### IDENTIFICATION

The individual, Mr. Gonzalez, was a 40-year-old English-speaking Latino man. He had a long history with the justice system, both as a juvenile and as an adult.

### PRESENTING COMPLAINTS

Mr. Gonzalez was admitted to a forensic psychiatric hospital because of his mental illness and for restoration of competency to stand trial on charges of grand theft auto, burglary, and receiving stolen property. Mr. Gonzalez has a long history of grandiose, religious, persecutory, and erotomanic delusions, but he denies he has mental illness. He claims to use marijuana, methamphetamine, LSD, and mushrooms.

### HISTORY

Little information is available on Mr. Gonzalez's early childhood. He dropped out of school in the fifth grade, was constantly in trouble with the law, and ended up in the juvenile justice system at age 10. His juvenile arrests involved drug-related offenses and burglaries. During his preteen and teenage years, he was frequently very violent toward his peers, including females. He continued to be very violent as he grew older, although the frequency of his violence decreased during the last 10 years. At least two of his 20 convictions as an adult involved sexual aggression toward females, but there is no record of his being convicted of a sexual assault. He was never married and, although he has had numerous relationships with females, he is currently not in a stable relationship. He reports fathering three children.

His first episode of schizophrenia was at the age of 16. There is no record of what precipitated the episode, but Mr. Gonzalez remembers being treated for several months in an inpatient adolescent psychiatric unit of a local general hospital. Since then he has had numerous psychiatric admissions, the most recent being immediately prior to his current arrest. His mental illness has been perpetuated by only partial response to medication, his very limited insight into his mental illness, and an unwillingness to participate in therapy and wellness activities.

Mr. Gonzalez has been on Clozaril for several years, but he is sometimes medication nonadherent, especially when in the community. Multiple medication regimens for controlling his delusional disorder have not been successful. During previous inpatient admissions, he has inconsistently participated in psychotherapy and psychoeducational interventions. He has been assault-free for short periods during his hospitalizations.

## PEER AND WORK ISSUES

Mr. Gonzalez has never had a formal job. He worked, however, as a drug dealer for many years and was apparently very successful at it. He has reported using and selling recreational drugs from an early age. He has very poor social interaction skills and antagonizes most people. He has no friends but has transient relationships with people involved in the recreational drug trade and with drug users.

## FAMILY ISSUES

Mr. Gonzalez has two brothers and three sisters. One of his brothers also suffers from schizophrenia, currently well controlled with medication and psychosocial interventions. His parents separated during his childhood, and he rarely saw his father during his teenage years. Mr. Gonzalez has lost touch with his family members and does not want to renew any contact with them. He is ashamed of his current status, especially his incarceration at a forensic psychiatric hospital.

## BEHAVIORAL ASSESSMENT RESULTS

The admission and integrated assessments were completed during the first 24 hours and first week of admission, respectively. The psychiatric diagnosis of Schizophrenia, Paranoid Type, Chronic, was confirmed by using clinical assessment and the Structured Clinical Interview for *DSM-IV* Axis I Disorders—Clinical Version (First, Spitzer, Gibbon, & Williams, 1996). The severity of Mr. Gonzalez's symptomatology was assessed with two standard measures: the Scale for the Assessment of Negative Symptoms (SANS; Andreasen, 1983) and the Scale for the Assessment of Positive Symptoms (SAPS; Andreasen, 1984). Scores on the five subscales of the SANS were summed into a global index of negative symptoms, and the scores on the four subscales of the SAPS were summed into a global index of positive symptoms. Mr. Gonzalez scored 8.4 and 7.6, respectively, on these scales, indicating that he experienced significant levels of treatment-refractory negative and positive symptoms at admission.

The Psychotic Symptom Rating Scales (PSYRATS; Haddock, McCarron, Tarrier, & Faragher, 1999) were used to measure dimensions of hallucinations and delusions that are not covered by the SAPS (i.e., frequency, duration, distress, and disruption). Mr. Gonzalez scored 18.3 on the delusion subscales and 32.6 on the hallucination subscales. The PSYRATS was used because it is sensitive to changes due to therapy and was used as a baseline measure of current status.

Scores on the Questions About Behavioral Functions—Mental Illness scale (Matson et al., 2003) indicated that the motivation for Mr. Gonzalez's violence was due mainly to internal stimuli, suggesting that his violence was primarily associated with his psychotic disorder. There was, however, a secondary instrumental component to his aggression that was motivated by tangibles; i.e., Mr. Gonzalez was aggressive sometimes when he could not get something he desired. Direct observations of his behavior showed poor social interaction skills and aloofness. Treatment adherence data showed that occasionally he refused to take his medication. His score on the University of Rhode Island Change Assessment scale (URICA; McConnaughy et al., 1983) indicated that he was at the precontemplation stage of readiness for change with regard to his schizophrenia, at the contemplation stage with regard to substance dependence, and at the preparation stage with instrumental aggression.


## ETHICAL AND LEGAL ISSUES OR COMPLICATIONS

Mr. Gonzalez was admitted as an inpatient for treatment of his mental illness as well as for restoration of competency to stand trial. Restoration of competency will involve his demonstrating (a) a rational and factual understanding of the nature and purpose of the criminal proceedings pending against him and his charges, (b) knowledge of court procedures, roles and functions of various courtroom officials, types of pleas available to him and possible sentence, if convicted, and (c) the ability to cooperate with his attorney in a rational manner and assist in preparing and conducting a defense.

## CONCEPTUALIZATION AND TREATMENT RECOMMENDATIONS

Mr. Gonzalez was poorly socialized as a child, came from a single-parent family, and faced multiple stressors as an adolescent. His psychiatric problems were further compounded by his substance dependence from a young age. The assessments showed that, to a substantial degree, his problems were either a result of or exacerbated by his mental illness, although there was an instrumental component, especially in his aggressive behavior. This suggested a primary disorder-based approach to the treatment of his chronic paranoid schizophrenia, supplemented by a target symptom approach to the treatment of his aggression.

It was recommended that Mr. Gonzalez continue with the current psychopharmacology plan, using Clozaril for controlling his hallucinations and delusions, but that the psychiatrist collaborate with him in individual therapy focused on improving medication adherence. Given that he was at the precontemplation stage of change in terms of his readiness to engage in psychosocial interventions for his psychotic behavior, his treatment team recommended that he engage in groups that would assist him in achieving the following objectives sequentially: (a) learn the signs and symptoms of mental illness; (b) learn the signs and symptoms of psychosis; (c) identify the signs and symptoms of hallucinations and delusions in another person; (d) identify and accept signs and symptoms of hallucinations and delusions in himself; (e) identify the stressors and triggers to his delusions and hallucinations; (f) learn self-management techniques to control these stressors and triggers; (g) use the self-management techniques to control the stressors and triggers so that the delusions and hallucinations do not interfere with the quality of his life; and (h) develop and implement a personal wellness recovery plan so that he can anticipate and control his psychotic behavior in multiple contexts in the community. Further, the treatment team recommended that Mr. Gonzales attend individual and group cognitive-behavior therapy for psychotic disorders designed especially for individuals in the chronic phase of their illness (Warman, Grant, Sullivan, Caroff, & Beck, 2005).

Mr. Gonzales and his treatment team jointly decided that he attend a substance dependence group at the contemplation stage of instruction. Finally, Mr. Gonzalez requested if he could learn a self-management technique because he wanted to control his instrumental violence. His treatment team recommended that he attend a mindfulness-based group for anger management (Singh, Wahler, Adkins, Myers, & the Mindfulness Research Group, 2003). Therapeutic milieu interventions were also prescribed so that staff could reinforce what he learned during individual and group therapies.

## SUMMARY

Psychotic behaviors require a systematic, multitechnique, and multi-informant holistic evaluation that includes behavior analytic assessments before a person-centered therapy and wellness plan can be developed. In this chapter, we outlined this process and provided examples of different assessments that can be used for this purpose. Furthermore, we indicated how the assessments can be used to develop a brief phenomenological case formulation that leads to recovery-oriented treatment recommendations.

## REFERENCES

Agras, W. S., Taylor, C. B., Feldman, D. E., Losch, M., & Burnett, K. F. (1990). Developing computer-assisted therapy for the treatment of obesity. *Behavior Therapy, 21,* 99–109.

American Psychiatric Association. (1987). *Diagnostic and statistical manual of mental disorders* (3rd ed. rev.). Washington, DC: Author.

American Psychiatric Association. (1994). *Diagnostic and statistical manual of mental disorders* (4th ed.). Washington, DC: Author.

American Psychiatric Association. (2000). *Diagnostic and statistical manual of mental disorders* (4th ed., text revision). Washington, DC: Author.

Andreasen, N. C. (1983). *Scale for the Assessment of Negative Symptoms* (SANS). Iowa City: University of Iowa.

Andreasen, N. C. (1984). Scale *for the Assessment of Positive Symptoms* (SAPS). Iowa City: University of Iowa.

Anthony, W., Cohen, M., Farkas, M., & Gagne, C. (2002). *Psychiatric rehabilitation* (2nd ed.). Boston: Center for Psychiatric Rehabilitation.

Becker, M., Diamond, R., & Sainfort, F. (1993). A new patient focused index for measuring quality of life in persons with severe and persistent mental illness. *Quality of Life Research, 2,* 239–251.

Cohen, M. R., Anthony, W. A., & Farkas, M. D. (1997). Assessing and developing readiness for psychiatric rehabilitation. *Psychiatric Services, 48,* 644–646.

Eells, T. (1997). *Handbook of psychotherapy case formulation.* New York: Guilford Press.

Endicott, J., Nee, J., Harrison, W., & Blumenthal, R. (1993). Quality of Life Enjoyment and Satisfaction Questionnaire: A new scale. *Psychopharmacology Bulletin, 29,* 321–326.

Ferrans, C. E., & Powers, M. J. (1985). Quality of Life Index: Development and psychometric properties. *Advances in Nursing Science, 8,* 15–24.

First, M. B., Spitzer, R. L., Gibbon, M., & Williams, J. B. W. (1996). *Users guide for the Structured Clinical Interview for DSM-IV Axis I disorders—Clinical version: SCID I.* Washington, DC: American Psychiatric Association.

Frisch, M. B. (1994). *Manual and treatment guide for the Quality of Life Inventory.* Minneapolis, MN: National Computer Systems.

Haddock, G., McCarron, J., Tarrier, N., & Faragher, E. B. (1999). Scales to measure dimensions of hallucinations and delusions: The Psychotic Symptom Rating Scales (PSYRATS). *Psychological Medicine, 29,* 879–889.

Haynes, S. N. (1998). Principles and practices of behavioral assessment with adults. In C. R. Reynolds (Ed.), *Comprehensive clinical psychology, Vol. 4: Assessment* (pp. 157–186). Amsterdam: Pergamon Press.

Haynes, S. N., & O'Brien, W. H. (1990). The functional analysis in behavior therapy. *Clinical Psychology Review, 10,* 649–668.

Haynes, S. N., & O'Brien, W. H. (2000). *Principles and practice of behavioral assessment.* New York: Kluwer Academic.

Heinrichs, D. W., Hanlon, T. E., & Carpenter, W. T. (1984). The Quality of Life Scale: An instrument for rating the schizophrenic deficit syndrome. *Schizophrenia Bulletin, 10,* 388–397.

Hogan, T. P., & Awad, A. G. (1992). Subjective response to neuroleptics and outcome in schizophrenia: A re-examination comparing two measures. *Psychological Medicine, 22,* 347–352.

Kay, S. R., Opler, L. A., & Fiszbein, A. (1994). *Positive and Negative Syndrome Scale manual.* North Tonawanda, NY: Multihealth Systems.

Kirkpatrick, B., Buchanan, R. W., McKenney, P. D., Alphs, L. D., & Carpenter, W. T., Jr. (1989). The Schedule for the Deficit Syndrome: An instrument for research in schizophrenia. *Psychiatric Research, 30,* 119–123.

Lehman, A. F. (1995). *Toolkit for evaluating quality of life for persons with severe mental illness.* Cambridge, MA: Evaluation Center at Human Services Research Institute.

Linehan, M. M. (1993). *Cognitive-behavioral treatment of borderline personality disorder.* New York: Guilford Press.

Lopez, S. J., & Snyder, C. R. (2003). *Positive psychological assessment: A handbook of models and measures.* Washington, DC: American Psychological Association.

Matson, J. L., & Vollmer, T. R. (1995). *User's guide: Questions About Behavioral Function (QABF).* Baton Rouge, LA: Scientific Publishers.

Matson, J. L., Vollmer, T. R., & Singh, N. N. (2003). *Questions About Behavioral Function—Mental Illness (QABF-MI).* Unpublished manuscript, ONE Research Institute, Richmond, VA.

McConnaughy, E. A., Prochaska, J. O., & Velicer, W. F. (1983). Stages of change in psychotherapy: Measurement and sample profiles. *Psychotherapy: Theory, research, and practice, 20,* 368–375.

McEvoy, J. P., Apperson, L. J., Appelbaum, P. S., Ortlip, P., Brecosky, J., Hammill, K. K., et al. (1989). Insight in schizophrenia: Its relationship to acute psychopathology. *Journal of Nervous and Mental Disease, 177,* 43–47.

Nezu, A., Nezu, C., Friedman, S. H., & Haynes, S. N. (1997). Case formulation in behavior therapy: Problem-solving and functional analytic strategies. In T. D. Eells (Ed.), *Handbook of psychotherapy case formulation* (pp. 368–401). New York: Guilford Press.

Oliver, J., Huxley, P., Bridges, K., & Mohamad, H. (1996). *Quality of life and mental health services.* New York: Routledge.

O'Neill, R. E., Horner, R. H., Albin, R. W., Sprague, J. R., Storey, K., & Newton, J. S. (1997). *Functional assessment and program development for problem behavior: A practical handbook.* Pacific Grove, CA: Brooks/Cole.

Overall, J. E., & Gorham, D. R. (1988). The Brief Psychiatric Rating Scale (BPRS): Recent developments in ascertainment and scaling. *Psychopharmacology Bulletin, 24,* 97–99.

Perkins, D. O., Stroup, T. S., & Lieberman, J. A. (2000). Psychotic disorders measures. In Task Force for the Handbook of Psychiatric Measures (Ed.), *Handbook of psychiatric measures* (pp. 485–513). Washington, DC: American Psychiatric Association.

Persons, J. B. (1989). *Cognitive therapy in practice: A case formulation approach.* New York: W.W. Norton.

Power, M. J. (2003). Quality of life. In S. J. Lopez & C. R. Snyder (Eds.), *Positive psychological assessment: A handbook of models and measures* (pp. 427–441). Washington, DC: American Psychological Association.

Prochaska, J. O., & DiClemente, C. C. (1983). Stages and processes of self-change of smoking: Toward an integrative model of change. *Journal of Consulting and Clinical Psychology, 51,* 390–395.

Prochaska, J. O., DiClemente, C. C., & Norcross, J. C. (1992). In search of how people change: Applications to addictive behaviors. *American Psychologist, 47,* 1102–1114.

Rabkin, J., Wagner, G., & Griffin, K. W. (2000). Quality of life measures. In Task Force for the Handbook of Psychiatric Measures (Ed.), *Handbook of psychiatric measures* (pp. 135–150). Washington, DC: American Psychiatric Association.

Rapp, C. A. (1998). *The strengths model: Case management with people suffering from severe and persistent mental illness.* New York: Oxford University Press.

Sandman, C. A., & Touchette, P. (2002). Opioids and the maintenance of self-injurious behavior. In S. R. Schroeder, M. L. Oster-Granite, & T. Thompson (Eds.), *Self-injurious behavior: Gene–brain–behavior relationships* (pp. 191–204). Washington, DC: American Psychological Association.

Singh, N. N. (1999). *Strengths-based assessment.* Chesterfield, VA: ONE Research Institute.

Singh, N. N. (2001). Holistic approaches to working with strengths: A goodness-of-fit wellness model. In A. Bridge, L. J. Gordon, P. Jivanjee, & J. M. King (Eds.), *Building on family strengths: Research and services in support of children and their families* (pp. 7–16). Portland, OR: Portland State University, Research and Training Center on Family Support and Children's Mental Health.

Singh, N. N., Sabaawi, M., & Singh, J. (2004). Developmental disabilities and psychopathology: Rehabilitation and recovery focused services. In W. L. Williams (Ed.), *Developmental disabilities: Etiology, assessment, intervention, and integration* (pp. 243–258). Reno, NV: Context Press.

Singh, N. N., Wahler, R. G., Adkins, A. D., Myers, R. E., & the Mindfulness Research Group. (2003). Soles of the feet: A mindfulness-based self-control intervention for aggression by an individual with mild mental retardation and mental illness. *Research in Developmental Disabilities, 24,* 158–169.

Singh, N. N., Wahler, R. G., Winton, A. S. W., Adkins, A. D., and the Mindfulness Research Group. (2004). A mindfulness-based treatment of Obsessive-Compulsive Disorder. *Clinical Case Studies, 3,* 275–288.

Touchette, P. E., MacDonald, R. F., & Langer, S. N. (1985). A scatter plot for identifying stimulus control of problem behavior. *Journal of Applied Behavior Analysis, 18,* 343–351.

Towns, A. J., Singh, N. N., & Beale, I. L. (1984). Reliability of observations in a double- and single-blind drug study: An experimental analysis. In K. D. Gadow (Ed.), *Advances in learning and behavioral disabilities* (Vol. 3, pp. 215–240). Greenwich, CT: JAI Press.

Townsend, W., Boyd, S., Griffin, G., & Hicks, P. L. (2000). *Emerging best practices in mental health recovery.* Columbus: Ohio Department of Mental Health.

Warman, D. M., Grant, P., Sullivan, K., Caroff, S., & Beck, A. T. (2005). Individual and group cognitive-behavior therapy for psychotic disorders: A pilot investigation. *Journal of Psychiatric Practice, 11,* 27–34.

Weiden, P., Rapkin, B., Mott, T., Zygmunt, A., Goldman, D., Horvitz-Lennon, et al. (1994). Rating of Medication Influences (ROMI) scale in schizophrenia. *Schizophrenia Bulletin, 20,* 297–310.

Wieseler, N. A., Hanson, R. H., Chamberlain, T. P., & Thompson, T. (1985). Functional taxonomy of stereotypic and self-injurious behavior. *Mental Retardation, 23,* 230–234.

# 17

# AGGRESSIVE BEHAVIOR

JENNIFER LANGHINRICHSEN-ROHLING

*Department of Psychology*
*University of South Alabama*
*Mobile, Alabama*

MATTHEW T. HUSS

*Department of Psychology*
*Creighton University*
*Omaha, Nebraska*

MARTIN L. ROHLING

*Psychology Department*
*University of South Alabama*
*Mobile, Alabama*

## INTRODUCTION

Consider "Bob and Sarah," a couple in their 40s who have been unhappily married for the majority of their 12 years together. They are now seeking marital therapy to help diminish the frequency and intensity of their "out-of-hand" arguments. Or consider "Betty," a 40-year-old woman who referred herself for outpatient mental health treatment because of continued difficulties managing her anger at home and at work. Or consider "Ted," a recently brain-injured 29-year-old man being taken care of by his parents. Prior to his motorcycle accident, Ted's parents had been concerned about his substance abuse and "periodic run-ins with the law." They now want professional help controlling Ted's aggressive outbursts. Or consider "Stan," a 30-year-old man with a diagnosis of paranoid schizophrenia. Stan has a history of violence and assault that has led to at least three past involuntary psychiatric hospitalizations. Most recently, Stan has been brought to the emergency room by relatives because he has discontinued his neuroleptics and is again decompensating. They are worried that he might hurt someone.

In all four scenarios, the consulting clinician should determine the extent to which ongoing aggression is a part of the clinical picture and exactly what types of aggression, if any, have transpired. The clinician is also often expected to determine the likelihood that each of these individuals will engage in future aggression and the potential danger each person poses to other individuals in their environment. To facilitate the clinician's ability to accomplish these purposes, in this chapter we first describe some of the ongoing controversies regarding the assessment of aggression. We then make recommendations as to how these controversies might best be solved in diverse types of cases. Next, we present a comprehensive assessment strategy that can be used for many different referral questions (i.e., to determine whether aggression is part of the clinical picture; to generate hypotheses about how to intervene with aggressive individuals; and to determine the client's level of dangerousness or to make a risk appraisal). Our proposed strategy can be used in nonforensic as well as forensic settings and is especially applicable to treatment providers.

We conclude the chapter by presenting two brief case studies. Each example was chosen to highlight the utility of conducting a functional analysis of aggressive behavior within the context of a nested ecological approach. A functional analysis of aggression considers the purpose of the behavior and emphasizes situational factors that might elicit, suppress, and/or maintain the aggression. The nested ecological approach considers how the individual is embedded in multiple levels of context, each of which may be exerting an influence on his or her expression of aggression. We chose this combined approach because of its clinical and theoretical utility. Due to the expertise of the current authors, particular attention will be given to the assessment of aggression occurring within the context of an intimate relationship (i.e., intimate-partner violence).

## CURRENT ISSUES WITH REGARD TO ASSESSING AGGRESSION

A number of issues complicate assessment of aggression. These include definitional concerns about the nature of aggression, complexities associated with measuring the intention underlying the behavior to determine its aggressive quality, difficulties using observational strategies to assess aggression in adults, problems with existing self-report measures of aggression, and political controversies centering on the degree to which we should identify victim behavior as an antecedent to aggression. There are also ongoing debates about how to integrate information derived from various aggression assessment strategies. Each of these issues is discussed in turn.

The first issue is how to operationally define *aggression*. Throughout the literature, a variety of terms have been used interchangeably with at least some aspect of the concept of aggression, a fact that has led to some confusion and consternation (e.g., violence, abuse, assault, maltreatment, patriarchal terrorism, anger, and hostility; DiGiuseppe, Tafrate, & Eckhardt, 1994; Suris et al., 2004). However, consistent with the behavioral focus of the current text, aggression has most consistently been defined as an overt act intentionally aimed toward a target, with the goal of hurting or harming another person (e.g., Giancola & Chermack, 1998). The strengths of this definition include its ability to subsume a variety of types of behaviors (i.e., physical, sexual, and verbal) and its exclusion of feelings, such as anger and hostility, that may need to be treated separately (DiGiuseppe et al.). This definition also excludes accidental behavior (e.g., he stepped on my foot because he didn't see it). Using this definition, the intention of the actor is an important determinant of whether the behavior was, in fact, aggressive (e.g., Miller, Smith, Turner, Guijarro, & Hallet, 1996). In many cases, however, the motives of the perpetrator and the purpose of the aggressive behavior have proven to be difficult to determine (Daffern & Howells, 2002). Thus, the sequence of events surrounding the behavior needs to be identified because it often provides important clues about the perpetrator's motivations and the function of the behavior. Unfortunately, this sequence often takes place in private.

Similarly, within the domestic violence literature, Straus, Gelles, and Steinmetz (1981) have behaviorally defined *domestic violence* as a form of aggression that manifests itself as an overt act carried out with the intention of causing physical pain or injury to another person. These authors then focused on assessing the occurrence of overtly violent behaviors in a specific context (i.e., at a time of conflict between intimates or family members). The Conflict Tactics Scale (CTS; Straus, 1979) and its revised version, the CTS-II (Straus, Hamby, Boney-McCoy, & Sugarman, 1996), were created to measure these behaviors. Straus and colleagues' behavioral and context-specific measure(s) enhanced clinicians' abilities to reliably and validly measure the perpetration of aggressive acts by intimates. Moreover, inspection of the acts included on the CTS-II indicates that aggressive the conflict tactics were operationally defined quite broadly to include acts that are psychologically and sexually aggressive as well as acts that are physically violent. However, the CTS and the CTS-II have been criticized because of the authors' neglect of such issues as the intention of the perpetrator, the function or purpose of the aggression (e.g., self-defense versus seeking power or control; Vivian, Langhinrichsen-Rohling, & Heyman, 2004), and the impact of the behaviors being assessed (e.g., less impact is attributed to women's aggression than men's; Cascardi, Langhinrichsen, & Vivian, 1992).

Consequently, in the current chapter we also are choosing to define aggression as an overt act (i.e., physical, sexual, or verbal). These acts are typically, but not exclusively, perpetrated in conjunction with feelings of anger or hostility; therefore, feelings were not included in our operational definition of aggression. The term *violence* is used to describe one type of behavioral manifestation of aggression, but the term *aggression* is broader and represents a higher-level construct (Suris et al., 2004). Aggressive acts must be perpetrated with the intention to harm or injure the victim. Therefore, we assert that an assessment of ongoing aggression must include measures of the intention or motivations of the perpetrator, if possible, as well as the function or purpose of the behavior as it occurs in a particular context (e.g., an episodic or situation-specific analysis).

Across a variety of domains (e.g., child maltreatment, rape, stalking) and not just within the domestic violence literature, behaviorally based measures have facilitated our ability to describe, identify risk factors, and to consider the effectiveness of various interventions for a number of types of aggression (e.g., Sexual Experiences Survey; Koss, Gidycz, & Wisniewski, 1987; Multidimensional Measure of Emotional Abuse; Murphy & Hoover, 1999; Unwanted Pursuit Behavior Inventory; Langhinrichsen-Rohling, Palarea, Cohen, & Rohling, 2000). These measures also have advanced our ability to detect subtypes of aggressive perpetrators (e.g., Covell, Huss, & Langhinrichsen-Rohling, in press; Holtzworth-Munroe & Stuart, 1994; Langhinrichsen-Rohling, Huss, & Ramsey, 2000).

However, limitations to these measures also have been noted. For example, the majority of the existing behaviorally based measures rely on the aggressor's self-report of perpetration. These measures are subject to memory biases, cognitive distortions, and social desirability concerns (Suris et al., 2004). Behavioral measures of aggression have frequently been used only to determine the presence/absence of particular acts of aggression or to categorize someone as either a perpetrator or not (Kroner, 2005). This practice leads to greater inaccuracies than if continuous or probabilistic indices are derived. Furthermore, few of the existing measures have been used to describe aggressive episodes sequentially to determine the function of the behavior, its antecedents, and its consequences. Instead, this type of assessment has generally been conducted through a clinical interview (e.g., Heyman & Schlee, 2003). Some of the already developed instruments do not even allow for a multidimensional understanding of the behaviors' properties (e.g., intensity, frequency, and duration). Yet these features of the aggression are quite relevant to the behaviorally oriented clinician.

Other existing measures of aggression rely on reports gathered from either the victim or the aggressor's significant other (e.g., Measure of Wife Abuse; Rodenburg & Fantuzzo, 1993; Severity of Violence Against Women Scale; Marshall, 1992). A potential problem with gathering information from these individuals is that they may be motivated either to minimize or to magnify the perpetrator's aggressive behaviors. They even may refuse to participate in the assessment process to avoid consequences related to the alleged perpetrator. Or they may be inaccessible to the evaluating clinician.

Yet another existing strategy to measure aggressive behaviors utilizes information obtained from collateral sources, such as law enforcement personnel and health care professionals. This method also has limitations, for police officers and health care providers often are aware of only a fraction of an individual's aggressive acts. They also tend to become involved only after an aggressive act has transpired and may have little information about the sequence of events that culminated in an aggressive act.

Finally, some existing measures are designed to elicit aggression-related behaviors within the laboratory or for direct clinical observation (e.g., video-taping marital couples' conflictual interactions to determine communication sequences that are associated with marital violence; the bobo doll modeling paradigm; the Taylor aggression paradigm). However, the validity of many of the laboratory aggression paradigms has been criticized (Tedeschi & Quigley, 1996). In addition, clinicians who would typically rely on direct observation of their target behavior have to contend with some of the properties of aggression that make it less amenable to observation. Both physical and sexual aggression generally are low-base-rate events that take place in private. Aggressive acts can be subject to suppression because of social desirability concerns or lack of insight by the perpetrator. It can also be unethical and/or dangerous to provoke acts of aggression or even aggression-related behaviors. Consequently, as a result of the various limitations of any one type of assessment, a multimodal and multi-informant data-collection strategy is often necessary for assessment of aggression in adults.

To further the complexity, even within categories such as self-report instruments, existing measures designed to assess aggression have differed substantially, depending on the type of aggression being considered. For example, already-created instruments tend to assess only physical violence, emotional or psychological aggression, sexual abuse, verbal aggression or threats, patriarchal terrorism, stalking, harassment, or rape. There are relatively few well-developed measures that comprehensively assess multiple forms of aggression (Suris et al., 2004). Perhaps this void is because there has been relatively little cross-pollination among researchers in the various subareas, in spite of the fact that many types of aggression tend to co-occur (Kilpatrick, 2004; McEllistrem, 2004).

This domain-specific segregation of facets of aggression also occurs in clinical settings. For example, a clinician who measures a husband's perpetration of physical violence against his wife might neglect to assess whether there is concurrent child abuse. Some marital therapists do not routinely assess for co-occurring domestic violence, even though research findings suggest that two-thirds of unhappily married couples seeking therapy are likely to be experiencing ongoing aggression (O'Leary, Vivian, & Malone, 1992). And even when domestic violence is obviously present within an intimate relationship, relatively few clinicians habitually assess the co-occurrence of stalking, sexual abuse, or relationship rape in spite of their known associations with intimate-partner violence. Treatment providers for male batterers may not routinely assess the degree to which the wife or victim is also engaging in aggression. This neglect is unfortunate, because the degree to which the aggression is bidirectional and whether it is confined to one victim or is more universal, includes victims who are strangers as well as intimates, or consists of other types of aggression in addition to physical violence have all been shown to be clinically relevant (e.g., Holtzworth-Munroe & Stuart, 1994; Vivian & Langhinrichsen-Rohling, 1994).

## ASSESSMENT STRATEGIES

Therefore, to aid clinicians, we have outlined a model that can be used to assess many types of co-occurring aggression. We believe this model to be flexible enough that it can be used with many different types of clients in various settings where aggression might be a clinically relevant issue. This model may be particularly relevant to nonforensic settings, because many forensic settings mandate use of existing actuarial or structured assessment strategies. Although the presented model is comprehensive (and correspondingly can be time consuming), we assert that the use of a comprehensive model is likely to facilitate a more integrative and effective strategy for assessing aggression for adult outpatients, such as "Betty," "Bob and Sarah," "Ted," and "Stan."

Our conceptual model is graphically presented in Figure 17.1. As illustrated, we suggest that the clinician perform a multilevel functional analysis of aggres-

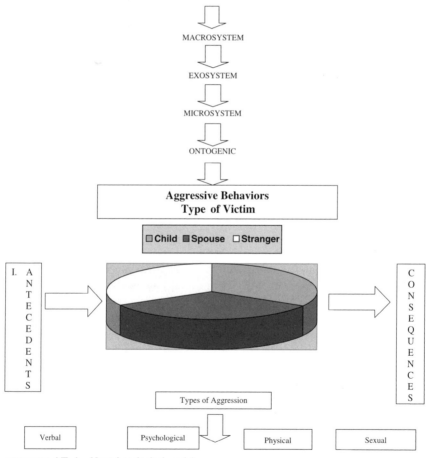

FIGURE 17.1    Nested ecological model.

sion, such as what can occur when aggression is considered within a nested ecological model. Dutton described the nested ecological model in reference to the production of domestic violence in 1995. More recently, Stith, Smith, Penn, Ward, and Tritt (2004) used this model to organize their meta-analytic findings of the risk factors for intimate-partner perpetration. They predicted there would be larger effect sizes for more proximate risk factors and smaller effect sizes for more distal risk factors. This hypothesis was partially supported. Distal factors did have the smallest effect sizes; however, the effect sizes for other levels of the nested ecological model did not differ as much in their associations with the perpetration of intimate-partner violence as predicted. Nonetheless, the Stith et al. paper provides specific data about which variables are most associated, and to what degree, with the perpetration of intimate-partner violence. Data about the risk factors for perpetrating other types of aggressive behavior could be used in a similar fashion (e.g., Hanson & Bussiere's [1998], meta-analysis of risk factors for sexual recidivism).

According to the nested ecological model, there are four levels of importance with regard to the assessment of aggression: (1) the macrosystem, (2) the exosystem, (3) the microsystem, and (4) the ontogenic. The *macrosystem* is the culture in which the individual is embedded and the general values and beliefs that are manifested within the culture. The *exosystem*, the next broadest level of the model, consists of the aggressors' social networks and structures, which would include their workplace, their peer group, and their interactions with the legal structure that connects them to the larger culture. The *microsystem* is the immediate environment in which the aggressive behaviors take place. The family, the marital or relationship dynamics, and the context-specific antecedents and consequences of the aggression are subsumed within the microsystem. Finally, the *ontogenic* level is specific to the perpetrator and, with respect to intimate-partner violence, includes his or her developmental history with respect to aggression and intimacy, alcohol and illicit drug use, ability to empathize, level of depression and anger/hostility, attitudes toward violence, and the degree to which he or she adheres to traditional sex roles (Stith et al., 2004).

Our model depicts how a functional analytic strategy can work in conjunction with a nested ecological approach. The two approaches are shown as orthogonal, to remind the clinician that antecedents can occur at any level in the ecological system, as can consequences. Finally, the model depicts some of the critical and nonoverlapping dimensions of aggression that need to be determined, including the nature of the victim or victims (e.g., stranger, child, spouse, or relationship partner); the type(s) of aggression being perpetrated (e.g., psychological, verbal threats, physical violence, or sexual violence), and the topography of the aggression (e.g., frequency, severity, and first occurrence).

Another important issue emerges, however, when this type of assessment strategy is used. Namely, the clinician will need to determine how to integrate data collected from this flexible assessment strategy. The available data will have been obtained from multiple instruments and informants. Historically, clinicians have

TABLE 17.1　Structured and Actuarial Strategies Used to Assess Aggression

| Name of Strategy | Authors | Type of Risk Assessment | Number of Items | Type of Violence |
|---|---|---|---|---|
| Psychopathy Checklist—Revised (PCL-R) | Hare (2003) | Diagnostic | 20 | Multiple |
| Violence Risk Appraisal Guide (VRAG) | Harris, Rice, & Quinsey (1993) | Actuarial | 12 | General |
| Historical, Clinical, Risk—20 (HCR-20) | Webster, Douglas, Eaves, & Hart (1997) | Structured | 20 | General |
| MacArthur Classification Tree Approach | Monahan et al. (2001) | Actuarial | 134 | General |
| Sexual Violence Risk—20 (SVR-20) | Boer, Hart, Kropp, & Webster (1997) | Structured | 20 | Sexual |
| Minnesota Sex Offender Screening Tool (MnSOST-R) | Epperson et al. (2000) | Actuarial | 16 | Sexual |
| Static—99 | Hanson & Thorton (2000) | Actuarial | 10 | Sexual |
| Sexual Violence Risk Appraisal Guide (SORAG) | Quinsey, Harris, Rice, & Cormier (1998) | Actuarial | 14 | Sexual |
| Danger Assessment Scale (DA) | Campbell (1986) | Actuarial | 12 | Domestic |
| Spousal Assault Risk Assessment (SARA) | Kropp, Hart, Webster, & Eaves (1999) | Structured | 20 | Domestic |
| Ontario Domestic Assault Risk Assessment (ODARA) | Hilton et al. (2004) | Actuarial | 13 | Domestic |
| Domestic Violence Screening Inventory (DVSI) | Williams & Houghton (2004) | Actuarial | 12 | Domestic |
| Rapid Risk Assessment of Sexual Offense Recidivism (RRASOR) | Hanson (1997) | Actuarial | 4 | Sexual |

integrated assessment data using either an actuarial strategy or their own professional and/or personal judgment. Actuarial assessment strategies for aggression or violence have received the bulk of researchers' attention. At the current time, a number of different actuarial strategies have been developed to aid the clinician who has been asked to assess a client's violence potential. Some of the most noteworthy of these strategies are shown in Table 17.1. Structured clinical models also are becoming more commonplace; some of these are also included in Table 17.1. These models are similar to actuarial strategies; however, in the structural assessment, it is recognized that the component of the assessment that is derived via an actuarial approach can be modified by the clinician in reference to idiosyncratic information about the client.

## RESEARCH BASIS

According to the research literature, across many domains, actuarial approaches have been identified as more accurate than clinical strategies of data integration (Dawes, Faust, & Meehl, 1989; Grove & Meehl, 1996).

There are many advantages to using an actuarial or structured assessment strategy. These include helping the clinician be less susceptible to a variety of cognitive biases, such as optimistic overconfidence, framing, and anchoring (Mills, 2005). As the field has advanced, it has become clear that actuarial approaches have significantly improved clinicians' ability to assess aggression and predict risk of future violence or recidivism (e.g., Harris, Rice, & Camilleri, 2004). Less is known about the performance of newer actuarial instruments and the degree to which allowing the clinician to exert judgment, as in the structured assessment approach, aids the prediction process. Structured assessment strategies combine actuarial approaches with clinical judgment. The clinician who can integrate idiosyncratic client-specific information with an existing actuarial risk appraisal determines the final risk estimate.

However, it has not yet been determined if structured assessment strategies will outperform pure actuarial approaches in clinical practice (Mills, 2005). Both approaches rely on empirical research to identify the most relevant risk factors for future aggression. These risk factors are then used to construct a specific instrument with which to conduct the aggression assessment. Thus, actuarial and structured instruments are consistent with the premises of the nested ecological model because they focus on a host of risk variables, including exosystem, microsystem, and ontogenic factors. Use of an existing actuarial instrument also has the advantage of giving clinicians a straightforward way to collapse data to derive an overall risk index, a piece of information that is frequently required in forensic settings and is becoming more standard in nonforensic settings. Also, there is not currently a clinician-friendly way to integrate information gathered from a flexible battery approach of aggression.

The Violence Risk Appraisal Guide (VRAG; Harris, Rice, & Quinsey, 1993) is an actuarial measure of aggression that consists of 12 items often gathered during a clinical interview and/or a thorough review of collateral information (e.g., personality disorder diagnosis, diagnosis of schizophrenia, age at index offense, marital status, and history of substance abuse). The items of the VRAG are weighted so that scores on individual items have a differential impact on the total score. Although the VRAG was originally constructed using the best predictors of violence among mentally ill Canadian offenders, it has since been used successfully with sex offenders (Harris, et al., 1993), criminal offenders awaiting release (e.g., Folino, Marengo, Marchiano, & Ascaziber, 2004), psychiatric patients (e.g., Doyle, Dolan, & McGovern, 2002), child molesters and rapists (Rice & Harris, 1997), and wife assaulters (Hilton, Harris, & Rice, 2001) throughout North America and Europe. Most recently, the VRAG has been used to predict violence committed by women as well as men (Harris, Rice, & Camilleri, 2004). Once the clinician has collected the necessary information, which consists of static and dynamic risk factors, a total score is derived. That score then represents the patient's risk for violence. Clinical judgment is not used to alter the VRAG index score.

The Hare Psychopathy Checklist (PCL-R; Hare, 2003) is a second instrument that has significantly advanced the aggression risk assessment field, though it was not designed to assess risk itself (Mills, 2005). This measure is designed to collect information in order to detect psychopathy. Higher levels of psychopathy have been shown to predict both general criminality and acts of violence (Hemphill, Hare, & Wong, 1998). Although psychopathy has historically been associated only with violent criminal offenders, evidence is mounting that psychopathy is a useful and necessary risk factor for aggression across a variety of populations (e.g., Huss & Langhinrichsen-Rohling, 2000). Psychopathy has been associated with aggression in civil psychiatric patients, rapists and child molesters, and substance abusers across North America, Australia, and Europe (e.g., Alterman, Rutherford, Cacciola, McKay, & Boardman, 1998; Skeem & Mulvey, 2001). Psychopathy has been shown to be a significant risk factor for aggression for women as well as for men and for juveniles as well as for adults (Salekin, Leistico, Neumann, DiCicco, & Duros, 2004; Warren, Burnette, & South, 2003). Consequently, it has been cogently argued that psychopathy should not only be assessed in cases of extreme violence, but it should be included in most comprehensive assessments of aggression (e.g., Huss, Covell, Langhinrichsen-Rohling, in press). Consistent with this premise, the presence of psychopathy comprises one of the 12 items on the VRAG.

Another recent advance in assessment approaches was developed in conjunction with the MacArthur Violence Risk Assessment study (Monahan, 2003). This multisite study examined over 1000 civilly committed psychiatric patients and assessed them with empirically identified risk factors for violence. These risk factors comprised four domains (i.e., dispositional, historical, contextual, and clinical). Responses were then included in an iterative classification tree (ICT). The ICT is based on an interactive model of aggression that allows for multiple and interactive combinations of static and dynamic risk factors. Interestingly, Banks et al. (2004) have found that combining the results of multiple ICTs in a simple unit-weighted model provides far better risk classification and prediction of violence than does any one model by itself. In fact, by combining the results of five ICTs and scoring them from −1 (low risk) to 0 (average risk) to +1 (high risk), these authors generated five separate groups whose sums ran from −5 to +5. Risk Class 1 (i.e., the lowest-risk group), comprised 36.5% of the sample. These individuals accounted for only 1.1% of the violent acts committed by the entire sample over a 20-week period. Risk Group 2 (i.e., a low-risk group) consisted of 26.4% of the sample; these individuals had committed just 7.9% of the violent acts that occurred over the 20-week period. Risk Class 3 (i.e., average risk) consisted of 19.5% of the sample. These individuals committed 23.7% of the violent acts. In Risk Class 4 (i.e., high risk), 10.9% of the sample was placed and they committed 33.8% of the total violent acts. Finally, only 6.7% of the sample fell in Risk Class 5 (i.e., the highest-risk group), but these individuals accounted for 33.5% of the violent acts committed over the 20-week period. Based on these data, the clinician who uses a simple linear combination of multiple actuarial models may substantially increase the accuracy of their violence prediction. This assertion is consistent with the model we are proposing, in that we are encouraging the clinician to assess multiple variables in a variety of contexts in order to generate more accurate aggression predictions and more client-specific treatment recommendations. However, we do not currently offer a precise model for the aggregation of the multiple sources of information, and we encourage clinicians to be mindful of how they use various types of objective data to arrive at a subjective clinical conclusion.

In terms of the model we are recommending, the clinician must rely on both empirical research and the individual characteristics of their patients to identify relevant risk factors. For example, the following have been shown to be high-risk personality traits for being an aggressive versus a nonaggressive substance abuser: impulsivity, novelty seeking, lack of ability to empathize, high levels of hostility, and low frustration tolerance. Cognitive skills related to the perpetration of aggression include: risk perception, conditionability, pain avoidance, lack of foresight, verbal learning ability, and differences in patterns of attention and arousal (Fishbein, 2002). Choices are then made as to which of these risk factors to assess in which patients under what particular clinical conditions.

Likewise, as to men's perpetration of intimate-partner violence, Stith and colleagues' (2004) meta-analysis yielded large effect sizes for five disparate risk factors (i.e., perpetration of emotional abuse, forced sex, illicit drug use, attitudes condoning marital violence, and decreased marital satisfaction). Moderate effect sizes were reported for six risk factors (i.e., traditional sex-role ideology, anger/hostility, history of partner abuse, alcohol use, depression, and career/life stress). A variety of other risk factors were shown to have small associations with perpetration. Typically, static risk factors have been featured in the actuarial strategies. In contrast, this meta-analytic research highlights the importance of assessing dynamic risk factors. Thus, our proposed model incorporates static, dynamic, and situation-specific risk factors in order to enhance the predictive process.

## CLINICAL UTILITY

Despite the research support for increased efficacy associated with utilizing an actuarial instrument to predict a client's potential for future aggression, clinicians, particularly those outside of forensic and correctional settings, have not fully embraced their utility. There are a number of possible reasons. Most of the existing actuarial instruments designate specific information that needs to be collected to generate a risk appraisal. In this way, they are similar to a fixed neuropsychological test battery (e.g., the Halsted Reitan Battery, or HRB), which must be given in a standardized fashion and in its entirety to derive an overall impairment index (e.g., HII: Reitan & Wolfson, 1985; GNDS: Reitan & Wolfson, 1988). Consequently, clinicians are likely to need additional training in order to utilize any of the actuarial strategies. Most are rather time consuming to administer, even after training.

Feasibility also is an issue (Gardner, Lidz, Mulvey, & Shaw, 1996). Information about past legal charges, complete psychiatric history, and the like are not always available to clinicians when violence predictions are imminently necessary (within 24 hours) or when institutional resources are finite. Elbogen, Calkins, Tomkins, and Scalora (2001) identified those risk factors that have been empirically supported. They then investigated whether these risk factors are generally available in clinical practice across several inpatient settings. They found several significant differences in the quantity and quality of information available across different types of settings and suggested that such differences should be taken into account in the construction and implementation of actuarial approaches.

Furthermore, actuarial instruments often do not have ways to include situation-specific risk markers (Hart, 1998). For example, a patient who fails to endorse many of the items related to future aggression on an actuarial measure but states that he will unequivocally act out violently if released would not be easy to quantify on most existing instruments. Many clinicians may also experience frustration because existing actuarial strategies are difficult to modify from one assessment context to another. In fact, this problem has led to research-based modifications of existing actuarial strategies for particular contexts. As shown in Table 17.1, domain-specific actuarial instruments have been constructed for use when assessing domestic violence. Specifically, the Danger Assessment Scale and Spousal Assault Risk Assessment Guide have been two of the more prominent measures identified in the literature (see Dutton & Kropp, 2000, for a review). Likewise, the Sexual Offense Risk Assessment Guide (SORAG) and several other new instruments have been developed for use with potential sex offenders. Though these modifications of existing actuarial strategies are likely to increase predictive accuracy because they are context specific, the proliferation of actuarial instruments may make it even less likely that any one of these instruments will receive widespread use among clinicians.

Another issue of concern is that the gap between empirically recommended guidelines (e.g., using multiple models; Banks et al., 2004) and typical clinical practice may be widening. For example, the risk appraisal literature is increasingly suggesting that simple univariate approaches to the assessment of aggression are faulty and do not represent reality. As a result, more complex methods, such as the MacArthur decision tree model, have been developed. Though these models accommodate the complex interchange and integration of the relevant univariate factors, no clinicians can currently use the complex ICT procedures that are necessary for this approach. The software to perform these operations in a general practice was not commercially available as of the writing of this chapter. Finally, actuarial and structured strategies to assess aggression have been shown to be most useful to help the clinician predict risk for violence or risk of recidivism; however, these strategies were not typically designed to yield suggestions for interventions. For these reasons and others, research has found that most well-known actuarial strategies to assess violence and aggression are infrequently used in nonforensic clinical settings (Elbogen et al., 2001).

Practicing clinicians have been shown to be more likely to use a flexible, client-specific battery for assessment purposes, rather than a fixed actuarial strategy that is time consuming and non-client-specific (e.g., Sweet, Moberg, & Suchy, 2000). Little has been written to date, however, about which existing self-report and observational data-collection strategies might best be utilized by a clinician who hopes to conduct a functional behavioral analysis of a patient's aggression. Even less has been written about how to help clinicians integrate data gathered from a variety of measures that might involve a number of different informants (i.e., information gathered via a flexible battery). This is important because accurate predictions are most likely to occur with the inclusion of both static and dynamic risk factors collected through a multimodal, multi-informant assessment strategy that is summarized in ways that minimize clinical biases (Hanson, 2005). However, recent research has demonstrated that when relevant self-report predictors are utilized, they produce comparable results to the most well-known risk-appraisal procedures, including the HCR-20, the PCL, and the VRAG (Walters, in press). This finding suggests that flexible assessment strategies for aggression may be more useful than was originally anticipated.

Historically, clinical judgment has been used to integrate data gathered from a flexible client-specific strategy. Proponents of clinical integration approaches point to research findings indicating that clinical judgments rise above chance levels for predicting future occurrences of both inpatient and outpatient violence (e.g., Lidz, Mulvey, & Gardner, 1993; McNiel & Binder, 1991). Furthermore, according to Mossman's (1994) meta-analysis of the clinical predictions studies, clinicians can distinguish violent from nonviolent patients at modest, yet above-chance, levels. Nonetheless, clinical judgments about which patient will be violent have continued to be criticized because, although they may be accurate in some instances, they appear to be inferior to actuarial predictions in the aggregate (Mills, 2005; Quinsey et al., 1998).

Recently, a few researchers from different fields have proposed strategies that rely on statistical methods to integrate data gathered via a flexible battery. In fact, two of the three authors of the present chapter have been collaborating on a system of data integration and interpretation in the area of neuropsychology. The Rohling Interpretive Method (RIM; Miller & Rohling, 2001; Rohling, Miller, & Langhinrichsen-Rohling, 2004) is designed to combine data from an individual patient that have been generated during a neuropsychological assessment, using meta-analytic techniques to improve on the diagnostic skills of neuropsychologists. This process will then lead to better treatment planning for individuals who may be impaired by a neurological disease or brain injury caused by trauma. Flanagan and colleagues have generated a similar approach (e.g., Flanagan & Ortiz, 2001; McGrew & Flanagan, 1998) in the field of academic assessment and learning disabilities. These researchers have called their system the Cattell–Horn–Carroll (CHC) Cross-Battery (CB) approach, which is similar to the RIM, in that it involves the combination of test scores across domains of assessment to improve the reliability and validity to individual assessments, particularly when the assessments involve the administration of multiple instruments designed to assess the same construct.

Therefore, using our couple "Bob & Sarah" as our first example, we will describe some of the assessment instruments that could be used to assess aggression by a behaviorally oriented clinician who is practicing in an outpatient setting and utilizing a flexible assessment battery. It should be noted that the specific details of this couple have been changed to protect their privacy and that it would be most accurate to consider this case an amalgam of clients this chapter's authors have treated. Because of the level of unhappiness in the marriage, the treating marital therapist is concerned about the potential presence of aggression within the marriage but is not planning to utilize an existing actuarial assessment strategy to determine risk of violence. Instead, if aggression is occurring, the clinician is planning to conduct a functional analysis of behavior of the aggressive acts to determine if this couple is appropriate for conjoint therapy. This assessment strategy will be demonstrated. We will then suggest some methods of integrating the obtained assessment data in order to answer the following referral questions: (1) Is there aggression occurring in this marriage? (2) Can this couple be safely treated using conjoint therapy? (3) What is the function of the aggression? (4) What sequence of events triggers aggressive episodes? (5) What strategies are recommended for intervention?

As shown in Table 17.2, the clinician would first assess the degree to which any of the following types of aggression are occurring in the marriage (physical, sexual, and verbal). For each occurring type of aggression, it will be important to determine the frequency of occurrence and the severity of the aggressive acts being perpetrated. Because the aggressive acts are occurring within the marital context, similar measures will be given to both spouses in order to determine whether the aggression is being perpetrated in a uni- or a bidirectional fashion. Assessing each spouse also provides the clinician with information about the congruence of perceptions between the spouses. Clinically, it will also be relevant to determine whether there are relatives (i.e., children, other adults, etc.) who are

TABLE 17.2  Nested Ecological Strategy to Assess Intimate-Partner Aggression Contextually in Adults

| | Self-Report | Victim Report | Observational | Collateral Information | Functional Assessment of Aggression |
|---|---|---|---|---|---|
| *Aggressive Behaviors* | | | | | |
| Frequency, intensity | CTS2, AQ | X | | | X |
| Types of behaviors, victims, triggers, impact | PAVE | X | | | X |
| | | | | | |
| *Ontogenic* | | | | | |
| Mental health/ personality | MMPI, MCMI | | | X | |
| Anger/hostility | MAI, AQ, Novaco, STAXI | | X | | |
| Attitudes/beliefs re violence | Acceptance of Interpersonal | | | | |
| | Violence Scale, Inventory of Beliefs about Wife Beating | | | | |
| Empathy, responsibility | Interpersonal Reactivity Index | | | | |
| Substance Use | MAST, SASSI, DAST | X | | X | X |
| | | | | | |
| *Microsystem* | | | | | |
| Level of marital distress | DAS, SMAT, IMS | X | 10 min. conflict interaction | | |
| Jealousy | IJS | X | X | | X |
| Stalking | UPBI | X | | | |
| History of childhood abuse | MCTS, CTQ | X | | X | |
| | | | | | |
| *Exosystem* | | | | | |
| Work history/career | X | X | | X | |
| Income | X | X | | X | |
| Age | X | X | | X | |
| History of legal involvement | | X | | X | |
| History of general violence | | X | | X | |
| | | | | | |
| *Macrosystem* | | | | | |
| Community response to domestic violence | | | X | X | |

involved in the marital problems and/or who are additional participants in the aggression. Most importantly, if particular types of aggression are occurring in the marriage, it will be necessary to determine (1) the context in which each type of aggression is taking place, (2) the function of the aggression, and (3) the antecedents and consequences of all the aggressive behaviors.

As shown in Table 17.2, one of the most prominent measures with which to begin a couple-oriented aggression assessment process would be the Conflict Tactics Scale-2 (CTS-2; Straus et al., 1996). However, another useful measure might be the Aggression Questionnaire (AQ; Buss & Warren, 2000). The AQ is relatively brief and has good psychometric properties. It yields a total score and five subscale scores that assess physical aggression, verbal aggression, anger, hostility, and indirect aggression. An inconsistent-response index can also be derived from the AQ. For a review of other existing measures of aggressive behavior that could be employed, see Feindler, Rathus, and Silver (2003) or Suris et al. (2004).

A functional assessment of aggression would be addressed via a clinical interview or with the aid of the Proximal Antecedents to Violent Episodes Scale (PAVE; Babcock, Costa, Green, & Eckhardt, 2004). The PAVE consists of 30 situations. For each item, the respondent answers the question "How likely are you to be physically aggressive in each of the following situations?" Research with 162 male batterers and 110 couples indicated that the PAVE differentiated among batterer subtypes. Factor analysis revealed three types of motivations among spouses who perpetrate aggression: using violence to control, violence that occurs out of jealousy, and violence following verbal abuse and relationship distress— including as consequence to the partner's threats of divorce. In a related article about battering incidents, Sirles, Lipchik, and Kowalski (1993) rank-order problems rated to violence. According to the perpetrators, they are alcohol abuse, jealousy, disagreements about children, sexual problems, rejection by their partners, and drug-related problems. Victims listed alcohol abuse, money problems, and jealousy as the top three problems leading to relationship violence.

The ontogenic level is next in the nested ecological model. With regards to intimate-partner aggression, important variables at this level include the spouses' level of anger and hostility, existing mental health issues such as depression, personality characteristics, attitudes and beliefs regarding violence, the degree to which each spouse can express empathy or take responsibility for his or her behavior, and the level of substance abuse that is occurring.

Regarding anger and hostility, some have suggested that there are distinct developmental pathways that lead to different types of aggression (i.e., authority conflict, overt aggression, and covert aggression; Loeber & Loeber, 1998). Anger and hostility may have different roles in these various developmental pathways (Buss & Warren, 2000). The State–Trait Anger Scale (STAXI; Spielberger, Jacobs, Russell, & Crane, 1983), the Multidimensional Anger Inventory (Siegel, 1986), and the Novaco Anger Scale (Novaco, 1994) are measures of anger that could be utilized in an aggression assessment, if the clinician wanted more than the anger scale of the AQ. Observational data could also be collected via

Eckhardt's articulated thoughts in stimulated situations; data garnered during this observation can also be coded for aggression (Eckhardt, Norlander, & Deffenbacher, 2004).

The relationship between violence and mental illness/psychopathology continues to be a subject of some controversy (e.g., Daffern & Howells, 2002). On the one hand, most mentally ill people are not violent. On the other hand, particular mental illnesses expressed at certain levels of severity have been shown to increase the risk of aggression (Swanson, 1994). In particular, psychosis has repeatedly been demonstrated to be a risk factor for violence. Depression is also associated with both perpetrating and being victimized by intimate-partner violence and should be assessed accordingly (Stith et al., 2004). There are a number of well-validated self-report and interview measures for this purpose.

Personality disorders also are related to the perpetration of intimate-partner violence. For example, abusers have been shown to have higher rates of antisocial, aggressive-sadistic, passive-aggressive, and narcissistic personality disorders than nonabusers (Craig, 2003). The presence and extent of psychopathology can be determined in a number of ways, including such self-report measures as the MMPI-2 and the MCMI-III (Craig), clinical interview, and by using a number of individual measures of aspects of personality or psychopathology.

Attitudes and beliefs about violence would generally be assessed with a self-report measure such as the Acceptance of Interpersonal Violence Scale (Burt, 1980) or the Inventory of Beliefs about Wife Beating (Saunders, Lynch, Grayson, & Linz, 1987). Recent research indicates that the ability to empathize with another and the ability to take responsibility for one's behavior may also be important protective factors for intimate-partner violence (Covell et al., in press). Specifically, overall emotional numbing appears to increase the risk for general violence (Covell et al.). These characteristics also can be assessed via existing self-report instruments (e.g., Interpersonal Reactivity Index; Davis, 1980) or a clinical interview.

Presence of substance abuse is another important ontogenic factor to assess, because of its ability to potentiate violence. The Michigan Alcohol Screening Test (MAST; Selzer, 1971), the Drug Abuse Screening Test (DAST; Skinner, 1995), and the Substance Abuse Subtle Screening Inventory—3 (SASSI-III; F. G. Miller & Lazowski, 1999) are all standardized measures useful in assessing substance abuse. Spouses should report their own drinking level and their partner's drinking level.

Other important variables occur at the microsystem level. With regard to the perpetration of intimate-partner violence, the co-occurrence of marital or relationship satisfaction emerges as important. The Dyadic Adjustment Scale (DAS; Spanier, 1976), the Short Marital Adjustment Test (SMAT; Locke & Wallace, 1959), and the Index of Marital Satisfaction (IMS; Hudson, 1982) are just some of the measures that can be used to assess relationship satisfaction.

Recent research also highlights the associations that jealousy and unwanted pursuit behaviors during times of separation have with the production of intimate-partner violence (Stith et al., 2004; Babcock et al., 2004). One commonly used measure of jealousy is the Interpersonal Jealousy Scale (IJS; Mathes & Severa, 1981). It is also possible to observe the client's responses to hypothetical jealousy producing scenarios (e.g., Murphy, Meyer, & O'Leary, 1994). Previous research also has related the perpetration of unwanted pursuit behaviors to intimate-partner violence. This type of behavior can be assessed with the Unwanted Pursuit Behavior Inventory (UPBI; Langhinrichsen-Rohling, Palarea, et al., 2000).

A large body of research indicates that a family history of child abuse or witnessing parental violence is another microsystem factor associated with the perpetration of intimate aggression (Stith et al., 2000). This history can be assessed via clinical interview or collateral sources or by using modifications of the Conflict Tactics Scale (Straus et al., 1996).

Several exosystem variables also have been shown to be associated with the perpetration of intimate-partner violence. These variables include current employment status and work history, age, history of legal involvement, and history of generalized violence. As shown in Table 17.2, these factors are most frequently assessed via simple self-report questions or by accessing collateral sources.

Macrosystem variables include the community's typical response to domestic violence, including standard interventions/sanctions imposed by the legal system. Knowledge of the person's ethnicity and that subculture's sex-role expectations and aggression-related attributions would also be important because these may function as antecedents and/or regulate the consequences to the aggressive behaviors.

The same assessment strategy used in our first case study will then be utilized with our second case "Betty," in order to demonstrate how this model can be modified for another type of clinical situation. For both cases, assessment data were collected via an intake interview, self-report measures, and observation; the purpose of the assessment was to aid the treating clinician. The intake interview gathered data related to the client's current symptoms (e.g., history of presenting problem, duration, onset, intensity, frequency, and context); coping strategies and resources; family, educational, and relational history; medical and mental health history; risk issues; prior trauma or abuse history; substance abuse history; past treatment; expectations of therapy; and co-occurring psychological problems not mentioned in the initial presenting problem (as recommended by Ey & Hersen, 2004). Consistent with research conducted by Hamberger and Lohr (1997), motivations for aggression were assessed with the following question: "What is or was the function, purpose, or payoff of your aggressive behavior?" Clarification was provided if this question was not immediately understood. With regard to the functional assessment, our model was that each spouse has certain vulnerabilities (both state and trait) to aggression, but aggression will only manifest itself given a certain sequence that includes a prompting event, or "trigger." The consequences of the event will, in turn, either increase or decrease the probabilities that those acts will occur again under similar situations.

## CASE STUDY 1

### IDENTIFICATION

Bob and Sarah are in their early 40s. They have been married for 12 years and have four young children of their own. Both have professional degrees. Bob owns a small company in town that has a history of being financially lucrative, whereas Sarah works from an office located in their home. They have been quite social and are well known in their community for being a "happy" couple.

### PRESENTING COMPLAINTS

In contrast to their public persona, the couple described the marriage as consisting of a long series of "out-of-hand" arguments with little emotional or physical intimacy. Their presenting complaints included a desire to stop the frequent and intense fighting, to increase their ability to communicate with each other, to reestablish physical intimacy (Bob), to increase trust (Sarah and Bob), and to parent their children more effectively.

### HISTORY

Sarah has been in individual therapy for depression and anxiety for a number of years. She indicated that she was currently "self-medicating" with alcohol and prescription anxiolytics. Recently, Sarah told Bob that she had had a long-lasting "affair" with a former colleague, who also was married. Sarah had terminated this relationship a year before her disclosure to Bob, but was unsure whether she had enough feelings left for Bob to rejuvenate their marriage. Bob stated that he blamed the affair on the colleague, who he believed exploited Sarah's respect for his professional accomplishments and her vulnerability due to depression and marital dissatisfaction. He assigned little blame to Sarah during the intake session. Bob also indicated that he had been married briefly before but that his first marriage had ended following his first wife's miscarriage. He said that he is desperate to make this second marriage last.

### PEER AND WORK ISSUES

Bob's job involved a great deal of responsibility and long hours. Sarah expressed dissatisfaction that she often did not seem to be a priority in Bob's life. Bob's career choice also required him to be the "expert" and someone who is often "in control." This was an interpersonal style that he generalized to other areas of his life, including his marriage. Historically, Bob had been the family's primary wage earner. However, due to changes in the local business climate, his income significantly decreased over the past two years. He expressed a great deal of concern regarding the couple's changing financial situation and stated that he was dissatisfied with his ability to provide his family the lifestyle to which they had become accustomed. He also was angry that Sarah seemed to be oblivious to their financial problems and spent large amounts of money without consulting him.

Sarah also worked long hours, but her work involved less interaction with other people and more creativity and artistic expression. She reported that she experienced a great deal of stress trying to carve out time for her work. Sarah felt lonely due to her lack of interaction with people outside of their home. As therapy began, however, Sarah's job had become increasingly financially successful and she was being offered greater professional opportunities. Sarah believed that Bob was threatened by this turn of events. Sarah had several friends, who also were quite artistic. Sarah socialized with these women infrequently and never with Bob alone.

## BEHAVIORAL ASSESSMENT RESULTS
### (INCLUDING FUNCTIONAL ASSESSMENT)

In the year prior to treatment, Bob had twice grabbed Sarah during an argument and forcibly held her down to prevent her from leaving their home. Sarah sustained red marks on her arms and shoulders during both of these episodes. However, she sought no medical attention for herself following these altercations. Furthermore, during the heat of one argument, Bob verbally threatened Sarah, saying, "I'll never let you leave me." As is common in many maritally aggressive couples, Sarah had also engaged in violence directed toward Bob. Specifically, on approximately five different occasions over this same time period, Sarah had thrown household objects (e.g., a cell phone, a book, a lamp) at Bob while they were arguing. Both spouses reported that no acts of sexual aggression had occurred in their marriage.

To consider the situational antecedents of these aggressive acts, both Bob and Sarah completed the PAVE (Babcock et al., 2004). Results indicated that Bob's aggressive behavior is most likely to occur in response to his feelings of jealousy. Specifically, Sarah's threats of leaving him and seeking a divorce preceded both of his acts of aggression. In contrast, Sarah's acts of aggression all followed verbal conflicts between her and Bob in which she felt invalidated and belittled.

In keeping with the nested ecological model, a variety of other self-report measures were administered to assess the relevant ontogenic and microsystem factors related to the aggression. These measures indicated that both Sarah and Bob were experiencing mild depression: Bob scored a 14 on the BDI-II and Sarah scored a 16. With regard to marital distress, Sarah's DAS scores were in the low

80s, which is in the distressed range. However, Bob's was just barely in the nondistressed range (DAS = 101) and was significantly discrepant from Sarah's. Alcohol use scores were elevated for both Bob and Sarah. Sarah reported drinking four to five glasses of wine during the day, every day. She stated that this helped her "numb out." Bob drank between four and six mixed drinks at least one night per week. He also drank a glass of wine every night with dinner. Both spouses agreed that their worse fights had occurred when Bob and Sarah had had considerable amounts to drink.

Bob scored high on jealousy; Sarah did not. Both scored high on measures of hostility and anger; however, neither partner endorsed attitudes indicating acceptance of interpersonal violence, and both were congruent in their reports of their own and their partner's aggressive behaviors.

According to Sarah, the consequences of Bob's aggressive acts are that she is afraid to leave him and yet feels more and more emotionally withdrawn. Furthermore, Sarah said that immediately after Bob's aggression she was more frightened of him and what he might do, particularly with regard to their children. Therefore, she would try harder to keep him calm. Bob said that the purpose of his aggression was to keep Sarah from leaving but that he felt very guilty afterwards. He attempted to make amends by expressing romantic interests toward Sarah, which Sarah consistently rebuffed. He realized that one of the consequences of his aggression was keeping Sarah in the marriage; this both pleased and saddened him.

According to Bob, there were no obvious consequences to Sarah's physical acts of aggression. He stated that she "has a weak arm" and none of her "throwing" could ever hurt him. Sarah indicated she felt frustrated following her aggressive acts, because she was trying to get Bob to pay more attention to her point of view. However, she thought that he never "got the point," despite her extreme behavior toward him. Despite this outcome, she too felt guilty about her violent behavior and frequently promised herself that it would never happen again. Bob found Sarah's verbal aggression the most distressing, particularly her threats of divorce.

## ETHICAL AND LEGAL ISSUES OR COMPLICATIONS

There are several issues of concern in this case. First, although aggression is a common concomitant of marital distress, intense debate exists about the degree to which violent couples should be treated conjointly. In fact, in some states conjoint treatment is prohibited if there is any evidence of marital violence (Heyman & Schlee, 2003). However, Vivian and Langhinrichsen-Rohling (1994) and others have argued that couples who present for treatment with bidirectional aggression may be candidates for conjoint therapy. Furthermore, proponents of conjoint therapy for couple violence argue that there are individual, dyadic, and social determinants for aggression and the most efficacious therapy will address all the determinants. Similarly, rewards for aggression occur both at the individual and at the dyadic level; therefore, changes must also occur at both of these levels (Heyman & Schlee).

Second, the presence of three children in the home raises concerns about co-occurring child abuse. At intake, both Bob and Sarah denied perpetrating any aggressive acts toward their children. However, Sarah is concerned that the children are being affected by the marital tension and frequent arguments. Bob believes that one of the children witnessed Sarah throwing her cell phone at him.

Third, one of the complications in this case, which is not unusual in marital cases similar to this, is that neither spouse considered the aggression to be the primary problem (Feldbau-Kohn, O'Leary, & Schumacher, 2000). Both spouses were more concerned about the lack of intimacy and affection, their poor communication skills, and the constant bickering. Both were also concerned about their children and felt they were ineffective parents.

## CONCEPTUALIZATION AND TREATMENT RECOMMENDATIONS

When working with a violent couple, safety issues must be addressed first, and, regardless of the patient's self-goals, cessation of the aggression must be a priority (Feldbau-Kohn et al., 2000). Couples that experience severe and/or unilateral aggression are typically best served by another approach. Goals of conjoint therapy for aggression would differ from those of traditional marital therapy (e.g., Physical Aggression Couples Program, PACT; Heyman & Schlee, 2003). This program works best in couples in which the aggression is linked to anger control, stress management, and communication deficits that include high levels of hostility and negative reciprocity patterns (Heyman & Schlee). The therapy would include a focus on how each spouse might be contributing to the escalation of discord into aggression. Skills training would involve recognizing and controlling self-angering thoughts, using self-calming and acceptance strategies in situations of intense emotion, increased communication skills, increased positive activities, and strategies to stop chains of negativity (e.g., time out). Although this format for treating intimate-partner aggression is controversial, researchers have demonstrated that this type of intervention is effective (O'Leary, Heyman, & Neidig, 1999). Furthermore, traditional marital therapy might be implemented after the cessation of the aggression.

## CASE STUDY 2

This next case highlights how this strategy can be used with an individual client (i.e., "Betty") in an outpatient setting.

# IDENTIFICATION

Betty is a single 42-year-old Caucasian woman who presented to therapy because of difficulties managing her anger and getting along with her mother. Betty is unemployed. She supports herself with a monthly disability check and with supplemental income from odd jobs completed for her mother.

# PRESENTING COMPLAINTS

Betty wanted help letting go of past grievances that she thought about constantly. She also wanted to be less angry and have a less volatile relationship with her mother. Betty also indicated that she was lonely and would like to develop a long-lasting and trustworthy intimate relationship. She thought this would be most likely to occur if she lost weight by starting an exercise program.

# HISTORY

Betty had been hospitalized twice for mental health problems, 3 years prior to intake and 7 years prior to intake. Both hospitalizations were inpatient. Both times, Betty was committed because she was judged to be a danger to others. At the time of the second hospitalization, Betty had driven onto a military base and assaulted a guard who was trying to help her. She grabbed him around the throat and screamed threats and obscenities at him.

Betty reports never knowing her father. Her mother raised Betty and her sister, who is two years older than Betty. Betty indicated that her sister is extremely bright but is currently working at a job that fails to utilize her capabilities. Betty never felt emotionally supported by her mother, who was physically and verbally abusive toward her. Betty also witnessed her mother being physically abused by several of her boyfriends. Despite their conflictual relationship, Betty's mother currently supports her financially and Betty indicated that she would not hesitate to hurt anyone who hurt her mother.

Betty has had several important romantic relationships. Each ended badly. The last one ended when Betty discovered that her live-in boyfriend was cheating on her in their home. During these relationships, Betty had gotten pregnant twice. She terminated both pregnancies because she believed she could not successfully nurture a child. Betty also has a dog that was a very important part of her social network.

# PEER AND WORK ISSUES

Betty is not currently working on a consistent basis. She has occasional odd jobs from her mother. She also receives a small monthly disability check that is related to the brief time she spent in the military. Betty reports having no close friends. Although she loves her sister, she believes that her sister and mother talk about her critically whenever they can. Therefore, she makes little effort to contact her sister. She also expresses resentment that her mother tells everyone about "her problems" and warns them about her temper and unpredictability. She feels that this information should be private and that it is interfering with her making any new friends.

## BEHAVIORAL ASSESSMENT RESULTS
### (INCLUDING FUNCTIONAL ASSESSMENT)

Though Betty denied any current acts of physical or sexual violence, her verbal aggression was apparent throughout the intake. For example, Betty used the pronoun "it" to describe people she disliked or had distain for; she also described having many urges of "throwing" people up against the wall and choking them. Betty indicated that her anger was intense, quick to occur, and long-lasting. Triggers for her anger include her mother complaining to Betty about her life, her mother interfering with Betty's life, and situations in which she perceived service people to be incompetent. Betty denied acting on her aggressive impulses; however, interviews with Betty's mother indicated that she felt quite frightened when Betty used highly aggressive language in a harsh and loud tone of voice. Betty seemed surprised and hurt that her mother indicated that she was afraid of her, for Betty felt confident she would never actually hurt anyone ("because the bad guy always gets caught and goes to jail"). Betty indicated that her aggressive words functioned to let people know she was "losing it." Threatening her mother also resulted in Betty's getting the space that she wanted, because after an angry exchange Betty's mother would withdraw from her for periods of days or even weeks.

At the macroscopic level, the proactive community-wide stance against violence served as a protective factor for Betty's aggression. At the exosystem level, Betty's history was positive for general violence and for legal involvement related to her aggression. However, her age was serving as a protective factor because she felt that she had been around long enough to know that assaulting someone was only going to get her locked up in the hospital or in jail. Her inability to support herself financially and her reliance on her mother for money constituted an exosystem risk factor. Self-report assessment of microsystem factors indicated risk generated by many ongoing and unspoken conflicts in Betty's relationship with her mother. Another microsystem risk factor was Betty's history of childhood abuse and maltreatment. At the ontogenic level, Betty's assertive communication skills were poor, as were her problem-solving and conflict-negotiation communication skills. Betty also endorsed many anger-producing distorted thoughts and scored high on multiple types of anger and hostility. Betty had a history of mental health problems, including psychosis, and had many personality disturbances; however, she did not use alcohol or other illicit substances and took her prescribed medication faithfully. On interview, Betty took relatively little responsibility for her behavior and was unable to consider other people's points of view.

## ETHICAL AND LEGAL ISSUES OR COMPLICATIONS

The main concern in this case was whether Betty posed a significant risk to others that would warrant inpatient intervention. Correspondingly, the clinician was concerned about whether there was a duty to warn individuals toward whom Betty was expressing violent thoughts. However, Betty consistently indicated that she would not act on her violent thoughts and felt confident she could control her aggressive impulses, as long as she was being appropriately medicated for her psychosis.

## CONCEPTUALIZATION AND TREATMENT RECOMMENDATIONS

Treatment consisted of helping Betty dispute her anger-producing thoughts. Alternative behaviors were generated for high-stress situations. Assertive (versus passive or aggressive) communication strategies were practiced, and their effects on other people were noted. Joint sessions were held with Betty's mother to help Betty express her concerns more openly and appropriately. Betty also developed a larger social support network, and she initiated a daily diet and exercise program.

## SUMMARY

Assessing aggression is a complex task that differs depending on the nature of the client being assessed, the type of aggression taking place, and the situations in which the aggression is occurring. Assessment also is affected by the role of the clinician (e.g., an assessor for the court or a treatment provider). In this chapter, we have provided a model that helps the clinician consider a variety of variables occurring at multiple levels that may be functioning either to increase or decrease the probability of aggression. Two divergent case studies predicated on this model were then described. Although a statistical strategy does not currently exist to help the clinician integrate data gathered via a flexible battery, this type of strategy has been developed in related areas and is likely soon to be applied to the assessment of aggression in adults.

## REFERENCES

Alterman, A. I., Rutherford, M. J., Cacciola, J. S., McKay, J. R., & Boardman, C. R. (1998). Prediction of 7 months methadone maintenance treatment response by four measures of antisociality. *Drug & Alcohol Dependence, 49,* 217–223.

Babcock, J. C., Costa, D. M., Green, C. E., & Eckhardt, C. I. (2004). What situations induce intimate partner violence?: A reliability and validity study. *Journal of Family Psychology, 18,* 433–442.

Banks, S., Robbins, P. C., Silver, E., Vesselinov, R., Steadman, H. J., Monahan, J., et al. (2004). A multiple-models approach to violence risk assessment among people with mental disorder. *Criminal Justice and Behavior, 31,* 324–340.

Boer, D. P., Hart, S. D., Kropp, P. R., & Webster, C. D. (1997). *Manual for the Sexual Violence Risk—20. Professional guidelines for assessing risk of sexual violence.* Vancouver, Canada: British Columbia Institute on Family Violence.

Burt, M. (1980). Cultural myths and supports for rape. *Journal of Personality and Social Psychology, 38,* 217–230.

Buss, A. H., & Warren, W. L. (2000). *Aggression Questionnaire.* Los Angeles: Western Psychological Services.

Campbell, J. C. (1986). Nursing assessment for risk of homicide with battered women. *Advances in Nursing Science, 8,* 36–51.

Cascardi, M., Langhinrichsen, J., & Vivian, D. (1992). Marital aggression: Impact, injury, and health correlates for husbands and wives. *Archives of Internal Medicine, 152,* 1178–1184.

Covell, C. N., Huss, M. T., & Langhinrichsen-Rohling, J. (in press). Empathic deficits among male batterers: A multidimensional approach. *Journal of Family Violence.*

Craig, R. J. (2003). Use of the Millon Clinical Multiaxial Inventory in the psychological assessment of domestic violence: A review. *Aggression and Violent Behavior, 8,* 235–243.

Daffern, M., & Howells, K. (2002). Psychiatric inpatient aggression: A review of structural and functional assessment approaches. *Aggression and Violent Behavior, 7,* 477–497.

Davis, M. H. (1980). A multidimensional approach to individual differences in empathy. *Catalog of Selected Documents in Psychology, 10,* 85.

Dawes, R. M., Faust, D., & Meehl, P. E. (1989). *Science, 243,* 1668–1674.

DiGiuseppe, R., Tafrate, R., & Eckhardt, C. (1994). Critical issues in the treatment of anger. *Cognitive and Behavioral Practice, 1,* 111–132.

Doyle, M., Dolan, M., & McGovern, J. (2002). The validity of North American risk assessment tools in predicting inpatient violent behavior in England. *Legal and Criminological Psychology, 7,* 141–154.

Dutton, D. G. (1995). The domestic assault of women: Psychological criminal justice perspectives. Vancovver, BC: UBC Press.

Dutton, D. G., & Kropp, P. R. (2000). A review of domestic violence risk instruments. *Trauma, Violence, & Abuse, 1,* 171–181.

Eckhard, C., Norlander, B., & Deffenbacher, J. (2004). The assessment of anger and hostility: A critical review. *Aggression and Violent Behavior, 9,* 17–43.

Elbogen, E. B., Calkins, C., Tomkins, A. J., & Scalora, M. (2001). Clinical practice and violence risk assessment: Availability of MacArthur risk cues in psychiatric settings. In D. Farrington, C. Hollins, & M. McMurran (Eds.). *Sex and violence: The psychology of crime and risk assessment,* (pp. 38–55). Routledge: London.

Epperson, D. L., Kaul, J. D., Huot, S. J., Hesselton, D., Alexander, W., & Goldman, R. (2000). *Minnesota Sex Offender Screening Tool—Revised: Development, performance, and recommended risk level cutoff scores.* Unpublished manuscript.

Ey, S., & Hersen, M. (2004). Pragmatic issues in assessment of clinical practice. In M. Hersen (Ed.), *Psychological assessment in clinical practice* (pp. 3–20). New York: Brunner-Routledge.

Feindler, E. L., Rathus, J. H., & Silver, L B. (2003). *Assessment of family violence.* Washington, DC: American Psychological Association.

Feldbau-Kohn, S., O'Leary, K. D., & Schumacher, J. A. (2000). Partner abuse. In V. B. Van Hasselt & M. Hersen (Eds.), *Aggression and violence* (pp. 116–134). Needham Heights, MA: Allyn & Bacon.

Fishbein, D. (2002, October). Neuropsychological and emotional functioning in substance abusers with and without aggression: Implications for treatment workshop presented at the 22nd Annual National Academy of Neuropsychology conference, Miami Beach, FL.

Flanagan, D. P., & Ortiz, S. O. (2001). *Essentials of cross-battery assessment.* New York: John Wiley & Sons.

Folino, J. O., Marengo, C. M., Marchiano, S. E., & Ascaziber, M. (2004). The Risk Assessment Program and the Court of Penal Execution in the Province of Buenos Aires, Argentina. *International Journal of Offender Therapy and Comparative Criminology, 48,* 49–58.

Gardner, W., Lidz, C. W., Mulvey, E. P., & Shaw, E. C. (1996). A comparison of actuarial methods for identifying repetitively violent patients with mental illnesses. *Law and Human Behavior, 20,* 602–609.

Giancola, P. R., & Chermack, S. T. (1998). Construct validity of laboratory aggression paradigms: A response to Tedeschi and Quigley (1996). *Aggression and Violent Behavior, 3,* 237–253.

Grove, W., & Meehl, P. (1996). Comparative efficacy of informal (subjective, impressionistic) and formal (mechanical, algorithmic) prediction procedures: The clinical-statistical controversy. *Psychology, Public Policy, and Law, 2,* 293–323.

Hamberger, L. K., & Lohr, J. M. (1997). An empirical classification of motivations for domestic violence. *Violence Against Women, 3,* 401–424.

Hanson, R. K. (1997). *The development of a brief actuarial risk scale for sexual offense recidivism.* Ottawa, Ontario, Canada: Department of the Solicitor General of Canada.

Hanson, R. K. (2005). Twenty years of progress in violence risk assessment. *Journal of Interpersonal Violence, 20,* 212–217.

Hanson, R. K., & Bussiere, M. T. (1998). Predicting relapse: A meta-analysis of sexual offender recidivism studies. *Journal of Consulting and Clinical Psychology, 66,* 348–362.

Hanson, R. K., & Thornton, D. (2000). Improving risk assessments for sex offenders: A comparison of three actuarial scales. *Law and Human Behavior, 24,* 119–136.

Hare, R. D. (2003). *Hare Psychopathy Checklist—Revised (PCL-R)* (2nd ed.). Toronto, Ontario, Canada: Multi-Health System.

Harris, G. T., Rice, M. E., & Camilleri, J. A. (2004). Applying a forensic actuarial assessment (the Violence Risk Appraisal Guide) to nonforensic patient. *Journal of Interpersonal Violence, 19,* 1063–1074.

Harris, G. T., Rice, M. E., & Quinsey, V. L. (1993). Violent recidivism of mentally disordered offenders: The development of a statistical prediction instrument. *Criminal Justice & Behavior, 20,* 315–335.

Hart, S. (1998). The role of psychopathy in assessing risk for violence: Conceptual and methodological issues. *Legal and Criminological Psychology, 3,* 121–137.

Hemphill, J. F., Hare, R. D., & Wong, S. (1998). Psychopathy and recidivism: A review. *Legal and Criminological Psychology, 3,* 139–170.

Heyman, R. E., & Schlee, K. (2003). Stopping wife abuse via physical aggression couples treatment. *Journal of Aggression, Maltreatment, & Trauma, 7,* 135–157.

Hilton, N. Z., Harris, G. T., & Rice, M. E. (2001). Predicting violence by serious wife assaulters. *Journal of Interpersonal Violence, 16,* 408–423.

Hilton, N. Z., Harris, G. T., Rice, M. E., Lang, C., Cormier, C. A., & Lines, K. J. (2004). A brief actuarial assessment for the prediction of wife assault recidivism: The Ontario Domestic Assault Risk Assessment. *Psychological Assessment, 16,* 267–275.

Holtzworth-Munroe, A., & Stuart, G. L. (1994). Typologies of male batterers: Three subtypes and the differences among them. *Psychological Bulletin, 116,* 476–497.

Hudson, W. W. (1982). *The clinical measurement package: A field manual.* Homewood, IL: Dorsey Press.

Huss, M. T., & Langhinrichsen-Rohling, J. (2000). Identification of the psychopathic batterer: The clinical, legal, and policy implications. *Aggression and Violent Behavior, 5,* 403–422.

Huss, M. T., Covell, C. N., & Langhinrichsen-Rohling, J. (in press). Clinical implications for the assessment and treatment of antisocial and psychopathic domestic violence perpetrators. *Journal of Aggression, Maltreatment, & Trauma.*

Kilpatrick, D. G. (2004). What is violence against women? Defining and measuring the problem. *Journal of Interpersonal Violence, 19,* 1209–1234.

Koss, M. P., Gidycz, C. A., & Wisniewski, N. (1987). The scope of rape: Incidence and prevalence of sexual aggression and victimization in a national sample of higher education students. *Journal of Consulting and Clinical Psychology, 55,* 162–170.

Kroner, D. G. (2005). Issues in violent risk assessment: Lessons learned and future directions. *Journal of Interpersonal Violence, 20,* 231–235.

Kropp, P. R., Hart, S. D., Webster, C. D., & Eaves, D. (1999). *Spousal Assault Risk Assessment (SARA) guide: User's manual.* Toronto, Ontario, Canada: Multi-Health System.

Langhinrichsen-Rohling, J., Huss, M. T., & Ramsey, S. (2000). The clinical utility of batterer pro-files. *Journal of Family Violence, 15,* 37–53.

Langhinrichsen-Rohling, J., Palarea, R., Cohen, J., & Rohling, M. L. (2000). Breaking up is hard to do: Unwanted pursuit behaviors following the dissolution of a romantic relationship. *Violence and Victims, 15,* 73–90.

Lidz, C., Mulvey, E., & Gardner, W. (1993). The accuracy of predictions of violence to others. *Journal of the American Medical Association, 269,* 1007–1011.

Locke, H. J., & Wallace, K. M. (1959). Short Marital Adjustment and Prediction tests: Their reli-ability and validity. *Marriage and Family Living, 21,* 251–255.

Loeber, R., & Loeber, M. S. (1998). Development of juvenile aggression and violence. *American Psychologist, 53,* 242–259.

Marshall, L. L. (1992). Development of the Severity of Violence Against Women Scales. *Journal of Family Violence, 7,* 103–121.

Mathes, E. W., & Severa, N. (1981). Jealousy, romantic love, and liking: Theoretical considerations and preliminary scale development. *Psychological Reports, 49,* 1227–1231.

McEllistrem, J. E. (2004). Affective and predatory violence: A bimodal classification system of human aggression and violence. *Aggression and Violent Behavior, 10,* 1–30.

McGrew, K. S., & Flanagan, D. P. (1998). *The Intelligence Test Desk Reference (ITDR): Gf-Gc cross-battery assessment.* Boston: Allyn & Bacon.

McNiel, D., & Binder, R. (1991). Clinical assessment of the risk of violence among psychiatric inpa-tients. *American Journal of Psychiatry, 148,* 1317–1321.

Miller, F. G., & Lazowski, L. E. (1999). *The Adult Substance Abuse Subtle Screening Inventory Manual* (2nd ed.). Springville, IN: SASSI Institute.

Miller, L. S., & Rohling, M. L. (2001). A statistical interpretive method for neuropsychological test data. *Neuropsychology Review, 11,* 143–169.

Miller, T. Q., Smith, T. W., Turner, C. W., Guijarro, M. L., & Hallet, A. J. (1996). A meta-analytic review of research on hostility and physical health. *Bollettino di Psicologia Apllicata, 220,* 3–40.

Mills, J. (2005). Advances in the assessment and prediction of interpersonal violence. *Journal of Inter-personal Violence, 20,* 236–241.

Monahan, J. (2003). Violence risk assessment. In A. Goldstein (Ed.), *Handbook of psychology: Foren-sic psychology* (pp. 527–540). New York: John Wiley & Sons.

Monahan, J., Steadman, H. J., Silver, E., Appelbaum, P. S., Robbins, P. C., Mulvey, E. P., et al. (2001). *Rethinking risk assessment: The McArthur study of mental disorder and violence.* New York: Oxford University Press.

Mossman, D. (1994). Assessing predictions of violence: Being accurate about accuracy. *Journal of Consulting and Clinical Psychology, 62,* 783–792.

Murphy, C. M., & Hoover, S. A. (1999). Measuring emotional abuse in dating relationships as a multifactorial construct. *Violence and Victims, 14,* 39–53.

Murphy, C. M., Meyer, S. L., & O'Leary, K. D. (1994). Dependency characteristics of partner assaultive men. *Journal of Abnormal Psychology, 103,* 729–735.

Novaco, R. W. (1994). Anger as a risk factor for violence among mentally disordered. In J. Monahan & H. J. Steadman (Eds.), *Violence and mental disorder: Developments in risk assessment* (pp. 21–60). Chicago: University of Chicago Press.

O'Leary, K. D., Heyman, R. E., & Neidig, P. H. (1999). Treatment of wife abuse: A comparison of gender-specific and couples approaches. *Behavior Therapy, 30,* 475–505.

O'Leary, K. D., Vivian, D., & Malone, J. (1992). Assessment of physical aggression against women in marriage: The need for multimodal assessment. *Behavioral Assessment, 14,* 5–14.

Quinsey, V. L., Harris, G. T., Rice, M. E., & Cormier, C. A. (1998). *Violent offenders: Appraisal and managing risk.* Washington, DC: American Psychological Association.

Reitan, R. M., & Wolfson, D. (1985). *The Halstead–Reitan Neuropsychological Test Battery: Theory and clinical interpretation.* Tucson, AZ: Neuropsychological Press.

Reitan, R. M., & Wolfson, D. (1988). *Traumatic brain injury volume II: Recovery and rehabilitation.* Tucson, AZ: Neuropsychological Press.

Rice, M. E., & Harris, G. T. (1997). Cross-validation and extension of the Violence Risk Appraisal Guide for child molesters and rapists. *Law and Human Behavior, 21,* 231–241.

Rodenberg, F. A., & Fantuzzo, J. W. (1993). The measure of wife abuse: Steps toward the development of a comprehensive assessment technique. *Journal of Family Violence, 8,* 203–228.

Rohling, M. L., Miller, L. S., & Langhinrichsen-Rohling, J. (2004). Rohling's Interpretive Method for neuropsychological data analysis: A response to critics. *Neuropsychology Review, 14,* 155–170.

Salekin, R. T., Leistico, A. R., Neumann, C. S., DiCicco, T. M., & Duros, R. L. (2004). Psychopathy and comorbidity in a young offender sample: Taking a closer look at psychopathy's potential importance over disruptive behavior disorders. *Journal of Abnormal Psychology, 113,* 416–427.

Saunders, J. B., Lynch, A., Grayson, M., & Linz, D. (1987). The Inventory of Beliefs about Wife Beating: The construction and initial validation of a measure of beliefs and attitudes. *Violence and Victims, 2,* 39–57.

Selzer, M. L. (1971). The Michigan Alcohol Screening Test: The quest for a new diagnostic inventory. *American Journal of Psychiatry, 127,* 1653–1658.

Siegel, J. M. (1986). The multidimensional anger inventory. *Journal of Personality and Social Psychology, 51,* 191–200.

Sirles, E. A., Lipchik, E., & Kowalsi, K. (1993). A consumer's perspective on domestic violence interventions. *Journal of Family Violence, 8,* 267–276.

Skeem, J. L., & Mulvey, E. P. (2001). Psychopathy and community violence among civil psychiatric patients: Results from the MacArthur violence risk assessment study. *Journal of Consulting & Clinical Psychology, 69,* 358–374.

Skinner, H. A. (1995). Drug Abuse Screening Test. *Addictive Behaviors, 7,* 363–371.

Spanier, G. B. (1976). Measuring dyadic adjustment: New scales for assessing the quality of marriage and similar dyads. *Journal of Marriage and the Family, 38,* 15–28.

Spielberger, C. D., Jacobs, G., Russel, S., & Crane, R. S. (1983). Assessment of anger: The State–Trait Anger Scale. In J. N. Butcher & C. D. Spielberger (Eds.), *Advances in personality assessment* (Vol. 2, pp. 159–187). Hillsdale, NJ: Erlbaum.

Stith, S. M., Rosen, K. H., Middleton, K. A., Busch, A. L., Lunderberg, K., & Carlton, R. P. (2000). The intergenerational transmission of spouse abuse. *Journal of Marriage and the Family, 62,* 640–654.

Stith, S. M., Smith, D. B., Penn, C. E., Ward, D. B., & Tritt, D. (2004). Intimate partner physical abuse perpetration and victimization risk factors: A meta-analytic review. *Aggression and Violent Behavior, 10,* 65–98.

Straus, M. A. (1979). Measuring the intrafamily conflict and violence: The Conflict Tactics (CT) Scales. *Journal of Marriage and the Family, 41,* 75–88.

Straus, M. A., Gelles, R. J., & Steinmetz, S. K. (1981). Violence in the home. In M. A. Straus, R. J. Gelles, & S. K. Steinmetz (Eds.), *Behind closed doors: Violence in the American family* (pp. 4–28). Newbury Park, CA: Sage.

Straus, M. A., Hamby, S. L., Boney-McCoy, S., & Sugarman, D. B. (1996). The Revised Conflict Tactics Scales (CTS2): Development and preliminary psychometric data. *Journal of Family Issues, 17,* 283–316.

Suris, A., Lind, L., Emmett, G., Borman, P. D., Kashner, M., & Barratt, E. S. (2004). Measures of aggressive behavior: Overview of clinical and research instruments. *Aggression and Violent Behavior, 9,* 165–227.

Swanson, J. W. (1994). Mental disorder, substance abuse, and community violence: An epidemiological approach. In J. Monahan & H. J. Steadman (Eds.), *Violence and mental disorder: Developments in risk assessment* (pp. 101–136). Chicago: University of Chicago Press.

Sweet, J. J., Moberg, P. J., & Suchy, Y. (2000). Ten-year follow-up survey of clinical neuropsychologists: Part I. Practices and beliefs. *The Clinical Neuropsychologist, 10,* 202–221.

Tedeschi, J., & Quigley, B. (1996). Limitations of laboratory paradigms for studying aggression. *Aggression and Violent Behavior, 1,* 163–177.

Vivian, D., & Langhinrichsen-Rohling, J. (1994). Are bidirectionally violent couples mutually victimized? A gender-sensitive comparison. *Violence and Victims, 9,* 107–124.

Vivian, D., Langhinrichsen-Rohling, J., & Heyman, R. E. (2004). The thematic coding of dyadic interactions: Observing the context of couple conflict. In P. K. Kerig & D. H. Baucom (Eds.), *Couple Observational Systems* (pp. 273–288). Mahwah, NJ: Erlbaum.

Walters, G. D. (in press). Risk-appraisal versus self-report in the prediction of criminal justice outcomes: A meta-analysis. *Criminal Justice and Behavior.*

Warren, J. I., Burnette, M., & South, S. C. (2003). Psychopathy in women: Structural modeling and comorbidity. *International Journal of Law & Psychiatry, 26,* 223–242.

Webster, C., Douglas, K., Eaves, D., & Hart, S. (1997). *HCR-20: Assessing the risk of violence. Version 2.* Burnaby, BC, Canada: Simon Fraser University and Forensic Psychiatric Services Commission of British Columbia.

Williams, K. R., & Houghton, A. B. (2004). Assessing the risk of domestic violence reoffending: A validation study. *Law & Human Behavior, 28,* 437–455.

# 18

## SLEEP DYSFUNCTION

SHAWN R. CURRIE

*Addiction Centre, Foothills Medical Centre*
*Calgary, Alberta, Canada*

## INTRODUCTION

### INSOMNIA

The ubiquitous nature of sleep difficulties is well established. Between 9% and 20% of the general adult population experiences chronic insomnia (Ancoli-Israel & Roth, 1999; Ohayon, 2002; Partinen & Hublin, 2000). The average rate across studies was recently estimated as 15.3% (Lichstein, Durrence, Reidel, Taylor, & Bush, 2004). Prevalence rates tend to vary from survey to survey due to the inconsistent use of strict diagnostic criteria for defining insomnia. Ohayon recently estimated the prevalence of *DSM-IV*–defined Insomnia Disorder as 6% in the general population. An additional 25% to 30% of adults complain of occasional or transient insomnia (Ancoli-Israel, & Roth; Ohayon). Insomnia is not limited to North America but appears to be an international problem. Twenty-seven percent of the 26,000 patients from 15 countries that participated in the World Health Organization (WHO) International Collaborative Study on Psychological Problems in General Health Care (Üstün et al., 1996) reported persistent sleep difficulties. At least 50% of patients followed up one year later still reported significant sleep problems. Prevalence rates of both chronic and transient insomnia increase with age, reaching as high as 50% in some studies (Lichstein et al., Ohayon). Furthermore, there is a higher prevalence of insomnia in women compared to men (18% vs. 12%, respectively) in the U.S. general population (Lichstein et al.). On the other hand, the severity of sleep dysfunction in men and women complaining of insomnia appears to be comparable (Lichstein et al.).

Insomnia frequently co-occurs with another medical or psychiatric disorder (Lichstein, McCrae, & Wilson, 2003; McCall & Reynolds, 2000). In epidemiological studies, the comorbidity of insomnia and psychiatric disorders occurs in 40% to 65% of cases (Lichstein, McCrae, et al., 2003; Ohayon, 2002). Specific patient groups have been identified as being particularly vulnerable to sleep disturbances. For example, up to 70% of treatment-seeking chronic pain patients report significant insomnia (Pilowsky, Crettenden, & Townley, 1985; Wilson, Watson, & Currie, 1998). High rates of insomnia are associated with major depression, anxiety disorders (McCall & Reynolds), and alcohol dependence (Brower, 2001; Currie, Clark, Rimac, & Malhotra, 2003). Historically, disturbed sleep in these populations has been considered a consequence or symptom of the primary disorder. However, insomnia often persists even after the primary disorder resolves (Currie et al.; Lichstein, McCrae, et al., 2003). Furthermore, there is compelling epidemiological evidence that insomnia is a risk factor for the later development of major depression, anxiety disorders, and alcohol abuse (Ford & Kamerow, 1989; Weissman, Greenwald, Niño-Murcia, & Dement, 1997; Wong, Brower, Fitzgerald, & Zucker, 2004).

## OTHER SLEEP DISORDERS

Insomnia is by far the most prevalent sleep disorder. Sleep apnea, characterized by the cessation of airflow through the mouth and nose during the sleep period, affects about 2% of adult women and 4% adult males (Partinen & Hublin, 2000). Because people with apnea generally breathe normally during the day, this potentially fatal disorder can go undetected for many years. Restless legs syndrome and periodic limb movement appear with approximately the same frequency as sleep apnea, although the majority of cases are considered mild with little functional impairment (Montplaisir, Nicolas, Godbout, & Walters, 2000). The *International Classification of Sleep Disorders—Revised* (ICSD; American Sleep Disorders Association, 1997) lists dozens of other sleep disorders, most of which are extremely rare (e.g., narcolepsy) or occur exclusively in children (Partinen & Hublin). The noninsomnia sleep disorders usually require medical assessment that is beyond the scope of practice for most psychologists. Hence, the bulk of this chapter will focus on assessment of the insomnia-spectrum disorders.

## DIAGNOSIS OF SLEEP DISORDERS

Two parallel classification schemes exist for diagnosing sleep disorders. The *DSM* system (4th edition, American Psychiatric Association, 1994) is the most widely known but is generally not preferred by sleep experts because the criteria do not include any specification for frequency or severity of insomnia symptoms. The *DSM-IV* criteria for primary insomnia specify a minimum duration of one month of difficulty initiating or maintaining sleep or of nonrestorative sleep. The sleep problem must interfere with the individual's ability to function during the day or cause clinically significant distress. The ICSD (American Sleep Disorders Association, 1997) definition of psychophysiological insomnia is comparable to the *DSM* system in terms of the duration and functional impairment criteria. Unlike the *DSM-IV*, the ICSD diagnostic description of psychophysiological insomnia specifies that the condition be maintained in part by learned cognitive and emotional arousal over the sleep experience. Although there is often a precipitating event, many learned sleep-inhibiting behaviors manifest in clients over time and are believed to play a dominant role in sustaining the insomnia. One of the goals of the assessment procedure is to identify these behaviors so that they may be targeted for change during treatment.

The ICSD criteria are also vague in the specification for frequency of symptoms (the sleep problem must occur "almost nightly"). Neither the *DSM* nor the ICSD system provides specific quantitative criteria for distinguishing normal from abnormal sleep. For many years, researchers have adopted the following quantitative criteria to identify insomniacs: The individual must have a sleep onset latency (SOL) or time awake after sleep onset (WASO) greater than 30 minutes for a minimum of three nights per week. In a rigorous sensitivity-specificity analysis, Lichstein, Durrence, Taylor, Bush, and Riedel (2003) provided empirical support for these criteria in identifying "research-grade" insomnia.

## DESCRIPTION OF ASSESSMENT STRATEGIES

### CLASSIFICATION SCHEMES

Several methods exist for measuring sleep, however, there is no universally accepted taxonomy of sleep assessment procedures. The trend in behavior therapy (and its medical cousin, behavioral medicine) over the last 20 years has been toward disorder-based assessment models and away from general models of human behavior (Haynes, 1998; Ollendick, Alvarez, & Greene, 2004). Accordingly, the evolution of sleep assessment has been driven and ultimately shaped by the need for clinicians and researchers to diagnose, quantify, and monitor treatment response for specific sleep disorders. Assessment methods for insomnia have been heavily influenced by the cognitive-behavioral model (Morin, 1993; Smith, Smith, Nowakowski, & Perlis, 2003). For example, increasing attention in recent years has been paid to the role of cognition in the maintenance of insomnia (Harvey, 2002).

Current sleep assessment methods can be categorized along several dimensions, including retrospective versus prospective, subjective versus objective, and observational versus self-report. Furthermore, one can assess insomnia as a symptom and as a distinct disorder (Harvey, 2001). The choice of measurement scheme will be influenced by the purpose of the assessment, the orientation of the clinician or researcher, and available resources. In most clinical settings, sleep is most often assessed on the basis of global, retrospective evaluations (e.g., "How are you sleeping?"). Global evaluations of sleep are not necessarily inaccurate (Monk et al., 2003), but they lack the depth of information that can be indispensable for proper diagnosis, planning interactions, and assessing treatment response.

## COMMON MEASURES OF SLEEP BEHAVIOR

Sleep is a multidimensional construct, but several parameters are regularly used to quantify the severity of dysfunction and assess response to treatment. The main dimensions of insomnia include:

1. Number of minutes it takes the client to fall asleep, commonly referred to as sleep onset latency (SOL)
2. Number of minutes the client spends awake throughout the night, known as wake after sleep onset (WASO)
3. How often the client wakes up, known as number of awakenings (AWK)
4. The total length of time spent asleep, known as total sleep time (TST—can be expressed in minutes or hours)
5. The client's satisfaction with his or her sleep, known as sleep quality (SQL—usually assessed with a numerical rating scale such as 0–10, with 0 being "extremely poor" and 10 being "extremely good")

The ratio of hours slept to time in bed, known as sleep efficiency (SEF), is another commonly reported outcome variable. Higher values of SEF indicate less sleep fragmentation. SOL is the main index of sleep initiation, TST the index of sleep duration, and SEF, AWK, and WASO the main indices of sleep continuity. With the exception of sleep quality, all these dimensions can be assessed via subjective sleep measures (questionnaires and sleep logs) and objective sleep measures. Normative thresholds have been defined for SOL, TST, WASO, and SEF for the purpose of distinguishing normal from abnormal sleep. As noted, a self-reported sleep onset latency (SOL) or time awake after sleep onset (WASO) greater than 30 minutes at least three nights per week is the usual definition of insomnia (Lichstein, Durrence, et al., 2003). For SEF the value of 85% has been routinely used (Morin, Hauri, et al., 1999), and for TST a cutoff of 6.5 hours has been proposed (Lacks & Morin, 1992; Smith, Nowakowski, Soeffing, Orff, & Perlis, 2003). Comprehensive normative data for AWK has only recently become available (Lichstein et al., 2004); however, no cutoff for distinguishing a normal from an abnormal number of awakenings has been established.

These parameters provide a means of quantifying sleep, giving sleep researchers and clinicians a common language to communicate regarding level of dysfunction. Determining insomnia-related impairment is more complicated. Both the *DSM-IV* and the ICSD define Insomnia Disorder on the basis of daytime functioning being compromised in some way. Hence, assessing the daytime consequences of sleep dysfunction is an important area of sleep assessment. However, there is a lack of consensus as to which domains of daytime functioning are most sensitive to the impairing effects of insomnia. Furthermore, there are no standardized tools for assessing insomnia-related impairment. Suggested domains include work performance, fatigue, depressive and anxious symptoms, reliance on sleep medication, and quality of life. Roth (2004) recently reviewed the evidence that TST and measures of sleep continuity are correlated with alertness, memory, psychomotor performance, risk of car accidents, and pain threshold. For example, decreases in TST are reliably associated with memory impairment, while increased TST was related to improved alertness. Similarly, impaired sleep continuity is associated with impaired alertness, psychomotor performance, and memory. Insomnia is also associated with increased depression (Breslau, Roth, & Rosenthal, 1996; Chang, Ford, & Mead, 1997; Ford & Kamerow, 1989), absenteeism (Zammitt, Weinera, & Damato, 1999), accidents (Balter & Uhlenhuth, 1992), and increased health care utilization (Simon & Von Korff, 1997). The successful treatment of insomnia should result in improvements in such areas of daytime functioning. Unfortunately, many outcome studies include minimal or no measures of change in for the consequences of insomnia.

## SPECIFIC ASSESSMENT METHODS AND
## RESEARCH BASIS

Mash and Hunsley (2004) recently defined behavioral assessment as the systematic application of scientific principles across the client's life domains for the purpose of gathering data that can inform decisions about the nature of problems and possible treatments. Like most specialities in behavior therapy, the assessment methods for insomnia have been heavily influenced by the research conducted by psychologists over the last 25 years. Furthermore, the assessment of sleep tends to be multimodal in nature. Over the next few pages, the most frequently used assessment methods for sleep will be reviewed.

### Sleep Behavior Questionnaires

Several retrospective sleep questionnaires have been developed for clinical and research applications. These multi-item instruments ask clients about their sleep habits over a specified time frame, typically 2–4 weeks. One such questionnaire is the 19-item Pittsburgh Sleep Quality Index (PSQI; Buysse, Reynolds, Monk, Berman, & Kupfer, 1989). This brief, self-rated questionnaire inquires about the individual's sleeping habits and sleep quality for the past month. The PSQI produces seven scale scores, sleep quality, sleep latency, sleep duration, habitual sleep efficiency, sleep disturbances, sleep medication, and daytime dysfunction, along with a global index score. Scores of 6 or more on the global index indicate poor sleep (maximum score possible is 21). The PSQI has been used as an outcome measure in several insomnia trials (Currie, Clark, Hodgkins, & el-Guebaly, 2004; Currie, Wilson, Pontefract, & de Laplante, 2000; Mimeault & Morin, 1999) demonstrating that it is sensitive to change following treatment. The psychometric properties of the PSQI have also been investigated by several independent groups (Backhaus, Junghanns, Broocks, Riemann, & Hohagen, 2002; Carpenter & Andrykowski, 1998; results summarized in Table 18.1), with

TABLE 18.1　Reliability and Validity of Different Methods of Assessing Sleep

| Method | Common Purpose | Norms | Test–Retest Reliability | Validity | AASM Recommendation[a] |
|---|---|---|---|---|---|
| | | | Prospective | | |
| Polysomnography | Diagnose and screen for noninsomnia disorders | *Good sleepers:* SOL = 10 min; TST = 7 hr; WASO = 10 min; SEF = 90%. *Insomniacs:* SOL = 56 min; TST = 5.9 hr; WASO = 45 min; SEF = 79%[b] | SOL = .58; AWK = .60; WASO = .72 (average *r* across three nights)[c] | Considered gold standard | Not required for routine diagnosis of insomnia |
| Diary | Quantify severity of insomnia; treatment monitoring and outcome | *Good sleepers:* SOL = 14.3 min; WASO = 10.9 min; TST = 433.2 min; AWK = 1.2[d]. *Insomniacs:* SOL = 42.3 min; WASO = 53.8 min; TST = 384.0 min; AWK = 2.2[d] | SOL = .76; SEF = .74; TST = .77; WASO = .74; SQL = .70 (2 weeks)[c,e,f] Cronbach's alpha = .85 (SQL) to .94 (WASO)[e] | Correlation with PSG: SOL = .62–.99; AWK = .27–.63; WASO = .83–.88; TST = .42–64[g] | Can assist in diagnosis and treatment monitoring |
| Actigraph | Treatment monitoring and outcome | None | SOL = .82; SEF = .78; TST = .80; WASO = .54 (5-day interval)[e] | Concordance with PSG: 97% (good sleepers) Correlation with PSG: *r* = .94 (good sleepers); *r* = .77 (insomniacs)[b] | Insufficient evidence for recommendation |
| Collateral reports | Diagnosis, treatment monitoring, and outcome | None | SOL = .78; AWK = NS; WASO = NS[c] | Sleep diary: SOL = .84–.99[g] SII: Total score = .39[e] | Can assist in diagnosis and treatment monitoring |

| Measure | Purpose | Normative data | Reliability | Validity | Clinical utility |
|---|---|---|---|---|---|
| Clinical interview | Diagnosis; functional analysis | Not applicable | No data | No data | Essential for diagnosis |
| Structured interview[h] | Diagnosis | Not applicable | Interrater reliability across diagnoses: kappa = .85[h] | Diagnosis confirmed by PSG in 90% of cases[h] | Can assist in diagnosis |
| Pittsburgh Sleep Quality Index[j] | Quantify severity of sleep dysfunction; treatment monitoring and outcome | Global score (0–21) *Insomnia:* 12.5 ± 3.8 *Control:* 3.3 ± 1.8 | *Retrospective* r = .86 (total score; 45-day interval); Cronbach's alpha = .85[j] | Sensitivity = 98.7% Specificity = 84.4% *PSG correlates:* SOL = .28; SEF = –.32; TST = –.32 *Diary correlates:* SOL = .71; TST = 81[j] | Can assist in diagnosis and treatment monitoring |

[a] AASM = American Academy of Sleep Medicine (as per practice guidelines published in Chesson et al., 2000); WASO = wake time after sleep onset; SEF = sleep efficiency; SOL = sleep onset latency; TST = total sleep time; SQL = sleep quality; PSG = polysomnography; NS = not significant.
[b] Smith, Nowakowski, et al. (2003).
[c] Coates et al. (1982).
[d] Lichstein et al. (2004).
[e] Currie et al. (2004).
[f] Haythornthwaite, Hegel, & Kerns (1991).
[g] Lacks (1988).
[h] Schramm et al. (1993).
[i] Buysse et al. (1989).
[j] Backhaus et al. (2002).

encouraging results for test–retest reliability and concordance with other sleep measures. A related scale is the Sleep Impairment Index (SII; Morin, 1993), a seven-item scale that covers similar dimensions of insomnia (sleep onset, sleep maintenance, early morning awakenings, satisfaction with sleep, interference with daily functioning, noticeability of sleep impairment to others, and concern over insomnia). Each dimension is rated on a 5-point scale, ranging from 1 ("not at all") to 5 ("extremely"), with a maximum possible score of 35. The SII has also been evaluated for its psychometric properties (Bastien, Vallieres, & Morin, 2001) and is sensitive to change following treatment (Morin, Colecchi, Stone, Sood, & Brink, 1999). Other sleep questionnaires include the Brock Sleep and Insomnia Questionnaire (Cote & Ogilvie, 1993), the Sleep Disturbance Questionnaire (SDQ; Espie, Brooks, & Lindsay, 1989), and recently the Rochester Sleep Continuity Inventory (Smith, Nowakowski, et al., 2003). These instruments include a similar range of items as the PSQI and SII.

Advantages of self-report questionnaires such as the PSQI and SII are (1) they are brief and easy to administer in a variety of clinical settings; (2) they require little explanation (hence, can also be used in mailed-out surveys or completed in the waiting room); (3) they are inexpensive; (4) they provide sufficient detail on a client's sleep behavior to make a preliminary evaluation of whether a sleep problem exists; (5) sleep parameters correlate reasonably well with the same information derived from sleep diaries (Smith, Nowakowski, et al., 2003); and (6) they appear to be sensitive to treatment effects (Currie et al., 2004; Edinger, Wohlgemuth, Radtke, Marsh, & Quillian, 2001; Mimeault & Morin, 1999) . On the negative side, retrospective questionnaires employ a single sample method of data collection (Smith, Nowakowski, et al.). Clients are asked to make broad judgments about their sleep quantity and quality using a long period of reference (e.g., 30 nights of sleep). Clients may selectively report on their most recent night of sleep or the "worst-case scenario" when making judgments rather than make a true personal average (Gehrman, Matt, Turigan, Dinh, & Ancoli-Israel, 2002). Furthermore, sleep questionnaires lack sufficient specificity concerning sleep disorders. As noted, the symptoms of insomnia overlap substantially with other sleep disorders. A high questionnaire score can indicate that a sleep disorder exists but not the type of sleep disorder. For these reasons, sleep questionnaires may be best used as screening tools, as indices of change following treatment, or as complementary tools for other assessment methods.

## Questionnaires Assessing Other Sleep-Related Domains

A variety of self-report instruments have been developed for specific purposes in sleep assessment other than measuring the nocturnal symptoms of insomnia. Two scales of daytime sleepiness are available: the Stanford Sleepiness Scale (SSS; Hoddes, Zarcone, Smythe, Phillips, & Dement, 1973) and the Epworth Sleepiness Scale (ESS; Johns, 1991). These brief self-administered scales are used to assess subjective propensity to fall asleep. Although daytime sleepiness is a common symptom of insomnia, several studies have found no significant difference between sleepiness ratings in insomniacs and good sleepers (Sateia, Doghramji, Hauri, & Morin, 2000), calling into question the discriminant validity of these scales. Reporting on a sample of over 700 good and bad sleepers, Lichstein et al. (2004) found that SSS and ESS scores correlated higher with ratings of sleep quality than with quantitative sleep measures such as SOL and TST.

The Dysfunctional Beliefs and Attitudes about Sleep Scale (DBAS; Morin, 1993) assesses negative thoughts and unrealistic expectations about sleep and insomnia. The DBAS has good psychometric properties (Espie, Inglis, Harvey, & Tessier, 2000) and has been used as an outcome measure for insomnia treatment that aims to correct faulty beliefs about sleep (Espie, Inglis, Tessier, & Harvey, 2001; Ström, Pettersson, & Andersson, 2004). The scale can be used clinically to assess and target specific dysfunctional thoughts about sleep to which an individual client subscribes. The client's highest score on the five subscales (misconceptions about the causes of insomnia, need for control over insomnia, magnifying consequences, unrealistic sleep expectations, faulty beliefs about sleep-promoting practices) can be used to initiate discussion about the behavioral consequences of holding such negative thoughts. Norms for the DBAS averaged across several studies of good and poor sleepers are presently in development (Colleen Carney, Nov. 2004).

The Insomnia Impact Scale (Hoelscher, Ware, & Bond, 1993) assesses both nocturnal symptoms of insomnia and impairment in daytime functioning related to sleep dysfunction. The questionnaire has 40 items (total score ranging from 40 to 200) covering problems such as mind racing at night, memory problems from sleep loss, calling in sick after a bad night of sleep, and excessive worry about insomnia. The scale has good discriminant validity (Hoelscher et al.). Lichstein et al. (2004) recently published norms on the scale (good sleepers: $M = 94.5$, $SD = 21.8$; insomniacs: $M = 114.7$, $SD = 25.0$).

The Sleep Behavior Self-Rating Scale (Kazarian, Howe, & Csapo, 1979), which provides an index of sleep-incompatible behaviors, such as reading, eating, and watching television in bed and engaging in negative thoughts prior to bedtime. Items on this scale inquire about the frequency of such behaviors (scale points range from "never" to "very often"). The scale demonstrates high test–retest reliability ($r = .88$) and internal consistency (.76). A related instrument is the Sleep Hygiene Awareness and Practice Scale (SHAPS; Lacks & Rotert, 1986), which examines both knowledge of and adherence to good sleep hygiene. For example, the caffeine knowledge section assesses the subject's awareness of the presence of caffeine in 18 common foods, beverages, and nonprescription drugs. There is little data on the psychometric properties of the SHAPS. Research conducted during the scale's development revealed that insomniacs actually demonstrated more sleep hygiene knowledge than good sleepers (Lacks & Rotert) but showed less adherence to the practice of good sleep hygiene. For example, insomniacs had near perfect knowledge of caffeine-containing substances but continued to drink more caffeinated beverages in the evening than good sleepers.

## Collateral Reports

Behavioral sleep assessment can also make use of collateral reports obtained from a spouse or roommate. Collateral reports can fall under the category of retrospective or prospective assessment, but they are generally viewed as retrospective because the collateral is asked about the client's recent sleep behavior. One tool available for third-party sleep observations of insomnia is the spouse version of the Sleep Impairment Index (SII; Morin, 1993). Spousal reports of insomnia severity using the SII appear to be sensitive to change following treatment (Currie et al., 2004; Mimeault & Morin, 1999; Morin, Colecchi, et al., 1999). There has been some research on the reliability and validity of collateral estimates of sleep measures. In an early report, Coates et al. (1982) reported that spousal estimates of sleep latency and sleep duration were consistent with those of good sleepers. Subsequent research with insomniacs has produced mixed results. Moderately high correlations between spouse and insomniac estimates of SOL were reported in two studies (Domino, Blair, & Bridges, 1984; Lacks, 1988). Two other studies reported very poor agreement between the insomniac's and the spouse's ratings of symptom severity (Currie, Malhotra, & Clark, 2004; Kump, Whalen, & Tishler, 1994). Currie et al. (2004) found better agreement on the SII items pertaining to sleep behaviors (e.g., time to fall asleep, frequency of awakenings) than on items assessing the consequences of insomnia (e.g., daytime fatigue). In other words, collaterals are better at approximating the severity of nocturnal insomnia symptoms than the associated daytime impairment and distress caused by the insomnia.

## Direct Observation

The use of observation in behavioral assessment has declined since the mid-1980s (Ollendick et al., 2004). The method is gradually being replaced with the proliferation of self-report measures. Nevertheless, watching a person sleep remains one of the most direct methods of assessing sleep. Although impractical for outpatient applications, this procedure is widely used in inpatient settings. Nurses are often required to check on patients at least once an hour to record their state of consciousness (awake or asleep) and any associated sleep problems. Smith, Nowakowski, et al. (2003) note that the judgment of sleeping state is typically made on the basis of the patient's body position, absence of movement, facial expression, and eyes (closed or open). Determining someone's sleeping status is also influenced by contextual factors, such as time of day (e.g., an immobile patient is more likely to be judged sleeping at 2:00 AM than at 2:00 PM) and location (e.g., bed versus chair). The reliability and validity of observational judgments of sleeping state have not been researched. Increasing the sampling rate (e.g., from every 60 minutes to every 15 minutes) will obviously increase the temporal resolution of direct observation, although a high-frequency sampling interval may prove to be impractical. Furthermore, sleep is by definition a behavior characterized by a low frequency of activity (sleep could also be defined as the absence of activity). Even with a high sampling rate, the validity of visual detection is still prone to the fundamental limitation that an individual lying down with his or her eyes closed may in fact be awake. Directing a response from the client (e.g., asking "Are you awake?") would obviously enhance the accuracy of observational assessment but also introduces a rather serious reactivity confound.

Direct observation would have greater utility if the focus were on identifying discrete problematic sleep events. For example, observers could watch for symptoms of sleep apnea (loud snoring with periods of interrupted breathing) or periodic limb movements. The frequency of these events is considered diagnostic. Given the expense and inconvenience associated with overnight polysomnography, initial screening for sleep apnea and the movement-based sleep disorders via direct observation would represent a cost-effective assessment strategy.

### Self-Monitoring

Sleep is a highly personal event that lends itself well to self-monitoring. In addition, most sleep experts agree that prospective monitoring via a sleep diary is the preferred assessment procedure for insomnia (Lacks and Morin, 1992; Smith, Smith, et al., 2003). Ollendick et al. (2004) identify three criteria for effective self-monitoring in behavioral assessment: (1) The behavior should be clearly defined; (2) prompts to use the procedure should be available; and (3) rewards should be provided to reinforce its use. These criteria can be easily satisfied in the application of self-monitoring for sleep. Sleep behaviors can be clearly delineated on the sleep diary for clients to complete daily. Although there is no standardized sleep diary, most diary forms include a core set of items considered critical for capturing nightly sleep habits. Patients typically record their (a) bedtime, (b) rising time, (c) total sleep time (in hours or minutes), (d) sleep onset latency (SOL), (e) number of awakenings, and (f) ratings of sleep quality (e.g., 0 = "extremely poor" to 10 = "extremely good"). Time in bed (TIB), wake time after sleep onset (WASO), and sleep efficiency (SEF; the ratio of hours slept to time in bed) are easily derived from the log data. Clients can also record the time and duration of any naps, consumption of caffeinated beverages, and the use of sleep aids such as hypnotic medication.

Clients are instructed to complete the diary each morning upon rising, thereby providing a salient temporal prompt that should enhance consistent recording. Administration of a sleep diary should ideally include a training period to ensure that clients complete the form accurately and understand the importance of daily monitoring of sleep (Espie, 1991). Thereafter, the clinician should check that all items are completed and make inquires about anomalous entries or evident gaps of missing data.

Throughout the assessment and certainly during treatment, clients should be asked to bring their completed diaries in for review and discussion with the therapist. Feedback on the diary (e.g., weekly averages for sleep measures) can be a powerful incentive for clients to continue using the diary. In two randomized controlled trials of CBT for insomnia, clients were provided with weekly progress charts depicting change in sleep measures throughout treatment (Currie et al., 2004; Currie et al., 2000). These charts were well received by clients and encouraged their continued self-monitoring. Despite the perceived benefits of regular self-monitoring of sleep, compliance with the methodology remains a big issue. Stone, Shiffman, Schwartz, and Hufford (2002) reported a large discrepancy between patients' self-reported compliance with paper logs (92% of clients reported completing the log within 30 minutes of the scheduled assessment time) and actual compliance assessed via an electronic monitor of which clients were unaware (the monitor indicated the dairy was not opened at all on 32% of days). It is important, therefore, for clinicians to routinely inquire about the frequency and time of day that clients actually complete the sleep diary.

An example of a sleep log from the lab of Drs. Célyne Bastien and Charles Morin (Bouchard, Bastien, & Morin, 2003) at Laval University is provided in Figure 18.1. This log is typical of many used in sleep research, employing a single-page, seven-day format to make the process of recording nightly sleep simple for patients. The log is also noteworthy because of the addition of several items for assessing compliance to stimulus control instructions, a core intervention in the behavioral treatment of insomnia (Morin, 1993). For example, clients are asked to report on the number of times they left the bed when unable to sleep. Success in CBT for insomnia depends on the regular practice of the behavior-change strategies (Bouchard et al.; Riedel & Lichstein, 2001); however, relatively few treatment-outcome studies have systematically monitored client adherence.

Until recently the only normative data on the sleep diary came from an early quantitative review by Lacks (1988). Pooling the results from several studies of good and poor sleepers, she arrived at average SOLs of 12.6 minutes for good sleepers and 56.7 minutes for insomniacs. More recently, Lichstein et al. (2004) conducted a large epidemiological study of insomnia that involved the use of sleep diaries as well as other instruments. A total of 772 individuals ranging in age from 18 to 98 were selected from the greater Memphis area using the random digit dialing procedure. Participants completed a sleep diary similar to Figure 18.1 for a 14-day period. Comprehensive norms for good sleepers and insomniacs stratified by age, gender, and ethnicity are now available. The overall norms for good and bad sleepers are provided in Table 18.1.

The concurrent validity of sleep diaries has been assessed in a number of ways. The subjective sleep estimates from insomniacs have been compared with those obtained for spouses and roommates. Lacks (1988) reported the correlation between insomniac and spousal estimates of SOL ranged from .84 to .99. When compared with polysomnography (PSG), the gold standard of sleep assessment, the convergent validity of sleep diaries is less encouraging. Studies have consistently shown that the subjective morning estimates of sleep measures exhibit poor concordance with polysomnographic recordings of the same measures. In a large-scale study of 122 drug-free insomniacs, Carskadon et al. (1976) found that

| | Sunday | Monday | Tuesday | Wednesday | Thursday | Friday | Saturday |
|---|---|---|---|---|---|---|---|
| 1. Yesterday, I drank ___ cups of coffee and ___ cups of tea. | 3/0 | 2/0 | 2/0 | 3/0 | 3/0 | 3/0 | 3/0 |
| 2. Yesterday, I took a nap between ___ and ___. | 1 PM/2 PM | 2 PM/3 PM | None | 12 PM/2 PM | 1:30 PM/2 PM | None | 1 PM/2 PM |
| 3. Yesterday, on the whole, I followed the seven good sleep habit rules. (1 = not at all, 5 = completely) ___. | 2 | 2 | 1 | 2 | 1 | 2 | 1 |
| 4. Last night, I used my bedroom for activities other than sleeping or sex (e.g., watching TV). | Yes | Yes | Yes | Yes | Yes | Yes | Yes |
| 5. Last night, I practiced my presleep routine. ("Yes" or "No") | Yes | No | Yes | No | Yes | Yes | Yes |
| 6. Last night, I turned off the lights to sleep at ___ o'clock. | 9 PM | 10:30 PM | 9:30 PM | 12 AM | 1 AM | 11:15 PM | 11:30 PM |
| 7. After I turned off the lights, it took me ___ minutes to fall asleep. | 2 hr | 90 min | 1 hr | 75 min | 2 hr | 3 hr | 45 min |
| 8. The total number of times I woke up last night and had trouble falling back asleep was ___. | 4 | 5 | 3 | 2 | 2 | 3 | 4 |
| 9. I spent a total of ___ minutes awake last night. | 2 hr | 3 hr | 1 hr | 75 min | 90 min | 1 hr | 1.5 hr |
| 10. I got out of bed ___ times last night when I could not fall asleep. | 0 | 2 | 1 | 0 | 1 | 1 | 0 |
| 11. This morning, I woke up at ___ o'clock. | 5 AM | 6 AM | 6 AM | 6 AM | 7 AM | 8 AM | 7 AM |
| 12. Last night, I slept a total of ___ hours. | 3 hr | 5 hr | 5 hr | 6 hr | 5.5 hr | 6.5 hr | 6.5 hr |
| 13. This morning, I got out of bed at ___ o'clock. | 8 AM | 9 AM | 6 AM | 10 AM | 11 AM | 9:30 AM | 9 AM |
| 14. Upon awakening this morning, I would rate my feeling of restedness as ___. (1 = exhausted to 5 = well rested) | 1 | 2 | 1 | 2 | 2 | 1 | 1 |
| 15. On the whole, I rate the quality of my sleep last night as ___ (0 = extremely poor to 5 = extremely good) | 0 | 1 | 2 | 2 | 1 | 1 | 1 |

FIGURE 18.1   Example of a sleep diary. (Adapted from Bouchard, Bastien, & Morin, 2003.)

insomniacs consistently overestimated time to fall asleep by an average of 30 minutes and underestimated sleep duration by an average of 40 minutes as compared to polysomnography of the same measures. On the other hand, subjective SOL estimates from sleep diaries appear to correlate significantly with PSG. Correlation coefficients range from .62 to .99 for SOL, .27 to .63 for AWK, .83 to .88 for WASO, and .42 to .64 for TST (Lacks, 1988). Freedman and Papsdorf (1976) further demonstrated that the correlation between sleep diary estimates and PSG increases with successive recording nights, suggesting that training and practice are required for subjects to become accurate self-monitors of their sleeping behavior.

## Polysomnography

Most clients presenting with symptoms of primary insomnia do not require overnight polysomnography to confirm diagnosis. The recent Practice Parameters for the Evaluation of Chronic Insomnia from the American Academy of Sleep Medicine (AASM; Chesson et al., 2000) clearly state that PSG is not indicated for the routine evaluation of insomnia. This consensus statement derives from accumulated evidence that the severity of self-reported sleep disturbances associated with insomnia often do not correspond with the severity of continuity disturbances found in one to two nights of PSG. Furthermore, it has been argued that symptoms and characteristics of insomnia do not lend themselves to accurate assessment using PSG (Morin, 2000; Reite, Buysse, Reynolds, & Mendelson, 1995; Smith, Smith, et al., 2003). The American Academy of Sleep Medicine does recommend PSG for individuals with symptoms of insomnia when (1) a sleep-related breathing disorder, narcolepsy, periodic limb movements, or a parasomnia is suspected, (2) an underlying neurological disorder is suspected, and (3) the client has shown to be refractory to all treatment for insomnia (Chesson et al.).

When PSG is indicated, assessment procedures tend to be highly standardized, although there is no universally accepted minimum number of nights required. Reason for referral will often dictate how many nights the clients will need to spend in the sleep lab. Sleep apnea, for example, can be detected in a single night. Adaptation nights are sometimes employed to attenuate the "first-night effect," in which the client reacts to the novel environment of the sleep lab and the intrusion of having many wires and electrodes attached to his or her body. A basic polysomnographic assessment would include (a) electroencephalogram (EEG); (b) electro-oculogram (EOG); (c) electromyogram (EMG) of chin muscles; (d) electrocardiogram (EKG); and (e) respiratory effort. In addition, oral and nasal airflow may be recorded if sleep apnea is suspected and an EMG recording taken for the detection of periodic leg movements. Paper recordings are hand-scored using a structured set of scoring rules (Rechtschaffen & Kales, 1968). Computerized sleep-scoring algorithms are also now available (Carskadon & Rechtschaffen, 2000). In addition to the standard sleep continuity values (TST, SOL, etc.), measures of interest from a PSG analysis include the relative proportion and distribution of sleep stages (stages 1–4 and REM sleep) and the presence of any sleep anomalies. Normative PSG data are available for good sleepers and insomniacs (see Table 18.1).

Although polysomnography is considered the gold standard for assessing sleep, there is surprisingly few published data on the internight reliability of traditional sleep measures. In an early study, Moses, Lubin, Naitoh, and Johnson (1972) demonstrated that, even with the inclusion of adaptation nights, the test–retest reliability of measures of TST, WASO, and SOL on consecutive recording nights is low (.13, .30, and .20, respectively). Coates et al. (1982) reported more encouraging reliability coefficients for both good and poor sleepers (see Table 18.1 for coefficients). Two factors likely contribute to the variability in internight reliability for PSG sleep measures. First, PSG research typically relies on small samples; studies involving more than a dozen subjects are rare. Second, the internight reliability of sleep measures is directly influenced by the interrater reliability of hand-scoring, which tends to peak around .85 even for trained scorers (Moses et al.).

## Actigraphy

A popular and cost-effective alternative to lab- and home-based PSG is emerging in actigraph technology. Because Chapter 5 (by Tryon) is devoted to the description of activity measurement, the present section will be limited to application in sleep disorders. It is worth noting that the principles and procedures involved in actigraphy are rooted in basic behavioral assessment. Actigraphy provides psychologists with the means to detect and quantify human movement, with the aim of inferring states of wake or sleep from the specific pattern of movement (Smith, Smith, et al., 2003). Parameters such as the rate of sampling, time frame (e.g., 1, 2, 7, to up to 30 days, depending on battery duration), and detection threshold are set by the researcher. The actigraph itself is a small, lightweight ($4.4 \times 3.3 \times .96$ cm, 57 g) self-contained unit worn on the nondominant wrist when used to assess sleep. Because the technology is completely automated, the rate of sampling can be set to a much higher rate (e.g., movement can be sampled every second) than would be feasible with traditional observation or self-monitoring.

Scoring programs are available to convert the activity data to dichotomous values indicating simple sleep versus wake state during each epoch. Internally reliable estimates of common indices of insomnia severity can be produced (Jean-Louis, Kripke, Mason, Elliot, & Youngstedt, 2001; Sadeh, Hauri, Kripke, & Lavie, 1995), which are sensitive to change after treatment (Brooks, Friedman, Bliwise, & Yesavage, 1993; Currie et al., 2000). When compared to the gold standard of PSG, however, the movement-based sleep estimates from the actigraph are prone to large measurement errors. In cases of insomnia, the disagreement between actigraph and PSG estimates of sleep duration can vary from only a few minutes to over an hour (Sadeh et al.). The precision of actigraphy also seems to vary with insomnia subtype (Hauri & Wisbey, 1992).

Although the technology has a promising future in the behavioral assessment of sleep disorders, actigraphy is still plagued with several limitations that reduce many users' enthusiasm for its application in assessing insomnia. Smith, Smith, et al. (2003) note that few validation studies have been conducted on insomniacs. Cross-validation studies with PSG, which show agreement rates of up to 97% for TST and WASO, have predominately used normal sleepers. The agreement rate for insomniacs is much lower (about 77%), with an average nominal discrepancy between actigraph and PSG estimates for TST of 25 minutes (Smith, Nowakowski, et al., 2003). The higher rate of discrepancy for insomniacs may be due to increased motor activity in sleep-disorder patients or, more fundamentally, to the fact that insomniacs spend more time awake at night than good sleepers (Morin, 2000). There may also be differences in the various scoring software that now exists, although Sadeh et al. (1995) concluded that various scoring algorithms show similar levels of precision for a range of sleep disorders. A comparison of actigraph and self-report estimates of sleep parameters also reveal discrepancies. Sleep onset latency from the actigraph was an average of 10 minutes less than the sleep diary estimate in a recent study of 56 insomniacs (Currie et al., 2004). The modalities were modestly correlated ($r = .64$).

Despite these limitations, actigraphs have an advantage over PSG in assessing insomnia because sleep can be studied over many nights in the patient's natural sleep environment with minimal inconvenience. The role of actigraphy may be to augment self-report data in treatment-outcome studies. The validity of a treatment outcome is enhanced when changes in sleep can be demonstrated in more than one modality. In addition, feedback from the actigraph can be clinically useful for individual assessment cases. In extreme cases of sleep state misperception, for example, feedback from several nights of actigraph recording may help to convince a client that he or she is indeed getting some sleep (Smith, Smith, et al., 2003). There may also be a role for actigraphy in increasing adherence to sleep schedule changes considered integral to the behavioral management of insomnia. Carney, Lajos, and Waters (2004) found that individuals were more likely to follow sleep rules such as refraining from napping and maintaining a regular sleep schedule if they were told the actigraph would be used to monitor adherence.

## CLINICAL UTILITY

### NORMS AND STANDARDIZATION

One issue that has received little attention until recently is the establishment of appropriate norms for comparing good and poor sleepers. The new publication *Epidemiology of Sleep* by Kenneth Lichstein and colleagues (2004) has provided the first comprehensive sleep norms derived from the use of prospective self-monitoring. Results of their large household survey confirmed several existing beliefs about the nature of sleep and produced some new findings. For example, sleep does become more fragmented with age, and women report insomnia to a greater degree than men. On the other hand, the impact of age on sleep appears to be limited to measures of sleep continuity. There was no significant change in SOL and TST with age, and sleep quality actually improved with age. Consistent with other research, the relationship between severity of sleep dysfunction and daytime functioning appears to be weak and inconsistent. In addition to providing norms on the sleep diary, this study provides the first age, gender, and ethnic stratified norms on the ESS, SSS, and Insomnia Impact Scale. The main limitation of this normative database is that all participants were selected from a single urban center in the southern United States.

The widely used normative thresholds for distinguishing good from bad sleep (i.e., SOL or WASO > 30 minutes for three nights per week) were also validated by this new epidemiological study (Lichstein et al., 2004). A significant advantage of these data is that researchers and clinicians cannot only apply the normative threshold, but can evaluate an individual's sleep within the entire range of normal and abnormal sleep parameters. Consider the hypothetical case of a 25-year-old male with a reported SOL of 25 minutes every night of the week. Applying the normative cutoff of 30 minutes, it would appear this individual has normal sleep and therefore does not require treatment. In reality, this client's sleep pattern is in the upper limit (approximately 90th percentile for males in this age range) of what would be considered normal sleep.

A prerequisite to the establishment of sleep norms is standardization of the measures. Mash and Hunsley (1990) note that standardization is often misconstrued as promoting the idea that there is one true method (or set of methods) of assessing a behavior and that the same measures need to be applied in all situations. Standardization actually refers to the uniform application of a measure across conditions of administration, holding constant variables such as time limits, instructions, and scoring criteria (Anastasi, 1997). Application of behavioral sleep measures falls short of standardization in several ways. For example, there is no universally agreed-on duration for the collection of sleep diary data. Textbooks on insomnia treatment and noted sleep experts recommend a baseline of one or two weeks (Morin, 1993; Smith, Smith, et al., 2003). Indeed, acceptable internal consistency and test–retest reliability coefficients can be achieved with a baseline of two weeks (Currie et al., 2004). On the other hand, other research on insomniacs suggests that a three-week baseline is needed to obtain a stable estimate of WASO (Wohlgemuth, Edinger, Fins, & Sullivan, 1999). Treatment-outcome studies also vary, in both the length of baseline data collection (Riedel & Lichstein, 1995) and the length of post-treatment data collection. Some studies use an additional two weeks of diaries after treatment ends as the post-treatment data (Currie et al., 2000; Mimeault & Morin, 1999); others include the last week of treatment as the post-treatment data (Espie et al., 2001), when clients could be implementing the treatment strategies. Similarly, follow-up assessments can include either one week (Currie et al., 2000) or two weeks

(Bastien, Morin, Ouellet, Blais, & Bouchard, 2004) of diary collection. Variability in data-collection periods undoubtedly has affected the reported treatment-effect sizes, typically represented as change from baseline to post-treatment or follow-up. The effect size for SOL is greater than that for WASO in the meta-analysis of psychological treatment for insomnia (Morin, Culbert, & Schwartz, 1994), which may reflect the greater within-subject variability in diary measures of WASO for poor sleepers.

Some progress has been made toward the standardization of methods for assessing chronic insomnia. The Standards of Practice Committee of the American Academy of Sleep Medicine (AASM) produced a set of practice parameters for evaluating complaints of persistent insomnia (Chesson et al., 2000; Sateia et al., 2000). Practice parameters, acknowledged in Table 18.1, include three standards and two guidelines. Unfortunately, the use of behavioral assessment tools (diaries, questionnaires, etc.) is presented as a guideline only. Chesson et al. note that the application of such tools in assessing individual clients is variable and left to the clinician's discretion. Furthermore, no specific standards or guidelines are advanced to direct the use of behavioral assessment tools. For example, there is no specific recommendation regarding the use of self-monitoring over a retrospective questionnaire to assess severity of sleep dysfunction, even though the former is preferred by most sleep experts. Nor is any recommended length of self-monitoring (one, two, or three weeks) advanced. Nevertheless, the publication of these practice guidelines represents significant progress in the field of behavioral sleep medicine.

## OBJECTIVE VERSUS SUBJECTIVE DISAGREEMENT

The discrepancy between subjective and objective sleep measures is a recurring theme in the field of behavioral sleep medicine. It is a point both of embarrassment and of scientific curiosity among sleep researchers that subjective and objective evaluations of the same sleep parameters (e.g., time to fall asleep) can sharply disagree. Insomnia specialists have argued that the gold standard objective measure, polysomnography, has limited utility in diagnosing and assessing response to insomnia treatment (Morin, 2000; Smith, Nowakowski, et al., 2003). Furthermore, the AASM has declared that PSG is unnecessary for the routine evaluation of insomnia (Chesson et al., 2000). Nevertheless, researchers have not been able to fully explain the sometimes-large discrepancy between PSG and diary estimates for standard sleep parameters. In a landmark study, Carskadon et al. (1976) reported that insomniacs overestimated time to fall asleep and underestimated sleep duration by approximately 30 minutes each. Several related studies have produced similar results (Edinger & Finns, 1995; Rosa & Bonnet, 2000; Wohlgemuth et al., 1999). Hence, the discrepancy is both large and reproducible. It is worth noting that good sleepers also overestimate SOL and underestimate TST. Summarizing across eight studies of good sleepers, Lacks (1987) found an average discrepancy between sleep diary and PSG estimates for SOL of about 15 minutes in normal sleepers. Additionally, Rosa and Bonnet reported that the objective–subjective discrepancy is largely independent of a self-reported sleep problem. In their comparison of 121 self-identified poor sleepers and 56 persons with no insomnia complaint, an objective finding of insomnia by EEG was better predicted by dysphoric mood and hyperarousal than by history of an insomnia disorder.

There are several plausible explanations for the lack of agreement between objective and subjective sleep assessments. The first explanation is that insomniacs tend to exaggerate their severity of sleep dysfunction. Insomniacs tend to score highly on personality measures of neuroticism and hypochondrias (Morin, 1993; Rosa & Bonnet, 2000). Hence, they may be prone to overreport symptoms of distress, including sleep pathology (Smith, Smith, et al., 2003). This view is generally acknowledged, but most insomnia experts fall short of accepting that insomnia is due solely to psychopathology and hence does not represent a real health problem. Insomnia is considered a psychophysiological disorder, with similar characteristics to chronic benign pain. That is, there are psychologically mediated factors that influence both the presentation and the course of the condition.

A second explanation is that there are many sources of error in both objective and subjective sleep-measuring devices and that to expect a high concordance between methods would be unrealistic. We have seen that test–retest reliability coefficients for both PSG and diary measures of SOL are modest at best. The equipment used in PSG is vulnerable to errors in recording, resolution, and transcription. The EEG tracings used to score sleep states derive from surface recordings of brain wave activity. Smith, Nowakowski, et al. (2003) point out that the voltage recordings from the surface represent highly degraded estimates of underlying neuronal electrical activity that had to pass through several inches of bone, brain matter, and cerebral spinal fluid to reach the recording electrodes. Hand-scored PSG recordings are also prone to error. Distinguishing the sleep stages necessitates reading not only the EEG but also the EMG and EOG tracings. Sleep diary estimates of time to fall asleep are also subject to several sources of error, most notably individual variability in being able to detect the passage of time, the retrograde amnesia that accompanies sleep onset, and the fact that estimates are made in the morning after the individual has been sleeping for several hours.

Another explanation for the discrepancy is that a sleep diary and PSG fundamentally measure different aspects of sleep behavior. With a parameter such as SOL, the diary is assessing the sleeper's memory of how long it took him or her to fall asleep. Polysomnography is primarily measuring the neurophysiological events that accompany the transition from wake to sleep. Similarly, the actigraph assesses sleep onset based on a predetermined algorithm that estimates the beginning of stage 2 sleep from the cessation of movement. Determining SOL from the actigraph also depends on the client's providing the exact time that he or she turned off the lights in preparation for sleep (using a sleep diary or the event marker feature on many actigraph units). In our use of the actigraph as an outcome measure, we have noticed variability in the accuracy that clients indicate the lights-out time. The actigraph estimate of SOL, therefore, is influenced by the mechanical operation of the unit, the precision with which the client indicates the lights-out time, and the validity of the scoring program.

It is worth noting that sleep dysfunction is one of very few mental health problems in which objective measurement is possible. There is limited application of true objective measurement with problems such as depression, anxiety, and marital discord. For example, studies of neuroimaging, blood assay analysis, and cerebrospinal fluid have failed to identify any definitive, reproducible biological markers for major depression that can be reliably used in diagnosis (Kaplan, Sadock, & Grebb, 2002). Furthermore, sleep is not the only mental health problem in which subjective and objective measures can disagree. A related conundrum in psychological assessment is that children and adults diagnosed with Attention-Deficit Hyperactivity Disorder can often score in the normal range on standard neuropsychological tests of attention, concentration, and learning ability. This finding does not invalidate the diagnosis but merely suggests that the presentation of objective symptoms may be extremely variable and not easily detected by standard psychological tests. The same may be true for insomnia.

## ASSESSMENT, CONCEPTUALIZATION, AND TREATMENT PLANNING

### MINIMAL AND OPTIMAL ASSESSMENT

The preceding section provided the fundamental knowledge necessary to implement a behavioral assessment protocol of insomnia. Given the wide range of assessment methods at one's disposal, it may be helpful to define both a minimal and an optimal assessment procedure for sleep dysfunction. A minimal sleep assessment for clinicians who are not specialists in the field would include a screening tool such as the PSQI or SII. Clients with a high score (e.g., exceeding the cutoff of 6 for the PSQI) should be interviewed regarding the nature and severity of their sleep problems. The presentation of breathing-related symptoms or features that are not typical of insomnia would be an indication for further assessment by a specialist in sleep disorders. An optimal assessment procedure for clients presenting with symptoms consistent with insomnia would be the PSQI, a detailed clinical interview including a functional analysis, and two weeks of self-monitoring using a sleep diary. Such an assessment would provide sufficient information to confirm a diagnosis of insomnia, identify the precipitating and perpetuating psychological factors, identify targets for behavior change, and establish a baseline of sleep habits before any interventions are initiated.

## CLINICAL INTERVIEW AND FUNCTIONAL ANALYSIS

The first face-to-face contact with the insomniac occurs during the clinical interview. The goals of a clinical interview can be broad or narrow, depending on the nature of the presenting complaint and the needs of the client. In general, the interview serves to document the severity and natural history of insomnia, screen for other sleep disorders, explore the contribution of psychological factors in the onset and maintenance of insomnia, and identify what additional assessment procedures are required. At a minimum, the clinical interview should collect sufficient information to make a preliminary diagnosis, screen for noninsomnia disorders, such as sleep apnea, and rule out other causes of the individual's sleep complaint. Ideally, the clinician should strive to complete a comprehensive evaluation of the history of the client's sleep problem, including but not limited to impact on daytime functioning, current sleeping habits, health behaviors (diet, exercise, substance use), medical history and medication use, history of psychopathology, and past treatment for sleep problems, including attempts at self-management.

Obtaining a differential sleep diagnosis can be challenging when many sleep disorders have the same nocturnal and daytime characteristics as insomnia. For example, unrefreshing sleep and daytime fatigue are symptoms of both insomnia and sleep apnea. For many sleep disorders, a definitive diagnosis cannot be made on the basis of interview data alone. Although the interview can screen for core symptoms, the formal diagnosis of obstructive sleep apnea, restless legs syndrome, and periodic limb movements and most parasomnias require overnight polysomnography. Apnea can also be assessed via the SnoreSat system, a portable sleep monitor that can detect sleep apnea with a high degree of accuracy (Flemons & Remmers, 1996).

The clinical interview can be structured or semistructured. Many clinics and clinicians have developed their own interview schedule. Charles Morin provides a template for a semistructured interview in his book *Insomnia: Psychological Assessment and Management* (1993). This interview is noteworthy because it encompasses a functional analysis, which is considered the hallmark of behavioral assessment (Ollendick et al., 2004). Within the context of sleep assessment, a functional analysis would encompass a detailed evaluation of the precipitants, antecedents, possible secondary gain (e.g., sick role), and perpetuating factors functionally related to the sleep complaint. A detailed behavioral analysis should identify key maintenance factors in the client's insomnia. For example, the client may reveal maladaptive sleeping behaviors, such as the use of the bedroom for activities other than sleep or sex (e.g., watching TV, reading). In many cases, the coping strategies insomniacs develop can serve to maintain rather than ameliorate the sleep disorder. The clinician should inquire whether such behaviors are recent additions to the client's routine and whether the activity is a new coping response to his or her sleep dysfunction. In addition to sleep behaviors and routines, the functional analysis should address potential sleep-incompatible cognitions. Oxford University researcher Alison Harvey (2002) has provided a useful cognitive model of insomnia that defines "safety behaviors" that occur in response to anxious sleep-related thoughts. For example, the fearful thought that a poor night of sleep will impair performance at work may lead the client to call in sick and to try to recover lost sleep by napping during the day.

In summary, a functional analysis should identify antecedents and other variables that are both directly and indirectly related to the client's sleep complaints. It is not uncommon for a functional analysis to reveal a more pressing mental health problem (e.g., major depression) in the client's life that may be causally linked to their insomnia. As noted, insomnia is a prominent symptom of many medical and psychiatric conditions and it is important to rule out physical illness or psychopathology as the primary cause of disturbed sleep. The diagnosis of primary psychophysiological insomnia is often made by exclusion of other causes. Note that medical or psychiatric comorbidity does not preclude focused treatment of insomnia. Behavioral treatment for insomnia can be initiated concurrently or following treatment of the primary disorder if the insomnia persists. Recent research suggests that targeting insomnia in treatment can alleviate depressive symptoms in the absence of any specific interventions for depression (Morawetz, 2003).

A structured interview for sleep disorders is also available to aid in diagnostic decision making. Schramm et al. (1993) developed the *Structured Interview for Sleep Disorders for DSM-III-R* (SIS-D) for use in psychiatric settings. The SIS-D consists of a structured inquiry about specific symptoms of sleep disorders as defined by the *DSM* classification scheme. Although it was originally developed using the *DSM-III-R* criteria (American Psychiatric Association, 1987), my colleagues and I have adapted the interview to include *DSM-IV* criteria in several research studies (Currie et al., 2000; Currie, et al., 2004; Wilson et al., 1998). Also worth noting is the Sleep-EVAL system (Ohayon, 1996), a computerized structured interview for assessing sleep disorders in epidemiological research. Like our adaptation of the SIS-D, the Sleep-EVAL system uses a combination of *DSM-IV* and ICSD criteria in the determination of insomnia disorder.


## CASE STUDY

The following case demonstrates a clinical application of multimodal sleep assessment. The case is also an illustration of the complicated nature of secondary insomnia in a client with medical comorbidity.


### IDENTIFICATION

Ms. K., a 40-year-old married woman, was referred by her rehabilitation specialist for assessment and treatment of insomnia.

## PRESENTING COMPLAINT

For the last two years, Ms. K. had experienced severe and persistent sleep problems. She also had chronic neck pain and migraines and was moderately depressed (Beck Depression Inventory score of 18) at the time of the assessment. Ms. K. reported that she came close to passing out from pain at least five times a week. Ms. K.'s initial self-report was that it took her an average of 2 hours to fall asleep each night. She reported getting only about 5 hours sleep each night, despite spending close to 10 hours lying in bed. She reported waking up from pain and then having trouble finding a comfortable sleeping position again. For medication, she was taking acetaminophen with codeine, fluoxetine, and trazodone for sleep.

## HISTORY

Ms. K. had been injured in a motor vehicle accident approximately 2.5 years previously. She sustained a whip-lash injury resulting in a small cervical fracture (not spinal cord damage) and soft tissue damage. Ms. K.'s sleep problems began approximately 6 months after the onset of her chronic pain. Ms. K. reported mild-to-moderate insomnia prior to her accident. She reported that "I've always been a light sleeper," just like her mother and sister. However, she reported that her sleep problems had never interfered with her ability to function to the same degree as present. Ms. K. described herself as a perfectionist. She often brought work home to complete at night. She did this to avoid "leaving things to the last minute." She was extremely sensitive to criticism and often ruminated about completing work tasks late, even though she admitted that had never happened. Ms. K. denied any history of abusing substances. She presently avoided alcohol because it made her headaches worse.

## PEER AND WORK ISSUES

Prior to her accident, Ms. K. was employed as an accountant for a large oil company. She enjoyed her work, although she found it stressful partly because of her perfectionist tendencies. Ms. K. went on short-term disability shortly after the car accident. After one year of partially successful rehabilitation, Ms. K. went on long-term disability.

## FAMILY ISSUES

Ms. K. reported a supportive relationship with her husband of 15 years. His income had always been higher than hers, such that the family experienced little financial hardship with Ms. K. on disability. Ms. K.'s husband did complain of her sleep problem. Specifically, he reported that she was extremely restless in bed, took a long time to fall asleep, woke up several times during the night, and seemed tired and irritable most of the day. Because of her sleep problem, he had begun to sleep in the spare room most nights. The couple had two children, ages 10 and 14 years. Ms. K. reported no problems getting along with her children.

## BEHAVIORAL ASSESSMENT RESULTS

Ms. K. was first interviewed to assess a probable diagnosis of insomnia secondary to chronic pain and to rule out other causes of her sleep problem. Her husband was also interviewed. He corroborated the severity of her sleep difficulties, although he noted that she did have good nights of sleep during the week, in which she woke up only a couple of times. He denied observing any breathing-related difficulties (e.g., loud snoring, periods of interrupted breathing) or periodic limb movements in Ms. K. at night.

Ms. K. scored an 18 on the PSQI. A detailed clinical interview revealed several sleep-incompatible behaviors. Ms. K. stated that she dreaded going to bed each night. Despite this fear, she had a habit of going to bed quite early, in a desperate effort to get more sleep. Ms. K. completed the sleep diary for 2 weeks (results are shown in Figure 18.1). Her bedtimes were extremely variable, ranging from 9:00 PM to 1:00 AM. Similarly, her rising time could range from 5:00 AM to 11:00 AM. She reported napping an average of once a day (average length of nap = 45 min). She reported taking between 90 and 120 minutes to fall asleep each night (average SOL = 98 min). During the presleep period, Ms. K. tended to ruminate about her many personal problems, including her lack of sleep. She perceived herself to be a burden to her family and worried that she would never work again. In the interview, Ms. K. also reported spending a great deal of time in her bedroom during the day not sleeping. She used her bed as a place to rest when fatigued from pain. About a year ago she placed a television in her bedroom, out of convenience, and she reported that she would sometimes eat her meals in bed.

## ETHICAL AND LEGAL ISSUES OR COMPLICATIONS

Given Ms. K.'s extended period away from work and her long-term disability status, there was some initial concern about possible financial disincentives for her getting better. However, she presented as being motivated to improve her sleep pattern and seemed genuinely dissatisfied with being on permanent disability. She had aspirations to return to work on a part-time basis.

## CONCEPTUALIZATION AND TREATMENT RECOMMENDATIONS

Ms. K. meets diagnostic criteria for insomnia secondary to chronic pain with a history of subthreshold insomnia prior to the onset of her pain. She also displayed many of the personality characteristics of insomniacs (perfectionistic, hyperaroused, and prone to anxiety and excess worry). The onset of chronic pain seemed to worsen her preexisting sleep difficulties. Ms. K. continued to experience insomnia after undergoing outpatient pain management education and rehabilitation. The presence of chronic pain was an obvious factor in the maintenance of her insomnia. However, several other perpetuating factors were identified from the functional analysis. For example, she spent 12–16 hours every day in her bedroom, despite sleeping an average of 5 hours per day. As a result of the excess time in bed, Ms. K. had formed a strong association between her bedroom environment and sleeplessness. She also used her bedroom as a place to ruminate about problems, contributing to a conditioned state of anxiety in the sleep environment. Her taking of naps during the day also led to problems of initiating sleep at night.

In light of these factors, Ms. K. is a good candidate for cognitive-behavioral treatment (CBT) for insomnia. The presence of moderate depression in this client raised the question of whether it would be better to focus treatment on her sleep disorder or the depression. The decision was left to Ms. K. She noted that her depression had been stable for some time and was not getting worse. She had received therapy for depression as part of her pain rehabilitation and was continuing to take fluoxetine. She also felt her depression was partially caused by her sleep difficulties. Therefore, she opted to focus treatment on the insomnia. Given the severity of her insomnia and the presence of a chronic medical problem, it is important in a case such as this to be realistic about the degree of improvement that could be expected. Ms. K. was informed that she would likely not become a "perfect sleeper" but could reasonably expect an improved sleep pattern with consistent application of the strategies. Her sleep diary revealed that at present she rarely applied stimulus control procedures, such as getting out of bed when unable to fall asleep. As treatment goals, Ms. K. desired a sleep onset latency of no more than 30 minutes and wished to wean off the trazodone, which she acknowledged was having little benefit for her sleep. The initial part of treatment would focus on core behavioral interventions for insomnia: stimulus control and sleep restriction (Morin, 1993). These interventions help to reestablish the bed as the dominant cue for sleep, regulate the sleep–wake schedule, and consolidate sleep over a shorter period of time. Cognitive interventions (e.g., cognitive restructuring of her anxious thoughts about sleep) would be integrated into every session. The CBT treatment for secondary insomnia would be implemented over seven sessions (cf. Currie et al., 2000).

## SUMMARY

The complaint of poor sleep is one of the most common client problems that clinicians working in mental health face. Relatively few health professionals feel confident to conduct a comprehensive assessment of sleep dysfunction. This chapter has provided a practical overview of models and procedures involved in assessing insomnia and related disorders. Although specialized training in sleep medicine is an asset, the main objective of the chapter was to put behavioral assessment methods used for sleep within the reach of the average psychologist or psychiatrist in practice. A significant strength in this area is that most assessment techniques are empirically derived. Most advances in sleep medicine have come from research applications of assessment models and specific techniques. These include use of diagnostic interviews, self-report inventories, the sleep diary, and portable assessment devices such as the actigraph. Norms have been developed for some of these tools, increasing both their clinical and their research utility. Furthermore, progress has been made in the last five years toward development of appropriate standards in the area of assessing insomnia. Future challenges will be monitoring adherence to these standards and further refinement of the standards as they relate specifically to behavioral assessment (e.g., use of the sleep diary). Finally, it should be noted that the field of behavioral sleep medicine represents a successful collaboration among the disciplines of psychology, psychiatry, respirologists, nursing, and researchers. It has become a truly multidisciplinary field.

## REFERENCES

American Psychiatric Association. (1987). *Diagnostic and statistical manual of mental disorders* (3rd ed. revised). Washington, DC: Author.

American Psychiatric Association. (1994). *Diagnostic and statistical manual of mental disorders* (4th ed.). Washington, DC: Author.

American Sleep Disorders Association (ASDA). (1997). *International classification of sleep disorders: diagnostic and coding manual.* Lawrence, KS: Allen Press.

Anastasi, A. (1997). *Psychological testing* (7th ed.). Toronto, Ontario, Canada: Prentice Hall.

Ancoli-Israel, S., & Roth, T. (1999). Characteristics of insomnia in the United States: Results of the 1991 National Sleep Foundation Survey. I. *Sleep, 22*(Suppl. 2), S347–S353.

Backhaus, J., Junghanns, K., Broocks, A., Riemann, D., & Hohagen, F. (2002). Test–retest reliability and validity of the Pittsburgh Sleep Quality Index in primary insomnia. *Journal of Psychosomatic Research, 53,* 737–740.

Balter, M. B., & Uhlenhuth, E. (1992). New epidemiologic findings about insomnia and its treatment. *Journal of Clinical Psychiatry, 53,* 34–39.

Bastien, C. H., Morin, C. M., Ouellet, M., Blais, F. C., & Bouchard, S. (2004). Cognitive-behavioral therapy for insomnia: Comparison of individual therapy, group therapy, and telephone consultations. *Journal of Consulting & Clinical Psychology, 72,* 653–659.

Bastien, C., Vallieres, A., & Morin, C. M. (2001). Validation of the Insomnia Severity Index as an outcome measure for insomnia research. *Sleep Medicine, 2,* 297–307.

Bouchard, S., Bastien, C. H., & Morin, C. M. (2003). Self-efficacy and adherence to cognitive-behavioral treatment of insomnia. *Behavioral Sleep Medicine, 1,* 187–199.

Breslau, N., Roth, T., & Rosenthal, L. (1996). Sleep disturbance and psychiatric disorders: A longitudinal epidemiological study of young adults. *Biological Psychiatry, 39,* 411–418.

Brooks J. O., Friedman, L., Bliwise D. L., & Yesavage, J. A. (1993). Use of wrist actigraphs to study insomnia in older adults. *Sleep, 16,* 151–155.

Brower, K. J. (2001). Alcohol's effects on sleep in alcoholics. *Alcohol Health & Research World, 25,* 110–125.

Buysse, D. J., Reynolds, C. F., Monk, T. H., Berman, S. R., & Kupfer, D. J. (1989). The Pittsburgh Sleep Quality Index: A new instrument for psychiatric practice and research. *Psychiatry Research, 28*, 193–213.

Carney, C. E., Lajos, L. E., & Waters, W. F. (2004). Wrist actigraph versus self-report in normal sleepers: Sleep schedule adherence and self-report validity. *Behavioral Sleep Medicine, 2*, 134–143.

Carpenter, J. S., & Andrykowski, M. A. (1998). Psychometric evaluation of the Pittsburgh Sleep Quality Index. *Journal of Psychosomatic Research, 45*, 5–13.

Carskadon, M. A., & Rechtschaffen, A. (2000). Monitoring and staging human sleep. In M. Kryger, T. Roth, & W. C. Dement (Eds.), *Principles and practice of sleep medicine* (3rd ed., pp. 1197–1216). Toronto, Ontario, Canada: W. B. Saunders.

Carskadon, M. A., Dement, W. C., Mitler, M. M., Guilleminault, C., Zarcone, V. P., & Spiegel, R. (1976). Self-reports versus sleep laboratory findings in 122 drug-free subjects with complaints of chronic insomnia. *American Journal of Psychiatry, 133*, 1382–1388.

Chang, P., Ford, D. E., & Mead, L. A. (1997). Insomnia in young men and subsequent depression: The Johns Hopkins Precursors Study. *American Journal of Epidemiology, 146*, 105–114.

Chesson, A., Hartse, K., Anderson, W. M., Davila, D., Johnson, S., Littner, M., et al. (2000). Practice parameters for the evaluation of chronic insomnia. *Sleep, 23*, 237–241.

Coates, T. J., Killen, J. D., George, J., Marchini, E., Silverman, S., & Thoresen, C. (1982). Estimating sleep parameters: A multitrait–multimethod analysis. *Journal of Consulting and Clinical Psychology, 50*, 345–352.

Cote, K., & Ogilvie, R. D. (1993). The Brock Sleep and Insomnia Questionnaire. *Sleep Research, 22*, 356.

Currie, S. R., Clark, S., Hodgins, D. C., & el-Guebaly, N. (2004). Randomized controlled trial of brief cognitive-behavioral interventions for insomnia in recovering alcoholics. *Addiction, 99*, 1121–1132.

Currie, S. R., Clark, S., Rimac, S., & Malhotra, S. D. (2003). Comprehensive assessment of insomnia in recovering alcoholics using daily sleep diaries and ambulatory monitoring. *Alcoholism: Clinical and Experimental Research, 27*, 1262–1270.

Currie, S. R., Malhotra, S. D., & Clark, S. (2004). Agreement among objective, subjective, and collateral reports of poor sleep in recovering alcoholics. *Behavioral Sleep Medicine, 2*, 293–296.

Currie, S. R., Wilson, K. G., Pontefract, A. J., & deLaplante, L. (2000). Cognitive-behavioral treatment of insomnia secondary to chronic pain. *Journal of Consulting and Clinical Psychology, 68*, 407–416.

Domino, G., Blair, G., & Bridges, A. (1984). Subjective assessment of sleep by sleep questionnaire. *Perceptual and Motor Skills, 59*, 163–170.

Edinger, J. D., & Fins, A. I. (1995). The distribution and clinical significance of sleep time misperceptions among insomniacs. *Sleep, 18*, 232–239.

Edinger, J. D., Wohlgemuth, W. K., Radtke, R. A., Marsh, G. R., & Quillian, R. E. (2001). Cognitive behavioral therapy for treatment of chronic primary insomnia: A randomized controlled trial. *JAMA, 285*, 1856–1864.

Espie, C. A. (1991). *The psychological management of insomnia.* Chichester, England: John Wiley & Sons.

Espie, C. A., Brooks, D. N., & Lindsay, W. R. (1989). An evaluation of tailored psychological treatment of insomnia. *Journal of Behavior Therapy & Experimental Psychiatry, 20*, 143–153.

Espie, C. A., Inglis, S. J., Harvey, L., & Tessier, S. (2000). Insomniacs' attributions: Psychometric properties of the Dysfunctional Beliefs and Attitudes about Sleep Scale and the Sleep Disturbance Questionnaire. *Journal of Psychosomatic Research, 48*, 141–148.

Espie, C. A., Inglis, S. J., Tessier, S., & Harvey, L. (2001). The clinical effectiveness of cognitive behavior therapy for chronic insomnia: Implementation and evaluation of a sleep clinic in general medical practice. *Behavior Research & Therapy, 39*, 45–60.

Flemons, W. W., & Remmers, J. E. (1996). The diagnosis of sleep apnea: Questionnaires and home studies. *Sleep, 19*, S243–S247.

Ford, D. E., & Kamerow, D. B. (1s989). Epidemiological study of sleep disturbances and psychiatric disorders. *JAMA, 262,* 1479–1484.

Freedman, R., & Papsdorf, J. D. (1976). Biofeedback and progressive relaxation treatment of sleep-onset insomnia: A controlled all-night investigation. *Biofeedback and Self-regulation, 1,* 253–271.

Gehrman, P., Matt, G., Turingan, M., Dinh, Q., & Ancoli-Israel, S. (2002). Towards an understanding of self-reports of sleep. *Journal of Sleep Research, 11,* 229–236.

Harvey, A. (2001). Insomnia: Symptom or diagnosis? *Clinical Psychology Review, 21,* 1037–1059.

Harvey, A. (2002). A cognitive model of insomnia. *Behavior Research & Therapy, 40,* 869–894.

Hauri, P. J., & Wisbey, J. (1992). Wrist actigraphy in insomnia. *Sleep, 15,* 293–301.

Haynes, S. N. (1998). The changing nature of behavioral assessment. In A. S. Bellack & M. Hersen (Eds.), *Comprehensive handbook of psychological assessment: Behavioral assessment* (4th ed., pp. 1–21). Boston: Allyn & Bacon.

Haythornthwaite, J. A., Hegel, M. T., & Kerns, R. D. (1991). Development of a sleep diary for chronic pain patients. *Journal of Pain and Symptom Management, 6,* 65–72.

Hoddes, E., Zarcone, V., Smythe, H., Phillips, R., & Dement, W. C. (1973). Quantification of sleepiness: A new approach. *Psychophysiology, 10,* 431–436.

Hoelschen, T. J., Ware, J. C., & Bond, T. (1993). Initial validation of the insomnia impact scale. *Sleep Research, 22,* 149.

Jean-Louis, G., Kripke, D. F., Mason, W. J., Elliot, J. A., & Youngstedt, S. D. (2001). Sleep estimation from wrist movement quantified by different actigraphic modalities. *Journal of Neuorscience Methods, 105,* 185–191.

Johns, M. W. (1991). A new method for measuring daytime sleepiness: The Epworth Sleepiness Scale. *Sleep, 14,* 540–545.

Kaplan, H. I., Sadock, B. J., & Grebb, J. A. (2002). *Synopsis of psychiatry* (9th ed.). Baltimore: Lippincott Williams & Wilkins.

Kazarian, S., Howe, M., & Csapo, K. (1979). Development of the sleep behavior self-rating scale. *Behavior Therapy, 10,* 412–417.

Kump, K., Whalen, C., & Tishler, P. V. (1994). Assessment of the validity and utility of a sleep-symptom questionnaire. *American Journal of Respiratory Critical Care, 150,* 735–741.

Lacks, P. (1987). *Behavioral treatment for persistent insomnia.* Toronto, ON, Canada: Pergamon Press.

Lacks, P. (1988). Daily sleep diary. In M. Hersen & A. S. Bellack (Eds.), *Dictionary of behavioral assessment techniques* (pp. 162–164). New York: Pergamon Press.

Lacks, P., & Morin, C. M. (1992). Recent advances in the assessment and treatment of insomnia. *Journal of Consulting & Clinical Psychology, 60,* 586–594.

Lacks, P., & Rotert, M. (1986). Knowledge and practice of sleep hygiene techniques in insomniacs and good sleepers. *Behavior Research & Therapy, 24,* 365–368.

Lichstein, K. L., Durrence, H. H., Riedel, B. W., Taylor, D. J., & Bush, A. J. (2004). *Epidemiology of sleep.* Mahwah, NJ: Erlbaum.

Lichstein, K. L., Durrence, H. H., Taylor, D. J., Bush, A. J., & Riedel, B. W. (2003). Quantitative criteria for insomnia. *Behavior Research and Therapy, 41,* 427–455.

Lichstein, K. L., McCrae, C. S., & Wilson, N. M. (2003). Secondary insomnia: Diagnostic issues, cognitive-behavioral treatment, and future directions. In M. L. Perlis & K. L. Lichstein (Eds.), *Treating sleep disorders: Principles and practice of behavioral sleep medicine* (1st ed., pp. 286–304). Toronto, Ontario, Canada: John Wiley & Sons.

Mash, E. J., & Hunsley, J. (1990). Behavioral assessment: A contemporary approach. In A. S. Bellack, M. Hersen, & A. E. Kazdin (Eds.), *International handbook of behavior modification and therapy* (2nd ed., pp. 87–106). New York: Plenum Press.

Mash, E. J., & Hunsley, J. (2004). Behavioral assessment: Sometimes you get what you need. In M. Hersen (Ed.), *Comprehensive handbook of psychological assessment: Behavioral assessment.* Hoboken, NJ: John Wiley & Sons.

McCall, W. V., & Reynolds, D. (2000). Psychiatric disorders and insomnia. In M. H. Kryger, T. Roth, & W. C. Dement (Eds.), *Principles and practice of sleep medicine* (3rd ed., pp. 640–646). Toronto, Ontario, Canada: W. B. Saunders.

Mimeault, V., & Morin, C. M. (1999). Self-help treatment for insomnia: Bibliotherapy with and without professional guidance. *Journal of Consulting & Clinical Psychology, 67,* 511–519.

Monk, T. H., Buysse, D., Kennedy, K. S., Potts, J. M., DeGrazia, J. M., & Miewald, J. M. (2003). Measuring sleep habits without using a diary: The Sleep Timing Questionnaire (STQ). *Sleep, 26,* 208–212.

Montplaisir, J., Nicolas, A., Godbout, R., & Walters, A. (2000). Restless Legs Syndrome and periodic limb movement disorders. In M. H. Kryger, T. Roth, & W. C. Dement (Eds.), *Principles and practice of sleep medicine* (3rd ed., pp. 742–752). Toronto, Ontario, Canada: W. B. Saunders.

Morawetz, D. (2003). Insomnia and depression: Which came first? *Sleep Research Online, 5,* 77–81.

Morin, C. M. (1993). *Insomnia: Psychological assessment and management.* New York: Guilford Press.

Morin, C. M. (2000). The nature of insomnia and the need to refine our diagnostic criteria. *Psychosomatic Medicine, 62,* 483–485.

Morin, C. M., Colecchi, C., Stone, J., Sood, R., & Brink, D. (1999). Behavioral and pharmacological therapies for late-life insomnia: A randomized controlled trial. *Journal of the American Medical Association, 281,* 991–999.

Morin, C. M., Culbert, J. P., & Schwartz, S. M. (1994). Nonpharmacological interventions for insomnia: A meta-analysis of treatment efficacy. *American Journal of Psychiatry, 151,* 1172–1180.

Morin, C. M., Hauri, P. J., Espie, C. A., Spielman, A. J., Buysse, D., & Bootzin, R. R. (1999). Nonpharmacologic treatment of chronic insomnia. *Sleep, 22,* 1134–1156.

Moses, J., Lubin, A., Naitoh, P., & Johnson, L. C. (1972). Reliability of sleep measures. *Psychophysiology, 9,* 78–82.

Ohayon, M. (1996). Epidemiological study on insomnia in the general population. *Sleep, 19,* S7–S15.

Ohayon, M. (2002). Epidemiology of insomnia: What we know and what we still need to learn. *Sleep Medicine Reviews, 6,* 97–111.

Ollendick, T. H., Alvarez, H. K., & Greene, R. W. (2004). Behavioral assessment: History of underlying concepts and methods. In M. Hersen (Ed.), *Comprehensive handbook of psychological assessment: Behavioral assessment* (pp. 19–34). Hoboken, NJ: John Wiley & Sons.

Partinen, M., & Hublin, C. (2000). Epidemiology of sleep disorders. In M. H. Kryger, T. Roth, & W. C. Dement (Eds.), *Principles and practice of sleep medicine* (3rd ed., pp. 558–579). Toronto, Ontario, Canada: W. B. Saunders.

Pilowsky, I., Crettenden, I., & Townley, M. (1985). Sleep disturbance in pain clinic patients. *Pain, 23,* 27–33.

Rechtschaffen, A., & Kales, A. (1968). *A manual of standarized terminology, techniques, and scoring system for sleep stages of human sleep.* Los Angeles: BIS/BRI, UCLA.

Reite, M., Buysse, D., Reynolds, C., & Mendelson, W. (1995). The use of polysomnography in the evaluation of insomnia. *Sleep, 18,* 58–70.

Riedel, B. W., & Lichstein, K. L. (1995). Sleep compression and sleep education for older insomniacs: Self-help versus therapist guidance. *Psychology & Aging, 10,* 54–63.

Riedel, B. W., & Lichstein, K. L. (2001). Strategies for evaluating adherence to sleep restriction treatment for insomnia. *Behavior Research & Therapy, 39,* 201–212.

Rosa, R. R., & Bonnet, M. H. (2000). Reported insomnia is independent of poor sleep as measured by electroencephalography. *Psychosomatic Medicine, 62,* 474–482.

Roth, T. (2004). Measuring treatment efficacy in insomnia. *Journal of Clinical Psychology, 65*(Suppl 8), 8–12.

Sadeh, A., Hauri, P. J., Kripke, D. F., & Lavie, P. (1995). The role of actigraphy in the evaluation of sleep disorders. *Sleep, 18,* 288–302.

Sateia, M. J., Doghramji, K., Hauri, P. J., & Morin, C. M. (2000). Evaluation of chronic insomnia. *Sleep, 23,* 243–308.

Schramm, E., Hohagen, F., Grasshoff, U., Riemann, D., Hajak, G., Hans-Gunther, W., & Berger, M. (1993). Test–retest reliability and validity of the structured interview for sleep disorders according to *DSM-III-R*. *American Journal of Psychiatry, 150,* 867–872.

Simon, A., & VonKorff, M. (1997). Prevalence, burden, and treatment of insomnia in primary care. *American Journal of Psychiatry, 154,* 1417–1423.

Smith, L. J., Nowakowski, S., Soeffing, J. P., Orff, H. J., & Perlis, M. L. (2003). The measurement of sleep. In M. L. Perlis & K. L. Lichstein (Eds.), *Treating sleep disorders: Principles and practice of behavioral sleep medicine* (1st ed., pp. 29–73) Toronto, Ontario, Canada: John Wiley & Sons.

Smith, L. J., Smith, L. J., Nowakowski, S., & Perlis, M. L. (2003). Primary insomnia: Diagnostic issues, treatment, and future directions. In M. L. Perlis & K. L. Lichstein (Eds.), *Treating sleep disorders: Principles and practice of behavioral sleep medicine* (1st ed., pp. 214–261). Toronto, Ontario, Canada: John Wiley & Sons Canada, Ltd.

Stone, A. A., Shiffman, S., Schwartz, J. E., & Hufford, M. R. (2002). Patient noncompliance with paper diaries. *British Medical Journal, 324,* 1193–1194.

Ström, L., Pettersson, R., & Andersson, G. (2004). Internet-based treatment for insomnia: A controlled evaluation. *Journal of Consulting & Clinical Psychology, 72,* 113–120.

Üstün, T. B., Privett, M., Lecrubier, Y., Weiller, E., Simon, A., Korten, A., et al. (1996). Form, frequency, and burden of sleep problems in general health care: A report from the WHO Collaborative Study on Psychological Problems in General Health Care. *European Psychiatry,* [Vol] *11*(Suppl. 1), 5S–10S.

Weissman, M. M., Greenwald, S., Nino-Murcia, G., & Dement, W. C. (1997). The morbidity of insomnia uncomplicated by psychiatric disorders. *General Hospital Psychiatry, 19,* 245–250.

Wilson, K. G., Watson, S. T., & Currie, S. R. (1998). Daily diary and ambulatory activitiy monitoring of sleep in patients with insomnia secondary to chronic pain. *Pain, 75,* 75–84.

Wohlgemuth, W. K., Edinger, J. D., Fins, A. I., & Sullivan, R. J. (1999). How many nights are enough? The short-term stability of sleep parameters in elderly insomniacs and normal sleepers. *Psychophysiology, 36,* 233–244.

Wong, M. M., Brower, K. J., Fitzgerald, H. E., & Zucker, R. A. (2004). Sleep problems in early childhood and early onset of alcohol and other drug use in adolesence. *Alcoholism: Clinical & Experimental Research, 28,* 578–587.

Zammit, G. K., Weiner, J., & Damato, N. (1999). Quality of life in people with insomnia. *Sleep, 22*(Suppl. 2), pp. 379–385.

# 19

## BORDERLINE
## PERSONALITY DISORDER

WENDI L. ADAMS
TRACY JENDRITZA
SOONIE A. KIM

*Portland Dialectical Behavior Therapy Program*
*Portland, Oregon*

### INTRODUCTION

Personality disorders are described in the *Diagnostic and Statistical Manual of Mental Disorders* (*DSM-IV*; American Psychiatric Association [APA], 1994) as an "enduring pattern of inner experience and behavior that deviates markedly from the expectations of the individual's culture, is pervasive and inflexible, has an onset in adolescence or early adulthood, is stable over time, and leads to distress or impairment" (page 629). Borderline Personality Disorder (BPD) was added to the *DSM-III* (APA, 1980) and represents a description of behavioral patterns that have been noted as resistant to traditional psychotherapy since at least 1938, when Adolf Stern first coined the term *borderline* (Linehan, 1993). The prevalence rate of BPD is estimated to be 0.5% to 2% of the general population, 10% of the outpatient treatment population, and 20% of the inpatient population (APA, 1994; Widiger & Trull, 1993). Prevalence rates are estimated to double when a subgroup of "high-utilizing" inpatients are considered (Linehan, Kanter, & Comtois, 1999). An estimated 75% of individuals diagnosed with BPD have engaged in parasuicidal behaviors either currently or historically and approximately 10% will die as a result of a completed suicide (Frances, Fyer, & Clarkin, 1986; Clarkin, Widiger, Frances, Hurt, & Gilmore, 1983; Cowdry, Pickar, & Davies, 1985). Linehan and Heard (1999) assert that BPD is one of the most financially and psychologically costly mental disorders. The financial costs of the disorder span beyond the mental health system and often involve the medical system, social service agencies, and the legal system. Additionally, the emotional costs of the disorder impact the client and his/her interpersonal world. Also, the comorbidity rates between BPD and Axis I disorders are high, with a prevalence of comorbid mood, anxiety, substance abuse, and eating disorders (Dolan-Sewell, Krueger, & Shea, 2001). Therefore, accurate assessment and diagnosis of BPD are important, given the prevalence, seriousness, and complexity of the disorder and the necessity of delivering effective treatment to this historically treatment-resistant population.

## DISCUSSION OF BORDERLINE PERSONALITY DISORDER

BPD is described in the *DSM-IV* (APA, 1994) as follows: "A pervasive pattern of instability of interpersonal relationships, self-image, and affect, and marked impulsivity beginning by early adulthood and present in a variety of contexts" (p. 654). Five of the following nine diagnostic criteria must be met for a client to be diagnosed with BPD: (1) frantic attempts to avoid abandonment, whether real or imagined; (2) unstable relationships, alternative between idealization and devaluation; (3) severely unstable self-image or sense of self; (4) potentially self-damaging impulsive behavior in at least two areas, such as binge eating, drinking, and spending; (5) suicidal or self-mutilating behavior; (6) severe reactivity of mood lasting a few hours to a few days; (7) chronic feelings of emptiness; (8) uncontrollable anger (subjectively experienced or outbursts); and (9) brief paranoid ideation or dissociative symptoms when under stress.

The *DSM-IV* (APA, 1994) requirement of five out of the total of nine symptoms just described raises the potential for numerous symptom presentations and permutations that ultimately meet diagnostic criteria for BPD, thereby resulting in heterogeneity among BPD clients and potential symptom overlap with multiple disorders (Comtois, Levensky, & Linehan, 1999). This potential for diversity in symptom presentation warrants the use of accurate, specific, and ongoing assessment focused on specific behaviors, as opposed to the general diagnostic construct of BPD, in an effort to accurately assess and ultimately deliver effective treatment for this historically difficult-to-treat population.

## REORGANIZED CRITERIA

Linehan (1993) developed a cognitive-behavioral model of BPD in an effort to deliver effective treatment and better understand the pathogenesis of this disorder. She reorganized the diagnostic criteria of the *DSM-IV* by summarizing the symptoms into five categories of dysregulation. The first category she describes is *emotional dysregulation*, characterized by highly unstable and reactive emotional responses, problems with anger and anger expression, and difficulty with episodic anxiety, depression, and irritability. The onset of emotional responses tends to be quick and of a high intensity, and the return to a normal mood is typically slow, once an emotional response has begun, as a function of intensity. *Interpersonal dysregulation*, the second category described, is characterized by unstable and intense relationships often marked with difficulties, and the BPD individual often engages in frantic efforts to stay in relationships. The third category, *behavioral dysregulation*, includes extreme and problematic impulsive behaviors as well as suicidal and parasuicidal behavior (i.e., self-harming behavior without the intent to die). The fourth category, *cognitive dysregulation*, is characterized by cognitive rigidity, often in the form of dichotomous thinking, and brief nonpsychotic forms of thought dysregulation, such as delusions and dissociative experiences, often precipitated by stress. The final category is *self-dysregulation*, which manifests in feelings of emptiness, an unstable self-image, and low self-esteem (Linehan).

## BIOSOCIAL MODEL

The pathogenesis of the problem areas associated with BPD is theorized by the biosocial model as articulated by Linehan (1993). The biosocial model posits that the combination, or rather transaction, over time of the biologic vulnerability to emotion dysregulation coupled with an invalidating environment results in the problem areas associated with BPD. Etiological factors of the biological vulnerability associated with BPD are postulated to range from genetic factors, disadvantageous intrauterine environments, to the neurological sequelae of childhood trauma (see Linehan for a review). This biologic vulnerability with multiple causal pathways results in heightened emotional sensitivity and heightened reactivity to emotional stimuli.

The invalidating environment is described as a social environment that fails to confirm, verify, or corroborate the individual's experience. Furthermore, the invalidating environment fails to teach the individual what responses are more likely or less likely to result in the individual obtaining his/her goals. In addition, the invalidating environment communicates that the individual's typical responses to events are not to be taken seriously and are fundamentally wrong and inappropriate. Problem solving is oversimplified and portrayed as easy by the invalidating environment and, as a result, the environment fails to teach the individual to form realistic goals and expectations or tolerate distress. As a result of the invalidating environment's punishing the communication of negative experiences and only responding to escalated emotional displays, the individual learns to oscillate between emotional inhibition and extreme emotional expression.

Over time the individual learns to distrust his/her own perceptions, emotions, and other internal experiences and instead search the environment for cues pertaining to how to react. Over time and in general, free operant behaviors are blocked, thereby resulting in behavior that is primarily under the direct control of immediate reinforcement or social consequences (Koerner & Linehan, 1997). This can result in the BPD individual lacking awareness of and/or engagement in behaviors that are intrinsically rewarding to him/her. The invalidating environment is generally the family; however, society can be an invalidating environment for those who differ from the dominant culture. The transactional nature of the biosocial model alludes to its compensatory nature. For example, in a highly invalidating environment where the individual is abused, only a slight degree of emotional vulnerability can lead to BPD. Conversely, an average-to-low level of invalidation can result in BPD when the individual is highly vulnerable to emotional dysregulation. The biosocial model also provides a lens through which the assessment process can be filtered, in an effort to understand the current factors in the environment that are maintaining maladaptive behaviors.

## TREATMENT STAGES AND HIERARCHY

It is highly likely that after assessing a client and arriving at a diagnosis of BPD, the clinician will be faced with a list of problematic behaviors, dysphoric states, relationship problems, systemic problems, existential crises, and, more than likely, comorbid psychological disorders. In dialectical behavior therapy (DBT), an empirically validated treatment for BPD, treatment is structured into stages, which enables the clinician to organize and treat multiple problem areas effectively (Linehan, 1993). Two primary goals are the focus of treatment regardless of stage: an increase in dialectical behavior patterns, which represent balanced versus extreme and dichotomous patterns in thinking and responding, and building adaptive skills in living and relating to others. These two goals result in responding to situations effectively despite current affective state, which poses a challenge for individuals prone to emotional dysregulation.

The pretreatment stage of DBT consists of assessment, orientation to treatment, and obtaining a commitment from the client to participate in therapy. In stage 1, following pretreatment, the goal is to reduce problematic behaviors, which are arranged hierarchically in terms of level of importance. Suicidal and parasuicidal behaviors are the first to be addressed, followed by behaviors that impede the progress of therapy and, finally, behaviors that interfere with the quality of one's life and the obtainment of important goals (e.g., impulsive behaviors, maladaptive interpersonal behaviors). The focus of stage 2 of treatment is on behaviors that are related to Post-Traumatic Stress Disorder (PTSD), for many, though not all, patients have a history of trauma (Herman, 1997). Exposure therapy and cognitive modification techniques are employed at this stage of treatment and require adequate distress-tolerance skills on behalf of the client. Treatment of PTSD sequelae is often started, stopped, and returned to throughout the course of treatment, because it requires adequate distress-tolerance skills. Stage 3 of treatment is focused on increasing the client's self-respect, in addition to other areas the client might want to work on. This stage often involves working on career-related issues, developing more rewarding relationships, and increasing meaning in one's life (Linehan, 1993; Kim & Goff, 2002).

An accurate and comprehensive behavioral assessment undoubtedly helps the clinician to organize targets and to structure treatment. Behavioral assessment of

BPD more often than not yields a list of target behaviors, the organization and prioritizing of which is extremely important. Treatment of life-threatening behaviors first, then therapy-interfering behaviors, and lastly behaviors that interfere with quality of life is based on the intuitive point that clients, first, need to be alive in order to be treated and, second, need to engage in the therapeutic process in a manner that does not destroy the relationship and/or impede the work; when the first conditions are met, the client is able to focus on behaviors that erode his/her quality of life (Linehan, 1993). The structure of treatment in DBT reflects the treatment hierarchy, which is determined on a session-by-session basis, informed by the treatment plan and contingent on the data revealed by self-monitoring procedures and, at times, follow-up from previous sessions. Ongoing assessment is crucial because new problems areas can emerge as crises abate, stage 2 treatment can result in an increase in stage 1 targets despite prior successful resolution, and the emergence of environmental problems all can impact the client's symptomology. In fact, ongoing assessment is the essence of risk management as life-threatening behaviors are monitored on a weekly basis, a collaborative crisis plan is in effect as needed, and changes in symptomology and behaviors are tracked, treated, and noted.

## ASSESSMENT STRATEGIES AND RESEARCH BASIS

A comprehensive behavioral assessment enables the clinician to better understand the idiosyncrasies of the individual. For diagnostic clarity, a behaviorally focused assessment is recommended, given the myriad of presentations and permutations that meet diagnostic criteria for BPD in addition to the high comorbidity rates with other psychological disorders (Comtois et al., 1999; Dolan-Sewell, Krueger, & Shea, 2001). Ultimately, the process of assessment enables us to understand the client with whom we work, guide treatment planning and the organization of client problems, monitor risk, and evaluate progress. A variety of assessment strategies and techniques enable the practitioner to ascertain baselines for presenting problems that encompass BPD in general and Linehan's (1993) reorganized symptom criteria in particular. Three general types of assessment strategies will be addressed and considered for use at intake, across sessions, and at outcome: Clinical interviews (structured and semistructured interviews, collateral information, and observations), behavioral measures, paper-and-pencil measures, and functional analyses.

### INTAKE

Accurate assessment at intake is important for diagnosis, treatment planning, establishing baseline measures of symptomology and for ongoing assessment of progress. As noted elsewhere, the reorganized diagnostic criteria for BPD as articulated by Linehan (1993) encompass five areas of dysregulation: emotional, interpersonal, behavioral, cognitive, and self. Assessment at intake will ideally address these five areas, which collectively subsume the *DSM-IV* criteria for the disorder (APA, 1994). The comorbidity rates between BPD and Axis I disorders are high, with a prevalence of comorbid mood, anxiety, substance abuse, impulse control, and eating disorders (Dolan-Sewell et al., 2001). The high comorbidity rates coupled with the lack of categorical specificity of BPD warrants the assessment of a wide range of behaviors. A variety of assessment methods will be considered for use at intake.

## Structured and Semistructured Interviews

A detailed clinical interview with a thorough family, relationship, work, and academic history and collateral information from other health care providers can enable the clinician to arrive at an accurate diagnosis. Sullivan (1954) describes the process of data collection in the clinical interview as "participant-observation," in which the clinician uses self as an instrument of observation and the data lie in the transaction between the clinician and client.

Evidence of an invalidating family environment or otherwise disadvantageous early experiences are ascertained through querying the client regarding the quality of relationships with his/her family of origin, assessing for abuse and trauma, the presence of marital discord, familial psychopathology, early losses, and frequent moves. As the biosocial model posits, the transaction between the individual's biologic sensitivity and degree of invalidation is compensatory; therefore the absence of blatantly difficult family-of-origin experiences does not necessitate the absence of BPD, nor does abuse necessitate its presence (Linehan, 1993). Rather, information regarding early experiences and family history of psychopathology must be weighed in conjunction with other data gleaned from the interview.

In exploring the client's relationship history, the clinician will ideally spend sufficient time in an effort to identify maladaptive and pervasive patterns of interpersonal functioning. Obtaining information about significant past and present relationships, how relationships typically begin and end, and the type of individuals the client is typically attracted to for friendship or partners can enable the clinician to identify possible themes and patterns (McClanahan, Kim, & Bobowick, 2001). Additionally, assessing how the client typically reacts to and attempts to resolve relationship problems can provide the clinician with important diagnostic information, which may reveal functional aspects to problematic behaviors (e.g., suicide threats). Individuals with BPD often fear abandonment, which can manifest behaviorally in a variety of ways, such as ending relationships abruptly in an effort to control what is believed to be inevitable, staying in hopeless relationships to circumvent feelings of abandonment or being alone, and hypersensitivity to disagreements in relationships. Additionally, individuals with BPD often view people they are in relationship with in extreme terms, oscillating between devaluing and idealizing, which can be gleaned from descriptions of important relationships and at times is apparent in the therapeutic relationship.

Assessment of work functioning may reveal disruptions to employment due to interpersonal conflict and/or frequent job changes due to impulsivity and/or a lack of clarity regarding interests and preferences. Additionally, exploring work attendance and reasons for missing work provides important diagnostic information, for frequent absences are often the result of dysphoric states (mood dependent), consequences of behavioral impulsivity (e.g., self-harm, alcohol abuse), and avoidance of anxiety, among other factors. Assessment of academic functioning can reveal similar information regarding interpersonal functioning, mood-dependent behavior, impulsivity, and/or difficulty knowing oneself.

Longitudinal data are preferred when available, given the high comorbidity between BPD and Axis I disorders. Information regarding the manifestation, course, and longevity of symptoms can aid the clinician in the difficult task of differential diagnosis between BPD and other disorders with overlapping symptoms. In addition, it is important to assess not only the presence of but also the function of behaviors associated with comorbid conditions, because the relationship between BPD and these behaviors may reflect attempts at affect regulation. For example, comorbid substance abuse or binge eating often reflects an attempt at regulating anxiety or other dysphoric states. Furthermore, problematic affective states are often a consequent reaction to other problems areas associated with the diagnosis, such as interpersonal problems (Goff, 2002).

A variety of semistructured and structured interviews can enable the clinician to assess the presence of a personality disorder in general and BPD in particular, all of which require some degree of training. The Structured Clinical Interview for *DSM-IV* Personality Disorders (SCID-II) was designed in an effort to efficiently diagnose Axis II conditions based on *DSM-IV* criteria and has adequate reliability and validity for use in clinical settings (First, Gibbon, Spitzer, Williams, & Benjamin, 1997; Rogers, 2001). Another structured interview is the International Personality Disorder Examination (IPDE). The IPDE takes between three and four hours to administer, which precludes its use in most outpatient settings (Pull & Wittchen, 1991). The Revised Diagnostic Interview for Borderlines (DIB-R) is a semistructured interview whose revised form was developed in order to increase its ability to discriminate between BPD patients and other Axis II diagnoses (Zanarini, Gunderson, Frankenburg, & Chauncey, 1989; Hurt, Clarkin, Koenigsberg, Frances, & Nurnberg, 1986).

A detailed risk assessment, the standard of practice for assessing any mental disorder, is paramount in the assessment of BPD, given the relatively high rates of completed suicide (10%) and lifetime prevalence rate of parasuicidal behaviors (75%) (Frances et al., 1986; Clarkin et al., 1983; Cowdry et al., 1985). Assessment of current risk factors involves assessing for the presence of suicidal ideation, suicide plan, and access to means, depression, drug and/or alcohol use, psychotic thought processes, recent losses, family history of suicide, lack of social support, and history of previous attempts. Lethality of past attempts is ascertained by a thorough assessment at intake. The lethality of means can be estimated by consulting the Scale Points for Lethality Assessment, a 10-point scale for adults reflecting the likelihood of death associated with means and contextual factors (Bongar, 1991). A comprehensive discussion of suicide risk assessment is beyond the parameters of this chapter. For a detailed discussion of suicide risk factors, see Bongar (1992) and Davis, Gunderson, and Myers (1999) for a discussion of risk factors in chronically suicidal BPD individuals. Parasuicidal behaviors can be assessed as part of the clinical interview by querying the client regarding method, whether or not medical attention was required, frequency, intensity, and history of behavior, typical antecedents, environmental context, and access to means. A thorough risk assessment allows the clinician to establish a pretreatment baseline regarding frequency and intensity of life-threatening behaviors and associated consequences (e.g., emergency room visits and hospitalizations). It also enables the clinician to predict future occurrences of parasuicidal behaviors and the level of actual risk, which informs the application of contingency management strategies for extinguishing operant parasuicidal behaviors.

The Parasuicide History Interview—2 (PHI-2) is a semistructured interview designed to obtain detailed information regarding parasuicidial behaviors (Linehan, 1996). The data collected from the PHI-2 can span a predetermined interval of time or across the individual's life. In general, the PHI-2 enables the practitioner to establish baseline measures around life-threatening behaviors commonly found among BPD clients, which are a necessary focus of treatment.

**Behavioral Measures**

Observational/empirical data gleaned from the clinical interview can, at times, reveal areas of dysregulation that are diagnostic of BPD. The *DSM-IV* diagnostic criteria for BPD require a minimum of five out of nine symptoms, which reflect the five areas of dysregulation as articulated by Linehan (1993). The maladaptive behaviors associated with BPD all represent forms of dysregulation (Waltz & Linehan, 1999). Interpersonal, behavioral, cognitive, and self-dysregulation are conceptualized as, more often than not, being precipitated by emotional dysregulation and all areas impact one another (Waltz & Linehan). For example, a client may experience episodic dysphoric states (emotion dysregulation) and in reaction engage in parasuicidial acts (behavioral dysregulation) to reduce distress, which in turn can impact his/her relationships in a negative manner (interpersonal dysregulation). The five areas of dysregulation can be assessed through behavioral observation and measurement at intake, which enables the clinician to establish baselines for maladaptive behaviors.

Difficulties with emotion dysregulation can often be observed in session as clients may display emotional lability, lack of eye contact, and reactivity of mood, among other observable presentations suggestive of problems in this area. Baseline rates of behaviors associated with emotion dysregulation are ideally established at intake and assessed across sessions. Examples of behavioral manifestations of emotion dysregulation include hours slept per night, cancellation of activities due to mood, incidents of verbal and physical aggression, and activity level. When establishing a baseline rate of a particular behavior, attention is paid to the frequency, intensity, duration, and outcome of the behavior (Kazdin, 2001). With high-frequency behaviors, attention is paid to the outcome of the behavior, which is used as a baseline measure and target for change.

Interpersonal dysregulation can become manifest in the interactions between the client and the clinician. Clients with BPD are often interpersonally sensitive and prone to perceiving the therapist's nonverbal cues or statements as negative. Attention to the process of interaction with the client can enable the clinician to identify the presence of maladaptive interpersonal behaviors. Examples of behavioral measures of interpersonal dysregulation include the number of conflicts with partner or others and active avoidance of relationships.

Behavioral dysregulation can be observed by noting scars resulting from parasuicidal behaviors, weight, and appearance and from client's statements regarding impulsive behaviors assessed during the clinical interview. Examples of behavioral dysregulation include frequency, intensity, and duration of drug and alcohol abuse, binge eating, parasuicidal acts, suicide attempts, impulsive shopping or gambling, number of emergency room visits, and number and length of hospitalizations.

Cognitive dysregulation can be observed through the client's use of language to describe his or her experiences (e.g., extreme, rigid, categorical descriptions, expression of hopelessness). Behavioral measures of cognitive dysregulation might include the number of suicide attempts when the behavior is precipitated by hopelessness, lack of goal-directed activity, and frequency, intensity, and duration of dissociative episodes.

Self-dysregulation is more difficult to observe than the other areas of dysregulation and is generally inferred from the clinical interview (e.g., unaware of preferences, feeling empty). Examples of behavioral measures of self-dysregulation include lack of hobbies, frequent job changes due to fluctuating interests, frequent college major changes, and avoidance of being alone (distract from emptiness). We recommend the clinician note observations and relate them to relevant mental status areas (e.g., appearance, thought process, attention) as part of a thorough clinical assessment for BPD.

## Paper-and-Pencil Measures

Paper-and-pencil measures help the clinician to assess for the plethora of potential symptoms and comorbid conditions often observed in BPD clients. Many individuals with BPD experience greater psychopathology than is evident from their behavioral presentation and verbal indication (Edell, Joy, & Yehuda, 1990). In addition, the administration of these measures affords the clinician a baseline or multiple baselines from which to evaluate treatment progress, which is often of interest to and/or a requirement of third-party payment systems (e.g., managed care). However, there are a few shortcomings to the use of paper-and-pencil measures to be reviewed. First, all have high face validity, thereby making them sensitive to response sets. Second, they require the ability to accurately describe one's inner experiences, which is arguably difficult for an individual with symptoms associated with BPD as a result of intense labile moods, the tendency toward dissociation, the memory problems associated with high levels of emotion and stress, and lack of self-awareness. Lastly, these measures take time to administer, which may ultimately preclude their use in nonresearch settings.

All of the paper-and-pencil measures to be noted are intended to be used in conjunction with a thorough clinical interview and collateral information and should not be used in isolation for the purposes of diagnosis. Baseline frequency and intensity of problematic behaviors are ideally established at intake and tracked throughout treatment whether or not paper-and-pencil measures are utilized to quantify current symptomology.

Measures of general symptomology can enable the clinician to cast a wide diagnostic net in a relatively short period of time. The Brief Symptom Inventory (BSI) was selected based on prior empirical validation, comprehensive symptom coverage, and ease of administration. The BSI is essentially a brief form of the Symptom Check List—90—Revised and is designed to reflect psychological patterns of psychiatric patients and nonpatient populations (Derogatis & Spencer, 1982; Derogatis & Melisaratos, 1983). In general, the BSI is useful for the purposes of establishing individual baselines and tracking change regarding symptom distress across sessions. The Outcome Questionnaire-45 (OQ-45) is another paper-and-pencil, self-report measure of general symptomology with adequate reliability and validity. The OQ-45 is designed to assess general distress due to anxiety, affective, and adjustment symptoms, interpersonal problems, and difficulties related to fulfillment of social roles (Lambert & Hill, 1994). We recommend the OQ-45 over the BSI for a general symptom measure because it assesses functioning in addition to degree of symptom distress.

The Inventory of Altered Self-Capacities (IASC) is paper-and-pencil questionnaire designed to assess areas more specific to BPD (Briere & Runtz, 2002). The IASC was designed to assess the construct of "altered self-capacities," which the authors purport reflects three tasks important for successful interpersonal functioning: The ability to maintain a stable sense of self and awareness across a variety of contexts and in lieu of affect, affect tolerance, and the ability to develop and maintain meaningful relationships with little to minimal problems as a result of fears, behaviors, and cognitive distortions. The measure was found to have adequate reliability, validity, and internal consistency regarding the assessment of problem areas associated with BPD and antisocial personality disorder in particular (Briere & Runtz).

The following paper-and-pencil measures have been divided based on Linehan's (1993) reorganization of BPD diagnostic criteria. Several paper-and-pencil measures fall under the rubric of emotional dysregulation, as demonstrated in Table 19.1 (Linehan). All measures were chosen based on their adequate reliability and validity and ease of administration. Depression and anxiety measures

TABLE 19.1   Paper-and-Pencil Measures[a]

---

**Emotion Dysregulation**

The Beck Depression Inventory—second edition (BDI-II; Beck, Steer, & Brown, 1996; Beck, Ward, Mendelson, Mock, & Erbaugh, 1961)

The Beck Anxiety Inventory (BAI; Beck & Steer, 1993)

Personal Feelings Questionnaire—revised (PFQ2; Harder & Lewis, 1987; Harder & Zalma, 1990) State–Trait Anger Scale (STAS; Spielberger, Jacobs, Russell, & Crane, 1983)

**Interpersonal Dysregulation**

Inventory of Interpersonal Problems (IIP; Horowitz, Rosenberg, Baer, Ureno, & Villasenor, 1988)

Social Adjustment Scale (SAS-SR; Weissman, Prusoff, Thompson, Harding, & Myers, 1978)

**Behavioral Dysregulation**

Suicidal Behaviors Questionnaire (SBQ; Linehan, 1996)

Substance Abuse Subtle Screening Inventory—3 (SASSI-3; Lazowski, Miller, Boye, & Miller, 1998)

Yale–Brown Obsessive-Compulsive Scale—Shopping Version (YBOCS-S; Monahan, Black, & Gabel, 1996)

Garos Sexual Behavior Index (GSBI; Garos & Stock, 1998a, 1998b)

Eating Disorder Inventory—3 (EDI-3; Garner, Olmstud, & Polivy, 1983; Garner, 2004)

**Cognitive Dysregulation**

Dissociative Experiences Scale (DES; Bernstein & Putnam, 1986)

Scale for Suicidal Ideation (SSI; Beck, Brown, & Steer, 1997)

Reasons for Living Inventory (RFL; Linehan, Goodstein, Nielsen, & Chiles, 1983)

Beck Hopelessness Inventory (BHI; Beck, Weissman, Lester, & Trexler, 1974)

**Self-Dysregulation**

Rosenberg Self-Esteem Scale (RSE; Rosenberg, 1965)

Inventory of Altered Self-Capacities—Identity Impairment, Susceptibility to Influence Subscales (IASC; Briere & Runtz, 2002)

---

[a]This list is not exhaustive. For a more comprehensive review, consult the test manuals.

were included due to the high comorbidiy rate between BPD anxiety and mood disorders (Dolan-Sewell et al., 2001).

A measure of shame and guilt was also included in Table 19.1 (PFQ2) because proneness to the emotions of shame and guilt is believed to play a role in difficulties with emotional self-regulation and the pathogenesis of Axis I and II disorders (Buss, 1980; Wright, O'Leary, & Balkin, 1989). Shame is also a common reaction to uncontrollable negative affect and a typical consequence of early environments in which the individual's emotional responses were invalidated (Linehan, 1993). Furthermore, the propensity for shame is observed in survivors of childhood sexual abuse and it is estimated that 81% of patients with BPD have experienced some form of childhood abuse, an extreme form of invalidation (Linehan; Herman, 1997). Therefore measures of shame and guilt can be useful in the assessment of BPD because shame is often a consequence and etiology factor of emotional dysregulation.

We have also included a paper-and-pencil measure of anger in Table 19.1 because it pertains to emotional dysregulation. The *DSM-IV* lists uncontrollable anger as a symptom of BPD, which underscores the importance of assessing anger as a possible manifestation of emotional dysregulation (APA, 1994).

Intense relationships marked with difficulties and frantic attempts to avoid the loss of relationship despite a plethora of relationship problems and/or abruptly ending relationships are defining characteristics of interpersonal dysregulation (Linehan, 1993). Table 19.1 lists paper-and-pencil measures of interpersonal dysregulation with adequate reliability and validity.

A variety of behaviors and comorbid diagnoses fall under the rubric of behavioral dysregulation, and many reflect attempts at affect regulation triggered by dysphoric states (Linehan, 1993; Goff, 2002). The *DSM-IV* includes behavioral impulsivity and parasuicide (deliberate self-harm without the intent to die) as symptoms of BPD, with an estimated 75% of individuals with BPD engaging in parasuicidal behaviors currently and/or historically (Frances et al., 1986; Clarkin et al., 1983; Cowdry et al., 1985). Table 19.1 lists reliable and valid paper-and-pencil measures of behavioral dysregulation.

Dichotomous thinking, cognitive rigidity, dissociation, delusions, and other brief thought disturbances, in addition to suicidal ideation, are subsumed under the rubric of cognitive dysregulation (Linehan, 1993). Table 19.1 lists paper-and-pencil measures of cognitive dysregulation with adequate reliability and validity.

Self-dysregulation is manifested by feelings of emptiness, an unstable self-image, and low self-esteem (Linehan, 1993). This area of dysregulation is arguably more challenging to measure than the aforementioned areas because it reflects constructs that are difficult to measure and observe. Table 19.1 lists two measures selected based on their purported ability to assess experiences that fall under the self-dysregulation rubric.

### ONGOING

An accurate behavioral assessment of BPD is not a static process; rather, it is a dynamic process conducted at each point of contact with the client, utilizing a variety of information sources. The primary assessment tool utilized in the ongoing assessment of behaviors associated with BPD is the functional analysis. Stated simply, a functional analysis involves defining the behavior of interest and identifying antecedents and consequences associated with the behavior. The process of functional analysis involves defining the target behavior, tracking the behavior via self-monitoring procedures, conducting analyses, and, finally, hypothesis testing regarding alternative behaviors and self-interventions.

### Operational Definitions

In behavioral assessment, defining targets for change operationally at intake enables the clinician to develop a baseline and track change across sessions and is a necessary precursor to functional analysis. Kazdin (2001) describes operational definitions to be the result of defining a concept based on specific data. He states (p. 74):

> Operational definitions refer to defining a concept on the basis of the specific operations used for assessment. Paper-and-pencil measures (questionnaires to assess the domain), interviews, reports from others in contact with the client, physiological measures, and direct observation are among the most commonly used measures in psychological research to operationally defined key concepts.

In developing an operational definition, the clinician can emphasize either topography or function. Topographically based operational definitions are focused on the movements corresponding to the response, observational data. Functionally based operational definitions look to the consequence of the behavior and are believed to be more useful with regard to the information they provide than are topographical definitions, but they are also more vulnerable to assumptions and inferences on behalf of the assessor than are topographical definitions (Hutt & Hutt, 1970; Rosenblum, 1978; Hawkins, 1982).

Operational definitions should provide meaningful data characterized by having convergent validity, namely, that the definition of the target behavior should be consistent with common uses of the label and other sources, such as the referral source and research on the target behavior (Cambell & Fiske, 1959). In addition, an operational definition of a target behavior should be replicable, meaning similar measurement results should be obtained in different settings or by a different observer (Barlow & Hersen, 1984). The aforemention potential definitional problems can be minimized by making the definitions objective, clear, and complete, as articulated by Hawkins and Dobes (1977). *Objective* definitions refer to the observed aspects of the target behavior, not private events, of the individual of interest. *Clear* refers to the use of understandable language, ease of paraphrasing, and language that lacks ambiguity. *Complete* definitions include a name, a description, critical aspects of behavior, examples of the behavior, and gray-area circumstances in which it is difficult to determine whether or not the behavior fits the definition (Barlow & Hersen).

Operational definitions of target behavior will ideally reflect Linehan's (1993) reorganized criteria of BPD. Behavioral dysregulation most readily lends itself to operational definitions; however, each of the five areas of dysregulation can be defined in the aforementioned described manner, and paper-and-pencil measures help the clinician establish a baseline measurement of certain areas of dysregulation less amenable to direct observation. When operationally defining target behaviors, a precise description favoring specifics over generalities in terms of its topography, frequency of occurrence, and intensity is ideally sought (Linehan).

## Self-Monitoring

Use of self-monitoring techniques involving daily recording are less vulnerable to bias than retrospective accounts of behavior days after its occurrence

(Hollon & Garber, 1990). Self-monitoring tools are most effective when they are easy to use, are accessible to the client, and are utilized on a daily basis, ideally as close to the event of interest as possible. Typically, the use of self-monitoring requires shaping the client's behavior in an effort to increase the frequency of monitoring. This can be achieved by reinforcing successful approximations to daily tracking and problem-solving obstacles that may impede more frequent use. Linehan (1993) incorporates the use of self-monitoring in the form of a "diary card" in the treatment of BPD. Diary cards are used in DBT, an empirically validated treatment for BPD, to monitor treatment-relevant behaviors and emotions. In addition, the diary cards also monitor the use of skills as a self-intervention, their effectiveness, and the particular type of skill employed (Linehan). Use of a self-monitoring tool (e.g., diary card) ultimately enables the client and the clinician to track change with unparalleled detail and precision when utilized at least daily and is an important tool for the process of functional analysis. In behavior therapy, clients are taught self-monitoring techniques and the principles of behavioral change. The Portland DBT Program has developed a self-management module aimed at teaching clients, many of whom meet diagnostic criteria for BPD, how to apply behavioral assessment and modification procedures to target behaviors they wish to change (Kim & Goff, 1999).

## Functional Analysis

The functional analysis begins with an operational definition of the target behavior, as described earlier. A chain analysis, the term used in DBT, is synonymous with functional analysis (Linehan, 1993). A functional analysis of target behaviors is used in DBT when a client is new to treatment, a new problem area emerges, there is evidence of a change in frequency and/or intensity of a target behavior or apparent difficulties with self-control interventions, or when a problem arises in the process of therapy (Linehan). The purpose of a functional analysis of target behavior is to get specifics regarding the nature of the problem and factors maintaining (reinforcing) and/or causing (eliciting) it, to identify the obstacles to problem resolution, and ultimately to teach the client how to perform his/her own analyses. Through the process of functional analysis, strategies to help solve the problem should it arise in the future (and it usually does) are sought and the effectiveness of the solution(s) are tested. The process of functional analysis requires collaboration between client and therapist. Linehan suggests the use of validation and contingency management to foster a collaborative stance. It also requires a sufficient level of detail in describing the internal and external events associated with the behavior of interest and therefore warrants a level of curiosity similar to that of detectives working to solve a mystery. Additionally, the conclusions derived from the analysis are regarded as hypotheses to be tested and later confirmed or disconfirmed (Linehan).

Functional analyses range from the clinician asking a few questions regarding the controlling factors related to the target behavior for problems that have been explored previously and for which antecedents and consequences (both short and long term) have been identified to in-depth moment-by-moment questioning that can take an entire therapy session. Linehan (1993) identifies several dysfunctional links that often precipitate target behavior in the BPD treatment population and reflect the five areas of dysregulation described earlier. She states (p. 356):

> Common dysfunctional links might include dysregulation of specific emotions, distress tolerance, punishment and perfectionistic self-regulation strategies, nondialectical thinking, crisis-generating behaviors, acitive-passivity, apparent competence, self-invalidation, and inhibited grieving.

The target behaviors subsequent to the dysfunctional links often function to regulate intense emotions and/or are an attempt to affect change in the environment. The analysis of consequences helps the client and the clinician develop hypotheses regarding the target behavior's function. In general, the data gleaned from an in-depth functional analysis enable the client and the clinician to test hypotheses regarding the controlling factors maintaining or exacerbating target behaviors (e.g., dysfunctional links at the antecedent level and contingencies at the consequent level). Interventions are then developed to ameliorate hypothesized skills deficits, emotional responses, cognitions, and contingencies (Linehan). The targeted dysfunctional links are based on the biosocial model, behavioral principles, and behavioral patterns related to dialectical dilemmas (for a review, see Linehan).

The paper-and-pencil measures described in the preceding section can be administered repeatedly throughout the course of treatment. We recommend the use of one or two reliable and valid measures to be administered at the highest frequency that is useful, possible, and consistent, which often translates into once a month or bimonthly. The BSI (Derogatis & Spencer, 1982) and OQ-45 (Lambert & Hill, 1994) are sound measures for the purposes of tracking progress across several areas of pathology. The OQ-45 has the advantage of its emphasis on functioning in addition to symptom severity. However, in some cases it may be useful to employ an additional measurement specific to a particular problems area (e.g., BDI-II for depression). Also, different managed-care companies may require and/or prefer an alternative self-report measure to track treatment effectiveness (e.g., Life Status Questionnaire for PacifiCare Behavioral Health).

## OUTCOME

The outcome of therapy is ascertained through multiple assessment strategies. Change in operationally defined behavioral goals is one measure of outcome. Additionally, the GAF score at discharge can be compared to the client's pretreatment score to obtain a general impression of outcome. The comparison of pretreatment and discharge paper-and-pencil measures such as the OQ-45 provides the clinician with a quantified measure of change, which is often preferred by managed-care companies. Additionally, target behaviors can be tracked and outcome assessed through the use of a single-subject case study design, to be described later.

## CLINICAL UTILITY

Accurate behavioral assessment of BPD offers much in terms of clinical utility. It informs one's diagnosis and treatment plan, including the organization of behavioral targets, is a form of risk management, and provides a basis from which to monitor and evaluate progress.

### DIAGNOSIS

Again, the potential diversity and seriousness of presenting problems among clients meeting *DSM-IV* criteria for BPD warrants specific and behaviorally focused assessment. Behavioral assessment aids the process of diagnosis of BPD in its emphasis on the functional aspects of behavior. The five areas of dysregulation, which subsume the *DSM-IV* criteria for BPD, often reflect functional relationships, with emotional dysregulation generally precipitating behavioral manifestations of the other areas of dysregulation (Waltz & Linehan, 1999). In exploring the function of a particular maladaptive behavior, the clinician can better ascertain the relationship between BPD and frequently co-occurring Axis I disorders (functional, consequent, overlap of criterion sets) through the use of behavioral assessment strategies.

### ASSESSMENT, CONCEPTUALIZATION, AND TREATMENT PLANNING

Behavioral assessment is contextual, in that it looks to the particulars of the individual and his/her environment, assuming the same principles of learning are involved in the development and maintenance of adaptive and maladaptive behaviors. Ultimately it informs the treatment plan and intervention format. Clients with BPD often present with what can seem like a deluge of problematic behaviors, all of which are potential targets for change, ideal candidates for functional analyses. Linehan's (1993) treatment hierarchy orders target behaviors and problem areas associated with BPD by level of importance. Life-threatening behaviors, for example, parasuicide, suicide attempts, and severe suicidal ideation, are analyzed via a functional analysis as are behaviors that impede the progress and delivery of therapy. Behaviors that interfere with quality of life (e.g., drug use, gambling, promiscuity, disordered eating) are addressed next, assuming a lack of higher-order targets, and their selection is based on whether or not they interfere with the client's long-term goals; again, the process of functional analysis is a collaboration between client and therapist (Linehan).

## RISK MANAGEMENT

An accurate risk assessment at intake and throughout the course of therapy is of paramount importance in the diagnosis and treatment of BPD, and behavioral assessment lends itself to this task. Again, BPD is associated with parasuicidal behaviors (intentional self-injury without the intent of death), with approximately 75% of individuals with BPD reporting current or historic parasuicide and approximately 10% dying by completed suicide (Frances et al., 1986; Clarkin et al., 1983; Cowdry et al., 1985). Risk management is a crucial component to any treatment of BPD. In DBT, risk is managed through the constant assessment (at each session) and immediate treatment of life-threatening behaviors (Linehan, 1993). Lethality of past attempts is ascertained by a thorough assessment at intake and is assessed on an ongoing basis should life-threatening behaviors occur during the course of therapy. The lethality of means can be estimated by consulting the Scale Points for Lethality Assessment a 10-point scale for adults, reflecting the likelihood of death associated with means and contextual factors (Bongar, 1991). In DBT, clients also have access to their therapist's 24-hour emergency number, and a crisis plan is in effect for all clients who present with life-threatening behaviors. Hospitalization, voluntary or involuntary, is sought when the life-threatening behaviors can no longer be managed on an outpatient basis.

## PROGRESS EVALUATION

Behavioral assessment also enables the clinician to evaluate progress through the analysis of change, or lack thereof, in target behaviors via the employment of a single-subject case study design. There are several types of single-subject case designs that can be used to assess change in target behaviors across sessions and ultimately outcome of treatment. The A-B-A withdrawal designs involve the introduction of the treatment variable and then its withdrawal, ending in either the treatment condition (A-B-A-B, B-A-B) or the withdrawal condition (A-B-A). The A-B design, which involves a pretreatment assessment of target behavior frequency and additional frequency assessment on the introduction of treatment with multiple target measures is a type of single-subject research design from which outcome can be ascertained with regard to multiple treatment targets. The withdrawal design, an arguably more sophisticated design in isolating treatment effects, involves the withdrawal of the treatment condition in various temporal orderings (Barlow & Hersen, 1984). This involves severely altering the way in which treatment is delivered and ultimately deprives the client of potentially effective treatment at various points in time; therefore, for the purposes of analyzing the outcome of a particular case, the A-B design with multiple baselines fits the realities of clinical practice. The clinician can develop multiple baselines for a given target behavior, reflecting the frequency of the behavior across different contexts, or, what is more likely, a separate A-B design can be applied to each target behavior. The A-B design is a quasi-experimental design, thereby limiting the employment of statistical analysis. However, Kazdin (1984) has reviewed statistical methods that can be utilized with a single-subject case study design, all of which require a large number of data points (see Barlow & Hersen for a review).

## CASE STUDY

This case study illustrates the aforementioned behavioral assessment strategies. It is a composite of clients seen at the Portland DBT Program and does not represent one particular client. Shannon is a 32-year-old Caucasian female, referred by her previous therapist after treatment proved ineffective. Shannon is attractive and arrives at sessions professionally dressed. Shannon presents as depressed and irritable during sessions and shows no signs of a florid thought disorder. Her attitude toward the treatment and the therapist vacillates between admiration and compliance and frustration leading to verbal aggression directed toward the therapist. Except when angry, she speaks in a meek voice and makes little eye contact. She is of average intelligence, and her memory and reasoning abilities appear to be intact. Her insight into her difficulties and her judgment are somewhat impaired. Shannon has been divorced for several years and is currently in an 8-month relationship. She resides alone in an apartment.

Shannon complains of long-standing problems with emotion dysregulation and describes her emotions as "out of control" much of the time. Her emotional expressions tend to be intense and quick and she has great difficulty calming down after an emotional experience. She reports the most difficulty with regulating anxiety, depression, and anger. Shannon occasionally experiences panic attacks and generally feels at least mildly down and depressed much of the time. Additionally, Shannon has a history of more debilitating depressive symptoms that tend to last months, at a frequency of once or twice a year. In retrospect, Shannon believes she was likely depressed and anxious as a child and has struggled with these symptoms all of her adult life. Shannon also reports irritation with periods of rage, usually associated with interpersonal conflict. Additionally, Shannon has difficulty falling and staying asleep. She is currently on medication for sleep, which she has found only somewhat helpful.

Shannon's difficulty with emotional dysregulation often leads to behavioral dysregulation. This manifests in impulsive behaviors that she later regrets and are typically in response to intense emotions. Shannon often engages in self-harm behaviors when agitated and distressed or numb and detached. She reports this behavior helps her reregulate her emotions. Her self-harm behaviors have waxed and waned over the years, but the relief she gets from her emotions after engaging in the behavior makes it difficult for her to stop. When Shannon feels she can no longer tolerate her emotions, she gets desperate enough to consider suicide. She has a history of suicidal behaviors of varying severity and requiring intervention ranging from none at all for superficial scratches to her wrists to several days in an intensive care unit after an overdose. Suicide attempts are often triggered by abandonment or shaming experiences. For example, many of her suicide attempts were prompted by her exhusband's threats to end the relationship.

Shannon also tends to go on spending sprees in response to emotional distress that have left her in financial difficulty. Additionally, Shannon occasionally engages in binge-eating behavior when bored or anxious. She reports "numbness" after engaging in binge eating. Shannon also evidences cognitive dysregulation, such as black-and-white thinking, extreme negative self-talk, and chronic suicidality.

Shannon has interpersonal dysregulation in the form of frequent heated arguments with her current partner, during which she occasionally throws objects and leaves without resolving the matter. Although she questions her current relationship, she reports, "I can't be alone." She fears her partner will leave her, which may precipitate target behaviors. Shannon has evidenced this pattern of interpersonal behaviors in intimate relationships her entire adult life. In terms of self-dysregulation, she reports often feeling numb and detached from herself. She additionally reports occasional dissociative experiences.

Academically, Shannon was bright and received above-average grades for much of her schooling. Her grades dropped significantly in high school, however. During high school she also became rebellious and frequently skipped classes, was promiscuous, frequently shoplifted, smoked marijuana, and engaged in binge drinking. She did, however, graduate from high school and went on to a local college. After attending college on and off for seven years, she received a degree in literature.

As a teenager, she was referred to outpatient treatment by a guidance counselor who contacted Shannon's mother regarding his concerns. This treatment was somewhat helpful, in that school attendance improved. Later, Shannon received treatment at the college counseling center after a suicide attempt precipitated by a difficult breakup with a boyfriend. She put in frequent crisis calls to her therapist at the time, and her suicidal threats were escalating. She was eventually referred outside the college counseling system for further treatment. Shannon reports a total of four past therapists, all of whom eventually felt they could not help her. Shannon was hospitalized for suicide attempts and gestures, three times while in college and receiving treatment at the college counseling center and twice since that time. She liked the hospital, in that it gave her a break from her life; however, she feels the treatment at the hospital did not adequately address her issues.

In friendships, Shannon tends to alternately idealize and devalue her peers. For this reason, she has had difficulty maintaining long-term friendships. In recent years, Shannon has avoided friendships, due to the seemingly inevitably painful outcome of her relationships, and currently reports no peer-based source of social support. After graduating from a local college with a degree in literature, Shannon had difficulty finding a job within her interest area. She took a job as an administrative assistant at a law office, but was often irritated with the lawyers and unhappy in the position. She stayed in that position for nine months and then took subsequent jobs at a car dealership, in retail, as a waitress, and at a call center. Shannon again was generally unhappy at these jobs. She tends to have interpersonal difficulties at work as well. Specifically, coworkers report feeling as though they are "walking on eggshells" around her, and her supervisors have difficulty giving her constructive feedback because she reacts so intensely to any hint of criticism.

Shannon would ideally like to work as a writer, but her efforts to break into the industry have been unsuccessful to date. She reports having given up on that career path and is now considering going back to school, but she is undecided about the direction to take. Additionally, her current financial difficulties require her to work full time. Currently Shannon is working at a doctor's office in the medical billing department. Her job duties include mostly data entry, which she finds very boring and not challenging enough. She has been at her current position for five months and reports that the relative isolation of the job has decreased interpersonal conflicts with coworkers but leaves her feeling isolated and lonely.

Shannon is the youngest of three children born to her now-divorced parents. They divorced when she was seven. She lived with her mother after her parents divorced, and she was subsequently sexually abused by her mother's live-in boyfriend for a period of several years during adolescence. Her reports to her mother about the abuse were ignored, and her mother eventually married this man. The abuse was never reported to officials. Despite this history, Shannon feels very attached to and dependent on her mother. She reports being faced with cues of her abuse weekly, for she is often at her mother's home and calls her daily.

Shannon had little contact with her father growing up, and her hopes during adolescence and young adulthood to reestablish a meaningful relationship were not reciprocated. Her father remarried and had two children and reported he needed to focus on his "current family." Shannon continues to desire a relationship with her father.

Shannon's brother, who is five years older, was very successful in athletics during high school and received a lot of attention from both their mother and father around these accomplishments. He later got deeply involved in drugs, but Shannon's father continues to support him when he gets into trouble. Her older sister is only 19 months her senior, and growing up they had a very close relationships. Shannon's sister was not abused by the mother's boyfriend, but she was aware of the abuse occurring in the home. Her sister is currently married to a corporate attorney and has two children. Shannon's sister stays at home with her children, and her family is well off financially. Since her sister's marriage, their relationship has become more distant. Shannon feels as though her sister is ashamed of her now that she has a more affluent lifestyle.

Shannon was assessed using three levels of evaluation: intake, across sessions, and outcome assessments. At intake the DIB-R (Zanarini et al., 1989; Hurt et al.,

1986) aided in clarification of the Axis II diagnosis of Borderline Personality Disorder. Additionally, a detailed history of her parasuicidal behavior was obtained using the PHI-2 (Linehan, 1996), which gave lifetime prevalence and a baseline level of the severity of the behavior. Results of the detailed clinical interview, in concert with the DIB-R (Zanarini et al., 1989; Hurt et al.), suggest the following diagnoses: Axis I, Dysthymic Disorder, Anxiety Disorder NOS; Axis II, Borderline Personality Disorder; Axis III, Headaches; Axis IV, Relationship problems, lack of social support, and work-related stressors; Axis V, current GAF of 45.

Shannon completed a number of pencil-and-paper measures at intake and these same measures were collected on an ongoing basis. Those related to generally symptomology included the OQ-45, in the severe range with a score of 107. Results of measures to assess Shannon's level of emotional dysregulation included BDI-II, in the moderate range with a score of 23, a moderate BAI of 24, and scores on the STAS in the clinical range above the 75th percentile. Shannon's level of cognitive dysregulation was assessed with the BHI, with a score of 15, suggesting significant hopelessness.

In addition to the pencil-and-paper measures, on an ongoing basis two other behavioral assessment tools were used: self-monitoring and functional analysis. The diary card, which is a self-monitoring device developed by Linehan (1993), was collected on a weekly basis. The diary card involves daily tracking of emotions and urges for target behaviors on a scale of 0 to 5, with 0 reflecting no emotion or urge and 5 reflecting intense emotion or urge. Additionally, the diary card tracks the target behaviors that are the focus of treatment. These target behaviors usually fall under the rubric of behavioral dysregulation. During the initial months of treatment Shannon's diary card showed significant emotional dysregulation, in that she rated most of her emotions (including sadness, anger, and fear) at a 4 or 5 on an almost-daily basis. Additionally, she rated her level of suicidal urges consistently at a 3–4 daily, and her urge for self-harm was generally a 3. Finally, Shannon had a baseline of one self-harm incident each week, no suicide attempts, two binge-eating episodes a week, and approximately monthly shopping sprees. Later in treatment her emotional self-ratings dropped slightly to 3s and 4s daily, but her suicidal thoughts changed more drastically and began to become less frequent and less intense. Her self-harm behavior remitted, and her shopping became less frequent, but her binge eating remained the same, with some weeks of increased incidence of the behavior.

Functional analyses were conducted on a regular basis during therapy sessions. The functional analysis often revealed a typical pattern. Most of Shannon's behavioral dysregulation was triggered by an interpersonal conflict or criticism from her social environment. These precipitating events routinely led to intense emotional reactions. Shannon often feels as though she cannot control or tolerate these emotional experiences, and she then engages in self-harm behavior, shopping, or binge eating. After engaging in any of these target behaviors, Shannon feels an immediate sense of relief from the emotional distress. In the case of self-harm, these behaviors often bring her boyfriend, who is often involved in the precipitating event, to her side to comfort her. After time has passed, she feels extremely guilty and regrets her behaviors. It is hypothesized that these behaviors are maintained by the negative reinforcement of the relief from intense negative emotion and the positive reinforcement of the boyfriend's response.

In addition to the self-monitoring and functional analyses being conducted on an ongoing basis, Shannon was administered the OQ-45, BDI-II, BAI, and BHI on an ongoing basis. To assess Shannon's therapeutic outcome, these same measures and semistructured interviews administered at intake were again administered. Results indicated improvements in all areas.

## ETHICAL AND LEGAL CONSIDERATIONS

There are several ethical and legal considerations in this case. Most importantly, Shannon is reporting suicidal ideation and has a history of suicide attempts with varying levels of lethality. Additionally, those with Borderline Personality Disorder generally comprise a high-risk population to treat. For these reasons, legal and clinical risk-management issues should be well understood while treating this population (Linehan, 1993). Linehan has detailed some of the important risk-management considerations for treating BPD using DBT. First, persons treating high-risk populations such as those with BPD should assess their level of competence to do so. An adequate level of competence would involve knowledge of the literature related to suicidal behavior, BPD, and the other presenting diagnostic categories evidenced in the client. Second, it is important to thoroughly document risk assessments, risk–benefit analyses, consultation, and informed consent about treatment. Third, the clinical record should include records from past and present medical and psychiatric treatment providers. Fourth, the therapist should work to involve the family in the treatment to facilitate the management of suicidal behaviors. Fifth, the therapist should frequently and on an ongoing basis consult with other clinicians. Finally, in the event of a client's suicide, postvention should be conducted. This may include addressing the needs of the staff involved with the client, working with the family of the client, and attending to the possible legal issues that may arise.

Other ethical considerations in working with BPD are abandonment and boundaries. It is not uncommon for clients with BPD to engage in therapy-interfering behaviors (Linehan, 1993). These behaviors have the potential to impact the therapist's clinical judgment. At one extreme, the therapist may loosen his or her boundaries in response to the client's pushing of the boundaries and therefore reinforce the very behaviors that have been problematic in therapy and in the client's life (Koocher & Keith-Spiegel, 1998). At the other extreme, these therapy-interfering behaviors may result in the therapist's unilaterally terminating treatment in a manner that may be considered abandonment. To safeguard against these ethical dilemmas, it is important to address these behaviors directly and quickly. Linehan suggests four strategies for dealing with therapy-interfering behaviors. First is to define the behavior of concern clearly and specifically. Next is to use the technique of chain analysis to explore completely the antecedents, the behavior, and the consequences of the behavior. Third, using the information obtained during the chain analysis, is to identify potential solutions to the various important issues. Finally, if the client refuses to engage in the treatment in such a way as to ameliorate the therapy-interfering behavior, the therapist may consider and discuss with the client a vacation from therapy or a referral to a new therapist. A therapy vacation in DBT is a contingency strategy involving suspending treatment for a specific duration or until an agreed-upon condition has been evidenced. This should only be used if all other contingencies have been unsuccessful and the behavior seriously impacts the therapist's ability to conduct the treatment as needed for success or impacts the therapist's willingness to work with the client (Linehan).

Working with clients with BPD is often challenging, but recent developments in treatment have given therapists effective structures and strategies for managing the difficult behaviors. Treatment in a DBT model suggests that problems are due to a lack of basic skills, including distress tolerance, emotion regulation, interpersonal effectiveness and self-management, and maladaptive behaviors being reinforced by the environment while adaptive behaviors are punished (Linehan, 1993). DBT has five functions: capability enhancement, motivational enhancement, enhancement of generalizations of gains, enhancement of capabilities and motivation of therapists, and structuring of the environment to support clinical progress (Linehan).

## SUMMARY

Borderline personality disorder (BPD) is a serious, complex, and often-chronic condition with a high comorbidity rate and symptom overlap with several mental disorders. Additionally BPD is associated with high-risk behaviors such as suicide attempts and deliberate self-harm in addition to behavioral impulsivity. The heterogeneity in presentation among individuals with BPD warrants a behaviorally based assessment process, as does the seriousness and complexity of the disorder and its associated behaviors.

The five areas of dysregulation as described by Linehan (1993) are related to one another, reflecting functional and consequent relationships between maladaptive behaviors subsumed under each area. The relationships between the various maladaptive behaviors associated with BPD, elucidated through a behavioral lens, highlight the clinical utility of ongoing behavioral assessment for the treatment of the problem areas associated with BPD. Additionally, given the pervasiveness of potentially life-threatening behaviors in this treatment population, continuous behavioral analysis, monitoring, and testing of interventions aimed at the reduction of the problem areas such behaviors is a form of risk assessment and management. DBT offers the clinician a structure based on behavioral therapy from which to organize, prioritize, and treat multiple symptoms and behaviors associated with BPD, a disorder once thought to be treatment resistant.

## REFERENCES

American Psychiatric Association. (1980). *Diagnostic and statistical manual of mental disorders* (3rd ed.). Washington, DC: Author.

American Psychiatric Association. (1994). *Diagnostic and statistical manual of mental* disorders (4th ed.). Washington, DC: Author.

Barlow, D. H., & Hersen, M. (1984). *Single case experimental designs* (2nd ed.). Boston: Allyn & Bacon.

Beck, A., Brown, G., & Steer, R. (1997). Psychometric characteristics of the scale for suicide ideation with psychiatric outpatients. *Behavior Research Therapy 35,* 1039–1046.

Beck, A. T., & Steer, R. (1993). Beck Anxiety Inventory manual. San Antonio, TX: Psychological Corporation.

Beck, A. T., Steer, R. A., & Brown, G. K. (1996). *Manual for the Beck Depression Inventory* (2nd ed.). San Antonio, TX: Psychological Corporation.

Beck, A. T., Ward, C. H., Mendelsen, M., Mock, J., & Erbaugh, J. (1961). An inventory for measuring depression. *Archives of General Psychiatry, 4,* 53–63.

Beck, A., Weissman, A., Lester, D., & Trexler, L. (1974). The measurement of pessimism: The hopelessness scale. *Journal of Consulting and Clinical Psychology, 42,* 861–865.

Benjamin, L. (1996). *Interpersonal diagnosis and treatment of personality disorders* (2nd ed.). New York: Guilford Press.

Bernstein, E., & Putman, F. (1986). Development, reliability, and validity of a dissociation scale. *The Journal of Nervous and Mental Disease, 174,* 727–735.

Bongar, B. (1991). *The suicidal patient: Clinical and legal standards of care* (pp. 277–283). Washington, DC: American Psychological Association.

Bongar, B. (1992). *Suicide: Guidelines for assessment, management, and treatment.* New York: Oxford University Press.

Briere, J., & Runtz, M. (2002). The Inventory of Altered Self-Capacities (IASC): A standardized measure of identity, affect regulation, and relationship disturbance. *Assessment, 9,* 230–239.

Buss, A. H. (1980). *Self-consciousness and social anxiety.* San Fransico: Freeman.

Cambell, D. T., & Fiske, D. W. (1959). Convergent and discriminant validation by the multitrait–multimethod matrix. *Psychological Bulletin, 56,* 81–105.

Clarkin, J. F., Widiger, T. A., Frances, A., Hurt, S. W., & Gilmore, M. (1983). Prototypic typology and the Borderline Personality Disorder. *Journal of Abnormal Psychiatry, 92,* 263–275.

Comtois, K. A., Levensky, E. R., & Linehan, M. M. (1999). Behavior therapy. In M. Hersen & A. Bellack (Eds.), *Handbook of comparative interventions for adult disorders* (2nd ed., pp. 555–583). New York: John Wiley & Sons.

Cowdry, R. W., Pickar, D., & Davies, R. (1985). Symptoms and EEG findings in the borderline syndrome. *International Journal of Psychiatry in Medicine, 15,* 201–211.

Cundick, B. P. (1989). Review of the brief symptom inventory. In J. Cooley & J. Kramer (Eds.), *Tenth mental measurements yearbook* (pp. 111–112). Lincoln: University of Nebraska Press.

Davis, T., Gunderson, J. G., & Myers, M. (1999). Borderline Personality Disorder. In D. G. Jacobs (Ed.), *The Harvard Medical School guide to suicide assessment and intervention* (pp. 311–331). San Francisco: Jossey-Bass.

Derogatis, L. R., & Melisaratos, N. (1983). The Brief Symptom Inventory: An introductory report. *Psychological Medicine, 13,* 595–605.

Derogatis, L. R., & Spencer, P. M. (1982). *Administration & procedures: BSI manual—I.* Baltimore: Clinical Psychometric Research, John Hopkins University School of Medicine.

Dolan-Sewell, R. T., Krueger, R. F., & Shea, M. T. (2001). Co-occurrence with syndrome disorders. In W. J. Lively (Ed.), *Handbook of personality disorders* (pp. 84–104). New York: Guilford Press.

Edell, W. S., Joy, S. P., & Yehuda, R. (1990). Discordance between self-report and observed psychopathology in borderline patients. *Journal of Personality Disorders, 4,* 381–390.

First, M. B., Gibbon, M., Spitzer, R. L., Williams, J. B. W., & Benjamin, L. S. (1997). *Structured clinical interview for DSM-IV Axis II personality disorders (SCID-II).* Washington, DC: American Psychiatric Press.

Frances, A., Fyer, M., & Clarkin, J. F. (1986). Personality and suicide. *Annals of the New York Academy of Science, 482,* 281–293.

Garner, D. M. (2004). *Eating Disorder Inventory—3: Professional manual.* Lutz, FL: Psychological Assessment Resources.

Garner, D. M., Olmstead, M. A., & Polivy, J. (1983). Development and validation of a multidimensional eating disorder inventory for anorexia nervosa and bulimia. *International Journal of Eating Disorders, 2,* 15–34.

Garos, S., & Stock, W. (1998a). Investigating the discriminant validity and differentiation capability of the Garos Sexual Behavior Index. *Sexual Addiction & Compulsivity, 5,* 251–267.

Garos, S., & Stock, W. (1998b). Measuring disorders of sexual frequency and control: The Garos Sexual Behavior Index. *Addiction & Compulsivity, 5,* 159–177.

Goff, B. C. (2002). Borderline Personality Disorder. In J. Thomas & M. Hersen (Eds.), *Handbook of mental health in the workplace* (pp. 291–309). Thousand Oaks, CA: Sage.

Harder, D., & Lewis, S. (1987). The assessment of shame and guilt. In J. N. Butcher & C. D. Spielberger (Eds.), *Advances in personality assessment* (Vol. 6, pp. 89–114). Hillsdale, NJ: Erlbaum.

Harder, D., & Zalma, A. (1990). Two promising shame and guilt scales: A construct validity comparison. *Journal of Personality Assessment, 55,* 729–745.

Hawkins, R. P. (1982). Developing a behavior code. In D. P. Hartmann (Ed.), *Using observers to study behavior: New directions for methodology of social and behavioral science* (pp. 21–35). San Francisco: Jossey-Bass.

Hawkins, R. P., & Dobes, R. W. (1977). Behavioral definitions in applied behavioral analysis: Explicit or implicit. In B. C. Etzel, J. M. LeBlanc, & D. M. Baer (Eds.), *New directions in behavioral research: Theory, methods, and applications. In honor of Sidney W. Bijou* (pp. 167–188). Hillsdale, NJ: Erlbaum.

Herman, J. (1997). *Trauma and recovery: The aftermath of violence—From domestic abuse to political terror* (2nd ed.). New York: Basic Books.

Hollon, S. D., & Garber, J. (1990). Cognitive therapy for depression: A social cognitive approach. *Personality and Social Psychology Bulletin, 16,* 58–73.

Horowitz, L. M., Rosenberg, S. E., Baer, B., Ureno, G., & Villasenor, V. (1988). Inventory of interpersonal problems: Psychometric properties and clinical application. *Journal of Consulting and Clinical Psychology, 56,* 885–892.

Hurt, S., Clarkin, J., Koenigsberg, H., Frances, A., & Nurnberg, H. (1986). Diagnostic interview for borderlines: Psychometric properties and validity. *Journal of Counseling and Clinical Psychology, 54,* 256–260.

Hutt, S. J., & Hutt, C. (1970). *Direct observation and measurement of behavior.* Springfield, IL: Charles C Thomas.

Kazdin, A. E. (1984). Statistical analyses for single-case experimental designs. In D. Barlow & M. Hersen (Eds.), *Single case experimental designs* (2nd ed., pp. 285–321). Boston: Allyn & Bacon.

Kazdin, A. E. (2001). *Behavior modification: In applied settings* (6th ed.). Belmont, CA: Wadsworth/Thomas Learning.

Kim, S. A., & Goff, B. C. (1999). *Self-management and relapse prevention skills training unit.* (Available from the Portland Dialectical Behavior Therapy Program, 5125 S.W. Macadam Ave., Portland Oregon 97239).

Kim, S. A., & Goff, B. C. (2002). Borderline Personality Disorder. In M. Hersen (Ed.), *Clinical behavior therapy for adults and children* (pp. 160–180). New York: John Wiley & Sons.

Koocher, G. P., & Keith-Spiegel, P. (1998). *Ethics in psychology: Professional standards and cases* (2nd ed.). New York: Oxford University Press.

Koerner, K., & Linehan, M. M. (1997). Case formulation in dialectical behavior therapy for Borderline Personality Disorder. In T. Eells (Ed.), *Handbook of psychotherapy case formulation* (pp. 340–367). New York: Guilford Press.

Lambert, M. J., & Hill, C. (1994). Assessing psychotherapy outcomes and processes. In A. E. Bergin, & S. L. Garfield (Eds.), *Handbook of psychotherapy and behavior change* (4th ed., pp. 72–113). New York: John Wiley & Sons.

Lazowski, L., Miller, F., Boye, M., & Miller, G. (1998). Efficacy of the Substance Abuse Subtle Screening Inventor—3 (SASSI-3) in identifying substance abuse disorders in clinical settings. *Journal of Personality Assessment, 71,* 114–128.

Linehan, M. M. (1993). *Cognitive-behavioral treatment of Borderline Personality Disorder.* New York: Guilford Press.

Linehan, M. M. (1996). *Parasuicide History Interview—2: Instructions and cards.* Seattle, WA: University of Washington.

Linehan, M. M., Goodstein, J. L., Nielsen, S. L., & Chiles, J. A. (1983). Reasons for staying alive when you are thinking of killing yourself: The Reasons for Living Inventory. *Journal of Consulting and Clinical Psychology, 51,* 276–286.

Linehan, M. M., & Heard, H. (1999). Borderline Personality Disorder: Costs, course, and treatment outcomes. In N. Miller & K. Magruder (Eds.), *The cost-effectiveness of psychotherapy: A guide for practitioners, researchers, and policy-makers* (pp. 291–305). New York: Oxford University Press.

Linehan, M. M., Kanter, J. W., & Comtois, K. A. (1999). Dialectical behavior therapy for Borderline Personality Disorder: Efficacy, specificity, and cost effectiveness. In D. S. Janowsky (Ed.), *Psychotherapy: Indications and outcomes* (pp. 93–118). Washington, DC: American Psychiatric Press.

McClanahan, J., Kim, S. A., & Bobowick, M. (2001). Diagnostic interviewing: Personality disorders. In M. Hersen (Ed.), *Diagnostic interviewing* (pp. 173–201). New York, NY: Kluwer.

Monahan, P., Black, D., & Gabel, J. (1996). Reliability and validity of a scale to measure change in persons with compulsive buying. *Psychiatry Research, 64,* 59–67.

Pull, C. B., & Wittchen, H. U. (1991). CIDI, SCAN and IPDE: Structured diagnostic interviews for ICD 10 and *DSM III-R. European Psychiatry, 6,* 277–285.

Rogers, R. (2001). *Handbook of diagnostic and structured interviewing.* New York: Guilford Press.

Rosenberg, M. (1965). *Society and the adolescent self-image.* Princeton, NJ: Princeton University Press.

Rosenblum, L. A. (1978). The creation of behavioral taxonomy. In G. P. Sackette (Ed.), *Observing behavior: Vol. 2. Data collection and analysis methods* (pp. 15–24). Baltimore: University Park Press.

Spielberger, C. D., Jacobs, G., Russell, S., & Crane, R. S. (1983). Assessment of anger: The State–Trait Anger Scale. In J. N. Butcher & C. D. Spielberger (Eds.), *Advances in personality assessment* (vol. 2, pp. 159–187). Hillsdale, NJ: Erlbaum.

Sullivan, H. S. (1954). *The psychiatric interview.* New York: W. W. Norton.

Taylor, J. A. (1953). A personality scale of manifest anxiety. *Journal of Abnormal and Social Psychology, 48,* 285–290.

Waltz, J., & Linehan, M. M. (1999). Functional analysis of Borderline Personality Disorder behavioral criterion patterns: Links to treatment. In Derksen et al. (Eds.), *Treatment of personality disorders* (pp. 183–206). New York: Kluwer Academic/Plenum Press.

Weissman, M., Prusoff, B., Thompson, D., Harding, P., & Myers, J. (1978). Social adjustment by self-report in a community sample and in psychiatric outpatients. *Journal of Nervous and Mental Disease, 166,* 317–326.

Widiger, T. A., & Trull, T. J. (1993). Borderline and narcissistic personality disorders. In P. Sutker & H. E. Adams (Eds.), *Comprehensive handbook of psychopathology*, (2nd ed., pp. 337–370). New York: Plenum Press.

World Health Organization. (1990). Mental and behavioral disorders (including disorders of psychological development). In *International classification of diseases* (10th revision). Geneva: Author.

Wright, F., O'Leary, J. O., & Balkin, J. (1989). Shame, guilt, narcissism, and depression: Correlates and sex differences. *Journal of Psychoanalytic Psychology, 6,* 217–230.

Zanarini, M., Gunderson, J., Frankenburg, F., & Chauncey, D. (1989). The Revised Diagnostic Interview for Borderlines: Discriminating BPD from other Axis II disorders. *The Journal of Personality Disorders, 3,* 10–18.

PART III

# SPECIAL ISSUES

# 20

## TECHNOLOGY INTEGRATION AND BEHAVIORAL ASSESSMENT

DAVID C. S. RICHARD

*Department of Psychology*
*Rollins College*
*Winter Park, Florida*

ANDREW GLOSTER

*Department of Psychology*
*Eastern Michigan University*
*Ypsilanti, Michigan*

### INTRODUCTION

In a recent review of computer applications in behavioral assessment, Richard and Lauterbach (2003) noted that technology was making its presence known in virtually all aspects of behavioral training, practice, and research. They came to this conclusion by observing an accelerating trend of publications in computerized behavioral assessment in each 5-year period from the early 1970s to the present. A wide variety of applications were reviewed, including training simulations in behavior analysis and case conceptualization, Internet-based training programs in behavioral assessment, software for conducting behavioral observations, ecological momentary assessment using handheld computers, and clinical case formulation software. Since then, all of these research areas have experienced continued growth and a number of reviews have been published on computerized assessment and technology integration (see Schulenberg & Yutrzenka, 2004; Butcher, Perry, & Hahn, 2004; Richard & Bobicz, 2003).

We use the term *technology integration* to refer to the broad spectrum of technology applications that are currently being evaluated in an assessment or treatment context. Although technology integration frequently involves client use of a computer in some capacity (e.g., therapy via the Internet, ecological momentary assessment with a personal digital assistant, and direct computerized assessment), the term also refers to the use of any electronic device that might mediate an assessment or therapeutic encounter. Thus, videoconferencing and telemedicine would be subsumed under the broad umbrella of technology integration. This chapter is concerned primarily with technology integration as it relates to behavioral assessment.

The purpose of this chapter is twofold. Given the recent publication of other reviews on computerized assessment and technology use, we decided yet another review would not be especially useful. Instead, we have opted to critically discuss two technological innovations relevant to behavioral assessment (ecological momentary assessment and telehealth). To supplement our discussion, we then report results of an attitude and utilization survey we gave nonprofessionals and members of the Association for Behavioral and Cognitive Therapies regarding technology integration. Although others have surveyed clinicians to assess the way technology is used in clinical practice (e.g., Farrell, 1989; Rosen & Weil, 1996; McMinn, Buchanan, Ellens, & Ryan, 1999), no research has addressed whether behaviorally oriented clinicians might hold more favorable attitudes toward technology integration. Additionally, we are not aware of any studies that have compared attitudes of practicing professionals toward technology integration with those of nonprofessionals. Identifying differences between these two groups should help mental health professionals anticipate sources of potential resistance or misunderstanding nonprofessionals may hold regarding technology integration.

## TWO EXAMPLES OF TECHNOLOGY INTEGRATION: ECOLOGICAL MOMENTARY ASSESSMENT AND TELEHEALTH

Although space limitations prevent us from addressing each of the myriad ways in which technology has been integrated into clinical assessment and treatment, a rich literature has developed in both mainstream and specialty journals. Table 20.1 contains a listing of relevant technologies and published reports of their integration into assessment and treatment.

### ECOLOGICAL MOMENTARY ASSESSMENT (EMA)

Technological advances in handheld computer technology have provided new opportunities for the collection of self-monitoring data. Ecological momentary assessment, or EMA, refers to real-time, periodic, naturalistic assessment of behavior (Stone & Shiffman, 1994). Consistent with the behavioral tradition, EMA emphasizes measurement of current momentary states that require low

TABLE 20.1   Selected Examples of Technology Integration in Assessment and Treatment

| Technology | Context of Use | |
|---|---|---|
| | Assessment | Treatment |
| Cellular phone | Calling clients over course of treatment to assess progress (e.g., Axelson et al., 2003); using an interactive voice response system to monitor alcohol use (Collins, Kashdan, & Gollnisch, 2003); assessing substance use in a homeless population (Alemagno et al., 1996) | No treatment studies to date |
| Desktop computers | Clinical assessment of target problems at a clinic (Farrell, 1999a, 1999b; Farrell, Camplair, & McCullough, 1987); presentation of interpersonal conflict scenarios to assess client reactions (Lauterbach & Newman, 1999); adaptation of existing paper-and-pencil substance use measure to computerized delivery system (Sarrazin, Hall, Richards, & Carswell, 2002) | Exposure treatment for spider phobia (Gilroy, Kirkby, Daniels, Menzies, & Montgomery, 2000, 2003); treatment of a broad spectrum of anxiety disorders (Newman, Consoli, & Taylor, 1997), bulimia (Murray et al., 2003), anxiety and depression (van den Berg, Shapiro, Bickerstaffe, & Cavanagh, 2004) |
| Handheld computers | Smoking urges (O'Connell et al., 1998); migraine headaches (Sorbi, Honkoop, & Godaert, 1996); use of coping strategies (Stone et al., 1998), eating disorders (Stein & Corte, 2003), Obsessive-Compulsive Disorder (Herman & Koran, 1998) | Delivery of a cognitive-behavioral intervention for Panic Disorder and Generalized Anxiety Disorder (Newman, Kenardy, Herman, & Taylor, 1996, 1997; Newman, Consoli, & Taylor, 1999); use of handheld computers as a memory aid for individuals with head injury (Wright et al., 2001) |
| E-mail | Adjunctive monitoring of patients with eating disorders during treatment (Yager & Freedman, 2003) | Use of e-mail to augment individual treatment, track client progress, and maintain client contact (McDaniel, 2003; Peterson & Beck, 2003); suicide crisis intervention (Wilson & Lester, 1998); delivery of cognitive-behavioral treatment to bulimic (Robinson & Serfaty, 2003) and anorexia nervosa patients (Yager, 2001) |

*(continues)*

TABLE 20.1  (*continued*)

| | Context of Use | |
| --- | --- | --- |
| Technology | Assessment | Treatment |
| Internet | Screening for medical or psychological disorders (Andersson, Carlbring, Kaldo, & Ström, 2004), alcohol abuse (Kypri et al., 2004), schizoaffective and bipolar disorder (Chinman, Young, Schell, Hassell, & Mintz, 2004) | Online treatment modules using behavioral and cognitive-behavioral techniques for Post-Traumatic Stress Disorder (Lange et al., 2003; Litz, Williams, Wang, Bryant, & Engel, 2004), nicotine dependence (Bock et al., 2004), fear of public speaking (Botella, Hofmann, & Muscovitch, 2001), panic and agoraphobia (Alcañiz et al., 2003; Richards, Klein, & Carlbring, 2003) |
| Teleconferencing or telephone consultations | Neuropsychological testing (Berns, Davis-Conway, & Jaeger, 2004); assessment of Post-Traumatic Stress Disorder (Aziz & Kenford, 2004); psychiatric diagnosis using the Structured Clinical Interview for Diagnosis (Cacciola, Alterman, Rutherford, McKay, & May, 1999); dementia screening (Go et al., 1995) | Group counseling for female cancer survivors (Rosenfield & Smillie, 1998); cognitive-behavioral treatment for insomnia (Bastien, Morin, Ouellet, Blais, & Bouchard, 2004); counseling for suicidal teens (King, Nurcombe, Bickman, Hides, & Reid, 2003); cognitive-behavior therapy for Obsessive-Compulsive Disorder (Yeh, Taylor, Thordarson, & Corcaran, 2003), depressive disorders (Simon, Ludman, Tutty, Operskalski, & Von Korff, 2004) |
| Videoconferencing | Speech disorders (Theodoros, 2003); cognitive functioning in the elderly (Ball & Puffett, 1998); child psychiatric assessments (Elford et al., 2000); neuropsychological assessment (Kirkwood, Peck, & Bennie, 2000); Obsessive-Compulsive Disorder (Baer et al., 1995) | Cognitive-behavior therapy for childhood depression (Nelson, Barnard, & Cain, 2003) and panic disorder (Cowain, 2001); breast cancer support group (Freddolino & Han, 1999); counseling with epileptic teens and their families (Hufford, Glueckauf, & Webb, 1999) |
| Virtual reality | Motor movement in Parkinson's patients (Albani et al., 2002); proficiency in activities of daily living among traumatic brain-injured individuals (Lee et al., 2003) | Virtual exposure therapy for fear of flying (Rothbaum, Hodges, Smith, Lee, & Price, 2000; Rothbaum, Hodges, Anderson, Price, & Smith, 2002), acrophobia (Rothbaum et al., 1995), spider phobia (Garcia-Palacios, Hoffman, Carlin, Furness, & Botella, 2002), public speaking anxiety (Harris, Kemmerling, & North, 2002), and Post-Traumatic Stress Disorder (Rothbaum et al., 1999) |

levels of inference, rather than reporting of global, retrospective judgments. Time frames for assessment are typically immediate (e.g., *Rate your mood at this very moment*) or span the recent past (e.g., *Rate your average mood over the last four hours*). Which format is appropriate depends on the rate and variability of the behavior, since behaviors that occur at higher rates are subject to greater retrospective bias.

Although the handheld computing technology that makes EMA studies possible is relatively new, self-monitoring as a behavioral assessment technique is not. Compared to other self-monitoring approaches (e.g., diary recording, journaling), EMA is a desirable option, for several reasons. Data may be easily collected on an interval, event-contingent, or random schedule. If a signal-contingent interval sampling strategy is used, data-collection periods can be scheduled at equal or random intervals using commercially available software. Collected data may be time-stamped and stored in a database accessible by routinely used statistical packages. In addition to facilitating the ease with which data may be analyzed, these features may increase an individual's compliance with the data-collection procedure. For example, Hermann, Peters, and Blanchard (1995) found that individuals who were aware of the time-stamping feature also showed greater compliance with the monitoring protocol.

Another advantage of EMA, and all computerized adaptive testing, is that branching algorithms may be programmed into the software to create sophisticated questionnaires that dynamically reconfigure based on an individual's prior response. For example, an individual monitoring frequency and intensity of panic attacks via EMA several times per day may be administered additional questions if a threshold level determined *a priori* to have clinical significance is exceeded. Branching algorithms may also be utilized to help individuals in a therapeutic capacity (e.g., by directing a person who reports hyperventilating to slow his or her breathing).

The validity of clinical inferences derived from data collected via EMA is directly proportional to the relevance of the method for assessing the problem. Because EMA is a self-monitoring, self-report method it is subject to recording biases that may operate regardless of how the data are collected. Populations that are notoriously unreliable using conventional self-monitoring methods [e.g., eating-disordered patients; see Wilson and Vitousek (1999) for a discussion of self-monitoring issues and Stein and Corte (2003) for an EMA study with this population] are unlikely to become more compliant, reliable, or accurate simply because a handheld computer has substituted for a diary or journaling procedure. This concern may be greater in treatment settings if clients have good reason to make inaccurate data entries. For example, veracity of self-report data for a court-ordered individual with a history of pedophilia should be viewed cautiously regardless of how data are collected. If case disposition is contingent on treatment progress and treatment progress is determined in part by inspection of self-monitoring data, then the validity of data-based clinical inferences will likely be compromised.

If the purpose of assessment is to understand functional relations, EMA is appropriate only insofar as the method facilitates data collection relevant to functionality. If the monitored variables are not related to variability in a problem behavior, it is unlikely that the EMA results will have clinical utility. A related problem may arise if variables or problem behavior(s) cannot be reliably self-monitored. For example, covert phenomena (e.g., cognitions) or high-rate behaviors (e.g., stuttering) may be especially difficult for a person to self-monitor with any accuracy (Marks & Hemsley, 1999). The clinical significance of inaccuracy, however, is a function of the purpose of the assessment. If the purpose is to provide accurate and reliable frequency counts of a target behavior or phenomenon, then inaccurate data have obvious consequences. However, if the purpose is to understand functionality, then understanding how variables covary may occur in the absence of perfectly accurate data so long as measurement error is randomly distributed across observations and variability in behavior covaries with changes in other monitored variables. In signal-detection terms, having noise in the system is permissible so long as a signal (i.e., covariance) is still observed.

For clinicians, the financial costs and logistics associated with the technology remain a significant problem. Minimally, a therapist must buy a personal digital assistant (PDA) and software in order to program the items. Although PDAs may be purchased for less than $100, replacing lost or stolen PDAs is an expense few clinicians are willing to incur. Once the start-up costs are invested, however, a single PDA may be used with several different clients for a variety of self-monitoring tasks.

Beyond the cost of the PDA itself, the costs of software packages—and their respective learning curves—may discourage clinicians from using PDAs routinely in practice. For example, three commonly used PDA programming tools are Intellisync MobileApp Designer (formerly Satellite Forms—$995), AppForge ($899), and Pendragon ($249). The costs of these programs represent a potential barrier to widespread use (see results of the study later) and may be difficult to justify when paper-and-pencil journal entries incur virtually no cost. Although Microsoft offers a free programming tool designed for PocketPCs, it requires a strong working knowledge of the Microsoft Visual Basic programming language.[1]

Another significant problem associated with routine clinical use of PDAs involves the ultimate disposition of the collected data. In addition to requiring a software program that *acquires* data, the utilization of momentary assessment methods in clinical practice requires rapid data *analysis*. Data must be uploaded from the handheld device to the clinician's computer and then analyzed in a way that helps answer questions about functional relations operating in a client's life. Although enormous amounts of useful data may be collected using EMA, the

---

[1] For those interested in learning how to program behavioral experiments or behavioral observation software, we recommend Dixon and MacLin's (2003) book, *Visual Basic for Behavioral Psychologists*.

utility of the data will be negligible if a busy clinician does not have the time to analyze them properly. To date, reports from EMA studies have focused exclusively on the data-acquisition end of the assessment process, with little attention given to streamlining clinically useful analyses.

A final problem surrounds data analysis and psychometrics. By definition, EMA involves repeated collection of data across multiple variables from one individual. For example, an EMA study with 40 observation sessions and 4 measured variables yields 160 observations. To complicate matters, most EMA studies do not limit themselves to just 4 variables. In addition to the large number of data points, parametric assumptions concerning independence of data may be violated if the data are serially dependent. Serial dependence, or autocorrelation, refers to the situation in which the value of an observation is dependent on the value of a prior observation (e.g., a person's mood at 3 PM will depend to some degree on the person's mood an hour before). Parametric statistics are highly susceptible to serial dependency (Stevens, 1990). Sideridis and Greenwood (1997) reported that even low autocorrelation (.10, .20) results in biased $t$ and $F$ ratios up to 22%; but as the autocorrelation rises, $t$ and $F$ ratios can be biased by over 300%. For further details, the interested reader is referred to an excellent review of appropriate data analytic strategies provided by Schwartz and Stone (1998).

Another data analysis issue concerns the insensitivity of commonly used statistics to behavioral changes. For example, indices of reliability (e.g., test–retest reliability, Chronbach's alpha) can provide the mistaken impression that EMA measurement is unreliable. One can easily imagine a scenario in which the reliability of measurement across observations may be low if the variability of behavior is high. Such would be the case if we were to measure the mood of an individual with rapidly cycling mood states. In Figure 20.1, the solid line reflects

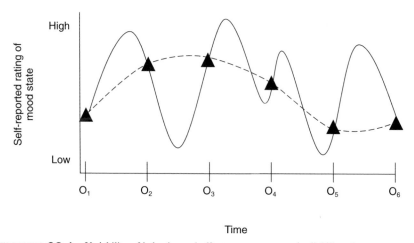

FIGURE 20.1   Variability of behavior and effects on accuracy and reliability of measurement.

a client's actual mood fluctuation over the course of a day. The triangles represent evenly spaced observation points one might expect using an interval sampling methodology with equal intervals. The broken line represents the trend implied by the EMA data. Several observations can be made from this example. First, reliability analyses may suggest that the EMA data are unreliable despite perfect accuracy of measurement (i.e., the fact that the triangles fall precisely on the solid line suggests accurate measurement). Second, the trend implied by the EMA data and the actual cycling of mood states are clearly different. The EMA data imply a much smoother wave function, whereas the client's actual behavior is much more variable. Although the EMA data would not suggest much of a change in mood between observations 2 and 3 or between observations 5 and 6, the client's actual change in mood was great and undetected. Thus, even EMA data could underestimate the magnitude of variability of the targeted mood or behavior if observations are infrequent. In cases where behavior variability is high and the purpose of measurement is to produce accurate estimates of behavior rates, more frequent observation periods would be warranted. However, in cases where behavior variability is high and the purpose of measurement is to assess how a behavior is functionally related to other variables in the environment, fewer observations may suffice so long as the number of observations is adequate to capture a representative amount of behavioral variability. Thus, EMA implies measurement of dynamic systems that require assessment procedures that emphasize accurate measurement of target behaviors or phenomena. Reliability, in the sense of classical test theory, is subordinate to accuracy.

### BEHAVIORAL TELEHEALTH

The term *behavioral telehealth* refers to a variety of technologies that permit remote assessment or treatment of behavioral problems (Nickelson, 1996). The technology may or may not have an explicit computer interface. For example, treatment via the Internet or e-mail would be subsumed under behavioral telehealth, as would videoconferencing or teleconferencing.

The way in which behavioral telehealth is executed has a large bearing on its relevance to behavioral assessment. To date, most discussion surrounding the use of the Internet for assessment purposes has focused on traditional clinical assessment (e.g., the adaptation of personality questionnaires, checklists). Because the focus has been on assessment of constructs rather than behavior, researchers have devoted considerable attention to the issue of *measurement equivalence*. Measurement equivalence refers to whether identical items presented in dissimilar delivery formats yield results that are psychometrically similar. Typically, measurement equivalence is implied by similar or identical factor structures, high pairwise correlations, failure to disprove the null hypothesis when power is adequate to detect differences, and confidence interval overlap between the two measures (see Rogers, Howard, & Vessey, 1993, for a discussion). For example, Baer et al. (1995) found that clinician ratings obtained via videoconference on the Yale–Brown Obsessive-Compulsive Scale (Y-BOCS) were equivalent to ratings by face-to-face interviewers using the same instrument.

Buchanan (2002, 2003) concluded that both personality and clinical assessment were feasible via the Internet but that new norms may need to be established for online versions of instruments. Some researchers have found a potentially problematic interaction between Internet assessment and negative affect, with Internet users reporting greater depression (Davis, 1999) and more variability in scores (Buchanan & Smith, 1999) relative to individuals completing standard paper-and-pencil versions of the same measure. In addition to measurement equivalence issues, administration variables that may affect ratings or scores may not be equivalent. For example, Kirkwood, Peck, and Bennie (2000) found that neuropsychological assessments conducted via videoconferencing were significantly longer in duration than their face-to-face counterparts. If longer administrations fatigue brain-injured individuals and cause a decrement in performance, equivalence of scores across dissimilar administration methods is unlikely.

Because behavioral assessors are more interested in the functionality of behavior than latent constructs implied by questionnaire results, concerns over measurement equivalence may not be especially pressing. A more critical question is whether telehealth technology can facilitate assessment methods relevant to measuring skill acquisition or the function of behavior. Although some questionnaires assess function, most do not. Thus, telehealth technologies that are most relevant to behavioral assessment will include those that permit remote observation of behavior. In this light, recent reports on the use of videoconferencing for treatment may foreshadow future efforts in behavioral assessment. For example, Bouchard and colleagues (2000) compared the effectiveness of 12-week cognitive-behavior therapy (CBT) for Panic Disorder with agoraphobia delivered via videoconference versus traditional face-to-face CBT. For both groups there were significant reductions in panic at post-treatment and 6-month follow-up. Differences between the face-to-face and videoconference conditions in symptom reduction were small.

To date, no study has examined the feasibility of conducting behavioral assessment using videoconferencing technology. In the most relevant study, Guilfoyle et al. (2003) had five allied health therapists (dietician, physiotherapist, podiatrist, speech pathologist, and occupational therapist) conduct an interdisciplinary videoconference assessment and face-to-face assessment with 12 elderly participants. With the exception of the dietician, the therapists rated the efficiency, suitability, and adequacy of care plan for the videoconferencing format significantly lower than for the face-to-face method. However, the authors concluded that the treatment care plans formulated by the therapists in the two conditions of reasonably similar quality.

Guilfoyle et al.'s (2003) results are similar to results by others, suggesting that health professionals prefer the face-to-face interviewing format over videoconferencing. Elford et al. (2000) had five child psychiatrists administer a psychiatric interview face-to-face and via videoconferencing. They found that although the psychiatrists considered the approach acceptable, a clear preference was indicated for the face-to-face format. Concerns were expressed by the psychiatrists over the possibility that the technology would fail, uncertainty about the approach when used in psychiatric emergencies, and an impersonal atmosphere or impeded rapport.

Whether or not videoconferencing technology can be usefully adapted for the purpose of direct observation remains to be seen. Research to date implies that most interview formats are amenable to videoconferencing, if not always psychometrically equivalent, but no study has concerned itself with remote coding of naturalistic or analogue behavior. One could imagine an analogue assessment study in which a camera sent a signal via a high-bandwidth Internet connection from a clinic in Maine to a remote observer coding the behavior in Los Angeles. Of interest would be the degree of agreement between the local and remote observers. Such an arrangement has both clinical and training implications. From a clinical standpoint, the services of behavioral specialists in one locale would be available to rural or impoverished areas. From a training perspective, students could learn how to code behavior as it occurred at a remote site. Since streaming video can be captured to a video file, an instructor could replay the session to assess coding accuracy.

### INTERNET RESOURCES

Although reports have been published concerning the use of the Internet in a therapeutic context or for adapting personality and diagnostic questionnaires to an online format, the Internet has not had a meaningful influence on the way behavioral assessors conduct assessments. Anecdotally, we have heard of therapists using Web sites to collect and aggregate self-monitoring data, but these activities are relatively rare. As with all data collected via the Internet, issues surrounding confidentiality and data security remain, especially if the Web site server is part of a larger commercial service. However, the Internet is home to a vast array of resources related to behavioral assessment. These resources run the gamut from supplementary educational tools for university-level courses in behavioral assessment to free observational software that may be downloaded. Table 20.2 includes a selected list of Internet resources that may be of interest to behaviorally oriented practitioners.

### WHY HAS TECHNOLOGY BEEN WEAKLY EMBRACED BY CLINICIANS?

Ample evidence suggests that clinicians have embraced some forms of technology integration but not others. In an early survey of clinicians, Farrell (1989) summarized his findings by noting that computer technology has had little effect on routine clinical practice. A later survey of 223 California professional psychologists by Rosen and Weil (1996) found that 20% of participants rated themselves as moderately to highly technophobic. In a multiple regression, four variables were found to predict use of computerized assessment technology: clinician age (older clinicians were less likely to utilize technology for assessment purposes), greater number of assessments conducted in a year, higher levels of comfort with technology, and greater number of managed-care clients.

McMinn and colleagues (1999) conducted one of the most comprehensive surveys of clinician utilization of technology. To begin with, they partitioned technology utilization into three waves. First-wave technology referred to the use of technology for routine clerical purposes that had no meaningful effect on delivery of clinical services (e.g., using a word processing program to write a report). Second-wave technologies were those that could have influence on clinical care and were already being used by many clinicians (e.g., computerized test administration and/or interpretation software). Third-wave technologies included newly emergent innovations that directly affected delivery of clinical services (e.g., virtual reality to treat anxiety disorders). They then surveyed 420 members of the American Psychological Association and found modest use of first-wave technologies, with significant clinician concerns regarding the routine use of second- and third-wave technologies. Specifically, one-third of all respondents viewed the adjunctive use of a computer in therapy as unethical. Both utilization rates and judgments of ethicality varied as a function of technology wave. Clinicians were less likely to use third-wave technologies in clinical practice and less likely to consider their use ethical.

Differences between therapists in receptiveness to technology integration occur for several reasons, not the least of which are differences due to one's theoretical orientation. Behavior analysts working with mentally retarded and autistic children have developed a long tradition of precise behavioral observation procedures that have been augmented by desktop and handheld software programs. Technology integration therefore represents an enhancement of data collection efficiency, not a paradigmatic shift regarding the necessity of observation to begin with. Other therapists may embrace a functional perspective but focus on problems that are difficult or impossible to observe directly (e.g., maladaptive thinking in a depressed individual). In a similar vein, humanistic psychotherapists may reject computerized assessment approaches altogether for fear of diminishing client–therapist rapport. Thus, readiness to use computer technology is a function not of one's experience with or attitudes toward technology, but of the value different orientations place on those assessment methods most augmented by technology integration.

Regardless of orientation, many clinicians are concerned that technology integration could increase rather than decrease a clinician's workload while contributing marginally, if at all, to incremental treatment gains. In other words, clinicians frequently do not perceive computerized assessment technology as

TABLE 20.2  Internet Sites with Behavioral Assessment Resources

| Site/Company | Internet Address | Description of Contents |
|---|---|---|
| *Educational Resources* | | |
| Center for Effective Collaboration and Practice | www.air.org/cecp/fba/default.htm | Reviews principles of functional behavioral assessment, video series. |
| Sopris West | sopriswest.com | CD-ROM: *Functional Behavioral Assessment, Third Edition.* Modules help participants learn how to conduct observations and develop functional hypotheses. |
| University of South Florida | http://www.fmhi.usf.edu/cfs/cfspubs/ pbsguide/facilitatorguidepbs.htm | Facilitator's Guide: Positive Behavioral Support. Online book in viewable PDF format developed by the staff of the Positive Behavioral Support Project at University of South Florida. Chapters cover goal identification, assessment procedures, and treatment implementation. |
| Center for Early Education and Development (CEED) | http://education.umn.edu/CEED/ publications/videos.html | Instructional video on conducting functional behavioral assessment with early childhood kids, $25. |
| *Online Web Course* | | |
| University of New Mexico | cdd.unm.edu/fbaps/ | Computer conferencing Web course in functional behavioral assessment offered by the Center for Development and Disability. |
| *Observational software* | | |
| ODLog (Version 2) | macropodsoftware.com | Observational software designed for Windows and MacIntosh. Trial version available for download. From $79. |
| TimerData | http://mfba.net/timerdata.pdf | Windows software that permits user to track behaviors over time. Can track up to 12 behaviors simultaneously and computes a variety of statistics (e.g., percentage of time engaging in target behavior, frequency of occurrence). $225 for an individual user. |

| | | |
|---|---|---|
| EthoLog 2.25 | http://www.geocities.com/ CapeCanaveral/Lab/2727/ethohome.html | Windows software for tracking discrete and continuous events over time. Generates an output file with summary information. Data may be exported to spreadsheet file. Freeware. |
| Spectator | http://www.biobserve.com/products/ spectator/index.html | Software that permits simultaneous collection and analysis of data for up to 10 subjects and 20 behaviors. Software can interface with video feeds for remote coding. No price provided on Web site. |
| Ecobehavioral Assessment Software Systems (EBASS) | http://www.jgcp.ku.edu/EBASS/ ebass_descrp.htm | Software designed to track parent–student interactions in a classroom setting. Functions for calculating interrater agreement, trend analysis, conditional probabilities, and conducting profile comparisons. $350. |
| *Handheld observational software* | | |
| !Observe from Sopris West | Sopriswest.com, psychsoft.com | Observational software for Palmos handheld computers. Desktop system can be MacIntosh or Windows. Variety of aggregating and analytic functions. $79. |
| Spectator Go! | http://www.biobserve.com/products/ spectator_go/index.html | Designed for Palm or PocketPC handheld operating systems. Desktop system can be MacIntosh or Windows. Allows simultaneous monitoring of 14 different behaviors across five different subjects. $299. |
| BASC Portable Observation Software | agsnet.com | Handheld software for Palm or PocketPCos. Works with Windows or MacIntosh desktop systems. Free program demonstration disk available on CD-ROM from Web site. $129.99. |
| *Report writing software* | | |
| TurboBehavior Plans | http://www.turbopsy.com/tbp2001.htm | Software that assists in generation of functional behavioral assessment reports. $250 for a five-user license. |
| *Other software* | | |
| Functional Skills Screening Inventory (WinFSSI) | http://www.winfssi.com/index.html | Observer rating system for assessing functional skills. Software facilitates ipsative assessment of skills over time using multiple raters. $450. |

being cost efficient or in the client's best interest or as possessing sufficient incremental clinical utility.

## TECHNOLOGY INTEGRATION: A SURVEY OF ABCT MEMBERS AND UNDERGRADUATES

### PURPOSE

Our study was based in part on the work of McMinn et al. (1999), who surveyed members of the American Psychological Association regarding their usage and ethical opinions of technology in private practice. In contrast, we surveyed members of the Association for Behavioral and Cognitive Therapies (ABCT) about their usage, intent to use, and ethical opinions of technology. In addition, we surveyed a student population to investigate whether the attitudes of ABCT members toward technology integration differed from those of nonprofessionals.

### METHOD

**Participants**

We collected data from two groups: members of the Association for Behavioral and Cognitive Therapies ($n = 93$) and undergraduate students ($n = 119$). We planned to report data from waiting room clients at the university's psychology clinic, but logistical obstacles prevented us from completing data collection by the publication deadline for this paper.

#### *ABCT Members*

ABCT members were recruited from ABCT's online referral network. All association members with a listed e-mail address were contacted and asked to participate in the study. A total of 940 e-mails were sent to association members. Of the 940, 169 e-mails were returned due to delivery failure (i.e., the e-mail address was not valid). Of the 771 e-mails that were not returned, a total of 99 responded. Six cases were removed due to missing data. Thus, our final sample consisted of 93 ABCT members, or 12.06% of all valid e-mail contacts. ABCT members who agreed to participate completed a copy of the survey and returned it by e-mail. The survey was embedded in the e-mail rather than attached, since previous research has found significantly higher response rates for embedded surveys (see Dommeyer and Moriarty, 1999–2000).

Of those who participated, 59.1% were male ($n = 55$) and 40.9% were female ($n = 38$). Half of the sample had received its highest degree within the last 18 years. Although the majority of respondents held a Ph.D. or Psy.D. (84.9%), other terminal degrees were reported: M.D. (3.2%), M.S.W. (3.2%), M.A. (1.1%), and other (6.5%). Respondents indicated a range of clinical orientations, including cognitive-behavioral (78.5%), behavioral (14.0%), behavior analytic (3.2%), existential (1.1%), and other (3.2%). Professional affiliations were reported as follows: private practice (29.0%), educational institution (24.7%), hospital (14.0%), university clinic (5.4%), community mental health (2.2%), Veterans Administration hospital (2.2%), consulting firm (2.2%), inpatient institution (1.1%), and other (19.4%). Finally, the vast majority of respondents (81.7%) indicated having not received graduate training in the use of computers or technology in a therapeutic or assessment context, while less than a fifth (17.2%) reported some training.

### Undergraduate Students

The second group of participants comprised 119 undergraduate students enrolled in psychology classes at a large midwestern state university. Of the respondents, 30.3% were male ($n = 36$) and 69.7% were female ($n = 83$). The sample was mostly Caucasian (77.3%), with African American (12.6%), Asian (2.5%), and other (5.8%) students represented. The mean age of the sample was 21.1 years ($SD = 5.3$ years; range = 18–46). Class extra credit was provided at the instructor's discretion. Questionnaires were administered in a paper-and-pencil format.

In addition to completing the student version of the survey, undergraduates completed the Beck Depression Inventory—II (BDI-II) and several questions about their own psychotherapy experiences.[2] We administered these measures because previous research has suggested that attitudes toward technology use in a therapeutic context may be a function of affect (i.e., greater negative affect has been associated with more negative attitudes toward technology integration; see Schulenberg and Yutrzenka, 1999). We were also curious about whether prior psychotherapy history moderated attitudes toward technology use.

The student sample was relatively free of depression. The mean BDI-II score for the sample was 9.8 ($SD = 7.8$; range = 0–43). This score is similar to that of the nondepressed normative sample reported for the BDI-II ($M = 7.65$, $SD = 5.9$; Beck, 1996). Fifteen students (12.6%) reported attending one or more psychotherapy sessions in the last year, and three students (2.5%) reported attending more than 10 psychotherapy sessions during the same time frame.

## Procedure

As noted earlier, the professional sample was contacted by e-mail. Each e-mail contained a brief introduction to the study, the survey, a demographic questionnaire, and the informed consent form. Participants were instructed to reply to the e-mail and place asterisks next to their desired responses. The student sample was recruited from undergraduate psychology courses in exchange for extra credit

[2] When used as a screening measure for depression, the following BDI-II cutoff scores can be used: 0–13, minimal depression; 14–19, mild depression; 20–28, moderate depression; and 29–63, severe depression.

provided by their instructors. Participants completed the questionnaires in groups of 2–10 individuals. Questionnaires were completed in counterbalanced order.

We created two versions of the survey: one for ABCT members and one for undergraduate students. The version for ABCT members included items tapping 19 possible uses of technology in clinical practice. The questions focused on what McMinn et al. (1999) termed second- and third-wave technologies. The survey did not assess attitudes toward technology used for routine clerical work (wave 1), since these uses are known to be routine and accepted. Specific technology uses that were queried in the survey are summarized in Table 20.3. For each technology application, the respondent answered three questions: (1) *Have you ever used this technology?* (2) *Do you intend to use the technology in the future?* (3) *Do you consider the use of this technology ethical?*

The student version of the survey was adapted from the survey provided ABCT members. The eight examples of technology integration included in the student version of the survey were selected based on their relevance to potential consumers of psychological services. Brief descriptions of each technology were included (a copy of the student survey is included in the appendix to this chapter). For each technology description, students answered two questions that assessed (1) whether the technology application was ethical and (2) their likely reaction if a clinician asked the student to use the technology in the stated manner. The term *ethical* was defined for students as behavior that is "professionally appropriate, justified, and in the best interest of the client."

### RESULTS

Participant responses are shown in Tables 20.3 (ABCT members) and 20.4 (undergraduates). For ABCT members, we summarized responses in terms of utilization, intent to use, and judgments of ethicality. For students, we summarized responses in terms of likely reactions to using the technology and judgments of ethicality.

### Technology Utilization Among ABCT Members

McMinn et al. (1999) defined a commonly used technology as one in which 90% or more of their sample endorsed having *ever* used the technology. Conversely, a rarely used technology was defined as one in which 10% or less of the sample *ever* used the technology. Similar to McMinn et al.'s prior results, our survey found that no technology was classified as commonly used. The most frequently used technologies[3] were computerized test-scoring software (79.6%), consultation with a colleague via e-mail (74.2%), computerized test-administration software (75.4%), and computerized test-interpretation software (67.8%). Our findings represent higher utilization rates than those reported by McMinn et al. (i.e., 55.8%, 12.2%, 40.3%, and 53.3%, respectively).

---

[3] Aggregated percentage indicating utilization from "rarely" to "very often."

Results of this study suggest that two technologies would be classified as rarely used (i.e., treatment via videoconferencing and virtual reality therapy). Seven technologies had never been used by at least 75% or more of the sample. For purposes of comparison, we report our results first, followed by those from McMinn et al. (1999) in italics: virtual reality (95.7%, *96.9%*),[4] treatment via videoconferencing (92.5%, *89.3%*), consultation via videoconferencing (84.9%, *78.1%*), supervision via videoconferencing (84.9%, *89.5%*), use of a computer in lieu of treatment (78.5%, *97.4%*), treatment via the Internet (80.6%, *98.1%*), and use of a handheld computer to help with the presenting problem (80.6%, *not measured*).

### ABCT Members' Ratings of Utilization Intent

We also asked ABCT members to rate whether they intended to use each technology in the future. Not surprisingly, responses varied with each item. Table 20.3 shows that most ABCT members intend to use computerized test-administration, test-scoring, and test-interpretation software in the future. In addition, most ABCT members intend to use e-mail for consultations with colleagues and computer programs between sessions to help clients with their problems. However, many of the technology applications received low marks with regard to utilization intent. For example, only a minority of ABCT members (17.2%) plan to use a computer in lieu of traditional therapy or plan to deliver treatment via the Internet. Even fewer have plans to deliver treatment via videoconferencing (11.8%).

These data should be interpreted cautiously, however, given that they may represent significant attitude shifts by ABCT members *in favor of* technology utilization. For example, the fact that nearly one-third of ABCT members intend to utilize virtual reality technology in the future could signal a trend *toward* technology integration. Recent development of the virtual reality research literature, almost all of which has been published in the last 6–10 years, probably has influenced a significant proportion of ABCT members who now consider virtual reality a viable treatment alternative for a variety of anxiety disorders. Similarly, close to half of ABCT members reported an intent to use handheld computers to help clients monitor behavior between sessions.

### Student Reactions to Technology Applications

Overall, students could best be described as guarded in their reactions to technology integration. Table 20.4 reports mean student reactions to various technologies and percentages for each response option. Students responded most favorably to using computer programs between sessions to help with a client problem ($M = 2.36$, $SD = .72$), using handheld computers to monitor behavior between sessions ($M = 2.37$, $SD = .74$), and using a computer to administer a test

---

[4] Percentages indicate proportion of respondents who have *never* used the technology in an assessment or treatment context.

TABLE 20.3  Professionals' Utilization, Intent, and Judgment of Ethics Regarding Various Technology Applications ($n = 93$)

| Technology Application | Have you used? (%) | | | | | Intend to use? (%) | | | Ethical? (%) | | | |
|---|---|---|---|---|---|---|---|---|---|---|---|---|
| | Never | Rarely | Sometimes | Fairly Often | Very Often | Yes | No | Undecided | Yes | No | Undecided | Y/N Ratio |
| Use computer to take notes during a session* | 73.1 | 11.8 | 2.2 | 4.3 | 8.6 | 26.9 | 61.3 | 10.8 | 69.9 | 19.4 | 10.8 | 3.60 |
| Use computer program between sessions to help with problem* | 58.1 | 8.6 | 22.6 | 6.5 | 4.3 | 50.5 | 21.5 | 28.0 | 84.9 | 4.3 | 10.8 | 19.74 |
| Use computer in lieu of traditional therapy | 78.5 | 12.9 | 7.5 | 0.0 | 1.1 | 17.2 | 61.3 | 21.5 | 48.4 | 15.1 | 35.5 | 3.21 |
| Treatment via Internet* | 80.6 | 14.0 | 4.3 | 1.1 | 0.0 | 17.2 | 57.0 | 25.8 | 31.2 | 23.7 | 44.1 | 1.32 |
| Consultation about a client with a colleague via e-mail | 25.8 | 29.0 | 34.4 | 10.8 | 0.0 | 69.9 | 15.1 | 15.1 | 80.6 | 10.8 | 8.6 | 7.46 |
| Supervisory consultation with a junior therapist via e-mail | 51.6 | 20.4 | 20.4 | 5.4 | 2.2 | 48.4 | 29.0 | 16.1 | 66.7 | 17.2 | 11.8 | 3.88 |
| Computerized test-administration software* | 24.7 | 28.0 | 23.7 | 15.1 | 8.6 | 62.4 | 21.5 | 16.1 | 91.4 | 4.3 | 4.3 | 21.26 |
| Computerized test-scoring software | 20.4 | 23.7 | 24.7 | 17.2 | 14.0 | 72.0 | 18.3 | 9.7 | 94.6 | 4.3 | 1.1 | 22.00 |
| Computerized test-interpretation software | 31.2 | 28.0 | 20.4 | 9.7 | 9.7 | 57.0 | 20.4 | 21.5 | 86.0 | 1.1 | 12.9 | 78.18 |
| Computer report services or automated report-generation software | 41.9 | 22.6 | 20.4 | 9.7 | 4.3 | 45.2 | 40.9 | 14.0 | 82.8 | 7.5 | 9.7 | 11.04 |

| | | | | | | | | | | | | |
|---|---|---|---|---|---|---|---|---|---|---|---|---|
| Treatment or consultation via teleconferencing* | 49.5 | 21.5 | 25.8 | 2.2 | 1.1 | 49.5 | 22.6 | 28.0 | 80.6 | 3.2 | 16.1 | 25.19 |
| Clinical supervision via teleconferencing | 68.8 | 17.2 | 11.8 | 2.2 | 0.0 | 19.4 | 26.9 | 33.3 | 86.0 | 0.0 | 14.0 | >86.00 |
| Treatment via videoconferencing* | 92.5 | 4.3 | 3.2 | 0.0 | 0.0 | 11.8 | 47.3 | 36.6 | 60.2 | 6.5 | 33.3 | 9.26 |
| Consultation via videoconferencing | 84.9 | 9.7 | 4.3 | 1.1 | 0.0 | 22.6 | 30.1 | 40.9 | 80.6 | 3.2 | 16.1 | 25.19 |
| Clinical supervision via videoconferencing | 84.9 | 10.8 | 2.2 | 1.1 | 0.0 | 25.8 | 34.4 | 34.4 | 78.5 | 5.4 | 16.1 | 14.54 |
| Virtual reality* | 95.7 | 2.2 | 1.1 | 1.1 | 0.0 | 29.0 | 28.0 | 41.9 | 87.1 | 5.4 | 7.5 | 16.13 |
| Multimedia technology for assessment or therapy | 68.8 | 9.7 | 16.1 | 4.3 | 1.1 | 33.3 | 29.0 | 37.6 | 79.6 | 2.2 | 18.3 | 36.18 |
| Biofeedback | 38.7 | 36.6 | 16.1 | 7.5 | 1.1 | 34.4 | 46.2 | 18.3 | 93.5 | 2.2 | 4.3 | 42.50 |
| Use handheld computer to monitor behavior between sessions* | 80.6 | 7.5 | 9.7 | 1.1 | 0.0 | 49.5 | 21.5 | 29.0 | 88.2 | 2.2 | 8.6 | 40.09 |
| Treatment or consultation via teleconferencing* | 49.5 | 21.5 | 25.8 | 2.2 | 1.1 | 49.5 | 22.6 | 28.0 | 80.6 | 3.2 | 16.1 | 25.19 |

Y/N Ratio is the ratio of Yes to No responses. If the value for "No" was zero, a 1 was entered in its place to avoid infinity when calculating the ratio. Responses sum to less than 100% due to rounding or missing data. An asterisk indicates an item that was replicated on the student version of the Technology Use Survey.

**TABLE 20.4** Student Reactions to Various Technology Applications ($n = 119$)

| Technology Application | Mean (SD) | How would you react? (%) | | | | | |
| --- | --- | --- | --- | --- | --- | --- | --- |
| | | Very Positively | Positively | Neutral | Negatively | Very Negatively |
| Use computer program between sessions to help with problem | 2.36 (0.72) | 7.6 | 55.5 | 30.3 | 6.7 | 0.0 |
| Use handheld computer to monitor behavior between sessions | 2.37 (0.74) | 11.8 | 47.1 | 37.0 | 4.2 | 0.0 |
| Computer-administered test | 2.58 (0.92) | 10.1 | 39.5 | 34.5 | 14.3 | 1.7 |
| Use computer to take notes during a session | 2.71 (1.04) | 11.8 | 31.1 | 37.8 | 13.4 | 5.9 |
| Treatment via videoconferencing | 3.06 (0.97) | 3.4 | 27.7 | 34.5 | 28.6 | 5.9 |
| Virtual reality | 3.28 (1.09) | 3.4 | 24.4 | 27.7 | 30.3 | 14.3 |
| Treatment via teleconferencing | 3.55 (0.81) | 0.0 | 9.2 | 37.8 | 42.0 | 10.9 |
| Treatment via Internet | 3.88 (0.88) | 1.7 | 6.7 | 14.3 | 56.3 | 21.0 |

Some responses sum to less than 100% due to rounding and missing data.

($M = 2.58$, $SD = .92$). Students responded least favorably to treatment via the Internet ($M = 3.88$, $SD = .88$), treatment via teleconferencing ($M = 3.55$, $SD = .81$), and the use of virtual reality ($M = 3.28$, $SD = 1.09$). With regard to the three most negatively viewed technologies, substantial proportions of students indicated they would have negative or very negative reactions: treatment via the Internet (76.3%), treatment via teleconferencing (52.9%), and virtual reality (44.6%).

### Self-Rated Depression and Student Reactions

We were also interested in whether the level of self-reported depression was related to student reactions. Individuals with negative affect or depression may respond less favorably to computerized assessment (Schulenberg & Yutrzenka, 1999). Students were divided into two groups, based on their BDI-II score: no self-reported depression (BDI-II scores ranging from 0 to 13; $n = 91$) and moderate to severe depression (BDI-II scores 20 and higher; $n = 14$). Individuals with scores from 14 to 19 were removed from the analysis in order to increase homogeneity of groups. Dependent variables were students' ratings of their reactions to the eight technology applications listed in Table 20.2. Reaction scores were on a 5-point Likert scale ranging from "very positively" to "very negatively," with higher scores indicating more negative reactions. A series of independent sample $t$-tests were run, with alpha adjusted to .01 to protect the experiment-wise error rate. None of the eight $t$-tests were statistically significant. In addition, BDI-II scores were not significantly correlated with reactions to any technology.

### Effect of Prior Therapy History

We then correlated estimated number of prior therapy sessions with student reactions to each technology. Only one correlation was significant: We found a mild positive correlation between number of prior therapy sessions and negative student reactions to using the Internet for therapy, $r(117) = .22$, $p < .05$. Thus, receptiveness to Internet-mediated treatment appears to be related to prior therapy history.

## Ethicality

### ABCT Members

ABCT members largely viewed a wide variety of technology integrations as ethical. The use of computer report services, teleconferencing for supervisory and treatment purposes, videoconferencing consultation and supervision, virtual reality treatment, multimedia treatment and assessment applications, handheld computer self-monitoring, test-scoring and -interpretation software, e-mail supervisory consultation, and the use of computer software to assist clients between sessions all were rated by a vast majority of ABCT members as ethical practices.

Two technology applications failed to receive a majority endorsement with regard to ethicality. These included the use of a computer in lieu of traditional therapy (48.4%) and treatment via the Internet (31.2%). Additionally, five technology applications were deemed unethical by 10% or more of the sample: treatment via the Internet (23.7%), using a computer to take notes during a session (19.4%), supervisory consultation with a junior therapist via e-mail (17.2%), using a computer in lieu of traditional therapy (15.1%), and consultation about a client with a colleague via e-mail (10.8%).

A rough index of ethicality may be created by dividing the proportion of ABCT members who found a technology ethical by the proportion who did not (i.e., the Y/N ratio reported in Tables 20.3 and 20.5). Higher ratios suggest greater agreement among ABCT members that the given technology integration is ethical. Table 16.3 shows that the highest Y/N ratios were for clinical supervision via teleconferencing (Y/N ratio = 86.0), computerized test-interpretation software (Y/N ratio = 78.18), biofeedback (Y/N ratio = 42.50), and the use of handheld computers to monitor behavior between sessions (Y/N ratio = 40.09). The lowest Y/N ratios were obtained for treatment via the Internet (Y/N ratio = 1.32), using a computer in lieu of traditional therapy (Y/N ratio = 3.21), using a computer to take notes during a session (Y/N ratio = 3.60), and providing supervisory consultation with a junior therapist via e-mail (Y/N ratio = 3.88).

### *Comparing ABCT Members' to Students' Judgments of Ethicality*

Table 20.5 reports the proportion of ABCT members and students that judged a technology application to be ethical (in percentages and only for items that overlapped across surveys). As with Table 20.3, the Y/N ratio is reported for both ABCT members and students. Comparison of item Y/N ratios across each item shows them to be larger, in every case, for the ABCT members.

We then conducted a $\chi^2$ test with Yates' correction for continuity to determine whether the proportion of ethicality judgments, expressed in percentage terms, differed between the two groups (MedCalc, 2004). The proportion of ABCT members that considered a technology integration ethical was compared to the corresponding percentage for students. To reduce experiment-wise error rate for multiple comparisons, alpha was set at .01. Three items showed significantly different proportional endorsements for ethicality (i.e., treatment consultation via teleconferencing, use of a computer to administer a test, and use of virtual reality for treatment purposes). In each case, the proportion of ABCT members judging the technology integration to be ethical exceeded the corresponding percentage of students.

### Comparison to McMinn et al. (1999) Results

Finally, we examined whether our results were similar to those obtained by McMinn et al. (1999) in their survey of 420 APA members who listed their

TABLE 20.5  ABCT Members' and Students' Judgments of Ethicality

| Technology Application | ABCT Members (%) | | | | Students (%) | | | | | |
| --- | --- | --- | --- | --- | --- | --- | --- | --- | --- | --- |
| | Yes | No | Undecided | Y/N Ratio | Yes | No | Undecided | Y/N Ratio | $\chi^2$ | $p$ |
| Use handheld computer to monitor behavior between sessions | 88.2 | 2.2 | 8.6 | 40.09 | 76.5 | 11.8 | 11.8 | 6.48 | 3.86 | .05 |
| Treatment or consultation via teleconferencing | 80.6 | 3.2 | 16.1 | 25.19 | 37.8 | 37.8 | 24.4 | 1.00 | 37.20 | <.001 |
| Computer-administered test | 91.4 | 4.3 | 4.3 | 21.26 | 72.3 | 16.8 | 10.9 | 4.30 | 11.16 | <.001 |
| Use computer program between sessions to help with problem | 84.9 | 4.3 | 10.8 | 19.74 | 82.4 | 6.7 | 10.9 | 12.30 | .09 | .76 |
| Virtual reality | 87.1 | 5.4 | 7.5 | 16.13 | 38.7 | 42.0 | 19.3 | 0.92 | 48.929 | <.001 |
| Treatment via videoconferencing | 60.2 | 6.5 | 33.3 | 9.26 | 54.6 | 25.2 | 21.1 | 2.17 | .459 | .50 |
| Use computer to take notes during a session | 69.9 | 19.4 | 10.8 | 3.60 | 64.7 | 22.7 | 12.6 | 2.85 | .429 | .51 |
| Treatment via Internet | 31.2 | 23.7 | 44.1 | 1.32 | 19.3 | 57.1 | 23.5 | 0.34 | 3.377 | .07 |

primary employment as private practice. Although comparing samples from different studies can be hazardous, we considered the analysis a useful starting point for understanding potential differences between ABCT members and mainstream clinicians regarding technology integration.[5]

For both samples we collapsed the proportion of respondents who indicated that they *fairly often* or *very often* used a technology in their practice. Percentage endorsements were then compared using the proportional $\chi^2$ test described previously. Significant differences in percentage endorsements, with ABCT members reported first, were found for the following items: using a computer to take notes during a session (12.9% vs. 2.4%, $\chi^2$ (1, $N = 119$) = 17.91, $p < .001$), consulting a colleague about a client via e-mail (10.8% vs. 0.7%, $\chi^2$ (1, $N = 119$) = 27.52, $p < .001$), providing clinical supervision via e-mail (7.6% vs. 0.0%, $\chi^2$ (1, $N = 119$) = 27.01, $p < .001$), and using computerized test-administration software (23.7% vs. 12.7%, $\chi^2$ (1, $N = 119$) = 6.50, $p < .01$). Significant differences were not found for the use of virtual reality technology, treatment via the Internet, use of computerized test-interpretation software,[6] or the use of a computer in lieu of traditional therapy. Again, some caution is warranted in interpreting these results, given that not all of the McMinn et al. (1999) questions mapped onto our survey, and vice versa. For example, our survey included questions regarding technologies that were either newly emergent six years ago (e.g., use of handheld computers, videoconferencing, multimedia technology) or omitted by McMinn and colleagues (e.g., biofeedback).

## DISCUSSION

The results imply increasing acceptance of technology use for some clinical duties and practices. This seems to be most true of assessment-related and consultation-related activities. However, the use of computers for conducting therapy (e.g., virtual reality) remains infrequent and probably localized to specialty clinics and research units. Although a healthy percentage of ABCT members consider virtual reality ethical (87.1%) and indicated some intent to use the technology in the future (29.0%), 97.9% reported rarely or never using it in practice. Our results also suggest that care should be taken in explaining the rationale of virtual reality to prospective clients. Fully 44.3% of students indicated that they would respond negatively or very negatively to virtual reality technology. Although it may be that students were reacting negatively to the exposure aspects of virtual reality, rather than the technology per se, it is apparent that the generally positive atti-

---

[5] We are also cognizant of the fact that both technology and the research surrounding it has advanced in the intervening time between McMinn et al.'s paper and our chapter. Thus, we proceed cautiously, with an understanding that our remarks should serve primarily as a heuristic for future research.

[6] The question regarding computerized test-interpretation *services* was not included in the McMinn et al. (1999) study.

tude toward virtual reality enjoyed by ABCT members may not generalize to those outside the profession or to mainstream clinicians.[7]

Our results with regard to the virtual reality item contrast with results published by Garcia-Pallacios, Hoffman, Kwong See, Tsai, and Botella (2001). They surveyed 162 students and found that the vast majority would prefer virtual reality treatment for spider phobia to *in vivo* exposure. Although we did not compare reactions to these two treatment options, the fact that 42% of students in our sample found virtual reality treatment to be unethical is interesting. It could be that students view the utility and ethicality of virtual reality differently as a function of the presenting problem. Our example described treatment for combat-related stress, whereas Garcia-Pallacios and colleagues concerned themselves with spider phobia. It could also be that the act of indicating a preference for virtual reality or exposure therapy in the prior study created a halo effect and mitigated negative reactions toward virtual reality.

Fifteen of the 19 technologies we surveyed were considered ethical by at least 75% of the behavior therapist sample, yet 11 of the 19 technologies have never been used by more than half the sample. With regard to utilization intent, only 4 of the 19 technologies were endorsed by more than half of the ABCT members as technologies they intend to use in the future. To understand low utilization rates by individual ABCT members, qualitative responses were examined to the open-ended question "Please list the major reasons and/or obstacles that may have discouraged you from using technology in your practice." Of the 54 responses to this question, four main themes emerged: cost of the technology and equipment, lack of clear evidence that the technology improves the effectiveness of treatment, lack of training, and the perception that the technology interferes with the therapeutic relationship.

Student participants held a somewhat more conservative view of utilizing these technologies in psychological practice. Students were especially skeptical of the Internet as a treatment vehicle, receiving treatment via teleconferencing, and the use of virtual reality. Although one might argue that the brief descriptions provided in the surveys did not do justice to the techniques and therefore resulted in lower judgments of ethicality, the results suggest at the very least that use of these technologies warrants a thorough justification to clients who may use them. With regard to virtual reality, providing a thorough rationale to a client for both exposure therapy and the use of the technology is warranted, given that the treatment may have low apparent face validity.

In contrast, four technologies were rated as *positive* or *very positive* by more than 40% of students. These were using a computer between sessions to help with a problem (63.1%), using a handheld computer to monitor behavior between ses-

---

[7] In McMinn et al.'s (1999) study, 38.8% of respondents considered virtual reality therapy ethical under "many circumstances" or "unquestionably." Fully 45.5% responded "don't know/not sure." In contrast, our sample was much more generous: 87.1% of respondents considered virtual reality therapy ethical and only 7.5% were undecided.

sions (58.9%), using a computer to administer a test (49.6%), and using a computer to take notes during a session (42.9%). We found it especially interesting that a line was drawn by students when it came to integrating technology in a therapeutic context. Using technology in an adjunctive or assessment capacity was viewed by students most positively. However, the moment technology mediated treatment (e.g., treatment via videoconferencing, treatment via teleconferencing, treatment via the Internet) or was responsible for treatment delivery (e.g., virtual reality), reactions became increasingly negative. Thus, students appeared to discriminate between technologies designed to collect data and those that showed potential to mediate, replace, or otherwise modify the therapeutic relationship.

Ethicality judgments among ABCT members and students showed some between-group differences. First, with the exception of using a computer in lieu of therapy and using the Internet for treatment purposes, a majority of ABCT members found most forms of technology integration to be ethical. Although the students agreed with the ABCT members with regard to treatment via the Internet, they did not consider treatment/consultation via teleconferencing or virtual reality technology to be ethical. These results are consistent with those reported by Rochlen, Beretvas, and Zack (2004), who found that participants were more comfortable with, and showed a greater preference for, face-to-face counseling rather than Internet-mediated counseling. Second, the Y/N ratios for students on all technology applications were lower than for ABCT members, suggesting less within-group certainty about the ethicality of technology integration.

Our study was limited by several factors. First, we are currently collecting a sample of clients referred to our university psychology clinic. It may be that client attitudes will differ from those of student participants on the dimensions we described here. Second, our final response rate from the ABCT membership was relatively small (12.16%) and consisted of individuals with e-mail addresses. Thus, we may have built in a bias toward individuals with some pro-technology bias to begin with. Third, the two samples differed not just with regard to their level of training in psychology, but also by gender. While the majority of our survey respondents in the behavior therapy sample were male, close to 70% of our student sample was female. Differences in responses may have reflected a more general gender difference in technology receptivity.

## SUMMARY

The purpose of this chapter was to introduce the reader to two forms of technology integration—ecological momentary assessment and telehealth—in order to illustrate important issues clinicians and researchers confront when technology mediates assessment and/or therapy. We then surveyed both ABCT members and undergraduates to assess between-group differences in receptiveness to technology integration. Overall, ABCT members were generally more at ease with the use of technology in clinical practice and expressed fewer concerns about the ethicality of use. Students were generally less positive and expressed greater concern as the technology appeared to play a larger role in the therapeutic process.

Whether or not technology will continue to play a role in the assessment and treatment of behavioral problems is really not the issue—one has a hard time imagining a reversal in technology integration, given the pressure from third parties to deliver empirically supported treatments and the great conveniences technology provides. The real question is whether each form of technology integration actually enhances assessment and treatment or is merely a convenient but inadequate substitute for appropriate practice. Further, some technology uses may be appropriate and well received for some assessment or treatment tasks but not for all. An obvious concern with technology integration thus becomes the degree to which technology starts to dictate the kinds of assessment or treatment behavior therapists conduct and the effects of those practices on client welfare. As we become increasingly better at creating sophisticated computer programs, high-fidelity video transmissions, and so forth, do we correspondingly run the risk of alienating the very consumers of our services who seek not technological sophistication but human compassion? In other words, is the appeal of technology integration greater for the therapist or for the client? These questions may be partly answered through survey data, but a full discussion of the long-term consequences of technology integration to the profession still needs to be undertaken.

## APPENDIX: STUDENT VERSION OF TECHNOLOGY UTILIZATION SURVEY

We are interested in your reaction to the use of certain kinds of treatment. Please read each of the following stories. After you have read each story, please answer the questions that follow. This survey asks you to judge how ethical certain treatments are. The term *ethical* means *professionally appropriate, justified*, and in the *best interest of the client*.

1. Imagine that as part of therapy you needed to keep track of certain events as they occurred to you throughout the week. To help with this, your therapist gave you a handheld computer that beeped periodically throughout the day and reminded you to record certain information. Your therapist is convinced that using the handheld computer will help in your treatment.

   1a. Would you consider using a handheld computer to monitor your behavior or emotions ethical?
       A. Yes
       B. No
       C. Undecided

1b. How would you react if you were asked to monitor your behavior or emotions with a handheld computer?
    A. Very positively
    B. Positively
    C. Neutral
    D. Negatively
    E. Very negatively

2. Imagine that when you visited your therapist, the therapist provided you a computer program that was designed to help you with your problem. You could complete the program either at the clinic or at home. You were instructed to complete the computer program during the week in between sessions.

    2a. Would you consider using a computer program in between sessions ethical?
        A. Yes
        B. No
        C. Undecided

    2b. How would you react if you were asked to use a computer program in between sessions?
        A. Very positively
        B. Positively
        C. Neutral
        D. Negatively
        E. Very negatively

3. Imagine that instead of seeing a therapist once per week in an office, you interacted with the therapist once per week over the Internet.

    3a. Would you consider this treatment ethical?
        A. Yes
        B. No
        C. Undecided

    3b. How would you react if treatment was delivered to you via the Internet rather than in an office setting?
        A. Very positively
        B. Positively
        C. Neutral
        D. Negatively
        E. Very negatively

4. Suppose your therapist wanted you to take a 90-minute test. Imagine that the entire test was administered by a computer.

    4a. Would you consider the use of a computer to administer a test ethical?
        A. Yes
        B. No
        C. Undecided

4b. How would you react if you were asked to complete a test on a computer?
  A. Very positively
  B. Positively
  C. Neutral
  D. Negatively
  E. Very negatively

5. Imagine that instead of seeing a therapist, you had regular contact with a therapist via *tele*conferencing (talking to a therapist through a telephone).

  5a. Would you consider conducting therapy over the telephone ethical?
    A. Yes
    B. No
    C. Undecided

  5b. How would you react if you were asked to use teleconferencing as a treatment approach?
    A. Very positively
    B. Positively
    C. Neutral
    D. Negatively
    E. Very negatively

6. Imagine that instead of seeing a therapist in an office, you had regular contact with a therapist via *video*conferencing (seeing and hearing a therapist through a closed-circuit television).

  6a. Would you consider videoconferencing therapy ethical?
    A. Yes
    B. No
    C. Undecided

  6b. Would this type of videoconferencing be acceptable to you?
    A. Very positively
    B. Positively
    C. Neutral
    D. Negatively
    E. Very negatively

7. Imagine that a former soldier who experienced live combat is now a client. During his time in the military, he was involved in a firefight that still haunts him today. As part of therapy, the client puts on a computer monitor that fits over his head. The computer monitor then produces images of a firefight that helps him relive his trauma so that he can work through his emotions.

  7a. Would you consider this kind of treatment ethical?
    A. Yes
    B. No
    C. Undecided

7b. How would you react if you were asked to complete this kind of treatment (imagine that it might be useful for treating your particular problem)?
    A. Very positively
    B. Positively
    C. Neutral
    D. Negatively
    E. Very negatively

8. Imagine that during a therapy session, your therapist used a computer to enter notes while you spoke to him/her.

    8a. Would you consider it ethical for your therapist to use a computer to take notes during therapy?
        A. Yes
        B. No
        C. Undecided

    8b. How would you react if your therapist used a computer to take notes during therapy?
        A. Very positively
        B. Positively
        C. Neutral
        D. Negatively
        E. Very negatively

## REFERENCES

Albani, G., Pignatti, R., Bertella, L., Priano, L., Semenza, C., Molinari, E., et al. (2002). Common daily activities in the virtual environment: A preliminary study in parkinsonian patients. *Neurological Sciences, 23,* S49–S50.

Alcañiz, M., Botella, C., Baños, R., Perpiñá, C., Rey, B., Lozano, J., et al. (2003). Internet-based telehealth system for the treatment of agoraphobia. *CyberPsychology & Behavior, 6,* 355–358.

Alemagno, S. A., Cochran, D., Feucht, T. E., Stephens, R. C., et al. (1996). Assessing substance abuse treatment needs among the homeless: A telephone-based voice interactive system. *American Journal of Public Health, 86,* 1626–1628.

Andersson, G., Carlbring, P., Kaldo, V., & Ström, L. (2004). Screening of psychiatric disorders via the Internet. *Nordic Journal of Psychiatry, 58,* 287–291.

Axelson, D. A., Bertocci, M. A., Lewin, D. S., Trubnick, L. S., Birmaher, B., Williamson, D. E., et al. (2003). Measuring mood and complex behavior in natural environments: Use of ecological momentary assessment in pediatric affective disorders. *Journal of Child and Adolescent Psychopharmacology, 13,* 253–266.

Aziz, M. A., & Kenford, S. (2004). Comparability of telephone and face-to-face interviews in assessing patients with Post-Traumatic Stress Disorder. *Journal of Psychiatric Practice, 10,* 307–313.

Baer, L., Cukor, P., Jenike, M. A., Leahy, L., O'Laughlen, J., & Coyle, J. T. (1995). Pilot studies of telemedicine for patients with Obsessive-Compulsive Disorder. *American Journal of Psychiatry, 152,* 1383–1385.

Ball, C., & Puffett, A. (1998). The assessment of cognitive function in the elderly using videoconferencing. *Journal of Telemedicine and Telecare, 4,* 36–38.

Bastien, C. H., Morin, C. M., Ouellet, M., Blais, F. C., & Bouchard, S. (2004). Cognitive-behavioral therapy for insomnia: Comparison of individual therapy, group therapy, and telephone consultations. *Journal of Consulting & Clinical Psychology, 72,* 653–659.

Berns, S., Davis-Conway, S., & Jaeger, J. (2004). Telephone administration of neuropsychological tests can facilitate studies in schizophrenia. *Schizophrenia Research, 71,* 505–506.

Bock, B. C., Graham, A. L., Sciamanna, C. N., Krishnamoorthy, J., Whiteley, J., Carmona-Barros, R., et al. (2004). Smoking cessation treatment on the Internet: Content, quality, and usability. *Nicotine and Tobacco Research, 6,* 207–219.

Botella, C., Hofmann, S. G., & Moscovitch, D. A. (2001). A self-applied, Internet-based intervention for fear of public speaking. *Journal of Clinical Psychology, 60,* 821–830.

Bouchard, S., Payeur, R., Rivard, V., Allard, M., Paquin, B., Renaud, P., et al. (2000). Cognitive behavior therapy for Panic Disorder with Agoraphobia in videoconference: Preliminary results. *CyberPsychology & Behavior, 3,* 999–1007.

Buchanan, T. (2002). Online assessment: Desirable or dangerous? *Professional Psychology: Research and Practice, 33,* 148–154.

Buchanan, T. (2003). Internet-based questionnaire assessment: Appropriate use in clinical contexts. *Cognitive Behaviour Therapy, 32,* 100–109.

Buchanan, T., & Smith, J. L. (1999). Research on the Internet: Validation of a World Wide Web–mediated personality scale. *Behavior Research Methods, Instruments, and Computers, 31,* 565–571.

Butcher, J. N., Perry, J., & Hahn, J. (2004). Computers in clinical assessment: Historical developments, present status, and future challenges. *Journal of Clinical Psychology, 60,* 331–345.

Cacciola, J. S., Alterman, A. I., Rutherford, M. J., McKay, J. R., & May, D. J. (1999). Comparability of telephone and in-person Structured Clinical Interview for *DSM-III-R* (SCID) diagnoses. *Assessment, 6,* 235–242.

Chinman, M., Young, A. S., Schell, T., Hassell, J., & Mintz, J. (2004). Computer-assisted self-assessment in persons with severe mental illness. *Journal of Clinical Psychiatry, 65,* 1343–1351.

Collins, R. L., Kashdan, T. B., & Gollnisch, G. (2003). The feasibility of using cellular phones to collect ecological momentary assessment data: Application to alcohol consumption. *Experimental and Clinical Psychopharmacology, 11,* 73–78.

Cowain, T. (2001). Cognitive-behavioural therapy via videoconferencing to a rural area. *Australian & New Zealand Journal of Psychiatry, 35,* 62–64.

Davis, R. N. (1999). Web-based administration of a personality questionnaire: Comparison with traditional methods. *Behavior Research Methods, Instruments, and Computers, 31,* 572–577.

Dixon, M. R., & MacLin, O. (2003). *Visual Basic for behavioral psychologists.* Reno, NV: Context Press.

Dommeyer, C. J., & Moriarty, E. (1999–2000). Comparing two forms of an e-mail survey: Embedded vs. attached. *International Journal of Market Research, 42,* 39–50.

Elford, R., White, H., Bowering, R., Ghandi, A., Maddiggan, B., St. John, K., et al. (2000). A randomized, controlled trial of child psychiatric assessments conducted using videoconferencing. *Journal of Telemedicine and Telecare, 6,* 73–82.

Farrell, A. D. (1989). Impact of computers on professional practice: A survey of current practices and attitudes. *Professional Psychology: Research & Practice, 20,* 172–178.

Farrell, A. D. (1999a). Development and evaluation of problem frequency scales from Version 3 of the Computerized Assessment System for Psychotherapy Evaluation and Research (CASPER). *Journal of Clinical Psychology, 55,* 447–464.

Farrell, A. D. (1999b). Evaluation of the Computerized Assessment System for Psychotherapy Evaluation and Research (CASPER) as a measure of treatment effectiveness in an outpatient training clinic. *Psychological Assessment, 11,* 345–358.

Farrell, A. D., Camplair, P. S., & McCullough, L. (1987). Identification of target complaints by computer interview: Evaluation of the Computerized Assessment System for Psychotherapy Evaluation and Research. *Journal of Consulting and Clinical Psychology, 55,* 691–700.

Freddolino, P. P., & Han, A. S. (1999). Direct service applications of videoconferencing technologies: Case examples from Korea and the United States. *Journal of Technology in Human Services, 16,* 19–33.

Garcia-Palacios, A., Hoffman, H., Carlin, A., Furness III, T. A., & Botella, C. (2002). Virtual reality in the treatment of spider phobia: A controlled study. *Behaviour Research and Therapy, 40,* 983–993.

Garcia-Palacios, A., Hoffman, H. G., Kwong See, S., Tsai, A., & Botella, C. (2001). Redefining therapeutic success of virtual reality exposure therapy. *Cyberpsychology and Behavior, 4,* 341–348.

Gilroy, L. J., Kirkby, K. C., Daniels, B. A., Menzies, R. G., & Montgomery, I. M. (2000). Controlled comparison of computer-aided vicarious exposure versus live exposure in the treatment of spider phobia. *Behavior Therapy, 31,* 733–744.

Gilroy, L. J., Kirkby, K. C., Daniels, B. A., Menzies, R. G., & Montgomery, I. M. (2003). Long-term follow-up of computer-aided vicarious exposure versus live graded exposure in the treatment of spider phobia. *Behavior Therapy, 34,* 65–76.

Go, R. C. P., Duke, L. W., Harrell, L. E., Cody, H., Bassett, S. S., Folstein, M. F., et al. (1995). Development and validation of a structured telephone interview for dementia assessment (STIDA): The NIMH Genetics Initiative. *Journal of Geriatric Psychiatry & Neurology, 10,* 161–167.

Guilfoyle, C., Wootton, R., Hassall, S., Offer, J., Warren, M., & Smith, D. (2003). Preliminary experience of allied health assessments delivered face to face and by videoconference to a residential facility for elderly people. *Journal of Telemedicine and Telecare, 9,* 230–233.

Harris, S. R., Kemmerling, R. L., & North, M. M. (2002). Brief virtual reality therapy for public speaking anxiety. *CyberPsychology & Behavior, 5,* 543–550.

Herman, S., & Koran, L. M. (1998). *In vivo* measurement of Obsessive-Compulsive Disorder symptoms using palmtop computers. *Computers in Human Behavior, 14,* 449–462.

Hermann, C., Peters, M. L., & Blanchard, E. B. (1995). Use of handheld computers for symptom monitoring: The case of chronic headache. *Mind/Body Medicine, 1,* 59–69.

Hufford, B. J., Glueckauf, R. L., & Webb, P. M. (1999). Home-based, interactive videoconferencing for adolescents with epilepsy and their families. *Rehabilitation Psychology, 44,* 176–193.

King, R., Nurcombe, B., Bickman, L., Hides, L., & Reid, W. (2003). Telephone counselling for adolescent suicide prevention: Changes in suicidality and mental state from beginning to end of a counselling session. *Suicide & Life-Threatening Behavior, 33,* 400–411.

Kirkwood, K. T., Peck, D. F., & Bennie, L. (2000). The consistency of neuropsychological assessments performed via telecommunication and face to face. *Journal of Telemedicine and Telecare, 6,* 147–151.

Kypri, K., Saunders, J. B., Williams, S. M., McGee, R. O., Langley, J. D., Cashell-Smith, M. L., et al. (2004). Web-based screening and brief intervention for hazardous drinking: A double-blind randomized controlled trial. *Addiction, 99,* 1410–1417.

Lange, A., Rietdijk, D., Hudcovicova, M., van de Ven, J., Schrieken, B., & Emmelkamp, P. M. G. (2003). Interapy: A controlled randomized trial of the standardized treatment of posttraumatic stress through the Internet. *Journal of Consulting and Clinical Psychology, 71,* 901–909.

Lauterbach, W., & Newman, C. F. (1999). Computerized intrapersonal conflict assessment in cognitive therapy. *Clinical Psychology and Psychotherapy, 6,* 357–374.

Lee, J. H., Ku, J., Cho, W., Won., Y. H., Kim, I. Y., Lee, S-M., et al. (2003). A virtual reality system for the assessment and rehabilitation of the activities of daily living. *CyberPsychology and Behavior, 6,* 383–388.

Litz, B. T., Williams, L., Wang, J., Bryant, R., & Engel, Jr., C. C. (2004). A therapist-assisted Internet self-help program for traumatic stress. *Professional Psychology, Research, and Practice, 35,* 628–634.

Marks, M., & Hemsley, D. (1999). Retrospective versus prospective self-rating of anxiety symptoms and cognitions. *Journal of Anxiety Disorders, 13,* 463–472.

McDaniel, S. H. (2003). E-mail communication as an adjunct to systemic psychotherapy. *Journal of Systemic Therapies, 22,* 4–13.

McMinn, M. R., Buchanan, T., Ellens, B. M., & Ryan, M. K. (1999). Technology, professional practice, and ethics: Survey findings and implications. *Professional Psychology: Research & Practice, 30,* 165–172.

MedCalc. (2004). *MedCalc for Windows: Statistics for biomedical research* (software manual). Belgium.

Murray, K., Pombo-Carril, M. G., Bara-Carril, N., Grover, M., Reid, Y., Langham, C., et al. (2003). Factors determining uptake of a CD-ROM-based CBT self-help treatment for bulimia: Patient characteristics and subjective appraisals of self-help treatment. *European Eating Disorders Review, 11,* 243–260.

Nelson, E., Barnard, M., & Cain, S. (2003). Treating Childhood Depression over videoconferencing. *Telemedicine Journal & e-Health, 9,* 49–55.

Newman, M., Consoli, A., & Taylor, C. B. (1997). Computers in assessment and cognitive behavioral treatment of clinical disorders: Anxiety as a case in point. *Behavior Therapy, 28,* 211–235.

Newman, M., Consoli, A., & Taylor, C. B. (1999). A palmtop computer program for the treatment of Generalized Anxiety Disorder. *Behavior Modification, 23,* 597–619.

Newman, M. G., Kenardy, J., Herman, S., & Taylor, C. B. (1996). The use of handheld computers as an adjunct to cognitive-behavior therapy. *Computers in Human Behavior, 12,* 135–143.

Newman, M. G., Kenardy, J., Herman, S., & Taylor, C. B. (1997). Comparison of palmtop-computer-assisted brief cognitive-behavioral treatment to cognitive-behavioral treatment for Panic Disorder. *Journal of Consulting and Clinical Psychology, 65,* 178–183.

Nickelson, D. W. (1996). Behavioral telehealth: Emerging practice, research, and policy opportunities. *Behavioral Sciences and the Law, 14,* 443–457.

O'Connell, K. A., Gerkovich, M. M., Cook, M. R., Shiffman, S., Hickcox, M., & Kakolewski, K. E. (1998). Coping in real time: Using ecological momentary assessment techniques to assess coping with the urge to smoke. *Research in Nursing and Health, 21,* 487–497.

Peterson, M. R., & Beck, R. L. (2003). E-mail as an adjunctive tool in psychotherapy: Response and responsibility. *American Journal of Psychotherapy, 57,* 167–181.

Richard, D. C. S., & Bobicz, K. (2003). Computers and behavioral assessment: 6 years later. *Behavior Therapist, 26,* 219–223.

Richard, D. C. S., & Lauterbach, D. (2003). Computers in the training and practice of behavioral assessment. In M. Hersen (Series Ed.), S. N. Haynes, & E. Heiby (Vol. Eds.), *Comprehensive handbook of psychological assessment: Vol. 3. Behavioral assessment* (pp. 222–245). New York: John Wiley & Sons.

Richards, J., Klein, B., & Carlbring, P. (2003). Internet-based treatment for Panic Disorder. *Cognitive Behaviour Therapy, 32,* 125–135.

Robinson, P., & Serfaty, M. (2003). Computers, e-mail and therapy in eating disorders. *European Eating Disorders Review, 11,* 210–221.

Rochlen, A. B., Beretvas, S. N., & Zack, J. S. (2004). The Online and Face-to-Face Counseling Attitudes Scales: A validation study. *Measurement & Evaluation in Counseling & Development, 37,* 95–111.

Rogers, J. L., Howard, K. I., & Vessey, J. T. (1993). Using significance tests to evaluate equivalence between two experimental groups. *Psychological Bulletin, 113,* 553–565.

Rosen, L. D., & Weil, M. M. (1996). Psychologists and technology: A look at the future. *Professional Psychology: Research & Practice, 27,* 635–638.

Rosenfield, M., & Smillie, E. (1998). Group counselling by telephone. *British Journal of Guidance & Counselling, 26,* 11–19.

Rothbaum, B. O., Hodges, L. F., Anderson, P. L., Price, L., & Smith, S. (2002). Twelve-month follow-up of virtual reality and standard exposure therapies for the fear of flying. *Journal of Consulting and Clinical Psychology, 70,* 428–432.

Rothbaum, B. O., Hodges, L. F., Kooper, R., Opdyke D., Williford, J. S., & North, M. (1995). Virtual reality graded exposure in the treatment of acrophobia: A case report. *Behavior Therapy, 26,* 547–554.

Rothbaum, B. O., Hodges, L. F., Smith, S., Lee, J. H., & Price, L. (2000). A controlled study of virtual reality exposure therapy for the fear of flying. *Journal of Consulting and Clinical Psychology, 68,* 1020–1026.

Rothbaum, B. O., Hodges, L. F., Alarcon, R., Ready, D., Shahar, F., Graap, K., et al. (1999). Virtual reality exposure therapy for PTSD Vietnam veterans: A case study. *Journal of Traumatic Stress, 12,* 263–271.

Sarrazin, M. S. V., Hall, J. A., Richards, C., & Carswell, C. (2002). A comparison of computer-based versus paper-and-pencil assessment of drug use. *Research on Social Work Practice, 12,* 669–683.

Schwartz, J., & Stone, A. (1998). Strategies for analyzing ecological momentary assessment data. *Health Psychology, 17,* 6–16.

Schulenberg, S. E., & Yutrzenka, B. A. (2004). Ethical issues in the use of computerized assessment. *Computers in Human Behavior, 20,* 477–490.

Sideridis, G. D., & Greenwood, C. R. (1997). Is human behavior autocorrelated? An empirical analysis. *Journal of Behavioral Education, 7,* 273–293.

Simon, G. E., Ludman, E. J., Tutty, S., Operskalski, B., & Von Korff, M. (2004). Telephone psychotherapy and telephone care management for primary care patients starting antidepressant treatment: A randomized controlled trial. *Journal of the American Medical Association, 292,* 935–942.

Sorbi, M., Honkoop, P. C., & Godaert, G. L. R. (1996). A signal-contingent computer diary for the assessment of psychological patients of the migraine attack. In J. Fahrenberg & M. Myrtek (Eds.), *Ambulatory assessment: Computer-assisted psychological and physiological methods in monitoring and field studies* (pp. 403–412).

Stein, K. F., & Corte, C. M. (2003). Ecologic momentary assessment of eating-disordered behaviors. *International Journal of Eating Disorders, 34,* 349–360.

Stevens, J. (1990). *Intermediate statistics: A modern approach.* Hillsdale, NJ: Erlbaum.

Stone, A. A., Schwartz, J. E., Neale, J. M., Shiffman, S., Marco, C. A., Hickcox, M., et al. (1998). A comparison of coping assessed by ecological momentary assessment and retrospective recall. *Journal of Personality and Social Psychology, 74,* 1670–1680.

Stone, A. A., & Shiffman, S. (1994). Ecological momentary assessment (EMA) in behavioral medicine. *Annals of Behavioral Medicine, 16,* 199–202.

Theodoros, D., Russell, T. G., Hill, A., Cahill, L., & Clark, K. (2003). Assessment of motor speech disorders online: A pilot study. *Journal of Telemedicine & Telecare, 9,* 66–68.

van den Berg, S., Shapiro, D. A., Bickerstaffe, D., & Cavanagh, K. (2004). Computerized cognitive-behaviour therapy for anxiety and depression: A practical solution to the shortage of trained therapists. *Journal of Psychiatric & Mental Health Nursing, 11,* 508–513.

Wilson, G., & Lester, D. (1998). Suicide prevention by e-mail. *Crisis Intervention & Time-Limited Treatment, 4,* 81–87.

Wilson, G. T., & Vitousek, V. T. (1999). Self-monitoring in the assessment of eating disorders. *Psychological Assessment, 11,* 480–489.

Wright, P., Rogers, N., Hall, C., Wilson, B., Evans, J., Emslie, H., et al. (2001). Comparison of pocket-computer memory aids for people with brain injury. *Brain Injury, 15,* 787–800.

Yager, J. (2001). E-mail as a therapeutic adjunct in the outpatient treatment of anorexia nervosa: Illustrative case material and discussion of the issues. *International Journal of Eating Disorders, 29,* 125–138.

Yager, J., & Freedman, J. (2003). Monitoring patients with eating disorders by using e-mail as an adjunct to clinical activities. *Psychiatric Services, 54,* 1586–1588.

Yeh, A. H., Taylor, S., Thordarson, D. S., & Corcoran, K. M. (2003). Efficacy of telephone-administered cognitive behaviour therapy for obsessive-compulsive spectrum disorders: Case studies. *Cognitive Behaviour Therapy, 32,* 75–81.

# 21

## EVALUATING OLDER ADULTS

BARRY A. EDELSTEIN
ERIN L. WOODHEAD
EMILY H. BOWER
ANGELA J. LOWERY

*Department of Psychology*
*West Virginia University*
*Morgantown, West Virginia*

### INTRODUCTION: DEMOGRAPHICS OF AGING

The field of geropsychology is challenged by the increasing number of older adults and our incomplete understanding of the aging brain. In 2002, people age 65 years and older comprised over 12% of the U.S. population (35.6 million). With the baby boomers entering the older adult cohort, these numbers are predicted to double to 71.5 million by 2030, or 20% of the U.S. population (U.S. Administration on Aging, 2003). As the group grows, the face of the "average" older adult will change and the cohort will be more diverse. While minorities make up over 17% of the elderly population today, they will comprise 26.4% in 2030 (U.S. Administration on Aging).

Population predictions aside, today's 65-year-olds are projected to lead another 18 years of life (U.S. Administration on Aging, 2003), and many will experience it with challenges underrecognized by the mental health community. Approximately 19% of those 85 years and older have depressive symptoms (Federal Interagency Forum on Aging-Related Statistics, 2004). However, many older adults with depressive symptoms are not being identified as needing mental health services. Physical health status may also be different than what providers anticipate. Nearly 38% of older adults live with severe disability, and most have at least one chronic medical condition (U.S. Administration on Aging). Yet 38.6% of noninstitutionalized older adults report their health as "excellent" or "very good" (U.S.

*Clinician's Handbook of Adult Behavioral*
*Assessment*

497

Administration on Aging), and indeed many who live long, live well (Poon et al., 1992).

The pluralistic reality is that older adults are very healthy and very sick; they are middle-class Latinos and white and raising a grandchild; their population is growing. The accuracy of assessment relies on full recognition of these characteristics.

In the following sections we provide a knowledge base for readers unfamiliar with the unique characteristics of older adults and a variety of factors that should be taken into consideration when assessing older adults.

## AGEISM AND MYTHS OF AGING

In an era when adults experience the stress of caring for children and parents simultaneously and businesses capitalize on pathologizing aging, it can be difficult to be open-minded or positive about growing old. Stereotypes about aging abound, reinforcing both true and false pictures (McHugh, 2003).

Rowe and Kahn (1998) delineated common myths about aging. The authors challenged the truthfulness of ideas such as older adults are unproductive and incompetent and that "to be old is to be sick." These myths contribute to ageism, defined by Butler (1969) as judgments or discriminatory beliefs about older adults based on age alone. Contemporary examples of ageism include differential treatment of older adults, compared to younger adults, in health care settings (Williams, 2000; Ward, 2000) and mandatory retirement policies not based on competence (Cardinali & Gordon, 2002).

Clients and clinicians alike hold such prejudices, and these can heavily influence assessment. For example, family members and physicians may dismiss forgetfulness as an insignificant and normal sign of aging. However, it is believed that many mental abilities, including learning and accessing learned information, are retained into old age (Park, 2000). Indeed, memory problems may indicate the presence of a general medical condition (American Psychological Association, 1998). This illustrates how, when adhering to socially acceptable stereotypes of aging, important assessment questions may be ignored. As the result of an incomplete assessment, a client could be prescribed medication he or she does not need, or opportunities for maintaining independence could be unnecessarily removed.

Another harmful negative stereotype is that older adults are, by definition, sick or disabled (Palmore, 1999). Yet it was estimated in 1999 that just 20% of Medicare recipients age 65 and older (6.8 million) were disabled (Federal Interagency Forum on Aging-Related Statistics, 2004). The Centers for Disease Control and Prevention, in a 2004 report, estimated the rate of disability to be 30% for all older adults and also stressed that disability is not indicative of sickness (Merck Institute of Aging and Health, 2004). Chronic conditions, as opposed to acute illness, are the leading cause of death for older adults (Merck Institute of Aging and Health; Palmore). Heart disease, cancer, and stroke top this mortality list (National Center for Health Statistics, 2002). Beyond resulting in lost lives, chronic conditions do diminish quality of life. The leading chronic conditions for older adults are hypertension, arthritic symptoms, and coronary heart disease (Merck Institute of Aging and Health; Federal Interagency Forum on Aging-Related Statistics), with 80% of older adults living with one condition and 50% living with two or more conditions (Merck Institute of Aging and Health). Forty-three percent of older adults report good or excellent health (Merck Institute of Aging and Health). While this indicates that chronic conditions are affecting older adults' daily lives, there is clearly no evidence that to be old is to be infirm or feeble.

## AGE-RELATED CHANGES AND ACCOMMODATIONS

Age-related sensory, cognitive, and biological changes present idiographic considerations in the assessment of older adults. For example, one might ask whether a client's slow responses are due to an age-related process (e.g., poor eyesight) or to a potential disease process (e.g., Parkinson's disease). Accordingly, one might then ask what accommodations can be made to take into consideration or perhaps maximize assessment performance in light of this slowing of responses. Each client presents a different constellation of these issues, which influences assessment and treatment.

### SENSORY CHANGES

Changes in the sensory systems, particularly vision and hearing, should be considered in a clinical judgment. A clinician may learn about these problems through self-report, but attending to proxy information and assessing how the client interacts with the environment are equally important. Age-related sensory changes tend to be progressive and can go unnoticed by the client. Due to space limitations, we will focus on vision and hearing impairments and their potential effects on assessment.

Ocular diseases are present for 18% of older adults, with an average of one-third of those over 85 being affected (Federal Interagency Forum on Aging-Related Statistics, 2004). Macular degeneration, open-angle glaucoma, and cataracts are the most prevalent (Mayo Foundation for Medical Education and Research, 2004; Federal Interagency Forum on Aging-Related Statistics). In particular, macular degeneration is the leading cause of severe vision loss, with nearly 40% of those over 75 years living with some degree of it (Klein, Klein, & Linton, 1992). Additionally, clinicians should be aware of glaucoma symptoms, for nearly half of people with glaucoma do not know they have it (Sommer et al., 1991). For those who avoid ocular disease, vision decrements are quite common. A quarter of people experience myopia, and over a half have astigmatism (Casser et al., 1997). Presbyopia, or thickening of the lens, affects nearly everyone by age 50. On a tissue level, the whole eye may change: The retina may become thinner, the iris stiffer, and the lens thicker, rendering the eye less able to focus and adjust to changes in lighting.

Depth perception, visual acuity, and peripheral vision are factors that can affect test performance (Edelstein, Whipple-Drozdick, & Null-Kogan, 1998). Depth perception is compromised at close proximity due to presbyopia, which may cause problems reading test materials with small print. These deficits may be noticeable by age 50 and should be accommodated with the use of large print (e.g., 16-point font) and corrective lenses. Lens thickening also results in a decreased ability to handle glare. In testing situations, care can be taken to minimize use of high-gloss paper (Storandt, 1994) and to angle lights to an optimal diffusion. Anticipating and addressing these biological changes will improve test validity by reducing error variance. While it is important to recognize the deficits for the purposes of mental status testing, it is also an opportunity for intervention. Vision impairments, when addressed early enough, are often amenable to improvement.

Hearing impairments affect nearly half of men and one-third of women over age 65 (Federal Interagency Forum on Aging-Related Statistics, 2004). The most common age-related change in the inner ear is the break down of the hair cells (cilia) or their ability to send communication through the nerves in the ear. This is experienced as an inability to hear high-pitched frequencies. Problems with distinguishing sounds in a crowded room or filtering background noise are also common and may be an issue for people who otherwise have good hearing. Earwax buildup can cause similar sensations and is easily remediable. People who have been exposed to loud noises, perhaps through their occupation, may show more inner ear damage. Finally, medication such as high doses of aspirin and illnesses that result in high fever may promote temporary or permanent inner ear damage (Mayo Foundation for Medical Education and Research, 2004).

Hearing loss may have wide-ranging effects on quality of life, including mobility, independence, social behavior, and self-concept (Edelstein et al., 1998). It may precipitate fewer interactions with friends. For some, effects will be so serious as to promote depression (Mulrow et al., 1990) and misleading diagnoses due to a clinician's focus on "zoning out" behaviors that are actually due to poor hearing (Mindel & Vernon, 1987). Accordingly, it is important to take advantage of the opportunity to address hearing deficits. A clinician might notice that a client asks for statements to be repeated, speech is louder than normal, or there is a focus on the speaker's mouth, which may be indications of hearing loss (Vernon, 1989). Hearing aids are very helpful for some—one in five people with hearing loss use them—but others find that they change the quality of sound in undesirable ways. In addition to amplification devices, clinicians with higher-pitched voices may consider lowering the pitch (Storandt, 1994). Directly facing the client and eliminating background noise should also be helpful.

## COGNITIVE CONSIDERATIONS

Colloquially, one of the most common fears about growing old is the loss of memory. An intact memory is equated with identity and personality and, ultimately, quality of life. However, the incidence of age-related memory impairment among older adults is lower than many people believe. Just 15% of men and 11% of women over 65 years have moderate or severe impairment (Federal Interagency Forum on Aging-Related Statistics, 2004). The prevalence rises in the cohort of 85-year-olds and older; 32% of the "oldest old" have moderate or severe impairment (Federal Interagency Forum on Aging-Related Statistics).

It is normal for some declines in memory to occur with age. Working memory, episodic memory, some facets of semantic memory, spatial memory (Craik, 2000), and cued and free recall (Park, 2000) all show declines. Additionally, some older adults have increased difficulty with abstract thinking, acquiring and storing new information, and remembering long strings of information (Edelstein et al., 1998). Processing time may be slower with age (Park), but not necessarily accuracy (Edelstein et al.). Notably, procedural memory, remote memory (Craik), and world knowledge (vocabulary) (Park) show little decline as compared to younger adults, exemplifying that not all areas of the brain experience age-related decline. Because assessment of these abilities is also important in circumscribing disease-related cognitive deficits, the clinician has the difficult task of identifying and accounting for age-related deficits before making a diagnosis.

While many dementias are not reversible or successfully ameliorated, they share cognitive symptoms with disease-related and age-related declines that may be treatable. The National Institute on Aging (as cited in American Society on Aging, 2004) has identified around 100 general medical conditions that may present similar symptomatology as dementia; depression is one example. Such conditions tend to be precipitated by stressors common to older adults: emotional distress, physical illness, medication interactions, social and cultural conflicts, nutrition deficiencies, alcohol abuse, and lack of physical activity (American Society on Aging). The latter three may account for 20% of memory complaints (American Society on Aging).

Age-related changes and accommodations, including sensory and cognitive influences, can directly affect the validity of mental status assessment. These normal processes can both mimic the symptoms of medical conditions and be exacerbated by them, making the clinician's job of diagnosis and treatment difficult. Through awareness of possible illness comorbidities and medication side effects, for example, clinicians can assess and eliminate noncausal factors. The aim of this thorough process is higher-quality assessment through improved validity and reliability.

## BEHAVIORAL VERSUS TRADITIONAL ASSESSMENT

Before discussing the mechanics and content of assessment, it is important to briefly discuss some conceptual and practical differences between behavioral and nonbehavioral/traditional assessment. The importance of this discussion will become more apparent as we later address specific assessment methods and instruments. The distinction between behavioral and nonbehavioral/traditional assessment instruments is unclear (see Edelstein, Martin, & Koven, 2003). They often share some of the same characteristics, even though each has evolved from different subparadigms (cf. Haynes & O'Brien, 2000). Behavioral and traditional paradigms can be distinguished in a variety of ways (see Barrios & Hartman, 1986; Cone, 1986; Haynes & O'Brien; Nelson & Hayes, 1986). Within the behavioral paradigm one finds instruments based on behavior-analytic, social learning, and cognitive-behavioral subparadigms (Kazdin & Wilson, 1978). Within the traditional paradigm one finds instruments that evolved from trait-oriented psychodynamic personality, intellectual, neuropsychological, diagnostic, and family systems subparadigms.

Behavioral and traditional paradigms can be distinguished in terms of their philosophical assumptions regarding descriptions and causes of behavior. Traditional approaches tend to emphasize descriptions of an individual's dispositional characteristics (e.g., personality traits) or what he or she *has* (cf. Mischel, 1968). The disposition is usually inferred from observed behavior and self-reports of feelings, attitudes, and behavior. The behavior of the individual tends to be explained by these personal characteristics. In contrast, behavioral approaches focus on the identification of environmental conditions that reliably produce the behaviors of interest. A lower level of inference is required in behavioral assessment because the focus is usually on behavior (including thoughts or cognitions) and not on dispositions inferred from the behavior.

Traditional and behavioral paradigms also can be differentiated on the basis of a distinction popularized by Allport (1937) in his discussions of personality: idiographic versus nomothetic approaches to assessment. In general, the nomothetic approach is used to examine commonalities among individuals, whereas the idiographic approach is used to ascertain the uniqueness of an individual. Nomothetic assessment typically involves use of assessment instruments that have been standardized with a large number of individuals. The same instrument is used to assess multiple individuals. The results of the assessment are compared against the results obtained with a standardization population (normative sample).

Idiographic assessment is an individualized approach to assessment that involves methods and measures used to examine the unique features of an individual's behaviors. The assessment results are often not compared with those obtained from other individuals. Mischel (1968) noted that "behavioral assessment involves an exploration of the unique or idiosyncratic aspects of the single case, perhaps to a greater extent than any other approach" (p. 190).

In practice, assessment methods and instruments of the traditional and behavioral paradigms are often combined (cf. Nelson-Gray, 1996). One might, for example, use a standardized, norm-based depression assessment instrument (e.g., Geriatric Depression Scale) to obtain a single score (nomothetic approach) and to ascertain information from individual test items for use in a behavioral analysis. The normative comparison of total scores may reveal that a client is depressed. The individual test items could then be used to gain an understanding of how the individual is experiencing depression, how it is manifested in his or her behavior, and the conditions under which these experiences and behaviors occur.

There is a necessary shift from more traditional, nomothetic to more behavioral, idiographic assessment approaches as one moves from cognitively intact to cognitively impaired individuals (Edelstein et al., 2003). The reliability and accuracy of the self-report method becomes questionable with moderate to severely cognitively impaired individuals. The clinician must rely more heavily on reports by others and on direct observation and analyses of controlling environmental variables to explain or account for the older adult's behavior.

## ASSESSMENT METHODS

Multiple methods and sources of information have repeatedly been strongly recommended in the behavioral assessment literature (e.g., Haynes & O'Brien, 2000) to ensure accurate, reliable, and valid information. Each method (e.g., interviews, direct observation, self-reports, reports by others, psychophysiological recordings) has strengths and weaknesses. One can avoid, to some degree, the weaknesses of any one method by using two or more assessment methods. In addition, each method can capture both unique and overlapping information. The strengths and weaknesses of some of these methods are discussed next.

### SELF-REPORT

The evidence supporting the accuracy, reliability, and validity of older adult self-reports is mixed. Schwarz (Schwarz & Knauper, 2000; Schwarz, 2003) has noted that the specific wording of questions, question format, and question context can influence self-reports of older adults. Older-adult estimates of their functional ability have been questioned, with some overestimating their functional ability (e.g., Rubenstein, Schairer, Weiland, & Kane, 1984) and others both under- and overestimating their abilities (e.g., Sager et al., 1992). Similarly, self-reports of memory impairment among older adults may be inaccurate (e.g., Perlmutter, 1978; Rabbitt, 1982; Sunderland, Watts, Baddeley & Harris, 1986; Zelinski, Gilewski, & Thompson, 1980). In contrast, several studies have provided evidence of good self-report reliability among older adults across a wide range of variables. Self-reports of activities of daily living by older adults in outpatient settings have been found to be strongly related to performance measures (Sager et al.). Resnick, Beckett, Branch, Scherr, and Wetle (1994) found the reliability of self-reported incontinence in community-based congregate-dwelling older adults to be moderate to strong (urinary incontinence questions .89–86; fecal incontinence questions .67–.69). Self-reported stroke was found to be valid among a group of Swedish community-dwelling older adults when participants with and without histories of strokes were reexamined following self-reports (Engstad, Bonaa, & Vitanen, 2000). Finally, good correspondence has been found between older-adult self-reports of insomnia and polysomnography results (e.g., Reite, Buysse, Reynolds, & Mendelson, 1995).

Unfortunately, some of the factors that can contribute to self-reports of questionable value are the very problems presented by older adults. For example, compromised physical and mental health, affective responses to acute illness, changes from previous levels of physical functioning occurring during hospitalization, and the presence of acute or chronic cognitive impairment (Sager et al., 1992) can all influence the quality of self-reports. Cognitively impaired older adults offer perhaps the greatest challenge for assessment through self-report. Notwithstanding the memory problems, cognitively impaired individuals are less likely to comprehend questions or the nature of information requested. Kiyak, Teri, and Borson (1994) found self-reports of functional health of demented individuals consistently rated as poorer than reports by family members. Older adults with dementia who deny memory impairment may also tend to deny other symptoms (e.g., Larrabee & Crook, 1989). On the more positive side, self-report inventories requiring only recent memory may be reliable and valid with individuals experiencing mild-to-moderate dementia (see Feher, Larrabee, & Crook, 1992).

Notwithstanding the caveats of older-adult self-report just noted, self-report inventories can be very useful in the assessment of older adults. Though many self-report inventories are used with older adults, few have sufficient psychometric support (i.e., norms, validity evidence, reliability evidence) with older adults. However, an increasing number of self-report instruments have been developed specifically for older adults for a variety of clinical variables, e.g., assertiveness (Northrop & Edelstein, 1998), worry (Wisocki, Handen, & Morse, 1986), fears (J. N. Kogan & Edelstein, 2004), and depression (Yesavage et al., 1983). In addition, several assessment instruments developed for younger adults have been shown to be reliable and valid with older adults (e.g., Beck Depression Inventory II: Beck, Steermm, & Brown, 1996; Beck Anxiety Inventory, BAI: Beck, Epstein, Brown, & Steer, 1988). The physical and cognitive demands of self-report inventories must be considered when selecting instruments. Problems with vision, reading comprehension, and perceptual-motor skills affect the reliability and validity of information obtained via questionnaires and inventories (Edelstein et al., 2003).

## REPORT BY OTHERS

The report-by-other (e.g., spouse, caregiver, adult child) assessment method can provide unique and converging data, particularly regarding contextual factors relating to the problem(s) in question (Edelstein, Martin, & McKee, 2000). Such reports can be particularly valuable when assessing cognitively impaired individuals. Reports by others are subject to the same potential problems of unreliability, invalidity, and inaccuracy as other assessment methods. For example, accuracy of caregiver reports of dementia patient ADLs can vary as a function of the caregiver's depressive symptoms and burden level (e.g., Zanetti, Geroldi, Frisoni, Bianchetti, & Trabucchi, 1999).

## INTERVIEW

The interview is a convenient and flexible assessment method that often varies in reliability as a function of its degree of structure. An unstructured or semi-structured interview permits rephrasing of questions and the exploration of a wide range of topic areas. Cognitively unimpaired older adults are generally as cooperative with interviews as younger adults, but there are some age-related differences that should be considered when interviewing older adults. For example, older adults are more likely than younger adults to be more cautious when responding (Okun, 1976), to give more acquiescent responses (N. Kogan, 1961), to refuse to answer certain types of questions (e.g., Gergen & Back, 1966), and to respond "don't know" (Colsher & Wallace, 1989). As with other assessment methods, the accuracy, reliability, and validity of information obtained must be considered in the context of the physical stamina, cognitive skills, and sensory deficits of older adults. Uncooperativeness can rise with the personality changes and increased suspiciousness that can accompany dementia. Involving a trusted individual (e.g., family member, caregiver) can oftentimes facilitate the interview, unless the "trusted" individual has been incorporated into a persecutory delusion.

A variety of semistructured and structured interviews have established psychometric properties with older adults (e.g., Comprehensive Assessment and Referral Evaluation: Gurland et al., 1977; Geriatric Mental State Schedule: Copeland et al., 1976).

## DIRECT OBSERVATION

Direct observation should always be considered as a source of assessment information. Direct observation data can provide convergent evidence in a multimethod assessment and offer clues to idiosyncratic variations in behavior that occur as a function of changes in environmental stimuli. Direct observation can be particularly useful when assessing older adults who are uncooperative, unavailable for self-report, or severely cognitively or physically impaired (Goga & Hambacher, 1977). Behavioral observation can be taught easily to individuals with little or no previous experience. Institutional settings (e.g., nursing homes, psychiatric hospitals) lend themselves to direct observation, where staff can observe behavior over time. However, one must balance the utility of data provided through direct observation with the competing demands of staff, who often do not consider systematic observation one of their responsibilities.

## PSYCHOPHYSIOLOGICAL ASSESSMENT

Psychophysiological assessment of older adults is typically employed when questions regarding sleep (discussed in a subsequent section) and autonomic nervous system arousal are considered. In our experience, formal psychophysiological assessment is rarely used in clinical settings, although this may change as telemetry devices become smaller and less expensive. Nevertheless, it is important for the clinician to appreciate the age-related changes in common psychophysiological indices, because some of the same content can be accessed through self-report. In general, autonomic arousal appears to diminish with age (Appenzeller, 1994), with resting heart rate and skin conductance levels in response to stressors diminishing with age (Anderson & McNeilly, 1991; Appenzeller; Juniper & Dykman, 1967; Lau, Edelstein, & Larkin, 2001). Older adults, however, exhibit a greater stress-induced blood pressure reactivity than younger adults (McNeilly & Anderson, 1997). These changes in autonomic arousal are believed to result from multiple age-related physiological and neurochemical changes (J. N. Kogan, Edelstein, & McKee, 2000). Therefore, one must be cautious when interpreting older adult reports of automatic arousal patterns and not assume that normative patterns will be comparable to those of younger adults.

## PSYCHOMETRIC CONSIDERATIONS

When selecting assessment instruments to use with older adults, one must realize that many common assessment instruments are inappropriate for use with older adults or their psychometric properties have yet to be examined with older adults. Inappropriate selection can yield missed diagnoses, misdiagnoses, and/or inappropriate treatment. Though all psychometric characteristics are important, of particular importance for the selection of older-adult assessment instruments are norms, content validity, and construct validity.

Attention to appropriate normative data is important because of age-related changes in item responses, as with younger adults, and because attention to normative data can help avoid the uniformity myth that older adults of all ages respond similarly to test items. Though one might not think twice about considering normative differences on a variety of psychological dimensions between 30- and 50-year-old adults, it is not uncommon for one to assume that 65- and 85-year-old individuals are the same or similar along these dimensions.

Content validity, the extent to which a variable accurately samples the domain in which one is interested (Cronbach, 1971), is particularly important when considering assessment instruments to use with older adults. It is not uncommon for representative subject content to change with age, as has been shown with depression (e.g., Yesavage et al., 1983), fears (e.g., J. N. Kogan & Edelstein, 2004), and assertiveness (e.g., Northrop & Edelstein, 1998).

As with content validity, the construct validity of measures obtained with assessment instruments can vary with age. For example, the nature and number of factors obtained through factor analysis of assessment instruments can differ across the age span (Kaszniak & Christenson, 1994). One must consider potential age-related changes in the construct validity of assessment instruments as the population for which one intends to use the instrument deviates from the population sample on which the instrument was standardized.

## MEDICAL CONSIDERATIONS: DISEASES

Several physical disorders can lead to biologically based psychological symptoms, others can present as psychological symptoms, and many engender psychopathological responses. In all cases, it is important for one working with older adults to appreciate the potential etiologies and contributions of these symptoms and to incorporate that knowledge into the assessment process. Most older adults have at least one chronic disease, most are taking multiple medications, and many of these medications can produce psychological symptoms.

### PARKINSON'S DISEASE

Symptoms of depression are often associated with Parkinson's disease (Frazer, Leicht, & Baker, 1996; Leentjens, 2004), with an estimated 41% of individuals with Parkinson's disease displaying either major depression (50%) or dysthmia (50%) (Starkstein, Preziosi, Bolduc, & Robinson, 1990). Depression in Parkinson's disease differs from that of other forms of depression by presenting with greater anxiety and "less self-punitive ideation" (Cummings, 1992). Depression can also be the initial presenting complaint of individuals with Parkinson's disease, with Starkstein et al. reporting that 29% of their participants with Parkinson's disease having history of depression prior to the appearance of any motor symptoms. Similar premorbid findings have been reported by Todes and Lee (1985). Anxiety is often associated with Parkinson's disease, particularly generalized anxiety, panic, and social phobia (Walsh & Bennett, 2001). Approximately 40% of individuals with Parkinson's disease experience anxiety disorders (Richard, Schiffer, & Kurlan, 1996).

## CANCER

Depression is a relatively common occurrence among cancer patients (McDaniel, Musselman, Porter, Reed, & Nemeroff, 1995), with the prevalence rates varying from 6% to 42%, depending on whether one includes the somatic criteria (Rodin, Craven, & Littlefield, 1993). The diagnosis of depression among cancer patients is complicated by the side effects of cancer treatment (e.g., anorexia, fatigue, insomnia; Frazer et al., 1996; Greenberg, 1989) and pain. The teasing apart of symptoms can be aided by knowledge of the presentations of cancer and depressive symptoms. For example, if fatigue is worse in the morning, depression may be the causal factor; if insomnia does not appear to be caused by pain, depression might be a likely cause (Edelstein et al., 2003). Symptoms of both anxiety (Passik & Roth, 1999) and depression (Gillam, 1990; Holland et al., 1986) can precede a pancreatic cancer diagnosis. Similarly, there is evidence that depression can precede lung (Hughes, 1985) head, and neck cancer (Davies, Davies, & Delpo, 1986).

## CHRONIC OBSTRUCTIVE PULMONARY DISEASE

Chronic obstructive pulmonary disease (COPD) comprises several degenerative diseases of the respiratory system, with chronic bronchitis and emphysema being the most common. The inability to obtain sufficient air is one of the more prominent symptoms. Both depression and anxiety are common psychological symptoms associated with COPD, with depression being the most common. Approximately 25–50% of individuals with COPD experience depressive symptoms (Murrell, Himmelfarb, & Wright, 1983). The anxiety associated with COPD is related to the hypoxia and dyspnea that accompanies the disease (Frazer et al., 1996). This anxiety places further demands on the respiratory system, which can, in turn, exacerbate respiratory distress and anxiety (Frazer et al.).

## MEDICAL CONSIDERATIONS: MEDICATIONS

Medication use is highest among those with chronic conditions (Federal Interagency Forum on Aging-Related Statistics, 2004), and its metabolism is understudied in the older-adult population. In addition to the high-prevalence of chronic conditions, often comorbid, older adults have normal, age-related changes that can affect metabolism. Specifically, differences in total body water, total body fat (Schneider, 1996), and liver and kidney function (Ferrini & Ferrini, 1993) render different effects as compared to younger controls. Also, adverse reactions can be more severe in older adults' changing bodies. Dizziness, numbness, dehydration, loss of appetite, nausea, and diarrhea in older adults can lead to falls, depression, and hallucinations (American Society on Aging, 2004). It is estimated that one-quarter of adverse drug reactions are avoidable, as was observed in a study (Committee on Quality of Health Care in America Report, Institute of Medicine, 1999) where preventable errors occurred in prescribing, monitoring, and patient adherence.

Complicating the juxtaposition of chronic diseases, normal drug side effects, and drug metabolism differences, the influence of multiple medications, or polypharmacy, is a consideration in assessment. Those over 65 years old take an average of 30 prescriptions, representing an increase from 18 prescriptions in the early 1990s (Federal Interagency Forum on Aging-Related Statistics, 2004). This growth is underscored by the fact that older adults comprise 13% of the country's population but take 34% of prescription medications (Merck Institute of Aging and Health, 2004). Negative drug interactions are a common problem (Lazarou, Pomeranz, & Corey, 1998), exacerbated by the use of multiple physicians and pharmacies. Older adults may be hesitant to use assertive behaviors with physicians (Andersen, Guthrie, & Urban, 2004), and declining abilities to accomplish self-care activities (e.g., taking medication on a schedule, being able to read expiration dates, making good decisions about insulin administration based on glucose levels) may be problematic (Park, 1999).

A thorough discussion of all assessment targets is beyond the scope of a single chapter. In the following sections we address some areas for which older-adult assessment questions are commonly raised. The reader is referred to Lichtenberg (1999) for a comprehensive treatment of older-adult assessment.

## COGNITIVE SCREENING

A brief discussion of cognitive screening is offered, with the assumption that a client can be referred to a neuropsychologist for more extensive evaluation. Cognitive impairment can result from a variety of factors that are not directly related to aging (e.g., drug side effects, cardiovascular disease, schizophrenia, dementia). Identification of potential sources of cognitive deficits is one of the more complex tasks in the multidimensional assessment of older adults. One typi-cally begins with the administration of a cognitive screening instrument. A variety of screening instruments have been used extensively with older adults, for example, the Mini-Mental State Examination (Folstein, Folstein, & McHugh,

1975), Mental Status Questionnaire (Kahn, Goldfarb, Pollack, & Peck, 1960), Dementia Rating Scale (Mattis, 1988), and The Short Portable Mental Status Questionnaire (Pfeiffer, 1975). The interested reader is referred to Macneil & Lichtenberg (1999) and Albert (1994) for thorough descriptions and evaluations of these and other screening instruments.

## DEPRESSION ASSESSMENT

Prevalence rates for major depression in community-dwelling adults over the age of 65 is approximately 2%, which is lower than the prevalence for younger adults. The rate for major depression among hospitalized older adults is approximately 11%, slightly higher for long-term-care residents (12%), and lower (5%) among nonpsychiatric outpatients (Blazer, 1994). Though the prevalence of major depression is higher among younger than older adults, older adults are more likely to experience subsyndromal depression, with estimates ranging from 15% to 30% (Montgomery et al., 2001). Older adults with subsyndromal depression do not meet criteria for a major depression or dysthymia diagnosis but still have some depressive symptoms that cause distress or impairment (Mossey, 1997). Rates of depressive symptoms range from 8% to 30% across various settings (e.g., communities, nursing homes, hospitals). Some life events for older adults, such as taking on the role of caregiver, may contribute to a period of transitory depression, though many older adults have had depression throughout much of their lives.

Depression that first occurs in old age is the most common late-onset psychological problem of older adults (Molinari, 2001), and it appears different from early-onset depression in several ways. Older adults with late-onset depression are less likely to have a family history of depression, are more likely to develop dementia, are more likely to show more impairment on neuropsychological tests, and tend to have more neurosensory hearing impairment (Alexopoulos, 1996).

When considering assessment of older adults, it is important to appreciate that older adults may differ from young adults in the presentation of depressive symptoms. Older adults are more likely to report depressed mood (Blazer, Crowell, George, & Landerman, 1986) and less likely to report feelings of guilt than younger adults. Musetti et al. (1989) found fewer reports of guilt and suicidal ideation among older than among younger adults. Norris, Snow-Turek, and Blankenship (1995) noted that while sleep disturbance, diminished energy levels, and strained effort are characteristic of depressed older adults, symptoms pertaining to appetite and sexual interest are not.

Fifteen to 30% of community-dwelling older adults (Blazer, Hughes, & George, 1987) and 23–40% of institutionalized older adults report elevated levels of depressive symptoms (Koenig, Meador, Cohen, & Blazer, 1988), which can result in slower recovery from illness, limitations in physical functioning, and an increased risk for major depression (Broadhead, Blazer, George, & Tse, 1990; Howarth, Johnson, Klerman, & Weissman, 1992).

Several self-report depression assessment instruments are suitable for older adults (see Edelstein, Kalish, Drozdick, & McKee, 1999), which include the Geriatric Depression Scale (GDS; Yesavage et al., 1983), the Beck Depression Inventory—II (BDI-II; Beck, Steer, & Brown, 1996), and the Center for Epidemiologic Studies Depression Scale (CES-D; Radloff, 1977). Though all of these instruments are suitable for older adults, each has unique characteristics that should be considered before being used with older adults. The GDS is presented in an easy-to-use yes/no format, with no somatic items. Though the CES-D has been used successfully to assess depression in community-dwelling older adults, its use as a diagnostic instrument has been discouraged (Eaton, Muntaner, Smith, Tien, & Ybarra, 2004). The BDI-II employs a Guttman scale, which can be difficult for cognitively impaired older adults to manage. Regardless of the instrument employed, each can be incorporated into a behavioral assessment by examining responses to individual items, with an eye to the conditions under which they are likely and unlikely to occur.

Depression assessment instruments that are appropriate for use with cognitively impaired adults include the Pleasant Events Schedule (Logsdon & Teri, 1997), the Cornell Scale for Depression in Dementia (Alexopoulos, Abrams, Young, & Shamoian, 1988), and the Dementia Mood Assessment Scale (Sunderland & Minichiello, 1996). The Pleasant Events Schedule is a behavioral self-report inventory of potentially reinforcing events, the results of which can be easily incorporated into a behavioral intervention for depression for cognitively impaired and unimpaired individuals. The Cornell Scale provides a severity rating of depression once a depression diagnosis has been established. The Dementia Mood Assessment Scale is a brief measure of mood for individuals with mild-to-moderate dementia.

Interview-based assessment instruments can also be used when diagnosing depression in older adults, including the Structured Clinical Interview for the *DSM-IV* Axis I disorders (SCID; First, Gibbon, Spitzer, & Williams, 1995) and the Hamilton Rating Scale for Depression (HRSD; Hamilton, 1967). However, as previously noted, the psychometric properties of these instruments with older adults must be considered when they are employed.

The Patient Health Questionnaire Nine-Item Depression Module (PHQ-9) has been suggested as an easy instrument for minor depression screening in primary care settings (Hegel, Stanley, & Arean, 2002).

Older adults are more likely than younger adults to experience chronic diseases (e.g., arthritis, diabetes, chronic obstructive pulmonary disease), which may have associated symptoms of depression. Additionally, symptoms of depression may result from medications used to treat such disorders. The clinician working with older adults must tease apart or at least account for the effects of diseases and medications when assessing an individual with symptoms of depression (Edelstein et al., 2003).

## SUICIDE ASSESSMENT

Older-adult suicide contributes a disproportionate share to the overall suicide rate. Adults over the age of 65 make up 13% of the population, yet suicides completed by this group account for 18% of all suicide deaths (National Center for Injury Prevention and Control, 2000). Among older adults, white males over the age of 85 are at the highest risk for completed suicide. The suicide rate for white males over age 85 is five times the national average (Hoyert, Airas, Smith, Murphy, & Kochanek, 2001).

Assessment of suicide risk among older adults is complicated by the fact that older adults are less likely than younger adults to report symptoms such as sad mood and depression. Younger adults are more likely to report suicidal ideation and previous attempts, whereas older adults are more likely to successfully complete suicide and less likely to report ideation or have previous attempts (Lyness, Cox, & Curry, 1995; Conwell, Duberstein, & Caine, 2002). In a recent survey, psychologists indicated that the top three suicide risk factors they would address when assessing older-adult suicide risk are history of suicide attempts, acute suicidal ideation, and seriousness of previous attempts (Brown, Bongar, & Cleary, 2004).

Few suicide assessment instruments have psychometric support when used with older adults. A comprehensive review of the current adult assessment instruments by Brown (2001) highlights instruments used with older adults, though these instruments do not have psychometric support for their use with that population. The instruments more likely to be valid for older adults are those that explore suicidal ideation with open-ended, relatively content-free questions regarding suicidal ideation (e.g., Scale for Suicide Ideation; Beck, Kovacs, & Weissman, 1979) and measures of constructs that have been found predictive of suicidal ideation, attempts, and completions (e.g., hopelessness, depression). Instruments based on younger-adult risk factors are less-likely to be valid for older adults, for risk factors can change with age.

The Reasons for Living Scale—Older Adults (RFL-OA; Edelstein, McKee, & Martin, 2000) is an unpublished scale that can be used with an older adult population to assess the reasons a patient may have for not committing suicide. This scale focuses on protective factors, instead of directly assessing suicide risk factors. Preliminary data (Edelstein, McKee, & Martin, 2000; Heisel & Duberstein, 2003) suggest good reliability with community-dwelling older adults and good reliability and validity with hospitalized depressed older adults. The Geriatric Scale for Suicidal Ideation (GSIS) is the second unpublished suicide assessment measure for older adults. Developed by Heisel and Flett (2001, 2004), the GSIS identifies and measures the nature and severity of suicidal thoughts. Preliminary evidence for its internal consistency, temporal stability, and construct validity is promising.

## ANXIETY ASSESSMENT

Anxiety disorders are the most prevalent of psychiatric problems among older adults, although they are less prevalent in older than in younger adults (Flint, 1994). Prevalence rates exceed 5.5% (Regier, Narrow, & Rae, 1990), with fears being the most prevalent of the anxiety disorders. Though this prevalence rate is lower than that of younger adults (7.3%), older adult anxiety disorder prevalence is twice that of mood disorders and four to eight times that of major depressive episode for adults over the age of 65 (Regier et al., 1988). Generalized Anxiety Disorder and phobias are the most common older adult anxiety disorders. Panic Disorder is rare among this population (Flint).

Our understanding of the development, experience, presentation, and appropriate assessment of anxiety among most age groups is quite good. However, this is not the case with older adults. Appropriate assessment of older-adult anxiety has been particularly neglected in the literature (Carmin, Pollard, & Gillock, 1999; J. N. Kogan et al., 2000). Age-related differences in the experience, presentation, and medically related complexities have contributed to this neglect. Evidence is growing that older adults experience arousing stimuli differently than younger adults, with older adults exhibiting less physiological arousal (e.g., Lau et al., 2001). Because such a large percentage (65%) of adults over the age of 65 have at least two chronic physical illnesses (Haley, 1996), one must be sensitive to the nature and potential etiologies of the anxiety symptoms presented by older adults. Symptoms of anxiety can precede, be associated with, and result from both physical illnesses and the medications used to treat them (see J. N. Kogan et al., 2000; Small, 1997).

Anxiety symptoms are often comorbid with depression symptoms. Among community-dwelling older adults, Lindesay, Briggs, and Murphy (1989) found that more than 90% who had a Generalized Anxiety diagnosis also displayed symptoms of an affective disorder (Lindesay et al.). Similarly, Beck, Stanley, and Zebb (1996) found that older adults with Generalized Anxiety Disorder reported higher levels of depressive symptoms than a matched control group.

Although there are numerous psychometrically sound assessment instruments for anxiety disorders, many lack psychometric support for use with older adults. Self-report anxiety assessment instruments for which there is adequate psychometric support with older adults include, for example, the Penn State Worry Questionnaire (PSWQ; Meyer, Miller, Metzger, & Borkovec, 1990), Beck Anxiety Inventory (BAI; Beck et al., 1988), Fear Survey Schedule for older adults (J. N. Kogan & Edelstein, 2004), and the Worry Scale (WS; Wisocki et al., 1986). As with the self-report measures of depression, these instruments may be used from a behavioral perspective by examining responses to individual items and exploring controlling variables.

## SLEEP DISORDER ASSESSMENT

Sleep disorders are prominent among older adults (Schubert et al., 2002) and can contribute to a variety of psychological and behavioral problems. Specific disorders that appear to be common among older adults include sleep apnea (Shochat & Pillar, 2003), insomnia (Morgan, 2000), and restless leg syndrome or periodic limb movements in sleep (Espie, 2000). The most common of these is insomnia, which occurs in 12–33% of older adults (Morgan). However, some of these cases of insomnia may be misdiagnosed. Lichstein, Riedel, Lester, and Aguillard (1999) discovered that in one community sample, 29% of older adults diagnosed with insomnia actually had sleep apnea. Men are more likely to have sleep apnea than women (13% versus 4%; Enright et al., 1996).

The architecture of sleep appears to change as adults age. For example, older adults appear to have more frequent shifts in sleep cycles during the night (Morgan, 2000). The total time spent sleeping and the amount of time spent in the rapid eye movement (REM) stage decrease with age as well. Older adults also have frequent complaints of trouble initiating and maintaining sleep (Schubert et al., 2002).

Several assessment instruments are used to evaluate sleep patterns and associated behavior in older adults (Espie, 2000). Polysomnography involves placement of electrodes on the face, neck, and, occasionally, limbs (Edinger, Hoelscher, Marsh, Lipper, & Lonescu-Pioggia; Lacks & Morin, 1992; Morin, Colecchi, Stone, Sood, & Brink, 1999; Morin, Kowatch, Barry, & Walton, 1993) for the recording of muscle movement, eye movement, brain activity, limb movement, and breathing rate. Actigraphy is another method for assessing sleep. An electrical recording device (actigraph) is attached to the wrist and measures physical activity (Friedman et al., 2000; Lacks & Morin; Schnelle et al., 1998). Low activity as measured by this device is associated with sleep. Measures obtained via actigraphy are strongly correlated with those obtained via polysomnography, the gold standard for sleep assessment. The Sleep Assessment Device measures sleep onset and interruption (Edinger et al.; O'Connor, Breus, & Youngstedt, 1998). This instrument emits a soft auditory tone at set intervals, telling the person to indicate whether her or she is still awake by saying something like "I'm awake" whenever they hear the tone. The device then records these utterances. The sleep diary is a popular behavioral self-assessment method that asks people to record items related to their sleep pattern and quality, such as bedtime, sleep quality, mood upon awakening, number of awakenings during night, and latency to sleep onset (Hoch et al., 2001; Lacks & Morin; Libman, Fichten, Bailes, & Amsel, 2000; Morin et al., 1993; Morin et al., 1999). This diary is usually completed in the morning. There are also questionnaires that ask the person about sleep quality and overall sleep pattern, such as the Pittsburgh Sleep Quality Index (PSQI; Buysse, Reynolds, Monk, Berman, & Kupfer, 1989). The PSQI has demonstrated adequate internal consistency, test–retest reliability, and construct validity.

## AGGRESSIVE BEHAVIOR ASSESSMENT

Aggressive behavior may be present in 6–22% of older adults with dementia (Holtzer et al., 2003). This includes behaviors such as hitting, kicking, threatening, insulting, biting, and spitting (Kopecky, Kopecky, & Yudofsky, 1998). Such behavior problems have a negative impact on the psychological and physical well-being of caregivers (Gaugler, Davey, Pearlin, & Zarit, 2000), and fellow residents of long-term-care facilities. This behavior tends to increase with cognitive decline (Holtzer et al.). African Americans and Latinos seem to be slightly more likely than Caucasians to have uncontrollable anger and combative behavior (Sink, Covinsky, Newcomer, & Yaffe, 2004).

Aggressive behavior lends itself to behavior analysis, for it can be reliably observed. It is important to consider the functional features of the behavior (Fisher, Swingen, & Harsen, 1998). In considering the function(s) of the behavior, observations should include setting events such as mood, antecedent stimuli, patient responses to stimuli, and environmental consequences of the behavior.

Several assessment instruments are commonly used to measure aggression in older adults with dementia (Fisher et al., 1998; O'Malley, Orengo, Kunik, Snow, & Molinari, 2002). The Cohen-Mansfield Agitation Inventory (CMAI; Cohen-Mansfield, 1986) is a 38-item measure assessing inappropriate verbal and motor behaviors, such as screaming, cursing, and biting (Shah, Evans, & Parkash, 1998). This scale has shown adequate internal consistency (Finkel, Lyons, & Anderson, 1992) and interrater reliability (Miller, Snowdon, & Vaughn, 1995). The Overt Agitation Severity Scale (OASS; Kopecky et al., 1998) objectively measures the severity and frequency of behaviors such as movements and vocalizations. It has shown adequate internal consistency, interrater reliability, and construct validity. Another method of assessing aggressive behavior in older adults with dementia is direct observation (Bridges-Parlet, Knopman, & Thompson, 1994; McCann, Gilley, Bienias, Beckett, & Evans, 2004). For example, observing and recording the number of hits that occur within one-minute time periods (Bridges-Parlet et al.).

The Rating Scale for Aggressive Behaviour in the Elderly (RAGE; Patel & Hope, 1992) is a 21-item scale measuring specific aggressive behavior over a three-day time period. It has demonstrated adequate test–retest reliability, interrater reliability, and concurrent validity.

## WANDERING ASSESSMENT

Wandering is one of the most serious and potentially hazardous of nursing care issues (Algase, Kupferschmid, Beel-Bates, & Beattie, 1997). Wandering behavior is prevalent in 39–57% of older adults with dementia (Holtzer et al., 2003). The likelihood that a dementia patient will develop wandering behavior increases over time and with cognitive decline (Hotzer et al.). One study found that in those with dementia, African Americans and Latinos were more likely than Caucasians to exhibit wandering behavior (Sink et al., 2004). Wandering may also be more common in men than in women (Nasman, Bucht, & Eriksson, 1993).

Several assessment methods have been identified to measure wandering-related behavior in dementia patients (Algase, 1998). Behavioral mapping can be used to assess patterns of wandering behavior (Snyder, Rupprecht, Pyrek, Brekhus, & Moss, 1978). In this method, individual location and movement are recorded for designated time periods. These movements are traced onto a map of the facility. This method helps to identify the locations where wandering is most likely to occur, the time periods when it is most likely to occur, and the amount of distance covered. Another method of assessing wandering behavior is with activity-monitoring devices, such as actigraphs and pedometers (Algase et al., 1997; Cohen-Mansfield, Werner, Culpepper, Wolfson, & Bickel, 1997). These electronic devices are worn on the wrist or waist and electronically measure the amount of movement over time. Counting and timing strategies involve counting the number of and timing the duration of wanderings (Algase, 1998). This information is then used to graph the wandering cycles over time. It can also be useful to conduct a functional analysis of the wandering behavior (Fisher, Harsin, & Hayden, 2000; Hussian, 1987). In a functional analysis, the controlling environmental variables of the behavior are identified. Hussian suggested guidelines for performing a functional analysis, including clarifying in what situations the person is oriented, identifying fluctuations in orientation across time, conducting observations, determining situations and stimuli that bring out the behavior, identifying the onset and course of the behavior, and determining if consequences of the behavior need to be altered.

## EATING DISORDERS ASSESSMENT

Eating patterns appear to change as adults age (Elsner, 2002). Many individuals may eat less as they age. Possible reasons for this phenomenon include depression, fewer social networks, reduced energy expenditure, problems chewing or swallowing, and medical problems (Donini, Savina, & Cannella, 2003; Elsner). The taste of food may change as well. Changes in the ability to smell food (Ship et al., 1996) and the density of taste buds (I. J. Miller, 1988) may decrease the amount of food that older individuals consume. Malnutrition puts older adults at risk for various physical problems, such as an increased likelihood of falls (Johnson, 2003). The prevalence of being underweight appears to increase with age. For example, for Caucasians in their 60s and 70s, the percentage of extremely underweight individuals [body mass index (BMI) < 18.5] increased from .8% in 1993 to 1.8% in 2000 in males and from 3.0% in 1993 to 7.6% in 2000 for females (Jenkins, Fultz, Fonda, & Ray, 2003). The percentage of overweight individuals appears to increase somewhat as well. In the same sample, the percentage of extremely obese men (BMI = 35–39.9) increased from

1.9% in 1993 to 2.2% in 2000. Obesity may actually shorten the life span of older adults (Fontaine, Redden, Wang, Westfall, & Allison, 2003).

Several methods can be used to assess nutritional health and eating in older adults. For instance, body weight and height can be used to calculate the body mass index, which can be an indication of an undernourished state or an over-weight state (Akner & Floistrup, 2003). Also, the DEXA is an X-ray machine that measures the amount of muscle, bone, and body fat (Lauque et al., 2004). To measure total food intake, a food diary can be used (Andersson, Gustafsson, Fjellstrom, Sidenvall, & Nydahl, 2001). This method requires the person to write down everything he or she eats or drinks and to estimate the sizes of the portions. The food diary may give an indication of whether the person is taking in too much or too little food. Several scales can be used to assess nutritional health. The Nutritional Form for the Elderly (NUFFE, Soderhamn & Soderhamn, 2002) is a 15-item measure of dietary history, current dietary assessment (e.g., appetite, food intake), and general questions (e.g., current medications, company at meals, ways to obtain food products). The NUFFE has demonstrated adequate internal consistency, construct validity, and predictive validity. The Mini-Nutritional Assessment (Guigoz, Lauque, & Vellas, 1996) questionnaire is an 18-item measure of malnutrition or well-nourishment that assesses things such as weight loss, number of meals, ability to eat, prescription drugs, and use of vegetables and fruits. It has shown adequate concurrent validity (Soini et al., 2004), internal consistency, and test–retest reliability (Bleda, Bolibar, Pares, & Salva, 2002). To assess problems with swallowing, physicians will often ask patients about the history and severity of the swallowing problem, feel the neck and oral cavity for masses or muscular abnormalities, and elicit a gag reflex (Palmer, Drennen, & Baba, 2000). A videofluorographic swallowing study can also be conducted in which the patient is given food mixed with barium so that the radiographic images of the swallowing process can be videotaped and assessed.

## SUMMARY

Projections of age demographics for this century clearly indicate an increase in the proportion of older adults in our society, with individuals 65 years of age and older being the fastest-growing segment of our population. Baby boomers nearing old age will soon tax available mental health resources, as an estimated one-quarter of these individuals will meet diagnostic criteria for mental disorders, and perhaps even more will require services for subsyndromal symptoms. With such growing numbers, it is becoming increasingly likely that the average adult clinician will encounter older-adult clients. It is our hope that this chapter serves clinicians and students who are seeking a modest overview of older-adult behavioral assessment.

## REFERENCES

Akner, G., & Floistrup, H. (2003). Individual assessment of intake of energy, nutrients, and water in 54 elderly multidiseased nursing-home residents. *The Journal of Nutrition, Health, and Aging, 7,* 2–11.

Albert, M. (1994). Brief assessments of cognitive function in the elderly. In M. P. Lawton & J. A. Teresi (Eds.), *Annual review of gerontology and geriatrics: Focus on assessment techniques* (pp. 93–106). New York: Springer Verlag.

Alexopoulos, G. S. (1996). Affective disorders. In J. Sadavoy, L. W. Lazarus, L. F. Jarvik, & G. T. Grossberg (Eds.), *Comprehensive review of geriatric psychiatry II* (pp. 563–592). Washington, DC: American Psychiatric Press.

Alexopoulos, G. S., Abrams, R. C., Young, R. C., & Shamoian, C. A. (1988). Cornell Scale for Depression in Dementia. *Biological Psychiatry, 23,* 271–284.

Algase, D. L. (1998). Wandering. In B. Edelstein (Vol. Ed.), *Comprehensive clinical psychology: Vol. 7. Clinical geropsychology* (pp. 371–412). Oxford, UK: Elsevier Science.

Algase, D. L., Kupferschmid, B., Beel-Bates, C. A., & Beattie, E. R. (1997). Estimates of stability of daily wandering behavior among cognitively impaired long-term care residents. *Nursing Research, 46,* 172–178.

Allport, G. W. (1937). *Personality: A psychological interpretation.* New York: Holt, Rinehart & Winston.

American Psychological Association, Presidential Task Force on the Assessment of Age-Consistent Memory Decline and Dementia. (1998). *Guidelines for the evaluation of dementia and age-related cognitive decline.* Washington, DC: American Psychological Association.

American Society on Aging. (2004). Live well, live long: Health promotion and disease prevention for older adults. Retrieved from http://www.asaging.org/cdc/index.cfm

Andersen, M., Guthrie, K. A., & Urban, N. (2004). Assertiveness with physicians: Does it predict mammography use? *Women & Health, 39*(2), 1–11.

Anderson, N. B., & McNeilly, M. (1991). Age, gender, and ethnicity as variables in psychophysiological assessment: Sociodemographics in context. *Psychological Assessment, 3,* 376–384.

Andersson, J. C., Gustafsson, K., Fjellstrom, C., Sidenvall, B., & Nydahl, M. (2001). Meals and energy intake among elderly women—An analysis of qualitative and quantitative dietary assessment methods. *Journal of Human Nutrition and Dietetics, 14,* 467–476.

Appenzeller, O. (1994). Aging, stress, and autonomic control. In M. L. Albert & J. E. Knoefel (Eds.), *Clinical neurology of aging* (pp. 651–673). New York: Oxford University Press.

Barrios, B., & Hartmann, D. P. (1986). The contributions of traditional assessment: Concepts, issues, and methodologies. In R. O. Nelson & S. C. Hayes (Eds.), *Conceptual foundations of behavioral assessment* (pp. 81–110). New York: Guilford Press.

Beck, A. T., Epstein, N., Brown, G., & Steer, R. A. (1988). An inventory for measuring clinical anxiety: Psychometric properties. *Journal of Consulting and Clinical Psychology, 56,* 893–897.

Beck, A. T., Kovacs, M., & Weissman, A. (1979). Assessment of suicidal ideation: The Scale for Suicide Ideation. *Journal of Consulting and Clinical Psychology, 47,* 343–352.

Beck, A. T., Stanley, M. A., & Zebb, B. J. (1996). Characteristics of Generalized Anxiety Disorder in older adults: A descriptive study. *Behaviour Research and Therapy, 34,* 225–234.

Beck, A. T., Steer, R. A., & Brown, G. K. (1996). *Manual for the Beck Depression Inventory* (2nd ed.). San Antonio, TX: Psychological Corporation.

Blazer, D. G. (1994). Epidemiology of late life depression. In L. S. Schneider, C. F. Reynolds, B. D. Lebowitz, & A. J. Friedhoff (Eds.), *Diagnosis and treatment of depression in late life* (pp. 9–19). Washington, DC: American Psychiatric Association.

Blazer, D. G., Crowell, B. A., Jr., George, L., & Landerman, R. (1986). Urban rural differences in depressive disorders: Does age make a difference? In J. Barrett & R. Rose (Eds.), *Mental disorders in the community: Progress and challenge* (pp. 32–46). New York: Guilford Press.

Blazer, D. G., Hughes, D. C., & George, L. K. (1987). The epidemiology of depression in an elderly community population. *The Gerontologist, 27,* 281–287.

Bleda, M. J., Bolibar, I., Pares, R., & Salva, A. (2002). Reliability of the Mini-Nutritional Assessment (MNA) in institutionalized elderly people. *Journal of Nutrition, Health, and Aging, 6,* 134–137.

Bridges-Parlet, S., Knopman, D., & Thompson, T. (1994). A descriptive study of physically aggressive behavior in dementia by direct observation. *Journal of the American Geriatrics Society, 42,* 192–197.

Broadhead, W. E., Blazer, D. G., George, L. K., & Tse, C. K. (1990). Depression, disability days, and days lost from work in a prospective epidemiologic survey. *Journal of the American Medical Association, 264,* 2524–2528.

Brown, G. (2001). A review of suicide assessment measures for intervention research with adults and older adults. Retrieved on 1/20/2005 from http://www.nimh.nih.gov/suicideresearch/adultsuicide.pdf.

Brown, L. M., Bongar, B., & Cleary, K. M. (2004). A profile of psychologists' views of critical risk factors for completed suicide in older adults. *Professional Psychology: Research and Practice, 35,* 90–96.

Butler, R. N. (1969). Ageism: Another form of bigotry. *Gerontologist, 9,* 243–246.

Buysse, D. J., Reynolds, C. F., Monk, T. H., Berman, S. R., & Kupfer, D. J. (1989). The Pittsburgh Sleep Quality Index: A new instrument for psychiatric practice and research. *Psychiatry Research, 28,* 193–213.

Cardinali, R., & Gordon, Z. (2002). Ageism: No longer the equal opportunity stepchild. *Equal Opportunities International, 21*(2), 58–68.

Carmin, C. N., Pollard, C. A., & Gillock, K. L. (1999). Assessment of anxiety disorders in the elderly. In P. A. Lichtenberg (Ed.), *Handbook of assessment in clinical gerontology* (pp. 59–90). New York: John Wiley & Sons.

Casser, L., Goss, D. A., Keller, J. T., Kneib, B. A., Moates, K. N., & Musick, J. E. (1997). *Optometric clinical practice guideline: Comprehensive adult eye and vision examination,* St. Louis, MO: American Optometric Association.

Cohen-Mansfield, J. (1986). Agitated behaviour in the elderly II: Preliminary results in the cognitively irritated. *Journal of the American Geriatrics Society, 34,* 722–727.

Cohen-Mansfield, J., Werner, P., Culpepper, W. J., Wolfson, M., & Bickel, E. (1997). Assessment of ambulatory behavior in nursing home residents who pace or wander: A comparison of four commercially available devices. *Dementia and Geriatric Cognitive Disorders, 8,* 359–365.

Colsher, P., & Wallace, R. B. (1989). Data quality and age: Health and psychobehavioral correlates of item nonresponse and inconsistent responses. *Journal of Gerontology: Psychological Sciences, 44,* P45–P52.

Committee on Quality of Health Care in America Report, Institute of Medicine. (1999). *To err is human: Building a safer health system.* Washington, DC: National Academy Press.

Cone, J. D. (1986). Idiographic, nomothetic, and related perspectives in behavioral assessment. In R. O. Nelson & S. C. Hayes (Eds.), *Conceptual foundations of behavioral assessment* (pp. 111–128). New York: Guilford Press.

Conwell, Y., Duberstein, P. R., & Caine, E. D. (2002). Risk factors for suicide in later life. *Biological Psychiatry, 52,* 193–204.

Copeland, J. R. M., Kelleher, M. J., Kellett, J. M., Gourlay, A. J., Gurland, B. J., Fleiss, J. L., et al. (1976). A semistructured clinical interview for the assessment of diagnostic and mental state in the elderly: The Geriatric and Mental State Schedule. I. Development and reliability. *Psychological Medicine, 6,* 439–449.

Cronbach, L. J. (1971). Test validation. In R. L. Thorndike (Ed.), *Educational measurement* (2nd ed., pp. 443–507). Washington, DC: American Council on Education.

Cummings, J. L. (1992). Depression and Parkinson's Disease: A review. *American Journal of Psychiatry, 149,* 443–454.

Davies, A. D. M., Davies, C., & Delpo, M. C. (1986). Depression and anxiety in patients undergoing diagnostic investigations for head and neck cancers. *British Journal of Psychiatry, 149,* 491–493.

Donini, L. M., Savina, C., & Cannella, C. (2003). Eating habits and appetite control in the elderly: The anorexia of aging. *International Psychogeriatrics, 15,* 73–87.

Eaton, W. W., Muntaner, C., Smith, C., Tien, A., & Ybarra, M. (2004). Center for Epidemiological Studies Depession scale: Review and revision (CESD and CESDR). In M. E. Maruish (Ed.), *The use of psychological testing for treatment planning and outcomes assessment* (pp. 363–377). Mahwah, NJ: Erlbaum.

Edelstein, B. A., & Drozdick, L. W. (1998). Falls among older adults. In B. A. Edelstein (Ed.), *Clinical geropsychology* (Vol. 7, pp. 349–369). Oxford, UK: Elsevier Science.

Edelstein, B. A., Drozdick, L. W., & Null Kogan, J. (1998). Assessment of older adults. In A. S. Bellack & M. Hersen (Eds.), *Behavioral assessment: A practical handbook* (4th ed., pp. 378–406). Needham Heights, MA: Allyn & Bacon.

Edelstein, B. A., Kalish, K., Drozdick, L. W., & McKee, D. (1999). Assessment of depression and bereavement in older adults. In P. Lichtenberg (Ed.). *Handbook of assessment in clinical gerontology* (pp. 11–58). New York: Wiley.

Edelstein, B. A., Martin, R. R., & Koven, L. P. (2003). Psychological assessment in geriatric settings. In J. R. Graham & J. A. Naglieri (Eds.), *Handbook of psychology: Vol. 10. Assessment psychology* (pp. 389–414). New York: John Wiley & Sons.

Edelstein, B. A., Martin, R. R., & McKee, D. R. (2000). Assessment of older adult psychopathology. In S. K. Whitbourne (Ed.), *Psychopathology in later adulthood* (pp. 61–88). New York: John Wiley & Sons.

Edelstein, B. A., McKee, D. R., & Martin, R. R. (2000, June). *Older adult reasons for living: Development of a suicide assessment instrument.* In J. Patrick (Chair), Psychological well-being in rural West Virginia. Symposium conducted at the meeting of the First International Conference on Rural Aging, Charleston, WV.

Edinger, J. D., Hoelscher, T. J., Marsh, G. R., Lipper, S., & Ionescu-Pioggia, M. (1992). A cognitive-behavioral therapy for sleep-maintenance insomnia in older adults. *Psychology and Aging, 7,* 282–289.

Elsner, R. J. (2002). Changes in eating behavior during the aging process. *Eating Behaviors, 3,* 15–43.

Engstad, T., Bonaa, K. H., & Vitanen, M. (2000). Validity of self-reported stroke. *Stroke, 31,* 1602.

Enright, P. L., Newman, A. B., Wahl, P. W., Manolio, T. A., Haponik, E. F., & Boyle, P. J. (1996). Prevalence and correlates of snoring and observed apneas in 5,201 older adults. *Sleep, 19,* 531–538.

Espie, C. A. (2000). Assessment and differential diagnosis. In K. L. Lichstein & C. M. Morin (Eds.). *Treatment of late life insomnia.* Thousand Oaks, CA: Sage.

Federal Interagency Forum on Aging-Related Statistics. (2004). *Older Americans 2004: Key indicators of well-being.* Washington, DC: U.S. Government Printing Office.

Feher, E. P., Larrabee, G. J., & Crook, T. J. (1992). Factors attenuating the validity of the Geriatric Depression Scale in a dementia population. *Journal of the American Geriatrics Society, 40,* 906–909.

Ferrini, A. F., & Ferrini, R. L. (1993). *Health in the later years* (2nd ed.). Dubuque, IA: Wm. C. Brown Communications.

Finkel, S. I., Lyons, J. S., & Anderson, R. L. (1992). Reliability and validity of the Cohen–Mansfield Agitation Inventory in institutionalized elderly. *International Journal of Geriatric Psychiatry, 7,* 487–490.

First, M. B., Gibbon, M., Spitzer, R. L., & Williams, J. B. W. (1995). *User's guide for the Structured Clinical Interview for DSM-IV Axis I disorders.* New York: Biometrics Research.

Fisher, J. E., Harsin, C. W., & Hayden, J. E. (2000). Behavioral interventions for patients with dementia. In V. Malinari (Ed.), *Professional psychology in long-term care: A comprehensive guide* (pp. 179–200). New York: Hatherleigh Press.

Fisher, J. E., Swingen, D. N., & Harsin, C. M. (1998). In A. S. Bellack & M. Hersen (Series Eds.) & B. Edelstein (Vol. Ed.), *Comprehensive clinical psychology: Vol. 7. Clinical geropsychology* (pp. 371–412). Oxford, UK: Elsevier Science.

Flint, A. J. (1994). Epidemiology and comorbidity of anxiety disorders in the elderly. *American Journal of Psychiatry, 151,* 640–649.

Folstein, M. F., Folstein, S. E., & McHugh, P. R. (1975). "A Mini-Mental State": A practical method for grading the cognitive state of patients for the clinician. *Journal of Psychiatric Research, 12,* 189–198.

Fontaine, K. R., Redden, D. T., Wang, C., Westfall, A. O., & Allison, D. B. (2003). Years of life lost due to obesity. *Journal of the American Medical Association, 289,* 187–193.

Frazer, D. W., Leicht, M. L., & Baker, M. D. (1996). Psychological manifestations of physical disease in the elderly. In L. L. Carstensen, B. A. Edelstein, & L. Dornbrand (Eds.), *The practical handbook of clinical gerontology.* Thousand Oaks, CA: Sage.

Friedman, L., Benson, K., Noda, A., Zarcone, V., Wicks, D. A., O'Connell, K., et al. (2000). An actigraph comparison of sleep restriction and sleep hygiene treatments for insomnia in older adults. *Journal of Geriatric Psychiatry and Neurology, 13,* 17–27.

Gaugler, J. E., Davey, A., Pearlin, L. I., & Zarit, S. H. (2000). Modeling caregiver adaptation over time: The longitudinal impact of behavior problems. *Psychology and Aging, 15,* 437–450.

Gergen, K. J., & Back, K. W. (1966). Communication in the interview and the disengaged respondent. *Public Opinion Quarterly, 30,* 385–398.

Gillam, J. H., III. (1990). Pancreatic disorders. In W. R. Hazzard, R. Andres, E. L. Bierman, & J. P. Blass (Eds.), *Principles of geriatric medicine and gerontology* (2nd ed., pp. 640–644). New York: McGraw-Hill.

Goga, J. A., & Hambacher, W. O. (1977). Psychologic and behavioral assessment of geriatric patients: A review. *Journal of the American Geriatrics Society, 25,* 232–237.

Greenberg, D. B. (1989). Depression and cancer. In R. G. Robinson & P. V. Rabins (Eds.), *Depression and coexisting disease* (pp. 103–115). New York: Igaku-Shoin.

Guigoz, Y., Lauque, S., & Vellas, B. J. (1996). Identifying the elderly at risk for malnutrition: The Mini-Nutritional Assessment. *Clinics in Geriatric Medicine, 18,* 737–757.

Gurland, B. J., Kuriansky, J. B., Sharpe, L., Simon, R., Stiller, P., & Birkett, P. (1977). The Comprehensive Assessment and Referral and Evaluation (CARE)—Rationale, development, and reliability. *International Journal of Aging and Human Development, 8,* 9–42.

Haight, B. K., Michel, Y., & Hendrix, S. (1998). Life review: Preventing despair in newly relocated nursing home residents, short- and long-term effects. *International Journal of Aging and Human Development, 47,* 119–142.

Haley, W. E. (1996). The medical context of psychotherapy with the elderly. In S. H. Zarit & B. G. Knight (Eds.), *Effective clinical interventions in a life-stage context: A guide to psychotherapy and aging* (pp. 221–240). Washington, DC: American Psychological Association.

Hamilton, M. (1967). Development of a rating scale for primary depressive illness. *British Journal of Social and Clinical Psychology, 6,* 278–296.

Haynes, S. N., & O'Brien, W. H. (2000). *Principles and practice of behavioral assessment.* New York: Kluwer Academic.

Hegel, M. T., Stanley, M. A., & Arean, P. E. (2002). Minor depression and "subthreshold" anxiety symptoms in older adults: Psychosocial therapies and special considerations. *Generations, 26,* 44–49.

Heisel, M. J., & Flett, G. L. (2001, August). *A psychometric analysis of the Geriatric Suicide Ideation Scale (GSIS).* Poster presentation at the annual conference of the American Psychological Association, San Francisco.

Heisel, M. J., & Flett, G. L. (2004). Assessing geriatric suicidality: The development and validation of the Geriatric Suicide Ideation Scale (GSIS). Manuscript submitted for publication.

Hoch, C. C., Reynolds, C. F., Buysse, D. J., Monk, T. H., Nowell, P., Begley, A. E., et al. (2001). Protecting sleep quality in later life: A pilot study of bed restriction and sleep hygiene. *Journal of Gerontology, 56B,* P52–P59.

Holland, J. C., Korzun, A. H., Tross, S., Silberfarb, P., Perry, M., Comis, R., et al. (1986). Comparative psychological disturbance in patients with pancreatic and gastric cancer. *American Journal of Psychiatry, 143,* 982–986.

Holtzer, R., Tang, M. X., Devanand, D. P., Albert, S. M., Wegesin, D. J., et al. (2003). Psychopathological features in Alzheimer's disease: Course and relationship with cognitive status. *Journal of the American Geriatrics Society, 51,* 953–960.

Howarth, E., Johnson, A. J., Klerman, G., & Weissman, M. M. (1992). Depressive symptoms as relative and attributional risk factors for first-onset major depression. *Archives of General Psychiatry, 49,* 817–823.

Hoyert, D. L., Smith, B. L., Murphy, S. L., & Kochanek, M. A. (2001). Deaths: Final Data for 1999. *National Vital Statistics Report, 49.* Hyattsville, MD: National Center for Health Statistics.

Hughes, J. E. (1985). Depressive illness and lung cancer. *European Journal of Surgical Oncology, 11,* 15–20.

Hussian, R. A. (1987). Wandering and disorientation. In A. P. Goldstein & L. Krasner (Series Eds.) & L. L. Carstensen & B. A. Edelstein (Vol. Eds.), *Handbook of clinical gerontology* (pp. 177–189). Elmsford, NY: Pergamon Press.

Jenkins, K. R., Fultz, N. H., Fonda, S. J., & Wray, L. A. (2003). Patterns of body weight in middle-aged and older Americans, by gender and race, 1993–2000. *Sozial und Praventivmedizin, 48,* 257–268.

Johnson, C. S. (2003). The association between nutritional risk and falls among frail elderly. *Journal of Nutrition, Health, and Aging 7,* 247–250.

Juniper, K., & Dykman, R. A. (1967). Skin resistance, sweat gland counts, salivary flow, and gastric secretion: Age, race, and sex differences and intercorrelations. *Psychophysiology, 4,* 216–222.

Kahn, R. L., Goldfarb, A. I., Pollack, M., & Peck, A. (1960). Brief objecative measures for the determination of mental status in the aged. *American Journal of Psychiatry, 117,* 326–328.

Kaszniak, A. W., & Christenson, G. D. (1994). Differential diagnosis of dementia and depression. In M. Storandt & G. R. VandenBos (Eds.), *Neuropsychological assessment of dementia and depression in older adults: A clinician's guide* (pp. 81–117). Washington, DC: American Psychological Association.

Kazdin, A., & Wilson, G. T. (1978). *Evaluation of behavior therapy: Issues, evidence, and research.* Cambridge, MA: Ballinger, 1978.

Keel, P. K., & Schwartz, M. B. (2001). Vulnerability to eating disorders across the lifespan. In R. E. Ingram & J. M. Price (Eds.), *Vulnerability to psychopathology.* New York: Guilford Press.

Kiyak, H. L., Teri, L., & Borson, S. (1994). Physical and functional health assessment in normal aging and in Alzheimer's disease: Self-reports vs. family reports. *The Gerontologist, 34,* 324–333.

Klein, R., Klein, B. E. K., & Linton, K. L. P. (1992). Prevalence of age-related maculopathy: The Beaver Dam Eye Study. *Ophthalmology, 99,* 933–943.

Koenig, H. G., Meador, K. G., Cohen, H. J., & Blazer, D. G. (1988). Depression in elderly hospitalized patients with medical illness. *Archives of Internal Medicine, 148,* 1939–1946.

Kogan, J. N., & Edelstein, B. A. (2004). Modification and psychometric examination of a self-report measure of fear in older adults. *Journal of Anxiety Disorders, 18,* 397–409.

Kogan, J. N., Edelstein, B. A., & McKee, D. R. (2000). Assessment of anxiety in older adults. *Journal of Anxiety Disorders, 14,* 109–132.

Kogan, N. (1961). Attitudes towards old people in an older sample. *Journal of Abnormal and Social Psychology, 62,* 616–622.

Kopecky, H. J., Kopecky, C. R., & Yudofsky, S. C. (1998). Reliability and validity of the Overt Agitation Severity Scale in adult psychiatric inpatients. *Psychiatric Quarterly, 69,* 301–323.

Lacks, P., & Morin, C. M. (1992). Recent advances in the assessment and treatment of insomnia. *Journal of Consulting and Clinical Psychology, 60,* 586–594.

Larrabee, G. J., & Crook, T. H. (1989). Dimensions of everyday memory in age-associated memory impairment. *Psychological Assessment: A Journal of Consulting and Clinical Psychology, 1,* 92–97.

Lau, A., Edelstein, B., & Larkin, K. (2001). Psychophysiological responses of older adults: A critical review with implications for assessment of anxiety disorders. *Clinical Psychology Review, 21,* 609–630.

Lauque, S., Arnaud-Battandier, F., Gillette, S., Plaze, J. M., Andrieu, S., Cantet, C., et al. (2004). Improvement of weight and fat-free mass with oral nutritional supplementation in patients with Alzheimer's disease and risk of malnutrition: A prospective randomized study. *Journal of the American Geriatrics Society, 52,* 1702–1707.

Lazarou, J., Pomeranz, B. H., & Corey, P. N. (1998). Incidence of adverse drug reactions in hospitalized patients. *Journal of the American Medical Association, 279,* 1200–1205.

Leentjens, A. F. G. (2004). Depression in Parkinson's disease: Conceptual issues and clinical challenges. *Journal of Geriatric Psychiatry and Neurology, 17,* 120–126.

Libman, E., Fichten, C. S., Bailes, S., & Amsel, R. (2000). Sleep questionnaire versus sleep diary: Which measure is better? *International Journal of Rehabilitation and Health, 5,* 205–209.

Lichstein, K. L., Riedel, B. W., Lester, K. W., & Aguillard, R. N. (1999). Occult sleep apnea in a recruited sample of older adults with insomnia. *Journal of Consulting and Clinical Psychology, 67,* 405–410.

Lichtenberg, P. (Ed.). (1999). *Handbook of assessment in clinical gerontology.* New York: John Wiley & Sons.

Lindesay, J., Briggs, K., & Murphy, E. (1989). Phobic disorders in the elderly. *British Journal of Psychiatry, 159,* 531–541.

Logsdon, R. G., & Teri, L. (1997). The Pleasant Events Schedule-AD: Psychometric properties and relationship to depression and cognition in Alzheimer's disease. *Gerontologist, 37,* 40–45.

Lyness, J. M., Cox, C., Curry, J., & Conwell, Y. (1995). Older age and the underreporting of depressive symptoms. *Journal of the American Geriatrics Society, 43,* 216–221.

Macneil, S., & Lichtenberg, P. (1999). Screening instruments and brief batteries for assessment of dementia. In P. Lichtenberg (Ed.), *Handbook of assessment in clinical gerontology* (pp. 417–441). New York: John Wiley & Sons.

Mattis, S. (1988). *The Dementia Rating Scale: Professional manual.* Odessa, FL: Psychological Assessment Resources.

Mayo Foundation for Medical Education and Research. (2004). Aging: What to expect as you get older. Retrieved [1/20/2005] from http://www.mayoclinic.com/invoke.cfm?id=HA00040

McCann, J. J., Gilley, D. W., Bienias, J. L., Beckett, L. A., & Evans, D. A. (2004). Temporal patterns of negative and positive behavior among nursing home residents with Alzheimer's disease. *Psychology and Aging, 19,* 336–345.

McDaniel, J. S., Musselman, D. L., Porter, M. R., Reed, D. A., & Nemeroff, C. B. (1995). Depression in patients with cancer. Diagnosis, biology, and treatment. *Archives of General Psychiatry, 52,* 89–99.

McHugh, K. E. (2003). Three faces of ageism: Society, image, and place. *Aging & Society, 23,* 165–185.

McNeilly, M., & Anderson, N. B. (1997). Age differences in physiological responses to stress. In P. E. Ruskin & J. A. Talbott (Eds.), *Aging and Post-Traumatic Stress Disorder* (pp. 163–201). Washington, DC: American Psychiatric Press.

Merck Institute of Aging and Health. (2004). *The state of aging and health in America 2004.* Washington, DC: Author.

Meyer, T. J., Miller, M. L., Metzger, R. L., & Borkovec, T. D. (1990). Development and validation of the Penn State Worry Questionnaire. *Behavioral Research and Therapy, 28,* 487–495.

Miller, I. J. (1988). Human taste bud density across adult age groups. *Journal of Gerontology, 43,* B26–B30.

Miller, R. J., Snowdon, J., & Vaughn, R. (1995). The use of the Cohen–Mansfield Agitation Inventory in the assessment of behavioral disorders in nursing homes. *Journal of the American Geriatrics Society, 43,* 546–549.

Mindel, E., & Vernon, M. (1987). *They grow in silence* (2nd ed.). San Diego, CA: College-Hill.

Mischel, W. (1968). *Personality and assessment.* New York: John Wiley & Sons.

Molinari, V. (2001). An interdisciplinary perspective on the assessment and treatment of depression in older adults. *Journal of Geriatric Psychiatry, 34,* 197–210.

Montgomery, S. A., Beekman, A. T. F., Sadavoy, J., Salzman, C., Thompson, C., Zisook, S., et al. (2001). Consensus statement on depression in the elderly. *Primary Care Companion to the Journal of Clinical Psychiatry, 2,* 46–52.

Morgan, K. (2000). Sleep and aging. In K. L. Lichstein & C. M. Morin (Eds.), *Treatment of late-life insomnia.* Thousand Oaks, CA: Sage.

Morin, C. M., Colecchi, C., Stone, J., Sood, B., & Brink, D. (1999). Behavioral and pharmacological therapies for late-life insomnia. *Journal of the American Medical Association, 281,* 991–999.

Morin, C. M., Kowatch, R. A., Barry, T., & Walton, E. (1993). Cognitive-behavior therapy for late-life insomnia. *Journal of Consulting and Clinical Psychology, 61,* 137–146.

Mossey, J. M. (1997). Subdysthymic depression and the medically ill elderly. In R. L. Rubenstein & M. P. Lawton (Eds.), *Depression in long-term care: Advances in research and treatment* (pp. 55–74). New York: Springer Verlag.

Mulrow, C. D., Aguilar, C., Endicott, J. E., Velez, R., Tuley, M. R., Charlip, W. S., et al. (1990). Association between hearing impairment and the quality of life of elderly individuals. *Journal of the American Geriatrics Society, 38,* 45–50.

Murrell, S. A., Himmelfarb, S., & Wright, K. (1983). Prevalence of depression and its correlates in older adults. *American Journal of Epidemiology, 117,* 173–185.

Musetti, L., Perugi, G., & Soriani, A. (1989). Depression before and after age 65: A re-examination. *British Journal of Psychiatry, 155,* 330–336.

Nasman, B., Bucht, G., & Eriksson, S. (1993). Behavioural symptoms in the institutionalized elderly—Relationship to dementia. *International Journal of Geriatric Psychiatry, 8,* 843–849.

National Center for Health Statistics, U. S. Department of Health and Human Services. (2002). *Mortality report.* Hyattsville, MD: Author.

National Center for Injury Prevention and Control (2000). *Fact sheet: Suicide.* Retrieved on 1/20/2005 from http://www.cdc.gov/ncipc/factsheets/suifacts.htm.

Nelson, R. O., & Hayes, S. C. (1986). The nature of behavioral assessment. In R. O. Nelson & S. C. Hayes, S. (Eds.), *Conceptual foundations of behavioral assessment* (pp. 3–41). New York: Guilford Press.

Nelson-Gray, R. (1996). Treatment outcome measures: Nomothetic or idiographic? *Clinical Psychology: Science and Practice, 3,* 164–167.

Norris, M. P., Snow-Turek, A. L., & Blankenship, L. (1995). Somatic depressive symptoms in the elderly: Contribution or confound? *Journal of Clinical Geropsychology, 1,* 5–17.

Northrop, L., & Edelstein, B. (1998). An assertive behavior competence inventory for older adults. *Journal of Clinical Geropsychology, 4,* 315–332.

O'Connor, P. J., Breus, M. J., & Youngstendt, S. D. (1998). Exercise-induced increase in core temperature does not disrupt a behavioral measure of sleep. *Physiology and Behavior, 64,* 213–217.

Okun, M. (1976). Adult age and cautiousness in decision: A review of the literature. *Human Development, 19,* 220–233.

O'Malley, K. J., Orengo, C. A., Kunik, M. E., Snow, L., & Molinari, V. (2002). Measuring aggression in older adults: A latent variable modeling approach. *Aging and Mental Health, 6,* 231–238.

Palmer, J. B., Drennan, J. C., & Baba, M. (2000). Evaluation and treatment of swallowing impairments. *American Family Physician, 61,* 2453–2462.

Palmore, E. B. (1980). The social factors in aging. In E. W. Busse & D. G. Blazer (Eds.), *Handbook of geriatric psychiatry* (pp. 222–248). New York: Van Nostrand Reinhold.

Palmore, E. B. (1999). *Ageism: Negative and positive.* New York: Springer Verlag.

Park, D. C. (1999). Aging and the controlled and automatic processing of medical information and medical intentions. In D. C. Park, R. W. Morrell, & K. Shifren (Eds.), *Processing of medical information in aging patients: Cognitive and human factors perspectives* (pp. 3–22). Mahwah, NJ: Erlbaum.

Park, D. C. (2000). The basic mechanisms accounting for age-related decline in cognitive function. In D. C. Park & N. Schwarz (Eds.), *Cognitive aging: A primer* (pp. 3–21). Philadelphia: Taylor & Francis.

Passik, S. D., & Roth, A. J. (1999). Anxiety symptoms and panic attacks preceding pancreatic cancer diagnosis. *Psycho-Oncology, 8,* 268–272.

Patel, V., & Hope, R. A. (1992). A rating scale for aggressive behaviour in the elderly—The RAGE. *Psychological Medicine, 22,* 211–221.

Perlmutter, M. (1978). What is memory aging the aging of? *Developmental Psychology, 14,* 330–345.

Pfeiffer, E. (1975). A short portable mental status questionnaire for the assessment of organic brain deficit in elderly patients. *Journal of the American Geriatrics Society, 23,* 433–441.

Poon, L. W., Clayton, G. M., Martin, P., Johnson, M. A., Courtenay, B. C., Sweaney, A L., et al. (1992). The Georgia Centenarian Study [Special issue]. *International Journal of Aging & Human Development, 34,* 1–17.

Proctor, E. K., Morrow-Howell, N. L., Doré, P., Wentz, J., Rubin, E. H., Thompson, S., et al. (2003). Comorbid medical conditions among depressed elderly patients discharged home after acute psychiatric care. *American Journal of Geriatric Psychiatry, 11,* 329–338.

Rabbitt, P. (1982). Development of methods to measure changes in activities of daily living in the elderly. In S. Corkin, K. L. Davis, J. H. Growdon, E. Usdin, & R. J. Wurtman (Eds.), *Alzheimer's disease: A report of progress.* New York: Raven Press.

Radloff, L. (1977). The CES-D Scale: A self-report depression scale for research in the general population. *Applied Psychological Measurement, 1,* 385–401.

Regier, D. A., Narrow, W. E., & Rae, D. S. (1990). The epidemiology of anxiety disorders: The Epidemiological Catchment Area (ECA) experience. *Journal of Psychiatric Research, 24,* 3–14.

Regier, D. A., Boyd, J. H., Burke, J. K., Rae, D. S., Myers, J. K., Kramer, M., et al. (1988). One-month prevalence of mental disorder in the U.S.: Based on five epidemiologic catchment area sites. *Archives of General Psychiatry, 45,* 977–986.

Reite, M., Buysse, D., Reynolds, C., & Mendelson, W. (1995). The use of polysomnography in the evaluation of insomnia. *Sleep, 18,* 58–70.

Resnick, N. M., Beckett, L. A., Branch, L. G., Scherr, P. A., & Wetle, T. (1994). Short-term variability of self-report of incontinence in older persons. *Journal of the American Geriatrics Society, 42,* 202–207.

Richard, I. H., Schiffer, R. B., & Kurlan, R. (1996). Anxiety and Parkinson's disease. *Journal of Neuropsychiatry and Clinical Neurosciences, 8,* 383–392.

Rodin, G., Craven, J., & Littlefield, C. (1993). *Depression in the medically ill.* New York: Brunner/Mazel.

Rowe, J. W., & Kahn, R. L. (1998). *Successful aging.* New York: Pantheon.

Rubenstein, L. Z., Schairer, C., Wieland, G. D., & Kane, R. (1984). Systematic biases in functional status assessment of elderly adults: Effects of different data sources. *Journal of Gerontology, 39,* 686–691.

Sager, M. A., Dunham, N. C., Schwantes, A., Mecum, L., Haverson, K., & Harlowe, D. (1992). Measurement of activities of daily living in hospitalized elderly: A comparison of self-report and performance-based methods. *Journal of the American Geriatrics Society, 40,* 457–462.

Schneider, J. (1996). Geriatric psychopharmacology. In L. L. Carstensen, B. A. Edelstein, & L. Dornbrand (Eds.), *The practical handbook of clinical gerontology.* Thousand Oaks, CA: Sage.

Schnelle, J. F., Cruise, P. A., Alessi, C. A., Ludlow, K., Al-Samarrai, N. R., & Ouslander, J. G. (1998). Sleep hygiene in physically dependent nursing home residents: Behavioral and environmental intervention implications. *Sleep, 21,* 515–523.

Schubert, C. R., Cruickshanks, K. J., Dalton, D. S., Klein, B. E., Klein, R., & Nondahl, D. M. (2002). Prevalence of sleep problems and quality of life in an older adult population. *Sleep, 25,* 889–893.

Schwarz, N. (2003). Self-reports in consumer research: The challenge of comparing cohorts and cultures. *Journal of Consumer Research, 29,* 588–594.

Schwarz, N., & Knauper, B. (2000). Cognition, aging, and self-reports. In D. Park & N. Schwarz (Eds.), *Cognitive aging: A primer* (pp. 233–252). Philadelphia: Taylor & Francis.

Shah, A., Evans, H., & Parkash, N. (1998). Evaluation of three aggression/agitation behaviour rating scales for use on an acute admission and assessment psychogeriatric ward. *International Journal of Geriatric Psychiatry, 13,* 415–420.

Ship, J. A., Duffy, V., Jones, J. A., & Langmore, S. (1996). Geriatric oral health and its impact on eating. *Journal of the American Geriatrics Society, 44,* 456–464.

Shochat, T., & Pillar, G. (2003). Sleep apnoea in the older adult: Pathophysiology, epidemiology, consequences, and management. *Drugs and Aging, 20,* 551–560.

Sink, K. M., Covinsky, K. E., Newcomer, R., & Yaffe, K. (2004). Ethnic differences in the prevalence and pattern of dementia-related behaviors. *Journal of the American Geriatrics Society, 52,* 1277–1283.

Small, G. W. (1997). Recognizing and treating anxiety in the elderly. *Journal of Clinical Psychiatry, 58,* 41–47.

Snyder, L. H., Rupprecht, P., Pyrek, J., Brekhus, S., & Moss, T. (1978). Wandering. *The Gerontologist, 18,* 272–280.

Soderhamn, U., & Soderhamn, O. (2002). Reliability and validity of the nutritional form for the elderly (NUFFE). *Journal of Advanced Nursing, 37,* 28–34.

Soini, H., Routasalo, P., & Lagstrom, H. (2004). Characteristics of the Mini-Nutritional Assessment in elderly home-care patients. *European Journal of Clinical Nutrition, 58,* 64–70.

Sommer, A., Tielsch, J. M., Katz, J., Quigley, H. A., Gottsch, J. D., Javitt, J., et al. (1991). Relationship between intraocular pressure and primary open-angle glaucoma among white and black Americans: The Baltimore Eye Survey. *Archives of Ophthalmology, 109,* 1090–1095.

Stanley, M. A., Beck, A. T., & Zebb, B. J. (1996). Psychometric properties of four anxiety measures in older adults. *Behavioral Research and Therapy, 34,* 827–838.

Starkstein, S. E., Preziosi, T. J., Bolduc, P. L., & Robinson, R. G. (1990). Depression in Parkinson's disease. *Journal of Nervous and Mental Disorders, 178,* 27–31.

Storandt, M. (1994). General principles of assessment of older adults. In M. Storandt & G. R. VandenBos (Eds.), *Neuropsychological assessment of dementia and depression in older adults: A clinician's guide* (pp. 7–31). Washington, DC: American Psychological Association.

Sunderland, A., Watts, K., Baddeley, A. D., & Harris, J. E. (1986). Subjective memory assessment and test performance in elderly adults. *Journal of Gerontology, 41,* 376–384.

Sunderland, T., & Minichiello, M. (1996). Dementia Mood Assessment Scale. *International Psychogeriatrics, 8,* 329–331.

Todes, C. J., & Lee, A. J. (1985). The premorbid personality of patients with Parkinson's disease. *Journal of Neurological and Neurosurgical Psychiatry, 48,* 97–100.

U.S. Administration on Aging. (2003). A profile of older Americans: 2003. Retrieved on [1/20/2005] from http://www.aoa.gov/prof/statistics/profile/2003/2_pf.asp

Vernon, M. (1989). Assessment of persons with hearing disabilities. In T. Hunt & C. J. Lindley (Eds.), *Testing older adults: A reference guide for geropsychological assessments* (pp. 150–162). Austin, TX: Pro-Ed.

Walsh, K., & Bennett, G. (2001). Parkinson's disease and anxiety. *Postgraduate Medicine, 77,* 89–93.

Ward, D. (2000). Ageism and the abuse of older people in health and social care. *British Journal of Nursing, 9,* 560–563.

Williams, B. O. (2000). Ageism helps to ration medical treatment. *Health Bulletin (Edinburgh), 58,* 198–202.

Wisocki, P. A., Handen, B., & Morse, C. K. (1986). The Worry Scale as a measure of anxiety among homebound and community active elderly. *The Behavior Therapist, 5,* 91–95.

Yesavage, J. A., Brink, T. L., Rose, T. L., Lum, O., Huang, V., Adey, M., et al. (1983). Development and validation of a geriatric depression screening scale: A preliminary report. *Journal of Psychiatric Research, 17,* 37–49.

Zanetti, O., Geroldi, C., Frisoni, G. B., Bianchetti, A., & Trabucchi, M. (1999). Contrasting results between caregiver's report and direct assessment of activities of daily living in patients affected by mild and very mild dementia: The contribution of the caregiver's personal characteristics. *Journal of the American Geriatrics Society, 47,* 196–202.

Zelinski, E. M., Gilewski, M. J., & Thompson, L. W. (1980). Do laboratory tests relate to self-assessment of memory ability in the young and old? In L. W. Poon, J. L. Fozard, L. S. Cermak, D. Arenberg, & L. W. Thompson (Eds.), *New directions in memory and aging: Proceedings of the George A. Talland memorial conference* (pp. 519–544). Hillsdale, NJ: Erlbaum.

# 22

---

# BEHAVIORAL

# NEUROPSYCHOLOGY

---

MICHAEL D. FRANZEN
GLEN E. GETZ

*Department of Psychiatry*
*Allegheny General Hospital*
*Pittsburgh, Pennsylvania*

KARIN SCHEETZ WALSH

*Mount Washington Pediatric Hospital*
*Baltimore, Maryland*

## INTRODUCTION

To some individuals the term *behavioral neuropsychology* may seem an oxymoron. Early behaviorists eschewed both abstract constructs, such as personality, and physiological mechanisms (e.g., the central nervous system). After all, behaviorism had its origins in a reaction to the large number of psychological theories that were propagated during the early part of the 20th century. The unit of study was behavior, and the issue was how environmental events related to behavior. Neuropsychologists, on the other hand, deemphasized the role of the environment and instead concentrated on the central nervous system as the main determinant of behavior. Behavior was invariant across environments as long as the central nervous system didn't change. In more recent times, however, behaviorists and neuropsychologists have begun to interact, either because more inclusive models, such as general systems theory, allow for different levels of explanation of the determinants of behavior or because, in the clinical realm, behaviorists and neuropsychologists have been working with patients with developmental disabilities or with acquired brain impairment.

In this chapter we provide an overview of some of the problems attendant on any attempts to merge these two areas of activity. After discussing the conceptual framework for the two types of assessment and measurement, we examine two constructs, each one having its origin in one of the assessment approaches

---

and each one being looked at from the alternate assessment system. Finally, we provide a model for combining the two types of assessment information.

## CONCEPTUAL FRAMEWORK

The Behavioral Neuropsychology Special Interest Group of the Association for Advancement of Behavioral Therapy first proposed behavioral neuropsychology in 1978 in an attempt to address the need of brain-injured persons for cognitive rehabilitation. The suggested definition at that time stated that behavioral neuropsychology is the combination of behavioral therapy techniques to treat organically impaired individuals, utilizing a neuropsychological assessment and intervention perspective (Horton, 1979). Throughout the 1980s and '90s, literature can be found discussing the development of this field, most notably the rehabilitation literature. Since the early 1990s, however, there has been little additional literature discussing the development and application of behavioral neuropsychology. In fact, the growth of this combined field appears to have been stunted. Horton (1997) reviewed developments in this field and concluded that it was premature to specify a behavioral neuropsychological assessment system and that, instead, the field should concentrate on intervention and treatment.

Why is there pessimism about the development of behavioral neuropsychological assessment? After all, there have been greater developments in behavioral treatment of neuropsychological deficits. Behavioral assessment and interventions are well integrated into treatment programs for individuals with acquired brain injury (H. A. Jacobs, 1993). As discussed in earlier chapters on the development of behavioral neuropsychology, there are notable differences in the basic theoretical conceptualizations between the fields of neuropsychology and behavioral psychology (Franzen, 1991, 2003; Franzen & Smith-Seemiller, 1998). There has yet to be a suggested overarching conceptualization to solidify this novel field, which indicates the difficulty in combining these fields. To review, Franzen (2003) discussed the distinct theories of measurement that drive behavioral and neuropsychological assessment: classical, representational, and operational theories. In classical theory, underlying much of neuropsychological assessment, abstract concepts are represented by assessment outcomes (scores). Behavioral assessment, in contrast, is based on operational theory, which posits that assessment outcomes (scores) result from those operations that are involved in the measurement process and have no specific meaning outside of the assessment. That is to say, the scores from neuropsychological assessment represents a quantity of an abstract construct, and the scores from behavioral assessment instead represent only the observable behavior and its definition as used by the clinician. The score from neuropsychological assessment represents the degree of memory skill. The score from a behavioral assessment represents some quantity of the behavior as defined and observed by the clinician.

For example, if a patient is being assessed for difficulties with attention and hyperactivity, the neuropsychological approach would utilize validated measures of attention and executive functions and, based on the scores the patient obtained through his or her performance, would make inferences as to an underlying defect in the attentional system and/or the frontostriatal circuit. However, in the behavioral approach these scores would be meaningless without the context of the assessment setting (task requirements, materials used, instructions given) as well as the interactions between the examiner and the patient. Both of these types of scores are frequently used in the clinical setting to draw some inferences regarding behavior outside the test situation. This is where potential for a partnership exists.

In addition to the underlying theory of measurement, several conceptual approaches inform neuropsychological assessment, including the normative developmental (Taylor & Fletcher, 1990), the neurodevelopmental systems (Bernstein, 2000), and the process approaches (Milberg, Hebben, & Kaplan, 1996). The differences among the three approaches relate to the core unit of analysis, which varies between the individual being assessed (neurodevelopmental systems), the individual's cognitive ability structure (normative developmental), and the individual's approach and/or errors in problem solution (process approach). The approach one takes guides the collection and interpretation of data. One can see that the process approach has the greatest potential and the most in common with the behavioral approach to data collection. When utilizing the process approach, the neuropsychologist collects qualitative data on how the individual being assessed approaches the task at hand and *why* errors were made. Thus, utilizing our earlier example, if a child is being assessed and demonstrates impairment on tests of attention and executive functions, the neuropsychologist utilizing the process approach would examine various factors, from the child's approach to the task to the environmental factors that may have contributed to his or her performance. For example, the child's errors may be described as related to his or her impulsive approach to tasks or to misunderstanding the directions of the task. Other factors may include reactivity to excessive noise near the assessment room, discomfort with surroundings, and performance or social anxiety.

As noted earlier, the issue of inferred variables, or variables that may not be observed, is one in which neuropsychology and behavioral psychology differ in the conceptualization. Neuropsychological data are considered to reflect hypothetical constructs. Not only are these constructs abstract, but they are thought to be mediated via actual physical manifestations or processes that are unobservable at the present time. This is noted as a concern of behaviorism, which in its most radical form functions from the idea that the rules governing behavior can be explained by observed stimulus–response relationships. Continued technological development has allowed clinicians to observe physical variations and processes that were previously unobservable (e.g., MRI, *f*MRI). Because the call for neuropsychological assessment to localize lesions is no longer so strong, there is the future potential to change the application of neuropsychological assessment data toward a more stimulus–response relationship. However, limitations continue to exist in the identification of neurotransmitter imbalances and abnormalities and the direct link to specific behavioral presentations.

There has also been work examining relations between radical behaviorism and neuropsychology on a theoretical level. Donohoe (1991) outlines the differing approaches to complexity of radical behaviorism and neuropsychology. Radical behaviorism follows a selectionist approach, in which complexity is not the result of an inherent quality or essence of the object (essentialism), but instead complexity is seen as the result of various processes operating at a molecular level (selectionism). Darwinian evolution is not the result of some essence of the object being manifested in a new species but is instead the result of various processes from the environment and from the minute genetic mutations to result in a new organism that is different from what preceded it. As an example of essentialism in neuropsychology, cognitive neuropsychology would propose that we remember because we have hierarchically organized semantic networks. Here the manifest complexity (memory) is the result of an underlying essence (semantic organization).

The thrust of selectionism is to look for the molecular processes that produce molar order. Complex environments engage in prolonged selection, resulting in complex behaviors. The process of selection is never obvious, but traces of the selection exist in the central nervous system and in the behavior controlled by the central nervous system. This supposition has congruence with aspects of developmental neuropsychology, in which cognitive skills (exemplified in certain behaviors) develop out of an interaction between the nervous system and the environment. Here the environment can be seen as the chemical environment of the central nervous system (produced by nutrition on the healthful side and by toxins on the teratogenic side) and the social physical environment of the person (produced by the success or failure of goal-directed behavior) and the social response of others when cognitive skill–related behaviors are exhibited. The development of verbal skills is the result of the central nervous system's response to verbal events processed by the developing individual, such as myelination of neuronal structures and strengthening of certain neuronal circuits when events are repeated, as well as the pruning of less frequently used circuits. Positive responses by significant others to emitted cognitive behaviors result in greater frequency of those reinforced behaviors and subsequent strengthening of the underlying neuronal circuits. To put it another way, the development of language skills requires intact central nervous system structures and physiology as well as an opportunity to observe and practice those skills. Language development may be hampered by damage to the underlying requisite central nervous system structures as well as a lack of exposure to the operation of those skills. This is particularly evident in language acquisition, in which there is evidence of critical periods during which the exposure to, and practice of, language skills is necessary for eventual optimal language function.

Selectionism is more consistent with the system's view of brain function than with the strict localizationism view. Systems theorists, of which Luria is an example, posit that behaviors that are complex enough to be observable are too complex to be the result of a single brain structure and are instead the result of multiple cooperating brain structures. Through practice and with feedback from the environment, an optimal functional system arises, probably subserved by a relatively strengthened neuronal circuit. Damage to a component of that system results in an attempt by the brain to substitute a less efficient system to produce the behavior of interest. Lurian conceptions of rehabilitation involve training another system to produce the behavior.

Taub and his associates have investigated the variables affecting brain reorganization in rehabilitation following traumatic damage (Morris & Taub, 2004; Taub, 2004; Taub, Uswatte, & Pidikiti, 1999; Taub et al., 1993). In general and simplistic terms, they have found that controlling events in the environment (neurorehabilitative training) can result in the emergence of new brain circuitry to produce the complex behaviors previously subserved by damaged brain structures.

Here is yet another instance of selectionism influencing neuropsychological thought: Clinical neuropsychologists frequently have to temper the interpretation of test results based on a consideration of the premorbid history of the patient. Educational experiences and occupational activities can play a role in the extent to which cognitive skills are developed as well as being a rough index of the innate ability of that individual's central nervous system to produce the cognitive skill behavior of interest.

The effects of central nervous system damage can then be seen as a function of the natural and social environment in which the cognitive skills were acquired. High-functioning individuals may show subtle deficits in executive skills or in abstract problem-solving skills following mild concussion, whereas individuals with less highly developed cognitive skills may not exhibit noticeable changes. Anecdotally, high-functioning individuals may report noticing changes in cognitive functioning early in the stages of a progressive, even before it is noticeable to others or before it is detectable on standardized tests. In both instances, because the environment and history of the high- and low-functioning individuals differ, the effects of the same central nervous system event also differ.

Neuropsychologists implicitly pay heed to this principle when they obtain a premorbid history in order to interpret the obtained test data. A score of 98 on the General Memory Index of the Wechsler Memory Scale—III has very different meanings when it is obtained by a law school professor and when it is obtained by an auto mechanic. In the former, that score may reflect decline; in the latter it may reflect normal performance.

## USE OF NEUROPSYCHOLOGIAL DATA TO INFORM TREATMENT PLANS

Greater use of neuropsychologists in rehabilitation settings can also be seen as an influence toward the merger of behavioral and neuropsychological assessment. Much of rehabilitation relies on behavioral interventions. Rehabilitation is frequently thought of as being the task of teaching the patient new ways of performing tasks. The clinical neuropsychologist in that setting is called on to describe assessment results in a way that lends itself to a behavioral operational intervention. Rourke, Fiske, and Strang (1986) offer a conceptual framework for relating neuropsychological assessment to treatment in children. Although this model was originally designed for children, it has broader applicability to the treatment of adults as well. They call this the *developmental neuropsychological remediation/habilitation model*. In this model there is still reliance on classical measurement theory, for one of the considerations in interpreting test results is the degree of overlap between brain lesion and ability structure. However, the clinician must also consider the demands of the environment in making predictions regarding short- and long-term behavioral outcomes. The authors suggest developing both the ideal short- and long-term remedial plans but then evaluating the availability of remedial resources in developing the realistic remedial plan. Finally, Rourke, Fiske, and Strang (1986) indicate there should be an ongoing reiterative relationship between neuropsychological assessment and intervention.

In a general sense, neuropsychological test data can help shape treatment plans by providing estimates of the degree of impairment, thereby suggesting the amount of support or environmental structure that would need to be employed in treating a given individual. Neuropsychological test data can also identify targets for intervention and identify relative cognitive strengths that can be capitalized on when designing alternate behavioral approaches to a task.

## USE OF BEHAVIORAL ASSESSMENT DATA TO INFORM NEUROPSYCHOLOGICAL ASSESSMENTS

As well as there being an important role for neuropsychological assessment results in the development of behavioral remediation plans, behavioral data play an important role in the interpretation of neuropsychological test results. The two main ways in which behavioral data can modify interpretation of test data is through consideration of qualitative features of performance and through the use of behavioral checklists to supplement the test data by providing information about the patient's behavior outside the test session. The process approach uses behavioral, nonstandardized observations to qualify the outcome of standardized test results, demonstrating another link between behavioral psychology and neuropsychology. Blind interpretation of test data is never a good idea because the context of premorbid history, concurrent medical status, and the assessment situation itself may all play a role influencing the performance of the patient. The approach used by the patient in performing the test task as well as the way in which any errors are made are important aspects of the process approach. It is not enough to know that a patient performed poorly on a visual-spatial construction task. The clinician must also know whether the task involved drawing from command or copying a design using three-dimensional blocks. The reason for the error score must also be investigated. Did the patient perform accurately although past the time limits, did the patient use a piecemeal approach that ignored the overall contour of the design, or did the patient accurately produce the overall contour and instead make errors in the internal details? These are all observations that would be recorded in the process approach and are similar to the types of data that might be employed in a behavioral assessment.

The clinical neuropsychologist is increasingly utilizing behavioral checklists and observational systems to complement the standardized test data. These observational instruments involve self-report or report by significant others. They do not supplant the standardized tests of cognitive function but instead are used to provide additional information to increase the accuracy of the generalizations drawn by the neuropsychologist. This can occur in two ways. First, the clinical neuropsychologist attempts to make statements about the behavior of the patient in the general, open environment based on test scores, and the accuracy of the reports can be enhanced by including information from people who have observed the patient in the open environment. Second, the effect of neuropsychological disorders may include neurobehavioral and emotional features. Assessing the degree of these noncognitive symptoms can both increase the diagnostic accuracy of the evaluation results as well as provide information that can modulate the interpretation of the test results.

For example, the cardinal cognitive features of Alzheimer's dementia include memory impairment in the form of rapid forgetting, visual spatial construction deficits, and a breakdown in semantic language relations. Standardized tests can be used to determine the presence of these cognitive features. However, Alzheimer's dementia also involves neurobehavioral features, such as wandering and sundowning (a worsening of cognitive symptoms late in the day). Additionally, the patient with Alzheimer's dementia may exhibit the psychiatric symptoms of paranoia and apathy. Neither the neurobehavioral nor the psychiatric symptoms will be as evident to the neuropsychologist in the assessment setting as they will be to the friends and relatives in the patient's environment. Systematically gathering information regarding these symptoms and their frequency will provide data that can be integrated into the assessment report.

Neuropsychologists are not simply utilizing assessments, including self-report measures or parental reports, to gather data about an individual's behavioral deficits rather than using the hard data of test scores. In fact, the integration of data collected from numerous sources is the hallmark of most neuropsychological assessments. These data sources include direct neuropsychological assessment, behavioral report measures from parents, teachers, and other caregivers, as well as behavioral observations made by the neuropsychologist during the time spent with the individual. Child neuropsychologists may spend time doing direct observation of a child within the classroom setting. It is how the clinical neuropsychologist uses the assessment results, rather than what type of test is used, that separates the neuropsychological assessment from the behavioral assessment. In distinction with the general psychologist or the behavioral psychologist, the clinical neuropsychologist will also include consideration of the status of the central nervous system in reaching conclusions and making predictions.

The advent of the process approach to neuropsychological assessment is concurrent with an increased appreciation of direct behavioral observations, for these are in part what allow the neuropsychologist to qualify performance on various measures of neurocognitive functioning. This combination of data-collection methodologies allows for a more accurate and complete picture of the patient and his or her strengths and weaknesses, leading to more specific and useful treatment planning. Additionally, such an interface has the potential to assist in making assessment more ecologically valid, including the potential for developing assessments based on behavioral principles.

On two different ends of the developmental spectrum, recent geriatric neuropsychologists and pediatric neuropsychologists have developed assessment instruments with a careful eye toward ecological validity. The Loewenstein Direct Assessment of Functional Status, or DAFAS (Loewenstein et al., 1989), and the Test of Everyday Attention in Children, or TEACH (Manly, Robertson, Anderson, & Nimmo-Smith, 1998), are both attempts to provide ecologically sound information pertinent to a neuropsychological assessment. The DAFAS requires the patient to engage in various behaviors relevant to everyday functioning, such as writing a check and addressing an envelope. The TEACH requires a child patient to engage in tasks that are more child friendly and more similar to environmentally relevant behaviors associated with attention. The information obtained from these instruments, when combined with information from standardized tests, can be used to make more accurate predictions about behavior in the open environment.

## INCREASING THE ECOLOGICAL VALIDITY OF NEUROPSYCHOLOGICAL TESTS CAN HELP BRIDGE THE GAP

Rating scales and inventories often are focused on a single diagnosis or constellation of problem behaviors. These tools tend to assist the clinician in diagnostic specification and can also assist in improving the ecological validity of the assessment battery as a whole. Numerous rating scales have been developed to assess the maladaptive behaviors associated with dementia (BEHAVE-AD, CBRS, DRS, GERRI), epilepsy, traumatic brain injury, psychiatric disorders (BASC, Achenbach CBCL, BDI/CDI, Anxiety scales, Millon scales, MMPI/MMPI-A, etc.), attention deficit disorders and executive dysfunction (BRIEF). These instruments have been developed for both adults and children and can be instrumental in informing the neuropsychological assessment and guiding treatment of problematic behaviors associated with specific disorders or deficits.

## SELF-MONITORING

*Self-monitoring* as a term has been used in the behavioral and the neuropsychological literature with somewhat different meanings. In general, self-monitoring can be described as the ability to evaluate and alter one's own behavior based on social norms and environmental cues. In behavioral assessment terms, the use of the term *self-monitoring* has been related mainly to the methods of monitoring. Reactivity to self-monitoring is sometimes used therapeutically in a behavioral setting. For example, a patient may be asked to self-monitor and record the frequency of anger outbursts in order both to provide a baseline of frequency before another intervention is applied and to reduce the frequency of occurrence of anger outbursts by increasing the awareness of these behaviors and by providing accountability by sharing that information with the behavior therapist. Generally, the effect of self-monitoring is to reduce negatively valenced behaviors and to increase positively valenced behaviors.

Self-monitoring takes on a somewhat different meaning in neuropsychological assessment. In children, it includes work-checking behavior, such as the ability of a child to assesses his or her ability to complete school-based assignments and chores at home. In adults, self-monitoring may include the capacity to evaluate the effect of one's behavior on others in the social environment and to modify one's behavior accordingly. In neuropsychological terms, self-monitoring is an executive-function skill modulated by connections between the orbital frontal and medial frontal lobes with limbic structures (Ward, 1948; Luu, Collins, & Tucker, 2000). Although self-monitoring appears to be independent of overall intelligence, it may be related to verbal intellectual reasoning and verbal mediation (Luria, 1961; Vygotsky, 1978). In order to increase understanding of the role of self-monitoring in neuropsychological assessment, we will consider the case of patients with deficient self-monitoring skills and then review some assessment instruments that have been suggested for use in this area.

### HEAD INJURY AND SELF-MONITORING

Individuals with closed head injury may exhibit some degree of impairment in self-monitoring accuracy. This may be particularly true of individuals with prefrontal lesions, who will demonstrate self-inhibitory difficulties. Thus, it is expected that self-monitoring skills are also negatively altered. As previously stated, the orbital and medial frontal lobes are integral in self-monitoring one's behavior. Specifically, the anterior cingulate has been shown to play an important role in self-monitoring tasks. The anterior cingulate has been shown to be involved in numerous executive functioning tasks, such as planning, novel behavior performance, and inhibition. Research using event-related-potential method-ology has discovered specific electrophysiological markers of self-monitoring, specifically in the anterior cingulate region (Dehaen, Posner, & Tucker, 1994; Miltner, Brown, & Coles, 1997). These authors have also suggested that the anterior cingulate modulates motivational processes that are related to self-monitoring one's behavior, particularly in terms of error monitoring. Case studies examining patients with lesions to these areas of the brain have consistently shown problems in recognizing social cues and controlling responses to situations.

For example, Eslinger and DeMasio (1985) described the behavior of a famous patient known as E.V.R. Premorbidly, this patient demonstrated no behavioral dif-ficulties and was a man of average to above-average intelligence. He reportedly exhibited no behavioral or emotional difficulties prior to sustaining an injury. After suffering bilateral lesions to the orbital and medial prefrontal lobe, he was unable to properly respond to emotionally significant stimuli, even though he con-tinued to demonstrate intact intelligence. This suggests that damage to this area of the frontal lobe produces executive dysfunction, in terms of diminished self-monitoring skills, without impairing other areas of cognition.

## SELF-MONITORING AND PSYCHIATRIC DISORDERS

Patients diagnosed with severe psychiatric disorders, such as schizophrenia and bipolar disorder, have been shown to exhibit impaired executive functioning. Numerous studies have examined the role of executive dysfunction in these pop-ulations, which, by clinical definition, demonstrate behavioral abnormalities. Studies have documented the relationship between executive dysfunction, specif-ically self-monitoring ability, and behavioral difficulties. For example, it appears that the inability to self-monitor behavior is related to impairment in social skill functioning. It has been well documented that patients diagnosed with schizo-phrenia, even during periods of syndromal recovery, exhibit difficulty in recog-nizing facial affect (Mueser et al., 1996; Penn, Spaulding, Reed, & Sullivan, 1996; Inhen, Penn, Corrigan, & Martin, 1996; Penn & Combs, 2000). The results indicated that this population was unable to recognize the emotional stimuli as effectively as nonpsychiatric populations. It has been suggested that deficits in facial affect processing may be associated with inappropriate behavior in patients diagnosed with Bipolar Disorder as well (Lembke & Ketter, 2002; Getz, Shear, & Strakowski, 2003). These studies conclude that it is likely that the inability to properly recognize affective responses and other social cues negatively affects one's own ability to monitor and alter behavior in order to make it consistent with social expectations. Therefore, the ability to recognize social cues limits self-monitoring behavior to the point of contributing to a classification of psychiatric illness.

The relation between self-monitoring performance and mood is probably present even in individuals who don't have a psychiatric diagnosis. Luu et al. (2000) examined the role of frontal lobe activation in the process of self-monitoring for errors in relation to levels of negative affect and negative emotionality in normal undergraduate students. These researchers found that negative mood was associated with less accurate awareness of errors and with the error-related negativity of the averaged EEG responses.

## SELF-MONITORING RATING SCALES

Rating scales have long been shown to be effective in quantifying the occurrence and severity of mood and anxiety-related difficulties. For example, the Beck Depression Inventory (Beck, 1978), Beck Anxiety Inventory (Beck, 1987, 1990), Hamilton Depression Rating Scale (Hamilton, 1960), and Young Mania Rating Scale (Young, Biggs, Ziegler, & Meyer, 1978) are just a few of the popular mood rating scales. Further, rating scales have also been utilized to describe behavioral difficulties. Gilliam's Aspergers Scale (Gilliam, 2001a), Gilliam's Autism Scale (Gilliam, 2001b), the Scale of Assessment of Negative Symptoms (Andreasen, 1989), and the Scale of Assessment of Positive Symptoms (Andreasen, 1984) are rating scales used to quantify behaviors. Behavior rating scales have also been developed to quantify observed behavior that is associated with cognitive functioning. For example, the development of rating scales (both self-report and others' report of patients) that contain items that reflect behavioral manifestations of self-monitoring attempts to help quantify this skill.

Rating scales have also been developed to help evaluate certain cognitive difficulties, such as attention and memory. Recently, scales to assess executive functioning have been developed in the attempt to quantify behaviors associated with this cognitive skill. Two commonly used measures include the Frontal System Behavioral Scale (FrSBe; Grace & Malloy, 2004) and Behavior Rating Inventory of Executive Functioning (BRIEF; Gioia et al., 2000). The FrSBe is used to compare executive functioning behaviors following a head injury to premorbid function and includes self-report as well as family-reported scales. Although it has no specific self-monitoring subscale, there are questions that explore this skill ("Apologizes for misbehavior, such as swearing").

The BRIEF, on the other hand, does specifically address self-monitoring skills, through multiple questions. The BRIEF is a rating scale for executive functioning skills in children between the ages of 6 and 18 years. Since these skills develop throughout childhood and adolescence, there are multiple versions and age-specific normative data. Items used to assess self-monitoring skills on the BRIEF include "Do not realize that certain actions bother others" and "Does not check work for mistakes." Items are scored, and a standard score for self-monitoring skill is created that compares this skill with that of others of a similar age. However, even rating scales may be limited in scope and interpretation and often do not correspond with data obtained from neuropsychological testing. For example, the BRIEF appears to be a sensitive measure of executive function in children with frontal lobe injuries (R. Jacobs, Anderson, Harvey, 2000). However, it should be noted that despite the construct validity of this tool, the self-monitoring scale is one of eight scales and incorporates only eight relatively subjective questions. Given the complexity of self-monitoring skills, it is possible that it does not examine this skill comprehensively, which may lead to inconsistency across test data.

At least one study has shown that children may be identified on the BRIEF as being impaired, but the performance on neuropsychological tests of executive function is relatively intact (Vreizen & Pigott, 2002). In this study, the BRIEF was administered to parents of 48 children who sustained moderate-to-severe traumatic brain injury. The children also underwent neuropsychological testing that examined areas of executive functioning. Results revealed that scores from the BRIEF did not correlate with any of the performance-based tests of executive functioning. There are several possible reasons for this inconsistency. The authors of the study suggest it is possible that the neuropsychological test is ecologically invalid and that the BRIEF is more sensitive to problems. It is also possible that the cognitive tests did not examine the same aspects of executive functioning as the BRIEF does, and therefore one would not expect similar results. Another possibility is rater bias. For example, it has been suggested by others that parents may overestimate the cognitive ability of their own children (Dewey, Crawford, Creighton, & Suave, 2000). Despite these limitations, the BRIEF remains one of the most valuable tools available to rate self-monitoring skills in children and provides valuable information in assessment. Because both the performance-based measures of executive function and the BRIEF have been separately validated as measures of executive function, the most likely explanation is that the two sets of instruments (and two types of assessment) provide different pieces of information, all of which may be helpful in the overall assessment of the individual. This study highlights the need to continue to develop ecologically valid protocols for assessment of monitoring and other executive function skills.

### SELF-MONITORING SUMMARY

Self-monitoring is one example of an executive-functioning ability that is difficult, but necessary, to quantify. Like most areas of executive functioning, it is observed in behavior demonstrated by individuals. However, there are limitations in testing protocols when clinically assessing this skill. Two common approaches to assess executive-functioning skills are through formal neuropsychological evaluations and utilization of behavior rating scales. However, both of these approaches have limitations. It is recommended that when evaluating these skills, behavioral reports as well as cognitive performance need to be implemented and examined in conjunction with each other.

## EXECUTIVE FUNCTIONING FROM A
## NEUROPSYCHOLOGICAL FRAMEWORK

The role of executive functions in the successful navigation of one's environment has become an important topic in recent years, and research continues to teach us more about the cortical involvement, including the intricate pathways and connections between the frontal lobes and numerous other cortical regions (Stuss & Benson, 1984). The degree of interconnectedness with virtually all other brain regions is such that damage to any cortical area may result in executive dysfunction, even without direct damage to the prefrontal cortex (Alexander & Stuss, 2000). Executive functions, from a neuropsychological perspective, include several behavioral domains: cognitive and behavioral inhibition, initiation, shift (cognitive, affective, behavioral), flexibility, working memory, planning, and organization. The executive domain of functions is generally understood to operate as the command center, managing and moderating the numerous functions of the brain. Lezak (1998) stated that executive functions are the abilities that allow for "independent, purposive, self-serving behavior," those behaviors that allow for the successful navigation of life.

Executive functions have been cited as playing a significant role in the behavioral disturbances observed in several disorders, including Attention-Deficit Hyperactivity Disorder, Tourette Syndrome, head injury, dementia, HIV/AIDS, depression, Bipolar Disorder, Obsessive-Compulsive Disorder, and schizophrenia. Not only have we begun to understand more fully the role of the frontal systems in these disorders, the construct has provided us an opportunity for more specific intervention, an excellent opportunity for the collaboration of neuropsychology and behavioral psychology.

Development of the frontal lobes and the cortical connections begins in infancy and progresses into adolescence and potentially into the second decade of life. Anderson (2002) presented an excellent review of the development of the executive system through adolescence. He presented a concise timeline of emerging executive functions, beginning with the immediate perinatal period. This highlights the importance of considering one's developmental status when approaching assessment and treatment of an individual of any age.

Besides the basic theoretical and conceptualization difficulties inherent in the development and implementation of this combined field, it is important to consider this merger of neuropsychology and behaviorism in the context of the individual's developmental status. Application of adult-based assessment tools and therapeutic techniques onto the pediatric population may be inappropriate and misleading. That being said, a discussion of the usefulness and applications of behavioral neuropsychology is presented.

Developmental neuropsychology provides a unique perspective on behavioral neuropsychology and brings a unique opportunity to consider this issue in a broader context than what has been discussed previously in the rehabilitation literature. Pediatric neuropsychology has incorporated behavioral explanations into the assessment of children. Bernstein (2000), in her discussion of the goals and purposes of clinical assessment, provides a framework for considering the joining of neuropsychology and behavioral psychology. It is especially important to the application of behavioral neuropsychology to the pediatric population. She stated that three interacting variables produce observable behavior: the brain, the context (environment), and development. She stated, "The necessary substrate for behavioral function of all types is the *brain*" (p. 402). However, Bernstein cautions that considering the brain alone is not sufficient for explaining observed behavior; environmental and psychological factors must be considered as well. This is important at all levels of the developmental life span, not just the pediatric. We are left with the question of how to integrate different types of data obtained from an assessment. How does one approach inform the other? What can we get from each other and combine to enhance the assessment and treatment of patients? We return to this question in a later section. For now we consider the flip side of examining the behavioral construct of self-monitoring from a neuropsychological perspective by examining a neuropsychological construct (memory) from a behavioral perspective.

## MEMORY AS A BEHAVIORAL CONSTRUCT

Memory is one of the most frequently used constructs in neuropsychology. Impaired memory is also one of the most frequently voiced complaints in referrals to clinical neuropsychologists. Memory is an abstract construct with mentalistic implications. Therefore, memory is not usually part of the behavioral conceptual framework. A discussion of memory will highlight some of the gap between neuropsychologists and behaviorists, but may also indicate a way to find some common ground. Neuropsychologists consider memory to be a process whereby an individual acquires information, procedures, or sensations from the environment in a way such that the individual demonstrates either awareness (explicit memory) or some systematic change in behavior without awareness (implicit memory). Memory is therefore some transient (allowing for forgetting) or lasting change in behavior. However, memory is conceptualized as being an abstraction that is responsible for that change in behavior. Memory is thought to be somehow encoded in the brain, and it is this engram that is responsible for the observed changes.

As Palmer (1991) points out, the behaviorist can study remembering but not memory. This distinction is because the behaviorist uses the behavioral unit as the locus of study. Broadly defined here, *behavior* is the act of an organism that is lawfully and systematically related to events in the environment or to other acts of the organism. Palmer goes on to say that nonvolitional, or automatic, recall can be seen as being under stimulus control; the presence of a stimulus evokes a sensory event from the past. Forgetting is not decay of the engram, as posited by neuropsychologists, but is instead due to incomplete re-creation of the eliciting stimulus situation or the influence of competing responses. Other aspects of memory, such as volitional recall, may be seen as aspects of problem solving rather than recalling. Remembering where we left an umbrella requires a variety of steps, with the eventual conclusion of either a correct or an incorrect response. Palmer states that in these intermediate steps, we provide ourselves with additional stimuli, which in turn elicit intermediate responses or pieces of information.

## SUMMARY

The challenge to the behavioral neuropsychologist is to combine the data from these types of assessments: behavioral observation and standardized testing. The process would be to use the information from one form of assessment to inform or interpret the data from the other form of assessment. If behavioral observation indicates that the patient spoke out loud, talking himself through the test procedure, scores on a test of problem solving may be interpreted as optimal performance when verbalization replaces or strengthens self-monitoring, usually thought to be subserved by the frontal lobes. A score near the intact range may be interpreted as reflecting impaired control of problem solving, because the verbal mediation was required, or as reflecting impaired working memory and concentration, because the verbal direction was required. As another example, if the patient is given a complex geometric figure to copy by drawing and he or she approaches the task by drawing various components, adding them one at a time to the design rather than first drawing the overall contour and then filling in the details, then an impairment in organization and construction may be interpreted even if the accuracy score was in the intact range.

Evaluation of the level of effort or malingering is an example of how neuropsychologists combine information from the two different realms to produce an interpretation. On the behavioral side, the clinical neuropsychologist will observe the outward signs of effort: whether or not the patient exhibited attending behavior and persisted at task, whether or not there appeared to be deliberate slowing of response. The clinical neuropsychologist will also look for inconsistencies (Franzen & Iverson, 1998). There might be an inconsistency between performances on different tests, where the patient performs poorly on a simple test of verbal attention but performs well on a computerized test of visual vigilance. There might be inconsistencies between the report of the patient and the performance of the patient on the standardized tests. For example, the patient may report that he lives alone and drove himself to the appointment but score in the severely impaired range on a test of memory. In addition, there are several standardized tests of effort, such as the Test of Memory Malingering (Tombaugh, 1997), and the neuropsychologist will use the scores from those tests to develop hypotheses about effort on the testing in general. Certain standardized tests, such as the Wisconsin Card Sorting Test, have indices that are associated with

less-than-optimal effort (Bernard, McGrath, & Houston, 1996). All of this information is combined in order to make a complex clinical decision about the validity of the scores obtained on the other standardized tests.

## REFERENCES

Alexander, M., & Stuss, D. (2000). Disorders of frontal lobe functioning. *Seminars in Neurology, 20,*
    427–437.
Anderson, P. (2002). Assessment and development of executive function (EF) during childhood. *Child
    Neuropsychology, 8,* 71–82.
Andreasan, N. C. (1984). The Scale for the Assessment of Positive Symptoms (SAPS). Iowa City:
    University of Iowa.
Andreasan, N. C. (1989). The Scale for the Assessment of Negative Symptoms (SANS): Conceptual
    and theoretical foundations. *British Journal of Psychiatry, 7,* 49–58.
Beck, A. T. (1978). *The Beck Depression Inventory (BDI).* San Antonio, TX: Psychological Corpo-
    ration.
Beck, A. T. (1987, 1990). *The Beck Anxiety Inventory (BAI).* San Antonio, TX: Psychological Cor-
    poration.
Bernard, L. C., McGrath, M. J., & Houston, W. (1996). The differential effects of simulating malin-
    gering, closed head injury, and other CNS pathology on the Wisconsin Card Sorting Test: Support
    for the "pattern of performance hypothesis." *Archives of Clinical Neuropsychology, 11,* 231–
    245.
Bernstein, J. H. (2000). Developmental neuropsychological assessment. In Yeates, K. O., Ris, M. D.
    (Eds.), et al. *Pediatric neuropsychology: Research, theory, and practice* (pp. 405–438). New York,
    NY: Guilford Press.
Dehaene, S., Posner, M. I., & Tucker, D. M. (1994). Localization of a neural system for error detec-
    tion and compensation. *Psychological Science, 5,* 303–305.
Dewey, D., Crawford, S. G., Creighton, D. E., & Suave R. S. (2000). Parents' ratings of everyday
    cognitive abilities in very low-birth-weight-children. *Journal of Developmental and Behavioral
    Pediatrics, 21,* 37–43.
Donahoe, J. W. (1991). The selectionist approach to verbal behavior: Potential contributions of neu-
    ropsychology and connectionism. In L. J. Hayes and P. N. Chase (Eds.), *Dialogues on verbal
    behavior* (pp. 146–177). Reno, NV: Context Press.
Eslinger, P. J., & Demasio, A. R. (1985). Severe disturbance of higher cognition after bilateral frontal
    lobe ablation. *Neurology, 35,* 1731–1741.
Franzen, M. D. (1991). Behavioral assessment and treatment of brain impairment. In M. Hersen and
    R. Eisler (Eds.), *Advances in behavior modification* (pp. 56–85). Beverly Hills, CA: Sage.
Franzen, M. D. (2003). Neuropsychological Assessment. In S. N. Haynes and E. Heiby (Eds.), *Com-
    prehensive handbook of psychological assessment—Behavioral assessment* (Vol. 3, pp. 386–401).
    New York: John Wiley & Sons.
Franzen, M. D., & Iverson, G. L. (1998). Assessment of malingered neuropsychological performance.
    In P. Snyder and P. D. Nussbaum (Eds.), *Handbook of hospital-based clinical neuropsychology*
    (pp. 88–101). Washington, DC: America Psychological Association Press.
Franzen, M. D., & Smith-Seemiller, L. (1998). Behavioral neuropsychology. In M. Hersen and A. E.
    Bellack (Eds.), *Behavioral assessment: A practical handbook* (4th ed., pp. 407–417). New York:
    Pergamon Press.
Getz, G. E., Shear, P. K., & Strakowski, S. M. (2003). Facial affect recognition deficits in bipolar dis-
    order. *Journal of the International Neuropsychological Society, 9,* 623–632.
Gilliam, J. E. (2001a). *Gilliam Asperger's Disorder Scale.* Austin, TX: Pro-Ed.

Gilliam, J. E. (2001b). *Gilliam Autism Rating Scale.* Austin, TX: Pro-Ed.

Gioia, G. A., Isquith, P. K., Guy, S. C., & Kenworthy, L. (2000). *Behavior Rating Inevntory of Exective Function.* Lutz, FL: Psychological Assessment Resources.

Grace, J., & Malloy, P. F. (2004). *Frontal Systems Behavior Scale (FrSBe).* Lutz, FL: Psychological Assessment Resources.

Hamilton, M. (1960). A rating scale for depression. *Journal of Neurology, Surgery, and Psychiatry, 23,* 56–61.

Horton, A. MacN. (1979). Behavioral neuropsychology: Rationale and research. *Clinical Neuropsychology, 1,* 2–23.

Horton, A. MacN. (1997). Behavioral neuropsychology: Problems and prospects. In A. MacN. Horton, D. Wedding, and J. Webster (Eds.), *The neuropsychology handbook* (2nd ed., pp. 73–97). New York: Springer Verlag.

Inhen, G. H., Penn, D. L., Corrigan, P. W., & Martin, J. (1996). Social perception and social skill in schizophrenia. *Psychiatry Research, 80,* 275–286.

Jacobs, H. E. (1993). *Behavioral analysis guidelines and brain injury rehabilitation: People, principles, and programs.* Gaithersburg, MD: Aspen.

Jacobs, R., Anderson, V., & Harvey, S. (2000). Behavior Rating Inventory of Executive Function ratings in children with documented brain lesions. Unpublished raw data cited in G. Gois, P. Isquith, S. Guy, & L. Kenworthy, *BRIEF—Behavior Rating Inventory of Executive Function,* professional manual. Odessa, FL: Psychological Assessment Resources.

Lembke, A., & Ketter, T. A. (2002). Impaired recognition of facial emotion in mania. *American Journal of Psychiatry, 159,* 302–304.

Lezak, M. D. (1998). *Neuropsychological assessment* (3rd ed.). New York: Oxford University Press.

Loewenstein, D. A., Amigo, D. A., Duara, R., Guterman, A., Hurwitz, D., Berkowitz, N. et al. (1989). A new scale for the assessment of functional status in Alzheimer's disease and related disorders. *Journal of Gerontology: Psychological Sciences, 44,* 114–121.

Luria, A. R. (1961). The role of speech in normal and abnormal behavior. New York: Liveright.

Luu, P., Collins, P., & Tucker, D. M. (2000). Mood, personality and self-monitoring: Negative affect and emotionality in relation to frontal lobe mechanisms of error monitoring. *Journal of Experimental Psychology, 129,* 43–60.

Manly, T., Robertson, I. H., Anderson, V., & Nimmo-Smith, I. (1998). Test of Everyday Attention for Children, the (TEA-Ch). Suffolk, England: Thames Valley Test Company.

Milberg, P., Hebben, N., & Kaplan, E. (1996). The Boston process approach to neuropsychological assessment. In I. Grant & K. Adams (Eds.), *Neuropsychological assessment of neuropsychiatric disorders* (2nd ed., pp. 58–80). London: Oxford University Press.

Miltner, W. H. R., Braun, C. H., & Coles, M. G. H. (1997). Event-related potentials following incorrect feedback in a time estimation task: Evidence for a generic neural system for error detection. *Journal of Cognitive Neuroscience, 9,* 787–797.

Mueser, K. T., Doonan, R., Penn, D. L., Blanchard, J. J., Bellack, A. S., Nishith, P., et al. (1996). Emotion recognition and social competence in chronic schizophrenia. *Journal of Abnormal Psychology, 105,* 271–275.

Palmer, D. C. (1991). A behavioral interpretation of memory. In L. J. Hayes and P,. N. Chase (Eds.), *Dialogues on verbal behavior* (pp. 261–279). Reno, NV: Context Press.

Penn, D. L., & Combs, D. (2000). Modification of affect perception deficits in schizophrenia. *Schizophrenia Research, 46,* 217–229.

Penn, D. L., Spaulding, W. D., Reed, D., & Sullivan, M. (1996). The relationship of social cognition to ward behavior in chronic schizophrenia. *Schizophrenia Research, 20,* 327–335.

Posner, M. I., & DiGirolama, G. J. (1998). Conflict, target detection and cognitive control. In R. Parasuraman (Ed.), *The Attentive Brain* (pp. 401–423). Cambridge, MA: MIT Press.

Rourke, B. P., Fiske, J. L., & Strang, J. D. (1986). *Neuropsychological assessment of children: A treatment-oriented approach.* New York: Guilford Press.

Stuss, D., & Benson, D. (1984). Neuropsychological studies of the frontal lobes. *Psychological Bulletin, 95,* 3–28.

Taub, E. (2004). Harnessing brain plasticity through behavioral techniques to produce new treatments in neurorehabilitation. *American Psychologist. 59,* 692–704.

Tombaugh, T. N. (1997). The Test of Memory Malingering (TOMM): Normative data from cognitively intact and cognitively impaired individuals. *Psychological Assessment, 9,* 260–268.

Vreizen, E. R., & Pigott, S. E. (2002). The relationship between parental report on the BRIEF and performance-based measures of executive function in children with moderate-to-severe traumatic brain injury. *Child Neuropsychology, 8,* 296–303.

Vygotsky, L. S. (1978). *Thought and language.* Cambridge, MA: MIT Press.

Ward, A. A. (1948). The anterior cingulated gyrus and personality. *Research Publications Association for Research in Nervous and Mental Diseases, 27,* 438–445.

Young, R. C., Biggs, J. T., Ziegler, V. E., & Meyer, D. A. (1978). A rating scale for mania; Reliability, validity and sensitivity. *British Journal of Psychiatry, 133,* 429–435.

# 23

# ETHICAL/LEGAL ISSUES

WILLIAM FREMOUW
JILL JOHANSSON-LOVE
ELIZABETH TYNER
JULIA STRUNK

*Department of Psychology*
*West Virginia University*
*Morgantown, West Virginia*

## INTRODUCTION

Adult psychological assessments focus on answering specific referral questions regarding an individual, not just the administration of psychological tests (Matarazzo, 1990). Assessment information is first gathered from multiple sources, such as interviews, observations, records, collateral reports, and standardized psychological tests, and is later integrated by the psychologist to answer the referral question. This process requires complex and sophisticated judgments regarding what types of information are (a) relevant, (b) reliable, and (c) reasonable for answering the referral question. After providing a general review of ethical guidelines, this chapter identifies and discusses both traditional and emerging ethical and legal issues that can arise in the process of adult assessment.

## ETHICAL AND LEGAL GUIDELINES

The professional activities of psychologists, including psychological assessment, are regulated by three types of guidelines: (1) broad, professional ethical principles, (2) narrower federal and state regulations, and (3) case law applicable to specific situations.

At the most general level of guidance, the "Ethical Principles of Psychologists and Code of Conduct" (American Psychological Association [APA], 2002) (hereinafter referred to as the Ethics Code) provides five aspirational general principles and 10 specific, enforceable ethical standards for professional practice. Assessment, the ninth ethical standard, consists of 11 substandards that outline the traditional areas of concern of assessment and form the foundation for examining the emerging areas of assessment, such as the Internet and "do-it-yourself" assessment. Deviations from these standards may lead to ethics complaints to the APA or to state licensing boards and form the basis for malpractice suits.

In 2003, the APA Ethics Committee received 274 initial inquiries regarding potential ethical violations. From those inquiries, the committee opened 25 new cases. That year, the committee also closed 36 and continued to investigate 66 cases. The majority (58%) of the 12 adjudicated investigations in 2003 resulted in recommendations for reprimand or censure, and an additional 33% resulted in loss of membership from APA (APA Ethics Committee, 2004). Ethics complaints may also be the basis for separate investigations by state licensing boards, which also regulate the field of psychology and can revoke licensure and the ability to practice. In 2004, the APA Insurance Trust estimated a 39% lifetime risk for psychologists being sued or reported to the licensing board over a 25-year professional career. In 2004, 1.6% of insured psychologists had legal action pending; 66% were licensing board complaints and 33% were malpractice lawsuits (APA Insurance Trust, 2004).

Clients may file malpractice civil suits in addition to formal complaints to the APA or state licensing boards. Malpractice cases are tort actions in which the plaintiff alleges that the psychologist caused damage or wrong (tort) by deviating from an ethical or legal standard of care in the context of a professional relationship. A deviation from the standard of care must be the proximate or direct cause of the damage. Most malpractice suits against psychologists concern sexual improprieties or dual relationship complaints. Fortunately, the probability of substantial financial loss from such civil actions is low. Since 1991, only 29 malpractice civil claims against psychologists have led to judgments exceeding $250,000 (APA Insurance Trust, 2004).

In psychology, standard of care not only applies to actual psychologist–client relationships, but also includes proper handling of health care information (e.g., client records, psychological test data). A new set of federal regulations was enacted on April 14, 2003, entitled Health Insurance and Portability and Accountability Act (HIPAA; U.S. Department of Health and Human Services, 2002), which created additional guidelines regarding the privacy, security, and electronic transmission of health information. These specific and narrow regulations govern the action of "covered entities" in terms of how they obtain, store, and disseminate health care and protected health care information (PHI). "Covered entities" are health care providers who transmit PHI electronically, such as by fax machine, even if for only one client. Knapp and VandeCreek (2003), authors of *A Guide to the 2002 Revision of the American Psychological Associ-*

*ation's Ethics Code*, recommend that all psychologists consider themselves a "covered entity," regardless of their current PHI electronic practices, and comply with these strict guidelines. HIPAA regulations have, at a minimum, altered consent procedures prior to services, increased security measures to ensure privacy of PHI, and guaranteed clients access to their records and the right to modify their records (except in forensic settings). Violations of HIPAA regulations can result in fines of up to $250,000 and prison sentences of up to 10 years (U.S. Department of Health and Human Services).

The narrowest form of legal regulation governing psychological practice arises from case law as applicable in federal and state courts. The case of *Daubert v. Merrell Dow Pharmaceuticals, Inc.* (1993) (hereinafter *Daubert*) has made a significant impact on psychological assessment procedures in terms of their admissibility in all federal and most state courts. Judges are provided criteria by which to decide the admissibility of expert testimony. The *Daubert* standard requires that all scientific evidence, such as psychological assessment results, be reliable, based on four criteria. The first area addressed is whether the scientific technique used to obtain the evidence is helpful and can be tested. This criterion has been operationalized as having a history of published validation studies with a variety of target samples and utilizing a variety of procedures. Second, the scientific technique is evaluated to determine if it has been subjected to peer review and publication. The error rate and standardization of the technique is considered as the third criterion. Finally, the overall general acceptance of the technique by the scientific community is factored into the decision for admissibility. Satisfaction of the *Daubert* standard is necessary for any test or measure to be admitted into testimony. Failure to meet this standard, based on a judge's opinion, leads to exclusion of the psychological assessment evidence.

For instance, a psychologist may be hired to present testimony based on informal behavioral observations of a husband–wife interaction. These observations may meet all of the APA ethical guidelines and HIPAA requirements, but they will not meet the *Daubert* standard unless the procedure of observation is widely accepted, peer reviewed, and standardized, with known error rates. The judge determines whether or not the *Daubert* standard is met; if the standard is not reached, the psychologist will not be permitted to testify. Although a psychologist may not be permitted to testify based on *Daubert* criteria, this does not necessarily mean that the psychologist violated ethical or legal standards. The subsequent U.S. Supreme Court ruling in *General Elec. Co. v. Joiner* (1997) established that trial judges have wide latitude in their application of the *Daubert* standard and can only be overruled if they abused their discretion. Clearly, this is the narrowest and strictest legal standard regarding psychological assessment and can vary from case to case, depending on the judge's application of the *Daubert* standard to a particular psychological assessment. Recent reviews have identified which psychological tests meet or do not meet the strict *Daubert* standard for admissibility, such as specific tests of cognitive functioning (Vallabhajosula & Van Gorp, 2001) or of parental fitness (Yañez & Fremouw, 2004).

Thus, ethical and legal guidelines governing psychological practice in general and psychological assessment in particular range from broad ethical standards with implications for professional association membership, state licensing, and/or malpractice civil suits, through specific HIPAA regulations with potential fines and imprisonment for violations, to the ability to testify about psychological assessments on a particular case in a particular court at a particular time. This can be conceptualized as levels of control from the broad ethical standards to the narrowest legal standards, such as *Daubert*, with varying consequences for violation of guidelines. The remainder of this chapter addresses traditional and emerging issues in adult psychological assessment that could raise ethical and legal challenges to practicing psychologists.

## TRADITIONAL ISSUES IN ASSESSMENT

Performing ethical and legal psychological assessments require adherence to all standards of the Ethics Code (APA, 2002), including competence, informed consent, privacy and confidentiality, release of test data, and record keeping, as well as the assessment standard.

### COMPETENCE

Ethical adult assessment requires that the psychologist be competent to perform the specific assessment procedure. As described in the Ethics Code Standard 2 (APA, 2002), psychologists only provide services within their "boundaries of competence," based on education, training, or experience. For example, a psychologist who specializes in anxiety disorders cannot ethically conduct a forensic evaluation on an adult sex offender without proper training in that area. Furthermore, psychologists should refer clients to appropriate professionals if the presenting problems are beyond their boundaries.

Psychologists must also be sensitive to their "cultural competence," or possession of knowledge and experience of individuals from cultures other than their own. When assessing a client from a cultural background with which they are not familiar, it is the duty of the psychologist to seek consultation if necessary (Knapp & VandeCreek, 2003). For instance, a psychologist assessing a person who "hears God" must consider the cultural context of such an experience, such as covered in the *Diagnostic and Statistical Manual of Mental Disorders (DSM-IV-TR*; American Psychiatric Association, 2000) cultural formulation outline, before concluding that the person has a mental illness. In certain cultures, "hearing God" is a normative, spiritual experience. Cultural sensitivity is an increasingly important area of focus for graduate and continued professional training.

# ADEQUACY OF ASSESSMENT DATA

Standard 9 of the Ethics Code (APA, 2002) pertains directly to the practice of assessment. Psychologists must form decisions based on "sufficient and substantial information." If a sufficient amount of information cannot be reasonably obtained, psychologists are required to acknowledge the limited validity and reliability of the assessment findings. For instance, it is not appropriate for a psychologist to diagnose an adult as mentally retarded on the sole basis of an interview, without an assessment of intellectual and functional impairment.

Regarding test administration, psychologists may only use assessment measures directly relevant to the current issue(s) of the client. The measures must be used properly, such as following administrative instructions from manuals and maintaining controlled testing environments. The measures are expected to have sound psychometric properties; however, if this is not the case, psychologists should acknowledge this on interpretation of results. Also, testing instruments must match clients' abilities (e.g., language, reading level). Only current measures are acceptable for use in any psychological assessment. The interpretation of results from obsolete and/or outdated measures is not appropriate. When new editions of measures are published, a specific transitional time period is established by the test publishers after which the earlier version is considered obsolete. (See the later section in this chapter on intellectual assessment and the death penalty for the serious implications of the use of obsolete assessment materials.)

# INFORMED CONSENT

Prior to beginning any psychological service, such as assessment, Ethics Code Standard 3.10 in general and 9.03 specifically (APA, 2002) require that the individual give informed consent to participate. Consent can only be given after the psychologist provides a description of the entire assessment. This includes a discussion of the actual measure(s) and the reason for use of the measure(s), the cost, the limits of confidentiality, third-party involvement (e.g., insurance company), and to whom the results will be made available. Additionally the individual is provided with an opportunity to ask questions and receive answers about the assessment prior to giving consent. However, there are several exceptions to this standard. First, if the assessment is mandated by law or by governmental regulations, psychologists are required to inform the person of the nature of the assessment (e.g., it is court ordered) as well as the limits of confidentiality before conducting the assessment. Second, in some instances the informed consent is implied instead of obtained, such as when the assessment is conducted as a routine educational, institutional, or organizational activity (e.g., psychological testing included in a job application). Finally, when the purpose of the assessment is to evaluate a person's capacity to make decisions, psychologists must adjust the reading level of all consent documents to that of the person being assessed and attempt to inform that person of all aspects of the assessment situation. Assent from the client should be obtained as well as consent from the person or entity with legal authority to do so.


## PRIVACY, PRIVILEGE, AND CONFIDENTIALITY

### Privacy

Psychologists may confuse the concepts of privacy, confidentiality, and privilege. Standard 4 of the Ethics Code (APA, 2002) addresses maintaining privacy and confidentiality, limits of confidentiality, and ethical disclosures of confidential information. Privacy is respected by refraining from disclosing the personal information and/or experiences of a client unless they are specifically "germane to the purpose" of the evaluation. For example, describing the sexual orientation of a client in a psychological assessment addressing a memory disorder would not be relevant or germane and would violate privacy. Client privacy is also maintained through appropriate physical settings. Psychological tests should not be administered in a busy hallway, and intake interviews should not be conducted in a crowded waiting room of psychologists' offices. HIPAA contains detailed privacy rules that address the providers' physical infrastructure, such as specifications for only certain individuals to have access to offices, files, fax machines, and security. Each place of business must have designated privacy officers and mandated staff training and must provide every client with privacy statements. To assist psychologists, the APA and APA Insurance Trust have developed documents (i.e., privacy statements and HIPAA-compliant forms) for use as models. Privacy is a basic client ethical right and is now a legal requirement of HIPAA.


### Privilege

Privilege and confidentiality are frequently confused and interchanged. *Privilege* is a legally defined special relationship, while *confidentiality* is an ethically defined professional relationship. Privilege, as defined by Black's law dictionary (Garner, 2001) refers to "a special right, exemption, or immunity granted to a person or class of persons; an exception to a duty." This is a legal concept that prohibits discussing confidential information divulged during legal proceedings, such as conversations between a lawyer and a client or a priest and a confessor (APA, 2003). In the case of a psychologist retained by a defense attorney to evaluate a client, the privilege between a defendant and the attorney will extend under an "umbrella" to incorporate the psychologist. If the psychologist is hired by the judge or prosecutor to conduct an evaluation, no legal privilege exists between that individual and the psychologist. Therefore, court-ordered psychological assessments are not privileged or protected from disclosure, since they are not part of an attorney's privileged work product.

## Confidentiality

Confidentiality is an important ethical guideline in clinical practice. If psychologists violate confidentiality, they may concurrently violate standards set forth by state licensing boards. Confidentiality violations may result in malpractice suits (Knapp & VandeCreek, 2003). Most states recognize that psychologists have a duty to maintain the confidentiality of client information (APA, 2003). Standard 4.01 of the APA Ethics Code (2002) state that a psychologist should take precautions to protect and maintain confidential information. The extent to which confidentiality can be maintained may be legally, institutionally, scientifically, or professionally regulated. According to Standard 4.02 of the Ethics Code, during the informed consent process, it should be explained to the client how confidentiality can be maintained or violated and how the information gathered during the assessment will be utilized (APA, 2002).

### DISCLOSURE

Psychologists may obtain consent from a legally appropriate party (individual, power of attorney, organization, etc.) to disclose confidential information about the concerned party. Standard 4.04 of the Ethics Code (APA, 2002) states that only the most pertinent information pertaining to the question for which the assessment was intended should be included in any form of communication, thus protecting privacy. Psychologists are also allowed to disclose confidential information, without the consent of the client, when legally mandated or legally permitted. Psychologists must always attempt to attain consent prior to breaching confidentiality, regardless of the circumstance. The APA Ethics Code standard 4.05 (2002) specifies that a psychologist may breach confidentiality in the following four areas: (1) to supply the required professional services, (2) to attain suitable consultations, (3) to ensure the safety of a client, the psychologist, or others, and (4) to collect payment for services rendered to a client. The Ethics Code (APA, 2002) also describes several federal and state laws that regulate breaches of confidentiality, specifically regarding psychologists' duty to warn and to protect. These laws require psychologists to disclose confidential information when a client (during assessment or more commonly during therapy) poses a risk to themselves or others.

## Danger to Self or Others

Psychologists have the duty to protect any identifiable victims from harm by clients, based on case and statutory laws (Knapp & VandeCreek, 2003). Although these protective responsibilities vary among states, the majority have adopted a "duty to protect" via case law, such as *Tarasoff v. Regents of the University of California* (1976), or "a duty to warn" statute (Knapp & VandeCreek). Psychologists must be aware of the legal responsibilities for the state in which they practice. The "duty to protect" requirement based on *Tarasoff* requires that psychologists or other mental health professionals attempt to protect any identifiable, intended victim. If a psychologist determines that there is serious potential danger from a client toward an identifiable victim, the psychologist is required, using reasonable means, to protect the intended victim by performing actions such as ensuring that the intended victim receives a direct warning about the potential harm, contacting law enforcement, initiating civil commitment/hospitalization, or engaging in other reasonable forms of intervention (Borum & Reddy, 2001).

The "duty to warn" statute requires psychologists to warn an identifiable and intended victim of potential harm, but it does not require any further action, such as notifying law enforcement. Psychologists should attempt, if possible, to involve the client in the decision to warn or protect the victim. If a client is suicidal, there is no "duty to warn." In this case the psychologist must decide if it is appropriate and necessary to breach confidentiality in order to protect the client. The psychologist should, of course, attempt to evaluate the seriousness of the threat and take the necessary precautions to protect his/her client (Knapp & VandeCreek, 2003).

### HIV-Positive Clients

Unlike the APA (American Psychological Association), the American Psychiatric Association has developed guidelines for determining if a "duty to warn" applies to HIV-positive clients, whose behavior is potentially dangerous to others. The guidelines encourage psychiatrists to actively persuade clients to cease problematic behavior and disclose the condition to the partners. The American Medical Association suggests reporting a client to the authorities if that individual is endangering a third party and refusing to disclose the condition to that third party (Melchert & Patterson, 1999). The APA has not adopted an official policy concerning disclosure and HIV-positive clients; however, in 1991 the organization released the following statements (APA, 1991):

1. A legal duty to protect third parties from HIV infection should not be imposed.
2. If, however, specific legislation is considered, then it should permit disclosure only when (a) the provider knows of an identifiable third party who the provider has compelling reason to believe is at significant risk for infection; (b) the provider has a reasonable belief that the third party has no reason to suspect that he or she is at risk; and (c) the client/patient has been urged to inform the third party and has either refused or is considered unreliable in his/her willingness to notify the third party.
3. If such legislation is adopted, it should include immunity form civil and criminal liability for providers who, in good faith, make decisions to disclose or not to disclose information about HIV infection to third parties.

Clearly, disclosure regarding HIV is controversial in the United States. Psychologists should be aware of state laws concerning disclosure of information about HIV-positive clients and should also be knowledgeable of criminal and/or civil liability for psychologists. Psychologists may legally submit a good-faith report to the local, state, or federal health departments concerning persons infected with

HIV. Usually, the health departments will notify individuals mentioned by the reporter of their risk of exposure to HIV (Melchert & Patterson, 1999).

## RELEASE OF TEST DATA

Standard 9.04 of the Ethics Code (APA, 2002) defines test data as raw and scaled scores, the specific answers provided by the clients, portions of test materials that include the responses, and any notes taken by psychologists regarding the verbal and nonverbal behavior of clients during the assessment. When presented with a written release from appropriate parties, psychologists are required to reveal the test data to that specified client or the client's designees. If a written release is not provided, psychologists may only reveal test data if ordered to do so by the law (Smith, 2003). A psychologist can withhold test data if this action protects the client or others from considerable harm or if inappropriate or inaccurate use of the data is anticipated, as noted in Standard 9.04 of the Ethics Code (APA, 2002). Test materials, defined as the actual instrument, stimuli, manuals, test questions, or protocols, are not considered to be test data and are not released along with the test data. Standard 9.11 of the Ethics Code (APA, 2002) requires psychologists to protect the integrity and security of the test materials.

### Subpoena/Subpoenas Duces Tecums

Psychological assessments can be objects of legal procedures for disclosure by a subpoena. Subpoenas are issued by court clerks instructing psychologists or psychologists' documents (subpoena duces tecums) to appear in court. Being issued a subpoena does not automatically require a psychologist to break confidentiality. If a client has not given permission to break confidentiality, the psychologist should maintain confidentiality until the client has provided written release of information or until ordered by the court to do otherwise (APA, 2003). Several situations exist in which special circumstances render a subpoena legally unenforceable. For example, a subpoena issued in a state different from the state in which the psychologist practices and a subpoena dropped off at a psychologist's office or served to a secretary without being directly served to the psychologist are instances that limit enforceability (APA Committee on Legal Issues, 1996).

After being properly served a subpoena, the psychologist should contact the client (and potentially the client's attorney). However, the psychologist may first wish to investigate the state guidelines for opposing or limiting the disclosure prior to contacting the client in order to present potential options to the client. The client may consent (although test security needs to be considered) or refuse to release the information. If a client refuses, the psychologist is advised to attempt a negotiation with the party requesting the information. If an agreement cannot be arranged, the psychologist can seek a ruling from the court compelling the disclosure. If a psychologist cannot or does not seek a ruling, the psychologist can encourage the client to file a motion to quash the subpoena (declare it invalid) or file a protective order (an order protecting against the negative consequences of disclosure) in an attempt to avoid legal repercussions (APA Committee on Legal Issues, 1996).

## Court Orders

Different from a subpoena, a court order is issued by a judge and specifies an action such as testifying or providing specific information. A failure to abide by a court order, because a judge issues it, can have more severe consequences than a failure to comply with a subpoena; in some instances, it can lead to financial or legal penalties (APA, 2003). As with a subpoena, the client should be informed of the court order to permit the client to contest the order.

## RECORD STORAGE AND DISPOSAL

Psychologists should maintain confidentiality throughout all aspects of the assessment process, including the storage and disposal of protected health information, according to Standard 6.02 of the Ethics Code (APA, 2002). Specifically, care should be taken with information that is stored on computers, such as excluding personal identifiers. Also, computers may only be accessed by persons who are included in the clients' informed consent. Psychologists should also plan for the maintenance of record confidentiality in the event of discontinuation of practice due to retirement, illness, or death. Ragusea (2002) suggests that psychologists create a will specifically to address the maintenance and disposal of records in the event of death. It is also recommended to assign this duty to another professional sensitive to ethical/legal issues.

The length of storage prior to disposal varies with material type, such as tax receipts and clinical records. The APA guidelines concerning clinical record storage suggest keeping full assessment records for 3 years after the last contact with the person. Additionally it is suggested to maintain, at a minimum, a summary of the record for an additional 12 years. This totals 15 years. If the client is a minor, the full record should be maintained until 3 years after the individual has turned 18. Thus, if the child is seen at age 1, these records must be maintained for 20 years. The APA may revise these guidelines to extend storage of full records to a 7-year period, a higher requirement than any state statute (APA Committee on Professional Practices and Standards, 1993). At this time, the most conservative practice would be to store adult records for a minimum of 15 years and child records for 21 years.

Records should only be disposed in a manner that guarantees their confidentiality and complete destruction, such as shredding or burning. This task should be delegated to individuals who will preserve the confidentiality of the records. Agencies that hire professional record disposal services should assign a staff member to oversee the record destruction and to ensure that records are not merely placed in a landfill or left in a warehouse.

## EMERGING ISSUES IN ASSESSMENT

The previous sections outlined traditional areas of legal/ethical concerns regarding assessment. The remainder of this chapter addresses four developing issues in the psychological assessment of adults.

### PSYCHOLOGICAL ASSESSMENT AND THE INTERNET

Information technology has advanced exponentially since the development of computers in the 1960s. Internet use in particular has grown with this trend, especially since the mid-1990s, with over 500 million individuals worldwide having Internet access. In our country, citizens spend an average of 26 hours per month surfing the Web at home and over 75 hours per month online at work. Almost one-quarter (23%) of U.S. citizens with online access have viewed information on the Internet regarding mental health (cited in Naglieri et al., 2004). The National Institute of Mental Health (NIMH) Web site is accessed approximately 7 million times each month (Taylor & Luce, 2003). The NIMH, along with other legitimate mental health resource Web sites, offers screening tests for psychological problems. Results from a study conducted by Houston et al. (2001) indicate that an online screening version of the Center for Epidemiological Studies' Depression Scale yielded 24,479 screenings completed within eight months. Of those, 58% had positive screens (indicating the presence of depression), and less than half had not received treatment for depression (cited in Taylor & Luce).

Using popular Internet search engines, any individual could easily find hundreds of Web sites that offer online screening tests for psychological problems such as depression, ADHD, and Alzheimer's disease, as well as tests of intelligence, personality, and romantic compatibility. The tendencies of some individuals to find fast and simple solutions to complex problems or issues, in addition to the rising cost of health care, are two reasons that individuals may be motivated to screen for psychological problems using Internet sites that offer quick results and minimal fees for services. While the Internet can be a useful tool for disseminating mental health information to many individuals, online screening of psychological problems raises several concerns.

Ethical issues arise for psychologists because Internet information is not always reliable and accurate. In many cases, Internet screening tests violate multiple standards of the Ethics Code (APA, 2002). Some Internet measures are advertised to have established reliability and validity; however, these claims are often based on a single study conducted by the test creators. This violates Standard 9.05 of the Ethics Code (APA, 2002) regarding psychometric soundness of instruments (Kier & Molinari, 2004). No clear information exists regarding whether or not the test developers are psychologists or if the tests developed are within their boundaries of competence. These issues may violate Standards 9.07 and 2 of the Ethics Code (APA, 2002), respectively. Furthermore, testing sites are not necessarily monitored in real time. Therefore, if an individual expresses suicidal/homicidal ideation in their responses during an online assessment, that individual may not receive necessary care. In the extreme situation of an individual committing suicide/homicide upon discovering the results of a test (e.g., meeting criteria for Alzheimer's disease), it is unclear if the test developer or Web site company is responsible in any manner for the death.

Two other ethical concerns stem from unreliable and inaccurate assessment information found on the Internet. First, individuals may be receiving false-positive or false-negative diagnoses. Second, if individuals are diagnosed with a disorder on an Internet Web site, emotional distress and adverse reactions may result that are not monitored. Most Web sites offer only telephone numbers for crisis intervention hotlines, not live therapists to assist with interpretation of assessment results. The absence of live, post-test feedback and assistance is one of the most problematic ethical aspects of Internet testing (Kier & Molinari, 2004). If referrals to mental health care providers are available, these services are typically near the location of the Web site, which is problematic since many users reside outside of the referral area. Another ethical issue involves the misuse/abuse of Internet testing. Individuals such as older adults could be forced by family members to complete online testing measures for dementia, and results could be used against them to justify admittance into nursing homes. Furthermore, employers could use invalid or questionable test results to force employees into early retirement (Kier & Molinari).

Currently, using the Internet for psychological screening is not illegal or unethical in our country (Kier & Molinari, 2004). In 1997, the APA Ethics Committee issued a statement regarding telephone, teleconferencing, and Internet services indicating that the earlier version of the Ethics Code (APA, 1992) does not directly address the previously listed services, and any complaints regarding these issues will be reviewed on a case-by-case basis. Psychologists are cautioned to review the code and determine if services violate any listed guidelines (APA, 1997). However, these procedures may violate many components of the revised APA Ethics Code (APA, 2002), which states that when ethical and legal guidelines conflict, the best practice is to be conservative by upholding the code while staying within legal limits.

While raising some ethical concerns, Internet testing does offer some advantages over direct assessment, such as increasing accessibility to mental health information for individuals who lack time and financial resources and reducing potential embarrassment from face-to-face inquiries about mental health issues. The Internet also allows anonymity of self-screening for psychological problems. These advantages, however, come at a cost that may not be apparent to the individual. Personal information such as psychiatric history, trauma history, or current mood states is not necessarily kept secure or confidential. Despite these areas of concern, it is likely that Internet testing for psychological problems will continue to grow with the expansion of the Internet.

## PSYCHOLOGICAL ASSESSMENT AND THE MEDIA

While the Internet provides one avenue for individuals seeking psychological assessment in a nontraditional manner, increased use of telecommunications among the general population has spawned an influx of media-driven public assessment. Call-in radio shows, such as Dr. Laura and Love Lines with Dr. Drew and Adam, receive calls from listeners with concerns ranging from problematic behavior of children to an inability to develop intimate relationships. From a 1- to 5-minute telephone conversation, these providers, often not licensed psychologists, formulate a hypothesis about the caller's problem, evaluate the seriousness of the issue, and propose solutions to the problem. Unlike crisis hotline services, these call-in shows serve an entertainment function, driven by advertisements and number of listeners. This type of reality-based psychological drama has made its way even to popular television shows, such as the Dr. Phil Show, which invites guests to appear and discuss a variety of topics, such as maladaptive family behaviors, eating disorders, affective disorders, and spousal concerns.

Numerous ethical issues arise when considering practices of large-scale media productions. In order to dispense sound psychological advice, some form of assessment of the individual's concern or problem must take place. Whether this assessment occurs primarily "off the air" or "on air," the brevity of callers' conversations or televised guest appearances calls into question the adequacy of the assessment to give informed opinions and advice. Standard 2.04 of the Ethics Code (APA, 2002) pertains to bases for scientific and professional judgments and states that psychologists should base their opinions "on established scientific and professional knowledge of the discipline." Advice should be given only if it falls within an individual's area or areas of competence and only if it is grounded in scientific study or well-established, accepted clinical practices (Fisher, 2003). For example, Dr. Laura's educational background is in physiology, making her level of competence in psychological areas questionable at best. When asked to render an opinion about an area outside of one's competence, referral to a more appropriate source is necessary.

Related to the standard on appropriate bases for scientific and professional judgment, Standard 5.04 of the Ethics Code (APA, 2002), regarding media presentations, states that

> when psychologists provide public advice or comment via print, Internet, or other electronic transmissions, they take precautions to ensure that statements (1) are based on their professional knowledge, training, or experience in accord with appropriate psychological literature and practice; (2) are otherwise consistent with this Ethics Code; and (3) do not indicate that a professional relationship has been established with the recipient.

When applied to radio call-in shows or brief televised exchanges, this standard requires that professionals make comments in a general format, not directing their advice toward the specific individual but referring to *typical* cases of a disorder or problem and *general* treatment options (Knapp & VandeCreek, 2003). Additional statements should specify that the brief exchange does not constitute therapy and that, if necessary, a therapist or mental health professional should be sought after the conversation is terminated. Individuals calling radio programs or appearing on shows must be made aware that they are not clients, in order to comply with ethical standards on media presentations and assessments. When dispensing psychological advice, the same standard of care is required as if providing direct treatment (Knapp & VandeCreek).

## PSYCHOLOGICAL ASSESSMENT AND COACHING CLIENTS

The Internet and other technology sources are used not only to obtain psychological evaluations and services, but also to locate and distribute information on psychological assessment instruments. Ruiz, Drake, Glass, Marcotte, and van Gorp (2002) note that 2–5% of Web sites found on the Internet using several popular search engines contained information considered to be a direct threat to test security. Approximately 20–25% of the Web sites contained indirectly threatening material. Of the sites that held material of direct threat to test security, information such as detectable signs of malingering, goals and procedures of evaluations, strategies used to detect deceptive responding, and even test stimuli were posted. Access to such detailed information is one method of coaching, or preparing, for how to respond to psychological evaluations. Independently looking for this type of information about symptoms or validity scales on assessment instruments is a form of self-coaching. Frequently, the motivation to develop such strategies arises in cases of malingering. The *DSM-IV-TR* (American Psychiatric Association, 2000) defines malingering as "the intentional production of false or grossly exaggerated physical or psychological symptoms, motivated by external incentives" (p. 739). Between 15% and 17% of cases presented in forensic settings have been found to involve malingering of symptoms (Rogers & Bender, 2003). Ethical concerns related to coaching on psychological assessment instruments impact psychologists in three different ways.

Internet sites, such as those previously described, clearly violate test security. As mentioned earlier in this chapter, Standard 9.11 of the Ethics Code (APA, 2002) clarifies that "test materials refer[s] to manuals, instruments, protocols, and test questions or stimuli and does not include test data." The standard further explains that the role of the psychologist is to "make reasonable efforts to maintain the integrity and security of test materials and other assessment techniques consistent with law and contractual obligations, and in a manner that permits adherence to this Ethics Code." The issue of giving clients psychological tests to take home raises one concern of test security. Knapp and VandeCreek (2003) suggest that in some cases, giving a client a test at home is appropriate, such as when logistical problems exist with seeing the client and in cases in which "there were no secondary gains that would encourage respondents to falsify results" (p. 144). In forensic settings, individuals being evaluated are not usually clients, since the evaluations are court ordered, and they stand to gain numerous external rewards, such as monetary compensation in civil litigation and reduced sentences in criminal trials. By displaying test stimuli on Web sites and, even more extensively, by providing strategies for how to avoid detection of deceptive responding, violations of test security lead to more sophisticated self-coaching.

Another ethical issue in the context of coaching and malingering involves attorney preparation, including informing clients about the assessment process and validity scales used in psychological testing. Wetter and Corrigan (1995) surveyed 70 practicing attorneys and 150 law students and found that almost 50% of the attorneys and over 33% of the students believe clients undergoing psychological evaluations should always or usually be informed of validity scales on psychological assessments. Validity scales designed to detect inconsistent responding or positive or negative impression management (faking good or faking bad) are effective, on the basis of individuals being unaware that certain test items are included only for detection of deceptive responding. When attorneys inform clients not to appear overly positive or extremely negative, clients become sensitive to questions or statements embedded in the assessment instrument that detect suspicious responding. Studies have found that individuals told to malinger perform significantly better, by avoiding detection on assessment instruments, when coached about validity scales (Suhr & Gunstad, 2000; Guriel et al., 2004). Lawyers, however, contend that they are ethically bound to advocate for their clients and that the existing Ethics Code standard (APA, 2002) regarding test security does not bind them, because they are not psychologists. Victor and Abeles (2004) present a detailed account of this ethical clash and offer suggestions on how psychologists can cope with this dilemma.

A final ethical issue regarding coaching involves clinical practice and research behavior of psychologists. Johnson and Lesniak-Karpiak's (1997) investigation on the effects of warning malingerers about the presence of detection strategies concludes in a recommendation that psychologists warn individuals that methods were being used to detect faking prior to testing. The authors state that this warning would serve to reduce malingering behavior. In response to this recommendation, Youngjohn, Lees-Haley, and Binder (1999) reviewed the literature on the impact of coaching and found that "coaching consistently shows that malingerers who are warned of the presence of symptom validity assessment techniques are able to feign deficits in a less exaggerated and more believable fashion and therefore elude detection" (p. 511). In addition to providing information that would assist an individual in their attempts to malinger, this advice may be in violation of Standard 9.11 of the Ethics Code (APA, 2002) involving test security. Ben-Porath (1994) raised an ethical question regarding coached malingering research itself. While researchers gain knowledge from studies designed to investigate strategies of malingerers and the effects of coaching, test security may also be compromised by the public dissemination of the research results. In sum, coaching clients in any form raises ethical and legal issues that should be considered in all psychological assessments.

## INTELLECTUAL EVALUATIONS AND THE
## DEATH PENALTY

Psychological assessments are conducted not only in the context of a clinical intake, educational placement, or diagnostic report, but also in the determination of whether an individual can be legally executed. In 2002, the Supreme Court ruled in *Atkins v. Virginia* that mentally retarded individuals could not be executed because it qualifies as "cruel and unusual punishment" under the Eighth Amendment. Justice Stevens, for the majority, wrote that those qualified as mentally retarded were "categorically less culpable than the average criminal" (*Atkins v. Virginia*, 2002). The criteria for determining mental retardation are established separately for each state; however, IQ score is almost always a major, if not sole, component (Kanaya, Scullin, & Ceci, 2003).

One ethical issue involving death penalty cases is the psychologist's participation in any aspect of the case, such as determining competency to stand trial or competency to be executed (Cunningham & Goldstein, 2003). Another ethical consideration for a psychologist involved in assessment aspects of death penalty cases concerns the "Flynn effect," which involves a tendency for cohort IQ scores to increase slowly but steadily with each passing year (Kanaya et al., 2003). Intelligence tests account for this well-documented phenomenon by periodically renorming the tests to ensure that average cohort performance scores center once again around a mean of 100. Tests are renormed approximately once every 15–20 years. The Flynn effect impacts test scores most dramatically at the beginning and end of each cycle (Kanaya et al.). For example, an individual who takes an IQ test shortly after a renormed version has been released will score lower than an individual with the same cognitive ability who takes the previous version of the test only months before. Examining school-age students who fall in the borderline and mild mental retardation ranges, Kanaya et al. report that an average of 5.6 points is lost when retesting occurs on a recently renormed test. When compared with peers who are retested after the same amount of time but who use the same test version, the first group of students is significantly more likely to be classified as mentally retarded.

The significance of the Flynn effect when administering intelligence tests is obvious. If older test versions are used, then individuals will score higher than someone of the same cognitive ability who is tested using a renormed, recent version of the test. A higher score could mean qualification for the death penalty. This discrepancy is particularly significant for individuals who score in the borderline range, where a difference of 5–6 points (the average lost when retested on a recently renormed test) could mean the difference between being executed and escaping execution. Implications are also evident for relying on old test scores, such as tests administered during childhood, based on the year the test was administered (Ceci, Scullin, & Kanaya, 2003). As previously mentioned, ethical obligations require that psychologists use current, updated versions of tests, particularly intelligence tests, and consider the impact of the Flynn effect when reviewing historical records and making current recommendations.

## SUMMARY

Adult psychological assessment requires knowledge, sensitivity, and the application of current ethical and legal standards. Ignorance of these standards is not an excuse for violations. These standards range from basic issues of the psychologist's competence to record storage and disposal. The 2002 Ethics Code provides detailed descriptions of the ethical requirements of the APA, and Knapp and VandeCreek (2003) explain and illustrate these guidelines in great detail. Legal issues are raised by high-risk clients who may be dangerous to others or themselves. These legal guidelines evolve from ongoing litigation and case law. The explosion of Internet access and information has created new ethical and legal problems. Similarly, the increase of "talk radio/TV" with on-air immediate assessment and advice pushes or exceeds the boundaries of ethical practice. Easily available information on psychological tests provides coaching information that threatens test security and validity of psychological assessments. Finally, results from psychological assessments often aid legal decisions. A difference between a life sentence in prison and execution could be at stake (e.g., *Atkins v. Virginia* (2002)). Obviously, the ethical, legal, and moral implications of psychological assessments are profound. All psychologists should be competent, cautious, and conservative in their assessment activities.

## REFERENCES

American Psychiatric Association. (2000). *Diagnostic and statistical manual of mental disorders* (4th ed., text revision). Washington, DC: Author.

American Psychological Association. (1991). *Legal liability related to confidentiality and the prevention of HIV transmission.* Washington, DC: APA Council of Representatives. Available from the APA Web site: http://www.apa.org/pi/hivres.html

American Psychological Association. (1992). Ethical principles of psychologists and code of conduct. *American Psychologist, 47,* 1597–1611.

American Psychological Association. (1997). *APA statement on services by telephone, teleconferencing, and Internet.* Retrieved September 12, 2004, from http://www.apa.org/ethics/stmnt01.html

American Psychological Association. (2002). Ethical principles of psychologists and code of conduct. *American Psychologist, 57,* 1060–1073. Available from the APA Web site: http://www.apa.org/ethics/

American Psychological Association. (2003). Legal issues in the professional practice of psychology. *Professional Psychology: Research and Practice, 34,* 595–600.

American Psychological Association, Committee on Legal Issues. (1996). Strategies for private practitioners coping with subpoenas or compelled testimony for client records or test data. *Professional Psychology: Research and Practice, 27,* 245–251.

American Psychological Association, Committee on Professional Practice and Standards. (1993). Recordkeeping guidelines. *American Psychologist, 48,* 984–986.

American Psychological Association, Ethics Committee. (2004). Report of the Ethics Committee, 2003. *American Psychologist, 59,* 434–441.

American Psychological Association, Insurance Trust. (2004). *Legal and ethical risks and risk management in professional practice.* Washington, DC: Author.

Atkins v. Virginia, 536 U.S. 304 (2002).

Ben-Porath, Y. S. (1994). The ethical dilemma of coached malingering research. *Psychological Assessment, 6,* 14–15.

Borum, R., & Reddy, M. (2001). Assessing violence risk in Tarasoff situations: A fact-based model of inquiry. *Behavioral Sciences and the Law, 19,* 375–385.

Ceci, S. J., Scullin, M., & Kanaya, T. (2003). The difficulty of basing death penalty eligibility on IQ cutoff scores for mental retardation. *Ethics & Behavior, 13,* 11–17.

Cunningham, M. D., & Goldstein, A. M. (2003). Sentencing determinations in death penalty cases. In A. M. Goldstein & I. B. Weiner (Eds.), *Handbook of psychology: Forensic Psychology* (pp. 407–436). New York: John Wiley & Sons.

Daubert v. Merrell Dow Pharmaceuticals, Inc., 113 S.Ct. 2786 (1993).

Epstein, J., & Klinkenberg, W. D. (2001). From Eliza to Internet: A brief history of computerized assessment. *Computers in Human Behavior, 17,* 295–314.

Garner, B. (Ed.). (2001). *Black's law dictionary.* St. Paul, MN: West Group.

General Elec. Co. v. Joiner, 522 U.S. 136 (1997).

Georgia Institute of Technology. (2000). *GVU's WWW User Surveys.* Available from: www.cc.gatech.edu.evu.user-surveys

Guriel, J., Yanez, R., Fremouw, W., Shreve-Neiger, A., Ware, L., Filcheck, H., et al. (in press). Impact of coaching on malingered posttraumatic stress symptoms on the M-FAST and the TSI. *Journal of Forensic Practice.*

Houston, T. K., Cooper, L. A., Vu, H. T., Kahn, J., Toser, J., & Ford, D. E. (2001). Screening the public for depression through the Internet. *Psychiatric Services, 52,* 362–367.

Johnson, J. L., & Lesniak-Karpiak, K. (1997). The effect of warning on malingering on memory and motor tasks in college samples. *Archives of Clinical Neuropsychology, 12,* 231–238.

Kanaya, T., Scullin, M. H., & Ceci, S. J. (2003). The Flynn effect and U.S. policies: The impact of rising IQ scores on American society via mental retardation diagnoses. *American Psychologist, 58,* 778–790.

Kier, F. J., & Molinari, V. (2004). Do-it-yourself testing for mental illness: Ethical issues, concerns, and recommendations. *Professional Psychology: Research and Practice, 35,* 261–267.

Knapp, S., & VandeCreek, L. (2003). *A guide to the revision of the 2002 American Psychological Association's ethics code.* Sarasota, FL: Professional Resource Press.

Matarazzo, J. D. (1990). Psychological assessment versus psychological testing: Validation from the school, clinic, and courtroom. *American Psychologist, 45,* 999–1017.

Melchert, T. P., & Patterson, M. M. (1999). Duty to warn and interventions with HIV-positive clients. *Professional Psychology: Research and Practice, 30,* 180–186.

Naglieri, J. A., Drasgow, F., Schmit, M., Handler, L., Prifitera, A., Margolis, A., et al. (2004). Psychological testing on the Internet. *American Psychologist, 59,* 150–162.

Pomerantz, A. M., & Handelsman, M. M. (2004). Informed consent revisited: An updated written question format. *Professional Psychology: Research and Practice, 35,* 201–205.

Ragusea, S. A. (2002). A professional living will for psychologists and other mental health professionals. In L. VandeCreek & T. L. Jackson (Eds.), *Innovations in clinical practice: A source book* (Vol. 20, pp. 301–305). Sarasota, FL: Professional Resource Press.

Rogers, R., & Bender, S. (2003). Evaluation of malingering and deception. In A. M. Goldstein & I. B. Weiner (Eds.), *Handbook of psychology: Forensic psychology* (pp. 109–129). New York: John Wiley & Sons.

Ruiz, M. A., Drake, E. B., Glass, A., Marcotte, D., & van Gorp, W. G. (2002). Trying to beat the system: Misuse of the Internet to assist in avoiding the detection of psychological symptom dissimulation. *Professional Psychology: Research and Practice, 33,* 294–299.

Smith, D. (2003). What you need to know about the new code: The chair of APA's Ethics Code Task Force highlights changes to the 2002 ethics code. *Monitor on Psychology, 34,* 62. Available from the APA Web site: http://www.apa.org/monitor/jan03/newcode.html

Suhr, J. A., & Gunstad, J. (2000). The effects of coaching on the sensitivity and specificity of malingering measures. *Archives of Clinical Neuropsychology, 15,* 415–424.

Tarasoff v. Regents of the University of California, 17 Cal. 3d 425, 551 P.2d 334 (1976).

Taylor, C. B., & Luce, K. H. (2003). Computer- and Internet-based psychotherapy interventions. *Current Directions in Psychological Science, 12,* 18–22.

U.S. Department of Health and Human Services. (2002, August 14). Standards for the privacy of individually identifiable health information: Final rule. *Federal Register, 67,* 53181–53273.

Vallabhajosula, B., & Van Gorp, W. G. (2001). Post-Daubert admissibility of scientific evidence on malingering of cognitive deficits. *Journal of the American Academy of Psychiatry and Law, 29,* 207–215.

Victor, T. L., & Abeles, N. (2004). Coaching clients to take psychological and neuropsychological tests: A clash of ethical obligations. *Professional Psychology: Research and Practice, 35,* 373–379.

Wetter, M. W., & Corrigan, S. K. (1995). Providing information to clients about psychological tests: A survey of attorneys' and law students' attitudes. *Professional Psychology: Research and Practice, 26,* 474–477.

Yañez, T., & Fremouw, W. J. (2004). The application of the Daubert standard to parental capacity measures. *American Journal of Forensic Psychology, 22,* 1–24.

Youngjohn, J. R., Lees-Haley, P. R., & Binder, L. M. (1999). Comment: Warning malingerers produces more sophisticated malingering. *Archives of Clinical Neuropsychology, 14,* 511–515.

# 24

# BEHAVIORAL ASSESSMENT
# OF WORK-RELATED ISSUES

DEREK R. HOPKO

*Department of Psychology*
*University of Tennessee, Knoxville, Tennessee*

SANDRA D. HOPKO

*Cariten Assist Employee Assistance Program*
*Knoxville, Tennessee*

C. W. LEJUEZ

*Department of Psychology*
*University of Maryland, College Park, Maryland*

## INTRODUCTION

Recent years have seen increased awareness and research into the multitude of factors that may interfere with one's ability to function effectively and efficiently in the workplace. These factors include emotional and behavioral problems, such as anxiety, depression, and substance abuse; job burnout; sexual harassment; workplace violence and aggression; employment uncertainty; and interpersonal conflict in the context of both the home and work environments (Kahn & Langlieb, 2003). In fact, estimates from two large-scale research surveys indicate that approximately 25% of the workforce experiences a mental disorder annually, with individuals between the ages of 18 and 24 (37% 12-month prevalence) being particularly vulnerable (National Comorbidity Survey, 1992; National Mortality Followback Survey, 1993). Other risk factors include employment in blue-collar occupations (i.e., service, operator, laborer), being female (with the exception of alcohol abuse/dependence and Bipolar Disorder), and being Caucasian or Hispanic (12-month prevalence: 24% vs. 20% of African Americans). The repercussions of mental health issues are staggering, affecting organizational commitment, employee absenteeism, work productivity, and job satisfaction, all of which factor into increased economic burden. Indeed, it is estimated that over 35 million workdays per year are lost among people with psychological problems (with major depression being most significant), resulting in economic losses of over $17 billion per year.

Accordingly, and with consideration for the fact that roughly 66% of employees with a mental health condition have never received psychological or pharmacological treatment for their problem(s) (National Comorbidity Survey, 1992), the importance of early problem identification and the development and implementation of reliable, valid, cost-effective, and efficient workplace assessment strategies has been highlighted as a pressing need (Hopko & Hopko, 2003; Pflanz & Heidel, 2003). It is assumed that utilization of such methods will facilitate primary prevention strategies, timely intervention, and potentially more accurate employee-treatment matching (Nielsen, Nielsen, & Wraae, 1998; Thornton, Gottheil, Weinstein, & Kerachsky, 1998). Behavioral assessment strategies may be ideal for these purposes, given the emphasis on time-efficient, psychometrically sound, and environmentally based methodologies as a means toward problem identification and resolution (Bellack & Hersen, 1988; Nelson & Hayes, 1979, 1986). In accordance with this premise, the objectives of the present chapter are to briefly summarize the nature and strategies of behavioral assessment, review the current status of workplace job skill assessment and the relationship of mental health problems with job attainment and sustained employment, review the prevalence and correlates of primary work-related emotional and behavioral problems, discuss the internal (e.g., employee assistance programs, I/O psychologists) and external (e.g., private practice, primary care) mechanisms through which behavioral assessment strategies may be implemented, present special considerations and practical issues of relevance to workplace assessment, and conclude with a case study that exemplifies a multimethod approach to the behavioral assessment of work-related issues.

## ASSESSMENT STRATEGIES

Behavioral assessment refers to the principles and procedures based on an ideographic, situational, empirical, and functional approach to human behavior. Grounded in these philosophical underpinnings, behavioral assessment strategies generally are designed to explicate the stimuli, organismic variables, behavioral responses (physiological, cognitive, and motoric), and consequences associated with problematic behaviors that require therapeutic intervention (Goldfried & Sprafkin, 1976). Numerous behavioral assessment strategies have been developed to accommodate these needs, and they generally may be characterized under the methods of unstructured or structured interviews, self-report measures, observational methods, and functional analysis (Thorpe & Olson, 1997). Although many resources theoretically are available, the appropriateness, required level of training, and clinical utility vary greatly across patients and assessment contexts (Alexopoulos et al., 2002; Bellack & Hersen, 1988; Cone, 1977). Before discussing assessment strategies specifically in the context of work-related issues and the occupational setting, this section briefly describes the primary methods of behavioral assessment.

## UNSTRUCTURED AND STRUCTURED INTERVIEWS

The structure of clinical interviews has tremendous variability, ranging from primarily unstructured and completely flexible approaches, to a semistructured approach that provides moderate direction and flexibility (e.g., intake form, Brief Psychiatric Rating Scale; Overall & Gorham, 1962), to structured methods that are more restrictive and goal directed. Largely due to concerns regarding the reliability and validity of unstructured interviews and efforts by managed care organizations to improve the efficiency and cost-effectiveness of assessment and treatment as well as the accountability of clinicians, increased focus has been placed on examining the utility of more structured procedures toward accomplishing these goals (cf. Groth-Marnat, 1997). Although typically not utilized in workplace settings, it is conceivable that structured interviews may prove valuable as an assessment strategy. For example, structured interviews may reduce gender biases among job applicants (Bragger, Kutcher, Morgan, & Firth, 2002), may prove useful in the screening of potential job candidates (Varela, Scogin, & Vipperman, 1999), generally are perceived as equitable by prospective employees (Lowry, 1994), and ultimately may be superior to more traditional, unstructured interviewing strategies (Wright, Lichtenfels, & Pursell, 1989).

## SELF-REPORT MEASURES

Self-report measures generally are designed to assess psychological or psychiatric symptoms, general health status and role functioning, quality of life, and service satisfaction (Maruish, 1999). These measures may be useful as screening instruments, as auxiliaries in the diagnostic process, as tools for monitoring incremental progress during treatment, and as outcome measures in assessing the efficacy and effectiveness of psychosocial and pharmacological interventions. Hundreds of scales have been designed to assess a tremendous range of content areas, including affective, verbal-cognitive, somatic, behavioral, and social symptoms of various clinical syndromes and psychosocial problems. In the context of the workplace environment and employee assessment, evidence is increasing of the utilization of self-report measures to assess mental health symptoms, job stress, interpersonal conflict, organizational constraints, employee workload, and work attitudes and job satisfaction (Harrison & McLaughlin, 1993; Kimball, Shumway, Korinek, & Arredondo, 2002; Spector & Jex, 1998; Spector, 2003; Stanton et al., 2002).

## OBSERVATIONAL METHODS

Observational assessment methods are used to describe and measure the qualitative properties as well as the frequency and duration of observable (overt motor) behaviors. Considering that direct assessment strategies intuitively should be a primary tool of behavioral therapists, compared to the rapid development of self-report and personality instruments and the increasing research base exploring structured assessment methods, remarkably minimal work has been done to expand the pioneering research of the 1970s and early '80s (Kanfer & Grimm, 1977). Although (formalized) direct observation strategies periodically have been used in workplace and home environments to evaluate variables such as job performance, adaptation to organizational change, and the impact of evening work on child behavior (Borman & Hallam, 1991; Heymann & Earle, 2001; Hoff, 2003), these methods generally are a greatly underutilized resource for assessing work-related issues.

## FUNCTIONAL ANALYSIS

Functional analysis generally refers to the process of identifying important, controllable, and causal environmental factors that may be related to the etiology and maintenance of problematic behaviors (Haynes & O'Brien, 1990). Rooted in behavioral theory, functional analysis is a strategy fundamental to initiating an appropriate behavioral intervention and may involve interviews with the patient and significant others, naturalistic observation, and/or the manipulation of specific situations that result in an increase or decrease of target behaviors (O'Neill, Horner, Albin, Storey, & Sprague, 1990). Often incorporating some form of daily monitoring, individuals may be asked to record problematic (target) behaviors, the context (time, place, surroundings) in which they occur, and the consequences that ensue. Strategies also may include the use of thought-monitoring logs or various thought-sampling methods (Csikszentmihalyi & Larson, 1987; Hurlburt, 1997). With all functional analytic strategies, the therapist works to identify the function (or maintaining reinforcers) of problematic behavior. Although functional analytic strategies may be quite useful in generating specific treatment goals and as a method of intervention, because the practice of conducting functional analyses requires extensive training, skill, and is based on complex causal behavioral models, the literature suggests that functional analyses are only infrequently conducted (Haynes, 1998; Haynes & O'Brien), with extremely rare implementation in workplace assessment (Gauthier, 2003; Horner, 1994).

## WORKPLACE JOB SKILL ASSESSMENT

Workplace job skill assessment often incorporates the aforementioned approaches and is a process by which job applicants are evaluated with regard to their suitability for the idiosyncratic demands of a given occupation. Largely based on the industrial/organizational literature, job skill assessment typically is conducted following a thorough job analysis, whereby the predominant skills, duties, and responsibilities of a job systematically are outlined (Brannick & Levine, 2002), potentially via incorporation of instruments such as the Position Analysis Questionnaire (McCormick, Jeanneret, & Meachem, 1969). Following the job analysis, many assessment strategies may be used to determine the most appropriate applicant to fulfill organizational needs. Among these strategies is the most common procedure of unstructured job interviews, a method of high utility when caution is taken to ensure equality across applicants with regard to question selection and presentation as well as sensitivity to individual differences and efforts to ensure equal opportunity. As an alternative assessment method, structured job interviews successfully have been used to minimize interviewer biases and more objectively rate job candidates (Ellis, West, Ryan, & DeShon, 2002). A more comprehensive, albeit time-intensive and expensive, process that may be used to supplement these interviewing strategies uses an *assessment center*, which generally involves the administration of tests and activities to a small number of applicants over a two- or three-day period (Lance, Foster, Gentry, & Thoresen, 2004). During this assessment phase, applicants may undergo unstructured and/or structured interviews, standardized tests, tests of cognitive ability, personality inventories, and potentially a work sample test. The work sample test is analogous to a direct observational assessment, whereby prospective employees are required to perform a sample of the duties they might be expected to perform while employed. In using these assessment strategies, job applicants' strengths and potential weaknesses are evaluated, with the end result being the selection of an employee perceived as most apt to perform job functions.

One of the factors that may dramatically impact job interview performance and the ability to acquire and maintain gainful employment is the experience of mental illness and associated interpersonal and behavioral problems (Cutler, 2004; Honey, 2003). Importantly, as indicated in the Americans with Disability Act (1990), the U.S. Equal Employment Opportunity Commission "prohibits private employers, state and local governments, employment agencies, and labor unions from discriminating against qualified individuals with disabilities in job application procedures, hiring, firing, advancement, compensation, job training, and other terms, conditions, and privileges of employment." Under this act, disability includes individuals who presently and/or historically have had mental health impairment that substantially limits one or more major life activities. As such, assuming individuals with mental illness can perform the essential functions of the job, nondiscriminatory consideration must be given toward hiring these individuals, a consequence of which involves the provision of assessment and treatment resources to assist employees in better understanding and coping with existing emotional and behavioral problems. Given the prevalence and impact of mental health problems in the workplace, along with the need to more efficiently assess, refer, and treat individuals who experience these problems, the remainder of the chapter discusses the behavioral assessment of primary emotional and behavioral problems in the workplace as well as mechanisms by which assessment strategies may be implemented.

## PRIMARY MENTAL HEALTH PROBLEMS AND WORK-RELATED ISSUES

### SUBSTANCE ABUSE AND DEPENDENCE

Alcohol abuse/dependence and clinical depression are the most prevalent psychiatric disorders in the workplace. Estimates suggest that up to 9% of the workforce may be diagnosable with alcohol abuse or dependence, with prevalence rates being higher among males (13%) than females (5%; Chima, 1995; National Comorbidity Survey, 1992). Although less common, drug abuse and dependence also affects a substantial number of American employees (3%). Perhaps even more troubling, the negative occupational, social, and physical consequences of substance disorders are compounded when you consider the frequency of other mental disorders and associated behavioral problems that often coexist with substance abuse (Mueser, Bennett, & Kushner, 1995). In addition to being male and experiencing comorbid psychiatric problems, other risk factors linked with substance disorders include occupation type, age, and perceptions of organizational wellness. For example, blue-collar workers are twice as likely as white-collar workers to have a significant alcohol problem, and male employees between the ages of 18 and 24 seem particularly vulnerable (24%; National Comorbidity Survey). Those employees who perceive their work environment to be less healthy and supportive also report considerably more alcohol-related problems (Bennett & Lehman, 1997). Importantly, even though the societal significance of substance disorders is highlighted in the form of increased absenteeism, decreased work productivity, and economic impact (second only to depression, with roughly $8.6 billion a year associated with absenteeism and lost productivity), alcohol-related disorders are the most highly unrecognized disorder in the workplace (74%; National Comorbidity Survey).

Considering the comorbidity of substance disorders with other mental illnesses, economic costs, underrecognition, and the substantial impact of substance-related disorders on occupational and social functioning, development and implementation of reliable and valid assessment strategies are essential for diminishing the magnitude of the problem. However, it also is true that many employees with substance disorders deny the existence of a problem, are fearful of the consequences of seeking out assessment and treatment resources that include employee assistance programs (EAPs), and lack the sufficient coping strategies to defend against work-life stressors (Browne, 1988). Behaviorally oriented mental health practitioners in a number of settings that include EAPs and private practice have many resources to increase employee and employer awareness, identify individuals in need of mental health treatment, decrease the fear and stigma associated with reporting substance problems, and provide the intervention components necessary to minimize the personal and organizational consequences of substance abuse. As a means to this end, behavioral assessment strategies may be quite valuable and have been nicely articulated in the extant literature, particularly as they pertain to alcohol-related disorders (Foy, Rychtarik, & Prue, 1988; L. C. Sobell, Breslin, & Sobell, 1997; L. C. Sobell, Sobell, & Nirenberg, 1988; L. C. Sobell, Toneatto, & Sobell, 1994).

A number of clinical interviewing strategies are utilized in assessing for substance abuse and dependence, all of which generally are based on criteria forwarded by the American Psychiatric Association (APA), World Health Organization (WHO), and the National Council on Alcoholism (NCA). These strategies vary greatly and may range from open-ended clinical interviews, diagnostic interviews such as the *Structured Clinical Interview for DSM-IV—Patient Version* (SCID-I/P; First, Spitzer, Gibbon, & Williams, 1996), to motivational interviewing strategies that primarily may be associated with the intervention process but also may be useful in providing valuable assessment information (W. R. Miller & Rollnick, 2002). These interviewing methods may be supplemented with data obtained through self-report instruments and self-monitoring exercises as well as more extensive personality inventories. Among the more commonly used and psychometrically strong self-report measures are the *Michigan Alcoholism Screening Test* (MAST; Selzer, 1971), *Drug Abuse Screening Test* (DAST; Skinner, 1982), *Lifetime Drinking History* (LDH; Skinner & Sheu, 1982), *timeline follow-back* (L. C. Sobell & Sobell, 1992), *Inventory of Drinking Situations* (IDS; Annis, 1982a), and both the brief and longer versions of the *Situational Confidence Questionnaire* (BSCQ; Breslin, Sobell, Sobell, & Agrawal, 2000; SCQ; Annis, 1982b). Personality inventories such as the *MMPI-2* (Butcher, Dahlstrom, Graham, Tellegen, & Kaemmer, 1989) and the *Personality Assessment Inventory* (PAI; Morey, 1991) also may be useful in assessing substance-related and other mental health problems.

Direct behavioral observations also have proven useful in assessing for substance disorders, including drink topography assessment in the natural environment and operant conditioning tasks. For example, it consistently has been demonstrated that compared with nonalcoholics, alcoholics consume more liquor, prefer straight drinks, and consume larger amounts per sip of alcohol (cf. Foy et al., 1988). Similar results have been obtained in the laboratory, where the *taste-testing task* has revealed that when alcoholic and nonalcoholic subjects are asked to compare alcoholic (and alcohol-free) beverages on various taste dimensions, the former group reliably consumes more alcohol and tastes a disproportionately greater number of alcoholic beverages (cf. L. C. Sobell et al., 1988, 1994). Operant laboratory tasks further indicate that alcoholics differ from social drinkers, in that they will work harder (e.g., on lever-pressing tasks) to obtain alcohol (Mello & Mendelson, 1971). While it is not necessarily practical to observe an employee's drinking behavior directly, employee health programs often utilize alternative but direct assessment strategies of substance intake that might involve biochemical measures, such as breath alcohol tests, urine samples, and liver function tests (cf. Foy et al., 1988; L. C. Sobell et al., 1988, 1994). Although the practicality of these strategies also might be questioned (e.g., time, costs) and there are certain limitations with regard to reliability and (external) validity indices of these strategies (L. C. Sobell et al., 1994), if these data were available they could reasonably be interpreted in the context of other available information to more accurately depict the significance of substance-related problems.

A final strategy in assessing for substance disorders involves functional assessment, long since considered a hallmark of the behavioral analysis of problematic behaviors and particularly useful in evaluating alcohol-related problems (M. B. Sobell, Sobell, & Sheahan, 1976; L. C. Sobell et al., 1994). In general, the functional analysis of substance-related behaviors is largely based on the SORC method of conceptualizing human behavior (Goldfried & Sprafkin, 1976; Kanfer & Grimm, 1977). Applied to substance use, this paradigm proposes that environmental *stimuli* present prior to substance use tend to elicit cognitive, affective, and physiological *organismic* reactions. The substance ingestion *response* follows and is maintained by a variety of positive *consequences*. Utilization of this model in a workplace setting (e.g., asking the employee to document the antecedents and consequences every time there is an urge to drink or drinking behavior) may be useful in identifying etiological and maintaining factors associated with substance abuse, which may include a number of contextual, affective, cognitive, familial, and other interpersonal variables.

## DEPRESSION

Prevalence of major depression in the workforce is approximately 9%, with women reporting depression (11%) at a higher rate than men (6%; National Comorbidity Survey, 1992). Among employees seeking mental health services, as many as 55–75% report significant problems with depression and anxiety (Fenrich, 2001; Poverny & Dodd, 2000). Mental health symptoms and work functioning are inversely related, and it is clear that increased depressive symptomology is associated with absenteeism, increased health care costs, decreased job performance, and slower return to work following medical procedures and the experience of significant physical problems (Fifield, Reisine, & Grady, 1991; Martin, Blum, Beach, & Roman, 1996; Soederman, Lisspers, & Sundin, 2003; Stewart, Ricci, Chee, Hahn, & Morganstein, 2003). It also is evident that increased job stress (as defined by high psychological demands), perceptions of increased workload, and decreased control or low decision authority are associated with a greater prevalence of depressive symptoms (Brief, Rude, & Rabinowitz, 1983; Griffin, Fuhrer, Stansfield, & Marmot, 2002; Mausner-Dorsch & Eaton, 2000). Some interesting gender differences also are apparent in the literature, with depression more strongly related to psychological demands and perceived equity in the performance of paid work for men, as opposed to increased physical demands and perceived equity in the performance of housework for women (Glass & Fujimoto, 1994; Wang & Patten, 2001). Although depression and decreased job performance appear intricately related, the positive news is that depressed individuals who receive psychiatric intervention appear to benefit substantially, as ascertained via decreased absenteeism, increased productivity and job satisfaction, and lower health care costs (Mintz, Mintz, Arruda, & Hwang, 1992; Simon et al., 2000, 2002). Given the potential benefits of psychiatric intervention for employees with clinical depression, behavioral assessment strategies may be useful in identifying those individuals most in need of these services.

A number of options are available to assess for symptoms of depression (Hopko, Lejuez, Armento, & Bare, in press; Rehm, 1988). Among the structured interviewing strategies with adequate-to-strong psychometric properties are the *SCID-I/P* (First et al., 1996), *Anxiety Disorders Interview Schedule* (ADIS-IV; Brown, DiNardo, & Barlow, 1994), *Schedule for Affective Disorders and Schizophrenia* (SADS; Endicott & Spitzer, 1978), and the *Hamilton Rating Scale for Depression* (HRSD; Hamilton, 1960). Self-report measures of depression also have proven useful as screening instruments, auxiliaries in the diagnostic process, as well as tools for monitoring treatment progress and outcome. Scales have been designed to assess a broad range of content areas, including affective, verbal-cognitive, somatic, behavioral, and social symptoms of depression. Among the most common self-report instruments are the *Beck Depression Inventories* (BDI; Beck & Steer, 1987; BDI-II; Beck, Steer, & Brown, 1996), *Center for Epidemiological Studies of Depression Scale* (CES-D; Radloff, 1977), *Harvard Department of Psychiatry/National Depression Screening Day Scale* (HANDS; Baer et al., 2000), and the *MMPI-2-D* (Butcher et al., 1989). Behavioral-monitoring logs or diaries also may be useful in assessing daily activities and sources of reinforcement, deficiencies in which may be associated with depressogenic symptoms (Hopko, Armento, Chambers, Cantu, & Lejuez, 2003; MacPhillamy & Lewinsohn, 1971). The majority of these self-report measures also have adequate-to-excellent psychometric properties (see Nezu, Ronan, Meadows, & McClure, 2000, for a comprehensive review).

Observational methods of assessing depressive symptoms may be used to measure the frequency and duration of observable (overt-motor) behaviors. In accordance with the Kanfer and Grimm (1977) model, depressed behaviors may include *excesses*, such as crying, irritable/agitated behaviors, and even suicidal behaviors, or *deficits*, such as minimal eye contact, psychomotor retardation, decreased recreational and occupational activities, as well as disruption in sleep, eating, and sexual behaviors (Kanfer & Grimm; Rehm, 1988). Pertaining to verbal behavior, several studies have demonstrated that depressed individuals exhibit a slowed and monotonous speech rate (Gotlib & Robinson, 1982; Libet & Lewinsohn, 1973; Robinson & Lewinsohn, 1973), take longer to respond to verbal behaviors of others (Libet & Lewinsohn), and exhibit an increased frequency of self-focused negative remarks (Blumberg & Hokanson, 1983; Gotlib

& Robinson). Nonverbal (motoric) differences between depressed and nonde-pressed individuals also are evident, in that depressed individuals smile less frequently (Gotlib & Robinson), make less eye contact (Gotlib, 1982; Ranelli & Miller, 1981), and are rated as less competent in social situations (Dykman, Horowitz, Abramson, & Usher, 1991).

In the context of depression, functional analysis involves assessing maintain-ing variables for undesirable (nonhealthy) depressive behavior(s), such as lethargy, social withdrawal, crying, alcohol abuse, and suicidality. Often incor-porating some form of daily monitoring, depressed patients may be asked to record depressive (target) behaviors, the context (time, place, surroundings) in which they occur, and the consequences that follow. Functional analytic tech-niques also may be useful for understanding maladaptive thought processes that cognitively oriented therapists believe to be a critical feature in eliciting depres-sive affect (Beck, Shaw, Rush, & Emery, 1979). For example, through strate-gies that include thought-monitoring logs or thought-sampling methods (Csikszentmihalyi & Larson, 1987; Hurlburt, 1997), functional analytic strategies can identify specific thought patterns elicited by certain environmental events and how these cognitions may correspond with depressive mood states. These same methods also may be utilized to assess change during and following therapeutic strategies that focus on challenging and restructuring the maladaptive or irrational cognitions. Although pretreatment functional analyses are only infrequently con-ducted among depressed patients (cf. Haynes & O'Brien, 1990), more traditional (Ferster, 1973; Lewinsohn, 1974) and contemporary behavioral theories and interventions for depression (Lejuez, Hopko, & Hopko, 2003; Martell, Addis, & Jacobson, 2001; McCullough, 2000), as well as treatments for other psychiatric conditions to a greater or lesser degree incorporate functional analytic techniques (Hopko & Hopko, 1999; Linehan, 1993).

## ANXIETY DISORDERS

Approximately 25% of Americans experience an anxiety disorder during their lifetime (Kessler et al., 1994), and roughly 56% of these individuals also can be expected to experience a comorbid depressive disorder (Mineka, Watson, & Clark, 1998). Within the workforce, 12-month prevalence rates range from 2% (Panic Disorder) to 7% (Social Phobia), with the former disorder associated with significant decreases in annual income and the latter anxiety disorder accounting for the most total days of lost productivity (National Comorbidity Survey, 1992). Anxiety disorders and coexistent symptoms have a significant negative impact on both the ability to obtain employment and workplace efficiency and produc-tivity. It has been demonstrated, for example, that individuals predisposed to develop anxiety or depression are significantly more likely to leave the labor force and, when these symptoms manifest, are about three to five times more likely to remain unemployed than individuals without mental illness (Sturm, Gresenz, Pacula, & Wells, 1999). Further, much like employees with a mood disorder, individuals who experience significant anxiety symptoms generally exhibit increased absenteeism, decreased work productivity and job satisfaction, interpersonal problems, and increased health problems (Dollard & Winefield, 1995; Hardy, Woods, & Wall, 2003; Lepine, 2002; Turnipseed, 1992). Although many environmental and biological factors may be associated with the etiology of anxiety symptoms, it is apparent that workplace factors such as role ambiguity, perceptions of workload and employer pressure, decreased control, and high-status jobs may play a major role (Caplan & Jones, 1975; Cherry, 1978; Griffin et al., 2002; Turnipseed).

The behavioral assessment of anxiety generally is conducted with reference to Lang's (1968) triple-response theory of emotion, which includes evaluation of cognitions, physiological responses, and observable behaviors. All three symptom clusters generally may be assessed via structured interviewing methods that include the *SCID-I/P* (First et al., 1996), *Anxiety Disorders Interview Schedule* (ADIS-IV; Brown et al., 1994), and the *Hamilton Rating Scale for Anxiety* (HRSA; Hamilton, 1959). In addition, several hundred self-report measures of anxiety and related constructs are available, many of which have very strong psychometric properties (Antony, Orsillo, & Roemer, 2001; Barlow, 2002). A few of these measures also are specific to work-based stress and the associated of work-related stress and familial conflict. These instruments include the *Work–Family Interface Scale, Interpersonal Conflict at Work Scale, Organizational Constraints Scale,* and the *Quantitative Workload Inventory* (Curbow, McDonnell, Spratt, Griffin, & Agnew, 2003; Spector, 2003). Administration of self-report measures also may be supplemented with other verbal report strategies, such as situational ratings and self-monitoring. The former method involves having patients subjectively report fear or anxiety intensity while the emotion is being elicited, perhaps through use of the *Subjective Units of Discomfort Scale* (SUDS; Wolpe & Lazarus, 1966). The latter technique requires that individuals observe and record behaviors and symptoms associated with an anxiety-eliciting situation, either through self-monitoring forms, daily thought records, or journals, a process that can provide valuable information in the context of functional assessment.

Behavioral observations of anxiety symptoms usually are conducted through behavioral avoidance or behavioral approach tests (BATs). These methods involve observation of behavior in the context of the feared object or event and may involve assessment on all three emotional domains. For example, individuals with agoraphobia may be asked to expose themselves to a naturalistic fear-inducing setting while their heart rate, SUDS ratings, and distance traveled may be recorded (Agras, Leitenberg, & Barlow, 1968). In addition to behavioral walks (e.g., for agoraphobic patients), other common BATs include driving, social encounters, and exposure to multiple objects or situations in which certain behaviors can be performed and measured (Craske, Barlow, & Meadows, 2000). Among the many advantages to incorporating such BATs in the assessment process are: (1) directly observing a patient's anxiety response system; (2) objective evaluation of avoidance and approach abilities and potentially more valid measurement of avoidance than self-report; and (3) identification of any safety behaviors that may be inhibiting exposure or the treatment process (Barlow, 2002). Finally, functional analytic strategies are a useful component of anxiety assessment, in that precise relationships may be highlighted among anxiety, avoidance, cognitions, and internal and external triggers, the identification of which may greatly facilitate positive treatment outcome (Emmelkamp, Bouman, & Scholing, 1992).

## INTERPERSONAL PROBLEMS: WORKPLACE AGGRESSION, EMPLOYEE CONFLICT, AND SEXUAL HARASSMENT

Problems in relationships may negatively affect the work environment and therefore are another important factor to consider when conducting an assessment of work-related issues. Examples of workplace interpersonal problems include employee conflict, workplace aggression, workplace violence, and sexual harassment. Employee conflict refers to tension between two or more employees that may affect the work performance of a small group or an entire department. Workplace aggression occurs when this tension escalates, which is defined as attempts by individuals to harm coworkers and/or their organization. The most extreme form of workplace aggression is workplace violence, which involves instances of direct physical assault (Neuman & Baron, 1998). Sexual harassment sometimes is considered a form of workplace violence and is defined by the Equal Employment Opportunity Commission (EEOC) as either *quid pro quo* harassment (job consequences such as hiring or promotion are made contingent on sexual cooperation) or as *hostile environment* (sexually related physical or verbal actions that are unwanted and offensive; EEOC, 1980).

Conflict among employees and aggressive behavior toward coworkers are the most common manifestations of interpersonal problems at work. Most often this tension and hostility occur between employees of equal rank within the organization rather than between employees and their supervisors or subordinates. Passive aggression is more frequent than active aggression and includes behaviors designed to obstruct coworkers' ability to do their job, prevent the company from meeting its goals, slow down work output, and waste resources. The most frequent type of overt aggressive behavior on the job is the expression of hostility via gestures, facial expressions, and verbal assaults (Neuman & Baron, 1998).

Incidence and prevalence of acts of workplace violence, especially those resulting in death, are the easiest to quantify. Workplace homicide is the fastest-growing category of murder in America and in 1993 was the second leading cause of death in the workplace and the leading cause of death for women (Neuman & Baron, 1998). According to national statistics, about 700 workplace homicides occur per year. These statistics are somewhat misleading, however, due to the fact that the majority of these homicides (80%) do not involve attacks from coworkers but rather are associated with robberies in high-risk occupations (Wilkinson, 2001). For example, the highest risk of occupational homicide is evident among taxicab drivers/chauffeurs, law enforcement officers, hotel clerks, gas station workers, security guards, stock handlers/baggers, store owners or managers, and bartenders (Neuman & Baron). Organizational and environmental factors that have been associated with workplace violence include unfair treatment, frustration-inducing events, increased workforce diversity, incongruence of needs/expectations and the organizational structure, and environmental conditions, such as extreme temperatures, high noise levels, and overcrowding (Neuman & Baron; Tobin, 2001). Acts of workplace violence cost American businesses approximately $4.2 billion annually in lost work time, employee medical benefits, and legal expenses (Mantell & Albrecht, 1994). Other "hidden" costs associated with physical and emotional consequences include disrupted sleep, cardiopulmonary problems, fatigue, hypertension, depression, family conflict, anger, and impaired coping (Hatch-Maillette & Scalora, 2002).

It is estimated that one of every two women will be subjected to some form of sexual harassment during her academic or working life. In one incidence study of female government employees, 33% reported experiencing repeated sexual remarks, 26% were victims of physical touching, 15% had been pressured for dates, and 10% had been pressured for sexual cooperation (Fitzgerald, 1993). Certain organizational characteristics are associated with an increased risk of sexual harassment. For example, sexual harassment takes place more frequently in companies where sex ratios are imbalanced, where there are high power differentials between male and female workers, where the workplace is highly sexualized, and where race-based or other forms of discrimination exist and in organizations in which harassment is never discussed, except as a topic of humor (Bell, Quick, & Cycyota, 2002). The impact of sexual harassment on the workplace includes tremendous financial costs, increased job turnover, lost productivity, damaged interpersonal relationships at work, decreased job satisfaction, and increased absenteeism (Hatch-Maillette & Scalora, 2002). Psychological consequences include anxiety, depression, headaches, sleep disturbances, gastrointestinal disorders, weight loss or gain, nausea, and sexual dysfunction (Fitzgerald).

Interviewing strategies to assess interpersonal problems in the workplace range from structured interviews that are part of a comprehensive evaluation (Buffone, 2001; Kausch & Resnick, 2001) to less formal approaches (Reddy, 1994). These interviews are conducted either proactively to prevent the development of problems or reactively after there has been an incident reported, most often the latter (Bell et al., 2002). If the problem involves conflict or tension among a group of employees, the services of a clinician (e.g., industrial/organizational psychologist) specializing in group appraisal methods may be sought out by the organization. This clinician generally conducts individual interviews with each of the employees in the department involved in the conflict to gather data about the functioning of the group, members' perceptions, areas of tension, major issues, goals, and interpersonal interactions. The next step involves providing feedback to the group with regard to the sources of tension and maintaining environmental contingencies. The third step in this process consists of problem-solving and team-building exercises, experiences that commonly include the development of occupational goals and objectives that employees can collabora-tively work toward (Lanza, 1985; Reddy, 1994; Munns, 1996).

For problems of workplace aggression and violence, interviewing strategies typically are focused on risk assessment. There are three types of risk assessment: preemployment screenings designed to avoid hiring problematic employees, fitness-for-duty evaluations to assess whether it is safe to return a high-risk employee to the job following a temporary suspension, and threat assessments designed to assess risk after an actual threat has been made (Fletcher, Brakel, & Cavanaugh, 2000). It has been suggested that certain key questions should be asked during a job interview to screen out employees with aggressive or violent tendencies. Examples of these questions include (Mantell & Albrecht, 1994): When have you felt that you were treated unfairly in your life? What did you do about it? What complaints have you had about your supervisors in the past? What has a supervisor done in the past to make you really angry? The clinician con-ducting a fitness-for-duty interview should be aware of research findings regard-ing particular warning signs that have been associated with perpetrators of workplace aggression and violence. However, there is a substantial gap in com-munication between researchers and clinicians on this issue, and clinicians do not always use the most accurate cues to make their evaluations (Hatch-Maillette & Scalora, 2002). The risk factors for dangerousness suggested by research include the following: discontent about perceived injustice at work, social isolation, poor self-esteem, fascination with military operations or guns, temper-control prob-lems, making threats, unstable family life (including childhood sexual or physi-cal abuse), complaints of heightened stress at work, being male and between the ages of 30 and 40, migratory job history, drug/alcohol abuse, and psychiatric impairment (Mantell & Albrecht; M. J. Miller, 2001; Douglas & Martinko, 2001). If an actual threat has been made, the interviewer should conduct a thorough threat assessment, including finding out exactly what was said, the tone of voice, facial expressions observed, context of the incident, and actions and reactions by observers (Wilkinson, 2001). The interviewer generally will also need to talk to the supervisor or human resources representative in addition to the employee to obtain accurate information regarding the incident.

For problems of sexual harassment, the interview is an important part of the investigative process after an accusation has been made. Both the accuser and the alleged perpetrator should be interviewed by human resources and possibly human rights legal and/or clinical consultants to obtain detailed information on the nature, severity, and frequency of the alleged harassment. The information gained from this interview process would then be used to determine whether harassment occurred and will assist in the decision-making process regarding disciplinary procedures (including termination) according to the company's sexual harassment policy (Schell, 2003).

Self-report instruments have been utilized in workplace settings to assess the type of conflict and the significance of particular issues among a group of employees. Some examples of instruments used in group assessment are: *Interpersonal Conflict Scale* (Nunns, Bluen, & King, 1989), *Team Orientation and Behavior Inventory, Myers–Briggs Type Indicator, Fundamental Interpersonal Relations Orientation—Behavior, Work Environment Scale, Group Environment Scale*, and *Group Styles Inventory* (for a review, see Reddy, 1994). Self-report instruments also are useful in providing feedback to companies on the prevalence of violent and sexual harassment behaviors (e.g., the *Violent Incident Form*; Arnetz, 1998; the *Sexual Experiences Questionnaire*; Fitzgerald, Gelfand & Drasgow, 1995). Preemployment screenings designed to identify employees with a propensity toward aggression or violence incorporate a variety of self-report instruments. These self-report measures range from traditional paper-and-pencil personality/ psychological tests to more specific personnel-selection batteries (e.g., *London House Personnel Selection Inventory, The Personnel Decisions Inc. Employment Inventory*, and the *Hogan Personnel Selection Series*; see Neuman & Baron, 1998). The incorporation of measurements of integrity (e.g., *Reid Report and Stanton Survey*), emotional intelligence (e.g., *Emotional Intelligence Questionnaire*), and problem-solving style (e.g., *Kirton Adaptation-Innovation Inventory* and the *Kolbe Index*) into the preemployment testing battery also may provide data on an employee's ability to manage interpersonal difficulties (see Hoffman, 2002).

Direct observation methods frequently are relied on during group assessments and team-building activities. The consultant continually observes interactions between various members of the group (in the natural setting or via videotape) and provides feedback on the progress being made and any problems that still need to be addressed. Particular areas for the observer to focus on include: who is conversing with whom and how frequently; who is considered to be of high or low influence or authority; issues regarding the general group climate and whether particular subgroups or cliques are being formed; issues of social support among employees and supervisors; what decision-making processes the group has adopted; and what norms have evolved around attendance, conflict, communication, gender, and race (Reddy, 1994). Direct observation as part of the preemployment screening is a useful strategy to aid in steering clear of perpetrators of aggression, violence, and sexual harassment. Ideally, a second interview with an applicant should be conducted in a different location from the first so that the potential employee can be observed interacting in different social situations. For example, a second interview done in a restaurant would provide an opportunity to observe how the applicant interacts with waiters and waitresses (Mantell & Albrecht, 1994). Gathering collateral information and background data, such as work history, military history, criminal records, credit reports, and driving records, also could be considered a form of behavioral observation (Neuman & Baron, 1998; Mantell & Albrecht).

Functional analysis of work-related interpersonal issues is not addressed specifically in the literature. However, there is some discussion of postincident analysis to review how incidents of violence and aggression were handled and how to prevent them in the future (Wilkinson, 2001). Clinicians trained in behavioral methods of assessment in general and who are comfortable performing functional analyses of other problems should find little difficulty generalizing this skill to work-related interpersonal issues. Some of the self-report instruments ask for information regarding the antecedents and consequences of an incident (e.g., the *Sexual Experiences Questionnaire—Specific Experience version*; Mazzeo, Bergman, Buchanan, Drasgow, & Fitzgerald, 2001) and thus might provide valuable information to the behavioral clinician performing the functional analysis.

## WORKAHOLISM AND JOB BURNOUT

The concept of workaholism often has been conceptualized within an addiction framework. It generally refers to a pattern of behavior that includes a strong drive toward work-related activities and perfectionism, engagement in work to reduce distress or guilt associated with not working, spending discretionary time in work activities, ruminations about work when not working, working beyond organizational or economic requirements, and deriving minimal pleasure from the work environment (Scott, Moore, & Miceli, 1997; Spence & Robbins, 1992). The work enthusiast, differing from the workaholic although highly involved in his or her work, generally does not experience the same degree of internal pressure, is more productive, and is much more satisfied with employment experiences (Bonebright, 2001; Spence & Robbins). The etiological factors associated with the development and maintenance of workaholism may be quite extensive, but it generally is hypothesized that behaviors of the workaholic may result from uncontrollable impulses and urges to engage in work activities (which may be a function of biological predispositions), a desire to escape personal issues outside of work, extreme desires to control one's environment, a highly competitive disposition, parental modeling of workaholic behaviors, and an impaired self-image and limited self-esteem (Seybold & Salomone, 1994). Approximately 25% of the workforce may be considered workaholic (Robinson, 1997), with males and females exhibiting comparable symptom patterns (Burke, 1999a). Many of these individuals experience significant problems with physical illness, anxiety, depression, substance abuse, and family and marital conflict (Bonebright, Clay, & Ankenmann, 2000; Burke, 1999a; Killinger, 1991; Robinson, Flowers, & Carroll, 2001). Adult children of workaholics also report increased depression, anxiety, an external locus of control, and a history of parentification (Carroll & Robinson, 2000; Robinson & Kelley, 1998).

Workaholism is strongly associated with the phenomenon of job burnout (Bonebright, 2000; Maslach, 1986). Originally proposed in the 1970s, the concept of job burnout has come to reflect a condition of emotional exhaustion, cynicism (depersonalization), and inefficacy (reduced personal accomplishment) that originates from experiences in the work environment and may over time characterize behavior and emotion external to the workplace (Maslach, 1982; Maslach, Schaufeli, & Leiter, 2001). Burnout is hypothesized to be a consequence of disproportional effort (time, emotional involvement, empathy), poor satisfaction (negative outcomes), and stressful and demanding working conditions, which ultimately may lead to the development of psychiatric problems that include clinical depression as well as decreased job performance, absenteeism, increased employee conflict, and negative health outcomes (Iacovides, Fountoulakis, Kaprinis, & Kaprinis, 2003; Maslach et al., 2001). A number of occupational and individual factors may increase the likelihood of experiencing job burnout. For example, increased workload, time pressure, role conflict with supervisors or coworkers, role ambiguity (i.e., ill-defined job responsibilities), and decreased social support are job characteristics consistently related to burnout (Maslach et al.). Although prevalence and process of burnout do not appear to differ between white- and blue-collar workers (Toppinen-Tanner, Kalimo, & Mutanen, 2002), occupations that require increased emotional commitment may account for significant variance in predicting burnout (Zapf, Seifert, Schmutte, Mertini, & Holz, 2001). Among the most pertinent individual factors related to burnout, younger age (under 30), being single, increased education (though potentially moderated with variables including occupation and status), and neuroticism (i.e., trait anxiety, depression, hostility, self-consciousness) have been implicated (Maslach et al. 2001). At this stage of research, neither gender nor ethnicity has been found to be a strong predictor of burnout.

Assessment of workaholism and job burnout has primarily involved self-report measures. In the workaholism area, the primary assessment measure has been the *Workaholism Battery*, which assesses three primary dimensions: work involvement, enjoyment, and drive (Spence & Robbins, 1992). Psychometric properties of the measure generally are strong across samples of varying demographic and occupational characteristics (Burke, 1999b, 2001; Burke, Richardsen, & Martinussen, 2002; Spence & Robbins). Although utilized less frequently, the *Work Addiction Risk Test* (WART; Robinson, 1999) also has been demonstrated to have adequate psychometric properties, with a recent discriminant validity study indicating that the total WART score correctly classified 86% of participants as being either a workaholic or a control participant (Flowers & Robinson, 2002). A brief new measure that assesses the dimensions of control in the work environment and tendencies to perform nonrequired work also may prove useful in workaholism assessment (Mudrack & Naughton, 2001). Although there are several self-report measures of job burnout (Shirom, 2003), the most widely used instrument is the *Maslach Burnout Inventory* (MBI-GS; Maslach, Jackson, & Leiter, 1996). The MBI-GS assesses burnout on the three dimensions of exhaustion, cynicism, and reduced professional efficacy and has been shown to have a reliable factor structure as well as strong reliability and validity indices across a variety of occupations and participant samples (Maslach et al., 2001). In addition to these self-report measures, considering the strong relations of workaholism, job burnout, anxiety, depression, substance abuse, and relevant contextual factors, which include the job environment, social support, and family dynamics, there is a clear need to further study the utility of existing observational assessment methods and functional analytic strategies as well as to develop more novel approaches toward identifying these work-related problems.

## MECHANISMS OF ASSESSING AND TREATING WORK-RELATED ISSUES

### INTERNAL MECHANISMS

Supervisors and coworkers usually are the first to recognize an employee's problematic behavior in the workplace. A pattern over time of decreased productivity, conflict with or withdrawal from coworkers, absenteeism, or increased errors often is indicative of a problem that may require mental health intervention. Depending on the company's policy, a supervisor may assess these problems via either informal strategies, such as direct observation and reviewing complaints from other coworkers or customers, or formal strategies, which include documenting work performance problems on a standardized observation checklist. Again depending on the particular company's written protocol, the next steps may include meeting with the employee face-to-face, making a contract for change, and reporting the issue to the human resources department. If the employee is unable to make improvements in job performance, he may be encouraged to seek the help of an employee assistance program (EAP) or an in-house psychologist.

EAPs, of increasing prominence in the workplace, originally were developed in the late 1930s as occupational alcohol programs designed to target employees with drinking problems. These early programs, influenced by the founding of Alcoholics Anonymous, consisted primarily of informal assessment and peer intervention. Over the years, it became evident that economic benefits were associated with the implementation of these programs, achieved through decreased absenteeism and increased productivity. At present, numerous EAPs that deal with a wide array of mental health issues have been established within large businesses and federal organizations (i.e., they have an *internal* EAP), and many smaller businesses also frequently contract for EAP services (i.e., they utilize an *external* EAP). While early EAPs generally functioned on an assessment and referral-based model (Van den Bergh, 2000), more contemporary EAPs have expanded their focus to encompass case management and intervention services that include ongoing assessment, crisis management, and critical incident stress debriefing, as well as brief psychotherapy (Oher, 1999; Summerall, Israel, Brewer, & Prew, 1999).

Among employees seeking EAP services, as many as 55–75% report significant problems with depression and anxiety (Fenrich, 2001; Poverny & Dodd, 2000) and approximately 40% report significant impairment associated with alcohol misuse (Thomas & Johnson, 1994). Perhaps more specific to the EAP environment as compared to conventional practice, clinicians also frequently address issues of job stress, organizational layoffs, and work addiction (Csiernik, Atkinson, Cooper, Devereux, & Young, 2001; Robinson, 1997; Worster, 2000). Employee Assistance Programs generally report great success in resolving mental health issues and their negative impact on job performance. Companies that utilize EAP services have a 75% reduction in inpatient substance abuse treatment costs and report 17% fewer accidents, 35% reduced turnover, 21% lower absenteeism, and 14% higher productivity (SAMSHA, 1995). Even when a referral is made to an outside resource, such as a private practice psychologist, employees that first have utilized an EAP are rated as better prepared for therapy, form better therapeutic relationships, and have better outcomes, regardless of the initial severity of the problem (Moore, Andreasen, & Nash, 2004).

Assessment strategies utilized by the majority of EAP clinicians, who generally are master's-level counselors or social workers, consist of demographic forms, informal interviews, conversations with supervisors and family members (with the employee's written consent), and occasionally self-report measurements, such as depression inventories or substance abuse screening instruments. However, more formalized and extensive assessment protocols have been implemented successfully by EAPs, for example, protocols designed to assist with identifying domestic violence (Falk, Shepard, & Elliott, 2002), substance abuse (Schneider, Casey, & Kohn, 2000), and crisis situations (Sussal & Ojakian, 1989).

Similar to an EAP, an in-house psychologist provides clinical and counseling services that include identifying and treating troubled employees as well as coordinating work adjustments appropriate to treatment needs, such as modifying an employee's schedule to accommodate outpatient therapy and assisting with reentry issues after an employee has been in an inpatient facility. In addition, an in-house psychologist can provide consultation to management, assist in making referrals, and interact with managed care organizations and can participate in organizational development (Broadbent, 1996; Feder, 1997).

## EXTERNAL MECHANISMS

In some cases workplace problems cannot be addressed internally. For example, in cases where there is not an EAP or an in-house psychologist or if the presenting problems are too severe, the company may seek assistance outside of the organization. In these situations the services of an industrial-organizational psychologist, a private practice psychologist, or other community agency may be utilized.

Industrial-organizational (I-O) psychologists have extensive training (graduate degree, internship) in workplace issues such as personnel selection, organizational development and change, and factors influencing individual, team, management, and business productivity (Thompson & Spector, 2003; Tharenou, 2001; Perrott, 1999). For example, the services of an I-O psychologist may be sought to assist companies in selecting candidates for various job openings (Hunter & Schmidt, 1983; Jackson & Schuler, 1990), to provide consultation regarding strategies to decrease organizational and occupational stress (Cooper, 1986), or to address more specific issues of employee health (Ilgen, 1990). Another common issue I-O psychologists are called on to assist with is that of employee conflict (Thompson & Spector). As described in the previous section on the assessment of interpersonal problems, the I-O psychologist will utilize a combination of individual and group appraisal methods to identify the source of conflict and work toward a resolution. Although a private practitioner generally will not have the specialized training of an I-O psychologist, with some training and experience he or she may assume some similar roles within an organization. These functions might include providing treatment for mental health problems, assessing employees' or job candidates' personality traits and abilities for employment or promotion, and organizational consulting (Lowman, 1982).

The I-O or other consulting practitioner will utilize a much more extensive and detailed assessment process than an EAP, due to the short-term nature of EAP services as well as the limits imposed by the licensure requirements of master's-level clinicians. The assessment battery performed by the I-O or clinical practitioner may include personality inventories, intelligence/aptitude testing, vocational preference measurements, assessment of emotional intelligence, projective tests, structured diagnostic interviews, and team appraisals (Lowman, 1982; Hoffman, 2002).

Other external resources commonly utilized by organizations for the assessment of workplace issues are inpatient psychiatric hospitals, alcohol and drug treatment facilities, and psychiatrists. Employees may be referred for assessment and treatment recommendations pertaining to severe mental illness, including suicidal/homicidal threats and/or substance abuse problems. Often employers will require a "fitness for duty" evaluation by one of these agencies before allowing employees to return to work. A common scenario is the employee that tests positive on a random or postaccident drug screen and is required by company policy to have an assessment with treatment recommendations before being released to return to work.

## SPECIAL CONSIDERATIONS

Internal and external mechanisms are not mutually exclusive. An employee initially seen at an EAP may be referred to a private practitioner for more specialized psychological testing. Conversely, an industrial-organizational or other consulting practitioner, in the process of doing a team assessment, may refer certain employees to the EAP for individual assessment and counseling. In these cases, fluid communication between all entities involved in the assessment process is particularly essential. Regardless of the mechanism (internal or external), the provider of the assessment services to an organization must always bear in mind the dual role of serving both the company as well as the individual employee (Shimmin, 1981). Issues of confidentiality should be addressed with the employer and the employee, and written permission should always be obtained before releasing any protected health information. Other considerations influencing the assessment process include the particular type of company, their organizational structure, and idiosyncratic employee characteristics and occupational requirements (Dallis, 1974). Prior to beginning the assessment process, the assessment provider should clarify the expectations of the company and develop a clear understanding of the characteristics and demands of the particular organization.

In addition to ethical concerns, which include issues of patient confidentiality, the nature and frequency of disclosures to employers and supervisors, and the potential involvement of multiple practitioners that might include internal and external service providers, an employee's emotional and behavioral problems should always be conceptualized, assessed, and treated with sensitivity to multiple contexts. For example, interpersonal problems and conflict within the workplace may be highly related to ongoing conflict in the home environment. Workaholic-type behaviors may serve an avoidance function, such that pressing problems in one's personal life are neglected and remain unresolved. Substance abuse behaviors may be triggered by a number of factors, which might include efforts to avoid unpleasant emotional states such as depression and anxiety, which in turn may be related to a number of situational antecedents that include negative employee-employer relations, poor job satisfaction, nonrewarding social relationships, and so forth.

Ultimately, emotional and behavioral problems that manifest in the workplace may be a product of underlying biological vulnerabilities and/or a complex system of situational factors and stressors that may be related to the work and/or home environments. As such, with recognition of the need for heightened ethical awareness, the necessity to evaluate behavioral problems in an ideographic and context-sensitive manner, and the importance of determining unique organizational characteristics that might be contributing to problematic behaviors, performing an effective and efficient workplace assessment can be quite challenging. Considering these factors, and given the extensive behavioral assessment strategies available and the potential information sources that may be utilized (employee, coworkers, employer, family, and significant others), care must be taken to ensure that an employee receives a comprehensive yet focused clinical assessment while simultaneously preserving the privacy of his/her information and rights afforded via the Americans with Disability Act (1990).

## CASE STUDY

John was a 24-year-old single Caucasian male with a twelfth-grade education. At the time of his intake evaluation he was a part-time student and full-time employee in a blue-collar company. Services offered by the company's EAP included education and training, workplace consulting, crisis intervention, assessment, short-term counseling, and referral for employees and their family members. The contract for this particular company allowed employees and their family members eight sessions of short-term counseling per person per year. John sought counseling on his own, so his attendance at the sessions was not reported to company management or human resources.

The primary methods of assessment utilized by the EAP therapist were an unstructured clinical interview, self-report measures, self-monitoring, and functional analysis. During the initial clinical interview, it became apparent that John was experiencing both anxiety and depressive symptoms. In particular, John was experiencing the following symptoms: feelings of hopelessness and worthlessness, fatigue, anhedonia, avolition, difficulty concentrating both at school and at work, panic attacks in social situations, persistent fear of having additional attacks, avoidance of social situations other than work or school, and chronic worry (8 hours per day) about his social performance. John was oriented on all spheres, with adequate grooming and hygiene. His mood was dysthymic, however, and psychomotor retardation was evident. John's thought process was logical and goal-directed, although his speech volume was low and his speech rate was slowed. There was no evidence of perceptual abnormalities. He was living with his girlfriend and her parents and had very limited social contact with anyone other than his girlfriend. Three events were proximal to the onset of these problems: (a) his father's passing away, (b) his mother's selling the house in which he was raised, and (c) a job transfer in which he had relocated from the midwest to a southwestern state. Prior to these events, John had experienced a depressed mood for approximately three years. Given these life stressors and the added demands of a more time-intensive job and part-time education, however, the severity of his negative mood increased substantially, prompting him to seek counseling services with the EAP. In addition to information obtained through the informal intake interview, John was administered the Beck Depression Inventory (BDI-II; Beck et al., 1996), Hamilton Rating Scale for Depression (HRSD; Hamilton, 1960), Beck Anxiety Inventory (BAI; Beck & Steer, 1993), and the Quality of Life Inventory (QOLI; Frisch, 1994). John scored a 38 on the BDI-II and a 36 on the HRSD, indicative of severe depression and consistent with interview data. The BAI indicated a moderate level of anxiety (20). On the QOLI, which assesses life satisfaction on various life domains (e.g., health, relationships, money), John scored in the "below average" range of life satisfaction (QOLI total = −3). An informal functional analysis revealed that avoidance of certain behaviors, which included calling his friends, engaging in social gatherings, and attending church services, was negatively reinforced via a reduction of anxiety associated with avoiding these activities. Avoidance of other behaviors, such as riding his bicycle, bowling, and studying, was more a consequence of depressive affect and avolition and less related to the anxiety-eliciting properties of these situations.

As part of the assessment process, John also was asked to complete a self-monitoring activity, in which he documented all activities and associated reward values over the course of one week (Hopko et al., 2003). This assignment was used to: (a) provide a baseline measurement by which to compare progress following treatment, (b) make John more cognizant of the quantity and quality of his activities, and (c) provide John with some ideas with regard to identifying potential activities to target during treatment. John also engaged in a monitoring exercise to encourage increased understanding of physiological, cognitive, and behavioral symptoms associated with his social anxiety. During this awareness training, John was educated about anxiety symptom domains with reference to personal experiences, increasing his insight and providing information that facilitated a functional analysis of his problematic symptoms. Results of these baseline measures were reviewed in the following session, revealing that John engaged in few activities other than working, sleeping, and spending time with his girlfriend. When queried about the reward (or reinforcement) value of such activities, John indicated that minimal pleasure was being experienced other than occasional satisfaction when interacting with his girlfriend. The anxiety awareness training exercise revealed reasonably high levels of discomfort over a range of social activities. In reviewing John's social experiences it became evident that elevated physiological responses and escape behavior largely were consequent to specific thoughts centered on feelings of inadequacy and perceptions that others had unrealistic expectations.

A brief behavioral activation treatment (BATD; Lejuez et al., 2003) was implemented, wherein John and the counselor worked together in establishing weekly goals arranged in a hierarchy according to their perceived difficulty. Behaviors targeted included social activities, such as calling friends and family or inviting friends to play golf; as well as studying, bowling, enrolling in an art class, and going mountain biking. John kept a weekly activity log of the duration and frequency of goals accomplished, and the counselor kept a master log of all activities as he progressed through the hierarchy. By the final session, John had accomplished all of his weekly behavioral goals for four consecutive weeks. In addition, brief cognitive therapy was implemented, whereby John could gain an increased understanding of his cognitive errors and maladaptive assumptions and work toward challenging these perceptions through behavioral experiments. Relaxation exercises also were incorporated into his weekly hierarchy, and imaginal exposure sessions were conducted to address his fears in social situations while incorporating relaxation and cognitive coping strategies. John's post-treatment BDI-II and HRSD scores indicated a decrease in depressive symptoms to a minimal and more tolerable level (BDI-II = 13; HRSD = 15), and the BAI indicated mild residual anxiety (score of 9). Quality of life also had improved, from $-3$ to $-1$. In addition, his verbal self-report revealed increased confidence in social situations, more energy and concentration at work and school, less time engaged in worrying, and increased feelings of self-esteem.

This case highlights the proactive role an employee assistance program can play in assessing and treating mental health issues prior to negative consequences, which might include increased absenteeism, decreased productivity, formal disciplinary measures on the job, and excessively high health care costs for the company. In addition, the utilization of behavioral assessment strategies, such as unstructured interviews, informal functional analysis, self-report instruments, and self-monitoring techniques, was presented as feasible within the EAP context. These strategies considered, we strongly advocate conducting a multimethod, ideographic assessment. However, we also acknowledge that the realities of clinical practice across settings often limit the feasibility of a comprehensive assessment approach. In the current case study, for example, utilization of a more structured interviewing strategy and administration of a personality measure such as the MMPI-2 or PAI may have provided additional information that might have proven useful in treatment planning. Accordingly, practitioners must evaluate potential restrictions and limitations (e.g., time, money, training, patient motivation) on a case-by-case basis and make a conscientious and well-informed decision on how well the available assessment options meet both the therapist's and the employee's goals and needs.

## SUMMARY

Data indicate that the one-year prevalence of psychiatric disorders in the workforce is approximately 25%, with a substantially larger number of employees exhibiting subclinical psychiatric symptoms or other behavioral problems nondiagnosable via current diagnostic nomenclature. Despite a significant number of internal and external assessment and treatment resources, only one-third of these individuals receive assistance for their emotional and behavioral problems. This situation is problematic, given the economic and social impact of work-related issues as well as the reciprocal relationship between work- and home-based problems. For example, family issues and the balancing of work and home life obligations contribute to worker stress (Zedeck & Mosier, 1990; Keita & Jones, 1990), and marital problems often spill over into the work environment, affecting job performance and sometimes contributing to workplace violence (Wilkinson, 2001). Given the multimethod approach and multicontext utility of behavioral assessment strategies, along with the need to conduct efficient and objective psychological assessments to meet the demands of a managed health care environment, behavior assessment may be an optimal means toward assessing work-related issues.

# REFERENCES

Agras, S., Leitenberg, H., & Barlow, D. H. (1968). Social reinforcement in the modification of agoraphobia. *Archives of General Psychiatry, 19,* 423–427.

Alexopoulos, G. S., Borson, S., Cuthbert, B. N., Devanand, D. P., Mulsant, B. H., Olin, J. T., et al. (2002). Assessment of late life depression. *Biological Psychiatry, 52,* 164–174.

Annis, H. M. (1982a). *Inventory of Drinking Situations (IDS-100).* Toronto, Ontario, Canada: Addiction Research Foundation.

Annis, H. M. (1982b). *Situational Confidence Questionnaire.* Toronto, Ontario, Canada: Addiction Research Foundation.

Antony, M. M., Orsillo, S. M., & Roemer, L. (2001). *Practitioner's guide to empirically based measures of anxiety.* New York: Kluwer.

Arnetz, J. E. (1998). The Violent Incident Form (VIF): A practical instrument for the registration of violent incidents in the health care workplace. *Work and Stress, 12,* 17–28.

Baer, L., Jacobs, D. G., Meszler-Reizes, J., Blais, M., Fava, M., Kessler, R., et al. (2000). Development of a brief screening instrument: The HANDS. *Psychotherapy and Psychosomatics, 69,* 35–41.

Barlow, D. H. (2002). *Anxiety and its disorders: The nature and treatment of anxiety and panic* (2nd ed.). New York: Guilford Press.

Beck, A. T., Shaw, B. J., Rush, A. J., & Emery, G. (1979). *Cognitive therapy of depression.* New York: Guilford Press.

Beck, A. T., & Steer, R. A. (1987). *Beck Depression Inventory: Manual.* San Antonio, TX: Psychological Corporation.

Beck, A. T., & Steer, R. A. (1993). *Beck Anxiety Inventory: Manual* (2nd ed.). San Antonio, TX: Psychological Corporation.

Beck, A. T., Steer, R. A., & Brown, G. K. (1996). *Manual for the BDI-II.* San Antonio, TX: Psychological Corporation.

Bell, M. P., Quick, J. C., & Cycyota, C. S. (2002). Assessment and prevention of sexual harassment of employees: An applied guide to creating healthy organizations. *International Journal of Selection and Assessment, 10,* 160–167.

Bellack, A. S., & Hersen, M. (1988). *Behavioral assessment: A practical handbook* (3rd ed.). New York: Pergamon Press.

Bennett, J. B., & Lehman, W. E. K. (1997). Employee views of organizational wellness and the EAP: Influence on substance abuse, drinking climates, and policy attitudes. *Employee Assistance Quarterly, 13,* 55–71.

Blumberg, S. R., & Hokanson, J. E. (1983). The effects of another person's response style on interpersonal behavior in depression. *Journal of Abnormal Psychology, 92,* 196–209.

Bonebright, C. A. (2001). *The Relationship of workaholism with stress, burnout, and productivity.* Unpublished doctoral dissertation. University of Iowa, Iowa City.

Bonebright, C. A., Clay, D. L., & Ankenmann, R. D. (2000). The relationship of workaholism with work-life conflict, life satisfaction, and purpose in life. *Journal of Counseling Psychology, 47,* 469–477.

Borman, W. C., & Hallam, G. L. (1991). Observation accuracy for assessors of work-sample performance: Consistency across task and individual difference correlates. *Journal of Applied Psychology, 76,* 11–18.

Bragger, J. D., Kutcher, E., Morgan, J., & Firth, P. (2002). The effects of the structured interview in reducing gender biases against pregnant job applicants. *Sex Roles, 46,* 215–226.

Brannick, M. T., & Levine, E. L. (2002). *Job analysis: Methods, research, and applications for human resource management in the new millennium.* Thousand Oaks, CA: Sage.

Breslin, F. C., Sobell, L. C., Sobell, M. B., & Agrawal, S. (2000). A comparison of a brief and long version of the Situational Confidence Questionnaire. *Behaviour Research and Therapy, 38,* 1211–1220.

Brief, A. P., Rude, D. E., & Rabinowitz, S. (1983). The impact of Type A behaviour pattern on subjective work load and depression. *Journal of Occupational Behavior, 4,* 157–164.

Broadbent, D. E. (1996). Counselling psychology in the workplace: Strategy or sticking plaster? *Counselling Psychology Quarterly, 9,* 37–45.

Brown, T. A., DiNardo, P. A., & Barlow, D. H. (1994). *The Anxiety Disorder Interview Schedule for DSM-IV.* Center for Stress and Anxiety Disorders. Albany: State University of New York.

Browne, A. C. (1988). Employee drug and alcohol use estimates: Assessment styles and issues. *Employee Assistance Quarterly, 3,* 265–278.

Buffone, G. W. (2001). Workplace violence: Assessment, prevention, and response. In T. L. Jackson & L. VendeCreek (Eds.), *Innovations in clinical practice: A source book, Vol. 19.* Sarasota, FL: Professional Resource Press/Professional Resource Exchange.

Burke, R. J. (1999a). Workaholism in organizations: Gender differences. *Sex Roles, 41,* 333–345.

Burke, R. J. (1999b). Workaholism in organizations: Measurement validation and replication. *International Journal of Stress Management, 6,* 45–55.

Burke, R. J. (2001). Predictors of workaholism components and behaviors. *International Journal of Stress Management, 8,* 113–127.

Burke, R. J., Richardsen, A. M., & Martinussen, M. (2002). Psychometric properties of Spence and Robbins' measures of workaholism components. *Psychological Reports, 91,* 1098–1104.

Butcher, J. N., Dahlstrom, W. G., Graham, J. R., Tellegen, A., & Kaemmer, B. (1989). *Minnesota Multiphasic Personality Inventory—2 (MMPI-2): Manual for administration and scoring.* Minneapolis: University of Minnesota Press.

Caplan, R. D., & Jones, K. W. (1975). Effects of workload, role ambiguity, and Type A personality on anxiety, depression, and heart rate. *Journal of Applied Psychology, 60,* 713–719.

Carroll, J. J., & Robinson, B. E. (2000). Depression and parentification among adults as related to paternal workaholism and alcoholism. *Family Journal Counseling and Therapy for Couples and Families, 8,* 360–367.

Cherry, N. (1978). Stress, anxiety, and work: A longitudinal study. *Journal of Occupational Psychology, 51,* 259–270.

Chima, F. O. (1995). EAP coordinators' perceptions of employees' problems pervasiveness. *Employee Assistance Quarterly, 11,* 71–80.

Cone, J. D. (1977). The relevance of reliability and validity for behavioral assessment. *Behavior Therapy, 8,* 411–426.

Cooper, C. L. (1986). Job distress: Recent research and the emerging role of the clinical occupational psychologist. *Bulletin of the British Psychological Society, 39,* 325–331.

Craske, M. G., Barlow, D. H., & Meadows, E. (2000). *Mastery of your anxiety and panic: Therapist guide for anxiety, panic, and agoraphobia (MAP-3).* San Antonio, TX: Graywind/Psychological Corporation.

Csiernik, R., Atkinson, B., Cooper, R., Devereux, J., & Young, M. (2001). An examination of a combined internal-external employee assistance program: The St. Joseph's Health Centre Employee Counselling Service. *Employee Assistance Quarterly, 16,* 37–48.

Csikszentmihalyi, M., & Larson, R. (1987). Validity and reliability of the experience sampling method. *Journal of Nervous and Mental Disease, 175,* 526–536.

Curbow, B., McDonnell, K., Spratt, K., Griffin, J., & Agnew, J. (2003). Development of the Work–Family Interface scale. *Early Childhood Research Quarterly, 18,* 310–330.

Cutler, D. L. (2004). A working life for people with severe mental illness. *Community Mental Health Journal, 40,* 276–277.

Dallis, C. A. (1974). Clients in business and industry. In N. R. Gamsky & G. F. Farwell (Eds.), *The counselor's handbook.* Oxford, England: Intext.

Dollard, M. F., & Winefield, A. H. (1995). Trait anxiety, work demand, social support and psychological distress in correctional officers. *Anxiety, Stress, and Coping: An International Journal, 8,* 25–35.

Douglas, S. C., & Martinko, M. J. (2001). Exploring the role of individual differences in the prediction of workplace aggression. *Journal of Applied Psychology, 86,* 547–559.

Dykman, B. M., Horowitz, I. M., Abramson, L. Y., & Usher, M. (1991). Schematic and situational determinants of depressed and nondepressed students' interpretation of feedback. *Journal of Abnormal Psychology, 100,* 45–55.

Ellis, A. P. J., West, B. J., Ryan, A. M., & DeShon, R. P. (2002). The use of impression management tactics in structured interviews: A function of question type? *Journal of Applied Psychology, 87,* 1200–1208.

Emmelkamp, P. M. G., Bouman, T. K., & Scholing, A. (1992). *Anxiety disorders: A practitioner's guide.* Oxford, England. John Wiley & Sons.

Endicott, J., & Spitzer, R. L. (1978). A diagnostic interview: The Schedule for Affective Disorders and Schizophrenia. *Archives of General Psychiatry, 35,* 837–844.

Equal Employment Opportunity Commission (EEOC) (1980). *Guidelines on Discrimination Because of Sex,* 29 C.F.R. 1604.11

Falk, D. R., Shepard, M. F., & Elliott, B. A. (2002). Evaluation of a domestic violence assessment protocol used by employee assistance counselors. *Employee Assistance Quarterly, 17,* 1–15.

Feder, J. (1997). Psychologists working for unions: Developing the United Federation of Teacher's Victim Support Program. *Professional Psychology: Research and Practice, 28,* 422–424.

Fenrich, E. W. (2001). *Impact of anxiety and depression of work-related problems and advancing intervention and prevention strategies for E.A.P.S.* Unpublished doctoral dissertation. The American University, Washington, D.C.

Ferster, C. B. (1973). A functional analysis of depression. *American Psychologist, 28,* 857–870.

Fifield, J., Reisine, S. T., & Grady, K. E. (1991). Work disability and the experience of pain and depression in rheumatoid arthritis. *Social Science and Medicine, 33,* 579–585.

First, M. B., Spitzer, R. L., Gibbon, M., & Williams, J. (1996). *Structured Clinical Interview for DSM-IV Axis I Disorders—Patient edition (SCID-I/P, Version 2.0).* New York: Biometrics Research Department, New York Psychiatric Institute.

Fitzgerald, L. F. (1993). Sexual harassment: Violence against women in the workplace. *American Psychologist, 48,* 1070–1076.

Fitzgerald, L. F., Gelfand, M. J., & Drasgow, F. (1995). Measuring sexual harassment: Theoretical and psychometric advances. *Basic and Applied Social Psychology, 17,* 425–445.

Fletcher, T. A., Brakel, S. J., & Cavanaugh, J. L. (2000). Violence in the workplace: New perspectives in forensic mental health services in the USA. *British Journal of Psychiatry, 176,* 339–344.

Flowers, C. P., & Robinson, B. (2002). A structural and discriminant analysis of the Work Addiction Risk Test. *Educational and Psychological Measurement, 62,* 517–526.

Foy, D. W., Rychtarik, R. G., & Prue, D. M. (1988). Assessment of appetitive disorders. In M. Hersen and A. S. Bellack (Eds.), *Behavioral assessment: A practical handbook* (2nd ed., pp. 456–483). New York: Pergamon Press.

Frisch, M. B. (1994). *Manual and treatment guide for the Quality of Life Inventory (QOLI).* Minneapolis, MN: National Computer Systems.

Gauthier, J. (2003). The use of knowledge from outside I/O psychology by I/O psychologists: A critique. *Canadian Psychology, 44,* 244–248.

Glass, J., & Fujimoto, T. (1994). Housework, paid work, and depression among husbands and wives. *Journal of Health and Social Behavior, 35,* 179–191.

Goldfried, M. R., & Sprafkin, J. N. (1976). Behavioral personality assessment. In J. T. Spence, R. C. Carson, & J. W. Thibaut (Eds.), *Behavioral approaches to therapy* (pp. 295–321). Morristown, NJ: General Learning Press.

Gotlib, I. H. (1982). Self-reinforcement and depression in interpersonal interaction: The role of performance level. *Journal of Abnormal Psychology, 91,* 3–13.

Gotlib, I. H., & Robinson, L. A. (1982). Responses to depressed individuals: Discrepancies between self-report and observer-rated behavior. *Journal of Abnormal Psychology, 91,* 231–240.

Griffin, J. M., Fuhrer, R., Stansfield, S. A., & Marmot, M. (2002). The importance of low control at work and home on depression and anxiety. Do these effects vary by gender and social class? *Social Science and Medicine, 54,* 783–798.

Groth-Marnat, G. (1997). *Handbook of psychological assessment* (3rd ed.). New York: John Wiley & Sons.

Hamilton, M. (1959). The assessment of anxiety states by rating. *British Journal of Medical Psychology, 32,* 50–55.

Hamilton, M. (1960). A rating scale for depression. *Journal of Neurology, Neurosurgery, and Psychiatry, 23,* 56–62.

Hardy, G. E., Woods, D., & Wall, T. D. (2003). The impact of psychological distress on absence from work. *Journal of Applied Psychology, 88,* 306–314.

Harrison, D. A., & McLaughlin, M. E. (1993). Cognitive processes in self-report responses: Tests of item context effects in work attitude measures. *Journal of Applied Psychology, 78,* 129–140.

Hatch-Maillette, M. A., & Scalora, M. J. (2002). Gender, sexual harassment, workplace violence, and risk assessment: Convergence around psychiatric staff's perceptions of personal safety. *Aggression and Violent Behavior, 7,* 271–291.

Haynes, S. N. (1998). The assessment-treatment relationship and functional analysis in behavior therapy. *European Journal of Psychological Assessment, 14,* 26–35.

Haynes, S. N., & O'Brien, W. H. (1990). Functional analysis in behavior therapy. *Clinical Psychology Review, 10,* 649–668.

Heymann, S. J., & Earle, A. (2001). The impact of parental working conditions on school-age children. The case of evening work. *Community, Work, and Family, 4,* 305–325.

Hoff, T. J. (2003). How physician-employees experience their work lives in a changing HMO. *Journal of Health and Social Behavior, 44,* 75–96.

Hoffman, E. (2002). *Psychological testing at work.* New York: McGraw-Hill.

Honey, A. (2003). The impact of mental illness on employment: Consumers' perspectives. *Work: Journal of Prevention, Assessment, and Rehabilitation, 20,* 267–276.

Hopko, D. R., Armento, M., Chambers, L., & Cantu, M., & Lejuez, C. W. (2003). The use of daily diaries to assess the relations among mood state, overt behavior, and reward value of activities. *Behaviour Research and Therapy, 41,* 1137–1148.

Hopko, D. R., & Hopko, S. D. (1999). What can functional analytic psychotherapy contribute to empirically validated treatments? *Clinical Psychology and Psychotherapy, 6,* 349–356.

Hopko, D. R., & Hopko, S. D. (2003). Employee assistance programs: Opportunities for behavior therapists. *The Behavior Therapist, 26,* 301–304.

Hopko, D. R., Lejuez, C. W., Armento, M. E. A., & Bare, R. L. (in press). Depressive disorders. In M. Hersen (Ed.), *Psychological assessment in clinical practice: A pragmatic guide.* New York: Taylor & Francis.

Horner, R. H. (1994). Functional assessment: Contributions and future directions. *Journal of Applied Behavior Analysis, 27,* 401–404.

Hunter, J. E., & Schmidt, F. L. (1983). Quantifying the effects of psychological interventions on employee job performance and work-force productivity. *American Psychologist, 38,* 473–478.

Hurlburt, R. T. (1997). Randomly sampling thinking in the natural environment. *Journal of Consulting and Clinical Psychology, 65,* 941–949.

Iacovides, A., Fountoulakis, K. N., Kaprinis, S., & Kaprinis, G. (2003). The relationship between job stress, burnout, and clinical depression. *Journal of Affective Disorders, 75,* 209–221.

Ilgen, D. R. (1990). Health issues at work: Opportunities for industrial-organizational psychology. *American Psychologist, 45,* 273–283.

Jackson, S. E., & Schuler, R. S. (1990). Human resource planning: Challenges for industrial/organizational psychologists. *American Psychologist, 45,* 223–239.

Kahn, J. P., & Langlieb, A. M. (2003). *Mental health and productivity in the workplace. A handbook for organizations and clinicians.* San Francisco: Jossey-Bass.

Kanfer, F. H., & Grimm, L. G. (1977). Behavioral analysis: Selecting target behaviors in the interview. *Behavior Modification, 1,* 7–28.

Kausch, O., & Resnick, P. J. (2001). Assessment of employees for workplace violence. *Journal of Forensic Psychology Practice, 1,* 1–22.

Keita, G. P., & Jones, J. M. (1990). Reducing adverse reaction to stress in the workplace: Psychology's expanding role. *American Psychologist, 45,* 1137–1141.

Kessler, R. C., McGonagle, K. A., Zhao, S., Nelson, B., Hughes, M., Eshleman, S., et al. (1994). Lifetime and 12-month prevalence of *DSM-III-R* psychiatric disorders in the United States. *Archives of General Psychiatry, 51,* 8–19.

Killinger, B. (1991). *Workaholics: The respectable addicts.* Toronto, Ontario, Canada: Key Porter Books.

Kimball, T. G., Shumway, S. T., Korinek, A., & Arredondo, R. (2002). Using the Satisfaction with Organization Scale (SOS): Two samples compared. *Employee Assistance Quarterly, 18,* 47–55.

Lance, C. E., Foster, M. R., Gentry, W. A., & Thoresen, J. D. (2004). Assessor cognitive processes in an operational assessment center. *Journal of Applied Psychology, 89,* 22–35.

Lang, P. J. (1968). Fear reduction and fear behavior: Problems in treating a construct. In J. M. Schlien (Ed.), *Research in psychotherapy* (Vol. III). Washington, DC: American Psychological Association.

Lanza, P. (1985). Team appraisals. *Personnel Journal, 64,* 46–51.

Lejuez, C. W., Hopko, D. R., & Hopko, S. D. (2003). *The brief Behavioral Activation Treatment for Depression (BATD): A comprehensive patient guide.* Boston: Pearson.

Lepine, J. P. (2002). The epidemiology of anxiety disorders: Prevalence and societal costs. *Journal of Clinical Psychiatry, 63,* 4–8.

Lewinsohn, P. M. (1974). A behavioral approach to depression. In R. M. Friedman and M. M. Katz (Eds.), *The psychology of depression: Contemporary theory and research.* New York: John Wiley & Sons.

Libet, J., & Lewinsohn, P. M. (1973). The concept of social skill with special reference to the behavior of depressed persons. *Journal of Consulting and Clinical Psychology, 40,* 304–312.

Linehan, M. M. (1993). *Cognitive-behavioral treatment of Borderline Personality Disorder.* New York: Guilford Press.

Lowman, R. L. (1982). Clinical psychology at work. *The Clinical Psychologist, 35,* 19–20.

Lowry, P. E. (1994). The structured interview: An alternative to the assessment center? *Public Personnel Management, 23,* 201–215.

MacPhillamy, D. J., & Lewinsohn, P. M. (1971). *Pleasant Events Schedule.* Eugene: University of Oregon.

Mantell, M., & Albrecht, S. (1994). *Ticking bombs: Defusing violence in the workplace.* New York: Irwin.

Martell, C. R., Addis, M. E., & Jacobson, N. S. (2001). *Depression in context: Strategies for guided action.* New York: W. W. Norton.

Martin, J. K., Blum, T. C., Beach, S. R. H., & Roman, P. M. (1996). Subclinical depression and performance at work. *Social Psychiatry, 31,* 3–9.

Maruish, M. (1999). Introduction. In Maruish, M. E. (Ed.), *The use of psychological testing for treatment planning and outcomes assessment* (2nd ed., pp. 1–39). Mahwah, NJ: Erlbaum.

Maslach, C. (1982). *Burnout: The cost of caring.* Englewood Cliffs, NJ: Prentice-Hall.

Maslach, C. (1986). Stress, burnout, and workaholism. In R. R. Kilburg & P. E. Nathan (Eds.), *Professionals in distress: Issues, syndromes, and solutions in psychology* (pp. 53–75). Washington, DC: American Psychological Association.

Maslach, C., Jackson, S. E., & Leiterm M. P. (1996). *Maslach Burnout Inventory Manual* (3rd ed.). Palo Alto, CA: Consulting Psychology Press.

Maslach, C., Schaufeli, W. B., & Leiter, M. P. (2001). Job burnout. *Annual Review of Psychology, 52,* 397–422.

Mausner-Dorsch, H., & Eaton, W. W. (2000). Psychosocial work environment and depression: Epidemiologic assessment of the demand-control model. *American Journal of Public Health, 90,* 1765–1770.

Mazzeo, S. E., Bergman, M. E., Buchanan, N. T., Drasgow, F., & Fitzgerald, L. F. (2001). Situation-specific assessment of sexual harassment. *Journal of Vocational Behavior, 59,* 120–131.

McCormick, E. J., Jeanneret, P. R., & Meachem, R. C. (1969). *Position Analysis Questionnaire*. West Lafayette, IN: Occupational Research Center, Purdue University.

McCullough, J. P., Jr. (2000). *Treatment for chronic depression: Cognitive behavioral analysis system of psychotherapy*. New York: Guilford Press.

Mello, N. K., & Mendelson, J. H. (1971). A quantitative analysis of drinking patterns in alcoholics. *Archives of General Psychiatry, 6,* 527–539.

Miller, M. J. (2001). The prediction and assessment of violence in the workplace: A critical review. *Dissertation Abstracts International: Section B: The Sciences and Engineering, 62,* 2070.

Miller, W. R., & Rollnick, S. (2002). *Motivational interviewing: Preparing people for change* (2nd ed.). New York: Guilford Press.

Mineka, S., Watson, D., & Clark, L. A. (1998). Comorbidity of anxiety and unipolar mood disorders. *Annual Review of Psychology, 49,* 377–412.

Mintz, J., Mintz, L. I., Arruda, M. J., & Hwang, S. S. (1992). Treatments of depression and the functional capacity to work. *Archives of General Psychiatry, 49,* 761–768.

Moore, M., Andreasen, D., & Nash, M. (2004, Spring). Preparing for Therapy, *EAP Digest*, pp. 26–29.

Morey, L. C. (1991). *The Personality Assessment Inventory professional manual*. Odessa: FL: Psychological Assessment Resources.

Mudrack, P. E., & Naughton, T. J. (2001). The assessment of workaholism as behavioral tendencies: Scale development and preliminary empirical testing. *International Journal of Stress Management, 8,* 93–111.

Mueser, K. T., Bennett, M., & Kushner, M. G. (1995). Epidemiology of substance use disorders among persons with chronic mental illnesses. In A. F. Lehman and L. Dixon (Eds.), *Double jeopardy: Chronic mental illness and substance abuse* (pp. 9–25). New York: Harwood Academic.

Munns, K. M. (1996). The effects of team-building interventions. *Dissertation Abstracts International: Section B: The Sciences and Engineering, 56,* 6436.

National Comorbidity Survey (NCS). (1992). Retrieved July 8, 2004, from http://www.hcp.med.harvard.edu/ncs/

National Mortality Followback Survey (NMFS). (1993). Retrieved July 8, 2004, from http://www.cdc.gov/nchs/about/major/nmfs/nmfs.htm

Nelson, R. O., & Hayes, S. C. (1979). Some current directions of behavioral assessment. *Behavioral Assessment, 1,* 1–16.

Nelson, R. O., & Hayes, S. C. (1986). *Conceptual foundations of behavioral assessment*. New York: Guilford Press.

Neuman, J. H., & Baron, R. A. (1998). Workplace violence and workplace aggression: Evidence concerning specific forms, potential causes, and preferred targets. *Journal of Management, 24,* 391–419.

Nezu, A. M., Ronan, G. F., Meadows, E. A., & McClure, K. S. (2000). *Practitioner's guide to empirically based measures of depression*. New York: Kluwer Academic/Plenum Press.

Nielsen, B., Nielsen, A. S., & Wraae, O. (1998). Patient treatment matching improves compliance of alcoholics in outpatient treatment. *Journal of Nervous and Mental Disease, 186,* 752–760.

Nunns, C. G., Bluen, S. D., & King, S. (1989). Behavioural assessment of interpersonal conflict in industry: Development of the Interpersonal Conflict Scale. *South African Journal of Psychology, 19,* 39–46.

Oher, J. M. (1999). *The employee assistance handbook*. New York: John Wiley & Sons.

O'Neill, R. E., Horner, R. H., Albin, R. W., Storey, K., & Sprague, J. R. (1990). *Functional analysis of problem behavior: A practical assessment guide*. Sycamore, IL: Sycamore.

Overall, J. E., & Gorham, D. R. (1962). The brief psychiatric rating scale. *Psychological Reports, 10,* 799–812.

Perrot, L. A. (1999). *Reinventing your practice as a business psychologist: A step-by-step guide*. San Francisco: Jossey-Bass.

Pflanz, S. E., & Heidel, S. H. (2003). Psychiatric causes of workplace problems. In J. P. Kahn and A. M. Langlieb (Eds.), *Mental health and productivity in the workplace. A handbook for organizations and clinicians* (pp. 276–296). San Francisco: Jossey-Bass.

Poverny, L. M., & Dodd, S. J. (2000). Differential patterns of EAP service utilization: A nine-year follow-up study of faculty and staff. *Employee Assistance Quarterly, 15,* 29–42.

Radloff, L. (1977). The CES-D scale: A self-report depression scale for research in the general population. *Applied Psychological Measurement, 1,* 385–401.

Ranelli, C. J., & Miller, R. E. (1981). Behavioral predictors of amitryptaline response in depression. *American Journal of Psychiatry, 138,* 30–34.

Reddy, W. B. (1994). *Intervention skills: Process consultation for small groups and teams.* San Diego, CA: Pfeiffer.

Rehm, L. P. (1988). Assessment of depression. In A. S. Bellack and M. Hersen (Eds.), *Behavioral assessment: A practical handbook* (3rd ed., pp. 313–364). New York: Pergamon Press.

Robinson, B. E. (1997). Work addiction: Implications for EAP counseling and research. *Employee Assistance Quarterly, 12,* 1–13.

Robinson, B. E. (1999). The Work Addiction Risk Test: Development of a tentative measure of workaholism. *Perceptual and Motor Skills, 88,* 199–210.

Robinson, B. E., Flowers, C., & Carroll, J. (2001). Work stress and marriage: A theoretical model examining the relationship between workaholism and marital cohesion. *International Journal of Stress Management, 8,* 165–175.

Robinson, J. E., & Kelley, L. (1998). Adult children of workaholics: Self-concept, anxiety, depression, and locus of control. *American Journal of Family Therapy, 26,* 223–238.

Robinson, J. C., & Lewinsohn, P. M. (1973). Behavior modification of speech characteristics in a chronically depressed man. *Behavior Therapy, 4,* 150–152.

Schell, B. H. (2003). The prevalence of sexual harassment, stalking, and false victimization syndrome cases and related human resource management policies in a cross section of Canadian companies from January 1995 through January 2000. *Journal of Family Violence, 18,* 351–360.

Schneider, R. J., Casey, J., & Kohn, R. (2000). Motivational versus confrontational interviewing: A comparison of substance abuse assessment practices at employee assistance programs. *Journal of Behavioral Health Services and Research, 27,* 60–74.

Scott, K. S., Moore, K. S., & Miceli, M. P. (1997). An exploration of the meaning and consequences of workaholism. *Human Relations, 50,* 287–314.

Selzer, M. L. (1971). The Michigan Alcoholism Screening Test: The quest for a new diagnostic instrument. *American Journal of Psychiatry, 127,* 89–94.

Seybold, K. C., & Salomone, P. R. (1994). Understanding workaholism: A review of causes and counseling approaches. *Journal of Counseling and Development, 73,* 4–9.

Shimmin, S. (1981). Applying psychology in organizations. *International Review of Applied Psychology, 30,* 377–386.

Shirom, A. (2003). Job-related burnout: A review. In J. C. Quick and L. E. Tetrick (Eds.), *Handbook of occupational health psychology* (pp. 245–264). Washington, DC: American Psychological Association.

Simon, G. E., Revicki, D., Heiligenstein, J., Grothaus, L., VonKorff, M., Katon, W. J., et al. (2000). Recovery from depression, work productivity, and health care costs among primary care patients. *General Hospital Psychiatry, 22,* 153–162.

Simon, G. E., Chisholm, D., Treglia, M., et al. (2002). Course of depression, health service costs, and work productivity in an international primary care study. *General Hospital Psychiatry, 24,* 328–335.

Skinner, H. A. (1982). The Drug Abuse Screening Test. *Addictive Behaviors, 7,* 363–371.

Skinner, H. A. & Sheu, W. J. (1982). Reliability of alcohol use indices: The Lifetime Drinking History and the MAST. *Journal of Studies on Alcohol, 43,* 1157–1170.

Sobell, L. C., Breslin, F. C., & Sobell, M. B. (1997). Substance-related disorders: Alcohol. In S. M. Turner and M. Hersen (Eds.), *Adult psychopathology and diagnosis* (3rd ed., pp. 128–158). New York: Wiley.

Sobell, L. C., & Sobell, M. B. (1992). Timeline follow-back: A technique for assessing self-reported alcohol consumption. In R. Z. Litten and J. Allen (Eds.), *Measuring alcohol consumption: Psychosocial and biological methods* (pp. 41–72). Totowa, NJ: Humana Press.

Sobell, L. C., Sobell, M. B., & Nirenberg, T. D. (1988). Behavioral assessment and treatment planning with alcohol and drug abusers: A review with an emphasis on clinical application. *Clinical Psychology Review, 8,* 19–54.

Sobell, L. C., Toneatto, T., & Sobell, M. B. (1994). Behavioral assessment and treatment planning for alcohol, tobacco, and other drug problems: Current status with an emphasis on clinical applications. *Behavior Therapy, 25,* 533–580.

Sobell, M. B., Sobell, L. C., & Sheahan, D. B. (1976). Functional analysis of drinking problems as an aid in developing individual treatment strategies. *Addictive Behaviors, 1,* 127–132.

Soederman, E., Lisspers, J., & Sundin, O. (2003). Depression as a predictor of return to work in patients with coronary heart disease. *Social Science and Medicine, 56,* 193–202.

Spector, P. E. (2003). Taking the measure of work: A guide to validated scales for organizational research and diagnosis. *Personnel Psychology, 56,* 813–816.

Spector P. E., & Jex, S. M. (1998). Development of four self-report measures of job stressors and strain: Interpersonal Conflict at Work Scale, Organizational Constraints Scale, Quantitative Workload Inventory, and Physical Symptoms Inventory. *Journal of Occupational Health Psychology, 3,* 356–367.

Spence, J. T., & Robbins, A. S. (1992). Workaholism: Definition, measurement, and preliminary results. *Journal of Personality Assessment, 58,* 160–178.

Stanton, J. M., Sinar, E. F., Balzer, W. K., Julian, A. L., Thoresen, P., Aziz, S., et al. (2002). Development of a compact measure of job satisfaction: The abridged Job Descriptive Index. *Educational and Psychological Measurement, 62,* 173–191.

Stewart, W. F., Ricci, J. A., Chee, E., Hahn, S. R., & Morganstein, D. (2003). Cost of lost productive work time among U.S. workers with depression. *Journal of the American Medical Association, 289,* 3135–3144.

Sturm, R., Gresenz, C. R., Pacula, R. L., & Wells, K. B. (1999). Labor force participation by persons with mental illness. *Psychiatric Services, 50,* 1407.

Substance Abuse and Mental Health Services Administration (SAMHSA) (1995). Prevalence and Treatment of Mental Health Problems: www.samhsa.gov

Summerall, S. W., Israel, A. R., Brewer, R., & Prew, R. E. (1999). The role of employee assistance programs in the era of rapid change in the health care delivery system. *International Journal of Emergency Mental Health, 1,* 251–252.

Sussal, C. M., & Ojakian, E. (1989). Crisis intervention in the workplace. *Employee Assistance Quarterly, 4,* 71–85.

Tharenou, P. (2001). The relevance of industrial and organizational psychology to contemporary organizations: How far have we come and what needs to be done post-2000? *Australian Psychologist, 36,* 200–210.

Thomas, J. C., & Johnson, N. P. (1994). Alcohol problems of employee assistance program populations. *Employee Assistance Quarterly, 10,* 13–23.

Thompson, L. F., & Spector, P. E. (2003). Industrial-organizational psychology. In W. G. Emenor & M. A. Richard (Eds.), *I'm a people person: A guide to human service professions* (pp. 131–144). Springfield, IL: Charles C Thomas.

Thornton, C. C., Gottheil, E., Weinstein, S. P., & Kerachsky, R. S. (1998). Patient-treatment matching in substance abuse: Drug addiction severity. *Journal of Substance Abuse Treatment, 15,* 505–511.

Thorpe, G. L., & Olson, S. L. (1997). *Behavior therapy: Concepts, procedures, and applications.* Boston: Allyn & Bacon.

Tobin, T. J. (2001). Organizational determinants of violence in the workplace. *Aggression and Violent Behavior, 6,* 91–102.

Toppinen-Tanner, S., Kalimo, R., & Mutanen, P. (2002). The process of burnout in white-collar and blue-collar jobs: Eight-year prospective study of exhaustion. *Journal of Organizational Behavior, 23,* 555–570.

Turnipseed, D. L. (1992). Anxiety and perceptions of the work environment. *Journal of Social Behavior and Personality, 7,* 375–394.

Van den Bergh, N. (2000). Where have we been? . . . Where are we going?: Employee assistance practice in the 21st century. *Employee Assistance Quarterly, 16,* 1–13.

Varela, J. G., Scogin, F. R., & Vipperman, R. K. (1999). Development and preliminary validation of the screening of law enforcement candidates. *Behavioral Sciences and the Law, 17,* 467–481.

Wang, J., & Patten, S. B. (2001). Perceived work stress and major depression in the Canadian employed population, 20–49 years old. *Journal of Occupational Health Psychology, 6,* 283–289.

Wilkinson, C. W. (2001). Violence prevention at work: A business perspective. *American Journal of Preventive Medicine, 20,* 155–160.

Wolpe, J., & Lazarus, A. A. (1966). *Behavior therapy techniques.* New York: Pergamon Press.

Worster, D. (2000). An EAP approach to managing organizational downsizing. *Employee Assistance Quarterly, 16,* 97–115.

Wright, P. M., Lichtenfels, P. A., & Pursell, E. D. (1989). The structure interview: Additional studies and a meta-analysis. *Journal of Occupational Psychology, 62,* 191–199.

Zapf, D., Seifert, C., Schmutte, B., Mertini, H., & Holz, M. (2001). Emotion work and job stressors and their effects on burnout. *Psychology and Health, 16,* 527–545.

Zedeck, S., & Mosier, K. L. (1990). Work in the family and employing organization. *American Psychologist, 45,* 240–251.

# 25

## ASSESSMENT OF VALUE CHANGE IN ADULTS WITH ACQUIRED DISABILITIES

ELIAS MPOFU

*Department of Counselor Education*
*Pennsylvania State University*
*University Park, Pennsylvania*

THOMAS OAKLAND

*Department of Educational Foundations*
*University of Florida*
*Gainesville, Florida*

### INTRODUCTION

People with acquired disabilities[1] (e.g., Diabetes Mellitus, major amputation, Multiple Sclerosis, Poliomyelitis, rheumatic conditions, spinal-cord injury, Traumatic Brain Injury) often experience considerable disruption of values. Moreover, the success of their rehabilitation often depends to a significant degree on their ability to examine and, if needed, revise their value system to accommodate their disability-related conditions (Menzel, Dolan, Richardson, & Oslen, 2002; Mpofu & Houston, 1998; Schwartz & Sprangers, 1999; Schwartz, Sprangers, Carey, & Reed, 2004; B. A. Wright, 1983). Similarly, people with the following conditions also face challenges to align their personal values in ways that are relevant to work and community participation: Guillain-Barré syndrome and other neuropathies, Muscular Dystrophy, Myasthenia Gravis, deep venous thrombosis, hip and leg fracture, deconditioning after abdominal surgery, pure motor stroke, and recovery from therapeutic procedures for lung and colon cancers. Patients

---

[1] Patients and people with disabilities are customers to providers of rehabilitation services. Therefore, the terms *patients, rehabilitation customers,* and *people with acquired disabilities* will be used interchangeably in this chapter.

displaying cognitive abnormalities associated with and secondary to their medical problems (e.g., patients with Multiple Sclerosis, Parkinson's Disease, and deconditioning after myocardial infarction or pneumonia) also are likely to face lifestyle-related value changes.

Assessment is a cornerstone of effective rehabilitation services. The primary purpose of assessment is to accurately describe behavior. In addition, assessment informs rehabilitation planning, implementation, monitoring, and evaluation. As noted throughout this chapter, assessment of values held by rehabilitation customers, their family and friends, and their health care providers can assist in rehabilitation efforts.

Most measures used in medical and psychosocial rehabilitation are provider centered (e.g., intended to inform providers) and deficient in customer-oriented outcomes (e.g., less likely to assist customers in improving self-understanding and assisting them in addressing important personal issues) (Gurka et al., 1999; Hobart et al., 2001; Simmons, Crepeau, & White, 2000). The need for "research to include outcome measures that map intraindividual change from premorbid status to current levels of functioning, rather than utilizing measures with fixed outcomes" is clear (Gurka et al., p. 255).

Value changes often constitute one of the most significant intraindividual changes that occur in a person after acquiring a disability (Mpofu, 2001; Mpofu & Houston, 1998; Schwartz & Sprangers, 1999; B. A. Wright, 1983). For example, patients with cancer may value small gains in physical functioning and quality of life (QOL) and minimize the significance of losses of equivalent magnitude. Patients with objectively deteriorating physical functioning report quality of life similar to those who are well (Albrecht & Devlieger, 1999). Despite its importance, value change following disability has received little empirical attention (Gibbons, 1999).

This chapter discusses self-report measures of values for use with individuals with acquired disabilities and suggests methods that could contribute to a new generation of such measures. A rationale for their use and models and methods for values measurement with people with acquired disabilities are presented. In addition, research on measures of values with this population and methods to improve the measurement of values for use in medical and psychosocial rehabilitation are discussed. Our review focuses on measures of values that are completed by rehabilitation customers or with the assistance of their significant others or rehabilitation professionals.

Patients' responses to chronic illness or disability early in its occurrence are critical to their long-term rehabilitation success, in that this information helps establish their attitudes and behaviors toward rehabilitation and rehabilitation planning (Antonak & Livneh, 1994; Rees, Waldron, O'Boyle, & MacDonagh, 2002). For example, changes in internal (or personal) health standards are more rapid early in the rehabilitation process with patients experiencing severe rather than mild symptoms of a chronic illness or disability. Knowledge of changes in patients' subjective experience of health is important for rehabilitation planning. Furthermore, self-reports by patients or people with disabilities generally are more reliable than reports by other persons (Schaefer, 2000; Sneeuw et al., 1997). Self-reports by patients complement performance (or objective) measures of health to enable the individualization of rehabilitation intervention (Daltry, Larson, Eaton, Phillips, & Liang, 1999; Daltry, Phillips, et al., 1995). Research on self-reports on value scales suggests that social desirability may not be a critical issue (Feather, 1988; Kristiansen, 1985).

## VALUES: DEFINITIONS AND SIGNIFICANCE TO REHABILITATION OUTCOMES

Values have been defined as need-based models of behavior that guide or influence an individual's goal setting and implementation (Veit & Ware, 1982; Neville & Super, 1986; Orbell, Johnston, Rowley, Davey, & Espley, 2001). They influence personal choices people make in various life roles (Neville & Super, 1986) and help establish the importance they attach to their choices (Gay, Weiss, Hendel, Dawis, & Lofquist, 1971; Kiresuk, Smith, & Cardillo, 1994; Neville & Super; Orbell, Johnston, Rowley, Davey, & Espley, 2001). Values express a preferred state of being and the activities or behaviors that lead to the attainment of preferred life goals (Rokeach, 1973). Values may be an expression of biologically based temperament preferences (Keirsey & Bates, 1984). Thus, they encompass instrumental behaviors (means), terminal goals (end states), personal preferences, and subjective importance (e.g., their importance to one's self) (Gay, Weiss, Hendel, Dawis, & Lofquist, 1971; Kane & Kane, 1982; Neville, & Super; Rokeach, 1973) (see Table 25.1).

Personal values are important to rehabilitation interventions in several ways. First, they play a significant role in the ways individuals interpret the meaning of a disability (J. G. Wright, Rudicel, & Feinstein, 1994; Schartz & Sprangers, 1999; Steinfeld & Danford, 2003) and therefore influence their participation in their family, work, and community (Mpofu, 2002; Sinclair, Fleming, Radwinsky, Clupper, & Clupper, 2002; Wright, 1993). Second, value preferences can help determine rehabilitation interventions that are acceptable to individuals (Hamblin, Beutler, Scogin, & Corbishley, 1993; Kane & Kane, 1982). For example, a customer's community reintegration plan is likely to be successful to the extent that it addresses activities that the customer considers important. Rehabilitation customers whose value preferences are consistent with rehabilitation interventions are likely to follow through with rehabilitation plans and strive to achieve rehabilitation goals (Ozer & Kroll, 2002). Third, given budgetary restraints for rehabilitation care, rehabilitation practices that are respectful of customer values are likely to be more cost effective. Fourth, values and other personal goals have a significant impact on rehabilitation success (e.g., their return to work, commu-

TABLE 25.1   Types of Values and Their Functions

| Rokeach (1973) | | Neville & Super (1986) |
|---|---|---|
| Instrumental Values | Terminal Values | Ability Utilization |
| Ambitious | A comfortable life | Achievement |
| Broadminded | An exciting life | Aesthetics |
| Capable | A sense of accomplishment | Altruism |
| Cheerful | A world at peace | Autonomy |
| Clean | A world of beauty | Creativity |
| Courageous | Equality | Economic rewards |
| Forgiving | Family security | Lifestyle |
| Helpful | Freedom | Physical activity |
| Honest | Happiness | Prestige |
| Imaginative | Inner harmony | Risk taking |
| Independent | Mature love | Social interaction |
| Intellectual | National security | Variety |
| Logical | Pleasure | Working conditions |
| Loving | Salvation | Cultural identity |
| Obedient | Self-respect | Physical prowess |
| Polite | Social recognition | Personal identity |
| Responsible | True friendship | Advancement |
| Self-controlled | Wisdom | Economic security |

nity reintegration) irrespective of the nature or severity of the impairment or disability (Orbell et al., 2001; Kivioja & Franklin, 2003). Attempts to incorporate rehabilitation customer values into rehabilitation planning presume a valid knowledge of the customer values, acquired directly from the customer's perspective.

## DOMAINS OF PARTICIPATION IMPACTED BY ACQUIRED DISABILITY

The National Institute on Disability and Rehabilitation Research considers "maximal participation of the individual with a disability in the community" the "ultimate goal of rehabilitation intervention" (Seelman, 2000, p. 1). Consequently, development of rehabilitation outcome measures that are sensitive to participation is important to rehabilitation intervention. Participation encompasses involvement in normal life activities, such as education, training, leisure, and work. Independent living and employment are two participation domains that often are especially important to long-term rehabilitation success (World Health Organization, 1999).

## INDEPENDENT LIVING

Independent living refers to the degree one has control over one's life, including the degree one must rely on others to organize and perform daily activities (Felce & Perry, 1995; Nosek & Fuhrer, 1992; Wehmeyer & Bolding, 2001). More specifically, independent living has been associated with a person's living arrangements—where and with whom a person chooses to or must live (DeJong, 1981; DeJong, Branch, & Corcoran, 1984; DeJong & Hughes, 1982; Boschen, 1996; Boschen & Gargano, 1996). The following participation outcomes commonly are found in literature on independent living: individual self-reliance, physical functioning, work and community participation, amount of perceived control, and characteristics of the physical and social environment (Nosek & Fuhrer, 1992; Wehmeyer & Bolding).

Rehabilitation customers were surveyed to determine the degree they desired alternative living arrangements, ranging from living with their immediate family to living in an institution (DeJong, 1981; DeJong et al., 1984). They rank-ordered their living arrangements in terms of perceived restrictiveness or hindrance to control over one's life. The customers identified living with their immediate family as least restrictive and living in an institution as most restrictive. Independent living also is characterized by one's ability to work or attend school, to have satisfying access to community resources, and to participate in desired social networks (Hutchinson & Pedlar, 1999; Kivioja & Franklin, 2003).

## EMPLOYMENT

People with disabilities who are employed generally have wider choices about their living arrangements and community participation (DeJong et al., 1984). Employment often helps provide the financial resources and autonomy that make independent living possible. Individuals with disabilities who enjoy the highest quality of life are those who are employed full time, have leisure time, and participate in schooling, homemaking, and social organizations (DeJong, 1981; Boschen, 1996; Boschen & Gargano, 1996).

Qualities associated with independent living and employment-related participation overlap and influence one another. Moreover, this overlap suggests that some personal values are common to several participation domains (e.g., work participation and independent living), may be measured by the same items, and may lead to the development of value measures that assess both shared and unique aspects of participation.

## VALUE CHANGE THEORY: CONSTRUCTS, OPERATIONALIZATION AND PROSPECTIVE MEASURES

Dissonance often occurs when an individual realizes incongruities between his or her lifestyle altered by the disability and his or her lifestyle based on premorbid or normative conditions. This dissonance often results in value changes that lead to acceptance of a disability and resulting lifestyle changes.

Disability-related value change (B. A. Wright, 1983) or response shift (Schwartz & Sprangers, 1999) involves value clarification (Mpofu & Houston, 1998; Scofield, Pape, McCracken, & Maki, 1980). Value clarification may be regarded as "helping clients place in perspective functional limitations imposed by disability" (Scofield et al., p. 186). Persons with disabilities who recalibrate their personal values, reprioritize goals and the ways to achieve them, and/or reconceptualize values in light of their disability are more likely to participate in work and community than are peers who attempt to continue to lead a lifestyle based on the pursuit of premorbid values.

B. A. Wright (1983) proposed a model of value restructuring that entails the enlargement of one's scope of values, subordination of physical qualities (e.g., agility, strength, beauty) to other personal qualities, containment of disability effects, and transformation of comparative values into asset values. Enlargement of the scope of values requires finding new meaning in events, abilities, and goals that may have held little interest prior to the onset of a disability. For example, if independence was a prior value and physical labor the idealized value mode, then an adjustment from independence to interdependence and valuing physical labor to valuing education may be required to facilitate personal adjustment. Subordination of physical qualities relative to other values involves giving nonphysical attributes (e.g., honesty, dependability) greater value than physical attributes. Containment of disability effects occurs when an individual sees the functional constraints of disability in perspective and separates the disability from other aspects of functioning.

Changes in personal values following disability have been described as a response shift (Schwartz & Sprangers, 1999). A response shift is characterized by a change of the meaning of one's self-evaluation of a target construct as a result of a (a) change in the consumer's internal standards (i.e., scale recalibration), (b) change in the consumer's values (i.e., relative importance of the domains constituting the target construct), and (c) redefining the target construct or value (i.e., reconceptualization) (Schartz & Sprangers). Self-comparisons, particularly in reference to others with more severe disabilities (e.g., a downward social comparison), may be associated with changes in one's internal standards (e.g., "Although I have a disability, others have more severe disabilities"). Group therapy with others who have disabilities may facilitate this effect, in part, by enabling one to view other's lives in intimate ways that lead one to reprioritize one's personal values. A consumer also may reconceptualize of the meaning of health as one learns that quality health is possible when one has a significant disability. Value reconceptualization subsumes goal reorientation and scale recalibration.

# FACTORS INFLUENCING VALUE CHANGE FOLLOWING DISABILITY

Multiple processes can impact value change following a personal experience of disability, including those held by the individual, his or her family and friends, sociocultural groups, the broader environment, and their interactions. At an individual level, the values held by the rehabilitation customer can influence his or her adjustment to the disability. Values prominent in one's social groups (e.g., family, friends), one's environment, as well as by one's rehabilitation service providers may impact one's disability-related value changes.

## INDIVIDUAL VALUES IN REHABILITATION

People with acquired disability seek to achieve rehabilitation outcomes that are important to their participation as individuals living with a disability. The impact of a disability on the degree to which people with similarly severe levels of disabilities participate in important life activities is not uniform (Albrecht & Devlieger, 1999; Boschen, 1996; Kivioja & Franklin, 2003). For example, the prediction that more than 75% of people with significant impairments returned to work could not be made on knowledge of their physical functioning (Kivioja & Franklin). Subjective factors (e.g., personal values) explain some of the differences in the degree to which people participate following an acquired disability. For example, presurgery goals predict disability at 9 months after knee-joint replacement (Orbell et al., 2001). Among those with a disability, participation in an environment depended, in part, on their subjective evaluation of the extent to which the values prominent in their environments are consistent with or violate their individual values, expectations, or abilities. Some decide to be as fully engaged as possible, while others decide to withdraw (Danford & Steinfeld, 2003). However, patients with poor health value intermediate outcomes to the same extent as those who achieve full recovery (Rees et al., 2002).

## SOCIOCULTURAL/ENVIRONMENTAL VALUES

At the sociocultural or environmental level, formative influences on an individual comprise the person's primary support systems, including the individual's family, significant others, and friends. The family constitutes a primary influence in an individual's value development and generally functions as a person's primary support network. Introduction of a disability into a family system often requires a family to examine its values and beliefs surrounding disability generally as well as its added responsibilities for caring for one with a disability (Rolland, 1994).

Individuals and families exist within communities. Thus, community views and values about disabilities are likely to influence the nature and extent of disability-related value changes. For example, a community's standards for behavior (e.g., perfectionism, beauty, independence, conformity, achievement, competition, gender) and environmental attitudes and associated responses toward people with disabilities (e.g., acceptance, supportive, stigmatization, devaluation, lower performance expectations, reinforcement of sick-role behavior) provide the context for and influence an individual's perceptions and responses toward his or her disability. Social norms and expectations that are negative may have a stronger deleterious impact on an individual's behavior than the actual disability (Smart, 2001). Thus, values prominent in an individual, his or her family system, and community interact to impact the trajectory and speed with which values may be recalibrated, redefined, and reconceptualized (Menzel et al., 2002; Schwartz & Sprangers, 1999). Measures of customer values for rehabilitation interventions and outcomes should be sensitive to the impact of perceived values emanating in a customer from his or her family, other important social groups, and the community. As noted elsewhere, values influence rehabilitation participation and success.

Values held by rehabilitation service providers often are overlooked yet can materially influence participation outcomes for individuals with acquired disability. Measures used in medical rehabilitation typically are directed narrowly toward issues important for achieving functional independence and resulting discharge rather than promoting global social functioning (e.g., Simmons et al., 2000). The narrow scope of medical rehabilitation measures may be justified by the fact that global social functioning builds on a successful physical rehabilitation regimen (Hobart et al., 2001). Furthermore, the current trend to reduce medical costs requires clinical and social rehabilitation outcome measures that support effective treatment resource allocation (W. P. Fisher, 1997).

The values held by medical rehabilitation practitioners toward the preeminence of promoting physical functioning may lead to optimistic beliefs about patient outcomes (e.g., once the disability is addressed physically, the patient's life will return more or less to normal). These attitudes may encourage patients and their significant others to form false hopes about social and emotional features of the patient's life after discharge. A convergence of values from the rehabilitation provider and those of the patient may form a foundation for the development of rehabilitation outcome measures that are more sensitive to the needs of the service providers, the patients, and their constituencies.


## CURRENT AND PROSPECTIVE MEASURES OF VALUE CHANGE WITH ACQUIRED DISABILITY

Despite the apparent importance of values and their restructuring to disability treatment outcomes and personal adjustment, the measurement of value change as a basis for rehabilitation outcome has received little attention (Gibbons, 1999; Mpofu, 2001; Mpofu & Houston, 1998; Schwartz & Sprangers, 1999). For example, a search for measures of values associated with employment and independent living using major databases on health measures (e.g., Health and Psychosocial Instruments and the Citation Index of Allied Health Literature) and the insertion of an array of word combinations (e.g., value(s), measurement, scales, patient, disability, employment, disability, independent, and living) lead to the identification of three scales: the Acceptance of Disability Scale (Linkowski, 1986), the Minnesota Importance Questionnaire (Gay et al., 1971), and the Thentest (Schwartz & Sprangers, 1999; Schwartz et al., 2004).

## THE ACCEPTANCE OF DISABILITY SCALE AND THE MINNESOTA IMPORTANCE QUESTIONNAIRE

The Acceptance of Disability Scale (ADS) is a self-report measure on which respondents indicate their agreement or disagreement to 50 items using a six-point Likert-type scale. The items were written to sample each of the disability-related value shifts as proposed by J. G. Wright and colleagues (1994). Item examples follow: to measure containment of disability effects ("A physical disability may limit a person in some ways, but this does not mean he/she should give up and do nothing with his/her life"), to measure enlargement of scope of values ("Though I am disabled, my life is full"), to measure subordination of physique ("There are many things a person with a disability is able to do"), and to measure transformation from comparative to assertive values ("Personal characteristics such as honesty and willingness to work hard are much more important than physical appearance and ability").

Construct validity was established though exploratory factor analysis. Principal components analysis of the 50 ADS items, using orthogonal rotations, yielded one factor that accounts for 44% of the variance. All items correlate positively and moderately with the principal factor. The ADS may be described most accurately as a global measure of value change following the experience of a disability. The measure has been adopted widely as a research instrument (Antonack & Livneh, 1994). However, its reliability in predicting vocational rehabilitation outcomes is low (McGuire, 2000), and the degree of its use within rehabilitation facilities is unknown.

The Minnesota Importance Questionnaire (MIQ) was developed to be consistent with a theory of work adjustment proposed by Lofquist, Dawis, and others (Weiss, 1967). The MIQ is not derived from value change theory (Mpofu & Houston, 1998). The MIQ consists of 20 need items presented in two forms.

In the paired form, each of the 20 items is matched with every other item, resulting in a total of 190 pairwise comparisons. Respondents indicate which one of two needs is more important in their ideal job or for a satisfying use of time. The paired form also presents the same list of 20 need items with directions that respondents make absolute judgments (i.e., whether each is or is not important) for their ideal job or satisfying use of leisure time. Persons without a disability complete the paired form in about 30–40 minutes.

The ranked form presents vocational need statements in groups of five, with respondents rank-ordering their importance within each set. The ranked form can be group administered in about 15–20 minutes by persons without a disability. Examples of values measured by the MIQ include ability utilization, achievement, creativity, advancement, social status, recognition, and responsibility.

One purpose of the MIQ is to assess "changes in the client's vocational needs ... which result from the onset of disability" and "satisfying use of nonwork time" (Gay et al., 1971). Therefore, the scale is intended to be directly relevant to the assessment of client values and counseling in rehabilitation settings. A client's vocational need changes can be understood best if there is premorbid information (e.g., premorbid work history) with which to compare the changes in vocational needs upon onset of a disability (Gay et al.).

The validity of the MIQ is supported from evidence that items similar to those on the MIQ tend to show low-to-moderate correlations with those on the Neville and Super (1986) Value Scale for students with hearing impairment (Hackbarth & Mathay, 1991). The MIQ correlated significantly with measures of work satisfaction for people with mental retardation (Melchiori & Church, 1997). However, the MIQ's grammar and comparative judgment format may present problems to students with hearing impairment and could be a source of unreliability when used with others who display significant disabilities (Hackbarth & Mathay).

## THE THENTEST

The Thentest (Schwartz & Sprangers, 1999; Schwartz et al., 2004) is a procedure for evaluating patient change. It is not a unitary psychometric instrument. A pretest–post-test design can be used to assess the degree to which patients recalibrate their subjective internal standards with regard to an area of functioning with a disability as well as the degree they reprioritize and reconceptualize their personal values following their disability. Using the Thentest procedures, people with an acquired chronic condition take a number of measures of rehabilitation outcome over a period of time during their rehabilitation (e.g., pretreatment, posttreatment, present or then time). Their current perceptions of health (as measured by one or more rehabilitation measures) are compared with retrospective reports of their previous health status (reflecting the *then* portion of the test's title). Mean differences between current and baseline scores are thought to reflect a value-related response shift.

For example, the Thentest was used to investigate standards recalibration, value reconceptualization, and reconstitution in 93 patients with multiple sclerosis (MS) at five years postillness. The best items from various rehabilitation outcome measures were used to assess perceived health, including the Sickness Impact Profile (Bergner et al., 1976), Multidimensional Assessment of Fatigue Scale (Belza, Henke, Yelin, Epstein, & Gilliss, 1993), and the Ryff Happiness Scale (Ryff, 1989). Mean score differences were used to estimate response shifts. Patients with MS who had lower self-standards for physical functioning over time (reflecting recalibration of internal standards) placed a different value on physical as compared to psychosocial functioning (reflecting reprioritization of values) and maintained a stable sense of well-being over time despite deteriorating physical functioning (reflecting reconceptualization of well-being) (Schwartz et al., 2004).

## OTHER MEASURES OF VALUES

Rokeach (1973) developed the Value Survey (RVS) basis on his theory of values (see Table 25.1). The RVS measures instrumental and terminal values in terms of their importance to the individual. The RVS lists 18 instrumental and 18 terminal values that respondents rank-order in terms of their importance to them as guiding principles in their life. The purpose of using the RVS with persons with disabilities is to enable them to better understand their value system and, if needed, to align their values to better reflect current physical and medical conditions and to achieve realistic aspired lifestyles. The reliability of the RVS with people without disabilities is satisfactory. Research on the reliability of the RVS and its validity for predicting outcomes in rehabilitation settings was not found. The RVS could be helpful as a measure of disability-related value change involving realignment of instrumental and terminal values in a manner that accounts for individual preferences.

Neville and Super's (1986) Value Scale (VS) uses 106 Likert-scaled items to measure 21 values (see Table 25.1). Examples include cultural identity, personal identity, physical prowess, aesthetics, physical activity, risk taking, lifestyle, advancement, economic security, and variety. The 21 values are clustered into seven major domains: authority, creativity, prestige, material, ability utilization, and sociability. Individuals rate the values in terms of their degree of importance now or in the future.

The VS has good potential as an instrument for directing rehabilitation interventions toward issues significant to the rehabilitation client and at various stages during the rehabilitation process. For example, the rehabilitation client may need to consider a wider range of potential ways of using his or her functional abilities. An examination of potential ways to utilize one's abilities implies placing a higher value on the scale's creativity and risk-taking dimensions. Discussions of client values related to client physical abilities may help identify accommodations a client might need in work and/or nonwork (e.g., recreation) settings.

## SUMMARY EVALUATION OF EXISTING
## VALUE MEASURES

Apart from a paucity of evidence on reliability and validity with people with disabilities, current measures of values impose a considerable burden on both customers and caregivers, in that they are quite lengthy and complex in wording. For example, administration of the 210-item MIQ averages 30–40 minutes for those without a disability. The sentence structure of the ADS (e.g., "I can see the progress I am making in rehabilitation and it makes me feel like an adequate person in spite of the limitations of my disability") makes it inaccessible to many people with cognitive impairments or other significant disability (Carl Pillar, District Manager, Pennsylvania Office of Vocational Rehabilitation—Personal Communication, December 8, 2003). The ADS does not report reliability estimates for a heterogeneous sample of people with acquired disabilities (Mpofu, 2004). The RVS has been criticized for assuming that all respondents will have the ability and motivation to reliably rank-order 18 values and that the perceived importance of a value will necessarily guide an individual's behavior. The Thentest lacks a standard battery with norms for disability categories or algorithms for determining significant response shift in applied settings. It also is based on the untested assumption that patients use the same internal standards for current (i.e., Thentest) as they did when completing the pretests and post-tests. A common limitation to all four measures is their attempt to assess values in a decontextualized or abstract manner, thus limiting perceptions of the practical relevance of values to real-life settings.

## VIEWS ON THE DEVELOPMENT
## OF MEASURES OF VALUES WITH
## ACQUIRED DISABILITY

A major limitation of value change theories (e.g., Menzel et al., 2002; B. A. Wright, 1983; Schwartz & Sprangers, 1999) lies in their relative neglect of environmental factors that impact ways a person learns, perceives, and forms his or her personal values. For example, value transformational theory articulates value changes that occur only in the individual, not as a function of the environment. Values are realized and acted on in particular contexts (e.g., work setting) and environments (e.g., institutional practices). As previously noted, the contexts or environments within which people with disabilities live are not value free. People with acquired disabilities may enjoy quality participation by recognizing and working to change those normative values in the environment or specific settings that compromise their participation. A conceptual model that combines constructs from extant theories of values, value change, and contextual/environmental enablers could significantly advance the quality of value change instrumentation and their relevance to rehabilitation intervention.

## TOWARD A SYSTEMS MODEL OF VALUE CHANGE

The practical usefulness of value measures could be enhanced by linking them to contexts and actions that enhance their recognition or as important guides to behavior. For example, previous discussion highlighted the fact that qualities that impact values come from several sources and systems, including the individual, family, friends, other social groups, community, and institutional practices, including health care providers.

A distinction has been made between perceived and enacted values (DeCarlo & Luthar, 2000; Kelly & Strupp, 1992). Perceived values are those goals, needs, and preferences that the individual believes to be important to self and others. Although such values may not have external objective criteria and may not be observable, they constitute part of a person's subjective reality and influence his or her behaviors in important ways. In contrast, enacted values are those acted on by the individual or performed by others in relation to the individual, partly for functional and instrumental purposes (e.g., to access services, to belong, for intrinsic satisfaction). The nature of relationships between perceived and enacted values deserves more empirical attention. Space limitations prohibit elaborate discussion of the model of values proposed here (see Figure 25.1). Nevertheless, we know that perceived and enacted values have a reciprocal influence. Environmental factors, individual differences, and their interactions influence both the strength and the direction of perceived and enacted values. Value reconstruction is possible at the individual, contextual, and environmental levels. The processes that influence value change at the individual level are understood better than those at the contextual or environmental levels. A challenge in designing values instruments is to construct them to be sensitive to the various levels at which values are apparent, owned, and acted on. This chapter discusses some strategies for developing measures of values that address values at both the individual and systems levels, together with their expressions in rehabilitation settings.

A review of the literature on systems models of value change suggests that an ideal values measure for use in rehabilitation settings should (a) be context sensitive, (b) be usable with people across a broad range of disabilities, (c) yield useful information to individual rehabilitation customers, not only to groups, (d) minimize burden of rehabilitation care to patients and service providers while achieving suitable psychometric standards, (e) locate and differentiate rehabilitation customer values on an interval rather than an ordinal scale, (f) be consumer driven in content and goals, and (g) be completed easily by a wide range of persons (Mpofu & Houston, 1998). The following discusses methods for developing measures of values following one's disability that are context sensitive, customer centered, and that use modern test theory.

## CONSTRUCTING A CONTEXT- AND CUSTOMER-
## SENSITIVE MEASURE OF VALUES

The next generation of measures of values should take into account the context of participation for which rehabilitation efforts are targeted as well as the values

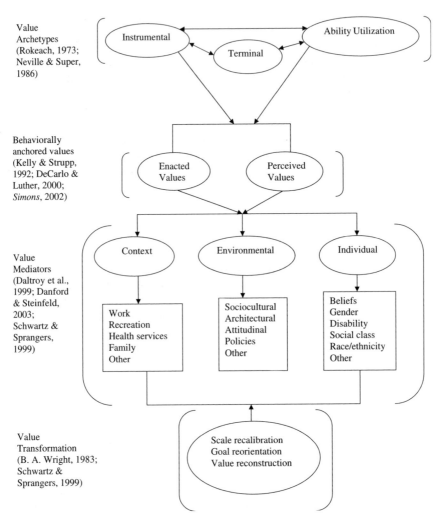

FIGURE 25.1    A systems model of values.

that are salient to rehabilitation customers, their families, and providers. Consensus-building approaches involving rehabilitation researchers, customers, and service providers are important to developing context- and customer-sensitive measures of values.

Measure development with consensus building was used successfully by Willer, Ottenbacker, and Coal (1994) to develop the Community Integration Questionnaire (CIQ). The CIQ is regarded as one of the best measures of community integration for use with persons with disabilities (Dittmar & Gresham, 1997), in part because it incorporated customer perspectives from its inception. Figure 25.2 presents a preliminary specifications chart for developing a context-

| | | Systemic Mediators | | | |
| --- | --- | --- | --- | --- | --- |
| Participation | Values | Individual | Family | Institution | Community |
| Work | *Perceived* | | | | |
| | Instrumental | | | | |
| | Terminal | | | | |
| | Ability utilization | | | | |
| | | | | | |
| | *Enacted* | | | | |
| | Instrumental | | | | |
| | Terminal | | | | |
| | Ability utilization | | | | |
| | | | | | |
| Independent Living | *Perceived* | | | | |
| | Instrumental | | | | |
| | Terminal | | | | |
| | Ability utilization | | | | |
| | | | | | |
| | *Enacted* | | | | |
| | Instrumental | | | | |
| | Terminal | | | | |
| | Ability utilization | | | | |

FIGURE 25.2    Matrix of Values for Rehabilitation Interventions: A Systems Approach.

sensitive measure of values for participation by persons with an acquired disability.

The following exemplifies an approach to using the values matrix of Figure 25.2 to explore values by institutional practices and type. Rehabilitation service providers could discuss perceived and enacted institutional values that influence their selection and use of rehabilitation outcome measures as well as how such values impact the long-term outcomes of the rehabilitation customer. Patients could discuss individual value change processes that initiate inpatient care and influence their employability and community reintegration. Patients also could compare their perceptions and values with those held by rehabilitation service providers, patients, and others. Patient views on important issues may be closer to those held by their significant others than to those held by their service providers (Heinemann, Bode, Cichowski, & Kan, 1998).

The content generated by the aforementioned discussion groups could allow a consumer conference to generate questions related to value change, items that could form a measure of values used by patients and others with disabilities at various points during rehabilitation: admission, discharge, outpatient, family, and community involvement. The issues and prospective questions for the value measure generated during the initial customers conference could be discussed with focus groups comprising consumers, as described later. A technical audit by seasoned practitioners and scholars in rehabilitation could help translate values content generated by rehabilitation customers and providers into scales that would be calibrated using both classical and more current psychometric methods, including item response theory (IRT).

Use of IRT methodology makes possible the development of measures of rehabilitation outcome that are unbiased by disability type, severity of disability, race, culture, gender, or age. This can occur because the items and tests are conceptualized as mapping an underlying construct rather than sample idiosyncrasies. Thus, measures that utilize IRT methods are likely to be useful with diverse populations (e.g., minority adults with disabilities).

### APPLYING ITEM RESPONSE THEORY TO
### REHABILITATION MEASURE DEVELOPMENT

Item response theory was developed initially for use in educational measurement. Its applications to the development of health care instruments are relatively recent yet becoming widespread. Item response theory allows one to determine the value of one test item or group of items by providing indexes that convey the degree an item or group of items contributes to estimating a person's ability on an underlying construct (or latent trait) (Andrich, 1988; Gierl, Henderson, Jodoin, & Klinger, 2001; Rasch, 1980).

Latent-trait estimation is possible because, with IRT, test item characteristics (e.g., test difficulty, item discrimination) and a person's ability (i.e., person ability) are placed on a common scale (or metric) using log-odd units, or logits, so that item statistics are established while taking ability estimation into account. Ability estimation is established through information from test item statistics. For example, the item difficulty parameter estimates the ability or trait level needed to correctly endorse an item. Item discrimination refers to the probability of a particular response to an item with a given difficulty level from a person of a specified ability level. Person ability is an estimate of the person's performance on a set of items that measure a single trait. A person who correctly responds to a particular item at a specified level of difficulty can be reliably said to possess a certain level of competence on the underlying trait the item measures. The interaction between a person's ability and a test's item difficulty allows one to create a model that enables the prediction of the likelihood that a person with a certain ability will answer a particular test item correctly.

The potential contribution of IRT to rehabilitation outcome research is attested to by its growing application to measure development (e.g., Bode, Lai, Cella, & Heinemann, 2003; W. P. Fisher, Harvey, Taylor, Kilgore, & Kelly, 1995; Hawley,

Taylor, Hellawell, & Pentland, 1999; Kilgore, Fisher, Silverstein, Harley, & Harvey, 1993; Linn et al., 1999). Related studies have investigated the following aspects: dimensionality (i.e., factor structure) of measures of functioning (e.g., Hawley et al.; Silverstein, Fisher, Kilgore, Harley, & Harvey, 1992), comparison of item difficulties as ability hierarchies on measures of physical functioning (D. Fisher et al., 1999; W. P. Fisher, Eubanks, & Marier, 1997), incremental value when predicting patient outcomes (e.g., Harvey et al., 1992; Hawley et al.; Linn et al.; Kilgore et al., 1993; Tesio & Cantagallo, 1998), rehabilitation measure equating (W. P. Fisher et al., 1995; W. P. Fisher et al., 1997), rehabilitation programming with various inpatient care facilities (Harvey et al.), construct equivalence across instruments and samples (Bode et al., 2003; W. P. Fisher, 1997; Stineman et al., 1996), and evaluating the reliability of measures of rehabilitation outcome training systems (Granger, Deutsch, & Linn, 1998; Turner-Stokes, Nyein, Turner-Stokes, & Gatehouse, 1999).

Studies by Bode et al. (2003) and W. P. Fisher et al. (1995) are among the few that demonstrate the use of IRT when establishing the applicability of a rehabilitation outcome measure across disability types. Specifically, Bode et al. investigated the usefulness of the Medical Outcomes Study 36-Item Short Form Health Survey (SF-36) for measuring physical functioning in four groups of patients who differed by illness: cancer ($n = 399$), HIV/AIDS ($n = 328$), stroke ($n = 328$), and Multiple Sclerosis ($n = 433$). The SF-36 was found to be reliable when used with persons who display these diverse chronic illness and disability profiles. W. P. Fisher (W. P. Fisher et al., 1995, 1997) demonstrated that various measures of physical and functional performance could be placed on a common metric using IRT procedures.

## SPECIFIC APPLICATIONS OF IRT TO CONSTRUCTING A MEASURE OF VALUES

IRT item statistics commonly are presented on an ordered hierarchy of a parameter (e.g., item difficulty, item discrimination), fit statistics, measures of dimensionality, and item information curves. The following suggests how a values measure could be constructed to take advantage of item informatics grounded in the use of IRT methodology.

### Person (Values) Abilities and Item Difficulty Hierarchies

Item difficulty could reflect the degree a particular value measure item is endorsed (i.e., how frequently an item is endorsed by a group of respondents). Person abilities could be estimated from performance on the set of items that measure values for participation (e.g., employment and independent living) with a disability group. Item difficulty and/or discrimination hierarchies could be interpreted as defining lower- to higher-level value change processes. For example, items toward the lower end of an item difficulty hierarchy (i.e., easier items) may be considered to reflect internal (or personal) health scale recalibration more than items at higher levels of difficulty. Items with higher difficulty levels could be regarded as measuring value transformation, that is, inclusive of internal scale recalibration and value reprioritization. Recalibration of internal standards occurs earlier (or is easier) than value transformation (Rees et al., 2002). Reprioritization of values from changes in their personal salience to the patient could be intermediate to the continuum comprising internal scale recalibration to value transformation. For example, with the experience of a threatening illness, a person may adapt by reprioritizing values without necessarily changing or transforming his or her core meanings. Moreover, persons who endorse higher-placed values (i.e., those that are endorsed less frequently) may be assumed to be capable of displaying lower placed values.

Gaps in item hierarchies could be interpreted to signify that the latent trait is measured inadequately by the existing item pool (Bond & Fox, 2001). Tests in which rank-ordered items display wide differences in difficulty values signal the need to construct additional items to fill the gaps. New items should be developed and pilot tested together with the other items to determine the extent to which the gaps have been filled.

### Unidimensionality of Values Measures

A majority of measurement models based on IRT require items to be unidimensional (i.e., measure one underlying construct). The degree of an item's unidimensionality can be used as a yardstick to determine the contribution of that test item to a pool of items thought to measure a construct.

Unidimensionality may be untenable when constructs are multilayered (Hayes, Morales, & Reise, 2000). For example, two dimensions rather than a single dimension may more adequately represent values for participation (e.g., employment and independent living are interrelated). However, theory-based test content specifications allow unidimensional measures to be constructed for the specific facets of a measure (e.g., separate items for values associated with employment and those associated with independent living).

When developing a context-sensitive measure of values, a unidimensional measure development strategy could be embedded within a multidimensional framework. The unidimensionality of a scale also can be established on the basis of comparative-fit indices using confirmatory factor analysis (CFA) methods. CFA also could be used to test for equality of covariance structures, as presumed by measures used to reflect response changes (e.g., as is used in the Thentest). For example, Schwartz & Sprangers (1999) considered changes in patterns of factor loadings on a Thentest measure to indicate a reconceptualization of values. The magnitude of the factor loading values is presumed to reflect reprioritization.

### Fit Statistics

IRT item statistics (e.g., item difficulty, item discrimination) commonly are presented in an ordered hierarchy. In IRT, fit statistics are used to determine the extent to which each item and a person's ability are consistent with others on the hierarchy of item difficulties or abilities. The statistics are particularly relevant to rehabilitation outcome measurement, in that unexpected deviations from an individual's ability may be clinically significant. For example, an observed deviation on a value item that is unexpected but close to a person's ability (using Infit statistics) may indicate potential for change with rehabilitation intervention. If the value deviation is unexpected and far from the person's ability (using Outfit statistics), the result may suggest that the person has unique values in that domain of functioning. These values may become a resource to use to support rehabilitation intervention in related areas or an area on which fewer rehabilitation resources need to be expended.

## Measure Equating

Measure equating refers to the practice of linking different measures by co-locating items that are common to both measures and have the same level of difficulty. Once the linked items are identified and located, then other items from two or more forms of the measure can be aligned on a common continuum and ordered relative to the location of the items that are common across scales. In this case, items that overlap the domains of values for participation (e.g., work and independent living) could be linked for creating a measure of values that combines the two domains. Items unique to each domain could be retained for a more detailed assessment within the specific domain.

## DETERMINING ANCHOR POINTS FOR FUNCTIONAL PARTICIPATION

IRT methods also can be used to establish anchor points that may serve as a transition point on the continuum of a latent trait that marks the difference between states of health (e.g., healthy and unhealthy) (Bond & Fox, 2001). Anchor-based applications can be important in rehabilitation outcomes measurement, in that people who score at a certain level on the trait continuum may evidence a unique health pattern and be responsive to an identifiable rehabilitation intervention. For example, an individual with a level of functioning at or above a certain point on a values continuum may have better potential for participation (e.g., due to education, employment, or level of independent living) as compared to someone at a lower level of functioning. Thus, anchor-based approaches also may enable the prediction of long-term rehabilitation outcomes (e.g., participation in work and independent living) on the basis of a current health status variable (e.g., personal values at admission). Anchor-based approaches to health outcome measurement have been applied infrequently in rehabilitation outcome measurement (Samsa et al., 1999; Testa, 2000).

## LIMITATIONS IN USING IRT MODELS

IRT models should be used with caution when developing values measures. First, high-item-discrimination indexes tend to be overestimates and could introduce error when estimating item difficulty (Hambleton, Jones, & Rogers, 1993). To rule out this possibility, one can hold out half of a sample to use later to verify the stability of an item hierarchy produced by the other half of the sample (W. P. Fisher et al., 1995; Hambleton et al.). Second, the larger the item bank, the shorter the test; the smaller the sample size, the larger the positive inflation of item difficulty values (Hambleton et al.). These limitations suggest a need to plan carefully during a measure's development, including item writing, participant recruitment, and item piloting.

## MAJOR ISSUES THAT NEED ATTENTION THROUGH RESEARCH AND OTHER FORMS OF SCHOLARSHIP

Issues that need attention include the use of qualitative measures, adopting customer-centered approaches to measure construction, establishing the external validity of the measures, and applying latent-trait methods. Each of these is considered next.

### THE USE OF QUALITATIVE MEASURES OF VALUES WITH PEOPLE WITH ACQUIRED DISABILITIES

Values are dynamic constructs and best assessed with measures that combine both qualitative and quantitative approaches (Mpofu & Houston, 1998). All value measures discussed in this chapter are quantitative in nature. Rapkin and Sprangers (2004) developed a Quality of Life Appraisal Profile (QOLAP) that could serve as a model for the construction of measures of patient values that combine qualitative and quantitative approaches. The QOLAP is a provider-administered measure of patients' perceptions of their quality of life with a chronic illness or disability in the following domains: life goals, threats, opportunities, strategies, reference groups, salient experiences, retrospective views, and recall of previous health status.

The reliability of qualitative measures to predict participation also would need to be established with the same rigor as that used with quantitative measures. Studies should include determining the reliability of raters, including those with acquired disabilities, their significant others, and/or rehabilitation service providers. The reliability of raters is particularly important with multidisciplinary teams, who may base rehabilitation intervention decisions on the assumption that measured statuses of clients are objective or independent of raters (Linacre & Wright, 1996).

The ability of service providers to reliably estimate important outcomes as perceived by their customers may be limited (J. G. Wright et al., 1994; Heinemann et al., 1998). Thus, the direct involvement of rehabilitation customers in the development and interpretation of measures may be needed. This orientation is consistent with authentic testing practices (Darling-Hammond, 1994). Authentic testing practices consider consumers as important stakeholders in the development and use of measures.

## A CUSTOMER-CENTERED APPROACH TO VALUES MEASURE DEVELOPMENT IS ADVOCATED

Research needs to compare the advantages and disadvantages of constructing measures of patient values using items preferred by those with disabilities, their significant others, and service providers as compared with those commonly used in current procedures. With the standard construction measure designs, experts unilaterally construct measures based on specific theories of values or on the need to cover important health status questions as determined by peer review. These methods are unlikely to be adequate when developing and interpreting measures of values for persons with disabilities.

Cognitive interviewing (Bassili & Scott, 1996; Presser & Blair, 1994; Sattler, 1998; Schober & Frederick, 1997) also may be used for validating whether the participant's responses to questions are consistent with the intent of the questions. Using cognitive interviewing methods (Sattler), participants are asked to verbalize the thoughts they use while responding to a question. Cognitive interviewing can be effective when mapping the mental routes participants may use in arriving at a response choice and may help explain atypical responses or typical responses arrived at for unexpected reasons. Studies that use cognitive interviewing in the design of rehabilitation-outcome measures could not be located. Evidence for using cognitive interviewing to assist in a test's development and validation is needed.

## EXTERNAL VALIDITY OF MEASURES SHOULD BE ESTABLISHED

Identification of sources of data needed to establish external validity should occur during the early stages of a measure's development. When establishing the purposes for which a measure may be used, test constructors should highly value and thus acquire data on external criteria predicted by the measure (Borsboom, Mellenbergh, & van Heerden, 2004). These criteria are not always self-evident and may be contaminated by the characteristics of the method of measurement, the rehabilitation customer (e.g., type of disability), the sociocultural environment (e.g., attitudes toward disability), and provider values (e.g., cost-reduction methods) (Rapkin & Sprangers, 2004). Better self-report measures of patient values will account for a significant proportion of the variance on the external measure.

Studies that document objective and acceptable external criteria for values measures with people with disabilities in various domains of participation are needed. For example, DeJong (DeJong, 1981; DeJong & Hughes, 1982; DeJong et al., 1984) and others operationalized measures of independent living as a participation outcome to include self-reported living arrangements, control of choice, and participation in normative community activities. People who report self-control of their living arrangements in normative (i.e., noncustodial) settings and have choices with regard to community participation are regarded as functionally independent. Use of these and similar criteria to validate measures of values that predict participation seemingly has not been investigated.

## USE OF LATENT-TRAIT MODELS IN CONSTRUCTING MEASURES OF PATIENT VALUES

The use of hierarchical linear models (HLMs) together with growth-modeling techniques and tests of mediation may enhance the quality of value measures for use with people with acquired disabilities. For the most part, the basic hierarchical structure involves people with disabilities nested within a disability group, within hospitals, and within communities. Depending on the research design, repeated measures analyses (e.g., nested within the individual patient) may be added to the hierarchy. Hierarchical linear models have been used to analyze repeated measures made on clusters of participants (Bryk & Raudenbush, 1992; Goldstein, 1995; Longford, 1993; Pinheiro & Bates, 2000). Participants within the same cluster are exposed to similar environmental conditions, while those from different clusters are exposed to different environmental conditions. Responses by participants from the same environment tend to be more similar than responses from those in different environments. When traditional methods for analysis are applied to these types of data, the results tend to be biased. However, HLMs accommodate the dependence in the data and yield unbiased parameter estimates.

IRT models can be embedded within an HLM framework (Adams, Wilson, & Wu, 1997; Raudenbush & Sampson, 1999). Using this data analysis strategy, one may designate responses as level-1 units, individuals as level-2 units, and the cluster as level-3 units (Cheong & Raudenbush, 2000; Raudenbush, Rowan, & Kang, 1991). Our objective in proposing studies that examine the utility of embedding an IRT model in the context of HLM is to study multilevel effects on the participant's latent values dimension. The three-level model could provide an examination of response patterns within individuals as well as the effect of different environments on the response patterns. This method could allow one to interpret item difficulty as an index of a compromise of a person's values following a disability. A person's ability corresponds to his or her values repertoire for participation in desired environments. Research that used HLMs to partition objective and subjective health conditions in the manner proposed could not be located.

Growth modeling could allow for charting changes in values over the rehabilitation period (e.g., from admission to community participation). Two models seemingly have potential for developing responsive measures of values (Rapkin & Schwartz, 2004; Taylor, Graham, Cumsille, & Hansen, 2000). Both models control for one's initial status. The first model provides information about average levels of change (e.g., growth) that may occur after an intervention. The second provides information about change over the observation period. Using a mixed design (e.g., combining cross-sectional and longitudinal components), the first model utilizes data from the cross-sectional design, whereas the second model utilizes data from the longitudinal design. Mixed models that involve a temporal design allow for the timing of observations to reflect the timing of stages of rehabilitation (i.e., from admission, discharge, outpatient, though community participation). A design that ties the timing and spacing of observations in longitudinal studies to intervention-related milestones could increase our understanding of the targeted changes (e.g., shifts in values) (Collins & Graham, 2002). In addition, this data-collection strategy involves shorter periods of time between measurement, thereby increasing reliability in self-reported measures (D. Fisher et al., 1999) and thus providing a more accurate and valid understanding of the processes of value change.

Both the cross-sectional and the longitudinal designs have several advantages when used to construct a measure of values for persons with acquired disabilities. The cross-sectional design could enable an assessment of the stability of item-difficulty or person-ability measures across groups, thus providing an important index of reliability. It could provide a test of the measure's empirical validity by benchmarking performance on the values measure to participation outcomes of known groups of individuals with disabilities (e.g., people with disabilities with and without employment, inpatients vs. outpatients). A longitudinal design could be used to map changes in values during the rehabilitation period. Longitudinal designs could be particularly useful for establishing the predictive validity of the values measure for individual customers. Studies that investigate the assumption of invariance of patients' internal standards across observation times with a longitudinal or a Thentest-type design are needed.

Mediation effects could be tested through a two-model structural equation modeling (SEM) analysis (Collins & Graham, 2002; Taylor et al., 2000). The first model could test the direct effects ($b_1$) of value changes on participation outcomes. The second model could add a mediator (e.g., changes in health, treatment, time since morbidity, life events) and assess the direct effect of the mediator on the outcomes ($b_2$) and the direct effect of the value changes on the mediator ($b_3$). In this second model, if $b_1$ declines and no longer is significant and $b_2$ remains significant, then the mediator explains the relationship between the intervention and the outcome. Partial mediation is possible. Statistical tests for partial mediation include assessing the difference in $b_1$ between the intervention and the first and second models (the mediation effect) by calculating the standard error (SE) of the mediation effect (Collins & Graham):

$$SE = \text{square root of } (b_2)^2(SEb_2)^2 + (b_3)^2$$

The significance of the observed test statistic is determined by dividing the mediation effect by its SE and comparing the result to critical values of the $t$-statistic. A third model to test the effects of antecedents (e.g., severity of disability, context of participation, gender) could be similarly constructed.

Rapkin and Schwartz (2004) propose a model that examines the effects of moderator variables on changes in the patient's subjective experience of health with chronic illness or disability. Moderator variables are the specific processes by which patients may change their health-related values (e.g., cognitive reappraisal, vicarious learning, socialization to sick role). Following Rapkin and Schwartz, moderator effects are estimated from the residual variance after excluding that accounted for by the antecedent and mediator variables. Expectancy tables and decision trees could be designed for predicting patient changes in values and taking into account the antecedent, mediator, and moderator variables. Such tools could facilitate the accurate and reliable interpretation of measures of values by patients, significant others, and rehabilitation service providers.


## SUMMARY

A person's values constitute one of his or her most fundamental qualities. Values help define one's personality, directly impact daily behaviors, and influence one's choice of friends and vocations, preferred leisure activities, and various life goals. Values typically are traits, that is, personal and stable qualities.

However, lifestyles often change for those with acquired disabilities. Their behaviors may become limited, their friends and family may treat them differently, and their work and preferred leisure activities often change. A review of the importance of values to rehabilitation interventions indicates that values influence the ways people interpret the impact and meaning of their disabilities. Moreover, values influence rehabilitation success. Therapeutic benefits are thought to increase when persons with acquired disabilities examine their values and, if needed, modify them in an effort to reflect current and future abilities and limitations and, through this process, redefine important life goals in realistic and positive ways.

Thus, values should be considered when planning and executing rehabilitation plans. A review of three measures and one process used to assess values in persons with acquired disabilities leads to the conclusions that they can be of some benefit, especially to professional caregivers. In contrast, persons with acquired disabilities may derive less value from their use. Moreover, in that existing measures assume values are static, such measures may not describe values accurately and be sensitive to various personal changes, including value changes, displayed by persons who experience life-changing disabilities.

A new generation of measures of personal values for use with persons with acquired disabilities is advocated. Seven qualities important to this new generation of tests were identified. Persons with acquired disabilities should assist in the design and development of value measures. These measures should enable them, their family, health care providers, and others to understand their personal values, to detect value changes, and to better understand the sources of these changes (e.g., the degree they are personal or emanate from family, friends, health care providers, and/or broader environmental influences). Additionally, value measures should assist persons with acquired disabilities to better understand the impact their values may have on their rehabilitation efforts.

Classical test theory and methods continue to be relevant to test development. In addition, modern test theory and methods, including the use of item response theory, hierarchical linear models, growth modeling, and mediation effects, hold particular promise for the development of value measures that are more sensitive to the needs for persons with acquired disabilities.

## REFERENCES

Adams, R. J., Wilson, M., & Wu, M. (1997). Multilevel item response models: An approach to errors in variables regression. *Journal of Educational and Behavioral Statistics, 22,* 47–76.

Albrecht, G. L., & Devlieger, P. (1999). The disability paradox: High quality of life against all odds. *Social Science and Medicine, 48,* 977–988.

Andrich, D. (1988). *Rasch models for measurement.* Newbury Park, CA: Sage.

Antonak, R. F., & Livneh, H. (1994). Instruments to measure psychosocial adjustment to illness and impairment: Part II. Specific illness and impairment measures. *Assessment in Rehabilitation and Exceptionality, 1,* 175–202.

Bassili, J. N., & Scott, B. S. (1996). Response latency as a signal to question problems in survey research. *Public Opinion Quarterly, 60,* 390–399.

Belza, B. L., Henke, C. J., Yelin, E. H., Epstein, W. V., & Gilliss, C. L. (1993). Correlates of fatigue in older adults with rheumatoid arthritis. *Nursing Research, 42,* 93–99.

Bergner, M., Bobbitt, R. A., Kressel, S., Pollard, W. E., Gilson, B. S., & Morris, J. R. (1976). Sickness impact profile: Conceptual formulation and development revision of a health status measure. *International Journal of Health Services, 6,* 393–415.

Bode, R. K., Lai, J., Cella, D., & Heinemann, A. W. (2003). Issues in the development of an item bank. *Archives of Physical Medicine and Rehabilitation, 84,* 52–60.

Bond, T. G., & Fox, C. M. (2001). *Applying the Rasch model: Fundamental measurement in the human sciences.* Mahwah, NJ: Erlbaum.

Borsboom, D., Mellenbergh, G. J., & van Heerden, J. (2004). The concept of validity. *Psychological Review, 111,* 1061–1071.

Boschen, K. A. (1996). Correlates of life satisfaction, residential satisfaction and locus of control among adults with spinal cord injuries. *Rehabilitation Counseling Bulletin, 39,* 230–243.

Boschen, K. A., & Gargano, J. (1996). Issues in the measurement of independent living. *Canadian Journal of Rehabilitation, 10,* 125–135.

Bryk, A. S., & Raudenbush, S. W. (1992). Hierarchical linear models: Application and data analysis methods. Newbury Park, CA: Sage.

Cheong, Y. F., & Raudenbush, S. W. (2000). Measurement and statistical models for children's problem behaviors. *Psychological Methods, 5,* 477–495.

Collins, L., & Graham, J. W. (2002). The effect of the timing and spacing of observations in longitudinal studies of tobacco and other drug use: Temporal design considerations. *Drug and Alcohol Dependence: An international Journal of Biomedical and Psychosocial Approaches, 68,* S85–S96.

Daltroy, L. H., Larson, M. G., Eaton, H. M., Phillips, C. B., & Liang, M. H. (1999). Discrepancies between self-reported and observed physical function in the elderly: The influence of response shift and other factors. *Social Science & Medicine, 48,* 1549–1561.

Daltroy, L. H., Phillips, C. B., Eaton, H. M., Larson, M. G., Patridge, A. J., Logigian, M., et al. (1995). Objectively measuring physical ability in elderly persons: The Physical Capacity Evaluation. *American Journal of Public Health, 85,* 558–560.

Danford, S., & Steinfeld, E. (2003). Measuring the influences of physical environments on the behaviors of people with impairments. In E. Steinfeld & G. S. Danford (Eds.), *Enabling environments: Measuring the impact of environment on disability and rehabilitation* (pp. 111–136). New York: Kluwer.

Darling-Hammond, L. (1994). Performance-based assessment and educational equity. *Harvard Educational Review, 64,* 5–32.

DeCarlo, L. T., & Luthar, S. S. (2000). Analysis and class validation of a measure of parental values perceived by early adolescents: An application of a latent class model for rankings. *Educational and Psychological Measurement, 60,* 578–591.

DeJong, G. (1981). *Environmental accessibility and independent living outcomes: Directions for disability policy and research.* East Lansing, MI: University Centers for International Rehabilitation.

DeJong, G., Branch, L. G., & Corcoran, P. J. (1984). Independent living outcomes in spinal cord injury: Multivariate analysis. *Archives of Physical Medicine and Rehabilitation, 65,* 66–73.

DeJong, G., & Hughes, J. (1982). Independent living: Methodology for measuring long-term outcomes. *Archives of Physical Medicine and Rehabilitation, 63,* 68–72.

Dittmar, S. S., & Gresham, G. E. (Eds.). (1997). *Functional assessment and outcomes measures for the rehabilitation health professional.* Gaithersburg, MD: Aspen.

Feather, N. T. (1988). The meaning and importance of values: Research with the Rokeach Value Survey. *Australian Journal of Psychology, 40,* 377–390.

Felce, D., & Perry, J. (1995). Quality of life: Its definition and measurement. *Research in Developmental Disabilities, 16,* 51–74.

Fisher, D., Stewart, A. L., Block, D. A., Lorig, K., Laurent, D., & Holman, H. (1999). Capturing the patient's view of change as a clinical outcome measure. *Journal of the American Medical Association, 282,* 1157–1162.

Fisher, W. P. (1997). Physical disability construct convergence across instruments: Towards a universal metric. *Journal of Outcomes Measurement, 1,* 87–113.

Fisher, W. P. (1998). A research program for accountable and patient-centered health outcome measures. *Journal of Outcomes Measurement, 2,* 222–239.

Fisher, W. P., Eubanks, R. L., & Marier, R. L. (1997). Equating the MOS, SF-36 and the LSU HIS physical functioning scales. *Journal of Outcomes Measurement, 1,* 329–362.

Fisher, W. P., Harvey, R. F., Taylor, P., Kilgore, K. M., & Kelly, C. K. (1995). Rehabits: A common language of functional assessment. *Archives of Physical Medicine & Rehabilitation, 76,* 113–122.

Gay, E. G., Weiss, D. J., Hendel, D. D., Dawis, R. V., & Lofquist, L. H. (1971). *Manual for the Minnesota Importance Questionnaire.* Minneapolis: University of Minnesota, Vocational Psychology Work Adjustment Project, Department of Psychology.

Gibbons, F. X. (1999). Social comparison as a mediator of response shift. *Social Science and Medicine, 48,* 1517–1530.

Gierl, M. L., Henderson, D., Jodoin, M., & Klinger, D. (2001). Minimizing the influence of item parameter estimation errors in test development: A comparison of three selection procedures. *The Journal of Experimental Education, 69,* 261–279.

Goldsmith, R. E., Stith, M., & White, J. D. (1987). The Rokeach Value Survey and social desirability. *Journal of Social Psychology, 127,* 553–554.

Goldstein, H. (1995). *Multilevel statistical models* (2nd ed.). New York: John Wiley & Sons.

Granger, C. V., Deutsch, A., & Linn, R. T. (1998). Rasch analysis of the Functional Independence Measure (FIM) Mastery Test. *Archives of Physical Medicine and Rehabilitation, 79,* 52–57.

Gurka, J. A., Felmingham, K. L., Baguley, I. J., Schotte, D. E., Crooks, J., & Marosszeky, J. E. (1999). Utility of the Functional Assessment Measure after discharge from inpatient rehabilitation. *Journal of Head Trauma and Rehabilitation, 14,* 247–256.

Hackbarth, J., & Mathay, G. (1991). An evaluation of two work value assessment instruments for use with hearing-impaired college students. *Journal of the American Deafness and Rehabilitation Association, 24,* 88–97.

Harvey, R. E., Silverstein, B., Venzon, M. A., Kilgore, K. M., Fisher, W. P., Steiner, M., et al. (1992). Applying psychometric criteria to functional assessment in medical rehabilitation: III. Construct validity and predicting level of care. *Archives of Physical Medicine and Rehabilitation, 73,* 887–892.

Hawley, C. A., Taylor, R., Hellawell, D. J., & Pentland, B. (1999). Use of the functional assessment measure (FIM + FAM) in head injury rehabilitation: A psychometric analysis. *Journal of Neural Psychiatry, 67,* 749–754.

Hambleton, R. K., Jones, R. W., & Rogers, H. J. (1993). Influence of item parameter errors in test development. *Journal of Educational Measurement, 30,* 143–155.

Hamblin, D. L., Beutler, L. E., Scorgin, F., & Corbishley, A. (1993). Patient responsiveness to therapist values and outcome in group cognitive therapy. *Psychotherapy Research, 3,* 36–46.

Hays, R. D., Morales, L. S., & Reise, S. (2000). Item response theory and health outcomes measurement in the 21st century. *Medical Care, 38,* 28–42.

Heinemann, A. W., Bode, R., Cichowski, K. C., & Kan, E. (1998). Measuring patient satisfaction with medical rehabilitation. In E. A. Dobrzykowski (Ed.). *Essential readings in rehabilitation outcomes measurement: Application, methodology, and technology* (pp. 92–103). Gaithersburg, MD: Aspen.

Heinemann, A. W., & Hamilton, B. B. (2000). Relation of rehabilitation intervention to functional outcome. *Journal of Rehabilitation Outcome Measures, 4,* 18–21.

Hobart, J. C., Lamping, D. L., Freeman, J. A., Langdon, D. W., McLellan, D. L., Greenwood, R. J., et al. (2001). Evidence-based measurement: Which validity scale for neurologic rehabilitation? *Neurology, 57,* 639–644.

Kane, R. L., & Kane, R. A. (Eds.). (1982). *Values in long-term care.* Toronto, Ontario, Canada: Lexington.

Keirsey, D., & Bates, M. (1984). *Please understand me.* Del Mar, CA: Prometheus Nemesis.

Kelly, T. A., & Strupp, H. H. (1992). Patient and therapist values in psychotherapy: Perceived changes assimilation. similarity, and outcome. *Journal of Consulting and Clinical Psychology, 60,* 34–40.

Kilgore, K. M., Fisher, W. P., Silverstein, B., Harley, J. P., & Harvey, R. F. (1993). Application of Rasch analysis to the Patient Evaluation Conference System. *Physical Medicine and Rehabilitation Clinics of North America, 4,* 493–515.

Kiresuk, T. J., Smith, A., & Cardillo, J. E. (Eds.). (1994). *Goal attainment scaling: Application, theory and measurement.* Hillsdale, NJ: Erlbaum.

Kivioja, A., & Franklin, R. D. (2003). Recovery of function. In R. D. Franklin (Ed.), *Prediction in forensic and neuropsychology: Sound statistical practices* (pp. 209–258). Mahwah, NJ: Erlbaum.

Korner-Bitensky, N., Mayo, N. E., & Poznanski, S. G. (1990). Occupational therapists' accuracy in predicting sensory, perceptual-cognitive, and functional recovery poststroke. *The Occupational Therapy Journal of Research, 10,* 237–248.

Kristiansen, C. M. (1985). Social desirability and the Rokeach Value Survey. *Journal of Social Psychology, 125,* 399–400.

Liang, M. H., Fossel, A. H., & Larson, M. G. (1990). Comparison of five health status instruments for orthopedic evaluation. *Medical Care, 28,* 632–642.

Linacre, J. M., & Wright, B. D. (1996). *Facets: Many facet Rasch analysis.* Chicago: MESA Press.

Linkowski, D. C. (1986). *The acceptance of disability scale: An update 1963–1983.* Unpublished manuscript.

Linn, R. T., Blair, R. S., Granger, C. V., Harper, D. W., O'Hara, D. W., & Maciura, E. (1999). Does the Functional Assessment Measure (FAM) extend the Functional Independence Measure (FIM) instrument? A Rasch analysis of stroke inpatients. *Journal of Outcome Measurement, 3,* 339–359.

Lipscomb, J. (1982). Value preferences for health: Meaning, measurement, and use in program evaluation. In R. L. Kane & R. A. Kane (Eds.), *Values and long-term care* (pp. 27–84). Lexington, MA: Lexington.

Longford, N. T. (1993). *Random coefficient models.* Oxford, UK: Oxford University Press.

McGuire, K. M. (2000). A study of selected factors affecting vocational rehabilitation outcomes for persons with disabilities: A one-year follow-up. *Dissertation Abstracts International, 60*(11-B), 5782.

Melchiori, L. G., & Church, A. T. (1997). Vocational needs and satisfaction of supported employees: The applicability of the theory of work adjustment. *Journal of Vocational Behavior, 50,* 401–417.

Menzel, P., Dolan, P., Richardson, J., & Oslen, J. A. (2002). The role of adaptation to disability and disease in health state valuation: A preliminary normative analysis. *Social Science and Medicine, 55,* 2149–2158.

Mpofu, E. (2001). Application of Bell's Transcription Convention to understanding disability experience: A case study. *Zimbabwe Journal of Educational Research, 13,* 1–23.

Mpofu, E. (2004). *Value changes that occur with acquired disability.* Unpublished manuscript.

Mpofu, E., & Houston, E. (1998). Assessment of value change in persons with acquired physical disabilities: Current and prospective applications. *Canadian Journal of Rehabilitation, 12,* 53–61.

Neville, D. D., & Super, D. E. (1986). *The Values Scale.* Palo Alto, CA: Consulting Psychologists Press.

Nosek, M. A., & Fuhrer, M. J. (1992). Independence and disabilities. A heuristic model. *Rehabilitation Counseling Bulletin, 36,* 6–20.

Orbell, S., Johnston, M., Rowley, D., Davey, P., & Espley, A. (2001). Self-efficacy and goal importance in the prediction of physical disability in people following hospitalization: A prospective study. *British Journal of Health Psychology, 6,* 25–40.

Ozer, M. N., & Kroll, T. (2002). Patient-centered rehabilitation: Problems and opportunities. *Critical Review in Physical and Rehabilitation Medicine, 14,* 273–289.

Pinheiro, J. C., & Bates, D. M. (2000). *Mixed-effects models in S and S plus.* New York: Springer Verlag.

Presser, S., & Blair, J. (1994). Survey pretesting: Do different methods produce different results? *Sociological Methodology, 24,* 73–104.

Rapkin, B. D., & Schwartz, C. E. (2004). Toward a theoretical model of quality-of-life appraisal: Implications of findings from studies of response shift. *Health and Quality of Life Outcomes, 2,* 1–12.

Rasch, G. (1980). *Probabilistic models for some intelligence and attainment tests.* Chicago: University of Chicago Press.

Raudenbush, S. W., Rowan, B., & Kang, S. J. (1991). A multilevel model for studying school climate with estimation via EM algorithm and application to U.S. high-school data. *Journal of Educational Statistics, 16,* 295–330.

Raudenbush, S. W., & Sampson, R. J. (1999). "Econometrics." Towards a science of assessing ecological settings with application to the systemic social observation of neighborhoods. *Sociological Methods, 29,* 1–41.

Rees, J. E., Waldron, D., O'Boyle, C. A., & MacDonagh, R. P. (2002). Response shift in individualized quality of life in patients with advanced prostate cancer. *Clinical Therapeutics, 24*(Suppl. B), 33–34.

Rokeach, M. (1973). *The nature of values.* New York: Free Press.

Rolland, J. S. (1994). *Families, illness and disability: An integrative treatment model.* New York: Basic Books.

Ryff, C. D. (1989). Happiness is everything, or is it? Explorations on the meaning of psychological well-being. *Journal of Personality and Social Psychology, 57,* 1069–1081.

Samsa, G., Edelman, D., Rothman, M. I., Williams, G. R., Lipscomb, J., & Matchar, D. (1999). Determining clinically important differences in health status measurement: A general approach with illustrations to the Health Utilities Index mark II: *Pharmacoeconomics, 15,* 141–155.

Sattler, J. (1998). *Clinical and forensic interviewing of children and families.* San Diego, CA: Author

Schaefer, N. C. (2000). Asking questions about threatening topics: A selective overview. In A. A. Stone, J. S. Turkkan, C. A. Bachrach, J. B. Jobe, H. S. Kurtzman, & V. S. Cain (Eds.), *The science of self-report: Implications for research and practice* (pp. 105–122). Mahwah, NJ: Erlbaum.

Schober, M. F., & Frederick, G. C. (1997). Does conversational interviewing reduce survey measurement error? *Public Opinion Quarterly, 61,* 576–602.

Schwartz, C. E., & Sprangers, M. A. G. (1999). Methodological approaches for assessing response shift in longitudinal health-related quality-of-life research. *Social Science and Medicine, 48,* 1531–1548.

Schwartz, C. E., Sprangers, M. A. G., Carey, A., & Reed, G. (2004). Exploring response shift in longitudinal data. *Psychology and Health, 19,* 51–69.

Scofield, M., Pape, A. A., McCracken, N., & Maki, D. (1980). An ecological model for promoting acceptance of disability. *Journal of Applied Rehabilitation Counseling, 11,* 183–187.

Seelman, K. (2000). Rehabilitation research and training centers on functional assessment and the evaluation of rehabilitation outcomes. Accomplishments to date and goals for the future: Introduction. *Journal of Rehabilitation Outcomes Measurement, 4*(4), 1.

Silverstein, B., Fisher, W. P., Kilgore, K. M., Harley, J. P., & Harvey, R. F. (1992). Applying psychometric criteria to functional assessment in medical rehabilitation: II. Defining interval measures. *Archives of Physical Medicine and Rehabilitation, 73,* 507–518.

Simmons, D. C., Crepeau, E. B., & White, B. P. (2000). The predictive power of narrative data in occupational therapy. *American Journal of Occupational Therapy, 54,* 471–476.

Sinclair, R. R., Fleming, W. D., Radwinsky, R., Clupper, D. R., & Clupper, J. H. (2002). Understanding patients' reactions to services: The role of personal service values in heart patient satisfaction and wellness. *Journal of Applied Social Psychology, 32,* 424–442.

Smart, J. (2001). *Disability, society, and the individual.* Austin, TX: Pro-Ed.

Sneeuw, K. C., Aaronson, N. K., Sprangers, M. A., Detmar, S. B., Wever, L. D., & Schornagel, J. H. (1997). Value of caregiver ratings in evaluating the quality of life of patients with cancer. *Journal of Clinical Oncology, 15,* 1206–1217.

Steinfeld, E., & Danford, E. (Eds.). (2003). *Enabling environments: Measuring the impact of environment on disability and rehabilitation* (pp. 111–136). New York: Kluwer.

Stineman, M. G., Shea, J. A., Jette, A., Tassoni, C. J., Ottenbacher, K. J., Fiedler, R., et al. (1996). The Functional Independence Measure: Tests of scaling assumptions, structure and reliability across 20 diverse impairment categories. *Archives of Physical Medicine and Rehabilitation, 77,* 1101–1108.

Taylor, B. J., Graham, J. W., Cumsille, P. E., & Hansen, W. B. (2000). Modeling prevention program effects on growth in substance use: Analysis of five years of data from the Adolescent Alcohol Prevention Trial. *Prevention Science, 1,* 183–197.

Tesio, L., & Cantagallo, A. (1998). The Functional Assessment Measure (FAM) in closed traumatic brain injury outpatients: A Rasch-based psychometric study. *Journal of Outcome Measurement, 2*(2), 79–96.

Testa, M. A. (2000). Interpretation of quality of life outcomes: Issues that affect magnitude and meaning. *Medical Care, 38,* 166–1774.

Turner-Stokes, L., Nyein, K., Turner-Stokes, T., & Gatehouse, C. (1999). The UK FIM+FAM: Development and evaluation. *Clinical Rehabilitation, 13,* 277–287.

Veit, C. T., & Ware, J. E. (1982). Measuring health and health-care outcomes: Issues and recommendations. In R. L. Kane & R. A. Kane (Eds.), *Values and long-term care* (pp. 233–260). Lexington, MA: Lexington.

Wehmeyer, M. L., & Bolding, N. (2001). Enhanced self-determination of adults with intellectual disability as 1–13 an outcome of moving to community-based work or living environments. *Journal of Intellectual Disability Research, 45,* 1–13.

Weiss, D. (1967). Manual for the Minnesota Satisfaction Scale. *Minnesota Studies in Vocational Rehabilitation XXII, Bulletin 45.* Minneapolis: University of Minnesota.

Willer, B., Ottenbacker, K. J., & Coad, M. L. (1994). The Community Integration Questionnaire: A comparative examination. *American Journal of Physical Medicine and Rehabilitation, 73,* 103–111.

World Health Organization (WHO). (1999). *ICIDH-2: International classification of impairments, disabilities and handicaps: A manual of classification relating to the consequences of disease.* Geneva, Switzerland: Author.

Wright, B. A. (1983). *Physical disability: A psychosocial approach* (2nd ed.). New York: Harper & Row.

Wright, J. G., Rudicel, S., & Feinstein, A. R. (1994). Ask patients what they want. *Journal of Bone and Joint Surgery, 76,* 229–234.

# AUTHOR INDEX

# SUBJECT INDEX